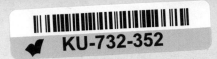

‘Indispensable for fans’ *Sunday Times*

‘Fascinating behind-the-scenes trivia’ *Sunday Express*

‘A classic reworking of the American dream: dream hard, work hard, aim high, let no one stand in your way’ Daily *Express*

‘As brick solid as its author’ *Independent on Sunday*

‘The revelations in its pages certainly pack a punch’ *HELLO!*

‘Schwarzenegger is extremely engaging company and a highly entertaining story teller’ *Empire*

‘Much hyped and much anticipated’ *Sunday Telegraph*

ALSO BY ARNOLD SCHWARZENEGGER

Arnold: The Education of a Bodybuilder

Arnold's Bodybuilding for Men

Arnold's Bodyshaping for Women

Encyclopedia of Modern Bodybuilding

The New Encyclopedia of Modern Bodybuilding

MY UNBELIEVABLY TRUE LIFE STORY

TOTAL RECALL

ARNOLD
SCHWARZENEGGER

with Peter Petre

SIMON &
SCHUSTER

London · New York · Sydney · Toronto · New Delhi

A CBS COMPANY

First published in Great Britain by Simon & Schuster UK Ltd, 2012
This paperback edition published by Simon & Schuster UK Ltd, 2013
A CBS COMPANY

10 9 8 7 6 5 4 3 2 1

Simon & Schuster UK Ltd
1st Floor
222 Gray's Inn Road
London WC1X 8HB

www.simonandschuster.co.uk

Simon & Schuster Australia, Sydney
Simon & Schuster India, New Delhi

Designed by Joy O'Meara
Photo editor: Audrey Landreth

A CIP catalogue record for this book is available from the British Library

ISBN: 978-1-84983-973-0
ISBN: 978-1-84983-974-7 (Ebook)

Printed and bound by CPI Group (UK) Ltd, Croydon, CR0 4YY

For my family

CONTENTS

TOTAL RECALL

America was as big as I'd always dreamed it would be while growing up in rural Austria. So I didn't have to fake my happiness and excitement when I played Hercules visiting Times Square in my first movie, Hercules in New York, *in 1969.*
Courtesy of Lionsgate

CHAPTER 1

Out of Austria

I WAS BORN INTO a year of famine. It was 1947, and Austria was occupied by the Allied armies that had defeated Hitler's Third Reich. In May, two months before I was born, there were hunger riots in Vienna, and in Styria, the southeastern province where we lived, the food shortages were just as bad. Years later, if my mother wanted to remind me about how much she and my father sacrificed to bring me up, she'd tell me how she'd foraged across the countryside, making her way from farm to farm to collect a little butter, some sugar, some grain. She'd be away three days sometimes. *Hamstern,* they called it, like a hamster gathering nuts; scrounging for food was so common.

Thal was the name of our very typical farm village. A few hundred families made up the entire population, their houses and farms clustered in hamlets connected by footpaths and lanes. The unpaved main road ran for a couple of kilometers up and down low alpine hills covered with fields and pine forests.

We saw very little of the British forces who were in charge—just an occasional truck with soldiers rolling through. But to the east, Russians occupied the area, and we were very conscious of them. The Cold War had begun, and we all lived in fear that the Russian tanks would roll in, and we'd be swallowed up into the Soviet empire. The priests in church would scare the congregation with horror stories of Russians shooting babies in the arms of their mothers.

Our house was on the top of a hill along the road, and as I was growing up, it was unusual to see more than one or two cars come through a day. A ruined castle dating back to feudal times was right across from us, one hundred yards from our door.

On the next rise were the mayor's office; the Catholic church where my mother made us all go to Sunday Mass; the local *Gasthaus*, or inn, which was the social heart of the village; and the primary school attended by me and my brother, Meinhard, who was a year older than me.

My earliest memories are of my mother washing clothes and my father shoveling coal. I was no more than three years old, but the image of my father is especially sharp in my mind. He was a big, athletic guy, and he did a lot of things himself. Every autumn we'd get our winter supply of coal, a truckload dumped in front of our house, and on this occasion he was letting Meinhard and me help him carry it into the cellar. We were always so proud to be his assistants.

My father and mom both originally came from working-class families farther north—factory laborers, mostly, in the steel industry. During the chaos at the end of World War II, they'd met in the city of Mürzzuschlag, where my mother, Aurelia Jadrny, was a clerk in a food-distribution center at city hall. She was in her early twenties, and a war widow—her husband had gotten killed just eight months after their wedding. Working at her desk one morning, she noticed my father passing on the street—an older guy, in his late thirties, but tall and good looking and wearing the uniform of the gendarmerie, the rural police. She was crazy about men in uniforms, so every day after that she watched for him. She figured out when his shift was so she would be sure to be at her desk. They'd talk through the open window, and she'd give him some food from whatever they had on hand.

His name was Gustav Schwarzenegger. They got married late in 1945. He was thirty-eight, and she was twenty-three. My father was assigned to Thal and put in charge of a four-man post responsible for the village and nearby countryside. The salary was barely enough to live on, but with the job came a place to live: the old forester's lodge, or *Forst-*

haus. The forest ranger, or *Forstmeister*, lived on the ground floor, and the *Inspektor* and his family occupied the top.

My boyhood home was a very simple stone and brick building, well proportioned, with thick walls and little windows to keep out the alpine winters. We had two bedrooms, each with a coal oven for heat, and a kitchen, where we ate, did our homework, washed ourselves, and played games. The heat in that room was supplied by my mother's stove.

There was no plumbing, no shower, and no flushing toilet, just a kind of chamber pot. The nearest well was almost a quarter mile away, and even when it was raining hard or snowing, one of us had to go. So we used as little water as we could. We'd heat it and fill the washbasin and give ourselves sponge or cloth baths—my mother would wash herself first with the clean water; next, my father would wash himself; and then Meinhard and I would have our turn. It didn't matter if we had slightly darker water as long as we could avoid a trip to the well.

We had wood furniture, very basic, and a few electric lamps. My father liked pictures and antiques, but when we were growing up, these were luxuries he couldn't afford. Music and cats brought liveliness to our house. My mother played the zither and sang us songs and lullabies, but it was my father who was the real musician. He could play all the wind and reed instruments: trumpets, flügelhorns, saxophones, clarinets. He also wrote music and was the conductor of the region's gendarmerie band—if a police officer died anywhere in the state, the band would play at the funeral. Often on Sundays in summer, we'd go to concerts in the park, where he would conduct and sometimes play. Most of our relatives on his side were musical, but that talent never made it to Meinhard or me.

I'm not sure why we had cats instead of dogs—maybe because my mother loved them and they cost nothing because they caught their own food. But we always had lots of cats, running in and out, curling up here and there, bringing down half-dead mice from the attic to show off what great hunters they were. Everyone had his or her own cat to curl up with in bed at night—that was our tradition. At one point, we had seven cats. We loved the cats, but never too much, because there was no such thing as going to the vet. If one of the cats started falling over from being too sick or too old, we'd wait to hear the shot from the backyard—the sound of my father's pistol. My mother, Meinhard, and I would then go out and make a grave with a little cross on top.

My mother had a black cat named Mooki that she constantly claimed was unique, although none of us could see why. One day when I was about ten, I was arguing with my mother about not wanting to do my homework. Mooki was nearby, curled up on the couch, as usual. I must have said something really uppity because my mother moved to smack me across the face. I saw it coming and tried to fend her off, but instead I hit her with the back of my arm. In a second, Mooki was off the couch—she leaped up between us and started clawing at my face. I pulled her off me and yelled, "Ow! What is this!?" Mom and I looked at each other and burst out laughing, even though I had blood running down my cheek. Finally, she had proof that Mooki was special.

After the turmoil of the war, my parents' big desire was for us to be stable and safe. My mother was a big, square-built woman, solid and resourceful, and she was also a traditional hausfrau who kept the house immaculately clean. She'd roll up the rugs and get down on her hands and knees with a brush and soap and scrub the planking, and then dry it off with rags. She was fanatical about keeping our clothes neatly hung and our sheets and towels precisely folded, with razor-sharp corners at the edge. Out back, she planted beets and potatoes and berries to keep us fed, and in fall she would put up preserves and sauerkraut in thick glass jars for the winter. Always when my father came home from the police station at twelve thirty, mom would be ready with lunch, and again with supper when he came home precisely at six o'clock.

The finances were her job too. Having been a clerk, she was very organized and was good at writing and math. Each month when my father brought home his pay, she'd leave him five hundred schillings for pocket money and take the rest for running the house. She handled all the family's correspondence and paid the monthly bills. Once a year, always in December, she took us shopping for clothes. We'd ride a bus to the Kastner & Öhler department store just over the next ridge, in Graz. The old building had only two or three floors, but in our minds it was as big as the Mall of America. It had escalators and a metal and glass elevator, so we could see everything as we rode up and down. Mom would buy just the absolute necessities for us, shirts and underwear and socks and so forth, and these would be delivered to our house the next day in neat brown paper bundles. Installment plans were new then, and she really liked being able to pay off a fraction of the bill each month until it was all paid. Liberating people like my mom to shop was a good way to stimulate the economy.

She took charge of medical problems too, even though my father was the one trained to deal with emergencies. My brother and I had every possible childhood illness, from mumps to scarlet fever to measles, so she got lots of practice. Nothing stopped her: one winter night when we were toddlers, Meinhard had pneumonia, and there was no doctor or ambulance to be had. Leaving me home with my dad, my mother bundled Meinhard on her back and hiked more than two miles in the snow to the hospital in Graz.

My father was a lot more complicated. He could be generous and affectionate, especially with her. They loved each other intensely. You could see it in the way she brought him coffee and in the way he was always finding small gifts for her, and hugging her and patting her on the behind. They shared their affection with us: we always got to cuddle up with them in bed, especially if we were scared by thunder and lightning.

But about once a week, usually on Friday night, my father would come home drunk. He'd been out until two or three or four in the morning, drinking at his usual table at the *Gasthaus* with the locals, often including the priest, the school principal, and the mayor. We'd wake up to hear him banging around in a rage and yelling at my mom. The anger never lasted, and the next day he'd be sweet and nice and take us to lunch or give us gifts to make up. If we misbehaved, however, he would smack us or use his belt on us.

To us, all this seemed totally normal: everybody's dad used physical punishment and came home drunk. One father who lived near us pulled his son's ears and chased him with a thin, flexible stick that he'd soaked in water to make it hurt more. The drinking seemed like just a part of the camaraderie, which was usually much more benign. Sometimes the wives and families would be invited to join their husbands at the *Gasthaus*. We kids always felt honored to sit with the adults and then be treated to dessert. Or we'd be allowed into the next room and drink a little Coca-Cola and play board games and look at magazines or the TV. We'd be sitting there at midnight thinking, "Wow, this is terrific!"

It took me years to understand that behind the *Gemütlichkeit* there was bitterness and fear. We were growing up among men who felt like a bunch of losers. Their generation had started World War II and lost. During the war, my father had left the gendarmerie to become a policeman in the German army. He'd served in Belgium and France, and in North Africa, where he caught malaria. In 1942 he barely escaped being captured at Leningrad, the bloodiest battle of the war. The building he was in was blown up by the Russians. He was trapped under rubble for three days. His back was broken, and he had shrapnel in both legs. It took months in a Polish hospital before he recovered enough to come home to Austria and rejoin the civilian police. And who knows how long it took his psychic wounds to heal, given all that he had witnessed? I heard them talk about it when they were drunk, and can imagine how painful it was for them. They were all beaten and also frightened that any day the Russians might come and take them away to rebuild Moscow or Stalingrad. They were angry. They tried to suppress the rage and humiliation, but disappointment was deep in their bones. Think about it: you are promised you will be a citizen of a great new empire. Every family will have the latest conveniences. Instead, you come home to a land in ruins, there's very little money, food is scarce, everything needs to be rebuilt. The occupying forces are there, so you're not even in charge of your country anymore. Worst of all, you have no way to process what you've experienced. How could you cope with that unbelievable trauma when no one was supposed to talk about it?

Instead, the Third Reich was being officially erased. All public servants—local officials, schoolteachers, police—had to go through what the Americans called denazification. You were questioned, and your record was examined to determine if you had been really hardcore or in a position to commit war crimes. Everything having to do with the Nazi era was confiscated: books, films, posters—even your personal journals and photographs. You had to give over everything: the war was supposed to be erased from your mind.

Meinhard and I were only faintly aware of it. In our house was a beautiful picture book that we would borrow to play priest and pretend it was the Bible because it was much larger than our actual family Bible. One of us would stand and hold it open while the other would say Mass. The book was actually a do-it-yourself album for promoting the mighty accomplishments of the Third Reich. There were sections for different categories, such as public works, tunnels and dams under construction, Hitler's rallies and speeches, great new ships, new monuments, great battles being fought in Poland. Each category had blank pages that were numbered, and whenever you went to the store and bought something or invested in a war bond, you would get a photo to match up with a number and paste into your book. When the collection was complete, you'd win a prize. I loved the pages that showed magnificent train stations and powerful locomotives spouting steam, and I was mesmerized by the picture of two men riding a little open flat handcar on the track, pumping the lever up and down to move themselves along—that seemed like adventure and freedom to me.

Meinhard and I had no idea what we were looking at, but one day when we went to play priest, the album was gone. We searched everywhere. Finally, I asked my mother where the beautiful book had disappeared: after all, that was our Bible! All she would say was, "We had to give it up." Later I would say to my father, "Tell me about the war," or ask him questions about what he did or went through. His reply was always, "There's nothing to talk about."

His answer to life was discipline. We had a strict routine that nothing could change: we'd get up at six, and it would be my job or Meinhard's to get milk from the farm next door. When we were a little older and starting to play sports, exercises were added to the chores, and we had to earn our breakfast by doing sit-ups. In the afternoon, we'd finish our homework and chores, and my father would make us practice soccer no matter how bad the weather was. If we messed up on a play, we knew we'd get yelled at.

My father believed just as strongly in training our brains. After Mass on Sunday, he'd take us on a family outing: visiting another village, maybe, or seeing a play, or watching him perform with the police band. Then in the evening we had to write a report on our activities, ten pages at least. He'd hand back our papers with red ink scribbled all over them, and if we had spelled a word wrong, we had to copy it fifty times over.

I loved my father and really wanted to be like him. I remember once when I was little, putting on his uniform and standing on a chair in front of the mirror. The jacket came down like a robe almost to my feet, and the hat was falling down on my nose. But he had no patience with our problems. If we wanted a bicycle, he'd tell us to earn the money for it ourselves. I never felt that I was good enough, strong enough, smart enough. He let me know that there was always room for improvement. A lot of sons would have been crippled by his demands, but instead the discipline rubbed off on me. I turned it into drive.

Meinhard and I were very close. We shared a bedroom until I was eighteen and left to join the army, and I never would have had it any other way. To this day, I'm more comfortable when there's someone to schmooze with until I fall asleep.

We were also supercompetitive the way brothers often are—always trying to outdo each other and win the favor of our dad, who, of course, was a competitive athlete himself. He'd set up races for us and say,

"Now let's see who's really the best." We were bigger than most of the other boys, but since I was a year younger, Meinhard usually won these head-to-head competitions.

I was always on the lookout for ways to gain the advantage. Meinhard's weak spot was fear of the dark. When he was ten, he finished elementary school in our village and graduated to the *Hauptschule*, which was over the ridge in Graz. To get there involved taking public transportation, and the bus stop was about a twenty-minute walk from our house. The problem for Meinhard was that school activities usually ran until well after sunset on the short winter days, so he had to make his way home after dark. He was too scared to do this alone, so it became my job to go to the bus stop and pick him up.

In fact I was scared too, going out in the dark alone at age nine. There were no streetlamps, and Thal was pitch black at night. The roads and paths were lined with pine forests like the ones in Grimm's fairy tales, so dense it was dark even in daytime. Of course we'd been raised on those horrible stories, which I would never read to my kids but which were part of the culture. There was always some witch or wolf or monster waiting to hurt the child. Having a policeman as a father also fed our fears. Sometimes he'd take us on foot patrol, and he'd announce he was looking for this or that criminal or killer. We'd come up to a hay barn standing by itself in a field, and he'd make us stand and wait while he pulled out his gun and checked inside. Or word would get around that he and his men had caught some thief, and we would run down to the station to look at the guy sitting there, handcuffed to a chair.

Reaching the bus stop was not a simple matter of following a road. The footpath wound past the castle ruins and downhill along the edge of the woods. One night I was walking on that path, keeping a close eye for threats in the trees, when suddenly, out of nowhere, a man was in front of me on the path. There was just enough moonlight to make out his shape and his two eyes shining. I screamed and stood frozen—it turned out to be just one of the local farmworkers headed the other way, but if it had been a goblin, it would have gotten me for sure.

I fought back my fear mainly because I had to prove that I was stronger. It was extremely important to show my parents "I am brave, he's not, even though he's a year and fourteen days older than me."

This determination paid off. For the trouble of picking up Meinhard, my father gave me five schillings a week. My mother took advantage of my fearlessness to send me to buy the vegetables each week at the farmers' market, which involved trekking through a different dark forest. This chore earned five schillings as well, money I happily spent on ice cream or my stamp collection.

The downside, however, was that my parents grew more protective of Meinhard and gave less attention to me. During the school holidays that summer of 1956, they sent me to work on my godmother's farm, but they kept my brother at home. I enjoyed the physical labor but felt left out when I got home and discovered they'd taken Meinhard on an excursion to Vienna without me.

Gradually our paths diverged. While I would be reading the newspaper's sports pages and memorizing athletes' names, Meinhard developed a passion for reading *Der Spiegel,* the German equivalent of *Time* magazine—in our family, that was a first. He made it his thing to learn the name and population of every world capital and the name and length of every significant river in the world. He memorized the periodic table and chemical formulas. He was a fanatic about facts and would challenge our father constantly to test what he knew.

At the same time, Meinhard developed an aversion to physical work. He didn't like to get his hands dirty. He started wearing white shirts to school every day. My mother went along with it but complained to me, "I thought I had my hands full washing your father's white shirts. Now *he* starts with *his* white shirts." Before long, it became the family prediction that Meinhard would be a white-collar worker, possibly an engineer, while I would be blue-collar, since I didn't mind getting my hands dirty at all. "Do you want to be a mechanic?" my parents would say. "How about a furniture maker?" Or they thought I might become a cop like my dad.

I had other ideas. Somehow the thought took shape in my mind that America was where I belonged. Nothing more concrete than that. Just . . . *America.* I'm not sure what triggered this. Maybe it was to escape the struggle of Thal and my father's iron rule, or maybe it was the excitement of going to Graz every day, where in autumn 1957, I followed Meinhard into the *Hauptschule* and started fifth grade. Compared to Thal, Graz was a giant metropolis, complete with cars and shops and sidewalks. There were no Americans there, but America was seeping into the culture. All the kids knew how to play cowboys and Indians. We saw pictures of American cities and suburbs and landmarks and highways in our textbooks and in grainy black-and-white documentaries shown on the clackety movie projector in our class.

More important, we knew that we needed America for safety. In Austria, the Cold War was immediate. Whenever there was a crisis, my father would have to pack his backpack and leave for the Hungarian border, fifty-five miles to the east, to help man the defenses. A year earlier in 1956, when the Soviets crushed the Hungarian revolution, he was in charge of taking care of the hundreds of people fleeing into our area. He set up the relocation camps and helped the refugees get where they wanted to go. Some wanted to go to Canada; some wanted to stay in Austria; and of course many wanted to go to America. He and his men worked with the families, and he had us kids come along and help feed them soup, which made a big impression on me.

Our education about the world continued at the NonStop Kino, a newsreel theater near the central square in Graz. It ran an hourlong show over and over all day. First would be a newsreel with footage from all around the world and a voice-over in German, then Mickey Mouse or some other cartoon, and then commercials consisting of slides of various stores in Graz. Finally, music would play, and the whole thing would start again. The NonStop wasn't expensive—just a few schillings—and each newsreel seemed to bring new wonders: Elvis Presley singing "Hound Dog." President Dwight Eisenhower making a speech. Clips of jet airliners and streamlined American cars and movie stars. Those are images I remember. There was also boring stuff, of course, and stuff that went right over my head, like the 1956 crisis over the Suez Canal.

American movies made an even deeper impression. The first one that Meinhard and I ever saw was a Tarzan film starring Johnny Weissmuller. I thought he was going to swing right out of the screen at us. The idea that a human could swing from tree to tree and talk to lions and chimpanzees was fascinating, and so was Tarzan's whole thing with Jane. I thought that was a good life. Meinhard and I went back to see it several times.

Two movie theaters we always went to faced each other across Graz's most popular shopping street. Mostly they showed Westerns but also comedies and dramas. The only problem was the strictly enforced rating system. A policeman assigned to the theater would check the ages of ticket holders going in. An Elvis movie, the equivalent of a modern PG-13, was pretty easy to get into, but all the movies I wanted to see—Westerns, gladiator movies, and war movies—were more like today's R-rated films and therefore were much harder to get into. Sometimes a friendly cashier would let me wait until the movie started and then signal with his head toward the aisle where the policeman was standing. Sometimes I'd wait by the side exit and walk into the auditorium backward.

I paid for my amusements with money I earned from my first entrepreneurial venture, selling ice cream at the Thalersee in summer 1957. The Thalersee was a public park, a beautiful lake nestled in the hills on the eastern end of Thal, about a five-minute walk from our house. The lake was easy to reach from Graz, and in summer thousands of people would come for the day to relax, to swim and row, or to play sports. By afternoon they'd be thirsty and hot, and when I saw people lining up at the ice-cream stand on the terrace, I knew this was a business opportunity. The park was big enough that, depending where your blanket was, going to the patio could mean a ten-minute hike, and your ice cream would be half melted by the time you got back. I discovered I could buy dozens of ice-cream cones for a schilling apiece and then walk around the lake and sell them for 3 schillings. The ice-cream proprietor welcomed the extra business and even loaned me a trunk to keep the cones cold. Selling ice cream, I could earn 150 schillings—almost $6—in an afternoon and get a nice tan walking around in my shorts.

Eventually my ice-cream earnings ran out, and being broke did not sit well with me. The solution I came up with that fall was panhandling. I would slip out of school and wander along Graz's main street, looking for a sympathetic face. It could be a middle-aged man or a student. Or maybe a farm lady who was in town for the day. I'd come up and say to her, "Excuse me, but I lost my money and my bus pass, and I need to go home." Sometimes she would chase me away, but most often she would say something like *"Du bist so dumm!"* or "How stupid can you be to do that?" That's when I knew I had her, because then she'd sigh and ask, "So, how much is it?"

"Five schillings."

And she'd say, "Okay. *Ja*."

I'd always ask the lady to write down her address so I could repay her. Usually she'd just tell me, "No, no, you don't have to send it back. Just be more careful next time," although sometimes she'd write it down. Of course, I had no intention of repaying. On my best days, I could beg 100 schillings—almost $4. That was enough to go to the toy store and go to the movies and really live it up!

The hole in my scheme was that a schoolkid alone on the street in the middle of a weekday was conspicuous. And a lot of people in Graz knew my father. Inevitably, somebody said to him, "I saw your son on the street in town today, asking a woman for money." This led to a huge uproar at home, with tremendous physical punishment, and that put an end to my panhandling career.

Those early excursions outside of Thal fired up my dreams. I became absolutely convinced that I was special and meant for bigger things. I knew I would be the best at something—although I didn't know what—

and that it would make me famous. America was the most powerful country, so I would go there.

It's not unusual for ten-year-old kids to have grand dreams. But the thought of going to America hit me like a revelation, and I really took it seriously. I'd talk about it. Waiting at the bus stop, I told a girl who was a couple of years older, "I'm going to go to America," and she just looked at me and said, "Yeah, sure, Arnold." The kids got used to hearing me talk about it and thought I was weird, but that didn't stop me from sharing my plans with everyone: my parents, my teachers, my neighbors.

The *Hauptschule,* or general school, was not geared to turn out the next world leader. It was designed to prepare children for the world of work. Boys and girls were segregated in separate wings of the building. Students got a foundation in math, science, geography, history, religion, modern language, art, music, and more, but these were taught at a slower pace than in academic schools, which prepared kids to go on to a university or technological institute. Completing *Hauptschule* generally meant graduating to a vocational school or an apprenticeship in a trade, or going straight into the workforce. Still, the teachers were very dedicated to making us smart and enriching our lives in every way they could. They would show movies, bring in opera singers, expose us to literature and art, and so on.

I was so curious about the world that school wasn't much of a problem. I learned the lessons, did the homework, and stayed right in the middle of the class. Reading and writing took discipline for me—they were more of a chore than they seemed to be for some of my classmates. On the other hand, math came easily; I never forgot a number and could do calculations in my head.

The discipline at school was no different from that at home. The teachers hit at least as hard as our parents. A kid was caught taking someone's pen, and the school priest hit him so hard with the catechism book that his ears were ringing for hours. The math teacher hit my friend in the back of the head so hard that his face bounced on the desk, and he broke two front teeth. Parent-teacher conferences were the opposite of today, where schools and parents go out of their way not to embarrass the kid. All thirty of us were required to sit at our desks, and the teacher would say, "Here's your homework. You work on it during the next couple of hours while your parents come through." One after the next, the parents would come in: the farm lady, the factory-worker dad. It was the same scene almost every time. They'd greet the teacher with great respect and sit while he showed them stuff on his desk and quietly discussed their child's performance. Then you'd hear the father say, "But sometimes he causes trouble?" And he'd turn, glare at his son, and then come over and smack the kid, hard, and go back to the teacher's desk. We'd all see it coming and be snickering like hell.

Then I'd hear my father coming up the stairs. I knew his footsteps, his police boots. He'd appear at the door in his uniform, and now the teacher would stand to show respect, because he was the inspector. They'd sit and talk, and it would be my turn: I'd see my father looking at me, and then he'd come over, grab me by the hair with his left hand, and *boom!* with his right. Then he would walk out without comment.

It was a tough time all around. Hardships were routine. Dentists did not use anesthesia, for instance. When you grow up in that kind of harsh environment, you never forget how to withstand physical punishment, even long after the hard times end.

When Meinhard got to be about fourteen and something at home didn't suit him, he would run away. He'd tell me, "I think I'm leaving again. But don't say anything." Then he would pack some clothes in his schoolbag so that nobody would catch on, and disappear.

My mother would go nuts. My father would have to phone all his buddies at the different gendarmerie stations in search of his son. It was an incredibly effective way to rebel if your father was the police chief.

After a day or two, Meinhard would turn up, usually at some relative's house or maybe just hiding out at a friend's place fifteen minutes away. I was always amazed that there were no consequences. Maybe my father was just trying to defuse the situation. He'd dealt with enough runaways in his police career to know that punishing Meinhard might compound the problem. But I'll bet it took every ounce of his self-control.

My desire was to leave home in an organized way. Because I was still just a kid, I decided that the best course for independence was to mind my own business and make my own money. I would do any kind of work. I was not shy at all about picking up a shovel and digging. During school vacation one summer, a guy from our village got me a job at a glass factory in Graz where he worked. My task was to shovel a big mound of broken glass into a wheeled container, cart it across the plant, and pour it into a vat for melting back down. At the end of each day, they gave me cash.

The following summer, I heard there might be work at a sawmill in Graz. I took my schoolbag and packed a little bread-and-butter snack to tide me over until I got home. Then I took the bus to the mill, got up my nerve, walked in, and asked for the owner.

They brought me to the office along with my satchel, and there was the owner, sitting in his chair.

"What do you want?" he asked.

"I'm looking for a job."

"How old are you?

"Fourteen."

And he said, "What do you want to do? You haven't learned anything yet!"

Still, he took me out into the yard and introduced me to some women and men at a machine for cutting scrap lumber into kindling. "You're going to work in this area here," he said.

I started right then and there and worked at the yard the rest of the holiday. One of my duties was to shovel great mountains of sawdust onto trucks that would take it away. I earned 1,400 schillings, or the equivalent of $55. That was a good amount in those days. What made me proudest was that even though I was a kid, they paid me a man's wage.

I knew exactly what to do with the money. All my life, I'd been wearing hand-me-downs from Meinhard; I'd never had new clothes of my own. I'd just started getting into sports—I was on the school soccer team—and as it happened, that year, the first tracksuits were coming into fashion: black long pants and black sweat jackets with zippers. I thought tracksuits looked wonderful, and I'd even tried showing my parents pictures in magazines of athletes wearing them. But they'd said no, it was a waste. So a tracksuit was the first thing I bought. Then with the cash I had left, I bought myself a bicycle. I didn't have enough money for a new one, but there was a man in Thal who assembled bikes from used parts, and I could afford one from him. Nobody else in our house owned a bike; my father had bartered his for food after the war and never replaced it. Even though my bike wasn't perfect, having those wheels meant freedom.

CHAPTER 2

Building a Body

WHAT I REMEMBER MOST about my last year of *Hauptschule* was the duck-and-cover drills. In the event of nuclear war, sirens would sound. We were supposed to close our books and hide under our desks with our heads between our knees and our eyes squeezed shut. Even a kid could figure out how pathetic that was.

That June of 1961, we'd all been glued to the TV watching the Vienna summit between the new US president, John F. Kennedy, and Soviet premier Nikita Khrushchev. Very few families had a television at home, but we all knew an electrical shop in the Lendplatz in Graz that had two TVs in the window. We ran down and stood on the sidewalk watching news reports on the meetings. Kennedy hadn't even been in office six months, and most experts thought that it was a big mistake to go up so soon against Khrushchev, who was blunt and articulate and wily as hell. We kids had no opinion about that, and since the TV was inside, we couldn't hear the sound anyway. But we watched! We were part of the action.

We were living in a frightening situation. Every time Russia and America argued about anything, we felt we were doomed. We thought that Khrushchev would do something terrible to Austria because we were right in the middle; that's why they had the summit in Vienna in the first place. The meeting didn't go well. At one point, after making a hostile demand, Khrushchev said, "It's up to the US to decide whether there will be war or peace," and Kennedy answered ominously, "Then, Mr. Chairman, there will be a war. It will be a cold, long winter." When Khrushchev put up the wall in Berlin that fall, you heard adults telling one another, "This is it." The gendarmerie was then the closest thing Austria had to an army, and my father had to go to the border with his military uniform and all his gear. He was away a week until the crisis cooled down.

In the meantime, we had lots of tension, lots of drills. My class of thirty or so adolescent boys was full of testosterone, but nobody wanted a war. Our interest was more in girls. They were a mystery, especially for kids like me who did not have sisters, and the only time we got to see them at school was in the courtyard before class because they were taught in their own wing of the building. These were the same girls we'd grown up with all our lives, but suddenly they seemed like aliens. How do you talk to them? We'd just reached the point where we were feeling sexual attraction, but it came out in odd ways—like the morning we ambushed them with snowballs in the yard before school.

Our first class of the day was math. Instead of opening the textbook, the teacher said, "I saw you guys out there. We better talk about this."

We worried we were in for it—this was the same guy who had broken my friend's front teeth. But today he was on a nonviolent track. "You guys want those girls to like you, right?" A few of us nodded our heads. "It is natural that you want that because we love the opposite sex. Eventually you want to kiss them, you want to hug them, and you want to make love to them. Isn't that what everyone wants to do here?"

More people nodded. "So don't tell me it makes sense to throw a snowball into a girl's face! Is that the way you express your love? Is that the way you say 'I really like you'? Where did you figure that out?"

Now he really had our attention. "Because when *I* think about the first move I made with girls," he continued, "I gave them compliments and kissed them, and I held them and made them feel good, that's what I did."

A lot of our fathers had never had this conversation with us. We realized that if you wanted a girl, you had to make an effort to have a conversation, not just drool like a horny dog. You had to establish a comfort level. I'd been one of the guys throwing snowballs. And I took these tips and carefully stored them away.

During the very last week of class, I had a revelation about my future. It came to me during an essay-writing assignment, of all things. The history teacher always liked to pick four or five kids and pass out pages of the newspaper and make us write reports discussing whatever article or photo interested us. This time, as it happened, I was picked, and he handed me the sports page. On it was a photo of Mr. Austria, Kurt Marnul, setting a record in the bench press: 190 kilograms.

I felt inspired by the guy's achievement. But what really struck me was that he was wearing glasses. They were distinctive; a little tinted. I associated glasses with intellectuals: teachers and priests. Yet here was Kurt Marnul lying on the bench with his tank-top shirt and tiny waist, an enormous chest, and this huge weight above his chest—and he had on glasses. I kept staring at the picture. How could someone who looked like a professor from the neck up be bench-pressing 190 kilos? That's what I wrote in my essay. I read it out loud and was pleased when I got a good laugh. But I came away fascinated that a man could be both smart and powerful.

Along with my new interest in girls, I was more conscious of my body. I was beginning to pay close attention to sports: looking at athletes, how they worked out, how they used their bodies. A year before, it meant nothing; now it meant everything.

As soon as school ended, my friends and I all made a beeline for the Thalersee. That was our big summer hangout; we'd swim and have mud fights and kick soccer balls around. I quickly started making friends among the boxers, wrestlers, and other athletes. The previous summer, I'd gotten to know one of the lifeguards, Willi Richter, who was in his twenties. He let me be his sidekick and help with his work. Willi was a good all-around athlete. When he wasn't on duty, I'd tag along as he worked out. He had this whole routine of using the park as his gym, doing chin-ups on the trees, push-ups and squats in the dirt, running up the trails, and doing standing jumps. Once in a while he'd hit a bicep pose for me, and it would look great.

Willi was friends with a pair of brothers who were really well developed. One was in university and one was a little younger. They were lifters, bodybuilders, and the day I met them, they were practicing shot put. They asked if I wanted to try, and started teaching me the turns and steps. Then we went up to that tree where Willi was doing chin-ups again. All of a sudden he said, "Why don't you try?" I barely could hold on because the branch was thick and you had to have really strong fingers. I managed one or two reps, and then I slipped off. Willi said, "You know, if you practice this the whole summer, I guarantee you will be able to do ten, which would be quite an accomplishment. And I bet your lats would grow a centimeter on each side." By *lats,* he meant the back muscles just below the shoulder blades, the latissimi dorsi.

I thought, "Wow, that's interesting, just from that one exercise." And then we followed him up the hill through the rest of his routine. From then on, I did the exercises with him every day.

The summer before, Willi had taken me to the World Weight Lifting Championship in Vienna. We rode up in a car with a bunch of guys, a four-hour drive. The trip took longer than we thought, so we only we got there for the last event, which was the super-heavyweight lifters. The winner was an enormous Russian named Yuri Vlasov. There were thousands of people in the auditorium yelling and screaming after he pressed 190.5 kilos, or 420 pounds, over his head. The weight lifting was followed by a bodybuilding contest, Mr. World, and this was my first time seeing guys oiled up and pumped and posing, showing off their physiques. Afterward we got to go backstage and see Vlasov in person. I don't know how we got in—maybe someone had a connection through the weight lifting club in Graz.

It was an adventure, and I had a great time, but at age thirteen, I didn't think any of it had to do with me. A year later, though, everything was starting to register, and I realized I wanted to be strong and muscular. I'd just seen the movie *Hercules and the Captive Women*, which I'd loved. I was so impressed with the star's body. "You know who that actor is, don't you?" Willi said. "That's Mr. Universe, Reg Park." I told Willi about my essay in school. It turned out that he had actually been present when Kurt Marnul set the record in the bench press. "He's a friend of mine," Willi said.

A couple of days later, Willi announced, "Tonight Kurt Marnul is coming to the lake. You know, the guy that you saw in the picture?"

"Great!" I said. So I waited around with one of my classmates. We were swimming and having our usual mud fights when finally Marnul showed up with a beautiful girl.

He wore a tight T-shirt and dark slacks and those same tinted glasses. After changing clothes in the lifeguard's shack, he came out in this tiny bathing suit. We were all flipping out. How unbelievable he looked! He was known for having gigantic deltoid and trapezius muscles, and sure enough, his shoulders were huge. And he had the small waist, the ridged abdominal muscles—the whole look.

Then the girl who was with him put on her bathing suit—a bikini—and she also looked stunning. We said hello and then just kind of hovered, watching while they swam.

Now I was definitely inspired. Marnul came to the lake all the time, it turned out, often with the most fantastic girls. He was nice to me and my friend Karl Gerstl because he knew he was our idol. Karl was a blond kid about my size and a couple of years older whom I'd introduced myself to one day after noticing that he had built up some muscle. "Do you work out?" I asked.

"Yeah, yeah," he said. "I started with chin-ups and a hundred sit-ups a day, but I don't know what else to do." So I'd invited him to work out every day with Willi and me. Marnul would give us exercises.

Soon a few more men joined: friends of Willi's and guys from the gym where Kurt worked out, all of them older than me. The oldest was a heavyset guy in his forties named Mui. He had been a professional wrestler in his heyday; now he just worked out with weights. Like Marnul, Mui was a bachelor. He lived on a government stipend and was a professional student at the university; a cool guy, very political and smart, who spoke fluent English. He played an essential role in our group because he translated the English and American muscle magazines as well as *Playboy*.

We always had girls around—girls who wanted to work out with us or just fool around. Europe was always far less puritanical than the United States. Dealing with the body was much more open—less hiding, less weirdness. It wasn't unusual to see nude sunbathers in private areas of the lake. My friends would vacation at nudist colonies in Yugoslavia and France. It made them feel free. And with its hillsides, bushes, and trails, the Thalersee was a perfect playground for lovers. When I was ten or eleven, selling ice cream around the lake, I didn't quite get why everyone was lying around on big blankets in the bushes, but by now I'd figured it out. Our group fantasy that summer was that we were living like gladiators. We were rolling back time, drinking pure water and red wine, eating meat, having women, running through the forest working out, and doing sports. Each week we'd build a big fire by the lake and make shish kebabs with tomatoes and onions and meat. We'd lie under the stars and turn the skewers in the flames until the food was just perfect.

The man who bought the meat for these feasts was Karl's father, Fredi Gerstl. He was the only real brain in the bunch, a solidly built guy with thick glasses who seemed more like a friend than a dad. Fredi was a politician, and he and his wife ran the two biggest tobacco and magazine kiosks in Graz. He was head of the tobacco sellers' association, but his main interest was helping young people. On Sundays he and his wife would put their boxer on a leash and walk around the lake, with Karl and me tagging along. You never knew what Fredi was going to come up with next. One minute he'd be talking about Cold War politics, and the next minute he'd tease us about not knowing anything yet about girls. He had been trained in opera, and sometimes he'd stand at the edge of the water and belt out an aria. The dog would howl in accompaniment, and Karl and I would get embarrassed and walk farther and farther behind him.

Fredi was the source of the gladiator idea. "What do you guys know about strength training?" he asked us one day. "Why don't you copy the Roman gladiators? *They* knew how to train!" Although he was pushing Karl to go to medical school, he was thrilled that his son had started working out. The idea of balancing the body and the mind was like a religion for him. "You have to build the ultimate physical machine but also the ultimate mind," he would say. "Read Plato! The Greeks started the Olympics, but they also gave us the great philosophers, and you've got to take care of both." He would tell us stories of the Greek gods, and about the beauty of the body and beauty in the ideal. "I know some of this is going in one ear and out the other," he'd say. "But I'm going to push you guys, and someday the penny will drop, and you will realize how important it is."

Right at that moment, though, we were more focused on what we could learn from Kurt Marnul. Kurt was totally charming and hip. He was perfect for us because he was Mr. Austria. He had the body and the girls and held the record in the bench press, and he drove an Alfa Romeo convertible. As I got to know him, I studied his whole routine. His day job was as the foreman of a road construction crew. He started work early in the morning and finished at three. Then he would put in three hours at the gym, training hard. He'd let us visit him so we would get the idea: you work, you make the money, and then you can afford this car; you train and then you win championships. There was no shortcut; you earned it.

Marnul was into beautiful girls. He knew how to find them anywhere: at restaurants, at the lake, at sports fields. Sometimes he'd invite them to stop by the job site where he'd be in his tank top, bossing the workers, directing equipment around. Then he'd come over and schmooze. The Thalersee was a key part of his routine. A typical guy would simply ask a girl out for a drink after work, but not Kurt. He'd drive her in his Alfa to the lake for a swim. Then they'd have dinner at the restaurant, and he'd get the red wine going. He always had a blanket and another bottle of wine in the car. They'd go back to the lake and pick some romantic spot. He'd put down the blanket and open the wine and sweet-talk the girl. The guy was smooth. Seeing him in action sped up the process in me that the math teacher had begun. I memorized Kurt's lines, and his moves, including the blanket and wine. We all did. And the girls responded!

Kurt and the others saw potential in me because in a short period of training, I grew and gained a lot of strength. At the end of the summer, they invited me to come work out in Graz where they had weights. The Athletic Union gym was down under the stands of the public soccer stadium; a big concrete room with overhead lights and the most basic equipment, barbells and dumbbells and chin-up bars and benches. It was full of big men puffing and heaving. The guys from the lake showed me how to do some basic lifts, and for the next three hours, I happily worked in, doing dozens upon dozens of presses and squats and curls.

A normal beginner's workout would be three sets of ten reps of each exercise, so your muscles just get a taste. But nobody told me that. The regulars at the stadium gym liked to trick the new guys. They egged me on so that I did *ten* sets of each exercise. After I finished, I joyfully took a shower—we didn't have running water at home, so I always looked forward to a shower at the soccer stadium, even though the water was unheated. Then I put on my clothes and walked outside.

My legs were feeling a little rubbery and sluggish, but I didn't think much about it. Then I got on my bike and fell off. This was strange, and I noticed now my arms and legs didn't feel connected to me. I got back on the bike, and I couldn't control the handlebars, and my thighs were shaking like they were made of porridge. I veered off to the side and fell into a ditch. It was pitiful. I gave up on riding the bike. I ended up having to walk it home, an epic four-mile hike. Still, I couldn't wait to get back to the gym and try weight training again.

That summer had a miraculous effect on me. Instead of existing, I started to live. I was catapulted out of the dull routine of Thal—where you get up, you get the milk from next door, come home and do your push-ups and sit-ups while your mother makes the breakfast and your father gets ready for work—the routine where there was really nothing much to look forward to. Now all of a sudden there was joy, there was struggle, there was pain, there was happiness, there were pleasures, there were women, there was drama. Everything made it feel like "now we are really living! This is really terrific!" Even though I appreciated the example of my father with the discipline and the things that he accomplished professionally, in sports, with the music, the very fact that he was my father took away from its significance for me. All of a sudden, I had a whole new life, and it was *mine*.

In the fall of 1962, at the age of fifteen, I began a new chapter in my life. I entered the vocational school in Graz and started my apprenticeship. Although I was still living at home, the gym in many ways replaced my family. The older guys helped the younger ones. They'd come over if you did something wrong or to correct your form. Karl Gerstl became one of my training partners, and we learned the joy of inspiring each other, pumping each other up, competing in a positive way. "I'm going to do ten reps of this weight, I guarantee you," Karl would say. Then he'd do eleven, just to stick it to me, and declare, "That was really great!" I'd just look at him and say, "Let me go for twelve now."

A lot of our ideas for training came from magazines. There were muscle-building and weight-lifting publications in German, but the US ones were by far the best, with our friend Mui providing the translations. The magazines were our bible for training, for nutrition, for different ways to make protein drinks to build muscles, for working with a training partner. The magazines had a way of promoting bodybuilding as a golden dream. Every issue had pictures of champions and details about their training routines. You'd see these guys smiling and flexing and showing off their bodies on Muscle Beach in Venice, California, of course surrounded by stunning girls in sexy bathing suits. We all knew the name of the publisher, Joe Weider, who was sort of the Hugh Hefner of the muscle world: he owned the magazines, had his picture and column in every issue, and included his wife, Betty, a gorgeous model, in almost every beach shot.

Soon life at the gym totally consumed me. Training was all I could think about. One Sunday when I found the stadium locked, I broke in and worked out in the freezing cold. I had to wrap my hands in towels to keep them from sticking to the metal bars. Week by week I would see the gains I was making in how much I could lift, the number of reps my muscles would tolerate, the shape of my body and its overall mass and weight. I became a regular member of the Athletic Union team. I was so proud that I, little Arnold Schwarzenegger, was in a club with Mr. Austria, the great Kurt Marnul.

I'd tried a lot of other sports, but the way my body responded to weight training made it instantly clear that this was where I had the greatest potential and I could go all out. I couldn't articulate what drove me. But training seemed something I was born for, and I sensed that it would become my ticket out of Thal. "Kurt Marnul can win Mr. Austria," I thought, "and he's already told me that I could too if I train hard, so that's what I'm going to do." This thought made the hours of lifting tons of steel and iron actually a joy. Every painful set, every extra rep, was a step toward my goal of winning Mr. Austria and entering the Mr. Europe competition. Then in November I picked up the latest issue of *Muscle Builder* at the department store in Graz. On the cover was Mr. Universe, Reg Park. He was wearing a loincloth, dressed as Hercules, and I realized with a start that *this* was the guy who'd starred in the movie I'd loved that summer. Inside were pictures of Reg posing, working out, winning as Mr. Universe for the second year in a row, shaking hands with Joe Weider, and chatting on Muscle Beach with the legendary Steve Reeves, an earlier Mr. Universe who had also starred in Hercules films.

I could barely wait to track down Mui and find out what the article said. It gave Reg's whole life story, from growing up poor in Leeds,

England, to becoming Mr. Universe, getting invited to America as a champion bodybuilder, getting sent to Rome to star as Hercules, and marrying a beauty from South Africa, where he now lived when he wasn't training on Muscle Beach.

This story crystallized a new vision for me. I could become another Reg Park. All my dreams suddenly came together and made sense. I'd found the way to get to America: bodybuilding! And I'd found a way to get into movies. They would be the thing that everyone in the world would know me for. Movies would bring money—I was sure that Reg Park was a millionaire—and the best-looking girls, which was a very important aspect.

In weeks that followed, I refined this vision until it was very specific. I was going to go for the Mr. Universe title; I was going to break records in power lifting; I was going to Hollywood; I was going to be like Reg Park. The vision became so clear in my mind that I felt like it had to happen. There was no alternative; it was this or nothing. My mother noticed right away that something was different. I was coming home with a big smile. I told her that I was training, and she could see I found joy in becoming stronger.

But as the months went by, she started to get concerned about my obsession. By spring, I'd hung up muscleman pictures all over the wall over my bed. There were boxers, professional wrestlers, weight lifters, and power lifters. Most of all, there were bodybuilders posing, especially Reg Park and Steve Reeves. I was proud of my wall. This was in the era before copying machines, and so I'd collected the images I wanted from magazines and then taken them to a shop to be photographed and reproduced as eight-by-tens. I'd bought soft felt-like matting, had it cut professionally, and glued the eight-by-tens on the mats and placed them on my wall. It looked really good, the way I had it all laid out. But it really worried my mom.

Finally one day she decided to seek professional advice and flagged down the doctor when he drove up the road on his usual rounds. "I want you to see this," she said and brought him upstairs to my room.

I was in the living room doing my homework but I could still hear most of the conversation. "Doctor," my mother was saying, "all the other boys, Arnold's friends, when I go to their homes, they have girls hanging on their walls. Posters, magazines, colored pictures of girls. And look at him. Naked men."

"Frau Schwarzenegger," said the doctor, "there is nothing wrong. Boys always need inspiration. They will look to their father, and many times this is not enough because he's the father, so they will look also to other men. This is actually good; nothing for you to worry about." He left, and my mother wiped tears from her eyes and pretended that nothing had happened. After that she would say to her friends, "My son has pictures of strongmen and athletes, and he gets so fired up when he looks at them, he trains every day now. Arnold, tell them how much weight you are lifting." Of course I'd started to have success with girls, but I couldn't share that with my mother.

That spring she discovered how much things had changed. I'd just met a girl who was two years older than me who was an outdoorsy type. "I like camping, too!" I said. "There's a really nice area on our neighbor's farm, right below our house. Why don't you bring your tent?" She came the next afternoon, and we had fun putting up this beautiful little tent. Some of the little kids from the neighborhood helped us pound in the stakes. It was just the right size for two people, and it had a zipper flap. After the kids went away, the girl and I went inside and started making out. She had her top off when suddenly I heard the sound of the zipper and turned just in time to see my mother's head stick into the tent. She made a big scene, called the girl a tramp and a whore, and stormed back up the hill to our house. The poor girl was mortified; I helped her pull down the tent, and she ran off.

Back at the house, my mother and I had a fight. "What is this?!" I yelled. "One minute you're telling the doctor that I have those pictures, and now you're worried about me having a girl. I don't get it. That's what guys do."

"No, no, no. Not around my house."

She was having to adjust to this whole new son. But I was really mad. I just wanted to live my life! That Saturday, I went into town and made up with the girl—her parents were away.

Apprenticeship was a big part of the training at the vocational school where I started in autumn 1962. Mornings we had class, and afternoons we would fan out across Graz to our jobs. This was lots better than sitting in a classroom all day. My parents knew I was good at math and enjoyed juggling figures in my head, and they had arranged for me to be in a business and commerce program rather than plumbing or carpentry or some other trade.

My apprenticeship was at Mayer-Stechbarth, a small building supply store in the Neubaustrasse with four employees. It was owned by Herr Dr. Matscher, a retired lawyer who always wore a suit to work. He ran the store with his wife, Christine. In the beginning, I was assigned mostly physical labor, from stacking wood to shoveling the sidewalk. I actually liked doing deliveries: carrying heavy sheets of composite board up customers' stairs was another form of strength training. Before long, I was asked to help take inventory, and that got me interested in how the store was run. I was taught how to write up orders and used what I'd learned in bookkeeping class to help with accounts.

The most important skill I acquired was selling. A cardinal rule was never to let a customer walk out the door without a purchase. If you did, it just showed what a poor salesman you were. Even if it was just one little bolt, you had to make a sale. That meant working every possible angle. If I couldn't sell the linoleum tiles, I'd push the floor cleaner.

I became buddies with the second apprentice, Franz Janz, based on our mutual fascination with America. We talked about it endlessly and even tried translating *Schwarzenegger* into English—we came up with "black corner," although "black plowman" would be closer. I brought Franz to the gym and tried to interest him in training, but it didn't take. He was more into playing guitar; in fact, he was a member of the Mods, Graz's first rock band.

But Franz understood how obsessed I was with training. One day he spotted a set of barbells somebody was getting rid of. He dragged them home on a sled and persuaded his father to sand off the rust and paint them. Then they brought them to my house. I converted an unheated area near the stairs into my home gym. From then on, I was able to step up my routine and train at home any day I didn't work out at the stadium.

At Mayer-Stechbarth, I was known as the apprentice who wanted to go to America. The Matschers were very patient with us. They taught us how to get along with customers and one another, and how to set goals for ourselves. Frau Matscher was determined to correct what she saw as gaps in our education. For instance, she thought we hadn't been exposed to enough elevated conversation and wanted to make us more worldly. She'd sit us down for long stretches and discuss art, religion, current affairs. To reward our efforts, she'd treat us to bread and marmalade.

Around the same time that Frau Matscher began feeding me culture, I got my first taste of athletic success. A beer hall might seem like a strange place to start a career in sports, but that's where mine began. It was March 1963 in Graz, and I was fifteen and a half, making my first public appearance in the uniform of the Athletic Union team: black training shoes, brown socks, and a dark unitard with narrow straps, decorated on the front with the club insignia. We were facing off against weight lifters from a rival club, and the match was part of the entertainment for a crowd of three hundred to four hundred people—all sitting at long tables, smoking and clinking their steins.

This was my first time performing in public, so I was excited and nervous when I walked out onstage. I put chalk on my hands to keep the weights from slipping, and right away did a two-arm press of 150 pounds, my normal weight. The crowd gave a big cheer. The applause had an effect like I'd never imagined. I could barely wait for my next turn in the rotation. This time, to my amazement, I lifted 185 pounds—35 pounds more than I ever had before. Some people perform better in front of an audience, some worse. A guy from the other team who was a better lifter than me found the audience distracting and failed to complete his last lift. He told me afterward that he couldn't concentrate as well as in the gym. For me, it was the opposite. The audience gave me strength and motivation, and my ego kicked in more. I discovered that I performed much, much better in front of others.

CHAPTER 3

Confessions of a Tank Driver

THE MILITARY BASE NEAR Graz was headquarters of one of the tank divisions of the Austrian army. I learned this because all young men in Austria were required to serve, and I was looking for a way to fit the army into my life goals. I realized that the logical thing for the army to do with somebody my size would be to put me in the infantry and have me carry machine guns and ammunition up mountains. But the infantry was based in Salzburg, and this was not consistent with my plan. I wanted to stay in Graz and continue with my training. My mission was to become the world champion in bodybuilding, not to fight wars. That wasn't really the mission of the Austrian army either. We had a military because we were allowed to have one. It was an expression of sovereignty. But it was a small military, and no one had any thought of engaging in real combat.

I was looking forward to joining the military and being away from home for the first time. I had just finished my education, and the sooner I completed my service, the sooner I could get a passport.

Being a tank driver sounded really good. Several friends who had joined the army were stationed in Graz, and I'd asked a thousand questions about jobs on the base. There were many positions for new recruits, including being in the administrative office or the kitchen, where you never touched a tank. My friends were in the armored infantry, which are troops trained to support tanks by riding on top of them into battle, jumping off, searching for antitank mines, and so on.

But it was the tanks themselves that fascinated me. I love big things, and the American-built M47 Patton, named after the World War II general, certainly fit that. It was twelve feet wide, weighed fifty tons, and had an 800-horsepower engine. It was so powerful that it could push through a brick wall and you'd hardly realize it if you were inside. It amazed me that someone would actually trust an eighteen-year-old with something this big and expensive. The other big attraction was that to qualify as a tank driver, you first had to be licensed in driving a motorcycle, a car, a truck, and a tractor-trailer. The army would supply the training for all that, which would have cost thousands and thousands of schillings in the civilian world. There were only nine hundred tanks in the whole Austrian army, and I wanted to stand out.

My father, who still had dreams of me becoming a policeman or military officer, was happy to put in a word with the base commander, a buddy of his from the war. He was a huge sports fan and was pleased to bring me into the fold. Once I'd completed basic training, he'd see to it that I could set up weight-lifting equipment on the base.

Everything would have worked out perfectly except for one miscalculation. I'd started winning trophies in weight lifting by now. I was the regional junior weight-lifting champ, and just that summer I'd won the Austrian power-lifting championship's heavyweight division, beating much more experienced men. Even though you could tell at a glance that I was still just an oversize kid, I was starting to compete successfully in bodybuilding too. I won a regional championship and actually placed third in the competition for Mr. Austria—good enough to share the stage with Kurt Marnul, who was still the king. Just before enlisting, I'd signed up for my first international competition, the junior version of Mr. Europe—a crucial next step in my plan. I hadn't realized that for the whole six weeks of basic training, there was no leaving Graz.

I didn't mind basic training. It taught me that something that seems impossible at the start can be achieved. Did we ever believe that we could climb a cliff in full field gear? No. But when we were ordered to do it, we did. And along the way, we even stuffed our pockets with mushrooms, which we turned over to the cook that night to make soup.

Still, I couldn't stop thinking about how much I wanted to compete for Junior Mr. Europe. I stole every minute I could to hit my practice poses in the latrine. I begged the drill sergeant to treat this like he would a family emergency and to let me go to Stuttgart, Germany, to compete. No chance. The night before the event, I finally decided fuck it and walked out of the gate.

A seven-hour train ride later, I was in Stuttgart, hitting my poses in front of a few hundred fans and soaking up the cheers. I won the title 1965 Best Built Junior Athlete of Europe. It was the first time I'd ever been outside Austria and the biggest audience I'd ever had. I felt like King Kong.

Unfortunately, I was punished when I returned to training camp. I was put into detention and made to sit by myself in a cell for twenty-four hours. Then my superiors got word of my victory, and I was freed. I kept my head down for the rest of basic training, and soon I was able to report to the tank unit my father's friend commanded. From then on, the army became a fantastic joyride. I set up a weight room in the barracks, where I was allowed to train four hours a day. Some of the officers and men also began training too. For the first time in my life, I could eat meat every day—real protein. I grew so fast that every three months I outgrew my uniform and had to be issued the next larger size.

Motorcycle training started right away, followed by cars the next month. We learned basic mechanics, because you always had to be able to fix your vehicle if something simple went wrong. Next was how to drive trucks, which turned out to be difficult because the military trucks had manual, unsynchronized transmissions. To shift up or down, you had to go into neutral *and* double clutch *and* rev the engine to the proper speed so that it could mesh with the next gear. This led to much gear grinding and big drama, because after only a little practice on the base, they took us out in real traffic. Until shifting became second nature, it was very hard to keep your eye on the road. I'd be distracted by the shift lever, and all of a sudden I'd see cars stopped in front of me and have to brake and downshift and do the thing with the clutch—all with the instructor yelling at me. By the time we came back to the base, I was always soaked with sweat; it was a great way to lose body fat.

The next stage, learning tractor-trailers, was hairy too, especially backing up using mirrors and opposite-direction steering. This took me a while to master and some crashing and banging into things. It really felt good when I finally graduated to tanks.

The M47 is built to be driven with one hand, using a joystick that controls the gears and the motion of the treads. You sit in the left front corner of the hull and have a brake and gas pedal for your feet. The metal seat can be raised and lowered; normally you drive with the hatch propped open and your head sticking out of the tank to see. But when you button up for battle, you drop the seat, close the hatch, and peer through a periscope. At night, there was a primitive form of infrared that let you just make out trees and bushes and other tanks. I could fit in the seat despite my size, but driving with the hatch shut could be very claustrophobic. I felt really proud to be learning this massive machine, something totally different than I had ever dealt with.

The nearest maneuver ground was a big tract of land along the ridge between Thal and Graz. To reach it, we had to leave the base and drive an hour and a half up a winding, gravel back road—a company of twenty tanks rumbling and clanking past houses and hamlets. Usually we drove at night, when civilian traffic was at a minimum.

I took pride in my driving ability, which meant being able to maneuver with accuracy and drive smoothly through holes and ditches so that my tank commander and crewmates didn't get banged around. At the same time, I was somewhat catastrophe-prone.

When we camped in the field, we had a regular routine. First, we'd work out: I had my weight plates and bars and exercise bench all stowed in compartments on top of the tank, where tools were usually kept. Three, four, or five other guys from the platoon would join me, and we'd exercise for an hour and a half before getting something to eat. Some nights the drivers had to stay with their tanks while the other guys went to the sleeping tent. We'd bed down by digging a shallow hole, putting down a blanket, and parking the tank overhead. The idea was to protect ourselves from wild boars. We were not allowed to kill them, and they roamed freely in the training area because I think they knew that. We also posted sentries who would stand on top of the tanks so the boars couldn't get at them.

One night we were camped near a stream, and I woke up with a start because I thought I heard the boars. Then I realized there was nothing on top of me. My tank was gone! I looked around and found it twenty or thirty feet away, sticking tail-up in the water. The nose was submerged, and the cannon was stuck down into the mud. I'd forgotten to apply the big brake, it turned out, and the ground was sloped just enough that the tank had slowly rolled away as we slept. I tried to get it out, but the treads just spun in the mud.

We had to bring in an eighty-ton towing unit, and it took hours to pull out my tank. Then we had to get it to the repair depot. The turret had to be taken off. The cannon had to be sent out to be specially cleaned. I had to sit in confinement for twenty-four hours for that one.

I could be a risk even in the tank garage. One morning I started my tank, adjusted my seat, and turned to check the gauges before pulling out. The readings were fine, but I felt the tank shaking a little, like the engine was running rough. I thought, "Maybe you should give it a little gas to smooth it out." So I gave it gas, keeping an eye on the gauges, but the shaking only got worse. This was very odd. Then I noticed that dust was coming down. I looked up out of the hatch and realized that instead of just revving the engine, I'd set the tank in motion and was pushing it through the garage wall. That's what was causing the shaking. Then a pipe burst, and water was spurting everywhere, and there was the smell of gas.

People were screaming "Stop! Stop!" so I shut off the tank. I got out and raced down the length of the garage to find the commanding officer, who knew my father. I figured he was my best hope. I'd seen him just that morning, and he'd said things like, "I ran into your dad the other day and told him how great you're doing."

I knocked on his door and said, "Sir, I think that I caused a little bit of a problem."

He was still in a great mood. "Oh, don't worry about it! What is it, Arnold?"

"Well, check it out; you've got to see."

And he said, "Come on." He patted me on the back as we walked outside, still in the spirit of the morning, as if to say, "You're doing well."

Then he saw the water spurting and guys milling around and the tank jutting through the wall.

He changed personality instantly: screaming, calling me every name he could think of, saying that he was going to call my father and tell him the opposite of what he'd said before. The veins on his neck were bulging. Then he went cold and snapped, "When I get back from lunch, I want everything to be fixed. That's the only way to redeem yourself. Get the troops together and *do it*."

The nice thing about the military is that it's self-sufficient. The division had its own bricklayers and plumbers and building supplies. Luckily, the roof hadn't fallen down or anything major, and my tank, of course, was made of steel, so it was fine. Guys thought my accident was so funny that they jumped right in to help, so I didn't have to organize much. By afternoon, we had the pipes fixed and the wall repaired and just had to wait for it to dry so we could put on the stucco outside. I was feeling good because I'd had a chance to learn about mixing cement and laying cinderblock. Of course I had to put up with the whole base teasing me, "Oh, I heard about your tank." And I had to spend a whole week on KP duty, peeling potatoes with all the other screwups right where everybody could see us when they came to get their food.

By spring 1966, I was starting to think the army wasn't necessarily practical for me. My victory in Stuttgart the previous fall had attracted a lot of attention. Albert Busek, one of the organizers of the competition and the editor of *Sportrevue* magazine, wrote a commentary predicting that bodybuilding was about to enter the Schwarzenegger era. I got several offers to become a professional trainer, including one from Busek's publisher, Rolf Putziger, who was Germany's biggest bodybuilding promoter. He offered me a job managing his gym in Munich, Germany, the Universum Sport Studio. It was extremely tempting: there would be a wonderful opportunity for training, and I'd have a better chance to become known. In Austria, bodybuilding was still a sideshow to weight lifting, but in Germany, it was more established in its own right.

In the bodybuilding world, word had continued to spread about my victory in Stuttgart. I'd been on the cover of several magazines because I made a good story: this Austrian kid who had come out of nowhere and was eighteen years old with nineteen-inch biceps.

I decided that it made sense to request an early discharge from the army. Along with the request, I submitted a copy of Putziger's job offer and some of the magazine stories about me. My commanding officers knew my ambition to become a bodybuilding champion, and I thought this would be a great step for me. But I wasn't holding my breath. While the minimum term of enlistment in the Austrian army was only nine months, tank drivers were required to serve three years because of the cost of their training. I'd heard of drivers getting discharged early because of family illness or because they were needed back on the farm, but I'd never heard of anybody getting discharged to pursue a dream.

It wasn't that I disliked the army. In fact, it was one of the best things that had ever happened to me. Being a soldier had done a lot for my self-confidence. Once I was living independently from my family, I found out I could depend on myself. I learned to make comrades of strangers and be a comrade in return. The structure and discipline seemed more natural than at home. If I carried out orders, I felt I'd accomplished something.

I'd learned a thousand little things in the course of nine months: from washing and mending shirts to frying eggs on the exhaust shield of a tank. I'd slept in the open, guarded barracks for nights on end, and found out that nights without sleep don't mean that you can't perform at a high level the next day and that days without food don't mean you'll starve. These were things I'd never even thought about before.

I aimed to be a leader someday, but I knew it was important to learn obedience as well. As Winston Churchill said, the Germans were the best at being at your throat or at your feet, and that same psychology prevailed in the Austrian army. If you let your ego show through, they'd put you in your place. Age eighteen or nineteen is when the mind is ready to absorb this lesson; if you wait till thirty, it's too late. The more the army confronted us with hardship, the more I felt like "Okay, it's not going to worry me; bring it on." Above all, I was proud to be trusted at age eighteen with a fifty-ton machine, even if I didn't always handle the responsibility as well as I might have.

My request for an early discharge sat around for months. Before it was acted on, there was one more blot on my military record. In the late spring, we were on a twelve-hour nighttime exercise from six o'clock at night till six in the morning. By two o'clock, the company had maneuvered into positions at the top of a ridge, and the order came down: "Okay, break for food. Tank commanders report for a briefing."

I was on the radio joking with a friend who'd just been given a newer version of the Patton tank, the M60, which was powered by diesel. He made the mistake of bragging that his tank was faster than mine. Finally I challenged him to prove it, and we both took off down the ridge. I would have stopped—a voice of reason in my head told me to—but I was winning. The rest of the guys in my tank were going nuts. I heard someone shouting at me to stop, but I thought it was just the other tank driver trying to get the advantage. When I got to the bottom of the ridge, I stopped and looked back for the M60. That was when I noticed a soldier clinging to our turret as if his life depended on it. He and a couple of other infantry had been sitting on the tank when I took off.

The others had either jumped off or fallen; he was the only one who'd been able to hang on to the end. We turned on our lights and went back up the hill—slowly, so that we wouldn't run over anybody—and collected the scattered troops. Fortunately, there were no serious injuries. When we arrived at the top, three officers were waiting in a jeep. I drove past and parked my tank as if nothing had happened.

No sooner had I climbed out of the hatch than the three officers all started screaming at me, like a chorus. I stood at attention until they were finished. After the yelling stopped, one of the officers stepped forward, glared at me for a moment, and then started to laugh. "Tank Driver Schwarzenegger," he ordered, "move your tank over there."

"Yes sir!" I parked the tank where he had pointed. Climbing out, I noticed that I was standing in deep, thick mud.

"Now, Tank Driver Schwarzenegger, I want you to crawl down under the length of your tank. When you come out the back, climb up on top, down through the turret, down through the hull, and out of your emergency hatch below. Then do it again." He ordered me to repeat that circuit fifty times.

By the time I had finished, four hours later, I was coated with twenty pounds of mud and could barely move. I must have smeared one hundred more pounds of mud inside the tank climbing through. Then I had to drive it back to base and clean it out. The guy could have thrown me in jail for a week, but I must admit that this was a more effective punishment.

I'll never know for sure, but I think the tank drag race may have worked in favor of my early-discharge request. A few weeks after the incident, I was called to a hearing with my superiors. The commander had the bodybuilding magazines and my job offer letter on his desk. "Explain this to us," he said. "You signed up to be a tank driver for three years, and then you requested a few months ago that you want to leave this summer, because you have this position in Munich."

I liked the army, I told them, but the Munich job was a giant opportunity for my career.

"Well," the officer said with a smile, "due to the fact that you are somewhat unsafe around here, we'll approve your request and let you go early. We can't have you crashing any more tanks."

CHAPTER 4

Mr. Universe

"**I CAN ALWAYS GET** you a job as a lifeguard at the Thalersee, so just remember if anything goes wrong, you never have to worry." That's what Fredi Gerstl told me when I visited him to say good-bye. Fredi was always generous about helping young people, and I knew he meant well, but I wasn't interested in a lifeguard job or any other safety net. Even though Munich was only two hundred miles from Graz, for me it was the first step on the way from Austria to America.

I'd heard stories about Munich: how every week a thousand trains came into its train station. I'd heard about the nightlife and the wild atmosphere of the beer halls and on and on. As the train came near to the city, I began seeing more and more houses, and then bigger buildings, and then up ahead the city center. I was wondering in a corner of my brain, "How will I find my way around? How will I survive?" But mostly I was selling myself on the mantra "This is going to be my new home." I was turning my back on Graz, I was out of there, and Munich was going to be my city, no matter what.

Munich was a boomtown, even by the standards of the West German economic miracle, which was in full swing by 1966. It was an international city of 1.2 million people. It had just landed the right to host the Summer Olympics in 1972 and the soccer World Cup finals in 1974. Holding the Olympic Games in Munich was meant to symbolize

West Germany's transformation and reemergence into the community of nations as a modern democratic power. Construction cranes were everywhere. The Olympic Stadium was already going up, as were new hotels and office buildings and apartments. All across the city were major excavations for the new subway system, designed to be the most modern and efficient in the world.

The *Hauptbahnhof*, or main station, where I was about to get off the train, was at the center of all this. The construction sites needed laborers, and they were streaming in from all over the Mediterranean and the Eastern bloc. In the station waiting rooms and on the platforms, you could hear Spanish, Italian, Slavic, and Turkish languages spoken more often than you heard German. The area around the station was a mix of hotels, nightclubs, shops, flophouses, and commercial buildings. The Universum Sport Studio, the gym where I'd been hired, was on the Schillerstrasse just five minutes from the station. Both sides of the street were lined with nightclubs and strip bars that stayed open till four in the morning. Then at five o'clock, the first breakfast places opened, where you could get sausage or drink beer or eat breakfast. You could always celebrate somewhere. It was the kind of place where a nineteen-year-old kid from the provinces had to get streetwise very fast.

Albert Busek had promised to have a couple of guys come meet me at the station, and as I walked up the platform, I saw the grinning face of a bodybuilder named Franz Dischinger. Franz had been the junior-division favorite in the Best Built Man in Europe competition in Stuttgart, the title I'd won the year before. He was a good-looking German kid, even taller than me, but his body had not filled out yet, which I think was why the judges had picked me instead. Franz was a joyful guy, and we'd hit it off really well, laughing a lot together. We'd agreed that if I ever came to Munich, we'd be training partners. After we grabbed something to eat at the station, he and his buddy, who had a car, dropped me off at an apartment on the outskirts of town where Rolf Putziger lived.

I had yet to meet my new boss, but I was glad he had offered to put me up, because I couldn't afford to rent a room. Putziger turned out to be a heavy, unhealthy-looking old man in a business suit. He was almost bald and had bad teeth when he smiled. He gave me a friendly welcome and showed me around his place; there was a small extra room that he explained would be mine as soon as the bed that he'd ordered for me was delivered. In the meantime, would I mind sleeping on the living room couch? It didn't bother me at all, I said.

I thought nothing about this arrangement until a few nights later, when Putziger came in late and instead of going into his bedroom lay down next to me. "Wouldn't you be more comfortable coming into the bedroom?" he asked. I felt his foot pressing up against mine. I was up off that couch like a shot, grabbing my stuff and heading for the door. My mind was going nuts: what had I gotten myself into? There were always gays among bodybuilders. In Graz, I'd known a guy who had a fantastic home gym where my friends and I would work out sometimes. He was very open about his attraction to men and showed us the section of the city park where the men and boys hung out. But he was a real gentleman and never imposed his sexual orientation on any of us. So I thought I knew what gay men were like. Putziger definitely didn't seem gay; he looked like a businessman!

Putziger caught up with me on the street as I stood trying to process what had happened and figure out where to go. He apologized and promised not to bother me if I came back in the house. "You are my guest," he said. Back inside, of course, he tried to close the deal again, telling me he could understand that I preferred women, but if I'd be his friend, he could get me a car and help my career and so on. Of course, I could have used a real mentor at that point, but not at that cost. I was relieved to get out of there for good the next morning.

The reason Putziger didn't fire me was that he needed a star for his gym even more than he needed a lover. Bodybuilding was such an obscure sport that there were only two gyms in Munich, and the larger of the two belonged to Reinhard Smolana, who in 1960 was the first Mr. Germany and who had won Mr. Europe in 1963. Smolana had also already placed third in Mr. Universe competition, so he was without any doubt the best-ranked German bodybuilder and the obvious authority on weight training. His gym was better equipped and more modern than Putziger's. Customers gravitated to Smolana; my job as the new sensation was to help the Universum Sport Studio compete. Albert Busek, the editor of *Sportrevue*, who had set all this in motion by suggesting me, turned out to be as honorable as Rolf Putziger was sleazy. When I told him about what had happened, he was disgusted. Since I now had no place to stay, he helped me convert a storeroom in the gym into sleeping quarters. He and I quickly became good friends.

Albert would have been a doctor or scientist or intellectual if anyone had ever told him to go to the university. Instead, he'd gone to engineering school. He discovered working out and then realized that he had talents for writing and photography. He asked Putziger if he could do some work for the magazine. "Yeah, give me an article, write something," Putziger said. After Albert and his wife had twins, and his student funding was cut, he ended up working for Putziger full time. Before long, Albert was running the magazine and had established himself as an expert on the bodybuilding scene. He was sure that I would become the next big thing, and because he wanted to see me succeed, he was willing to be the buffer between Putziger and me.

Apart from my troubles with the owner, the job was ideal. Putziger's establishment consisted of the gym, the magazine, and a mail-order business that sold nutritional supplements. The gym itself had several rooms instead of one big hall; it also had windows and natural light rather than the damp concrete walls I had gotten used to at the stadium in Graz. The equipment was more sophisticated than any I'd ever had access to. Besides weights, there was a full set of machines for shoulders, back, and legs. That gave me the opportunity to add exercises that would single out muscles, add definition, and refine my body in ways that are impossible to achieve with free weights alone.

I'd learned in the army that I loved helping people train, so that part of the job came easily. Over the course of the day, I would teach small groups and do one-on-one sessions with a wild assortment of guys: cops, construction workers, businessmen, intellectuals, athletes, entertainers, Germans and foreigners, young and old, gay and straight. I encouraged American soldiers from the nearby base to train there; the Universum Sport Studio was the first place I'd ever met a black person. Many of our customers were there simply to boost their fitness and health, but we had a core group of competitive weight lifters and bodybuilders whom I could imagine as serious training partners. And I realized that I knew how to rally and challenge guys like that. "Yeah, you can be my training partner; you need help," I'd joke. As the trainer, I liked being the ringleader, and even though I had very little money, I would take them out for lunch or dinner and pay.

Being busy helping customers meant that I had no time to train the way I was used to, with an intense four- or five-hour workout each day. So I adopted the idea of training twice a day, two hours before work and two hours from seven to nine in the evening, when business slacked off and only the serious lifters were left. Split workouts seemed like an annoyance at first, but I realized I was onto something when I saw the results: I was concentrating better and recovering faster while grinding out longer and harder sets. On many days I would add a third training session at lunchtime. I'd isolate a body part that I thought was weak and give it thirty or forty minutes of my full attention, blasting twenty sets of calf raises, say, or one hundred triceps extensions. I did the same thing some nights after dinner, coming back to train for an hour at eleven o'clock. As I went to sleep in my snug little room, I'd often feel one or another muscle that I'd traumatized that day jumping and twitching—just a side effect of a successful workout and very pleasing, because I knew those fibers would now recover and grow.

I was training flat out because in less than two months I knew I would be going up against some of the best bodybuilders alive. I'd signed up for Europe's biggest bodybuilding event, Mr. Universe, in London. This was a brash thing to do. Ordinarily, a relative novice like me wouldn't have dreamed of taking on London. I'd have competed for

Mr. Austria first, and then if I won, I'd have aimed for Mr. Europe. But at that rate, being "ready" for London would have taken years. I was too impatient for that. I wanted the toughest competition I could get, and this was the most aggressive career move I could make. Of course, I wasn't an idiot about it. I didn't expect to win in London—not this time. For now, though, I was determined to find out where I stood. Albert loved the idea, and since he knew English, he helped me fill out the application.

For a regimen as fanatical as mine, I needed more than one training partner. Luckily, there were enough serious bodybuilders in Munich who got a kick out of my Mr. Universe dream, even if they thought I was a little nuts. Franz Dischinger trained with me regularly, and so did Fritz Kroher, who was a country boy like me, from a small town in the Bavarian woods. Even Reinhard Smolana, owner of the rival gym, joined in. Sometimes he invited me to train at his gym or he came to mine to work out after hours. After just a few weeks, I felt like I'd found my buddies, and Munich was starting to seem like home.

My favorite training partner was Franco Columbu, who quickly became my best friend. I'd met him in Stuttgart the year before; he'd won the European championship in power lifting on the same day that I won Mr. Junior Europe. Franco was an Italian from the island of Sardinia, where he grew up on a farm in a tiny mountain village that sounded even more primitive than Thal when he described it to me. He spent much of his boyhood herding sheep, and at age ten or eleven, he'd be out in the wilderness alone for days at a time, finding his own food and fending for himself.

Franco had to drop out of school at thirteen to help on the family farm, but he was very hardworking and smart. He'd started out as a bricklayer and amateur boxer and made his way north to Germany to earn his living in construction. In Munich, he learned the language and the city so well that he qualified to be a taxi driver. The Munich taxi driver exam was hard even for natives, and for an Italian to pass it amazed everyone.

Franco was a power lifter, I was a bodybuilder, and we both understood that these sports were complementary. I wanted to add bulk to my body, which meant having to work with heavy weights, and Franco knew how to do that. Meanwhile, I understood bodybuilding, which Franco wanted to learn. He told me, "I want to be Mr. Universe." Others laughed at him—he was only five foot five—but in bodybuilding, perfection and symmetry can beat sheer size. I liked the idea of us training together.

Maybe because he'd spent so much time in the wild, Franco was quick to pick up on new ideas. He loved my theory of "shocking the muscle," for instance. It always seemed to me that the biggest obstacle to successful training is that the body adjusts so quickly. Do the same sequence of lifts every day, and even if you keep adding weight, you'll see your muscle growth slow and then stop; the muscles become very efficient at performing the sequence they expect. The way to wake up the muscle and make it grow again is to jolt it with the message "You will never know what's coming. It will always be different from what you expect. Today it's this, tomorrow it's something else." One day it's ultraheavy weights; the next day high reps.

A method we developed to shock the muscle was "stripping." In a normal weight training sequence, you do your first set with lighter weight and then work your way up. But in stripping, you do the reverse. For example, in preparation for London, I needed to bulk up my deltoids. So I'd do dumbbell presses, where you hold a dumbbell in each hand at shoulder height and then raise them up above your head. With stripping, I'd start at my top weight: six repetitions with 100-pound dumbbells. Put those down, take the 90-pound dumbbells and do six reps. And so on, all the way down the rack. By the time I reached the 40s, my shoulders would be on fire and six reps would feel like each arm was lifting 110 pounds, not 40. But before putting down the weights, I'd shock the deltoids further by doing lateral raises, lifting the 40s from hip level out to shoulder height. After that, my shoulder muscles would be so totally berserk that I did not know where to put my hands. It was agony to let them hang by my sides and impossible to lift them. All I could do was drape my arms on a table or a piece of equipment to relieve the excruciating pain. The deltoids were screaming from the unexpected sequence of sets. I'd shown them who was boss. Their only option now was to heal and grow.

After training hard all day I wanted to have fun at night. And in Munich in 1966, fun meant beer halls, and beer halls meant fights. I'd go with my buddies to these places where every night people would be sitting at long tables laughing and arguing and waving their mugs. And getting drunk, of course. People started fights all the time, but it was never like "I'm going to murder this guy." As soon as a fight ended, one guy would say, "Oh, let's have a pretzel. Can I buy you a beer?" And the other guy would say, "Yeah, I lost, so you can at least buy me a beer. I don't have any money anyway." Soon you'd be drinking together as if nothing had happened.

The beer itself didn't really appeal to me because it would interfere with training; I rarely drank more than one in a night. But I was totally into the fights. I felt like I was discovering new power every day and was huge and strong and unstoppable. There was not a lot of thinking involved. If a guy looked at me in a weird way or challenged me for whatever reason, I'd be in his face. I'd give him the shock treatment: I'd rip off my shirt to reveal my tank top underneath and then I'd punch him out. Or sometimes when he saw me he'd just say, "Oh, what the hell. Why don't we just get a beer?"

My friends and I backed each other up, of course, if the fight turned into a brawl. The next day, we'd pass around the stories at the gym and laugh. "Oh, you should've seen Arnold. He banged these two guys' heads together and then their friend came at him with a beer mug, but I caught him with a chair from behind, that fucker . . ." We were fortunate because even when the police came, which happened several times, they would just dismiss us. The only time I remember ever being taken in to the police station was when a guy claimed it was going to cost a lot of money to replace his teeth. We were arguing so much about what the teeth would cost that the police thought we'd start fighting again. So they took us in and held us until we agreed on an amount.

Even better than the fights were the girls. Right across the Schillerstrasse from the gym was the Hotel Diplomat, where airline stewardesses stayed. Franco and I would lean out the window in our tank tops and flirt with them when they spotted us from the street. "What are you doing up there?" they'd call out. "Well, we have a gym here. Do you want to train? Come on up."

I also would go across to the hotel lobby and introduce myself to the little groups of stewardesses as they came and went. To get them interested, I would combine my very best methods from the Thalersee and from years of selling hardware. "We have a gym across the street," I'd say, and I'd compliment the girl and tell her how she might enjoy working out. In fact, I thought it was foolish and stupid that gyms almost never encouraged women to train. So we would let them work out for free. And whether they came because they were interested in the men or purely to train, I was happy either way.

The girls came mostly at night. Our regular customers were usually gone by eight, but you could use the equipment until nine. I would be doing my second workout with my partners. If the girls just wanted to train, they could take a shower and be out by eight thirty. Otherwise they were welcome to stay, and we'd go out or have a party. Sometimes Smolana would show up with some girls, and then the night could get quite wild.

For the first few months in Munich, I let myself get carried away by nightlife and fun. But then I realized I was losing focus, and I started disciplining myself. The goal was not to have fun but to become the world champion in bodybuilding. If I was going to get my seven hours of sleep, I had to be in bed by eleven. There was always time to have fun, and we always had fun anyway.

My boss turned out to be a bigger threat to my Mr. Universe prospects than any beer hall drunk swinging a stein. With just a few weeks to go, I still hadn't heard back about my application to the contest. Finally, Albert called London, and the organizers said they'd never gotten anything from me. Finally, Albert confronted Putziger, who admitted that he'd found my application in the outgoing mail and thrown it away. He was jealous that I would get discovered and move to England or America before he could make money off me. I'd have been sunk except for Albert's command of English and his desire to stick up for me. He called London again and persuaded the organizers to consider my application, even though the deadline had passed. They agreed. Just days before the contest, the papers came through, and I was added to the list.

The other bodybuilders in Munich also rallied in my support. Putziger should have paid my way to London, of course, because any success I might have there would bring attention to his gym. But when word of his sabotage got around, it was his competitor Smolana who passed the hat and raised the three hundred marks I needed for a ticket. On September 23, 1966, I boarded a London-bound flight. I was nineteen, and it was the first time I'd ever taken an airplane. I'd been expecting to take a train, so I was ecstatic. I was sure that nobody I'd gone to school with had flown at this point. I was sitting on an airliner with businessmen, and it had all happened through bodybuilding.

The first Mr. Universe contest was held the year after I was born, 1948. It took place in London every September. The English speakers dominated, as in all of bodybuilding—especially the Americans, who probably won eight out of every ten years. All the great bodybuilders I'd idolized growing up had won the Mr. Universe title: Steve Reeves, Reg Park, Bill Pearl, Jack Delinger, Tommy Sansone, Paul Winter. I remembered seeing a photograph from the contest when I was a kid. The winner stood on a pedestal, trophy in hand, while everyone else stood below him on the stage. Being on that pedestal was always my vision of where I would end up. It was very clear: I knew what it was going to feel like and look like. It would be like heaven to make that real, but I didn't expect to win this year. I'd gotten the list of the bodybuilders I'd be competing against in the amateur class, looked at photos of them, and thought, "Jesus." Their bodies were better defined than mine. I wanted to finish in the top six because I felt like I couldn't beat the numbers two, three, and four from the last year. I felt they were too defined and I was not quite there. I was still in the slow process of building up to my ideal muscle mass; the idea was to get the size and then cut down and chisel and perfect it.

They held the competition in the Victoria Palace Theatre, an old ornate place decorated with marble and statues a few blocks from Victoria Station. Major competitions always followed a set routine. In the morning would be the preliminaries, or technical rounds. The bodybuilders and judges assembled in the auditorium—reporters could sit in, but the public wasn't allowed. The aim was to give the judges the chance to evaluate the contestants' muscular development and definition, body part by body part, and systematically compare each man with the rest. You'd stand in a line, along the back of the stage, with all the other men of your class (mine was "amateur tall"). Everyone had numbers pinned to their posing briefs. A judge would say, "Number fourteen and number eight, please step forward, give us a quadriceps." Those two bodybuilders would walk to the center of the stage and strike a standard pose that showed off the four muscles at the front of the thigh as the judges made notes. The results of these technical rounds were factored into the decisions later in the day. Then, of course, the big show would be the finals in the afternoon: a posing competition for each of the classes and ultimately a pose-off among the class winners to crown the overall amateur and professional champs.

Compared to the other competitions I'd seen, Mr. Universe was the big time. The Victoria Palace was completely sold out: more than fifteen hundred seats filled with applauding and cheering bodybuilding fans, and dozens more outside hoping to squeeze in. The show itself was as much circus as contest. The stage was professionally lit, with spotlights and floods, and they'd brought in a whole orchestra to help set the mood. The two-hour program included entertainment between the rounds of competition, like a bikini contest, acrobats, contortionists, and two troupes of women in leotards and mod boots who paraded and struck poses holding little barbells and weights.

To my amazement, in the technical round that morning, I'd discovered that I'd overestimated my competition. The top "tall amateur" bodybuilders were indeed better defined, but put us all together on stage, and I still stood out. The truth is that not all bodybuilders are strong, especially those who have done most of their training with weight machines. But years of power lifting and working with free weights had given me massive biceps and shoulders and back muscles and thighs. I simply looked bigger and stronger than the rest.

By showtime, word had gotten around that this monster teenager had shown up from out of nowhere with an unpronounceable name, and he was a goddamn giant. So the crowd was especially noisy and enthusiastic when our group came on. I didn't win, but I came much closer than I or anyone else would have expected. By the final pose-off, the contest was down to me and an American named Chester Yorton, and the judges decided for Chet. I had to admit that was the right call: although Chet was at least twenty pounds lighter than me, he was truly chiseled and beautifully proportioned, and his posing was smoother and more practiced than mine. Besides, he had a great suntan that made me look like bread dough next to him.

I was ecstatic being the surprise runner-up; I felt like I'd won. It threw me into the spotlight, so much so that people started to say, "Next year he's going to win." Muscle magazines in English started mentioning me, which was extremely important because I had to become known in England and America to reach my goal.

The giddiness lasted only until I had time to think. Then it hit me: Chet Yorton had ended up on that pedestal, not me. He'd earned the victory, but I thought I'd made a big mistake. What if I had gone to London intending to win? Would I have prepared better? Would I have performed better? Would I have won and now be Mr. Universe? Instead, I'd underestimated my chances. I didn't like the way this made me feel and worked myself into quite a state. It really taught me a lesson.

After that, I never went to a competition to compete. I went to win. Even though I didn't win every time, that was my mind-set. I became a total animal. If you tuned into my thoughts before a competition, you would hear something like: "I deserve that pedestal, I own it, and the sea ought to part for me. Just get out of the fucking way, I'm on a mission. So just step aside and gimme the trophy."

I pictured myself high up on the pedestal, trophy in hand. Everyone else would be standing below. And I would look down.

Three months later, I was back in London, laughing and horsing around on a living room rug with a jumble of kids. They belonged to Wag and Dianne Bennett, who owned two gyms and were at the center of the UK bodybuilding scene. Wag had been a judge at the Mr. Universe contest, and he'd invited me to stay with him and Dianne in their house in the Forest Gate section of London for a few weeks of training. Although they had six kids of their own, they took me under their wing and became like parents to me.

Wag had made it clear that he thought I needed a lot of work. At the top of his list was my posing routine. I knew there is a huge difference between hitting poses successfully and having a compelling routine. Poses are the snapshots, and the routine is the movie. To hypnotize and carry away an audience, you need the poses to flow. What do you do between one pose and the next? How do the hands move? How does the face look? I'd never had a chance to figure very much of this out. Wag showed me how to slow down and make it like ballet: a matter of posture, the straightness of the back, keeping the head up, not down.

This I could understand, but it was harder to swallow the idea of actually posing to music. Wag would put the dramatic theme from the movie *Exodus* on the hi-fi and cue me to start my routine. At first I couldn't think of anything more distracting or less hip. But after a while I started to see how I could choreograph my moves and ride the melody like a wave—quiet moments for a concentrated, beautiful three-quarter back pose, flowing into a side chest pose as the music rose and then *wham!*, a stunning most muscular pose at the crescendo.

Dianne concentrated on filling me up with protein and improving my manners. Sometimes she must have thought I'd been raised by wolves. I didn't know the right way to handle a knife and fork or that you should help clear up after dinner. Dianne picked up where my parents and Fredi Gerstl and Frau Matscher had left off. One of the few times she ever got mad at me was when she saw me shove my way through a crowd of fans after a competition. The thought in my head was "I won. Now I'm going to party." But Dianne grabbed me and said, "Arnold, you don't do that. These are people who came to see *you*. They spent their money, and some of them traveled a long way. You can take a few minutes and give them your autograph." That scolding changed my life. I'd never thought about the fans, only about my competitors. But from then on, I always made time for the fans.

Even the kids got in on the Educating Arnold project. There's probably no better way to learn English than to join a lively, happy London household where nobody understands German and where you sleep on the couch and have six little siblings. They treated me like a giant new puppy and loved teaching me words.

A photo of me during that trip shows me meeting my boyhood idol Reg Park for the first time. He's wearing sweats, looking relaxed and tan, and I'm wearing my posing trunks looking starstruck and pale. I was in the presence of Hercules, of the three-time Mr. Universe, of the star whose picture I kept on my wall, of the man on whom I'd modeled my life plan. I could barely stammer out a word. All the English I'd learned flew right out of my head.

Reg now lived in Johannesburg, where he owned a chain of gyms, but he came back to England on business several times a year. He was friends with the Bennetts and had generously agreed to help show me the ropes. Wag and Dianne felt that the best way for me to have a good shot at the Mr. Universe title was to became better known in the United Kingdom. Bodybuilders did that in those days by getting on the exhibition circuit—promoters all over the British Isles would organize local events, and by agreeing to appear, you could make a little money and spread your name. Reg, as it happened, was on his way to an exhibition in Belfast, Northern Ireland, and offered to bring me along. Making a name for yourself in bodybuilding is a lot like politics. You go from town to town, hoping word will spread. This grassroots approach worked, and the enthusiasm it created would eventually help me to win Mr. Universe.

One night I found myself standing in the wings and watching Reg pose onstage for a crowd of several hundred cheering exhibition fans. Then he went to the microphone and called me to the stage. He moderated while I showed off my strength: I would perform a two-arm curl of 275 pounds and deadlift 500 pounds five times. I finished by posing and received a standing ovation. I was ready to leave the stage when I heard Reg say, "Arnold, come over here." When I got to the microphone, he said, "Say something to the people."

So I said, "No, no, no."

"Why not?"

I said, "I don't speak English that well."

"Hey!" he says. "That's very good! Let's give a little applause. That takes a lot of nerve for a guy who doesn't speak English to say a sentence like that." He started clapping, and then they were all applauding.

All of a sudden I felt, "Gee, this is amazing. They liked what I said!"

Reg went on: "Say to them, 'I like Ireland.' "

"I like Ireland." Applause again. He said, "I remember you telling me earlier that this is the first time you're in Belfast, and you couldn't wait to get here. Right?"

"Yes."

"So tell them! 'I couldn't wait . . .' "

"I couldn't wait . . ."

" '. . . to get here.' "

". . . to get here." Wow, again applause. And every sentence he said for me to repeat, I got applause.

If he had told me the day before, "I'm going to bring you onstage and ask you to say a few words," I would have been scared to death. But here I was able to practice public speaking without the pressure. I didn't have to sweat about the audience accepting me or caring what I said. That fear was not there, because the body was the focus. I was lifting, I was posing. I knew they accepted me. This was just extra.

After that, I studied Reg at a bunch of shows. The way he spoke was unbelievable. He could entertain people. He was outgoing. He told stories. And he was Hercules! He was Mr. Universe! He knew about wine, he knew about food, he spoke French, he spoke Italian. He was one of those guys who really had his act together. I watched the way he held the mike, and I said to myself, "That's what you've got to do. You can't just pose on stage like a robot and then walk off so people never get to know your personality. Reg Park talks to them. He's the only bodybuilder I've seen who talks to people. That's why they love him. That's why he's Reg Park."

Back in Munich, I concentrated on building up business at the gym. Old man Putziger was almost never around, which was totally fine with Albert and me. He and I made a great team. Albert managed everything—the mail-order nutritional supplements business, the magazine, and the gym—doing the work of several men. My job, besides training, was to recruit new members. Our business goal, of course, was to overtake Smolana's and become the city's top gym. Advertising was an obvious first step, but we couldn't afford much of it, so we had some posters printed up. We'd wait until late at night and then work our way across the city—pasting them up at construction sites, where we figured the workers would be interested in bodybuilding.

But this strategy wasn't as successful as we hoped. We were scratching our heads about why until Albert passed one of the construction sites in daylight and noticed a Smolana poster on the wall in the exact spot where one of ours had been. It turned out that Smolana had been sending his guys around town pasting their posters over ours before the glue could dry. So we changed our routine. We'd poster once at midnight and then make a second pass at four in the morning to make sure that when the construction workers showed up for work, our gym would be the poster on top. Everybody got a kick out of the poster war, and slowly our membership started to grow.

Our pitch was that while Smolana's had more room, we had more spirit and more fun. We also had the wrestlers going for us. Today professional wrestling is a giant TV sport, but back then wrestlers would travel from city to city and put on bouts. When they came to Munich, they'd perform at the Circus Krone, which had a huge permanent arena as its home base. Whenever there was a wrestling match, the place was packed.

The wrestlers were always looking for somewhere to work out, and they picked our gym when they heard about me. I trained with guys like Harold Sakata, from Hawaii, who'd played the villain Oddjob in the 1964 James Bond movie *Goldfinger*. Like a lot of professional wrestlers, Harold started out as a lifter; he'd won a silver medal for the United States at the 1956 Summer Olympics in Melbourne, Australia. We also had Hungarian wrestlers, French wrestlers—guys from all over the world. I'd open up the gym at times when it was normally closed just to accommodate them, and at night I would go watch their matches. They wanted in the worst way to make me a wrestler too, but of course that was not my agenda.

Still, I was proud that our gym was becoming a little like the United Nations, because I planned to go global with everything that I wanted to do. American and British bodybuilders passing through town would stop by, and word got around among the American troops stationed nearby that the Universum Sport Studio was a good place to train.

Having a big range of customers was the perfect sales tool. If someone said to me, "Well, I was over at Smolana's gym, and they have more machines than you," I would say, "Well, they have one more room than we have, you're absolutely right. But think about why it is that everyone wants to come here. When any American bodybuilder comes from overseas, they train here. When the military looks for a gymnasium, they train here. When the professional wrestlers come into town, they train here. We even have women wanting to join!" I built it into a whole routine.

My initial success in London had reassured me that I was on the right track and that my goals were not crazy. Every time I won, I became more certain. After the 1966 Mr. Universe contest, I won several more titles, including Mr. Europe. Even more important for my local reputation, during the March beer festival I won a round of the Löwenbräukeller's stone-lifting competition, hoisting the old beer hall's 558-pound stone block higher than every other contestant that day. (The weight was in German pounds, equivalent to 254 kilos, or 558 English pounds.)

I knew I was already the favorite to win the 1967 Mr. Universe competition. But that didn't feel like enough—I wanted to dominate totally. If I'd wowed them with my size and strength before, my plan now was to show up unbelievably bigger and stronger and really blow their minds.

So I poured my energy and attention into a training plan I'd worked out with Wag Bennett. For months I spent most of my earnings on food and vitamins and protein tablets designed to build muscle mass. The drink of choice in this diet was like a nightmarish opposite of beer: pure brewer's yeast, milk, and raw eggs. It smelled and tasted so vile that Albert sampled it once and threw up. But I was convinced that it worked, and maybe it did.

I read everything I could find about the training methods of the East Germans and the Soviets. Increasingly, there were rumors that they were using performance-enhancing drugs to get superior results from their weight lifters, shot-putters, and swimmers. As soon as I figured out that steroids were the drugs in question, I went to the doctor to try them myself. There were no rules against using anabolic steroids then, and you could get them by prescription, yet already people seemed to feel two ways about their use. Bodybuilders didn't talk about steroids as freely as they talked about weight routines and nutritional supplements, and there was an argument about whether the bodybuilding magazines should educate people about the drugs or ignore the trend.

All I needed to know was that the top international champions were taking steroids, something I confirmed by asking the guys in London. I would not go into a competition with a disadvantage. "Leave no stone unturned" was my rule. And while there wasn't any evidence of danger—research into steroids' side effects was only getting under way—even if there had been, I'm not sure I would have cared. Downhill ski champions and Formula One race drivers know they can get killed, but they compete anyway. Because if you don't get killed, you win. Besides, I was twenty years old, and I thought I would never die.

To get the drugs, I simply went to see a local general practitioner. "I heard this will help muscle growth," I said.

"It's supposed to, but I wouldn't oversell it," he replied. "It's meant for people in rehab after surgery."

"Can you let me try it?" I asked, and he said sure. He prescribed an injection every two weeks and pills to take in between. He told me, "Take these for three months and stop the day the competition is over."

Steroids made me hungrier and thirstier and helped me gain weight, though it was mostly water weight, which was not ideal because it interfered with definition. I learned to use the drugs in the final six or eight weeks leading up to a major competition. They could help you win, but the advantage they gave was about the same as having a good suntan.

Later on, after I retired from bodybuilding, drug use became a major problem in the sport. Guys were taking doses of steroids twenty times the amount of anything we took, and when human growth hormone came on the scene, things really got out of hand. There were instances where bodybuilders died. I've worked hard since then with the International Federation of Bodybuilding and other organizations to get drugs banned from the sport.

The total effect of all these training refinements was that by September 1967, when I got on the plane again for London, I was packing another ten pounds of muscle.

That second Mr. Universe competition was every bit as good as I imagined. I went up against bodybuilders from South Africa, India, England, Jamaica, Scotland, Trinidad, Mexico, the United States, and dozens of other countries. For the first time, I heard people chanting "Arnold! Arnold!" I'd never experienced anything like that before. As I stood on the pedestal, holding my trophy, just the way I'd envisioned, I actually was able to deliver the right words in English to show some class and share the fun. I said into the microphone, "It is my lifetime ambition realized. I am very happy to be Mr. Universe. I say it again, it sounds so good. I am very happy to be Mr. Universe. My thanks to everyone in England who have helped me. They have been very kind to me. Thank you all."

Being Mr. Universe brought me a lifestyle beyond a young man's wildest dreams. In warm weather, the bodybuilders would pile into our old cars and head for the countryside and do the gladiator thing—grill fresh meat and drink wine and occupy ourselves with girls. At night I was hanging out with an international crowd of bar owners, musicians, bar girls—one of my girlfriends was a stripper and one was a gypsy. But I was wild only when I was wild. When it was time to train, I never missed a session.

Reg Park had promised that if I won Mr. Universe, he would invite me to South Africa for exhibitions and promotions. So the morning after the competition, I sent him a telegram saying, "I won. When am I coming?" Reg was as good as his word. He sent a plane ticket, and over the holiday season of 1967, I spent three weeks in Johannesburg with him, his wife Mareon, and their kids Jon Jon and Jeunesse. Reg and I traveled all over South Africa, including Pretoria and Cape Town, giving exhibitions.

Up until then, I had only the dimmest idea of what success in bodybuilding and movies and business really meant. Seeing Reg's happy family and prosperous life inspired me as much as seeing him play Hercules. Reg had started as a working-class kid in Leeds and was a bodybuilding star in America by the time he fell in love with Mareon in the 1950s. He took her to England and married her, but Leeds depressed her, so they moved back to South Africa, where he started his gymnasium chain. The business had done very well. Their house, which he called Mount Olympus, overlooked the city and had a swimming pool and gardens. The interior was roomy, beautiful, comfortable, and filled with art. As much as I was loving my hard-training, fun-loving, brawling, girl-chasing lifestyle in Munich, living with the Parks reminded me to keep my sights set higher than that.

Reg would wake me up at five o'clock each morning; by five thirty we'd be at his gym at 42 Kirk Street working out. I never even got up at that hour, but now I learned the advantage of training early, before the day starts, when there are no other responsibilities and nobody else is asking anything of you. Reg also taught me a key lesson about psychological limits. I'd worked my way up to three hundred pounds of weight in calf raises, beyond any other bodybuilder I knew. I thought I must be near the limit of human achievement. So I was amazed to see Reg doing calf raises with *one thousand* pounds.

"The limit is in your mind," he said. "Think about it: three hundred pounds is less than walking. You weigh two hundred fifty, so you are lifting two hundred fifty pounds with each calf every time you take a step. To really train, you have to go beyond that." And he was right. The limit I thought existed was purely psychological. Now that I'd seen someone doing a thousand pounds, I started making leaps in my training.

It showed the power of mind over body. In weight lifting, for many years there was a 500-pound barrier in the clean and jerk—kind of like the four-minute barrier in the mile, which wasn't broken until Roger Bannister did it in 1954. But as soon as the great Russian weight lifter Vasily Alekseyev set a new world record of 501 in 1970, three other guys lifted more than 500 pounds within a year.

I saw the same thing with my training partner Franco Columbu.

One afternoon years later we were taking turns doing squats at Gold's Gym in California. I did six reps with 500 pounds. Even though Franco was stronger than me in the squat, he did only four reps and put the bar back. "I'm so tired," he said. Just then I saw a couple of girls from the beach come into the gym and went over to say hello. Then I came back and told Franco, "They don't believe you can squat five hundred pounds." I knew how much he loved showing off, especially when there were girls around. Sure enough, he said, "I'm gonna show them. Watch this." He picked up the 500 pounds and did ten reps. He made it look easy. This was the same body that had been too tired ten minutes before. His thighs were probably screaming "What the fuck?" So what had changed? The mind. Sports are so physical that it's easy to overlook the mind's power, but I've seen it demonstrated again and again.

The immediate challenge for me back in Munich was how to use being Mr. Universe to attract more customers to our gym. Bodybuilding was still so obscure and considered so weird that winning the championship made no splash at all outside the gyms. I'd gotten more celebrity from lifting the heavy stone in the beer hall.

But Albert came up with an idea. If we had asked the newspapers to write a story about me winning Mr. Universe, they'd have thought we were nuts. Instead he had me walk around the city on a freezing day in my posing briefs. Then he called some of his newspaper friends and said, "You remember Schwarzenegger who won the stone-lifting contest? Well, now he's Mr. Universe, and he's at Stachus square in his underwear." A couple of editors thought that was funny enough to send photographers. I led them all over the city: from the market to the Hauptbahnhof, where I made a point of chatting up little old ladies to show I was friendly and nice and not some kind of monster. This is what politicians do all the time, but it was very unusual for a bodybuilder. In spite of the cold, I was having fun. The next morning a picture ran in one of the papers of me in my briefs and at a construction site, where one of the workers who was all bundled up against the cold was gawking at me in amazement.

After more than a year of effort, and stunts like these, we succeeded in doubling the gym membership to more than three hundred—but this was in a city of over a million people. Albert called bodybuilding a subcult of a subcult. We would have long conversations trying to figure out why the sport wasn't better known. We thought the answer must be in the mentality of most bodybuilders; they are hermits who want to hide under an armor of muscles. So they do everything in secret and train in dungeons and come out only when their muscles make them feel safe. There had been famous strongmen in history, such as Prussian-born Eugen Sandow, often called the father of modern bodybuilding, and Alois Swoboda, but that was at the beginning of the twentieth century, and there had been nobody like them since. No contemporary bodybuilder was enough of a showman to make training really catch on.

The competitions held in Munich were a depressing example of this. They weren't held in beer halls like the old strongman exhibitions. Instead, they took place in gyms where there would be just bare walls and a bare floor with a few dozen chairs, or in auditoriums on a bare stage. And this was Munich, a city full of people and entertainment and life. The sole exception was the Mr. Germany contest, held each year in the Bürgerbräukeller, a beer hall that catered to workers.

Albert and I had the idea of bringing bodybuilding competition upscale. We got together a little money and bought the rights to produce Mr. Europe for 1968. Next, we went to the owners of the Schwabinger Bräu, an elegant old beer hall in a classy neighborhood, and asked, "How about having the bodybuilders' contest here?"

The unusual choice of location helped us publicize the event, and we drew more than a thousand spectators, compared to a few hundred the previous year. Of course, we invited the press and made sure that the reporters understood what they were watching so they could write good stories.

The whole thing could have failed. We could have sold too few tickets, or somebody could have started a riot by leaping up onstage and cracking Mr. Europe over the head with a beer stein. But instead we packed the hall with unbelievable screaming and enthusiasm and life against the background of people drinking and clinking their steins. The energy of our event set a new standard in German bodybuilding.

That year's Mr. Europe contest had an especially big impact on bodybuilders from Eastern Europe because it coincided with the Soviet invasion of Czechoslovakia. On August 21, less than a month before the event, tanks rolled in to crush the democratic reforms that had been instituted during the so-called Prague Spring in early 1968. As the news spread, we got in touch with the bodybuilders we knew there and picked up many in our cars at the border. The Czechs were unusually well represented at Mr. Europe that year because they were able to use the competition as a pretext to flee. They went on afterward from Munich to Canada or to the United States.

I wondered when my turn would come to get to America. One corner of my brain was always focused on the question. In the Austrian army, for example, when I found out that they were sending tank drivers to the States for advanced training, I fantasized about staying in uniform for that. The problem, of course, was that when the training in America ended, I'd have to come back to Austria, and I'd still be in the army.

So I stuck with my original vision: a letter or a telegram would come, calling me to America. It was up to *me* to perform well and do something extraordinary, because if Reg Park had gotten to go there by doing something extraordinary, then I also would get to go by doing something extraordinary. In judging my progress, I used him and Steve Reeves as my benchmarks. Just like Reg, I'd gotten a very early start—earlier even than him, because he'd begun at seventeen just before he went into the military, and I'd started at fifteen. Winning Mr. Universe at the age of twenty got me this initial bang of publicity in the bodybuilding world, because I'd beaten Reg's long-standing record—he'd won at twenty-three, back in 1951.

When I first became obsessed with bodybuilding, I dreamed that winning Mr. Universe in London would guarantee my fame and immortality. But in reality, the competitive scene had grown much more complex. Like boxing today, bodybuilding had multiple federations that were constantly competing for control of the sport. They ran the championships that attracted bodybuilding's elite: the Mr. Universe contest in Britain; the Mr. World competition, which moved from country to country; the Mr. Universe contest in the United States; and the Mr. Olympia, a new event intended to crown the professional bodybuilding champion of the world. Fans needed scorecards to keep track of all this, and the important point for me was that not all the top bodybuilders competed at a given event. Some of the top Americans skipped the Mr. Universe competition in London and competed only in the American version, for instance. So the only real way for a bodybuilder to become the undisputed world champ was to rack up titles in all the federations. Only after he had challenged and defeated all rivals would he be universally acknowledged as the best. Reg Park had dominated in his day by winning the London Mr. Universe competition three times in fourteen years. Bill Pearl, a great California bodybuilder, had dominated by winning three Mr. Universe titles at that point plus Mr. America and Mr. USA. Steve Reeves had been Mr. America, Mr. Universe, and Mr. World. I was anxious not to just beat their records but also to run over them; if somebody could win Mr. Universe three times, I wanted to win it *six* times. I was young enough to do it, and I felt like I could.

Those were my dreams as I trained for the Mr. Universe contest to be held in London in 1968. To get to America, first I would have to thoroughly dominate the European bodybuilding scene. Having won Mr. Universe in the amateur class the year before was a great start. But it automatically elevated me to professional status, opening a whole new field of competitors. That meant that I had to go back and win the professional title even more decisively than I'd won as an amateur. That would make me a two-time Mr. Universe, and I'd really be on my way.

I made sure nothing else interfered. Not recreation, not my job, not travel, not girls, not organizing the Mr. Europe contest. I took time for all those things, of course, but my first priority remained working out a hard four or five hours per day, six days per week.

While I used the tips I'd learned from Wag Bennett and Reg Park, the focus of my training stayed the same. I was still growing physically, and I wanted to take advantage of my natural gift: a body frame that could handle more mass than the frames of any of the guys I was going to face. My goal was to show up at the Victoria Palace even bigger and stronger than the year before and just blow away the competition. At six foot two and 250 pounds, I was more impressive than I'd ever been.

The day before the contest did not start well. On my way to the airport, I went to the gym expecting Rolf Putziger to hand me my regular pay, which I was counting on as spending money for London. Instead, he presented a piece of paper and a pen. "Sign this, and you'll get your money," he said. It was a contract that named him as my agent and guaranteed him a cut of all my future earnings! I got over my shock enough to say no, but I left the gym reeling. I had only the money in my pocket and wasn't even sure I still had a job. Albert had to lend me five hundred marks so I could go to London. Of course, the trip ended much better than it began, with me winning Mr. Universe for the second time, decisively, the next day. There were photos of me in the muscle magazines hoisting a bikini-clad girl on my left arm while showing off my right biceps. But even better was the telegram I found waiting for me back at the hotel. It was from Joe Weider.

"Congratulations on your victory," it read. "You are the new young sensation. You are going to become the greatest bodybuilder of all time." It went on to invite me to come to America the next weekend to compete in his federation's Mr. Universe contest in Miami. "We will cover expenses," the telegram said. "Colonel Schuster will provide details."

I was thrilled to get a telegram from the undisputed kingmaker of bodybuilding champions. Being the biggest impresario in American bodybuilding meant that Joe Weider was the biggest bodybuilding impresario in the world. He had built an international empire of muscle-building exhibitions, magazines, equipment, and nutritional supplements. I was getting closer to my dream, not just of being a champion but also of going to America. I couldn't wait to call my parents and share the news that I was on my way. I hadn't expected this, but maybe I could rack up a third Mr. Universe title! That would be incredible, at age twenty-one. I was in competition shape, I had the momentum. I would overwhelm them in Miami.

Colonel Schuster turned out to be a medium-sized guy in a business suit who came to my London hotel later that day. He was, in fact, a colonel in the US National Guard, and he made his living as the European marketing agent for Weider's company. He gave me the airline ticket, but we hadn't gotten very far talking about the trip plans when he realized that I had no US visa.

I stayed at Schuster's house cooling my heels while the colonel went to the American embassy and pulled strings. The paperwork ended up taking a week. I filled the time as best I could, although I didn't really have a proper diet or a gym where I could train for five hours a day. I made do by going to the Weider warehouse, where they assembled dumbbells and barbells, and worked out with those. But I was distracted, and it wasn't the same.

The minute I set foot on the plane, all the frustration fell away. I had to change flights in New York, and circling over the city and seeing for the first time the skyscrapers, New York Harbor, and the Statue of Liberty was fantastic. With Miami, I wasn't sure what to expect, and it was raining when I got there. But it was impressive too, not just the buildings and palm trees but also the October heat and how happy it seemed to make people feel. I loved the tourist places with their Latin music. And the mixture of Latinos and blacks and whites was fascinating: I'd seen it in bodybuilding circles but never in Austria growing up.

Joe Weider had launched the American version of Mr. Universe ten years before to boost the popularity of bodybuilding in the United States, but this was the first time the contest had been held in Florida.

They'd taken over the Miami Beach Auditorium, a big, modern hall with 2,700 seats, which was normally home to TV's popular *Jackie Gleason Show*. I'd missed the run-up to the event—the interviews, cocktail parties, film and TV shoots, and promotions—but even so, the production felt big and American sized. There were bodybuilding legends everywhere, like Dave Draper and Chuck Sipes, each of whom had been Mr. America and Mr. Universe.

For the first time, I laid eyes on the world bodybuilding champ, Sergio Oliva. Sergio was an immigrant to the United States from Cuba who was the first member of a minority to win Mr. America, Mr. World, Mr. International, Mr. Universe, and Mr. Olympia. He'd just won his second consecutive Mr. Olympia title the previous week. Even though I wasn't yet in his league, Oliva knew we'd be competing soon. "He's very, very good," he told a reporter about me. "Next year will be tough. But that's okay with me. I do not like to compete with babies." When I heard about that, I thought, "Already the psych games are beginning."

Two dozen guys were in the competition, divided into two groups, tall and short. In the daytime rounds of preliminary judging, I beat the other tall men easily. But the top guy in the short-men category was Mr. America, Frank Zane, and he'd shown up in the best shape of his career. He'd just won the Mr. America competition in New York the week before. I was as big, well shaped, and powerful as I'd been in London, with the same impressive mass. But a week of twiddling my thumbs waiting for my visa had left me a little heavier than my ideal, which meant that when I posed, my body looked smooth and less sharply defined. Worse, besides being perfectly proportioned, muscular, and cut up, Zane had a serious tan, while I was as white as a soccer ball. Going into the evening finals, he was ahead of me on points.

That night in front of the crowd, I felt I looked 100 percent better because flexing and posing under stage lights all day had melted off the excess pounds. That helped make the competition between Frank Zane and me so close that we tied in the judges' final vote. But Frank's higher point score from earlier in the day made him the winner, not me. I stood by onstage trying not to look stunned while a guy five inches shorter than me and fifty pounds lighter took the prize.

It was a blow. I'd finally made it to America, just as I had envisioned. But then I lost Mr. Universe in Miami. To a lighter and shorter man. I thought the competition had been fixed because he was just not big enough to win against me. Even though I lacked the definition, he was a scrawny little guy.

That night, despair came crashing in. My cheerfulness almost never deserts me, but it did then. I was in a foreign country, away from my family, away from my friends, surrounded by strange people in a place where I didn't speak the language. How had I even made it this far? I was way out of my depth. All of my belongings were in one little gym bag; I'd left behind everything else. My job was probably gone. I had no money. I didn't know how I'd get home.

Worst of all, I'd lost. The great Joe Weider had brought me across the Atlantic to give me this opportunity, but instead of rising to the occasion, I'd embarrassed myself and failed to perform. I was sharing the room with Roy Callender, a black bodybuilder based in England who had also been in the London competition. He was very sweet, talking to me about my loss. He was much more mature than I was and was talking about things I did not quite understand. He was talking about feelings.

"Yeah, it's hard to lose after such a big victory in London," he said. "But remember that next year you will win again, and everyone will forget about this loss."

This was the first time that a man had ever been that nurturing with me. I knew that women were nurturing: my mother was nurturing, other women were nurturing. But to get real empathy from a guy was overwhelming. Up till then, I'd thought that only girls cry, but I ended up crying quietly in the dark for hours. It was a great relief.

When I woke up the next morning, I felt much better. Sunlight was pouring into the room and the phone next to the bed was ringing.

"Arnold!" said a raspy voice. "It's Joe Weider. I'm out by the pool.

You want to come down and order some breakfast? I'd like to interview you for the magazine. We want to do a cover story about you, exactly how you train . . ."

I went out to the pool, and there was Joe, wearing a striped bathrobe, waiting at a table with a typewriter right there. I couldn't believe it. I'd grown up on his magazines, in which Joe Weider always portrayed himself as the Trainer of Champions, the man who invented all the training methods and made bodybuilding happen and created all the greats. I idolized him, and here I was sitting with him by a pool in Miami. Suddenly the fears of the night before washed away. I felt important again.

Joe was in his midforties, clean shaven with sideburns and dark hair. He wasn't big—more medium height—but he was husky. I knew from the magazines that he worked out every day. He had a voice you couldn't miss: strong and penetrating with strange vowels that sounded different from the accents of other English speakers even to me. I later discovered that he was Canadian.

He asked everything about how I trained. We talked for hours. Even though my English made it slow going, he felt I had more to offer in the way of stories than the rest of the bodybuilders. I told him all about working out in the woods in the gladiator days. He enjoyed listening to all that. He interviewed me in great detail about the techniques I'd developed: the "split routine" method of training two or three times a day, the tricks that Franco and I had come up with to shock the muscles. Meanwhile I had to keep pinching myself. I was thinking, "I wish my friends in Munich and in Graz could see this, me sitting with Mr. Joe Weider, and he is asking me how I train."

By noon he seemed to make up his mind. "Don't go back to Europe," he said finally. "You need to stay here." He offered to pay my way to California and get me an apartment, a car, and living expenses so that I could concentrate on training for an entire year. By the time the same competitions came around again the next fall, I'd have another shot. Meanwhile, his magazines would report on my training, and he would supply translators so I could write about my programs and express my ideas.

Joe had plenty of opinions about what I needed to do to get to the top. He told me I'd been focusing on the wrong things; that even for a big man, power and bulk weren't enough. I had to train harder for muscle definition on top of these. And while some of my body parts were fantastic, I was still lacking in back, abs, and legs. And my posing needed more work. Training schemes were Joe Weider's specialty, of course, and he couldn't wait to start coaching me. "You are going to be the greatest," he said. "Just wait and see."

That afternoon at the gym, I thought more about my loss to Frank Zane. Now that I'd stopped feeling sorry for myself, I came to harsher conclusions than those I'd reached the night before. I still felt the judging had been unfair, but I discovered this wasn't the real cause of my pain. It was the fact that I had failed—not my body, but my vision and my drive. Losing to Chet Yorton in London in 1966 hadn't felt bad because I'd done everything I could to prepare; it was just not my year. But something different had happened here. I was not as ripped as I could have been. I could have dieted the week before and not eaten so much fish and chips. I could have found a way to train more even without access to equipment: for instance, I could have done one thousand reps of abs or something that would have made me feel ready. I could have worked on my posing—nothing had stopped me from doing that. Never mind the judging; I hadn't done everything in my power to prepare. Instead, I'd thought my momentum from winning in London would carry me. I'd told myself I'd just won Mr. Universe and I could let go. That was nonsense.

Thinking this made me furious. "Even though you won the professional Mr. Universe contest in London, you are still a fucking amateur," I told myself. "What happened here never should have happened. It only happens to an amateur. You're an amateur, Arnold."

Staying in America, I decided, had to mean that I wouldn't be an amateur ever again. Now the real game would begin. There was a lot of work ahead. And I had to start as a professional. I didn't ever want to go away from a bodybuilding competition like I had in Miami. If I was going to beat guys like Sergio Oliva, that could never happen again. From now on if I lost, I would be able to walk away with a big smile because I had done everything I could to prepare.

CHAPTER 5

Greetings from Los Angeles

THERE'S A PHOTOGRAPH OF me arriving in Los Angeles. I'm twenty-one years old, it's 1968, and I'm wearing wrinkled brown pants, clunky shoes, and a cheap long-sleeved shirt. I'm holding a beat-up plastic bag containing just a few things and waiting at the baggage claim to get my gym bag, which holds everything else. I look like a refugee, I can't speak more than a few phrases of English, and I don't have any money—but on my face is a big smile.

A photographer and a reporter, freelancers for *Muscle & Fitness* magazine, were on hand to chronicle my arrival. Joe Weider had assigned them to pick me up, show me around, and write about what I did and said. Weider was promoting me as a rising star. He offered to bring me to America to train with the champions for a year. He would provide a place to stay and spending money. All I had to do was work with a translator to write stories about my techniques for his magazines while training to achieve my dream.

The new and marvelous life I had dreamed about easily could have ended just a week later. One of my brand-new gym friends, an Australian strongman and crocodile wrestler, lent me his car, a Pontiac GTO with over 350 horsepower. I'd never driven anything so incredible, and it didn't take long before I was flying up Ventura Boulevard in the San Fernando Valley at autobahn speed. It was a cool and misty October morning, and I was about to learn that the streets of California get very slippery when it starts drizzling.

I got ready to downshift for an upcoming curve. Shifting was something I was good at because all the vehicles in Europe had manual transmissions, including the trucks I drove in the army and my banged-up old car in Munich. But downshifting the GTO slowed the rear wheels abruptly, breaking their hold on the road.

The car spun wildly around two or three times, completely out of control. I was probably down to about thirty miles per hour when momentum took me into the oncoming lanes—which were, unfortunately, very busy with morning traffic. I watched as a Volkswagen Beetle T-boned me on the passenger side. Then some American car hit me, and four or five more vehicles joined the pileup before everything came to a stop.

The GTO and I ended up about thirty yards down from my destination, Vince's Gym, where I was going to train. The car door on my side worked so I climbed out, but my right leg felt like it was on fire—the impact had wrecked the console between the two front seats, and when I looked down, a big splinter of plastic was sticking out of my thigh. I pulled it out, and now blood started running down my leg.

I was really scared, and all I could think of was to go to the gym for help. I limped in and said, "I just had a big accident." A few of the bodybuilders recognized me, but the one who took charge was a man I didn't know, who happened to be a lawyer. "You better get back out to your car," he said. "Don't leave the scene of an accident. It's called a hit-and-run here; hit-and-run, you understand? And you get in a lot of trouble. So go out there, stay with your car, and wait for the police."

He understood I'd just arrived in the United States and that my English wasn't good.

"But I'm here!" I said. "And I can look right over there!" I meant that I would easily see when the police arrived and go meet them.

"Trust me, just go back to your car."

Then I showed him my leg. "Do you know a doctor who can help me with this?"

He saw the blood and muttered, "Oh Christ." He thought for a second. "Let me call some friends. You don't have health insurance or anything?" I had trouble understanding what this meant, but we figured out that I didn't have insurance. Someone gave me a towel to hold against my leg.

I went back to the GTO. People were shaken up and hassled that they had to be late for work and that their cars were damaged and they were going to have to deal with their insurance companies. But nobody jumped all over me or made accusations. Once the cop was sure that the lady in the Volkswagen was okay, he let me go without a citation and just said, "I see you're bleeding; you ought to get that looked at." A bodybuilder friend named Bill Drake took me to a doctor and kindly paid the bill to get me stitched up.

I'd been an idiot to cause the wreck, and I wish I had everyone's names so I could write to them today and apologize.

I knew I'd been lucky: the police in Europe would have been incredibly strict in a situation like this. Not only could I have been arrested but also, as a foreigner, I could very well have ended up in jail or getting deported. The incident definitely would have cost me a lot of money in fines. But the cops in LA took the view that the roads were slick, this was an accident, there were no serious injuries, and the key thing was to get traffic flowing again. The cop who talked to me was very polite; he looked at my international driver's license and asked, "Do you want an ambulance, or are you okay?" Two guys from the gym told him I'd been in the country only a few days. It was pretty clear I couldn't really speak English, although I tried.

I went to sleep that night feeling optimistic. I still needed to work things out with the crocodile wrestler, but America was a great place to be.

My first view of Los Angeles was a shock. For me, America meant one thing: size. Huge skyscrapers, huge bridges, huge neon signs, huge highways, huge cars. New York and Miami had both lived up to my expectations, and somehow I'd imagined that Los Angeles would be just as impressive. But now I saw that there were only a few high-rises downtown, and it looked pretty skimpy. The beach was big, but where were the huge waves and the surfers surfing?

I felt the same disappointment when I first saw Gold's Gym, the mecca of American bodybuilding. I'd been studying Weider's bodybuilding magazines for years without realizing that the whole idea was to make everything seem much bigger than it was. I'd look at scenes of famous bodybuilders working out at Gold's, and my vision was of a huge sports club that had basketball courts, swimming pools, gymnastics, weight lifting, power lifting, and martial arts, like the giant clubs you see today. But when I walked in, there was a cement floor, and the whole place was very simple and primitive: a single two-story room about half the size of a basketball court, with cinder-block walls and skylights. Still, the equipment was really interesting, and I saw great power lifters and bodybuilders working out, lifting heavy weights—so the inspiration was there. Also, it was just two blocks from the beach.

The neighborhood of Venice around Gold's seemed even less impressive than the gym. The houses lining the streets and alleys looked like my barracks in the Austrian army. Why would you build cheap wooden barracks in such a great location? Some of the houses were vacant and run-down. The sidewalks were cracked and sandy, with weeds growing alongside the buildings, and some stretches of sidewalk weren't even paved.

"This is America!" I thought. "Why wouldn't they pave this? Why wouldn't they tear down this abandoned house and build a nice one?" One thing I knew for sure: back in Graz, you would never find a sidewalk that was not only paved but also totally swept and immaculate. It was inconceivable.

It was a challenge moving to a country where everything looked different, and the language was different, and the culture was different, and people thought differently and did business differently. It was staggering how different everything was. But I had the big advantage over most newcomers: when you are part of an international sport, you're never totally alone.

There's amazing hospitality in the bodybuilding world. No matter where you go, you don't even have to know people. You always feel you are part of a family. The local bodybuilders will pick you up at the airport. They will greet you. They will take you into their homes. They will feed you. They will take you around. But America was something else.

One of the bodybuilders in Los Angeles had an extra bedroom where I could stay at first. When I showed up to start training at the gym, guys greeted me and hugged me and made it clear that they were happy to have me over here. The guys found me a little apartment, and as soon as I moved in, this friendliness turned into "We've got to help him." They organized a drive and showed up one morning carrying packages and boxes. You have to picture a bunch of big, muscular guys: huge bears you'd never want near anything delicate or made of glass, who you'd hear in the gym every day saying, "Look at that chest, oh man!" or "I'm gonna squat five hundred pounds today—fuck it." Suddenly, here they were carrying boxes and packages. One of them says, "Look what I brought you," opens up this little box, and takes out some silverware. "You need some silverware so you can eat here." Another one unwraps a bundle and says, "My wife told me that these are the plates I can take; they're our old plates, so now you have five plates." They were very careful to name things and give simple explanations. Someone else brought a little black-and-white TV with an antenna sticking out the top and helped me set it up and showed me how to adjust the antenna. They also brought food that we sat around and shared.

I said to myself, "I never saw this in Germany or Austria. No one would even think of it." I knew for a fact that, back home, if I'd seen somebody moving in next door, it wouldn't have crossed my mind to assist them. I felt like an idiot. That day was a growing-up experience.

The guys took me over to see Hollywood. I wanted to have my photo taken there and mail it to my parents, as if to send the message "I've arrived in Hollywood. Next will be movies." So we drove until one of the guys said, "All right, that's Sunset Boulevard."

"When do we get to Hollywood?" I asked.

"This *is* Hollywood."

In my imagination, I must have confused Hollywood with Las Vegas, because I was looking for giant signs and neon lights. I also expected to see movie equipment and streets blocked off because they were shooting some big stunt scene. But this was nothing. "What happened to all the lights and stuff?" I asked.

They looked at one another. "I think he's disappointed," one guy said. "Maybe we should bring him back at night."

The others said, "Yeah, yeah, good idea. Because there's nothing to see during the day, really."

Later that week, we came back at night. There were a few more lights, but it was just as boring. I had to get used to it and learn the good places to hang out.

I spent a lot of time finding my way around and trying to figure out how things worked in America. In the evening, I often hung around with Artie Zeller, the photographer who'd picked me up at the airport. Artie fascinated me. He was very, very smart, yet he had absolutely no ambition. He didn't like stress, and he didn't like risk. He worked behind the window in the post office. He came from Brooklyn, where his father was an important cantor in the Jewish community; a very erudite guy. Artie went his own way, getting into bodybuilding in Coney Island. Working as a freelancer for Weider, he'd become the best photographer of the sport. He was fascinating because he was self-taught, endlessly reading and absorbing things. Besides being a natural with languages, he was a walking encyclopedia and an expert chess player. He was a die-hard Democrat, liberal, and total atheist. Forget religion. To him, it was all bogus. There was no God, end of story.

Artie's wife, Josie, was Swiss, and even though I was trying to stay immersed in English, it was helpful to be around people who knew German. This was especially true when it came to watching TV. I'd arrived in America during the last three or four weeks of the 1968 presidential campaign, so when we turned on the set, there was always something about the election. Artie and Josie would translate from speeches by Richard Nixon and Vice President Hubert Humphrey, who were running against each other. Humphrey, the Democrat, was always going on about welfare and government programs, and I decided he sounded too Austrian. But Nixon's talk about opportunity and enterprise sounded really American to me.

"What is his party called again?" I asked Artie.

"Republican."

"Then I'm a Republican," I said. Artie snorted, which he often did both because he had bad sinuses and because he found a lot in life to snort about.

Just as Joe Weider had promised, I got a car: a secondhand white Volkswagen Beetle, which made me feel at home. As a way of learning the area, I would visit different gyms. I made friends with a guy who managed a gym in downtown LA, at what was then called the Occidental Life Building. I drove inland and also down to San Diego to see the gyms there. People would take me places, too, which was how I got to know Tijuana, Mexico, and Santa Barbara. At one point, I drove with four other bodybuilders to Las Vegas in a VW microbus. It couldn't even get up to sixty miles per hour with all the muscle on board. Las Vegas itself, with its giant casinos and neon lights and endless gaming tables, really lived up to my expectations.

A lot of champions trained at Vince's Gym, such as Larry Scott, who was nicknamed "the Legend" and who had won Mr. Olympia in 1965 and 1966. Vince's had carpeting and plenty of nice machines, but it wasn't a power lifter's gym: they thought basic strength-training exercises like the full squat, bench press, and incline press were old-fashioned strongman stuff that didn't chisel the body.

The scene was totally different at Gold's. It was very rough, and monsters trained there: Olympic shot-put champions, professional wrestlers, bodybuilding champions, strongmen off the streets. There was almost no one in a workout outfit. Everyone trained in jeans and plaid shirts, tank tops, sleeveless wife-beater shirts, sweatshirts. The gym had bare floors and weight-lifting platforms where you could drop a thousand pounds and no one would ever complain. It was closer to the atmosphere where I came from.

Joe Gold was the genius of the place. He'd been part of Santa Monica's original Muscle Beach scene as a teenager in the 1930s, and after serving as a machinist in the merchant marine in World War II, he came back and started building gym equipment. Just about every machine in the place was Joe's design.

There was nothing delicate here: everything Joe built was big and heavy, and it worked. His cable rowing machine was designed with the footrests exactly high enough for you to work your lower lats without feeling like you were about to launch right out of the seat. When Joe designed a machine, he did it with everybody's input rather than going off on his own. So on all of it, the angles of pulling down were perfect, and nothing got stuck. And he was there every day, which meant that all the equipment was maintained continuously.

Sometimes Joe would simply invent new machines. He'd created one to do donkey raises. This calf exercise was essential for me because compared to the rest of me, my calves were congenitally puny and hard to build up. Normally you did a donkey raise by placing the balls of your feet on a bar or plank with your midfoot and heels suspended. Then you bent at the waist 90 degrees, braced your arms on a bar, had one or two training buddies climb up and sit on your back and hips as if you were a mule, and worked your calves by lifting them up and down. But with Joe's machine, you didn't need riders. You loaded it with any amount of weight you wanted, went underneath it in a donkey stance, and took off the lock. Now you had, say, seven hundred pounds on top of you, and you could do the donkey raises.

Gold's quickly became home for me because that's where I felt grounded. There was always a bunch of guys hanging around the desk, and all the regulars had nicknames, like Fat Arm Charlie and Brownie and Snail. Zabo Koszewski worked there for many years and was Joe Gold's close friend. They called him "the Chief." He had the best abdominals—he did one thousand reps of abs every day—and was re-

After coming to California, I posed for Joe Weider's bodybuilding magazines at Muscle Rock in the heights above Malibu. Bodybuilders like this spot because the ridges in the distance seem little and your muscles look bigger than the mountains. *Art Zeller*

Aurelia and Gustav Schwarzenegger, my mother and father, on their wedding day in 1945. He's wearing the uniform of the Austrian rural police.

Schwarzenegger Archive

My brother Meinhard was born in 1946, and then one year and fourteen days later came me. Our mother had her hands full with two young boys. Here we're on the unpaved main road outside our house in Thal.

Schwarzenegger Archive

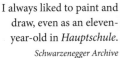

I always liked to paint and draw, even as an eleven-year-old in *Hauptschule*.

Schwarzenegger Archive

At age sixteen, I loved working out at the local lake, the Thalersee, with buddies like Karl Gerstl, Willi Richter, and Harry Winkler.
Schwarzenegger Archive

Hitting a front bicep pose in my first bodybuilding competition, at the Steirerhof Hotel in Graz, at age sixteen. Bodybuilding was so obscure that the contest organizers thought they needed a band onstage to help attract an audience.
Stefan Amsüss

I drove this fifty-ton M47 during my year in the Austrian army; my fellow crew members and I were responsible for its daily maintenance.
Schwarzenegger Archive

I could press 185 pounds at age sixteen as a member of the Graz Athletic Union weightlifting team—the applause of a crowd made me stronger.
Schwarzenegger Archive

I finally got to meet my idol Reg Park while training at the London gym of Wag Bennett in1966 (the W I'm wearing stands for Wag).
Schwarzenegger Archive

My dream became reality at London's Victoria Palace Theatre in 1967, when I became the youngest ever Mr. Universe at age twenty.
Albert Busek

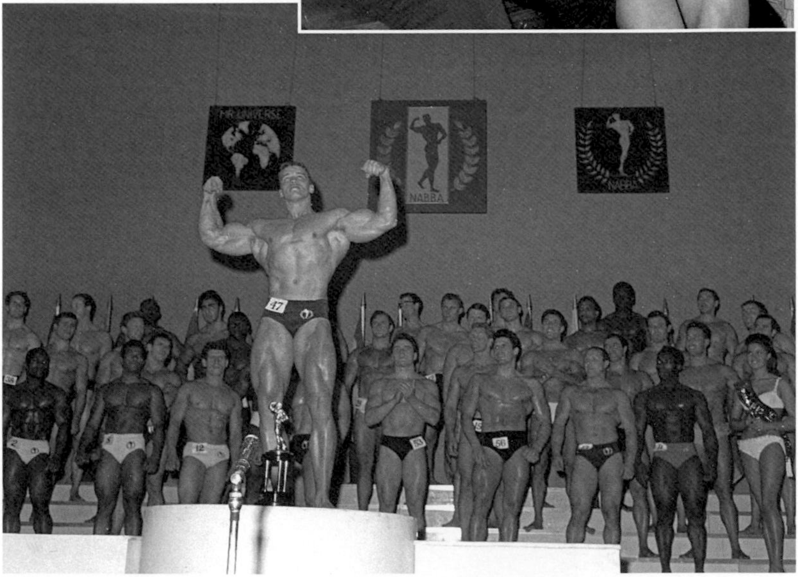

I walked around downtown Munich on a November day in my posing briefs to publicize bodybuilding and attract customers to the gym.
Rolf Hayo / Roba Press

My second Mr. Universe victory, in London in 1968, brought me an invitation and a plane ticket to America. I won the professional class and Dennis Tinerino the amateur class.
Schwarzenegger Archive

On occasional visits home to Austria, I'd work out in the attic with my dad, a national ice-curling champ. *Albert Busek*

I sat down with Joe Weider, the kingmaker of bodybuilding, on a hotel patio in Miami, hoping to pump him for training advice; I could hardly believe it when he started interviewing *me* instead. *Jimmy Caruso / Courtesy of Weider Health and Fitness*

California's Venice Beach was an amazing scene where gymnasts, circus performers, and bodybuilders loved to show off. Here we put on an impromptu acrobatics show. *Art Zeller*

My training partners (from top) Franco Columbu, Frank Zane, and Pete Caputo at Gold's Gym piled on as I did donkey raises to build up my calves.
Art Zeller

Joe Weider's wife Betty and I often posed for ads in his magazines. The pitch was simple: if you get muscles, you can go to the beach and pick up girls.
Art Zeller

Franco Columbu and I billed ourselves as European experts in construction and hired other bodybuilders to help in our first business doing masonry and repairs. *Art Zeller*

Joe Weider and I pore over photographs, working on magazine layouts.
Albert Busek

Doing my homework at the Santa Monica City College library.
Schwarzenegger Archive

On my way to rehab after major knee surgery in 1972, as my girlfriend Barbara Outland and Joe Weider supervise. The bodybuilding championships were just a few months away and I knew I had to bounce back fast.
Art Zeller

I tried to convince my mother to move to America after my father and brother died.
Schwarzenegger Archive

Believe it or not, chess, the brainiest game, has always been part of the scene at Muscle Beach. Here Franco and I square off.
Art Zeller

I'm squatting 500 pounds in preparation for the 1971 Mr. Olympia competition as Franco and Ken Waller stand by to help in case I lose balance or get stuck. *Art Zeller*

Going onstage at Madison Square Garden's Felt Forum to defend my Mr. Olympia crown in 1974. Those are Franco and Frank Zane behind me, and Lou Ferrigno, the wunderkind, in front keeping a close eye. *Art Zeller*

Hundreds of fans followed me to my hotel after my Mr. Olympia victory at Madison Square Garden. *Albert Busek*

I was getting to know lots of people in Hollywood. Here, drinks on my patio with directors Roman Polanski and Bob Rafelson and friends. *Art Zeller*

An advertising photo shoot for a Joe Weider product—the spring-loaded exercise bar I'm holding—gets filmed for the *Pumping Iron* documentary.

George Butler / Contact Press Images © 1975

Pumping Iron creators Charles Gaines and George Butler relax with me in South Africa in 1975.

George Butler / Contact Press Images © 1975

I work with a New York City ballet teacher to perfect my posing.

George Butler / Contact Press Images © 1977

On Muscle Beach, Franco and I lived the life we'd dreamed about as adolescents.
George Butler / Contact Press Images © 1973

Fooling around in the pool with Nastassja Kinski and others at the home of Frances Schoenberger of the Hollywood Foreign Press.
Michael Ochs Archives / Getty Images

I went to visit Andy Warhol at The Factory, his famous studio in Midtown Manhattan.
Fred W. McDarrah / Getty Images

I posed for a standing-room-only crowd at the Whitney Museum in New York. That's Candice Bergen at the foot of the podium, taking photos for the *Today* show.
Schwarzenegger Archive

With my idol Muhammad Ali in New Orleans 1978, after he beat Leon Spinks for his third world heavyweight title.
Schwarzenegger Archive

Meeting Senator Teddy Kennedy the night before the 7th Annual RFK Pro Celebrity Tennis Tournament. (Ethel Kennedy, Bobby's widow, is on Teddy's right.) A few minutes later, Tom Brokaw introduced me to Maria. *Ron Galella / Getty Images*

After my turn on the courts, I sat with Maria and her mother, Eunice Kennedy Shriver, at the RFK Pro Celebrity Tennis Tournament. *Ron Galella / Getty Images*

Maria, Franco, and I added to the local color on a Venice, California, sidewalk. *Albert Busek*

I was so lovestruck that I let Maria and her friend Bonnie Reiss commandeer my Jeep during the 1980 Teddy for President campaign. *Schwarzenegger Archive*

Joe Gold ran the best gym in America for bodybuilders. *Albert Busek*

Peter Brenner

Above right and below: When production of *Conan the Barbarian* got delayed, I trained all-out and shocked the bodybuilding world by coming out of retirement to win a record sixth Mr. Olympia title at the Sydney Opera House. *Neal Nordlinger*

ally ripped. My abs weren't like that, and the first thing Zabo told me when we met was that I needed to go on a diet. "You know?" he observed. "You're chubby." Joe Gold nicknamed me "Balloon Belly," and from then on, I was known as "Balloon Belly" and "Chubby."

Zabo, who came from New Jersey and whose first name was Irvin, had a whole collection of hashish pipes. We went over to his house every so often to get stoned. He read science-fiction novels day and night. Everything was, "Hey, man, wow!" and "Groovy!" and "Far out!" But that was normal around Venice. To smoke a joint was so casual it was like drinking a beer. You would go to someone's house, no matter who it was, and he'd light up a joint and say, "Have a hit." Or light up a hashish pipe, depending on how sophisticated he was.

I learned quickly what people meant when they said, "This is groovy." "This is cool." I found out that astrology was a big deal while trying to chat up this gorgeous girl. I said, "You and I, it seems like we really belong together; we should go out for dinner."

But she said, "Whoa, whoa, whoa, what sign are you?"

So I said, "Leo."

"That's not for me. That's really not for me. Thank you, but no thank you."

And she was gone. I went to the gym the next day and said, "Guys, I have a little problem here. I'm still learning." And I told them the story.

Zabo knew just what to do. He said, "Man, you got to say, 'I'm the *best* sign.' Try that."

It took only a few weeks before another situation came up. I was talking to a girl at lunch, and she asked, "What sign are you?"

And I said, "What do you guess?"

"Well, what?"

"The best!"

So she said, "You mean . . . Capricorn?"

"Yes!" I exclaimed. "How did you know?"

"I'm telling you, it's amazing because that fits so well with me, and I get along so well with you, I mean, this is like, wow!" She was excited and so happy. So I started reading up on the zodiac signs, all the characteristics associated with them, and how they match up together.

Using Gold's as my base, it was easy to make friends. The place was a melting pot of characters from all over the world: Australians, Africans, Europeans. I'd work out in the morning and say to a couple of guys, "Hey, do you want to go to lunch?" We'd go, and they'd tell me about their lives, and I'd tell them about mine, and we'd become buddies. At night I'd come back to train again, meet a different set of guys, go out with them for dinner, and get to know them too.

I was amazed by how readily people invited me to their homes and by how much Americans liked to celebrate. I'd never celebrated a birthday until I came to America; I had never even seen a cake with candles. But a girl invited me to her birthday party, and when my birthday came the following summer, the guys at the gym had a cake and candles for me. A guy would say, "I have to go home because it's my sister's first day of school, so we're going to celebrate." Or "Today is my parents' anniversary." I could not remember my parents ever even *talking* about their anniversary.

When Thanksgiving came, I had nothing planned because I didn't understand the tradition of this American holiday. But Bill Drake brought me to his house. I got to meet his mom, who served this extraordinary meal, and his dad, who was a professional comedian and was very, very funny. We have a saying in Austria: "You're so sweet I could eat you!" But because of the translation problem, when I tried using that to compliment Mrs. Drake, it came out really lewd. The whole family burst out laughing.

I felt even more amazed when a girl I dated invited me to her parents' house for Christmas. I said to myself, "God, I don't want to disrupt the family holiday." Not only did they treat me like a son but also every family member gave me a gift.

All of this hospitality was new and welcome, but it bothered me that I did not know how to respond. For instance, I'd never heard of sending a thank-you note, and yet Americans seemed to send them all the time.

"That is so weird," I thought. "Why can't you just say thank you over the phone or in person?" That's the way we did it in Europe. But here Joe Weider would invite me and a girlfriend to dinner, and afterward she'd say, "Give me his address because I want to write him a thank-you note."

And I would say, "Nah, come on, we already thanked him when we left."

"No, no, no, no, I grew up with manners."

I realized I'd better get with the program and learn American manners. Or maybe they were also European manners and I'd just never noticed. I checked with friends back in Europe in case I'd missed something. No, I had not; America really was different.

As a first step, I made it a rule to date only American girls; I did not want to hang out with girls who knew German. And I immediately signed up for English classes at Santa Monica Community College. I wanted my English to be good enough so that I could read newspapers and textbooks and go on to classes in other subjects. I wanted to speed up the process of learning to think, read, and write like an American. I didn't want to just wait till I picked it up.

One weekend a couple of girls took me up to San Francisco, and we stayed in Golden Gate Park. I said to myself, "This is unbelievable, how free people are in America. Look at this! Now we're sleeping at night in the park, and everyone is friendly." I didn't realize until much later that I had arrived in California at a totally crazy cultural moment. It was the late sixties, there was the hippie movement, free love, all this incredible change. The Vietnam War was at its peak. Richard Nixon was about to be elected president. Americans at the time felt like the world was turning upside down. But I had no idea that it hadn't always been this way. "So this is America," I thought.

I never heard many conversations about Vietnam. But personally I loved the idea of America pushing back on Communism, so if anybody had asked me, I'd have been for the war. I'd have said, "Fucking Communists, I despise them." I grew up next door to Hungary, and we always lived under the threat of Communism. Were they going to push through Austria just like they did Hungary in '56? Were we going to get caught in a nuclear exchange? The danger was so close. And we saw the effect that Communism had on the Czechs, the Polish, the Hungarians, the Bulgarians, the Yugoslavs, the East Germans—everywhere there was Communism around us. I remember going to West Berlin for a body-building exhibition. I'd looked across the Berlin Wall, across the border, and seen how dismal life was on the other side. It was literally like two different weathers. It felt like I was in sunshine and when you looked across the wall at East Berlin, there was rain. It was horrible. Horrible. So I felt very good that America was fighting Communism big-time.

It never struck me as strange that the girls I was dating weren't putting on makeup or lipstick or painting their nails. I thought having hairy legs and underarms was normal because in Europe none of the women waxed or shaved. In fact, I got caught by surprise by it one morning the following summer. I was in the shower with a girlfriend—we'd watched the Apollo astronauts make the first moonwalk on my little black-and-white TV the night before—and she asked. "Do you have a razor?"

"Why do you need a razor?"

"I hate these nubs on my legs." I didn't know what "nubs" meant, so she explained.

"What?" I said. "You shave?"

"Yeah, I shave my legs. It's so gross." I'd never heard that expression either. But I gave her my razor and watched her soap her legs, her calves, her shins, her knees, and shave them like she'd been doing it for five thousand years. Later that day I said to the guys at the gym, "Today a chick shaved in my fuckin' shower. Have you ever seen that?"

They looked at one another solemnly, nodded, and said, "Yeaaah." Then everybody cracked up. I tried to explain: "Oh, because in Europe, girls are all with the Bavarian look, you know, with the hair all over." That just made them laugh harder.

Eventually I pieced it together. Some of the girls I dated didn't shave: this was their protest against the establishment. They felt the beauty market was all about exploiting sex and telling people what to do, so they were rejecting that by being more natural. It was all part of the hippie era. The flowery dresses, the frizzy hair, the food they ate. They all wore beads, lots of beads. They brought incense to my apartment, so the whole place stank. That was bad, but I felt they were on the right track with the freedom of smoking a joint and the naturalness of nudity. All that was wonderful. I'd grown up a little bit like that myself, with the uninhibited scene at the Thalersee.

All that laid-back stuff was great, but my mission in America was clear. I was on a path. I needed to train like hell, diet like hell, eat well, and win more major titles the following fall. Weider had promised me a year, and I knew that if I did those things, I'd be on a roll.

Winning a couple of Mr. Universe contests in London didn't make me anywhere near the best bodybuilder in the world. There were too many overlapping titles, and not everyone was competing in the same place. Being the best would really come down to beating champions like the guys whose pictures I had hanging all over the walls of my room: Reg Park, Dave Draper, Frank Zane, Bill Pearl, Larry Scott, Chuck Sipes, Serge Nubret. They had inspired me, and I said to myself, "These are the kinds of people I have to go through eventually." My victories had put me in their league, but I was the newcomer with a lot left to prove.

At the very top of the pedestal was Sergio Oliva, the 230-pound, twenty-seven-year-old Cuban emigré. By now the muscle magazines simply called him the Myth. He'd taken his most recent Mr. Olympia title that fall in New York *unopposed*: not one of the other four bodybuilding champions invited to compete even showed up.

Oliva's background was even more unusual than mine. His father was a sugarcane laborer in pre-Castro Cuba, and during the revolution in the 1950s, Sergio enlisted in General Fulgencio Batista's army alongside his dad. After Fidel Castro and his rebel forces prevailed, Sergio established himself as an athlete. He was an Olympic weight lifter of much higher caliber than me, ending up on the Cuban team in the 1962 Central American and Caribbean Games. He would have led the team in the 1964 Olympics if he had not hated Castro's regime so much that he defected to the United States along with many of his teammates. He was also a terrific baseball player. That's what had helped him refine his waist: tens of thousands of reps twisting to swing a bat.

I'd met Sergio at the 1968 Mr. Universe contest in Miami, where he gave a posing demonstration that drove the audience wild. As one of the muscle magazines put it, his posing split the concrete. There was no question that Sergio was still way out of my reach. He was really ripped and pound for pound thicker, with more muscle intensity than I had. He had the rare ability among bodybuilders to look fantastic just standing relaxed. His silhouette was the best I'd ever seen: a perfect V-shape tapering from very wide shoulders to a naturally narrow, tubular waist and hips. The "victory pose," Sergio's trademark, was a move that very few bodybuilders in competition would even attempt. It involved simply facing the audience with the legs together and the arms extended straight overhead. It exposed the body completely: the huge, sweeping thighs built up from Olympic lifting, the tiny waist, and the near-perfect abdominals, triceps, and serratus. (The serrati are muscles on the sides of the rib cage.)

I was determined to beat this man eventually, but I was still far from having the kind of body I would need. I'd come to America like a hundred-carat diamond that everyone was looking at and saying, "Holy shit." But the diamond was only rough cut. It was not ready for display, at least not by American standards. Building a totally world-class body typically takes ten years at least, and I'd been training for only six. But I came on strong, and people were saying, "Look at the size of this young kid. What the hell? This guy, to me, has the most potential." So I'd won my victories in Europe as much on promise and courage as on the fine points of my physique. A huge amount work still remained to be done.

The ideal of bodybuilding is visual perfection, like an ancient Greek statue come to life. You sculpt your body the way an artist chisels stone. Say you need to add bulk and definition to your rear deltoid. You have to choose from an inventory of exercises for that muscle. The weight, the bench, or the machine becomes your chisel, and the sculpting could take a year.

This means you have to be able to see your body honestly and analyze its flaws. The judges in the top competitions scrutinize every detail: muscle size, definition, proportion, and symmetry. They even look at veins, which indicate an absence of fat under the skin.

In the mirror I could see plenty of strong points and plenty of weaknesses. I'd succeeded in building a foundation of power and mass. By combining Olympic lifting, power lifting, and bodybuilding, I'd developed a very thick and wide back, close to perfect. My biceps were extraordinary in size, height, and muscle peak. I had ripped pectoral muscles, and the best side-chest pose of anybody. I had a real bodybuilder's frame, with wide shoulders and narrow hips, which helped me achieve that ideal V shape that is one element of perfection.

But I also had some shortcomings. Relative to my torso, my limbs were too long. So I was always having to build the arms and legs to make the proportions seem right. Even with massive twenty-nine-inch thighs, my legs still looked on the thin side. My calves fell short compared to my thighs, and my triceps fell short compared to the biceps.

The challenge was to take the curse off all those weak points. It's human nature to work on the things that we are good at. If you have big biceps, you want to do an endless number of curls because it's so satisfying to see this major bicep flex. To be successful, however, you must be brutal with yourself and focus on the flaws. That's when your eye, your honesty, and your ability to listen to others come in. Bodybuilders who are blind to themselves or deaf to others usually fall behind.

Even more challenging is the biological fact that, in every individual, some body parts develop more readily than others. So when you start working out, you might find yourself saying after two years,

"Gee, isn't it interesting that my forearms never got really as muscular as the upper arms," or "Isn't it interesting that my calves somehow aren't growing so much." That was my particular bugaboo—the calves. I started out training them ten sets three times a week just like the other body parts, but they did not respond the same way. Other muscle groups were way ahead.

Reg Park gave me the wake-up call on that. He had perfect twenty-one-inch calves, so fully developed that each one looked like an upside-down valentine heart under the skin. When I trained with him in South Africa, I saw what he did to achieve that. He trained his calves every day, not just three times a week, and with a mind-blowing amount of weight. I was proud that I'd worked up to calf raises with three hundred pounds, but Reg had a cable system that let him apply one thousand. I said to myself, "This is what I need to do. I have to train my calves totally differently and not give them even a chance of not growing." When I got to California, I made a point of cutting off all my sweatpants at the knees. I would keep my strongpoints covered—my biceps, my chest, my back, my thighs—but I made sure that my calves were exposed so everyone could see. I was relentless and did fifteen sets, sometimes twenty sets, of calf raises every single day.

I knew all the muscles I needed to focus on systematically. In general, I had better muscles for pulling motions (biceps, lats, and back muscles) than for pressing motions (front deltoids and triceps). It was one of those hereditary things that meant I had to push those muscles much harder and do more sets. I'd built the big back, but now I had to think about creating the ideal definition and separation between the lats and the pecs and the serratus. I had to do exercises for the serratus, so that meant more closed-grip chin-ups. I had to lower the lats a little, which meant more cable raises and one-arm raises. I had to get the rear deltoids, which meant more lateral raises, in which you hold a dumbbell in each hand while standing and lift them straight out to the sides.

I had a whole list of muscles to attack: the rear deltoid and the lower latissimus and the intercostals and the abdominals and the calves, and blah, blah, blah! These all had to be built and chiseled and separated and brought into proper proportion to one another. Each morning, I'd get breakfast with one or two training buddies, usually at a deli called Zucky's on the corner of Fifth Street and Wilshire Boulevard. They had tuna, they had eggs, they had salmon, all the things I liked. Or we would go to one of those family breakfast places like Denny's.

Unless I had English class, I would go straight to Gold's and work out. Afterward, we might hit the beach, where there would be more exercises on the open-air weight-lifting platform, plus swimming and jogging and lying on the sand to perfect our tans. Or I'd go over to Joe Weider's building and work with the guys cooking up stories for the magazine.

I always split my routine into two training sessions. On Monday, Wednesday, and Friday mornings, I would focus on, say, chest and back. At night I would come back and work on my thighs and calves, and then practice posing and do other exercises. On Tuesdays, Thursdays, and Saturdays, it was shoulders, arms, and forearms. Of course, calves every day, abs every day except Sunday, which was a rest day.

Often for lunch or dinner we'd hit one of the local smorgasbords. Growing up in Europe, I'd never even heard of a smorgasbord. The idea of a restaurant where you could eat all you wanted would have been incomprehensible. The bodybuilders would start with five, six, or seven eggs, after which we'd go to the next station and eat all the tomatoes and vegetables. Then we would have the steak, and then the fish. Muscle magazines in those days were always warning that you had to have your amino acids, and that you had to be careful because the amino acids in certain foods weren't complete. "Hey," we said, "let's not even think about it; let's just eat all the proteins. We have the egg, the fish, the beef, the turkey, the cheese—let's just have it all!" You would think the owners of the smorgasbord would have charged us more at least. But they treated us no different from any other customer. It was as if God had created a restaurant for bodybuilders.

During those first months in Los Angeles, everything was going so well that it was hard to believe. There were surprisingly few consequences from my car crash, apart from the gash in my thigh. The crocodile wrestler who owned the GTO scarcely batted an eye about the damage. He worked for a dealership where he had his pick of the used cars, and his reaction was "Don't worry about it." In fact, he hired me. One of the dealer's specialties was exporting used cars, and I earned pocket money that fall by driving cars down to Long Beach and onto a freighter headed for Australia.

A few insurance companies called the gym to talk about damages to the other cars, but the conversations were too hard for me to understand, so I'd hand the phone to a workout partner. He'd explain that I was new to America and had no money, and the companies gave up. The only dramatic effect of the accident was that it made me frantic about getting health insurance. In Europe, of course, everybody was insured: you fell into a certain category if you were a student; if you were a child, you were covered by your parents' insurance; if you had a job, you had workers' coverage—even the homeless were covered. It scared me not to be covered here. I kept worrying, "If I get sick, what do I do?" I had no idea that you could go to an emergency room and receive free medical care. And even if I'd known, I wanted no handouts. Though it took me six months, I made sure that I paid back Bill Drake for my doctor bill.

It so happened that Larry Scott, a former Mr. Olympia who was retired from bodybuilding but still worked out every day, was now a regional sales manager for a big insurance company.

"I hear you're looking for insurance," he said to me. "Let me help you."

He came up with a policy that cost $23.60 a month, plus another $5 for disability, which sounded expensive to me because I earned only $65 a week from Weider. But I bought it and must have been one of the few new immigrants in LA with health insurance.

Around Thanksgiving 1969 I got an invitation to a December bodybuilding competition and demonstration in Hawaii. The crocodile wrestler had been planning to go home for the holidays, and he said, "I love Hawaii. Why don't I come with you and hang out and train with you for a few days, and then I'll go on to Australia from there?" The plan sounded good to me. Besides the obvious attractions of the beaches and the girls, Hawaii offered the chance to get to know Dr. Richard You, a US Olympic team physician who practiced there, and to visit weight-lifting legends like Tommy Kono, Timothy Leon, and Harold "Oddjob" Sakata (whom I already knew from Munich). So my buddy and I went to Joe Weider and asked if he knew the promoters and what he thought about me going. He was all for it. I could use the experience, he said, and the pressure of an upcoming competition would make me train harder.

CHAPTER 6

Lazy Bastards

JOE WEIDER CALLED THE hard-core bodybuilders lazy bastards. From what I could tell, he was mostly right. The typical customers at Gold's Gym were guys with day jobs: construction workers, cops, professional athletes, business owners, salesmen, and, as time went by, actors. But with a few exceptions, the bodybuilders *were* lazy. A lot of them were unemployed. They wanted to lie on the beach and have somebody sponsor them. It was always, "Hey, Joe, can you give me an airline ticket to fly to New York to the contest?" "Hey, Joe, can you give me a salary so I can train in the gym?" "Hey, Joe, can I have the food supplements for free?" "Hey, Joe, can you get me a car?" When they didn't get the handouts they felt entitled to, they were pissed. "Be careful of Joe," I'd hear them say. "That cheap son of a bitch doesn't keep his promises." I saw him completely differently. It's true Joe had a hard time parting with money. He came from a poor background where he had to fight for every nickel. But I didn't see any reason why he should just hand out money to any bodybuilder who asked.

Joe was a master at knowing exactly how to appeal to young and vulnerable males. When I first picked up his magazines at age fifteen, I was wondering how I would be strong enough to defend myself. How could I make sure that I'd be successful with the girls? How could I make sure that I would earn a great living? Joe sucked me into a world where I would feel special right away. It was the old Charles Atlas message: Send away for my course, and no one will be kicking sand in your face. You will be a great man in no time, you will be picking up girls, you will be walking around on Venice Beach!

Joe gave all the great bodybuilders nicknames in his magazines, like superheroes. Dave Draper, who trained at Gold's, was the Blond Bomber. I'd seen him in the 1967 Tony Curtis movie *Don't Make Waves.* That fired my imagination even more: here was another bodybuilder who'd gotten into movies! Weider's magazines photographed Dave with a surfboard walking around on the beach. That looked cool. In the background was a Volkswagen dune buggy, with the exposed wheels, and that looked cool too. He was surrounded by beautiful girls who gazed at him in awe.

Other pictures in the magazine showed scientists and technicians in white lab coats developing nutritional supplements in the Weider Research Clinic. "Weider Research Clinic," I would say to myself, "this is unbelievable!" And there were pictures of airplanes with "Weider" painted on the side in big letters. I'd imagined an outfit the size of General Motors, with a fleet of planes flying around the globe delivering Weider equipment and food supplements. The writing in the magazine sounded fabulous too when my friends translated it for me. The stories talked about "blasting the muscles" and building "deltoids like cannonballs" and "a chest like a fortress."

And now here I was, six years later, on Venice Beach! Just like Dave Draper, only now it was me with the dune buggy and the surfboard and the adoring girls. Of course, by this time I was aware enough to see that Weider was creating a whole fantasy world, with a foundation in reality but skyscrapers of hype. Yes, there were surfboards, but the bodybuilders didn't really surf. Yes, there were pretty girls, but they were models who got paid for the photo session. (Actually, one of the girls was Joe's wife, Betty, a beautiful model whom he didn't have to pay.) Yes, there were Weider supplements and, yes, some research took place, but there was no big building in Los Angeles called the Weider Research Clinic.

Yes, Weider products were distributed around the world, but there were no Weider planes. Discovering the hype didn't bother me, though. Enough of it was true.

Not only was I fascinated to be in the middle of this, I couldn't wait to see what happened next. "I have to pinch myself," I would think. I told my friends that my worst nightmare would be to feel somebody shaking me and hear my mother's voice say, "Arnold, you overslept! You have to get up! You're going to be two hours late for work. Hurry! You have to get to the factory!" And I'd be saying, "Noooo! Why did you wake me up? I was having the most incredible dream. I want to see how it turns out."

Joe himself wasn't the easiest guy to like. Starting in the Great Depression, he and his younger brother, Ben, had clawed their way out of the slums of Montreal and built their businesses from scratch. The Weider magazines, equipment, nutritional supplement businesses, and competitions were bodybuilding's biggest empire, bringing in about $20 million a year, which made Joe and Ben the men to know in what was still a money-starved sport. The only other people who actually made a living out of bodybuilding were a few promoters and gym owners; none of the bodybuilders themselves did, and I was the only one I'd ever heard of getting paid just to train.

Joe and Ben were always pushing to expand, and they didn't mind invading other people's turf. In 1946 they created their own association, the International Federation of Body Building (IFBB), to challenge both the American Athletic Union, which controlled Olympic weight lifting and bodybuilding in North America, and the National Amateur Body-Builders' Association (NABBA), which regulated bodybuilding in the United Kingdom. They started feuds by promoting their own versions of the Mr. America competition, which belonged to the AAU, and Mr. Universe, which belonged to NABBA. Just like in boxing, the duplication of titles caused a lot of confusion but helped bodybuilding to expand.

Joe was also the first to offer a cash prize for winning a bodybuilding championship. When he invented Mr. Olympia in 1965, the prize was $1,000 and an engraved silver plate. In any of the other contests, like Mr. Universe, all you got was a trophy. Joe's competitions also offered the best deal for contestants. He'd pay for your hotel and plane fare. But he would always hold onto the return ticket until you'd done your stint posing for his photographers after the event. Actually, Joe would have preferred to shoot the bodybuilders before the event, but the bodybuilders usually didn't feel ready to be photographed beforehand and Franco Columbu and I were the only ones who would agree. We liked it because being photographed forced us to be in good shape and gave us a chance to practice posing.

Mr. Olympia itself was sheer promotional genius. The idea was to choose a champion of champions and Mr. Olympia was by invitation only, and you had to be a present or past Mr. Universe to qualify. So Joe was cashing in on the proliferation of titles he'd created! No wonder the Weiders drove people crazy. Their latest campaign was lobbying the International Olympic Committee to recognize bodybuilding as an international sport.

I liked the fact that Joe Weider was a hustler. He had magazines. He had a federation. He had knowledge. He shook things up and wanted to make bodybuilding really big. He had something to offer that I needed, and he felt I had something to offer that he needed.

Plus, I was not a lazy bastard. The first thing I told him when I got to California was "I don't want to hang around. I don't want to take your money for nothing. Give me something to do where I can learn." He had a retail store on Fifth Street in Santa Monica that sold nutritional supplements and weight-lifting equipment. So I asked if I could work there. "I want to help customers," I told him. "It helps me to learn business and practice my English, and I like dealing with people."

Joe loved hearing this. "You see, Arnold," he said in his Canadian accent, "you want to work, you want to build yourself, you are German, you are a machine, you are unbelievable. *You are not like these lazy bastards!*"

I loved the way Joe's mind worked. He had already spun a whole myth about me: that I was this German machine, totally reliable, there's no malfunction, it always works. And he was going to apply his know-how and power to make this machine come to life and walk around like Frankenstein. I thought this was very funny. I didn't mind him thinking of me as his creation because I knew that meant that Joe Weider would love me. This fit right in with my goal of becoming the world champion, and the more he thought about me that way, the more generous he was.

Right from the beginning, I felt that he looked at me as the son he never had. I felt that this was a unique opportunity to learn. My own father gave me advice about being disciplined, tough, and brave, but not advice on how to succeed in business. I was always searching for mentors who could pick up where my father left off. Having Joe around was like having a father who appreciated what I was trying to do.

The company was still based back east in Union City, New Jersey, but the Weiders were building a new headquarters in the San Fernando Valley. Joe would come out every few weeks to supervise. He took me along to the construction meetings and let me hang around with him to see how the business worked. When it came to the publishing side of his business, he was always looking for printers who could do a better job and charge less, and he'd include me in those discussions, too. I'd visit him in New York and sit in on meetings there also. After my English improved, he took me on a business trip to Japan, to learn how he conducted negotiations overseas and see how essential distribution is—not just in magazines but in the success of any business.

Joe emphasized the importance of going global rather than doing business in just one country. He knew that was where the future was headed. On every trip, he had multiple goals: in Japan, for example, we also met with the national bodybuilding federation, and Joe advised them on how to improve their contests. Long plane rides with Joe were always stimulating. He'd talk about business, art, antiques, sports. He was a student of world history and Jewish history. He was also heavily into psychology. He must have gone to a shrink.

I was in heaven, since I'd always felt that my future would be in business. No matter what I was involved in, part of my mind was always wondering, "Is this what I'm meant for? What is the mission here?" I knew I was meant for something special, but what was it? Being a businessman, to me, was the ultimate. And now this leader was taking me on business trips, and I was learning just what I needed. Maybe I could end up marketing and selling food supplements, home equipment, and equipment for gyms, owning a gymnasium chain, and running a business empire—like Reg Park but on a global scale. How wild would that be! I knew I looked at business differently than other bodybuilders did. If Weider had offered the Japan trip to one of the other guys, he would have said, "Nah, Japan sounds boring. What gyms do they have over there? I want to work out," or something stupid like that. So maybe becoming the next generation Weider really was my destiny. Joe clearly was taking great joy in teaching me. He'd say, "You are really into this!"

What I learned from him went way beyond business. He was a collector of fine furniture and art, which I found fascinating. When I stayed at his apartment in New York, I looked at all the art and antiques. He talked about auctions, saying, "I bought this for this amount. Now it is worth this amount."

That was the first time I understood that old furniture can go up in value. Up until then, I'd just looked at it as old junk, like we had in Austria. So now Joe was saying, "Look at this from the French Empire period. This wood is mahogany. See the swans carved in the armrests? The swans were the emblem of Napoléon's wife the Empress Joséphine. And see, it has this sphinx made of brass embedded in the back? The French were really into Egyptian motifs." I started going with him to art auctions in New York at Sotheby's, Christie's, and other houses.

The Napoléon chair was one of Joe's prize pieces. He kept it in the guest room. The first time I stayed there, he made a big fuss about it: "It's very fragile, and very, very expensive. Make sure you don't sit on it or even touch it, okay?" I wanted to be careful with the chair, but that night when I was taking off my pants to go to bed, my foot got stuck, and I lost my balance and fell right onto it. The chair collapsed under my weight—it looked like it had exploded. I went to find Joe and said, "You have to see this. I just destroyed the chair."

He rushed into the room, and when he saw the pieces all over the rug he almost fainted. Then he started cursing. "*Oh! Bastard!* That's an expensive chair!" But he caught himself because he realized it sounded cheap to be complaining so much. It doesn't matter what chair it is, when they break, you can put them together again. It's not like it was gone, because it only really broke where it was glued together; where the joints were. It just fell apart when I landed on top of it.

I felt guilty, of course, but I still couldn't resist saying, "I can't believe that I hurt my knee, I hurt my hip, and you never asked, 'How are you feeling?' or said, 'Don't worry about that, I'm more concerned about you.' You are supposed to be like my father figure here in America! Here you are only concerned about this chair."

This made Joe feel really terrible. "Aw, Christ," he said, "you're right. Look at this! How cheap they put this together." And then he called *them* the bastards, the Napoléon guys who built the chair.

After that visit to New York, I flew to Chicago to see the AAU's Mr. America contest and spend a week training with Sergio Oliva. We'd be competing that fall, but that didn't get in the way of his hospitality. He and his wife had me to dinner at their apartment, and I received my first exposure to black Cuban Latino culture. Sergio had a jive way of talking and dressing and a different way of relating to his wife than I'd ever seen, with lots of temper and hollering on both sides. Even so, he was a true gentleman.

I was on a secret reconnaissance mission: I thought that you have to sneak into the enemy camp and experience how he sees the world! What is it that makes him a champion? What does he eat, how does he live, what is there to learn from the way he trains? How does he practice his posing? What is his attitude about competition? None of this information would give me the body to beat him, but it would motivate me and show me what I needed to win. Could I find a weakness I could use psychologically? I was convinced that sports are not just physical but also psychological warfare.

The first thing I discovered was that Sergio worked even harder than me. He had a full-time job at a steel mill, and, after spending all day in the heat of the furnaces, he'd go to the Duncan YMCA and train for hours. He was one of those guys that just didn't burn up easily. Every day, to start his routine, he would complete ten sets of twenty chin-ups. That wasn't for training his back. That was *just to warm up*. Every day. He had a number of unusual techniques that I could pick up. He did his bench press as half reps without ever locking out his elbows. That kept full tension all the time on the pectoral muscle, and he had beautiful, full pecs. There were also things I learned in the way that he practiced his posing.

Now, I also understood that what worked for Sergio wasn't necessarily going to work for me. We were more like mirror opposites. I had great biceps and back muscles, but his front deltoids, triceps, and pecs were better than mine. To beat him, I would have to work those muscles much, much harder and do more sets. His other great advantages were years of experience and great natural potential—he was truly an animal. But above all it was the fire in Sergio that inspired me. I said to myself that I would have to step it up.

I knew who would help me do that. I had world-class training partners in California, but almost from the minute I set foot there, I lobbied Joe to bring over my friend Franco. I missed many of my Munich buddies, and they must thought it was strange how I'd disappeared to California. But I missed Franco especially because we were like brothers, and he was the perfect training partner for me. Franco was a foreigner like me, and even in Munich, we both had the immigrant mentality and the same kind of hunger. Hard work was the only thing we could count on. I thought America would be great for Franco like it was for me.

Joe was never going to buy the sentimental argument, so I put it in commercial terms. "Bring Franco," I told him, "and you're going to have professional bodybuilding locked up. For years! You're going to have the best tall man in the heavyweight division"—meaning me—"and the best small man in the lightweight division." I described how pound for pound Franco was the most powerful lifter in the world (it was true; he could deadlift more than four times his weight) and how he'd been reshaping himself for bodybuilding.

Second, I told Joe, Franco was my ideal training partner, and if we could work together, I'd be an even more successful star. And third, I assured him, Franco was a hardworking guy who wouldn't take advantage of being in California just to loaf on the beach. He'd been a shepherd, a bricklayer, and a taxi driver. "He is no lazy bastard," I said. "You'll see."

Joe dragged his heels. Whenever I brought up Franco, he'd act like he'd never heard the name, and I'd have to make all the arguments again. But finally, in mid-1969, he caved and agreed to invite Franco and pay him the same $65 a week he was paying me. Then right away he started to brag about this fantastic small guy he was bringing from Europe. Except that he was not good with names and still could not quite remember Franco's. "Guess who we're bringing over now?" he announced at lunch. "Francisco Franco!"

Artie Zeller, the photographer who'd met me at the airport the year before, happened to be there and corrected him. "That's the dictator of Spain."

"No. I mean Columbus is his name."

"Are you sure?" asked Artie. "Columbus discovered America."

"No, wait, I mean Franco Nero."

"He's an Italian actor. He's in Westerns."

"Arnold! Who the hell are we bringing?" Joe finally asked.

"Franco *Columbu*."

"Aw, Jesus. Bastard! Italians! Why do Italians have such weird names? They all sound the same."

I picked up Franco at the airport in my white VW bug. I'd dressed it up with a racing steering wheel by this time, and it looked great. To welcome my friend to America and celebrate his arrival, I thought a marijuana cookie would be best. Frank Zane, the bodybuilder who'd beat me in Miami, had become a good friend and was into baking his own. Every so often he gave me one. "This will be funny," I thought. "I'm picking up Franco, he's going to be hungry after his long flight, so I'll give him half of the cookie." I wasn't going to give him the whole cookie because I didn't know how his body would react.

So when Franco got in the car, I asked, "Are you hungry?"

"Yes, I'm starving."

"Well, luckily, I have a cookie here. Let's share it." The first place I took him was Artie's apartment. Artie's wife, Josie, was Swiss, and I thought Franco might feel more comfortable around people who knew German. He spent the first hour after we arrived lying on the rug in their living room laughing.

"Is he always this funny?" Artie asked.

"He must have drunk a beer or something," I said. "But he is a funny guy."

"Oh, he's hilarious." Artie and Josie were both laughing like hell too. A few days later, I asked Franco, "You know why you were laughing so much?" and told him about the cookie.

"I knew there was something!" he said. "You've got to give me more of that because it felt so good!"

It turned out, though, that Franco had developed a severe reaction to a smallpox vaccination he'd received just before leaving Munich. His arm swelled up, he had fever and chills, and he couldn't eat. This went on for a couple of weeks. I was making him protein drinks every few hours. I ended up bringing a doctor to the apartment, because I was scared Franco was going to die. The doctor promised that Franco would eventually be fine.

I'd done such a great sales job with Joe Weider that he was eager to meet Franco and see how muscular he was. But my friend had shrunk from 170 pounds down to around 150. Joe would come over, and I'd hide Franco in the bedroom and tell Joe, "Oh, Franco, he's so busy, he went over to Gold's again to work out." Or "Yeah, yeah, he really wants to meet you, and he wants to look perfect, so he's on the beach getting a tan."

The plan was always for Franco to room with me. My apartment had only one bedroom, however, so I kept the bedroom and he slept on the pull-out couch. The place was so small that there wasn't even enough wall space to put up posters. But in Munich, I'd lived in a closet in the gym, so this was pure luxury to me. Franco felt that way too. We had a living room *and* a bedroom, and there were curtains. The beach was only three blocks away. Our bathroom had a sink, a toilet, and a bathtub with a shower, far better than what we'd had in Europe. No matter how small the place was, we felt like we'd really arrived.

I had visited Franco many times at his room in Munich. He always kept the place extremely clean. So I knew he'd be a great roommate, and that's how it worked out. Our place was immaculate. We vacuumed regularly; the dishes were always done, with nothing piling up; and the bed was always made, military style. We were both into the discipline of getting up in the morning and straightening up before you leave the house. The more you do it, the more automatic it becomes, and the less effort it takes. Our apartment was always way cleaner than anyone else's I went to, men or women. Especially women. They were like piglets.

Franco was the chef and I was the dishwasher, that was the deal. It didn't take him long to find all the Italian joints to buy his spaghetti and his potatoes and his meat. As far as supermarkets were concerned, though, he turned up his nose. "Ah, the Americans," he'd say. "You gotta go in the little store, the Italian store." He was always coming home with small food packages and jars and saying, "You only get this in an Italian store."

We were very happy in the apartment—until the landlord kicked us out. He knocked on the door one day and said we had to leave because it was only a one-bedroom. It was considered suspicious in those days in Southern California to have two guys sleeping in a one-bedroom place. I explained how Franco slept on the living room couch, but he just insisted, "It's really intended for one person." We wanted a bigger place anyway, so we didn't care. We found a beautiful two-bedroom apartment nearby and moved there.

The new place had wall space for us to decorate, but we had nothing to put up; I sure didn't have the money to buy art. Then one day in Tijuana, I saw this cool black-and-white poster of a cowboy with two guns drawn. It cost just $5, so I bought it. When I got home, I put it up on the wall with Scotch tape. It looked beautiful hanging there.

Then Artie came over. As soon as he saw it, he started snorting and acting pissed off. "Ugh," he said, "what a fool."

I said, "What's the matter?"

"Oh, Reagan, I mean, Jesus."

"That's a great picture. I found it in Tijuana."

He said, "Do you know who this is?"

"Well, it says below, 'Ronald Reagan.' "

"He's the governor of the state of California."

I said, "Really! That's amazing. That's twice as good. I have the governor of the state of California hanging here."

"Yeah, he used to be in Westerns," Artie said.

With Franco as my training partner, I could concentrate on my competition goals. I was determined to win the IFBB Mr. Universe title that I'd failed to get in Miami. That loss to Frank Zane still stung so much that I didn't want to just win the contest; I wanted to win it so decisively that people would forget I'd ever lost.

Then I planned to go over to London and win the NABBA Mr. Universe again. That would give me, at age twenty-two, four Mr. Universe titles on both sides of the Atlantic, more than anyone ever in the sport. It would gain me back the momentum I thought I'd lost, the halo of inevitability that put me in the spotlight and blew people's minds. And most important, it would broadcast that the only two bodybuilding champions the world should be looking at were Sergio Oliva and me. That was my goal: to make the leap from being one of the six or eight top guys to one of only two. It was my responsibility to pull this off; it was what I'd come to America to do. If I accomplished it and solidified my position in the bodybuilding world, from then on, I would be on a roll. Nobody would stop me.

After that, the next big goal would be to beat Sergio and win the Mr. Olympia title. I wasn't going to make the mistake I made going into Miami, where I thought I could coast to a victory. I trained as hard as I could.

Holding the Mr. Universe competition in Miami had been an experiment for the Weiders, and for 1969 they moved it back to New York. To pump up the excitement, they'd also scheduled the Mr. America, Mr. Universe, and Mr. Olympia competitions to take place on the same day, back-to-back-to-back in the Brooklyn Academy of Music, the largest performance venue in Brooklyn.

I'd been featured and hyped nonstop all year along with the other top bodybuilders in Joe's magazines, but Mr. Universe was my first major competition since the previous fall. I was eager to see how my newly Americanized body would go over with the judges and fans. The contest went even better than I'd planned. In one of the strongest fields ever, I ran over all the rest. Thousands of sets on Joe Gold's machines had helped me define my muscles to the point where neither the big guys nor the small guys were much of a threat. Plus I had a California tan!

Winning was such a high that I thought again about the Mr. Olympia event. What if I'd underestimated the progress I'd made? If I beat Sergio in that, I would be king!

The morning of the contest, he showed up in his trademark flashy clothes: a custom-tailored checked suit and vest, dark tie, black leather shoes, a mod hat, and lots of gold jewelry. We teased each other while we sat watching the Mr. America preliminaries.

"Hey, Monster, you in shape?" I asked.

"Hey, baby, you gonna see somethin' tonight, I tell you," Sergio said. "You gonna see it, but you ain't gonna believe it. Ain't nobody gonna believe it."

Finally, we were warming up backstage. Sergio was famous for his lengthy pumping-up routine, during which he always wore a long butcher's coat so the rival bodybuilders couldn't see his muscles. When the time came for us to go onstage, he took off the coat and walked ahead of me down the hall. Of course, he knew I'd be checking him out. Very casually, he lifted a shoulder and spread out the biggest lat muscle I'd ever seen. It was the size of a giant manta ray. Then he did the same thing with the other shoulder. His back was so huge it looked like it was blocking all the light in the hall. It was a really effective psych. I knew right then that I was going to lose.

We each posed, first me and then Sergio, and we each had the house screaming and stomping. Then the judges, announcing that they couldn't decide, called us back onstage to pose simultaneously. Someone shouted, "Pose!" but for a minute, neither of us budged—like we were daring each other to go first. Finally, I smiled and hit my double-biceps pose, one of my best. That brought a roar from the crowd. Sergio answered with his trademark two-arm overhead victory pose. Again the crowd went nuts, chanting "Sergio! Sergio!" I executed a chest pose, which he started to match but then thought better of it, shifting to a "most muscular" shot. More screams for Sergio. I did my best trademark pose—the three-quarters back—but that wasn't enough to turn it. He was simply still ahead of me.

I just kept smiling and hitting poses. I'd already done what I came to do, and I was much better off than the year before. I'd run over everybody except him. I could say to myself, "You did great, Arnold, and Sergio's days are numbered." But for now he was still clearly the champ, and when the judges declared for him, I gave him a big hug onstage. I thought Sergio deserved all of the attention. I was much younger, and I'd be number one in no time, and then I would enjoy all of this attention. In the meantime, he should have it. He was better.

That fall, Joe Weider launched me on phase two of my American dream: getting into movies. When word got around that some producers needed a bodybuilder to star in a film, Joe recommended me.

What happened with *Hercules in New York* was like one of those Hollywood fantasies. You come off the boat and walk down the street, and somebody says, "You're the one! You have the exactly the look!" and offers you a movie role. You hear it all the time, but no one knows if it's true.

As a matter of fact, former Mr. America Dennis Tinerino, whom I'd upset in 1967 to win my first Mr. Universe competition, had already been offered the part. Dennis was a legitimate champ: he had bounced back to win the amateur Mr. Universe title in 1968. But Joe didn't want him to get the role because Dennis worked mostly with the other bodybuilding federations. So he called the producers and told them that in Vienna I had been a Shakespearean actor, and they should dump Dennis and take me. "I know Tinerino won the Mr. Universe, but Schwarzenegger won it three times," he said. "You will get the best bodybuilder in the world. Schwarzenegger is your guy. He is extraordinary. His stage presence is outstanding."

There is no such thing as an Austrian Shakespearean actor. It doesn't exist. I didn't know what the hell Joe was talking about, but he told them he was managing me and didn't allow them to talk to me. He was worried that I couldn't speak English well enough, so when they said they wanted to meet me, he said, "No. Arnold's not around yet. He will be coming soon." All this really cracked me up. Eventually we went to see the producers, and Joe told me not to say much. The next thing I knew, I got the job. Joe knew how to sell.

After the Mr. Olympia competition, Franco and I went to London, where I won the NABBA Mr. Universe competition again, setting the record as the first bodybuilder to win four Mr. Universe crowns. Then I flew back to New York to become the new Hercules.

Hercules in New York was a low-budget spoof on the big sword-and-sandal epics. The idea was that Hercules gets bored living on Mount Olympus and rides a stray lightning bolt to present-day New York, even though his father, Zeus, forbids him to leave. He makes friends with a guy named Pretzie, a nebbishy character who runs a pretzel cart in Central Park. Pretzie tries to help Hercules adjust as he gets mixed up with gangsters, fights a grizzly bear, rides his chariot through Times Square, descends into hell, figures out how to buy lunch from the vending machines at the Automat, and gets involved with the pretty daughter of a mythology professor. Just as Hercules is adapting to life in the big city, Zeus runs out of patience and sends some other gods to fetch him back.

It was not a bad concept, putting Hercules in modern New York City, and the movie was very funny, especially Arnold Stang, the comedian who played Pretzie. He was so little and I was so big. I found the experience daunting, I have to admit. I thought it would take me at least until I was thirty to be in a movie. But here I was at twenty-two, in America, starring as Hercules. How many people got to live this kind of dream? "You should be happy!" I told myself.

At the same time I thought, "But I'm not ready. I haven't even learned about acting!"

If I'd had acting experience, it would have been a lot better. The producers hired an acting coach and a dialogue coach, but two weeks with them couldn't make up for my lack of English and lack of experience. I wasn't up to par. I had no clue what this type of performance should involve. I couldn't even understand all the sentences in the script.

The guy who played Zeus was a TV soap opera veteran named Ernest Graves. I remember cracking up in the middle of filming a scene because he produced this huge God voice for a speech he was supposed to give, and it was so different from the voice of the guy I'd met in the makeup trailer. He really got into it, and that was funny to me. But, of course, you're not supposed to laugh on the set. You're supposed to help the other performers and really buy into what they say. That's the whole concept of being supportive. When you're not on camera, and the camera is behind your shoulder, you stay in character, act your part, giving it everything you have in order to draw the best out of the actor who is being filmed. That is so important, but I had no clue. When something struck me as funny, I just laughed.

On the second-to-last day, I finally felt it, what acting is about. We were shooting a sentimental scene where Hercules and Pretzie are saying good-bye. I really got into it, just like they always talk about in acting. The director came over afterward and said, "I got goose bumps when you did that."

"Yeah, it was strange," I said. "I really felt that scene."

"You're going to be good. I think you'll have an acting career because as time went on with this project, you really started to get how to do it."

One of the producers asked if they could bill me as Arnold Strong—nobody could pronounce Schwarzenegger, he said, it was a ludicrous name, and besides putting Arnold Strong and Arnold Stang on the poster would be funny. When they edited the film, they dubbed another actor's voice over mine, because my accent was too thick for anybody to understand. Maybe the best thing about *Hercules in New York* was that for many years it wasn't even shown in the US: the production company went bankrupt, so the film went on the shelf before it could be released.

But even so, starring as Hercules was way beyond any dream for me. And they paid me $1,000 a week. Best of all, I got to send photographs home to my parents and write, "You see? I told you the whole thing was going to work. I came to America, won Mr. Universe, and now I'm in the movies."

I headed back to California a very happy guy. Joe Weider had promised to stake me for a year, and that time was up. But there was no question he wanted me to stay. As I became more and more successful, he kept thinking up new ways to feature me in the stories and advertisements in his magazines. He asked if I would take a tape recorder and interview the other bodybuilders. I didn't have to write the stories, just make the tapes, and the writers would turn them into a series of articles giving readers the inside scoop. All I had to do was talk to the others about their training routines, their diet, what vitamins they took, and so on. The guys came over, and Franco cooked them a big Italian meal—paid for by Joe, of course, as were the gallons of wine we opened. After everyone was loosened up, I brought out the tape recorder. Somehow we didn't get around to the subject of training and nutrition. First I asked, "We want to know all your girlfriends. Have you ever been out with boyfriends? What do you do when you go to bed?"

Joe's eyes got wider and wider when we played the tape for him the next day. "Dammit! Dammit!" he exploded. "Idiots! Clowns! There's nothing here I can use!" Franco and I were cracking up, but I promised to do the interviews again.

I started taping the bodybuilders one by one. Most bodybuilders don't have very interesting insights or routines. But I'd noticed that Joe's writers could make a story out of anything. So after the first few times, I'd just stop the interview if I got bored, and the tapes I gave Joe kept getting shorter and shorter. He would grumble, but he really wanted those interviews, and I would say innocently, "I can't help it if these guys don't have any ideas." The last couple of interviews were like five minutes and eight minutes, and Joe finally threw up his hands. "Aw hell," he growled. "Just give me back my machine."

CHAPTER 7

Experts in Marble and Stone

THE MONEY JOE PAID me never went very far. I was always looking for ways to earn more. As my English got better, and I could explain how to train, I would give seminars at Gold's and other gyms. Each netted $500.

I also launched a mail-order business out of my apartment. It grew out of the fan mail I was getting. People wanted to know how I trained my arms, my chest. And they asked how they could get fit themselves. I couldn't answer all these letters, so in the beginning, I got the writers at the magazine to help me with standard letters that I could send out. That gave me the idea of selling a series of booklets.

In America, unlike Europe, there weren't a million obstacles to starting a business. All I had to do was go down to city hall and pay $3.75 for a permit, and then rent a post office box to receive the orders. Next came the California Board of Equalization and the IRS. They'd ask, "How much do you think you'll make?"

"I hope a thousand dollars a month." So you'd pay $320 for the first estimated payment. There was no interrogation. They were kind, sweet, accommodating. When Franco and I started a bricklaying business, it was the same thing. We walked out shaking our heads, and Franco said, "This is why they call this the land of opportunity." We were so happy.

Basically, my booklets were the articles I'd been writing for Joe, which the writers and photographers helped me flesh out by adding more details and photos. We made a booklet for arms, one for chest, one for back, one for calves and thighs, how to get a more symmetrical body, how to gain weight, how to pose, and so on—ten different courses. You could order the whole set for $15 or $20 or pick and choose for $1 or $2 each. People asked for photos of me also, so I had an album printed up of my favorite shots. Joe Weider was big in mail order, of course, but he didn't really see his bodybuilders as competition. I talked him into giving me free advertising space in his magazines. "You can always start paying me for using me in your ads," I said, "but I'd like it if you just give me an opportunity." I figured Joe would go for this because he always hated to part with cash. And he agreed, and he was very supportive: he said I could start with a full-page ad that we would make into a double page if the thing really took off.

Many bodybuilders failed at mail order because they'd accept the money but not get it together to mail the product. You had to fill your orders within a certain time by law. If the post office received complaints, it would take away your post office box, and your business would be gone. You might even go to jail. But I was superefficient. I took the doors off my bedroom closet to make an alcove and had a friend build shelves and a little fold-down desk. Each booklet had its own numbered niche, and there were bins for incoming mail, checks, envelopes, and outgoing orders.

My booklets were a success. Soon I added an Arnold Schwarzenegger weight-lifting belt and other products, enough for a double-page ad. That brought in even more business. It built to the point where I could afford to hire a secretary to come in a few days a week and handle most of the mail.

I always showed Joe any ad I wrote before putting it in the magazine because he was a merchandising genius. He would pick apart my language almost word by word. "Why didn't you write 'fill within days'?" he'd ask. "Put that in the ad! People want to know you're dependable.

And you should say 'This booklet is a limited edition.' People love limited editions."

I loved being an American entrepreneur. With mail order I was doing what Charles Atlas had done!

Soon I started another business, this time with Franco. His idea was that we should work in construction, because he'd done that in Italy and Germany, and it seemed like people would want to hire two strong guys. But when we went to the union hall, we found out it could take months to join.

I said to Franco, "Why don't we just start our own company?" Franco knew bricklaying, and I knew business. So that's what we did. We put an ad in the newspaper that said "European bricklayers. Experts in marble and stone." We got our first job right away, building a wall for a guy in Venice whose house once belonged to the silent-film star Rudolph Valentino.

Franco and I had noticed that Americans loved foreign names: Swedish massage, Italian design, Chinese herbs, German ingenuity. We decided that we should highlight being European. The fact that Franco was Italian was especially good. Look at the Vatican! You can't beat Italian architecture. I'd also noticed that Americans like to bargain a little bit and feel like they're getting a deal—unlike Germans, who are more willing to accept the quoted price. So Franco and I had a whole routine. I'd bring a tape measure and take measurements and come up with the estimate—which was always in meters and centimeters, adding to the European mystique. Then I'd show it to Franco, and we would start arguing in German in front of the client.

The guy would ask, "What's going on?"

"Well, I don't have to tell you about Italians," I'd say, rolling my eyes. "I don't get it why he thinks this patio will cost eight thousand dollars. He wants to order *x* number of bricks, which is way more than we're going to need. I mean, between you and me, I think we can build it for seven thousand. We'll have all these extra bricks, and we can return them and get the thousand dollars back."

The guy would start to trust me right away. "That's really nice that you're trying to give me the best price."

"Well, we want to be competitive. I'm sure you got other estimates, right?"

"Oh, yes, yes."

"You see, Franco?" I'd say. Then we would argue some more in German, and the guy would be happy with the $7,000 deal.

We loved bricklaying and felt very productive. We also had a lot of fun. One time a woman had a competing bid for $5,000 to get her chimney replaced. That included $1,000 to demolish the old one. "A thousand dollars?" said Franco. "Let me look at this." He climbed up on the slope of the roof, braced his back against the shingles, and did a leg press that pushed over the whole chimney. It almost landed on the woman standing below. But instead of getting mad, she was grateful. "Oh, thank you so much for helping us! This was very dangerous. It could have fallen on somebody's head." She not only gave us the job but let us keep the old bricks, which I then sold to another customer as "vintage bricks."

Another customer wanted to replace a wall around his house. We had the idea that demolishing the old wall would be strenuous enough to serve as our workout that day. We rented the biggest sledgehammers we could find. I told Franco that we should make it a contest. "You start at that end and I'll start at this end," I proposed, "and let's see who gets to the middle first." We were hammering like maniacs, and I would have won except that a chunk flew off the wall and broke the customer's antique stained-glass window. There went our profit.

Franco and I hadn't even been in business a year when a big earthquake hit the San Fernando Valley on February 9, 1971. Patios heaved up. Walls cracked. Chimneys fell down. You could not have asked for a better opportunity. Franco and I ran our advertisement in the *Los Angeles Times* right away, and we were busy around the clock. For extra hands, we recruited bodybuilders off the beach—at one point, we had fifteen of them mixing cement and carrying bricks. It was a very funny sight, but we couldn't depend on the bodybuilders. They couldn't handle working every day. Just like Joe said, some of those guys were lazy bastards.

With the money we made, Franco and I were able to buy better cars and pay for more college classes. We were also able to afford our first investment. In those days, the airlines were planning to introduce supersonic planes, and there was a proposal to build a supersonic airport in Palmdale, right over the mountains fifty or sixty miles northeast of Los Angeles.

I wanted to be rich very quickly. When I heard that, I said to myself, "This could be a great investment." Sure enough, a month or two later, we got a copy of the local paper, the *Antelope Valley Press*, and right there on the front page was a magnificent rendering of the proposed airport: monstrous, very futuristic, exactly what I envisioned America was all about. To think big! In Graz, they used to worry about whether the airport should have three or four planes land a day. I said to myself, "This is major."

I figured that when you build an airport on that scale, you've got to have warehouses around it, and shopping malls, restaurants, housing developments, government buildings—growth, growth, growth. So I said to Franco, "Let's find out if there's anything for sale." It didn't take long before the *Antelope Valley Press* had another front-page story about how companies were buying up huge plots and subdividing and selling the land.

A gentleman from a development company took us out to see a piece of property. At that time, Antelope Valley was undeveloped, just desert. It took us two hours to get there on the bus, and the whole way, the guy talked about the plans. He explained how they were going to build a freeway into Palmdale, and that the airport would be intercontinental. Ultimately, it might even be used for space planes. We were impressed. When we got there, he showed us where the power and water would go, which confirmed my sense that the opportunity was real. I bought ten acres for $1,000 apiece and Franco bought five, right next to where the runway was going to be and near where a complex of high-rises might be built. We didn't have $15,000 in cash, so we agreed to $5,000 down and $13,000 in principal and interest payments over the next several years.

Of course, none of this took into account the issue of sonic booms and how they would affect people living under the flight paths. It became a huge fight, not just in the United States but around the world. Eventually governments concluded that airliners should go supersonic only over the oceans—and Franco and I ended up stuck with acres of desert. The developer kept insisting that all this was just a temporary setback. "Don't sell it," he said. "Your grandchildren are going to benefit."

I wasn't lying to Joe Weider when I said that Franco and I would both be champions. The speed with which Franco transformed himself into a world-class bodybuilder was truly amazing. As training partners, we had a big advantage. When we started working out together in Munich, there was no way for us to know much about what American bodybuilders were doing, so we had to learn on our own from scratch. We discovered dozens of training principles and techniques that we would write down. We were constantly on the lookout for new exercises and variations: it could be something as significant as the thousand-pound calf presses I learned from Reg Park, or as subtle as doing a curl with the wrist turned a certain way. Once each week we would choose an unfamiliar exercise and each do sets and reps until we couldn't do any more. Then we'd analyze the next day which muscles and sections of muscles were sore, and note it down. Working this way, we spent an entire year making a systematic survey of our bodies and building an inventory of hundreds of exercises and techniques. (Eventually this provided the basis for the *Encyclopedia of Modern Bodybuilding*, which I published in 1985.)

A key discovery we made was that you can't just copy someone else's routine, because everyone's body is different. Everyone has different proportions of torso and limb and different hereditary advantages and disadvantages. You can take an idea from another athlete, but you have to understand that your body may respond very differently from his or hers.

Experimenting like this helped us find ways to fix particular weaknesses. For instance, Franco had bowlegs, and we figured out how to fill out his inner thighs by having him do squats in a wider stance. Then we figured out techniques to build up his inner calves. He would never fool the judges into thinking his legs were perfectly straight. But they would be impressed by how he'd toned down the problem.

For the showdown with Sergio Oliva, I was determined to take my posing to a new level. Franco and I practiced our routines for weeks. To win, you have to be able to hit every pose for minutes at a time. Most bodybuilders will be able to do a vacuum pose, for example, which involves sucking in your stomach to call attention to the development of your chest. But often they can't hold the pose, either because they've pumped up too much backstage or because they're out of breath from previous poses. Or they have to let the pose go because they cramp up or start shaking.

So one of us would hold a pose for minutes while the other called out what needed to be done. I would be in a bicep pose, and Franco would say, "I see your arm shaking. Stop shaking." So I'd stop it from shaking. Then he'd say, "Okay, smile," and "Give me a little bit of twist in the waist," and then, "Okay, now go into a three-quarter-back pose. Ah, you took an extra step. No good. Start again."

You practice every pose and every transition because that extra step is the very thing that could make you lose in front of the judges. They'll think, "That's unprofessional. You're not ready for the big time. You are a fucking idiot; get off the stage. You can't even stand still in the pose. You haven't even practiced the simplest things."

At the Mr. Olympia level, what is most important is not necessarily what goes on in the middle of a pose. The judges assume you know how to do that. What becomes crucial is what you do between one pose and the next. How do the hands move? How does the face look? What is the posture? It's like in ballet. It's all about the straightness of the back, the head up, not down. Never, ever take an extra step. As you move from pose to pose, you have to visualize yourself as a tiger, slow and smooth. Everything smooth. And precise, without ever looking as if you are straining, because that too shows weakness. You have to be in total command of your face. Maybe you are struggling and completely winded, but you must breathe through your nose while keeping your mouth relaxed. Panting would be the worst. Then when you come back for the next shot, you need to look confident and exactly the way you're supposed to look.

My preparation for going up against Sergio didn't stop at the gym. I bought a movie projector. I assembled a whole collection of his performances in competition, and I watched those films at home again and again. Sergio really did have a stunning physique, but I realized that he had been using the same posing routine for several years. This was knowledge I could use to plan for the final one-on-one pose-off at Mr. Olympia. I memorized his moves in the order in which he hit them, and I got ready for each one with three poses of my own. I rehearsed this and visualized it over and over: "When he hits this, I will do this, and this, and this!" My goal was to overwhelm every move Sergio made.

Late that summer, the phone rang one day in Gold's Gym, and the manager called out from the desk, "Arnold, there's a guy on the phone by the name of Jim Lorimer."

"What does he want?"

"He wants to talk to you about the Mr. World competition."

"Tell him to call back. I'm in the middle of working out."

That call turned out to be one of those magical things that happened to me that I never could have planned. Jim still laughs about it today. When I called him, he explained that he was the organizer of the world weight-lifting championships, which were being hosted that year by the United States in Columbus, Ohio, and that after the championships, there would be a bodybuilding competition for the title of Mr. World. He wanted me to enter.

I'd never heard of Jim Lorimer and called around to see if anybody knew him. It didn't take long to learn he was for real. Jim was a former FBI agent, about twenty years older than me, and an important force in American sports. He'd been chairman of the United States Olympic Committee. He'd been a pioneer in building up the women's teams to compete against the Soviet bloc. He made his living as an executive at Nationwide Insurance, the largest employer in Columbus, and was a suburban mayor and a very well-connected politician. He'd been running the US weight-lifting championships and the Mr. America contest in Columbus on behalf of the AAU for years, and my friends said that those events were always very well organized. That was a big reason that Columbus had been chosen to host the 1970 world championship, and Jim had been asked to step up and run it.

I looked at the calendar and realized that the Mr. World event was on September 25, the Mr. Universe competition in London was on September 24, and the Mr. Olympia contest was in New York on October 7. I thought, "Wow, I could, theoretically, go and win the Mr. Universe in London, then come to Columbus, Ohio, and win the Mr. World, and then go to the Mr. Olympia. That would be unbelievable." In the space of just two weeks, I could cover the three federations that controlled all the bodybuilding competitions. Winning all three would be like unifying the heavyweight title in boxing: it would make me the undisputed world champ.

I was totally excited until I dug into the airline schedules. Then I called Jim Lorimer. "I want to come," I began. "But there is no way to make it from Mr. Universe to Mr. World in time. The earliest plane from London after Mr. Universe doesn't get to New York until two in the afternoon. And there's no connecting flight from New York to Columbus until five o'clock, which is when your competition already starts.

"Unless you can perform miracles, there is no way I can make it. I've talked to the other top bodybuilders from the Mr. Universe contest, like Franco Columbu, Boyer Coe, and Dave Draper, and they'd all be willing to come with me. But we don't see how it's possible.

"I hear you're a big-league organizer and you're very well connected. So let's see if you can pull it off."

It took Jim only a day. He called back and said, "We're sending a jet." It was a corporate jet belonging to Volkswagen, one of the event sponsors. "They'll fly to New York and pick you up."

I couldn't believe it when my idol Reg Park signed up to compete in the London Mr. Universe contest. I thought he was on my side! When a reporter asked me how it would feel to compete against the greatest Mr. Universe ever, I lost my usual happy-go-lucky attitude. "Second greatest," I corrected him. "I've won the title more times than him."

Ex-bodybuilding champs come out of retirement all the time to show off their training or refresh their image or who knows why. Reg had won his Mr. Universe titles at widely spaced intervals, in 1951, 1958, and 1965, and maybe he wanted to put a final stamp on the event. Or maybe I was receiving so much attention that he wanted to show that the older generation was still in charge. Whatever was motivating him, it put us at odds in a way I'd never expected.

When we saw each other in the warm-up room, we barely said hello. The competition felt awkward for everybody. The judges were uncomfortable. The fans were uncomfortable. Normally before a contest, other bodybuilders will come up and tell you, "You're looking great, you're going to win." But the people who liked us both didn't know what to say to one of us with the other man standing right across the room.

The reality is that a bodybuilder simply cannot train as hard when he's over forty as he can when he's twenty-three. I was in better shape than Reg—not even necessarily because of effort but just because of youth. His skin wasn't as fresh, his muscles were slightly in decline rather than in bloom. A few years earlier, it might have been different, but now it was my turn to be king. Reg was good enough that day to beat all the other contestants, including a former Mr. Universe who was only twenty-eight. But he was not good enough to beat me.

I felt good about winning but at the same time sad. My sights were set on Sergio Oliva, and I didn't need to defeat Reg Park to reach my dream.

The Volkswagen jet that Jim Lorimer had promised was waiting for us on the tarmac in New York the next day. Private jets were much less common than they are now, and for me and the other bodybuilders, it was a thrilling moment; we felt like we were finally getting the royal treatment like other big-time athletes. We flew to Columbus and drove to the Veterans Memorial Auditorium, walking in as the other bodybuilders were already in the middle of pumping up.

I was totally shocked to find Sergio Oliva there. He was a secret entry that nobody had told us about. "Fuck!" I said to myself. He looked like he was in top form, too. I was expecting a showdown with him in two weeks, not now.

It took me a few minutes to snap out of it and figure out what an opportunity this was. Although I hadn't known that Sergio was coming, I realized he had known about me. That meant he had come to Columbus in order to surprise me and take me out, so that I'd be beaten even before we reached New York, and he would have a clear victory in Mr. Olympia.

But, I reasoned, what could work for him could also work for me. "If I beat him today," I thought, "that's it for him in New York."

I needed to kick it into a higher gear. It was like when you have a superfast sports car with a nitrous injector on the engine: you press a button and get an extra hundred horsepower when you need it. I needed to hit that racing button now.

I took off my clothes, put on the oil, and started pumping up. They called us, and we went out on stage.

Mr. World was by far the biggest bodybuilding event I'd ever seen. Five thousand spectators packed the hall, twice the size of the crowd at the championships in London and New York. What was more, there were lights and cameras and announcers from *ABC's Wide World of Sports*; this was the first bodybuilding competition ever to be taped for national TV.

It did not matter if it was five thousand or five hundred seats, I knew that if I could get the crowd going using my salesmanship and charm, that would influence the judges and give me the edge. Sergio was playing the same game, strutting and waving and blowing kisses to his fans; he had a big following, and it was obvious that several dozen had shown up. The four top competitors were me, Sergio, Dave Draper, and Dennis Tinerino. We all came onstage at the same time to let the panel of seven international judges get a first look at us. The emcee asked each of us to show off a few of our favorite poses. The crowd clapped and cheered seeing us all perform at the same time. The energy was tremendous.

Compared with all the other bodybuilders I'd ever faced, Sergio really was in a class by himself. I was struck by that again the minute we were onstage. It was so hard to look impressive next to him with those extraordinary thighs, that impossibly tiny waist, those incredible triceps. I thought that I might have a little extra edge in the judges' minds because I'd just come from winning Mr. Universe. Or maybe Sergio had a slim edge because he was much more accomplished in Olympic weight lifting, and most of the judges came from that world.

To psych myself up, I looked for the slightest possible advantage. Now that we were in the bright TV lights, Sergio seemed a little soft to me. That was encouraging. I found that I really could anticipate his moves, and I started matching each pose. The crowd loved it, and you could see the TV cameras swiveling from him to me and back again. When we left the stage, I felt like I'd won that round.

It only got better from there. Sergio had been too free with the oil backstage, it was dripping off him when he posed and made him look more smooth than cut. Also, during his individual routine, he went through the poses a little too fast for people to fully take them in. When my turn came, I made sure I took the time to connect with crowd, so that each pose made them cheer a little louder, and they didn't want me to leave. It was like Sergio was onstage competing for the first time, and I was totally composed and comfortable.

In the final pose-off, I was 100 percent on. No matter what shot Sergio did to show his strength, I had a matching shot to show my strength. More important, I was the one who was willing to go all out. I was more eager than Sergio. I wanted the title more than he did.

The judges gave me first place unanimously. That shouldn't have been a surprise, but Sergio had been the champ for so long that he was really shocked. I stood there for a minute repeating to myself, "I can't believe it. I can't believe it. I just beat Sergio." The prize was a huge silver trophy, a high-tech electric watch, and $500 in cash—and new popularity and momentum to carry to New York.

When I walked offstage with my trophy, I was careful to do two things. First, I thanked Jim Lorimer. "This is the best organized competition I've ever seen," I told him. "When I retire from bodybuilding, I'm going to call you, and you and I will be partners. We'll be right here on this stage running the Mr. Olympia contest." Jim just laughed and said, "Okay, okay." It was probably the weirdest compliment he had ever heard, especially from a kid.

Second was to mess with Sergio's head. It's foolish to leave anything to chance when you're trying to unseat a three-time reigning Mr. Olympia. If the contest in New York was close, I told myself, the judges would give it to him. I had to blow him away onstage and make it easy for them to pick me. So I told him I thought I'd won today because I'd gained a lot of muscle size since he'd beaten me in New York the previous year. He was a little light, and that's why he lost, blah, blah, blah. I wanted him going away thinking he'd have to gain a few pounds to compete. He was soft today, and I wanted him softer in New York.

Mr. Olympia was scheduled two weeks later for a cushy Manhattan theater, and around noontime that day a bunch of us got together at the nearby Mid City Gym. The minute I saw Sergio, I started teasing him about eating, and Franco joined in, asking him if he'd lost weight. That made everybody laugh except Sergio. In fact, as I was soon to see, he had taken the bait. He'd added ten pounds in the two weeks since Columbus, and nobody can gain ten pounds in two weeks and still look cut.

The Town Hall theater had 1,500 seats, and it probably had never seen a crowd as rowdy as this. His fans were chanting "Sergio! Sergio! Sergio!" and mine trying were to outshout them, chanting "Arnold! Arnold! Arnold!" At the end of a long afternoon, the judges called us back for a final pose-off onstage. Sergio went through his standard repertoire, and, just as I'd planned, I went into high gear, ripping off three poses to every one of his. The crowd really loved this.

But the judges kept calling out poses until finally I was thinking, "We've been posing a long time." It seemed like it wasn't because the judges were uncertain about their decision; it was just because people were on their feet and going berserk, and the judges were saying, "Let's keep this going; the people love it."

We were exhausted. That's when I went for the kill. An idea came into my head, and I said to Sergio, "I've had it. I think those guys ought to know now, however the chips fall."

He said, "Yeah, you're right." He walked off one side of the stage and I started to walk off the other—but I walked only two steps. Then I stopped and hit another pose. And I turned toward his side and shrugged as if to say, "Where'd he go?"

Sergio came right back onstage a little confused. But by this time "Arnold!" was the only name they were chanting, and some of the fans were even booing him. I used the moment to execute my best professional posing and shots. Then it was over. The judges held a little meeting backstage, and the emcee came out and announced that I was the new Mr. Olympia.

Sergio never said anything to me about how I'd mocked him, but he told other people he felt he'd been had. That's not how I saw it. It was a primal moment. I'd finished him off by instinct in the heat of a competition that I'd dominated by then all the same.

Still, the next morning was strange, because Sergio, Franco, and I were sharing a hotel room. As soon as Sergio woke up, he amazed me by doing all kinds of push-ups and exercises. He was such a fanatic. Even the day after competition, he was pumping up in the hotel!

I have to admit that then I felt sorry that he'd lost. He was a great champion and an idol for many people. For years my mind had been fixed on wanting to destroy him, take him out, make him second, make him the loser. But the morning after beating him, I woke up and saw him next to me and felt sad. It was too bad he had to lose to make way for me.

CHAPTER 8

Learning American

IN BODYBUILDING I WAS king of the mountain, but back in everyday LA I was still just another immigrant struggling to learn English and make a life. My mind was so fixed on what I was doing in America that I rarely gave a thought to Austria or Germany. If I was competing in Europe, I'd go home to visit, and I kept in touch with Fredi Gerstl in Graz and Albert Busek in Munich. Often I would cross paths with Albert and other European friends on the bodybuilding circuit. I regularly sent pictures and letters home to my parents, telling them what I was doing. Whenever I won a championship, I'd send them the trophy, because I didn't need it in my apartment, and I wanted them to be proud. I'm not sure any of this meant much to them at the start, but after awhile they put up the photos and built a special shelf in their home to show off the trophies.

My dad would answer my letters for both of them. He always enclosed my original letter marked up in red ink—correcting my mistakes in spelling and grammar. He said this was because he thought I was losing touch with the German language, but he'd done the same thing with the essays he required Meinhard and me to write for him as kids. This kind of thing made it easy to believe that my parents and Austria were frozen in time. I was glad to be away living my own life.

Meinhard and I hardly kept in touch. Like me, he'd finished trade school and served a year in the army. Then he'd gone to work for an electronics company, first in Graz and later in Munich while I was living there. But our paths rarely crossed. He was an elegant dresser and a hard partyer and had a wild life with girls. Lately he'd been transferred to Innsbruck, Austria, and he'd gotten engaged to Erika Knapp, a beauty who was the mother of his three-year-old son, Patrick, and he showed signs of finally settling down.

He never got the chance. The spring after I won Mr. Olympia, in 1971, the phone rang in our apartment one day when I was out of town. It was my mother calling with the terrible news that my brother had been killed in a car accident. Meinhard crashed while driving alone drunk on a mountain road near the Alpine resort of Kitzbühel. He was just twenty-five years old.

I was away in New York, and Franco took the call. For some reason, the news made him feel so stricken that he couldn't tell me. It wasn't until three days later, when I came back to LA, that he said, "I have to tell you something, but I have to tell you after dinner."

Eventually I got it out of him that my brother had died.

"When did it happen?" I asked.

"Three days ago I got the phone call."

"Why didn't you tell me this earlier?"

"I just didn't know how to tell you. You were in New York and you were doing your business. I wanted to wait until you got home." If he had called me in New York, I could have been halfway to Austria already. I was touched by his worry for me, but also frustrated and disappointed.

I called my parents right away. My mother was sobbing on the phone and was barely able to speak at first. But then she told me, "No, we're not going to have the burial here; we're going to keep Meinhard in Kitzbühel. We're going tomorrow morning, and we'll have a very small service."

"I just found out about it," I said.

She said, "Well, I wouldn't try to come now, because even if you get the first plane, with the nine-hour time difference and the long flight, I don't think you'll get here in time."

It was a terrible blow to the family. I could hear the devastation in both my parents' voices. None of us was good at communicating feelings, and I didn't know what to say. I'm sorry? It's terrible? They knew that. The news left me numb. Meinhard and I were no longer close—I'd seen him only once in the three years since I'd moved to America—but still my mind flooded with memories of us playing as kids, going on double dates when we were older, laughing together. We would never have that again. I would never see him again. All I could think to do was push this out of my mind so I could go on with my goals.

I threw myself into my Los Angeles life. Going to school, training five hours a day at the gym, working in the construction and mail-order businesses, making appearances, and going to exhibitions—all of it was happening at the same time. Franco was just as busy. We both had incredibly full schedules, and some days stretched from six in the morning until midnight.

Becoming fluent in English was still the hardest thing on my to-do list. I envied my photographer friend Artie Zeller, who was the kind of person who could visit Italy for a week with Franco and come back speaking Italian. Not me. I couldn't believe how difficult learning a new language could be.

At the beginning, I'd try to translate everything literally: I would hear or read something, convert it in my head back into German, and then wonder, "Why do they have to make English so complicated?" There were things that I seemed unable to grasp no matter who explained them to me. Like contractions. Why couldn't you say "I have" or "I will" rather than "I've" and "I'll"?

Pronunciations were especially dangerous. As a treat, Artie took me to a Jewish-Hungarian restaurant where the dishes were the same as Austrian food. The owner came to take our order, and I said, "I saw this one thing here on the menu which I like. Give me some of your garbage."

"What did you call my food?"

"Just bring me some of your garbage."

Artie jumped in right away. "He's from Austria," he explained. "He means the *cabbage*. He's used to the cabbage from Austria."

Gradually, though, I started making progress, thanks to my classes at Santa Monica College. Going there really fired me up to learn. On my very first day in English as a Second Language, all of us foreigners were sitting in the classroom, and the teacher, Mr. Dodge, said, "Would you guys like to be inside or outside?"

We all looked around trying to figure out what he meant.

He pointed out the window and explained, "See that tree over there? Well, if you want, we can all sit in the shade and have our class there."

We went out and sat on the grass under the tree in front of the college building. I was so impressed. Compared to the way school worked in Europe, so formal and structured, this was unbelievable! I thought, "I'm going to take a college course sitting under the tree outside, as if I was on vacation! After this semester, I'm signing up for another class!" I called Artie and told him he should come by the next week and take a picture of us sitting outside.

In fact, the next semester I signed up for two classes. A lot of foreign students feel intimidated by the idea of jumping into college, but the community college dealt with me in such a low-key way and the teachers were so cool that it was a lot of fun.

Once Mr. Dodge got to know me a little bit and I told him about my goals, he introduced me to a counselor. The guy said, "Mr. Dodge suggested I should give you some other classes besides English. What do you like?"

"Business."

"Well, I have a good beginning business course where the language is not that difficult—a lot of foreigners take that class—and you have a good teacher who understands foreign students."

He put together a little program for me. "Here are eight classes you should take besides English. They're all business courses. If I were you, I would also take some math. You need to hear the language of math so that when someone says 'division,' you know what that means. Or 'decimal,' or 'fraction.' These are the terms you hear, and you may not understand them."

And I said, "You're absolutely right, I don't." So I added a math class where we did some decimals and easy algebra, and I started relearning the language of math.

The counselor also showed me how to fit classes into my life. "We understand you are an athlete, and some semesters maybe it doesn't work out. Since the fall is when you have your big competitions, then maybe you only take one class in the summer. You could go one night a week, from seven to ten, after your training. I'm sure you can handle that." I thought the way he worked with me was terrific. It felt great to add getting an education to my goals. There was no pressure, since nobody was saying to me, "You better go to college. You better get a degree."

I also had a math tutor at Gold's Gym: Frank Zane, who had been an algebra teacher in Florida before coming to California to train. I don't know why, but as a matter of fact, several of the bodybuilders had been teachers. Frank helped with my assignments and translations, explaining and taking the time when I didn't understand. In California, he had gotten deeply into Eastern philosophy and meditation and relaxing the mind. But that didn't rub off on me until later.

If I'd thought there would be a serious challenge to my dominance, I'd have stayed 100 percent focused on bodybuilding. But there was nobody on the radar. So I diverted some of my energy to other ambitions. I always wrote down my goals, like I'd learned to do in the weight-lifting club back in Graz. It wasn't sufficient just to tell myself something like "My New Year's resolution is to lose twenty pounds and learn better English and read a little bit more." No. That was only a start. Now I had to make it very specific so that all those fine intentions were not just floating around. I would take out index cards and write that I was going to:

- get twelve more units in college;
- earn enough money to save $5,000;

- work out five hours a day;
- gain seven pounds of solid muscle weight; and
- find an apartment building to buy and move into.

It might seem like I was handcuffing myself by setting such specific goals, but it was actually just the opposite: I found it liberating. Knowing exactly where I wanted to end up freed me totally to improvise how to get there. Take that twelve more college credits I needed, for example. It didn't matter which college they would come from; I would figure that out. I'd look at which courses were available and what the credits cost and whether they fit my schedule and the rules of my visa. I didn't need to worry about the exact details now, because I already knew I was going to get those dozen credits.

Immigration status was one of the obstacles I had to work around putting myself through college. I had a work visa, not a student visa, so I could only go part-time. I could never take more than two classes at once in any one school, so I had to jump all over. In addition to Santa Monica College, I went to West Los Angeles College and took extension courses at the University of California at Los Angeles. I realized this would be a problem if I wanted to earn a degree, because I'd have to link all those credits to make them all count. But a degree wasn't my objective; I only needed to study as much as I could in my available time and learn how Americans did business.

So at Santa Monica College, those English classes became English classes, math classes, history classes, and business administration. At UCLA, I took courses from the business school in accounting, marketing, economics, and management. I'd studied accounting in Austria, of course, but here it was a whole new thing. Computers were just happening: they were using big IBM machines with punch cards and magnetic tape drives. I liked learning about that, which I thought of as the American way of doing things. College appealed to my sense of discipline. I enjoyed studying. There was something really nice about having to read books in order to write reports and participate in class. I also liked working with the other students, inviting them over to my apartment to have some coffee and do our homework together. The teachers often encouraged that, so that if one person didn't know something, the others could explain it to him. It made the classroom discussions much more effective.

One course required us to read the business news every day and be prepared to talk about the headlines and stories in class. That became the first thing I did every morning: open the newspaper to the business page. The instructor would say, "Here's an interesting article about how the Japanese bought an American steel mill and dismantled it and set it up back in Japan. Now they're producing steel more cheaply than we can and selling it to us at a profit. Let's talk about that." I never could predict what was going to make a big impression on me. A guest lecturer at UCLA told us that in sales, the larger the salesman, the more he tended to sell. I found this fascinating, since I'm a big guy. I thought, "Well, I'm two hundred fifty pounds, so when I go out to sell something, my business ought to be huge."

I also found a steady girlfriend, which was a settling influence in my life. Not that meeting women was hard. Bodybuilding had its groupies just like rock 'n' roll. They were always there, at the parties, at the exhibitions, sometimes even backstage at contests offering to help guys oil up. They'd come to the gym and the beach to watch us work out. You could tell right away who was available. You could go down to Venice Beach and collect ten phone numbers. Barbara Outland was different because she liked me as a human being—she didn't even know what bodybuilding was. We met at Zucky's Deli in 1969. She was a college kid a year younger than me, waitressing for her summer job. We started hanging out together and having long conversations. Pretty soon my buddies at the gym started teasing, "Arnold is in love." When she went back to school, I thought about her, and we even wrote letters—a first for me.

I liked having a girlfriend; someone you saw more often. I could enjoy Barbara's life, her teaching career, her school, her goals. I could share my ambition and my training and my ups and downs.

She was much more of a girl-next-door type than a femme fatale:

blonde, tan, and wholesome. She was studying to be an English teacher and obviously wasn't just looking for a fun time. Her girlfriends who were dating guys in law school and med school thought I was strange, but Barbara didn't care. She admired me for writing down goals on index cards. Barbara's parents were wonderful to me. At Christmas, each family member had a gift for me—and later, when I brought Franco with me, gifts for him too. Barbara and I went to Hawaii, London, and New York together.

When Barbara graduated in 1971 and came to LA to start work, Franco was getting ready to move out. He was settling down too; he was studying to be a chiropractor and he'd gotten engaged to a girl named Anita, who was a full-fledged chiropractor already. When Barbara suggested moving in with me, it seemed totally natural, since she was already spending a lot of time at my place.

She was totally on board with my habit of saving every penny. We had barbecues in the backyard and spent days on the beach instead of going someplace fancy. I wasn't the best candidate for a relationship because I was so wrapped up in my career, but I liked having a partner. It was great to have someone there to go home to.

The fact that Barbara was an English teacher was great. She helped me a lot with the language, and she helped when I wrote papers for school. She was also very helpful with the mail-order business and writing letters, but I hired a secretary early on. Even so, we learned that when you have a relationship in a foreign language, you have to be extra careful not to miscommunicate. We'd get into ridiculous fights. One time we went to see the movie *Death Wish*, and she said afterward, "I like Charles Bronson because he's very rugged, very masculine."

I said, "I don't think Charles Bronson is that masculine. I mean, he's a skinny guy! I would call him more athletic than masculine."

"No," she said. "You think I'm saying he's *muscular*, but that's not what I mean. I'm saying he's *masculine*. Masculine is something else."

"Masculine, muscular, same fucking thing, I think that he's athletic."

"But to me he's very masculine."

I said, "No, that's the wrong . . ." and kept arguing. I went straight to the dictionary the minute we got home. Sure enough, she was right. Being masculine meant something totally different from being muscular—it meant that Bronson was manly and rugged, which he was. I said to myself, "How stupid. Oh God, you've got to learn this language! It is so stupid that you argue over something like that."

After I won Mr. Olympia, Weider started sending me on sales trips all over the world. I'd climb on a plane and make shopping mall appearances wherever he had distribution or was trying to expand. Selling was one of my favorite things. I'd stand in the middle of a shopping mall with a translator lady—for instance, the Stockmann shopping center in Finland—surrounded by a few hundred people from local gyms, because they'd have advertised my visit in advance. I'd be selling, selling, selling. "Vitamin E gives you fantastic extra energy for training hours every day to get a body like mine! And of course I don't want even talk about the sexual power it gives you . . ." People would be buying, and I was always a huge hit. Joe sent me because he knew that the hosts would then say, "We sold a lot of stuff. Let's make a deal."

I'd be wearing a tank top and hitting poses every so often while I made my pitch. "Let me talk about the protein. You could eat as many steaks as you want, or as much fish as you want, but the body can only take seventy grams at a time. That's the rule: a gram for every kilo of body weight. Muscle-building shakes are the way to fill the hole in your diet. So you can have five times the seventy grams if you want! You can't eat enough steak to make up for protein powder, because it's so concentrated." I would mix the shake in a chrome shaker, like the kind used to make martinis in bars, drink it, and say to someone in the crowd, "You try it." It was like selling vacuum cleaners. I'd get so excited that I'd rush ahead of the translator.

Then I'd move on to selling vitamin D, vitamin A, and special oil. By the time I finished, the sales manager would see all the interest. He would order Weider food supplements for the coming year. Plus barbell sets and dumbbells made by Weider. And Weider would be in heaven. Then a month later, I'd travel to another mall in another country.

I always went by myself. Joe would never pay for anyone else because he felt it was a waste of money. Traveling alone was perfectly fine, though, because no matter where I went, there was always someone to pick me up and treat me as if we were brothers because of bodybuilding. It was fun to go around the world and train in different gyms.

Weider wanted me to get to the point where I could sit down with the mall management to make the deal myself, and meet with publishers to line up more foreign-language editions of his magazines, and eventually take over the business. But that was not my goal. The same with the offer I received in the early seventies to manage a leading gymnasium chain for $200,000 a year. It was a lot of money, but I turned it down because it would not take me where I wanted to go. Managing a chain is a ten- to twelve-hour-a-day job, and that would not make me a bodybuilding champion or get me into movies. Nothing was going to distract me from my goal. No offer, no relationship, nothing.

But getting on a plane and selling was right up my alley. I always saw myself as a citizen of the world. I wanted to travel as much as I could because I figured if the local press was covering me there now as a bodybuilder, eventually I would be back as a movie star.

So I was on the road several times a year. In 1971 alone, I flew to Japan, Belgium, Austria, Canada, Britain, and France. Often I would add paid exhibitions to my itinerary to make extra cash. I was also giving free exhibitions and seminars in prisons around California. That started when I went to visit a friend from Gold's who was doing time in the federal prison on Terminal Island near LA. He was serving two years for auto theft and wanted to continue his training. I watched him and his friends work out in the prison yard. He had made a name for himself as the strongest prisoner in California by setting the state prison record in the squat with six hundred pounds. What impressed me was that he and the other serious lifters were all model prisoners, because that was how they won training privileges and permission to bring in protein from outside to help them become these strong animals. Otherwise the prison authorities would say, "You're just training to beat up on guys," and take away the weights. The more popular bodybuilding grew in prisons, I thought, the more guys would get the message to behave.

Being weight lifters also helped them after they got out. If they came to Gold's or other bodybuilding gyms, it was easy to make friends. Whereas most prisoners were dropped off at the bus station with $200 and ended up wandering around with no job and no connection to anybody, people at Gold's would notice if you could bench press three hundred pounds. Somebody would say, "Hey, do you want to train with me?" and you'd have made a human connection. On the bulletin board at Gold's there were always cards offering work for mechanics, laborers, personal trainers, accountants, and so on, and we would help the ex-prisoners find jobs as well.

So in the early 1970s, I went to men's and women's prisons all over the state to popularize weight training: from San Quentin, to Folsom, to Atascadero, where they kept the criminally insane. It never would have happened if the guards had thought it was a bad idea, but they supported it, and one warden would recommend me to the next.

In the fall of 1972, my parents came to Essen, Germany, to watch me in the Mr. Olympia contest, which was being staged in Germany for the first time. They'd never seen me compete at the international level, and I was glad they were there, although it was far from my best performance. They'd seen me in only one competition—Mr. Austria, back in 1963—and they'd come to that because Fredi Gerstl invited them. He'd helped line up sponsors and trophies.

It was a great experience to see them in Essen. They were very proud. They saw me crowned Mr. Olympia for the third time, breaking the record for the most bodybuilding titles. And they realized, "This is what he used to talk about—his dream that we didn't buy into." My mother said, "I cannot believe you are up there on the stage. You're not even shy! Where did you get that from?" People were congratulating them on my success, saying things like, "You sure put some discipline into that boy!" and giving them the credit they deserved. I handed my mother the trophy plate to take home. She was very happy. It was an important moment—especially for my father, who'd always said about my weight training, "Why don't you do something useful? Go chop wood."

At the same time, my parents seemed to feel out of place. They didn't know what to make of this scene of giant musclemen, one of them their son, parading in little briefs before thousands of cheering fans. When we went for dinner that evening and during breakfast the next morning before they left, it was hard for us to relate. My head was still in the competition, while they wanted to talk about matters much closer to home. They were still struggling with the devastation of Meinhard's death, and now their grandson was without a dad. And it was difficult for them that I was so far away. There wasn't much I could say to them, and I felt depressed after they left.

My parents didn't realize that I wasn't in the best shape for the Mr. Olympia contest. I'd been spending too much time on school and not enough time in the gym. My businesses and the sales trips and exhibitions had taken bites out of training. On top of it, Franco and I had been getting lazy, skipping workouts or reducing our sets by half. To get the most out of my workouts, I always needed specific goals to get the adrenaline pumping. I learned that staying on top of the hill is harder than climbing it.

But I had no such motivations leading up to Essen because defending the championship had been so easy up to now. I'd coasted to my second title as Mr. Olympia, in Paris in 1971. The only possible challenger had been Sergio—nobody else was in my league—and he'd been barred from the contest because of a dispute between federations. But in Essen, it seemed like all the top bodybuilders turned up at their very best except for me. Sergio was back, even more impressive than I remembered. And a new sensation from France, Serge Nubret, was also in top form, huge and really defined.

It was the hardest competition I'd ever been through, and if we'd been before American judges, I might well have lost. But German judges were always more impressed by sheer muscular mass, and fortunately I had what they were looking for. Winning narrowly did not make me feel good, however. I wanted my dominance to be clear.

After any competition, I always sought out the judges to ask for their input. "I appreciate that I won, but please tell me what were my weak points and what were my strong points," I'd say. "You're not going to hurt my feelings. I will still do a posing exhibition for you if you produce a show or anything like that." One judge at Essen, a German doctor who'd followed my career ever since I was nineteen, told me bluntly, "You were soft. I thought you were massive and still the best up there, but you were softer than I would like to see you."

From Germany, I went to do exhibitions in Scandinavia, and from there to South Africa to do seminars for Reg Park. Seeing him again was great; we'd gotten past the hard feelings from my having beaten him in London. However, the trip didn't turn out too well. I was scheduled for an exhibition near Durban, but when I arrived, I discovered that nobody had given any thought to supplying a posing platform. But I was in construction, right? So I said what the hell and built one myself.

Midway through my routine, the whole thing collapsed with a scary crash. I landed flat on my back with my leg pinned under me and a badly wrecked left knee—the cartilage was torn and the kneecap was pulled way out of place under the skin. The South African doctors patched me up enough to finish the tour with bandages. Except for this mishap, it was a wonderful trip. I went on safari and gave exhibitions and seminars, and coming back I stuffed thousands of dollars of earnings into my cowboy boots so nobody would steal it while I slept on the plane.

On my way home through London, I called Dianne Bennett to say hello.

"Your mother has been trying to find you," she said. "Call her. Your father is ill." I called my mother and then went home quickly to Austria to stay with them. My father had suffered a stroke.

He was in the hospital when I got there, and he recognized me, but it was terrible. He couldn't talk anymore. He was biting his tongue. I kept him company, and he seemed aware, but he was off in upsetting ways. He was smoking, and he'd become confused and try to put out the cigarette on his hand. It was painful and upsetting to see a man who had been so smart and so strong—an ice-curling champion—lose his coordination and his ability to think.

I stayed in Austria for quite a while, and he seemed stable when I left. Around Thanksgiving, back in Los Angeles, I had surgery on my knee. I'd just gotten out of the hospital on crutches, with my entire leg in a cast, when a call came from my mother. "Your father has died," she told me.

It was heartbreaking, but I didn't cry or freak out. Barbara, who was with me, got upset that I didn't seem to react at all. Instead, I focused on practical matters. I called my surgeon, who told me not to fly with the heavy cast—so once again I couldn't attend a family funeral. At least I knew that my mother had an enormous support system to organize the service and attend to all the details. The gendarmerie would close ranks to bury one of its own, and the band that my dad had led for many years would play, just as he had played at many funerals. The local priests, whom my mother was close to, would handle the invitations. Her friends would comfort her, and our relatives would come. Nevertheless I wasn't there, my parents' only surviving child, and that was the bottom line. I know she really missed me.

I was in shock and paralyzed. Yet frankly, I was also glad that the knee injury kept me from going, because I still wanted to separate myself from that whole side of my life. My way of dealing with the situation was deny and try to move on.

I didn't want my mother to be alone. In less than two years, both my father and brother had died, and I felt like our family was rapidly coming apart, and I could scarcely imagine the grief she must have felt. So now I had to take on responsibility for her. I was still only twenty-five, but it was time to step up and make her life wonderful. Now it was time for me to pay her back for the endless hours and days of nurturing and everything she'd done for us as babies and growing up.

I couldn't give my mom what she most wished for: a son close to home who would become a cop like Dad, marry a woman named Gretel, have a couple of kids, and live in a house two blocks from hers. That was the way in most Austrian families. She and my father had been okay with my move to Munich, which was 250 miles away and reachable by train. But I now realized that when I'd left for America without warning in 1968, I had shocked and hurt them. I wasn't going back, of course, but I wanted to make up for that too.

I started sending her money every month and calling her all the time. I tried to convince her to move to the United States. She didn't want to. Then I tried to have her fly over to visit. She didn't want to do that either. Finally, in 1973, about six months after my father died, she did come, and stayed with Barbara and me for a few weeks. She returned the next year too, and every year after that. I also found more and more of a connection with Patrick, my nephew. When he was little, and I went to Europe, I made sure to visit him and Erika and her husband, a military man who was a devoted stepfather. Then when Patrick got to be about ten, he became fascinated with the idea of his uncle living in America. He started collecting my movie posters. Erika would ask me for memorabilia; I sent him a dagger from *Conan* and T-shirts from *The Terminator* and other movies, and wrote letters for him to show off at school. In high school he would periodically ask me to mail him twenty or thirty autographed photos, which he used for who knows what entrepreneurial purpose. I helped send him to an international school in Portugal and, with Erika's permission, promised that if he kept up his grades, he could come to Los Angeles for college. He became my pride and joy.

Even though the supersonic airport no longer looked superpromising, and Franco and I were still making payments on fifteen acres of desert, I continued to believe that real estate was the place to invest. Many of our jobs entailed fixing up old houses, and it was eye opening. The owners would pay us $10,000 to fix up a house they'd bought for $200,000. Then they'd turn around and sell it for $300,000. Clearly there was real money to be made.

So I put aside as much money as I could and started looking around for investment possibilities. Two of the bodybuilders who had escaped from Czechoslovakia and come to California just before me had taken their savings and bought a little house to live in. That was fine, but they still had to pay the mortgage. I wanted an investment that would earn money, so that I could cover the mortgage through rents instead of having to pay it myself. Most people would buy a house if they could afford it; it was very unusual then to buy a rental property.

I liked the idea of owning an apartment building. I could picture starting with a small building, taking the best unit for myself to live in, and paying all the expenses by renting out the rest. That would let me learn the business, and as the investment paid off, I could expand from there.

Over the next two or three years, I did research. Every day I would look at the real estate section in the newspaper, studying the prices and reading the stories and ads. I got to where I knew every square block of Santa Monica. I knew how much the property values increased north of Olympic Boulevard versus north of Wilshire versus north of Sunset. I understood about schools and restaurants and proximity to the beach.

This wonderful real estate lady named Olga Asat took me under her wing. She might have been Egyptian; she'd emigrated from somewhere in the Middle East. Olga was older, short and heavyset, with frizzy hair, and she always wore a black outfit because she thought it made her appear leaner. You might look at someone like that and think, "Why am I dealing with her?" But I was drawn to the human being, the heart, the motherly love: she saw me as a fellow foreigner and really wanted to see me do well. She was such a pistol.

We ended up working together for years. Eventually, with Olga's help, I knew every building in town. I knew every transaction: who was selling, at what price, how much the property had appreciated since it last changed hands, what the financial sheet looked like, the cost of yearly upkeep, the interest rate on the financing. I met landlords and bankers. Olga was a miracle worker. She would try so hard, going from building to building to building until we found the right opportunity.

The math of real estate really spoke to me. I could tour a building, and as I walked through it, I would ask about the square footage, the vacancy factor, what it would cost per square foot to operate, and quickly calculate in my mind how many times the gross I could afford to offer and still be able to make the payments. The selling agent would look at me in a weird way as if to say, "How did he figure that out?"

It was just a talent I had. I'd get out a pencil and say, "I cannot go any higher than ten times gross because I think the average maintenance expense on a building like this is 5 percent. You have to leave that 5 percent available. And the interest rate is now 6.1 percent, so the loan will cost such and such annually." I would write it all down for the agent.

Then he or she would argue, "Well, you're right, but don't forget that the value of the property is going to rise. So maybe you have to put in a little bit of your own money along the way. At the end of the day, the value goes up."

"I understand," I'd say, "but I never pay more than ten times gross. If the value goes up in the future, that's *my* profit."

Interesting bargains began to appear after the Arab oil embargo of 1973 and the start of the recession. Olga would call and say, "This seller is in trouble financially," or "They really extended themselves, I think you should make a quick offer." In early 1974 she found a six-unit apartment house on Nineteenth Street just north of Wilshire—the more desirable side of Wilshire. The owners were trading up to a bigger building and wanted to sell fast. Even better, their deal on the bigger building was so good that they were willing to come down on price.

The building cost me $215,000. It took every dollar I'd saved—$27,000—plus another $10,000 borrowed from Joe Weider to make the down payment. The place wasn't much to look at: a sturdy early-1950s two-story structure of wood and brick. But I was happy with it from the minute Barbara and I moved in. It was in a nice neighborhood, and the apartments were roomy and well maintained. Mine was 2,400 square feet, extra large, and had a balcony in the front, a two-car garage underneath, and a little patio out back. It had other benefits too: I rented the other apartments to entertainment people. Actors I met in the gym were always looking for places to stay, so eventually there were four actors living there. It was a way to build connections in the business I wanted to get into. Best of all, I'd moved out of an apartment where I had to pay $1,300 a month in rent and into a property that paid for itself from Day One, just as I'd planned.

Seeing me pull off a $215,000 deal left my old friend Artie Zeller in shock. For days afterward, he kept asking how I had the balls to do it. He could not understand because he never wanted any risk in his life.

"How can you stand the pressure? You have the responsibility of renting out the other five units. You have to collect the rent. What if something goes wrong?" Problems were all he could see. It could be terrible. Tenants would make noise. What if somebody came home drunk? What if somebody slipped, and I got sued? "You know what America is like with the lawsuits!" and blah, blah, blah.

I caught myself listening. "Artie, you almost scared me just now." I laughed. "Don't tell me any more of this information. I like to always wander in like a puppy. I walk into a problem and then figure out what the problem really is. Don't tell me ahead of time." Often it's easier to make a decision when you don't know as much, because then you can't overthink. If you know too much, it can freeze you. The whole deal looks like a minefield.

I'd noticed the same thing at school. Our economics professor was a two-times PhD, but he pulled up in a Volkswagen Beetle. I'd had better cars for years by that time. I said to myself, "Knowing it all is not really the answer, because this guy is not making the money to have a bigger car. He should be driving a Mercedes."

CHAPTER 9

The Greatest Muscle Show Ever

AS MR. OLYMPIA, I WAS the three-time winner of a world championship that 99 percent of Americans had never heard of. Not only was bodybuilding obscure as a sport, but if you asked the average American about bodybuilders, all you'd hear was the negative stuff: "Those guys are so muscle-bound and uncoordinated, they can't even tie their shoes."

"It will all turn to fat and they'll die young."

"They all have inferiority complexes."

"They're all imbeciles."

"They're all narcissists."

"They're all homosexuals."

Every aspect of its image was bad. One writer said that the sport was about as easy to promote as midget wrestling.

It's true that bodybuilders look in the mirror as they train. Mirrors are tools, just like they are for ballet dancers. You need to be your own trainer. When you do dumbbell curls, for example, you need to see if one arm trails the other.

The sport was so far down, it was nowhere. To me bodybuilding had always seemed so American that I was still surprised when people couldn't guess what I did. "Are you a wrestler?" they'd ask. "Look at your body! No, no, I know, you're a football player, right?" They'd pick everything but bodybuilding.

In fact, the audiences were much larger in third world countries. A crowd of twenty-five thousand turned out to see Bill Pearl at an exhibition in India, while ten thousand showed up in South Africa. Bodybuilding was one of the most popular spectator sports in the Middle East. A great milestone in Joe Weider's career came in 1970, when the international community agreed to certify bodybuilding as an official sport. From that point on, bodybuilding programs qualified for state support in dozens of nations where athletics are subsidized.

But I'd been in the United States for four years, and basically nothing had changed. Each big city still had one or two gyms where the bodybuilders would train. The biggest competitions never aimed for more than four thousand or five thousand fans.

This bugged me because I wanted to see bodybuilding thrive, and I wanted to see the athletes and not just the promoters make money. I also felt that if millions of people were going to come to my movies someday, it was very important that they know where the muscles came from and what it meant to be Mr. Universe or Mr. Olympia or Mr. World. So there was a lot of educating to do. The more popular the sport became, the better my chances of becoming a leading man. It was easy for, say, New York Jets quarterback Joe Namath to get into commercials and films. In the major sports—football, baseball, basketball, and tennis—the stars would just cross over and make a lot of money. I knew that would never happen to me. I had to do more. I wanted to promote the sport, both so that more people would take part and to benefit my career.

Joe Weider was pretty set in his ways, though. He didn't want to try broadening his audience beyond the bodybuilding fans and fifteen-year-old kids—no matter how much I teased. "These are comic books!" I'd say about his magazines. " 'How Arnold Terrorized His Thighs'? 'This Is Joe's Biceps Speaking'? What kind of silly headlines are those?"

"It sells the magazine," Joe would say. His approach was to keep the products consistent and take every opportunity to expand their distribution around the world. Probably that was smart, because the business kept growing. But I realized that if I wanted to promote bodybuilding to a new audience, I'd have to find my own way.

I was passing through New York on the way to Europe in the fall of 1972 when I met the two people who would set me on the path: George Butler and Charles Gaines. Butler was a photographer and Gaines was a writer, and they were working as freelancers for *Life* magazine. They were on their way to cover the Mr. Universe contest that Joe Weider was staging in Iraq. They'd been told that they should talk to me to get background on bodybuilding.

I couldn't believe my good luck. These were the first journalists I'd ever really talked to from outside the bodybuilding world. They had access to maybe a million readers who'd never heard of the sport. They were about my age, and we hit it off really well. Gaines already knew quite a bit about bodybuilding, it turned out: he'd just published a novel called *Stay Hungry,* which centered on a bodybuilding gym in Alabama. It was a bestseller. That summer, he and Butler had teamed up on a story for *Sports Illustrated* about a contest called Mr. East Coast in Holyoke, Massachusetts. And they were already talking about continuing with the subject after the *Life* story and doing a book. They knew they were onto a fascinating subject that was unfamiliar to most Americans.

I wasn't going to be in Baghdad, but I promised that if they wanted to check out the bodybuilding scene in California, I'd make the arrangements and show them around. Two months later, they were sitting in my living room in Santa Monica getting acquainted with Joe Weider. I'd just introduced them, and it was somewhat confrontational at first. The visitors came on like cocky young guys who knew it all, even though Charles had been involved in bodybuilding for only three or four years, and George for less than that. They kept asking Joe why he wasn't pushing the sport in this or that direction, why he wasn't signing up corporate sponsors, and on and on. Why didn't he get *ABC's*

Wide World of Sports to cover his events? Why didn't he hire publicists? I could see that Joe thought they knew absolutely nothing, they were journalists, they saw everything from the outside. They had no understanding of the characters and personalities in the sport or what a challenge it was to try to bring in the big companies. You couldn't just snap your fingers and say, "Here's bodybuilding!" and have it be equal to tennis or baseball or golf.

But the discussion ended up being productive. Weider invited them out to his headquarters in the San Fernando Valley the next day, and they hung out with him and observed his operation. It was the start of bodybuilding going mainstream. I think at first it was a struggle for Joe. He was trying to figure out how to deal with a whole new kind of attention and not feel like someone was trying to take away his business, outdo him, or steal his athletes. I think there was a certain fear there. But he came to appreciate their way of looking at bodybuilding from the outside. Pretty soon he was including photos taken by Butler and stories by Gaines in his magazines.

I was right in the middle. I could see both sides, and I welcomed this development because I knew the sport needed fresh blood. I wondered if by working with Butler and Gaines, I could step into the mainstream too—get enough distance to reimagine bodybuilding and find ways to raise its public profile.

Over the coming months, the book they'd envisioned began to take shape. Doing research for *Pumping Iron: The Art and Sport of Bodybuilding*, George and Charles became familiar faces at Gold's. They were fun to hang out with and added a completely different dimension to the usual cast of characters. Charles Gaines was a good-looking, self-confident guy from a rich family in Birmingham, Alabama, where his dad was a businessman and his friends were part of the country club. He'd had a wild adolescence, dropped out of college for a while, and hitchhiked around the country. He always said that discovering bodybuilding helped settle him down. Eventually Charles became a teacher and outdoorsman. By the time we met, he lived in New England with his wife, a painter.

He'd figured out that there was a whole world of fascinating sports subcultures that weren't getting covered broadly: not only bodybuilding but also ice climbing and ice skiing. He was athletic, so he would try these sports himself and then write about them. Charles could convey what it felt like to improve as a weight lifter; to be able to bench thirty pounds more than he could a month earlier.

George Butler seemed even more exotic. He was British and had been raised in Jamaica, Kenya, Somalia, and Wales. His father was very British, very strict. George told stories about what a tough disciplinarian he was. He also described how, as a little boy, he'd spent half his time in the Caribbean with his mother while his father was off someplace. Then at a young age, he was sent away to boarding school. Later on, he went to Groton and the University of North Carolina and Hollins College, and he came out of it all with a million connections in New York society.

Maybe because of his background, George could strike you as cold and kind of prissy. He complained about little things. He always had over his shoulder an L.L. Bean bag containing his camera and a journal in which he wrote down things twenty-four hours a day. It seemed artificial to me, as if he had copied Ernest Hemingway or some famous explorer.

But George was exactly what bodybuilding needed to forge its new image. He was able to photograph it in a way that would make people say, "Wow, this is wild, look!" He didn't do straight-on muscle poses, which didn't excite the general public; instead, he'd photograph a bodybuilder as a little figure against the background of a huge American flag. Or he'd photograph the astonished faces of Mount Holyoke girls watching the bodybuilders compete. The Weider brothers did not think of things like that.

George could make something out of nothing. Or maybe it wasn't nothing; maybe it was just nothing to me because I saw it every day and I was part of it, whereas to him it was really something. Once, after a day spent shooting photos at Gold's, he asked me, "How do you walk around so fast in the gym and never touch anybody?"

To me the answer was obvious: when someone comes by, you move out of the way! Why bump into them? But George saw much more going on. A few weeks later, I heard him turn it into a story at a dinner party with his intellectual friends. "When Charles and I were in the gym, we watched very carefully the way these men moved around. And would you believe that in the four hours we spent there, we never saw any of these enormous bodybuilders bump into one another? Even though it was tight and there was a lot of equipment and not enough room, no one ever bumped. They just went by one another, just like big lions in a cage; they gracefully went by without touching."

His listeners were mesmerized. "Wow, they never bumped into each other?"

"Absolutely not. Here's another fascinating thing: Arnold never, ever had an angry look while he was training. He was lifting huge amounts of weight. He's always smiling. I mean, think about that. What must be inside his head? What must he know about his future, that he is always smiling?"

I thought, "This is brilliant. I would never be able to articulate it this way. All I would say is that I find joy in the gym because every rep and every set is getting me one step closer to my goal." But the way George expressed it, the scene he created of it, and the psychology he used made me say to myself, "This is perfect marketing."

Once he realized that I was funny and that I liked meeting new people, George started introducing me around New York City. I met fashion designers, heiresses, and people who made art movies. George loved bringing together worlds. He made friends at one point with a guy who published a magazine for firefighters. "This will be the new thing," George told everybody, "specialty magazines that cater to firemen, or law enforcement, or plumbers, or the military." He was way ahead of that trend.

In addition to being a photographer, George had aspirations as a filmmaker too, and he really liked the idea of putting me on the screen. He made short films of me training or going to school or interacting with other people and would show them to acquaintances and say, "Wouldn't it be interesting to put this guy in a movie?" He started trying to raise money for a documentary on bodybuilding to build on the book's success.

Charles Gaines, meanwhile, was making friends in Hollywood. He introduced me to Bob Rafelson, the director of *Five Easy Pieces*, who had bought the movie rights to *Stay Hungry*. While Charles was working with George on the *Pumping Iron* book project, he also started collaborating with Rafelson on the screenplay. I met Rafelson when Charles brought him to watch me work out on Venice Beach. Bob's wife, Toby, came along and took a bunch of pictures of Franco and me training, and she just loved it.

Connecting with Bob Rafelson suddenly swept me up into a whole different orbit. With him came a lot of the "New Hollywood" crowd: actor Jack Nicholson and director Roman Polanski, who were in the process of making *Chinatown*; as well as actors Dennis Hopper and Peter Fonda, who had made *Easy Rider* with Rafelson's producer Bert Schneider.

Gaines and Butler were pushing Rafelson to cast me in *Stay Hungry*. There was a main part for a bodybuilder named Joe Santo. Rafelson was a long way from making up his mind, but I remember sitting hypnotized in my apartment one night in early 1974 listening to him talk about what that would mean for me. "If we did this movie, I want you to know it will be a life changer for you. Remember what happened with Jack when he did *Five Easy Pieces*? Remember what happened to Dennis Hopper and Peter Fonda when they did *Easy Rider*? They all became superstars! I have a very good feeling for picking people, so when we do this movie, it will change your life. You won't be able to go anywhere where people don't recognize you."

I was dazzled, of course. One of the hottest directors in Hollywood was talking about making me a star! Meanwhile, Barbara was sitting next to me on the couch staring into space. I could sense the wheels turning. What would this do to our relationship and to me? My career was pulling me away from her. She wanted to settle down, get married, and have me open a health food store. She could see a huge storm coming.

Of course, her instinct was right. My focus was on training, acting, and making sure Rafelson hired me, not on getting married and having a family. But after Bob left, I told Barbara not to worry about what he'd said; it was just the marijuana talking.

I liked getting swept up into a cloud of celebrities. Nicholson's house was part of a "compound" up on Mulholland Drive next door to Polanski, Warren Beatty, and Marlon Brando. They'd invite me and some of the other bodybuilders up for parties, and sometimes people from that crowd would come to my building and we'd have barbecues on the little patio. It was hilarious: neighbors walking past on the sidewalk couldn't believe it when they saw who was there. But at the same time, I told myself not to get carried away. I was barely scraping the outside of that world. At that point, I was only a fan of those people.

I was being exposed to a world I didn't know. It was good to hang out, to watch them, to see how they operated and made decisions, and to hear them talk about movie projects, or building their homes, or building a house on the beach, or girls. I asked about acting and about the secret to becoming a leading man. Nicholson and Beatty, of course, were big proponents of method acting. They talked about how they prepared, how many times they rehearsed a role, and how they were able to live in the moment and improvise. Jack was shooting *One Flew Over the Cuckoo's Nest*, and he described how challenging it was to play a patient in an asylum. Meanwhile, Polanski, who had directed Nicholson in *Chinatown*, told of the differences between making a movie in Hollywood and making one in Europe: in America, the opportunity was grander, but the moviemaking was more formulaic and less artistic. They all had such enormous passion for their profession.

I thought that maybe down the road I'd get a chance to be in movies with them, in some kind of supporting role. But mostly I was thinking, "What a great promotion for bodybuilding, that this crowd now is accepting the sport."

—

My Hollywood career might never have taken off if not for a chain of events that started with Franco and me organizing a bodybuilding competition in Los Angeles that summer. I was still focused on wanting to see bodybuilding go mainstream. It frustrated me that bodybuilding shows were never advertised to the general public. That seemed totally wrong. I mean, what did we have to hide? People complained that reporters were always negative about bodybuilding and wrote stupid stories. Well, that was true, but who was talking to the press? Had anyone ever sat down and explained what we were doing? So Franco and I decided that if bodybuilding in LA was ever going to break out of its little shell, we had to promote it ourselves. We rented a big auditorium downtown and arranged the rights to host the Mr. International competition for 1974.

There were little signs that the time was right to do this. Lots of actors were starting to work out at Gold's. Gary Busey came regularly. Isaac Hayes, who'd won an Oscar for writing the *Shaft* theme song, would pull up in his Rolls every day and train. Up till then, the only actors working out in public were ones who reinforced the gay stereotype about bodybuilding. Actors like Clint Eastwood and Charles Bronson were muscular and had terrific bodies onscreen. They were working out, but in secret. Whenever somebody commented on their muscles, they'd say, "I was born this way." But that was starting to change, and weight training was becoming more acceptable.

Another positive sign was that more women were turning up at Gold's—not to ogle the guys but to ask about joining. At first, they weren't allowed. From a practical standpoint, it would have been hard for Joe Gold to let them in, because there was only one set of toilets and showers. But the real truth was that the guys were not yet ready for it. Bodybuilding was too much of a man's world. The last thing you wanted was to worry about what you said in the gym. There was a lot of cursing and a lot of man talk. I told Joe that he should include women.

I'd seen the benefits in Munich: having women in the gym made us train harder, even if you had to watch your language a little.

Sometimes the women who asked to join were sisters of bodybuilders or girlfriends. Sometimes they were girls who were already working out at the beach. If a woman needed to train for a physical test—to join the police or the fire department, say—Joe would always give special permission. He would tell her, "Come in at seven in the morning when there are fewer guys here, and you can work out. Be my guest; you don't have to pay anything."

Joe never made a decision without the bodybuilders' consent. Should there be a radio playing? Should he carpet the floor? Or would that ruin the dungeon effect? This was a hard-core gym that catered to the hard-core guys. We had endless discussions about letting women join. Finally we agreed to open the membership, but only to the hard-core women who signed a statement that said in effect: "We understand there's crude language, we understand there are weights dropping on feet and there are injuries, we understand there is only one set of bathrooms, and we will use the bathrooms on the beach." I wanted bodybuilding to open up completely to women, including women's championships. At least this was a start, and you could see the interest was there.

We felt bodybuilding contests were never big enough—it was always the same five hundred or one thousand spectators—and it felt very disorganized. Sometimes there was no music or the emcee was bad or the lighting was shitty. No one came to meet us at the airport. Everything was wrong. There were exceptions, like the Mr. World event in Columbus and the Mr. Universe event in London, but most competitions were amateurish. We made a list of everything we wanted to see fixed and started calling people for advice.

Franco and I scheduled our show for August 17. The hall we rented was a grand, old 2,300-seat theater in downtown LA called the Embassy Auditorium. The next thing we did was hire a publicist, Shelley Selover, who had an office right in Venice. When Franco and I went to see her, I doubt that she'd ever given bodybuilding a thought. But after asking a lot of questions and listening for a while, she agreed to take us on. "I can do something with this," she said. That was an important vote of confidence.

Shelley hooked us up right away with a veteran *Sports Illustrated* writer named Dick Johnston, who flew over from his home in Hawaii to check out our sport. Shelley coached us carefully before we met. "He wants to make the case to his editors that bodybuilders are athletes, serious athletes, and do a big story," she said. "You think you can help him with that?" So I went into the interview with all kinds of examples about how if this athlete hadn't picked bodybuilding, he'd have been a baseball star, and that guy would have been a boxer. They would be athletes anyway, but it happened that bodybuilding was their passion and was where they thought they had the most potential. Dick Johnston liked the idea and arranged to come back to cover our event.

Franco and I really hustled to put together the show. We knew we could never make ends meet with ticket sales alone. We had to pay the airfares for the bodybuilders coming in from around the world, we had to pay the judges, we had to pay for the hall and for advertising and promotion. So we looked for sponsors. Isaac Hayes suggested that we talk to his friend the great boxer Sugar Ray Robinson, who had a foundation. "He'll be into this," he told me. "His foundation is really for the underdog, you know? He gives money to inner city kids and minorities. So you just have to explain that as an Austrian in California and a bodybuilder, you're a minority!" Franco and I thought that was pretty funny, that we should be minorities. Franco was thrilled at the idea of meeting one of the greatest fighters of all time. I was excited too—I remembered seeing Robinson in newsreels as a kid. By 1974, he'd been retired for almost ten years.

When we arrived at his foundation, there were many people in the waiting room. I thought about everybody who must be hitting him up, and how great he was, as an ex-champ, to be spending his time on his foundation.

Finally, it was our turn. Sugar Ray brought us into his office and was incredibly warm. We were in such awe that we didn't even hear what he said the first few seconds. He took his time and listened to our pitch asking for money to purchase trophies for our event. By the end, he was laughing. It was just so weird, two foreigners trying to run an international championship in bodybuilding in LA. He gave us $2,800 for the trophies—which was a lot in those days. We went out and bought really nice ones with little plaques that said, "Donated by the Sugar Ray Robinson Youth Foundation."

We discovered that people really weren't negative about bodybuilding. They were open to it, but nobody was talking to them. This was open-minded America, ready to learn something new. Our approach was to educate the people. I had the personality. I knew Gaines's stories had gotten a good reception. You know how real estate people say "Location, location, location"? Our motto was "Presentation, presentation, presentation."

As Mr. International drew near, we put up posters headlined THE GREATEST MUSCLE SHOW EVER in YMCAs and gathering places all over town. The poster featured pictures of me (five times Mr. Universe, four times Mr. Olympia), Franco (Mr. Universe, Mr. World), Frank Zane (Mr. America, Mr. Universe), Lou Ferrigno (Mr. America, Mr. Universe), Serge Nubret (Europe's greatest bodybuilding star), and Ken Waller (Mr. America, Mr. World).

To my amazement, Shelley not only lined up newspaper interviews but also succeeded at getting me invited onto nationwide talk shows, including *The Merv Griffin Show*, *The Tonight Show*, and *The Mike Douglas Show*. That was when we realized we were right: there was actually an interest here; it wasn't like we were just imagining it.

Of course, given bodybuilders' stereotypical image, nobody was going to put me on the air without a preinterview well in advance. I had to go to the studio in the afternoon, hours before the show, so they could check out whether this muscleman could open his mouth and make sense. So I'd chat with the preinterviewer, who after awhile would say, "This is great! Now, can you say all this stuff when you're under pressure and in front of an audience?"

I would tell him, "Well you know, the interesting thing is, I don't see the audience. I'm so into it that I don't see them. So don't worry; I can block it out."

"Great, great."

The first show I did was *Merv Griffin*. The comedian Shecky Greene was the guest host that day. I sat down, and we exchanged a few lines, and then Shecky went quiet for a beat just looking at me. Then he burst out, "I can't believe it! You can talk!" That got a big laugh.

When somebody sets the bar that low, you cannot go wrong. Shecky kept complimenting me. He was very funny, and he made me funny as a result. This wasn't just a boost for me, it was a boost for bodybuilding in America: the viewers were getting to see a bodybuilder who looked normal when he was dressed, who could talk, who had an interesting background and a story to tell. All of sudden the sport had a face and a personality, which made people think, "I didn't realize these guys are funny! This isn't weird, it's great!" I was happy too, because I got to promote Mr. International.

Franco and I felt pretty nervous about our upcoming event especially after we talked to George Eiferman, one of the ex-bodybuilding champions we'd lined up as judges. George was an elder statesman of the sport (Mr. America 1948 and Mr. Olympia 1962) who now owned gyms in Las Vegas. A week before the contest, he came to visit and give advice. He met with Franco, Artie Zeller, and me at Zucky's.

George said, "Now make sure you that you have everything there."

"What do you mean?" I asked.

"I ran these competitions in the past. Sometimes we forget the simplest things."

"Like what?" I started sweating, wondering what it could be. I'd been concentrating so much on selling seats that maybe I'd overlooked some important details.

"For instance, do you have the chairs for the judges at the front table? Who is going to get you those chairs?"

I turned to Franco. "Did you take care of those chairs?"

Franco said, "You're such an idiot. How do I know about chairs for the judges?"

I said, "Okay, let's write this down." So I made a note that the next time we went to the auditorium, we had to figure out where to get this table to put in front of the stage and where to get nine chairs.

George went on: "You need a nice tablecloth on the table—a green one preferably, so it looks official. Also, have you thought about who is going to buy the notepads for the judges?"

"No."

He said, "Make sure the pencils you bring have erasers."

"Oh, shit."

George walked us through the whole thing. We had to figure out how the stage should look, how to arrange the backstage area and have weights there ready for pumping up, where those weights would come from, and how to get them into the back of the auditorium. "Have you worked that out?" he asked. "I'm sure this auditorium is governed by unions, so what are you allowed to lift and carry and what has to be done by the union guys?"

Franco and I, of course, didn't like the idea of having to obey union work rules. But we reminded ourselves that everything was much easier to do here compared to what it would be in Europe. Getting the permits and paying the taxes were much simpler, and the taxes were lower. Also, we had a lot of enthusiasm from the people who ran the auditorium.

In the end the competition was packed. Franco and I personally picked up all the bodybuilders from the airport, and we treated them exactly the way we would have wanted to be treated. The top bodybuilders were there. There was good, experienced judging. We invited judges, sponsors, and contestants to a reception the night before, which Franco and I paid for. All our publicity efforts really filled the hall, so that we ended up having to turn away two hundred people. Most important, the seats were filled by people from all walks of life, not just bodybuilders.

The ripples from my success on *The Merv Griffin Show* extended into the fall. Shelley booked me onto more talk shows. It was always the same. Since there was no expectation at all, I'd be spontaneous, and the host would respond, "This is fascinating!" Pretty soon I realized that in an entertainment interview, you could just make up stuff! I'd say things like, "In 1968 *Playboy* did a survey, and eighty percent of women hated bodybuilders. But now it's turned around, and eighty-seven percent of women love guys with muscles." They loved it.

Being on *Merv Griffin* led to another unexpected payoff. The morning after the show, I got a call at the gym from Gary Morton, the husband and business partner of Lucille Ball. "We saw you last night," he said. "You were funny. She has a job for you." Lucille Ball was then the most powerful woman in television. She was world famous for her sitcoms *I Love Lucy, The Lucy Show*, and *Here's Lucy*, and was the first woman in TV to break from the studios and run her own production company, which made her rich. Morton explained that she was working on a TV special with Art Carney, best known as Ed Norton on the 1950s sitcom *The Honeymooners*. She wanted me to play the part of a masseur. Would I come in that afternoon and read from the script? All of a sudden Lucy was on the phone. "You were fabulous! You were great! We'll see you later, right? Come in, we love you."

I went to their office, and somebody handed me the script. The show was called *Happy Anniversary and Goodbye*. I got really excited as I read it. Lucille Ball and Art Carney were playing a middle-aged couple named Norma and Malcolm. Their twenty-fifth anniversary is coming up, but instead Malcolm declares he's tired of Norma and suggests they get a divorce. Norma is tired of Malcolm, too. So they agree on a trial separation, and Malcolm moves out. But he goes back to the apartment to pick up something he forgot, and there is Norma, lying half naked on a table getting a massage. She plays it up to make him jealous, which leads to a hilarious fight, with the masseur, whose name is Rico, caught in the middle.

That masseur would be me. It was a seven-minute part of the hour-long show, and I thought, "*This* is great exposure; I will be on camera with Lucille Ball and Art Carney!" Since *Hercules in New York* had never been released, this would be my screen debut, and it would have an audience in the millions.

I was daydreaming about it when they called me in to read. Lucy, Gary Morton, and the director were all there, and she was very welcoming. "You were really funny last night!" she said. "Here, let's read."

The whole thing was so foreign to me, I had no idea that reading from a script means that you are supposed to actually act out the role. I sat and literally spoke my lines word for word, as if I was showing the teacher I knew how to read. "Hello my name is Rico and I'm from Italy and I was a truck driver there but now I'm a masseur."

And she said "*Oooo*-kay." I noticed the director looking at me. Under normal circumstances, they would have said, "Thank you very much; we'll call your agent." In my case, they couldn't have done that, because I didn't *have* an agent. But this wasn't an ordinary audition because Lucy really wanted me to play the part and nobody else was auditioning. I was there just so she could get Gary and the director on board.

She jumped right in to try to save me. "Great!" she said. "Now, do you know what the scene is about?" I said yes, and she said, "Tell me, just briefly."

And I said, "Well, it seems to me that I'm coming into your apartment because you've asked me to come and give you a massage, and you are getting divorced or a separation, or something like that, and I have these muscles because I was a truck driver in Italy, and I came to America, and I made some money not as a truck driver but as a masseur."

"That's *exactly* what it is. Now, can you tell me this again at the right moment when I ask you?" This time we played out the scene, starting with me ringing the doorbell, walking in with the massage table, and setting it up. She's gaping at my muscles and saying, "How did you get like that?"

"Oh, I actually come from Italy. I was a truck driver and then I became a masseur guy, and I'm very happy to be here today to massage you"—she is losing it as I'm saying this—"and after that I have another massage someplace else. I make a little bit of money massaging, and it's also good for the muscles."

"Now let's improvise," she said. So I made up a line. "Lie down so I can work you over."

She said, "Great, great! What do you think, guys?"

"That was funny, the way he explained it, and the Italian accent," the director said.

I said, "No, it's a German accent, but to you guys, it all sounds the same." They laughed and told me, "Okay, you've got the job."

Art Carney, Lucy, and I rehearsed that scene every day for a week. Carney had just won an Academy Award for his leading role in the movie *Harry and Tonto*. He was a very funny actor who turned out to have even more trouble than me memorizing lines. Finally, on Friday they told me, "On Monday when you come back, we're going to shoot live." I felt ready and said great.

Monday I waited backstage in the green room with some of the other actors. Then somebody came in and said, "Your scene is ready." They led me behind the stage to the door I was supposed to go through. "Stand here, and when the green light goes on, ring the doorbell and take it from there, just like we rehearsed."

So I waited, holding my massage table by the handle. I had on shorts and sneakers and a jacket I was supposed to strip off during the scene to reveal my tank top and my muscles underneath all pumped up and oiled up.

The green light came on, I rang the bell, Lucy opened the door, and I stepped onstage and said my first line, "I am Rico."

All of a sudden there was laughter and applause.

Which we hadn't rehearsed. I had no idea that "We're going to shoot live" in this case meant that we would be videotaping in front of three cameras and a studio audience. I'd never heard the expression before—what did it mean to me, a bodybuilder who had never been involved in TV? Meanwhile, Lucy was in character as Norma, acting hypnotized by my bulging legs and getting a big laugh by saying, "Oh, y-yes . . . won't you come in . . . Oh, you are in," and hurrying behind me to shut the door.

My next line was supposed to be "Where do we do it, here or in the bedroom?" But I'm standing frozen, holding the massage table and looking into the lights and listening to the applause and laughter of a thousand people filling this studio up to the rafters.

Being a total pro, Lucy saw what was happening and ad-libbed. "Well, don't just stand there looking at the art! You came to give me a massage—*right?*" I remembered my line, and from there the scene went great. There was applause throughout.

She was so good that I really thought she was asking me questions that I had to answer; I didn't feel like I was acting. It was a real lesson, and instead of getting paid, I should have paid them. Lucy followed my career like a mom for many years after that. As tough as she was by reputation, she was a sweetheart to me and would write me a letter of praise whenever a new movie came out. I ran into her many times at celebrity events, and she always gave me a big hug and just went off the deep end. "I take full credit for this man. He's going to become a big star," she'd say.

Lucy gave me advice about Hollywood. "Just remember, when they say, 'No,' you hear 'Yes,' and act accordingly. Someone says to you, 'We can't do this movie,' you hug him and say, 'Thank you for believing in me.' "

I had to be careful not to let my adventures in television sidetrack me from training. In July, Franco and I shifted to workouts at maximum effort twice a day to get ready for the competitions of the fall. I was defending my Mr. Olympia title for the fourth straight year, but in some ways it was far from routine. For the first time, the contest was going to be at Madison Square Garden, New York City's top location for rock concerts and sports. True, we were in the 4,500-seat Felt Forum rather than the 21,000-seat arena. But still, Madison Square Garden was where people came to see Muhammad Ali and Joe Frazier fight for the first time and to watch Wilt Chamberlain and Willis Reed play. It was where they came to listen to Frank Sinatra and to the Rolling Stones. It was the place for championships and major tournaments in college sports.

So bodybuilding was taking a big step up. People had seen me on TV. The book *Pumping Iron* was about to come out. And thanks to George Butler's tireless networking, the 1974 Mr. Olympia contest was getting buzz like it never had before. Charles Gaines's friend Delfina Rattazzi, an heiress to the Fiat fortune and later Jacqueline Kennedy Onassis's assistant at the Viking Press, would be hosting a book party at her apartment after the competition. She was inviting dozens of hip and trendy people who would have turned up their noses at bodybuilding before. I didn't know where it would all lead, but I knew I wanted to be in top form.

Joe Weider's magazine writers outdid themselves working to whip up excitement for this event, calling it "the Super Bowl of bodybuilding." The venue was a "modern Roman Colosseum." The contestants were "gladiators in a mortal vascular combat." The event itself was "the great muscle war of '74" and "the battle of the titans."

This year's drama revolved around bodybuilding's new wunderkind, Lou Ferrigno, a six-foot-five, 265-pound giant from Brooklyn. He was only twenty-two and getting better and better each year. He'd won both Mr. America and Mr. Universe in 1973, and now he was training to knock me off as Mr. Olympia. They were hyping Lou as the new Arnold. He had a terrific frame, wide shoulders, incredible abs, out-of-this-world potential, and nothing else on his mind except training and winning. To be precise, Lou was training for six hours a day, six days a week—more than even my body could stand. I loved being the champ. But how much more was there to prove after winning Mr. Olympia four straight years? Plus, my businesses were growing, and maybe I had the start of a movie career. As we trained for New York, I made up my mind that this Mr. Olympia would be my last.

Ferrigno had won the Mr. International contest that Franco and I had organized in Los Angeles. He was massive and symmetrical, and if I'd been a judge, I'd have picked him too, even though he was still undefined—like me when I first came to the America—and his posing needed work. If I'd had his body, I could have shaped it in a month to beat anyone—even me. I liked Lou, a nice, quiet guy from a sweet, hardworking family. He'd been partly deaf from the time he was a kid and had a lot to overcome growing up. Now he made a living as a sheet-metal worker, and his coach was his father, a New York City police lieutenant who drove him really hard. I could see how bodybuilding gave Lou pride. It made him somebody with a body. I loved the idea of a guy beating all the obstacles. I knew how he must have felt about me. He'd been a fan of mine growing up, and so he now saw me the way that I had once seen Sergio Oliva: as the champion he would ultimately have to beat.

But I didn't think he'd be ready. This wasn't going to be his year. So I trained carefully and kept things low-key and took it lightly when people would say to me, "Arnold, you've gotta be careful. If the judges want to look for a new face . . ." Or "Maybe Weider thinks you're too independent. Maybe he wants a new star."

Lou showed up in New York a few days before the competition, fresh from defending his Mr. Universe title in Verona, Italy. His father boasted at a press preview that if Lou won, he'd hold the title for a decade. "There is nobody on the horizon to challenge him." But Lou skipped a talk show on the morning of the competition to which he'd been invited along with Franco and me. "He's shy, he must be really *shvitzing*," I guessed. On the air I joked, "He is probably sitting at home watching my body and moving around his television set, posing, to see if he should compete."

At Madison Square Garden that night, it wasn't even close. By the final pose-off Lou was looking depressed, like a rookie who'd made a mistake. And he had. He'd tried so hard to add muscle definition that he'd lost too much weight, so his big body actually looked stringy and less muscular than mine. Onstage in front of a capacity crowd, I copied his poses, doing each one better than him. Then came a moment when we were face to face in matching biceps poses, and I gave Lou a little smile that said, "You are beaten." He knew it, the judges knew it, and so did the crowd.

Franco and I didn't stick around for very long after the contest; we ducked out with the Weiders and my old friend Albert Busek, who had flown from Munich to cover the event, to go to the *Pumping Iron* book party at Delfina's. The moment I walked in the door, *I* was the rookie. Delfina had a giant three-floor apartment, very decorated, very hip. There were paintings on the ceilings rather than on the walls so you could lie around getting stoned and look up and see the art.

An endless stream of people filled the huge rooms. The party was catered and seemed really well done, although I had never witnessed anything like this before, so I had no way to know. It was extraordinary. I had never seen this quality of people, the elegance, the high heels, the jewels, the extraordinary looking women, actors, directors, people from the art scene, people from fashion, and a lot of people I did not know at all. I could see that it was kind of a Euro-thing, with people very sophisticated, with their clothes, or lack thereof, gay people, strange people—everything was there.

All I could do was shake my head and say, "This is going to be an interesting life." I did not at all expect this. I was getting my first taste of what came with show business and fame in New York. No matter how many times you go there as a tourist or on business, you're never an insider. But now I felt I was being accepted—or at least like I was watching the show from the front row.

CHAPTER 10

Stay Hungry

BOB RAFELSON WAS STAYING at director-producer Francis Ford Coppola's apartment in the Sherry-Netherland Hotel facing Central Park, and the day before the Mr. Olympia contest, he brought me up to see it. I didn't know an apartment could be like that. It was as big as a house. It made quite an impression. I'd stayed only at Holiday Inns and Ramadas. And to have such a place and not even be there! Coppola was using it just for friends to stay in. The apartment had beautiful paintings and furniture, plus full hotel services day and night. I was amazed by his library of videotapes: an entire wall of movies categorized by genre—musical, action, drama, comedy, history, prehistoric, animated, and so on.

The next night at the book party, Rafelson's friends were all hanging out and watching me. Bob had brought them because he wanted to know what they thought. Did they like my personality? Would I be good for his movie?

Gaines and Butler had been pushing all along for him to cast me in the lead bodybuilder role in *Stay Hungry*. I'd been pushing too. "Where else are you going to find a body like this?" I asked him. "Looking for a professional actor is bullshit! I can do all that stuff! I'm sure I can act if you direct me right." The plot of the movie sounded like fun the way that Charles described it to me. He'd set the story in the city of Birmingham, Alabama, where he grew up. The hero, Craig Blake, is a young southern aristocrat who has inherited a lot of money and needs to find himself. He's stuck in the country club set, and he's working as the front man for crooked developers who are secretly trying to take over a block of downtown. One of the businesses they need to buy out is a bodybuilding gym.

The minute Craig walks into the gym, his world starts to change. There's a pretty receptionist he likes, a country girl named Mary Tate Farnsworth. And he becomes fascinated by the bodybuilding scene. The lead bodybuilder, Joe Santo, is a Native American training for the Mr. Universe contest. He's a playful, funny guy who sometimes works out in a Batman costume. Meeting him and the other bodybuilders inspires the hero, and he starts to buy into Joe Santo's philosophy: "You can't grow without burning. I don't like to be too comfortable. I like to stay hungry." Once Craig gets involved with the people at the gym, he realizes that he can't sell them out, and the plot takes off from there.

Rafelson had already hired his friend Jeff Bridges as Craig—which was very exciting because Bridges was a hot new talent who had starred in *The Last Picture Show* and Clint Eastwood's new movie *Thunderbolt and Lightfoot*. Charles thought I would be perfect as Joe Santo, and changed the character from an American Indian to an Austrian.

Maybe it was seeing me in the television skit with Art Carney and Lucille Ball that finally caused Rafelson to make up his mind. He called me after *Happy Anniversary and Goodbye* aired in late October and told me the part was mine. "You're the only one who has the body and the personality," he said. "But before you start to celebrate, we've got to get together tomorrow and talk."

When we sat down at Zucky's in Santa Monica the next day for lunch, Bob was all business. I'd never seen him in movie-director mode. He took charge of the conversation, and he had a lot to say. "I want you to play this lead role in the film, but I'm not going to give it to you," he began. "You have to earn it. Right now I feel you are not capable of being in front of the camera and selling all the different beats that I need." I didn't know what a beat was, but as he continued, I began to catch on.

"Most people think of a bodybuilder as a guy who will walk into a room and crash into everything and break it. When he talks, it'll be rough talk.

"But I bought the book partly because this guy, besides being powerful, is sensitive. You'll see him lifting hundreds of pounds of weight, but in the next scene, he might pick up a glass and say, 'Do you know what this is? This is Baccarat crystal. Look how gorgeous it is, how delicate it is.' That's just one example. He loves music. He plays the fiddle. He can get off on the quality of a guitar. He has a sensitivity and intuition that are almost like a woman's. That's what makes the character; he's able to shift gears. That's very hard to pull off." I made a mental note: I would have to take a few fiddle lessons.

"For instance," Bob was saying, "you've told me that bodybuilding is an art. But I want you to be able to sit with the leading lady, and when she says, 'Wow, look at your calves!' and say, 'Well, the calf is a very important body part. To win the competition, you cannot just have a blob of muscle there. It needs to be a heart shape; an inverted heart shape. See? And the measurements of the calf and the upper arm and the neck all have to be the same. It goes back to the Greeks. When you see Greek sculptures, they are beautifully proportioned—not just big biceps but also big shoulders and calves.' "

Bob said he wanted me to be able to explain all that not as a bodybuilder would explain it, but with feeling, more like an artist or art historian. "*And* you have to do it on camera. I've heard you talk like this sometimes, but can you pull it off when I say, 'Action'? Can you pull it off when I do the close-up, and the cross-angle shot, and the master shot, and the top shot? Can you stay in character for that, and then snap into the same character the next day when the script calls for you to do a wild training session where you and the other guys bounce around with huge weights? That's what makes this part unique."

He wasn't finished with his list of requirements.

"Also, if you're Joe Santo, you have to deal with the southern country club scene, where they have big parties and where all these silly people are drunk all the time. Everything you have you've earned through hard work. Now here's this new acquaintance, Craig Blake, who inherited a lot of money, walking around in a nice suit, and he wants to be your friend. How do you feel about that?

"I think you can learn to do all this. But I want you to take acting classes before we shoot."

Bob must have been expecting me to put up a fight because he seemed surprised when I agreed. I was excited. Not only was somebody finally explaining to me what movie acting was actually about, but also he was making it a challenge. I wasn't being hired just because he'd watched me win Mr. Olympia and I got along with his movie-star friends. I had to earn it, which was what I liked to do.

Bob had another condition, and this one was harder: he wanted me to cut down to 210 pounds from 240. "The camera makes the body look bigger," he explained, "and I don't want you to overwhelm the other actors with your size. You can weigh two-ten and still sell the idea of being Mr. Universe."

This was a big request. I knew that the only way I could get down to 210 was to let go of my vision of myself as the world's most muscular guy. I couldn't have it both ways. So I was forced to make the decision I'd been leaning toward anyway: to retire from competition. I'd been bodybuilding for twelve years already, and the philosophy of the movie spoke to me. I liked the idea of staying hungry in life and never staying in one place. When I was ten, I wanted to be good enough at something to be recognized in the world. Now I wanted to be good enough at something else to be recognized again, and even bigger than before.

The teacher Rafelson sent me to, Eric Morris, had been Jack Nicholson's acting coach. He had an LA studio, and I still remember the address and phone number by heart because I sent so many people to him in the following years. As you walked into the studio, there was a sign next to the entrance that read DON'T ACT. I wondered about that the first time I saw it. But the production company was paying for three months of private lessons and classes, and I was ready to give it a chance.

Morris turned out to be a skinny guy in his late thirties, with shaggy blond hair and penetrating eyes. His full motto was "Don't act. Only be real." He was always talking with great enthusiasm about the discoveries he'd made and what was missing from other theories of acting. I didn't know any other theories of acting. But I did know that the world he opened up to me was mind blowing.

It was the first time I'd heard anybody articulate ideas about the emotions: intimidation, inferiority, superiority, embarrassment, encouragement, comfort, discomfort. A whole new world of language appeared.

It was like going into the plumbing business and suddenly hearing about parts and tools that you need, and you say to yourself, "I don't even know how to spell the things we are talking about here." It was like a whole new sea of words that you're hearing over and over until you finally ask, "What does that mean?"

It was broadening my horizons to things that I'd ignored. In competition, I'd always walled off emotions. You have to keep your feelings under control or you can be knocked offtrack. Women always talked about emotions, but I considered it silly talk. It did not fit into my plan. Not that I usually admitted this to them, because it did not make them happy—instead I'd half listen and just say, "Yeah, I understand." Acting was just the opposite. You had to let things affect you and keep your defenses down because that was how you became a better actor.

If you had to enact an emotion in a scene, Morris would get you to go back and connect to some sense memory. Let's say that you associated the smell of coffee brewing with a time when you were six years old and your mother was making coffee, probably not for you but maybe for your dad. You visualized being in the kitchen, the way it looked with your father and mother there, and that got you into a certain emotional state. It was the smell of coffee that took you there.

Or the smell of a rose: maybe the first time you got flowers for some girlfriend. You could see her in front of you, how she smiled, how she kissed, and that got you into a certain mood also. Or if you heard sixties rock 'n' roll, that took you back to a time when somebody was playing the radio in the gym while you lifted. Morris was trying to help me identify the triggers for specific emotions I might need in *Stay Hungry*. He'd say, "When you were competing and winning, were you exhilarated, over-the-top excited? Maybe we can use that in a scene."

I had to explain that actually I was not especially exhilarated when I won, because to me, winning was a given. It was part of the job. I had an obligation to win. So I did not feel "Yeah! I won!" Instead I'd say to myself, "Okay, did that. Let's move on to the next competition."

I said that I always found surprises much more exhilarating. If I passed all my classes at UCLA, I would walk out ecstatic because even though I expected to pass, it was still a pleasant surprise. Or going to a Christmas party and getting an unexpected gift. I explained that to him. Then Morris would simply say, "Okay, let's go back to those moments."

He probed and probed. When did I feel in love? When did I feel excluded? How did I feel when I left home? How did I feel when my parents told me it was time to start paying them *Kostgeld*—food money—if I wanted to keep living in their house? Americans don't usually do that, so how did it feel? He would latch onto different things until he found the emotion.

I hated it at first. I told him, "I have not dealt with any of this stuff that you are talking about until now. It's not the way I live." He didn't believe a word of it. "You sell yourself as being the kind of guy who doesn't experience emotion, but don't delude yourself. Not paying attention to it or dismissing it doesn't mean that it is not part of you. You actually have the emotion because I see it in your eyes when you say certain things. You can't fool a fooler."

He was teaching me to access all the emotions that were stored in my mind. "Everyone has them," he said. "The trick in acting is to summon them up in the quickest way. Why do you think certain actors can cry when they want? Not just mechanical crying, but real crying, where your whole face contracts and your lip quivers. It means that the actor can recall something very, very upsetting very quickly. And it's very important for the director to capture that in the first two takes, because the actor can't do it again and again without it becoming mechanical. You can't mess with the mind that often," he said. "But I'm not worried about that with Bob Rafelson because he is definitely the right director. He's very much aware of all this."

There is a scene in *Five Easy Pieces* where Jack Nicholson cries. Eric told me how Rafelson stopped filming and talked to Nicholson for two hours until he saw him getting choked up. They were talking about something in his life, too quietly for the other people on the set to hear. Then Bob announced, "Great, Jack, stay with that," the other actors moved in, they shot the scene, and he cried. "Bob got him into that," Eric said. "Sometimes it's difficult, sometimes it's easy, sometimes it doesn't happen and then you have to try another day.

"What I'm trying to do is give you the tools," he continued. "Maybe you didn't cry when your brother died, you didn't cry when your dad died. But is it upsetting to you that here you are, they died, and now you and your mother are left alone?" He was trying every angle. But we hit a wall there. I couldn't figure it out. Nothing worked. We decided that crying on cue had to wait.

Besides the private lessons, I also took his group classes three nights a week from seven to eleven. It was twenty people, and you all worked on scenes or did exercises, and some of it was fun. He would pick a topic like, say, anger and frustration. "I want everyone to talk about it. What makes you frustrated?" For the first hour, we'd all tell stories of when we were angry and frustrated. Next he'd say, "Good. Let's save that emotion. Now somebody give me some lines, make up some lines that show that frustration." We would ad-lib frustration. The next class might revolve around reading from a script cold, or auditioning, and on and on.

Those nights were a lot less fun when Morris would take stuff I'd told him in private lessons and trot it out in front of the whole acting class. It was his way of going for the raw nerve. He didn't hesitate to push me or embarrass me. I might be reading lines we'd rehearsed from the *Stay Hungry* script, and he'd interrupt me and say, "What the fuck was that? Really, that's all you have in you? This afternoon when you and I did it, I felt goose bumps. Now I feel no goose bumps. Now I feel like you're trying to do a show or you're trying to do the Arnold shtick here. This is not Arnold shtick. This is something totally different. Do it over."

The private lessons all focused in one way or another on the script. Morris told me, "We're going to go through it line by line and analyze even the scenes that have nothing to do with you, because you'll see, in fact, that they do. We've got to figure out why you are in the South; what it means when you meet the country club people who are throwing around their inherited money and having their cocktails at night. We've got to understand the weather, and the bodybuilding gym, and the crooks who are ripping off everyone." So we worked through the script page by page, line by line. We would talk about each scene, and I'd start learning the dialogue, and then we'd analyze it again. I'd do the dialogue for him and then again in the class at night in front of the twenty people—he'd assign one of the girls to read the lines of Mary Tate.

Then he'd bring me to read for Bob Rafelson. I got to see the parade of actors, men and women, passing through Bob's office auditioning for the other parts. In case I was wondering, that reminded me how big a deal this movie was. Rafelson made a point of showing me the ropes and teaching me lessons that went beyond just acting. He was always explaining why he did things. "I picked this guy because he looked like a country club boy," and "We're shooting in Alabama because in California we'd never get lush green landscape and oyster bars and the backdrop we need to make the story authentic."

When he picked Sally Field to play Mary Tate, he wanted to make that a big teaching point. "You see?" he said. "I've been auditioning all these girls, and the one who is actually the best is the Flying Nun!"

"What is the flying nun?" I asked.

He had to back up and explain he meant Sally Field, and that everybody knew her as the flying nun because she'd played the part of Sister Bertrille for years on a TV sitcom. After we got that straight, he had a bigger point to make. "Everybody thinks they know what a girl has to do to get the part," he said. "The perception is that you get the job by banging the director. And there were girls with big tits and great hair and great bodies who came in and offered that to me. But in the end the Flying Nun got the job. She doesn't have big tits, she doesn't have a curvaceous body, she didn't offer to fuck me, but she has what I needed most in this part, which is talent. She was a serious actor, and when she came in and performed, I was blown away."

Because this was my first big movie and I wasn't an actor by profession, Bob also felt it would be good for me to hang out and see movies actually being made. So he called a few sets to arrange for me to come by to watch for an hour. It was good to experience how silent it gets on the set when they say, "We're rolling." It was good to learn that "action" doesn't necessarily mean action—the actors still might be adjusting and asking, "What's my first line?"

This was Bob's way of teaching me that, yes, there will be thirteen takes, and, yes, this is normal, but just remember only one will be seen. So don't worry when I say for the thirteenth time, "Let's do it again." No one will know. And don't worry if you cough in the middle of a scene, he told me. "I'd cut around it, I'd cover it from this angle and that angle."

The more I hung out on the set, the more comfortable I felt.

After he cast Sally Field, Bob became especially fanatic about the need for me to lose weight. She's so petite he worried that if I didn't slim down, I'd make her look like a shrimp. "When we get to Birmingham, if I put you on a scale the day before shooting and you're not two hundred ten, you are not in the picture," he threatened. There was no

Eric Morris class for a star bodybuilder to get rid of muscle, so I was on my own. First I had to redo myself mentally—let go of the 250-pound image of Mr. Olympia that was in my head. I started visualizing myself instead as lean and athletic. And all of a sudden what I saw in the mirror no longer fit. Seeing that helped kill my appetite for all the protein shakes and all the extra steak and chicken I was used to. I pictured myself as a runner rather than a lifter, and changed around my whole training regimen to emphasize running, bicycling, and swimming rather than weights.

All through the winter, the pounds came off, and I was pleased. But at the same time, my life was getting too intense. I was working on my mail-order business and on my acting classes, going to college, training for three hours a day, and doing construction. It was a lot to juggle. I often felt overwhelmed and started asking myself, "How do I keep it all together? How do I not think about the next thing while I'm still doing this thing? How can I unplug?"

Transcendental meditation was popular with people on the beach in Venice. There was one guy down there I liked: a skinny guy who was into yoga; kind of the opposite of me. We would always chat, and eventually I found out that he was a Transcendental Meditation instructor. He invited me to one of his classes at this center near UCLA. There was a little bit of hokum involved: you had to bring a piece of fruit and a handkerchief and perform these little rituals. But I paid no attention to that. Hearing them talk about the need to disconnect and refresh the mind was like a revelation. "Arnold, you're an idiot," I told myself. "You spend all this time on your body, but you never think about your mind, how to make it sharper and relieve the stress. When you have muscle cramps, you have to do more stretching, take a Jacuzzi, put on the ice packs, take more minerals. So why aren't you thinking that the mind also can have a problem? It's overstressed, or it's tired, it's bored, it's fatigued, it's about to blow up—let's learn tools for that."

They gave me a mantra and taught me to use a twenty-minute meditation session to get to a place where you don't think. They taught how to disconnect the mind, so that you don't hear the clock ticking in the background or people talking. If you can do this for even a few seconds, it already has a positive effect. The more you can prolong that period, the better it is.

In the middle of all this, Barbara was going through changes too. She and Franco's wife, Anita, signed up for EST (Erhard Seminars Training), a popular self-help seminar. They asked if we wanted to come, but Franco and I felt we didn't need it. We knew where we were going. We knew what we wanted. We had control over our lives, which is what EST claimed to teach.

As a matter of fact, the gimmick in the opening session was that no one could leave the room to go to the bathroom. The idea was if you cannot even control your own piss, how are you ever going to get control over yourself or have control over anybody else around you?

I was amazed that people would pay for that! Still, if Barbara and Anita wanted to try it, I didn't mind.

Barbara and Anita were all sunny and positive when they came home after the first weekend they went. Franco and I were thinking that maybe we should go to EST too. But the second weekend, something happened that sent Barbara and Anita both off the deep end. They came back all angry and negative, thinking everything was wrong with their lives and ready to blame everybody around them for it. Barbara was furious with her father. She was the third of three daughters, and she thought he treated her like the son he never had. I gave her hell for that. I really liked her father and wasn't sophisticated enough to understand. To me there was no indication that he treated her like a boy. Then she accused me of being on a power trip and not paying enough attention to her.

We usually got along very well and had lived together for more than three years. But she was a normal person who wanted normal things, and there was nothing normal about me. My drive was not normal. My vision of where I wanted to go in life was not normal. The whole idea of a conventional existence was like Kryptonite to me. When Barbara saw me moving away from bodybuilding and into acting, I think she realized we had no future. Right after I left for Alabama to start shooting *Stay Hungry*, she moved out.

I felt really sad about the whole thing. Barbara was part of my life. I'd developed feelings I'd never had. The comfort of being with someone and sharing our lives, so I wasn't just putting up my own pictures on the wall but sharing the wall space and choosing the furniture and rugs together. Feeling included in her family was comforting and wonderful. We'd been a unit, and all of sudden it was ripped apart. I struggled to understand. I thought at first that maybe Bob Rafelson had told her, "I need Arnold to get more sensitive. I need to see him cry. If you want to help our movie, move out and fuck him up bad." Otherwise it seemed crazy that she split.

I knew I was losing something valuable. My emotions told me we should stay together, while rationally I could see her point. It wouldn't work in the long run. Barbara wanted to settle down, and I needed to be free to change and grow. The years with Barbara taught me a great lesson: how having a good relationship can enrich your life.

Birmingham turned out to be a small industrial city about the size of Graz, and the shooting of *Stay Hungry* was the biggest excitement in town. We got there in April 1975, and within a few weeks, you could already feel the sticky summer heat. I loved it there. We shot for three months and got to know the city very well, all the bars and oyster bars and restaurants. The hotel the cast stayed at was great. The people were extraordinarily friendly, and, of course, Charles Gaines was a native son, so we were invited to a lot of parties. Having just broken up with Barbara, I was glad to spend some time away from home.

As soon as I started rehearsing with Sally Field, I saw what Rafelson had been talking about. She was in total command of her craft, and within seconds she could cry or get angry or whatever was required. She was fun to be around too, always bubbly and full of energy. I was grateful to her and to Jeff Bridges for helping me learn. Jeff was very low-key, a little bit of a hippie, into playing his guitar, a comfortable person to hang out with, and very, very patient. I worked hard holding up my end of the deal. I invited other cast members to critique my acting, and I made Jeff promise to tell me what he really thought.

At first it was hard not to take criticisms personally. But Rafelson had warned me that changing careers would be tough. In this world, I wasn't number one in the universe; I was just another aspiring actor. He was right. I had to surrender my pride and tell myself, "Okay, you're starting again. You're nothing here. You're just a beginner. You're just a little punk around these other actors."

Yet I liked the fact that a movie is the effort of dozens of people. You need the people around you for you to look good, whereas bodybuilding is much more *me* oriented. You have your training partner, of course, but in competition you always want to throw a little shit on the other diamonds to make sure you're the only one who sparkles. I was ready to get away from that.

In bodybuilding, you try to suppress your emotions and march forward with determination. In acting, it's the opposite. You look for the sense memories that would serve as emotional keys. To do that, you have to strip away the calluses. It takes a lot of work. I'd remember the flowers I picked for my mother for Mother's Day, which would remind me of being at home, being part of the family. Or I'd tap into my anger at Joe Weider for reneging on a promise to pay for something. Or I'd think back to when my father didn't believe in me and said, "Why don't you do something useful? Go chop some wood." To live your life as an actor, you can't be afraid of someone stirring up your emotions. You have to take the risk. Sometimes you'll be confused, sometimes you'll cry, but that will make you a better actor.

I could tell that Bob Rafelson was happy with the way things were going because after the first two or three weeks, he stopped checking my weight. I was already back up to 215 by the time we shot the Mr. Universe pose-off. That sequence comes near the film's end: the bodybuilders in the Mr. Universe contest suspect Joe Santo of having stolen the prize money, and they all spill out onto the Birmingham streets. Once the real bad guy is caught, the bodybuilders notice that they've attracted a crowd and spontaneously start a posing exhibition. The crowd gets so into it that soon everybody's posing in this big, happy climax. Shooting the scene was just like that: the extras and the onlookers in Birmingham got mixed up, and everybody was laughing and doing muscle poses, and Rafelson was on his megaphone shouting, "Please do *not* touch the bodybuilders."

George Butler came to Alabama in the middle of all this to turn all my new plans upside down. He'd always talked about turning *Pumping Iron* into a documentary, but he wasn't able to raise the money while they were finishing the book. Now things had changed. With all the publicity around Mr. Olympia, the book had become a surprise bestseller. And because I was making a movie with Bob Rafelson, the money was easier to raise. Also, George's wife, Victoria, was a smart investor, and as long as I was in the film, she was willing to put in money.

"So we can do it!" he announced when we sat down to talk. His idea was to make the documentary hinge on me competing in the next Mr. Olympia contest, which was scheduled for November in Pretoria, South Africa. I had to remind him that I'd shifted my goal to acting and completely changed my training routine. "I'm retired," I said. "Look, I've taken off all this muscle." The conversation grew pretty heated.

"Well, there *is* no *Pumping Iron* if you're not in it," George insisted. "The other guys can't carry the movie with their personalities. You're really the only one in bodybuilding who brings life to the sport. I need you to be in it. Otherwise I can't raise the money." Then he claimed that working on the project would be good for my acting career.

"I don't need it for my career," I said. "You can't get any better than this movie with Bob Rafelson. As soon as I go back, I want to continue with my acting—that's where the opportunity is."

George tried playing another card: "We're prepared to pay you fifty thousand dollars to do this." This was a number he'd thrown around already the previous year. Back then it sounded good because I was just buying the apartment building in Santa Monica and taking on a lot of debt. And I still liked the idea of that kind of money coming in. At this moment, however, it rubbed me the wrong way. "I don't really want to go back into competition," I said.

I didn't owe George anything, but there was a lot to sort out. He was the best promoter I'd ever met, and I knew he would throw himself into this project. A *Pumping Iron* film by him would be an opportunity, maybe a great opportunity, to present bodybuilding as a sport to people who normally would never pay any attention. I felt that I couldn't turn my back on bodybuilding. So much of my life was wrapped up in it and so many friends.

There were business dimensions to think about too. Backstage in Columbus, Ohio, years before, I'd told promoter Jim Lorimer that I wanted to partner with him someday to produce bodybuilding events. After my last Mr. Olympia tournament, I'd called him. "Remember how I said when I retired from competition I'd get in touch?" I asked. We agreed to go into business together, and we were putting together a bid with other investors he knew to make Columbus the home of future bodybuilding competitions. If anyone had the business skill and the connections to bring bodybuilding into the heartland and the American sports mainstream, it was Jim. Of course I still had the Arnold mail-order business, which was now bringing in $4,000 a year and growing.

And I was still attached to Joe Weider. Joe and I had battled—for example, at times he'd gotten mad when I signed up for a competition that he didn't sponsor. But there was always that father-and-son bond. Joe adjusted to my movie career by covering the filming of *Stay Hungry* in his magazines. All the fans knew I was retiring, and the way he framed it was "Arnold is going into this other arena, and he is going to carry bodybuilding with him no matter what movie he does, so let's follow him and support him." When he realized I was serious about acting, Joe gave up gracefully on the dream of having me take over his business. But he would have freaked if he'd thought he would totally lose me, because I was the goose that laid the golden egg.

Finally, George convinced me to compete again. I looked at what

I wanted to accomplish. Besides being the bodybuilding champion I was by now convinced that bodybuilding itself was ready for a big push. George and Charles had started the ball rolling with their articles and book. The seminars I taught were full. Working with reporters, I'd made the media a support system for whatever I wanted to sell. I felt it was my responsibility, as the bodybuilder with personality and the large following, to carry that on. I shouldn't think only about my own career but also about the big picture: the need for fitness in the world and how weight training could make you a better tennis or football or soccer player. And we could make bodybuilding fun.

A *Pumping Iron* film could have a huge impact. Documentaries such as *Marjoe,* about an evangelist named Marjoe Gortner, and *The Endless Summer,* about two young surfers traveling the world in search of the perfect wave, were very hip at that point. The films would move from city to city, using money from the last showing to finance the next screening.

I told George that to get my body back into shape for competition was like turning the *Titanic.* Mechanically, it was an easy decision; I knew all the training steps I would have to take. But it was much harder to buy into psychologically. I'd deprogrammed myself from being onstage in competition and from needing that glory. Now starring in movies was the motivating thing. That shift had involved months of adjustment. So to go back now was a real challenge. How would I convince myself again that that body was the most important thing?

Still, I thought I would be able to win. I'd have to increase from 210 pounds back to competition weight, but I'd done something like this before, after my knee surgery in 1972. My left thigh atrophied from twenty-eight inches down to twenty-two or twenty-three, yet I'd built it back up bigger than ever in time for Mr. Olympia that year. My theory was that muscle cells, like fat cells, have a memory, so they can grow back quickly to where they were. There was some uncharted territory, of course. I would want to perform even better than I did at Madison Square Garden, so should I come all the way back to 240 pounds, or should I come in leaner? Whatever the answer, I thought it was doable.

The idea of constantly having Butler's cameras on me while I trained was tempting. You always want to look better when the camera's on you, so it's a great motivator. I thought that maybe the camera crew would eventually feel like just part of the woodwork, and I'd no longer be self-conscious around it— and that would be great for my acting career.

For at least a week, I'd sit in the hotel weighing the pros and cons, and then I'd go shoot another scene of *Stay Hungry*. Then I'd go back and think about it some more, and hang out and talk to other people. Charles Gaines had decided to move on to other writing projects and not work on the documentary with George. He thought my returning to competition would be a mistake. "You are on your acting mission now," he told me. "You need to show the community that you're serious about it. After this movie, they'll want to see you continue with acting classes with talented actors and directors. But if now all of a sudden you're competing again, it'll look like you have one foot in and one foot out so that you can go back to bodybuilding in case acting doesn't work. Is that the impression you want to give?"

All my life, my goals had been simple and linear, like building up a muscle with hundreds of thousands of reps. But this situation wasn't simple at all. Yes, I had committed 100 percent to becoming a lean and athletic-looking actor—how could I undo that and refocus myself on winning Mr. Olympia again? I knew the way my mind worked, and that to accomplish anything, I had to buy in completely. The goal had to be something that made total sense and that I could look forward to every day, not just something I was doing for money or some other arbitrary reason, because then it wouldn't work.

In the end I realized I had to think about the problem a different way. It could not be solved from a purely selfish point of view. I felt that even though I was on the trajectory to launch an acting career, I owed too much to bodybuilding to reject it. So I had to do *Pumping Iron* and compete for Mr. Olympia again—not for myself, but to help promote bodybuilding. I would pursue my acting career at the same time, and if my actions were confusing to people like Charles, I'd just have to explain.

—

A month after I got back from Alabama, my friends threw a twenty-eighth birthday party for me at Jack Nicholson's house. The organizer was Helena Kallianiotes, who looked after his property and who had a small part in *Stay Hungry.* She was a dancer and understood the hard training and dedication involved in bodybuilding. In Birmingham, she'd become a good friend, helping me rehearse and showing me around the oyster bars. Later, when I wrote *Arnold's Bodyshaping for Women*, Helen was the first person I consulted to get more into a woman's mind about training.

The party was a great success. Many people from Hollywood came, as well as my friends from Venice Beach—this amazing mix of actors, bodybuilders, weight lifters, karate guys, and writers, plus visitors from New York. There were about two hundred altogether. For me, this was heaven because I could introduce myself to so many new people.

I got to know Nicholson, Beatty, and the rest of the Mulholland Drive crowd a little better now that I was back. They were so hot in those days, with movies like *Chinatown*, *The Parallax View*, and *Shampoo*. They were on the covers of magazines, they went to the trendiest nightclubs. They were always together, and in winter, the whole clique would fly to Gstaad, Switzerland, to ski. I was not inside enough to be partying with them all the time, but I did get exposed to how stars at that level lived and operated, what they were into, and how they moved around, and it inspired me to be there myself in a few years.

Jack Nicholson was very casual and low-key. You would always see him with his Hawaiian shirt, shorts or long pants, sunglasses, and disheveled hair. He owned the most expensive Mercedes, a maroon 600 Pullman, with all-leather interior and extraordinary woodwork. The person who actually used this car was not Jack but Helena. Jack himself drove a Volkswagen Beetle, and that was his shtick: "I'm so rich that I'm going to sell myself like an ordinary person. I'm not into money at all." He would drive his little Beetle to the studio lot on the way to a media interview or a discussion about a film. The guard at the gate would say, "Oh, Mr. Nicholson, of course. Your parking spot is right over there," and Jack would putt-putt in as if the car could barely get there. It was genuine. He was more comfortable in the VW than in the Mercedes. I would have loved the Mercedes.

A photographer friend from New York visited and took me to Warren Beatty's house on the beach. Warren wanted the photographer to see the plans for the new house he was building on Mulholland Drive. Beatty was famous for never making up his mind and debating every decision for thousands of hours. He was accomplishing a lot: he'd recently starred in *The Parallax View* directed by Alan Pakula, and was cowriting and starring in *Shampoo*, and was directing scenes for the Russian Revolution movie that eventually became *Reds*. But hearing him talk, you wondered how he got anything done at all. I thought this was not the way I would operate if I were at that level. But I was also learning that born actors are always a little artsy and strange. You can identify the type. When you hang out with businessmen, they act like businessmen. Politicians act like politicians. These guys were entertainers, and they acted like entertainers. They were Hollywood. It was a different thing.

The one who did not fit this picture was Clint Eastwood. The Mulholland Drive bunch liked to go for dinner at Dan Tana's restaurant on Santa Monica Boulevard. They would sit together, and Clint would be there eating at his own table on the other side of the room. I went up to him and introduced myself, and he invited me to sit for a minute and chat. He was a bodybuilding fan and worked out regularly himself. He wore a herringbone tweed jacket, very similar to the one he'd worn in his 1971 movie *Dirty Harry*. Later I learned it wasn't just similar, it was the same jacket. Clint was a very frugal guy. After we became friends, he told me that he always kept the clothes from his movies and wore them for years and never bought anything new. (Nowadays, of course, he likes to deck himself out in beautiful clothes. Maybe he still gets them for free.) It made a lot of stars uncomfortable to see a celebrity eating alone. But, in fact, Clint was totally at ease and un-self-conscious.

Costarring in a soon-to-be-released Bob Rafelson movie didn't get me very far when I tried to find an agent. One guy who approached me was Jack Gilardi, who represented O. J. Simpson, the top running back in the National Football League. O.J. was at the peak of his athletic career, and Gilardi was getting him parts on the side in movies like the disaster flick *The Towering Inferno*. The studios liked to have O.J. in there just for the name, so football fans would go to see the movie. That's how you manufactured an audience. But it was never the starring role, and nobody who mattered in Hollywood paid attention.

Jack wanted to do the same thing for me. He figured if I was in a movie, then all the bodybuilding fans would buy tickets. "As a matter of fact," he said, "I have a good Western script and a meeting with the producers, and there's something in here for you." It was maybe the sixth or seventh most important role.

This was not at all what I had in mind. Whoever represented me had to buy into the big vision. I didn't want an agent who would say, "I'm sure you must have something in your movie for Arnold, maybe a minor supporting part with a few lines where he can be listed in the cast." I wanted an agent who would pound the table on my behalf. "This guy has leading-man potential. I want to groom him for that. So if you can offer us one of the top three parts, we're interested. If not, let's just move on."

I couldn't find anyone at the big agencies who saw it this way. William Morris and International Creative Management were the dominant agencies in town, and that was where I wanted to be because they always got first look at the big movie projects, they handled all the big directors, and they dealt with the top people at the studios. An agent from each place was willing to meet with me because I'd just shot a picture with Bob Rafelson.

They both said the same thing: there were too many obstacles. "Look, you have an accent that scares people," said the guy from ICM. "You have a body that's too big for movies. You have a name that wouldn't even fit on a movie poster. Everything about you is too strange." He wasn't being mean about it, and he offered to help in other ways. "Why don't you stay in the gym business, and we can develop a chain of franchises? Or we can help you in lining up seminars and speaking engagements. Or with a book or something like that about your story."

I understand it better today that there's so much talent all over the world that these big agencies don't really have the time or the desire to groom someone and nurture him to the top. They're not in the business of doing that. It has to happen or not happen. But at the time, I felt stung. I knew I had a strange body. I knew my name was hard to spell—but so was Gina Lollobrigida's! Why should I give up my goal because a couple of Hollywood agents turned me down?

The accent was an issue I could do something about. That summer I added accent removal lessons to my schedule, along with acting classes, college courses, running my businesses, and training for Mr. Olympia. My teacher was Robert Easton, a world-famous dialect coach whose nickname was the Henry Higgins of Hollywood. He was a gigantic guy, six foot three or four, with a big beard, a tremendous voice, and the most precise enunciation. The first time we met, he showed off by speaking English first with a High German accent and then a Low German accent. Next, he shifted into an Austrian accent and then a Swiss accent. He could do English accents, southern accents, and accents from Brooklyn and Boston. Robert had been a character actor mainly in Westerns. His diction was so perfect, I was scared to open my mouth. His house, where I went to practice with him, contained thousands of books about language, and he loved each one. He would say, "Arnold, the book over there on the fourth shelf from the bottom, third book in, pull it out, will you? It's about the Irish," and off he would go.

Easton had me practice saying "A fine wine grows on the vine" tens of thousands of times. It was very difficult with the *f*, the *w*, and the *v* together, because the German language doesn't have a *w* sound, only the *v*. When we drink wine, we spell it *wein* and pronounce it "vine." So now I had to say "wuh, wuh, wuh, *wine.* Why. What. When." Then there was *v*, as in "We're going to vuh, vuh, *Vegas.*" Also, German doesn't have the same *s* and *z* as English: "the sink is made of zinc." Bob explained it was the harshness of my accent that made people feel threatened, so rather than get rid of it completely, I only had to soften it and be smoother.

Meanwhile, George Butler had launched into filming *Pumping Iron* like a wild man. He made a big impression on the bodybuilders by darkening the skylights at Gold's because it was too bright for the movie cameras. He and his crew shot scenes at Venice Beach. They followed Franco to Sardinia on a visit to his childhood village way up in the mountains and shot footage of his humble roots. They came with me to Terminal Island, where I did a posing exhibition and gave weight-training lessons for the prisoners. He lined up a New York City ballet instructor and filmed her coaching Franco and me on our posing in the New York studio of Joanne Woodward, the Academy Award–winning actress and wife of Paul Newman.

Every movie has to have an element of conflict, and George decided that *Pumping Iron* would focus on the rivalry between Lou Ferrigno and me in the 1975 Mr. Olympia competition, and the suspense of whether or not Lou would knock me off as champion. He was fascinated by Lou's relationship with his father, and the fact that we were both sons of policemen. The contrasts between us were perfect. George went to shoot Lou working out in his small, dark gym in Brooklyn, the exact opposite of Gold's. Lou's personality was dark and brooding, while mine was sunny and beachy. Normally, Lou came to California to train and get a tan before major competitions, but George persuaded him to stay in Brooklyn to heighten the contrast even more. That was fine with me because it would make him even more isolated and easier to beat.

My job, of course, was to play myself. I felt that the way to stand out was not just to talk about bodybuilding, because that would be one-dimensional, but to project a personality. My model was Muhammad Ali. What separated him from other heavyweights wasn't only his boxing genius—the rope-a-dope, the float like a butterfly, sting like a bee—but that he went his own way, becoming a Muslim, changing his name, sacrificing his championship title by refusing military service. Ali was always willing to say and do memorable and outrageous things. But outrageousness means nothing unless you have the substance to back it up—you can't get away with it if you're a loser. It was being a champion combined with outrageousness that made Ali's whole thing work. My situation was a little different because bodybuilding was a much less popular sport. But the rules for attracting attention were exactly the same.

Coming up with outrageous things to say was easy because I was always thinking them to keep myself entertained. Besides, George was egging me on. During one interview, I made bodybuilding sound sexy by comparing the pump, when you inflate your muscles with oxygenated blood, to an orgasm. I claimed I'd skipped my father's funeral because it would have interfered with my training. I philosophized that only a few men are born to lead, while the rest of humanity is born to follow, and went from that into discussing history's great conquerors and dictators. George had the good sense to cut such stuff from the movie, especially my remark that I admired Hitler's speaking ability, though not what he did with it. I still didn't know the difference between outlandish and offensive.

It was stressful having the cameras on me all the time: not just when I was working out but also when I was at home, visiting friends, attending business school or acting class, evaluating real estate, reading scripts. Again, I was grateful for Transcendental Meditation, especially because the TM centers wouldn't allow cameras inside.

Putting the psych on Lou and his father was part of the drama for the movie. I started setting them up that autumn by pretending to be scared.

"I hope that you screw up your training," I told Lou's father. "Otherwise he's going to be very dangerous for me at the Olympia."

"Oh, we're not going to screw anything up."

Lou himself was easy to rattle, like Sergio Oliva, Dennis Tinerino, or any of the bodybuilders who were so inward that they'd didn't pay that much attention to the world. You could say casually to Lou, "How have you been doing with your abs?"

And he'd say, "Fine. Why? Actually, I feel pretty ripped."

"Well, it's . . . No, never mind, don't worry about it, they look great." As you said it, he'd start looking at his abs, and then afterward, Lou would pose in the mirror as the insecurity took hold.

You can see in *Pumping Iron* how I kept teasing him and his dad right up to the moment of the competition. Like when I tell Lou, "I already called my mother and I told her that I won, even though the competition is tomorrow." Or, on the morning of the event, when he and his parents invite me to breakfast at the hotel, and I say, "I can't believe this. You ignore me all week, and now you want to have breakfast on the morning of the competition? You are trying to psych me out!" I pretend I'm so scared that my scrambled egg is shaking on my fork. All this was mainly show, so that audiences would walk away from *Pumping Iron* saying, "Can you believe that guy? He literally talked his opponent into losing." But it also had its effect on Lou, who came in third as I won the Mr. Olympia title for a record sixth time straight.

CHAPTER 11

Pumping Iron

***PUMPING IRON* WAS ONLY** half finished, and George was out of cash. Rather than give up on the project, he hit on the idea of staging a posing exhibition in a New York City art museum to try to attract wealthy patrons. We weren't sure whether this idea was stupid or really brilliant. The Whitney Museum of American Art, which was known for unconventional stuff, leaped at the opportunity.

The event was advertised as *Articulate Muscle: The Male Body in Art*, and the museum stayed open to host it on a Friday night in February 1976. The idea was to present live posing by Frank Zane, Ed Corney, and me next to slides of Greek statues and great works by Michelangelo, da Vinci, and Rodin. A panel of professors and artists would add commentary along the way and afterward. This was the first time anyone had a serious public discussion about the meaning of bodybuilding.

George was hoping for a few hundred people, but despite a snowstorm that night, more than 2,500 showed up and the line stretched around the block. The museum's fourth-floor gallery overflowed with people standing and sitting on every inch of floor space. In the middle was a raised, revolving platform on which we were to take turns posing.

Probably two-thirds of the crowd had never even seen a bodybuilder before. They were from the media and the New York art scene:

critics, collectors, patrons, and avant-garde artists like Andy Warhol and Robert Mapplethorpe. *People* magazine, *The New Yorker*, the *New York Times*, and the *Daily News* all had reporters there, and actress Candice Bergen was shooting photographs for the *Today* show. She was a great photographer and of course very beautiful. All of sudden, bodybuilding was hip. We'd made it out of the sports world and the carnival world and into international pop culture.

Frank, Ed, and I were proud to be posing at a real museum. We'd planned our exhibition to be artistic, leaving out hard-core bodybuilding poses like the "most muscular." We wanted each pose to look like a sculpture, especially because we were on a rotating platform. When my turn came, Charles Gaines narrated as I hit the standard shots and showed off some of my trademark poses, like the three-quarters back shot. Gaines said, "Arnold owns this pose. And in it you see all the muscles in the back; you see the calf; you see all the thigh muscles." I wrapped up my ten minutes with a perfect simulation of *The Thinker* by Rodin and got a lot of applause.

We put on our clothes after we finished posing and went back out and joined the discussion with the art experts. Their talks were fascinating, in a way. For one thing, they showed that you can make a debate out of anything. One professor said this gathering marked "the entry of the highly developed, beautiful masculine form into the sphere of official culture." The next guy thought that because of Vietnam, America was looking for a new definition of virility, which was us. But then he tied bodybuilding to Aryan racism in 1920s Europe and the rise of the Nazis and warned that we symbolized the possible growth of fascism in the United States. Another professor compared our poses to the worst Victorian-era kitsch. He got booed.

The whole thing was mainly a publicity stunt, of course. But I thought that talking about the body as sculpture made sense. My Joe Santo character in *Stay Hungry* described it that way. Art fascinated me, and if the comparison to sculpture attracted outsiders and helped them understand, then great! Anything was better than the stereotype of bodybuilders as stupid, gay, narcissistic, muscle-bound freaks.

Unfortunately, much less was happening in Hollywood than in New York. *Stay Hungry* was my first experience in how movie marketing can go wrong. Upon the film's April release, it received good reviews but fizzled at the box office, playing for ten or twelve weeks before disappearing. The problem was that the publicists and marketing people at United Artists could not figure out how to promote it. Rafelson let me sit in on a meeting before the release, and they were talking about putting posters in gyms. Then when the film came out, they had Sally Field and me on *The Mike Douglas Show* showing the fifty-year-old host how to exercise. Each time we did something like that, I felt like we were moving in the wrong direction. *Stay Hungry* should have been sold as a Bob Rafelson picture—"from the director of *Five Easy Pieces*!"—and they should have let the exercise dimension be a surprise. Then moviegoers would have walked away saying, "That's Rafelson. He always introduces us to some weird world."

Although my instincts told me that the marketing was embarrassing, I didn't have the sophistication or confidence to say it. I assumed that the studio would have its act together much more. Of course, later on, I realized that studios work by formulas. If you're even a little outside the box, they don't know what to do with you.

Rafelson wasn't happy either, but the problem with directors when they get a big reputation is that they can be their own worst enemy. They just want to do everything themselves, cut the trailers, do the advertising. You can't tell them anything. Then the big battles begin, and the fine print in the contract usually dictates who wins. In this case, it was the studio. Bob butted heads with the marketing people but never got anywhere. They thought he was not a team player.

One good thing did come of it, though. I finally found an agent on the strength of having costarred in *Stay Hungry*: Larry Kubik, whose small talent agency Film Artists Management also represented Jon Voight and Sylvester Stallone. His phone was ringing for me, but with the wrong kinds of offers. He was searching for leading roles where I might fit, and in the meantime, we were turning down lots of junk. Somebody asked me to play a bouncer. They wanted me to play a Nazi officer, a wrestler, a football player, a prisoner. I never took jobs like that because I would say to myself, "This isn't going to convince anybody that you're here to be a star."

I was very glad I could afford to say no. With the income from my businesses, I didn't need money from acting. I never wanted to be in a financially vulnerable position, where I had to take a part I didn't like. I saw this happen all the time to the actors and musicians who worked out at the gym. An actor would complain, "I've been playing this part as a killer for three days, and I'm so glad it's over."

"If you hated it, why did you do it?" I'd ask.

"They gave me two thousand dollars. I have to pay for my apartment."

You could argue that, no matter what the part, being in front of a camera was always good practice. But I felt that I was born to be a leading man. I had to be on the posters, I had to be the one carrying the movie. Of course I realized that this sounded crazy to everybody but me. But I believed that the only way you become a leading man is by treating yourself like a leading man and working your ass off. If you don't believe in yourself, then how will anyone else believe in you?

Even before *Stay Hungry*, I had a reputation at the gym for turning down film work. Someone would call and say, "Can we have a few strong guys come over for an interview?" Some of us would go, and the stunt coordinator or director's assistant would say, "What we want you to do is pull yourself up onto this roof, sprint across, have this fistfight, and then jump off the roof into a stunt pad . . ." I would say to myself, "That's not really what builds a leading man's career" and tell them I wasn't interested.

"But we love you. The director loves you. You are the biggest guy, you have the right face, you're the right age. We'll give you seventeen hundred dollars a day."

"I'd love the seventeen hundred a day, but I don't really need the money," I'd say. "Give it to one of my friends here; they need it much more."

Larry agreed that I should be picky, but it drove his business partner, Craig Rumar, crazy to see us turn jobs away. I always got worried when Larry was on vacation. Craig would get on the phone with me and say, "I don't know if I can get you anything. No one is doing movies now. Everything has gone foreign. It's really tough out there. Why not do commercials?"

Larry's biggest triumph that year was that after an endless number of tries, he got me an appointment to see Dino De Laurentiis. Dino was a legend in the movie business for producing classics like Federico Fellini's *La Strada* (1954) and campy hits like *Barbarella* (1968), as well as lots of flops. He'd gotten rich and then gone broke making movies in Italy and then started over in Hollywood. Lately, he'd been on an incredible roll with *Serpico, Death Wish, Mandingo,* and *Three Days of the Condor*. He liked to adapt comic books to the screen and was looking for somebody to play Flash Gordon.

When Larry and I showed up at Dino's office, it was just like a setup from *The Godfather*. Dino sat behind his desk at one end of the room, and at the other end of the room, behind us, was a connection of De Laurentiis's from Italy, a producer named Dino Conte.

De Laurentiis was like an emperor. He had this huge, ornate antique desk: long and wide and maybe even a little taller than a standard desk. "Wow, look at this desk," I thought. Dino himself was a little guy, very short, and I had this urge to say something complimentary but also funny. What popped out of my mouth was "Why does a little guy like you need such a big desk?"

He looked at me and said, "You havva an accent. I cannot use-a you. You can-a not be Flasha Gordon. Flasha Gordon is American. Ah."

I thought he must be joking. "What do you mean *I* have an accent?" I said. "What about *you*?" The whole thing was going south. De Laurentiis announced, "The meeting is over," and Larry and I heard Dino Conte stand up behind us and say, "This way, please."

Larry exploded as soon as we got to the parking lot.

"One minute and forty seconds!" he screamed. "This was the shortest meeting I've ever had with any producer, because *you* decided to fuck it up! Do you know how long I worked on this fucking meeting? Do you know how many months it took to get into this fucking office? And you say to the guy that he's little instead of saying maybe the opposite? That he is tall; that he's much, much taller than you thought he was? He's a monster! He's as big as Wilt Chamberlain! And maybe forget about the desk and just sit down and talk to him about your acting career?"

I realized he had a point. My mouth got in the way. Again.

"What can I tell you?" I said to Larry. "You're right. That was a real forehead move. I'm sorry." *Forehead* was a term I'd picked up from my bodybuilder friend Bill Drake, who used it all the time. "Look at that Archie Bunker over there," he'd say. "What a forehead!" Meaning, What a lowbrow idiot.

It was more than a year after shooting *Stay Hungry* before I landed another lead role: this one in an episode of a popular TV series called *The Streets of San Francisco,* starring Karl Malden and Michael Douglas as police detectives. In the episode "Dead Lift," they have to track down my character, a bodybuilder who loses it and unintentionally breaks the neck of a girl who mocks his body. The investigation leads them deep into a fictional San Francisco bodybuilding and arm wrestling scene, which meant that I was able to get bit parts for Franco and a lot of my other friends. Having the whole Gold's Gym gang on the set was very funny. As it happened, the 1976 Mr. Universe and Mr. Olympia competitions were only a few weeks away, so the guys were more focused on preparing than on performing for the cameras. They drove the director crazy by wandering off to go train.

I knew that *The Streets of San Francisco* was a good credential that would help get Hollywood to take me more seriously. It was also a way to build up recognition among the television audience. The scene where I kill the girl was intimidating, though. Hurting a woman, yelling, ripping down paintings, and throwing around furniture was not me at all. Reading the script, I thought, "Jesus Christ, how did I ever get into this?" Considering how many hundreds of people I went on to wipe out in the movies, that's funny in retrospect. In the end I just did the scene, not thinking too much about it, and the director was pleased.

My deeper worry was about getting typecast. I thought that playing a villain or an ass kicker onscreen was the worst thing for me. When Robert De Niro kills in *Taxi Driver,* he's the little guy, and people are 100 percent behind him, so it's good for his career. But for a man of my size and with my looks and accent, bad-guy roles seemed like a dead end. I asked Bob Rafelson about this, and he agreed. His suggestion was that I do the unexpected and play against type. I grew fascinated with the idea of doing a remake of the "The Killers," an Ernest Hemingway story in which an ex-boxer named the Swede is hunted down by a couple of Mafia hit men. I imagined myself playing the victim, the Swede. But the idea never went anywhere.

Luckily, the buzz for *Pumping Iron* kept building. George Butler had raised the money he needed to finish it, and now he was hustling nonstop to promote it. Probably his smartest move was hiring Bobby Zarem, the king of New York publicists. Bobby was a balding guy of about forty who grew up in Georgia and went into the PR business straight out of Yale. He liked to come across as a crazy professor, with his tie missing, his shirt out, and his hair sticking out in tufts on the sides. He always talked like he was completely confused and the world was coming to an end. He'd moan, "I don't know what I'm doing, I've never seen it this bad, I have to go to my shrink, this guy's not returning my phone calls, and I think the whole project is coming down." Hearing him talk that way about *Pumping Iron* scared me until I realized it was shtick. Inevitably, somebody would say to him, "No, no, Bobby, everything's okay. You're going to pull this off," and he loved that.

Bobby had set up his own firm only a year or two before, and I think he took on *Pumping Iron* partly to prove what he could do. Certainly George Butler wasn't paying him very much. But in the eleven months from the Whitney show until *Pumping Iron*'s release, Zarem worked behind the scenes, building the buzz. He'd arrange for a screening room, invite twenty or so serious hitters from the worlds of art, literature, and finance, and play scenes from the work in progress. He always made sure that one or two members of the media were at these events, even though they were off the record. Often I'd go with him—that's how I met TV journalist Charlie Rose, for example, whose then wife, Mary, became a financial supporter of the film. Bobby would always introduce the screening with a short talk about bodybuilding as a fascinating link between sports and art or as a leading indicator of the trend to fitness—just enough hype to make the guests feel they were in the vanguard. Afterward, there would be a thousand questions.

I was in awe watching Bobby work the media. He taught me that ordinary press releases were a waste of time, especially if you were trying to get the attention of TV reporters. "They don't read!" he said. Instead, he knew dozens of journalists and their editors personally. He would customize a story for a particular reporter, call, and say, "I'm sending this over. Please call me back as soon as you get it. If you don't call back, I'm going to assume you don't want the story, and then you won't have much." Bobby was famous for his long, old-fashioned handwritten proposals. He let me read a four-page letter to the editor of *Time* explaining why the magazine should do a major story on bodybuilding. Editors and news directors all over New York were willing to meet with him and talk seriously. And if newspapers or TV stations were competing on a story, he would brew up a different angle for each, so they weren't just following one another. He would study the story, work on it, and talk to people at night—he hung out at Elaine's, the Upper East Side mixing spot for literati, journalists, and celebrities.

Bobby's job was promoting *Pumping Iron,* but I took a page from his book to get recognized for my work in *Stay Hungry*. Even though the movie had missed at the box office, I'd been nominated for a Golden Globe award for best debut by a male actor. (*Hercules in New York* had been such a wipeout that *Stay Hungry* counted as a debut film!) There were four other nominees—including Harvey Spencer Stephens, the five-year-old who played Damien in the horror film *The Omen*, and author Truman Capote for his part in the comedy whodunnit *Murder by Death.* Of course this brought out the competitor in me. How could I make sure I stood out? The strategy I hit on was to take out ads in the show business trade papers *Variety* and the *Hollywood Reporter* thanking the Hollywood Foreign Press Association, whose members select the Golden Globe winners, for nominating me.

I also invited association members to a dinner and an advance screening of *Pumping Iron.* Bobby Zarem didn't really like this idea because my nomination was for *Stay Hungry,* not *Pumping Iron,* and he thought that *Pumping Iron* was too cutting edge for the Hollywood foreign press. But I felt it could only help. For one thing, critics like to see your latest work, even if it's not actually what's being judged, because they like to feel they're voting for someone who is on a roll. Also, in *Pumping Iron* I was able to be myself much more, so why not give them both: *Stay Hungry* with my acting and *Pumping Iron* with my outrageousness? Besides, I figured that the foreign press automatically would be sympathetic toward an immigrant struggling with a sport in America. And even if none of these reasons held up, I was very proud of the work I'd put into *Stay Hungry* and wanted to do everything possible to call attention to it. A lot of the writers came to the screening, and when it ended, people gave me a big hug and said things like "You were terrific!" and "This is wonderful!" so I knew it had worked.

A week before the January 1977 premiere, *Pumping Iron* was in the gossip columns because of a lunch that Bobby masterminded at Elaine's. Delfina Rattazzi was the hostess, I was the guest of honor, and celebrities such as Andy Warhol, George Plimpton, Paulette Goddard, Diana Vreeland, and the editor of *Newsweek* showed up. But the woman who stole the show was Jackie Onassis. She was known for keeping a low profile and never giving interviews, and I was flattered that she came in spite of the fact that she knew the press would be writing about it. I think she did it partly as a favor—Delfina was now her editorial assistant at Viking Press—and partly out of curiosity, because she enjoyed being involved with art, trends, and new things.

She stayed for the entire lunch, and I got to talk with her for fifteen minutes. JFK had been synonymous with America to me as a kid growing up, so meeting Jackie was like a dream. What impressed me most was her sophistication and grace. She'd obviously come prepared, because she didn't ask anything clumsy or vague, like "What is this movie about?" Instead, she made me feel that *Pumping Iron* was important and that she appreciated what we were trying to do. She asked all kinds of specific questions: How do you train? How do you judge a competition? What's the difference between Mr. Olympia and Mr. America? Would this be something beneficial for my teenage son? At what age can you start with a workout routine? I was predisposed to liking her before we met, and that conversation made me a big fan.

Of course people of her caliber have the social skills to make it seem like they are very much aware of you and that they know a lot about what you are doing. It was very hard to say whether she was truly interested. My guess was that she probably was a naturally curious person. Or maybe she really did think that John F. Kennedy Jr. might like to train. Or maybe she was just doing a favor for Delfina. But she certainly gave *Pumping Iron* a big publicity boost, and the fact that she brought her son to the New York premiere a week later convinced me that she was genuine.

For the premiere, Bobby Zarem and George Butler pulled out all the stops. They invited five hundred people to the Plaza Theater on East Fifty-eighth Street. There were photographers, TV cameras, police barricades, limos pulling up, searchlights crisscrossing the sky—the works. The temperature was near zero, but a dozen teenage fans were waiting for me and started chanting, "Arnold! Arnold!" when I showed up. I got there early with my mom, who'd flown over from Austria for the event, because I wanted to circulate and kiss all the pretty girls and welcome people as they arrived. For the first time in my life, I wore a tux. I had to get it specially tailored because even though I'd slimmed down to 225 pounds, nobody had a rental that would fit a fifty-seven-inch chest and thirty-two-inch waist.

The crowd was a fantastic medley of writers, socialites, hipsters, entertainers, executives, critics, artists, fashion models, and bodybuilding fans—including Andy Warhol; Diana Vreeland; actresses Carroll Baker, Sylvia Miles, and Shelley Winters; actor Tony Perkins and his wife, fashion photographer Berry Berenson; writer Tom Wolfe; the model Apollonia van Ravenstein; porn star Harry Reems; and half the cast of *Saturday Night Live*. James Taylor came with his wife, Carly Simon, who was pregnant. She flexed a biceps for the cameras and told a reporter that her hit song "You're So Vain" wasn't about a bodybuilder.

The bodybuilders themselves made a dramatic entrance. While everybody was milling around in the lobby sipping white wine, in swept six of the giants from the film, including Franco, Lou Ferrigno, and Robby "the Black Prince" Robinson, who was decked out in a black velvet cape and wearing a diamond earring.

Pumping Iron was finally doing what we'd hoped: bringing bodybuilding into the mainstream. I'd been interviewed in the media all week. And lots of good reviews showed that the critics were getting the message. "This deceptively simple, intelligent movie humanizes a world that has its own cockeyed heroism," wrote *Newsweek*, while *Time* called the movie "beautifully shot and edited, intelligently structured and—to risk what will surely seem at first a highly inappropriate term—charming. Yes, charming."

The audience at the Plaza liked the movie too, applauding wildly at the end. They stayed in their seats for the bodybuilding demonstration that followed. My main job for the night was to be the emcee. We led off with Franco's strongman routine, which included bending a steel bar with his teeth and blowing up a rubber hot-water bottle with his lungs. Just before the hot-water bottle exploded, you could see people in the front rows covering their ears. Then the other bodybuilders joined Franco onstage and demonstrated poses as I narrated. At the end, actress Carroll Baker in a slinky dress ran up onstage and started feeling everyone's triceps, pectorals, and thighs before pretending to faint with ecstasy right into my arms.

My new tuxedo had its second major outing two weeks later at the Golden Globes. The ceremony was at the Beverly Hilton hotel, and again my mom was my date. She spoke only a few words of English and could barely understand what was being said unless I translated. But the hoopla in New York had amused her, and when the photographers yelled, "Pose with your mother!" she grinned and let me give her a big hug. She was impressed that the studio sent a limo to bring us to the Golden Globes. She was really excited about seeing Sophia Loren.

A lot of stars showed up for the Golden Globes because it was less stuffy and more fun than the Oscars. I spotted actors Peter Falk, Henry Fonda, and Jimmy Stewart over near the bar. Actresses Carol Burnett, Cybill Shepherd, and Deborah Kerr were there. I traded jokes with Shelley Winters and flirted with the gorgeous Raquel Welch. Henry Winkler came over to say nice things about *Stay Hungry*, and I explained to my mom in German that he was the Fonz, star of a big TV sitcom called *Happy Days*. When we sat down to dinner, I spotted Dino De Laurentiis with Jessica Lange. She was the sexy leading lady in *King Kong*, which Dino had produced, and was up for the best debut by an actress award. Dino took no notice of me.

Also sitting near us was Sylvester Stallone, whom I knew a little bit because Larry Kubik was his agent too. His movie *Rocky* was the blockbuster of the year—at the box office, it had blown away all the other hits that were up for awards, including *Network*, *All the President's Men*, and *A Star Is Born*—and was nominated for Best Film. I congratulated him, and he told me enthusiastically that he was writing a new movie about wrestlers and that there might be a part for me.

After dinner Harry Belafonte, who was emceeing, came onstage. I felt my competition calmness come over me—here, like in bodybuilding, I knew I could relax because I'd done everything in my power to win. When my category came and I won, Sylvester Stallone led the applause. Then *Rocky* won, and he went nuts, kissing every woman he could reach on his way to the stage.

It was an incredible feeling to get my first award for acting. Winning the Golden Globe confirmed for me that I wasn't crazy; I was on the right track.

I was spending almost as much time in Manhattan as in LA. For me, New York was like a candy store. Hanging out with all of these fascinating characters was so much fun. I was proud and happy to be accepted, and I felt lucky to have the kind of personality that put people at ease. They didn't feel threatened by my body. Instead, they wanted to reach out to me, help me, and understand what I was trying to do.

Elaine Kaufman, the owner of Elaine's, was known for being tough and difficult, but she was a sweetheart to me. She made herself my mother on the New York scene. Every time I came in, she would escort me from table to table and introduce me—we'd go to director Robert Altman's table, and then Woody Allen's table, and then Francis Ford Coppola's table, and then Al Pacino's table. "You guys have got to meet this young man," she'd say. "Arnold, why don't I pull out a chair for you, sit down here, let me get you some salad or something." Sometimes I felt extremely uncomfortable, because she'd have interrupted their conversation, and maybe I wasn't even welcome. But there I was.

I made some dopey mistakes—like telling the great ballet dancer Rudolf Nureyev that he shouldn't lose touch with his home country and he ought to go back and visit, not realizing that he'd defected from Russia in 1961. But Elaine's regulars were usually curious and friendly. Coppola asked a lot of questions about the bodybuilding scene. Andy Warhol wanted to intellectualize it and write about what it meant: How can you look like a piece of art? How can you be the sculptor of your own body? I connected with Nureyev because we were each having our portrait painted by Jamie Wyeth, a well-known artist in his own right and the son of the famous painter Andrew Wyeth. Sometimes Nureyev would invite Jamie and me to join him at Elaine's. He'd sweep in late at night, after one of his performances, wearing an extraordinary fur coat with a big collar and a flowing scarf. He was not tall, but he commanded the room with his attitude. He was the king. You saw it in the way he walked, the way he took off the coat, with every movement striking and perfect. Just like onstage. At least it seemed that way to me: in the presence of someone like that, your imagination takes over, and they become bigger than life. He was a sweet guy to talk to, and he told me about his love for America and the New York scene. Still, I was in awe. Being the top ballet dancer was different from being the top bodybuilder. I could be Mr. Olympia for four thousand years and never be as big as Nureyev. He was on a different plane, like Woody Allen, who could show up for a black-tie event wearing a tux and white tennis shoes, and nobody would object. It was his way of saying "Fuck you. The invitation said black tie, so I wore the black tie, but I also came as Woody Allen, on my feet." I admired the audacity that he and Nureyev shared.

As for downtown, the Greenwich Village restaurant One Fifth was a great spot. Late on Saturday nights, following *Saturday Night Live*, that was where cast members John Belushi, Dan Aykroyd, Gilda Radner, and Laraine Newman would hang out. Often I'd watch them perform the show at NBC Studios in Rockefeller Plaza, and then meet them down at One Fifth—after which we'd all head back uptown to Elaine's.

The best downtown parties were thrown by Ara Gallant, a skinny little guy in his midforties who always wore tight leather or denim, high-heeled cowboy boots with silver toes, a little black cap with jingling gold charms, black sideburns, and, at night, eyeliner. In the fashion world, he was famous as a photographer and as the hair and makeup stylist who created the seventies disco look: red lips, spangly clothes, big hair. He'd invite every model he could think of to his parties in his big, exotic apartment, which had red lights, thumping music in the background, and a constant haze of pot smoke. Dustin Hoffman would be there, along with Al Pacino, Warren Beatty, and Gallant's best friend, Jack Nicholson—all the major players from the movie world. To me it was heaven. I went to every party I was invited to and was always one of the last to leave.

Andy Warhol had loaned Jamie Wyeth space in his famous studio, the Factory, to paint a portrait of me. Usually late in the afternoon I'd go there to pose, and by eight or nine o'clock Jamie would be finished, and we'd head for dinner. But one night Warhol said, "If you want to stay, you are more than welcome. I'm doing some photos in a half hour or so."

I was fascinated by Warhol, with his blond spiky hair, his black leather, his white shirts. When he talked to you, even at a party, he always had a camera in one hand and a tape recorder in the other. It made you feel like he might use the conversation in his magazine, *Interview.*

I said yes; I was curious to see him at work. A half-dozen young men came in and took off all their clothes. I thought, "I may be part of something interesting here." I was always ready for a discovery or new experience. If it got flaky, I would tell myself, "God has put me on this path. He means me to be here, or else I'd be an ordinary factory worker in Graz."

I didn't want to stare at the naked guys, so instead I casually walked around talking to Andy's assistants. They were putting up old-fashioned spotlights around a table in the middle of the studio. It was a big, sturdy table with a white cloth on top.

Now Andy asked a few of the naked guys to climb up on it and form a pile. Then he started moving them around. "You lie there. No, you lie across him, and then you lie across him. Perfect. Perfect." Then he stepped back and asked the other naked guys, "Who is flexible here?"

"I'm a ballet dancer," somebody said.

"Perfect. Why don't you climb up, get one leg underneath here and one leg on top, and then we will build it sideways . . ."

Once he had the pile just the way he wanted, he started snapping Polaroids and adjusting the lights. The shadows had to be just so—he was fanatical about it. "Come over here, Arnold. See? This is what I'm trying to get. It's not there yet. I'm frustrated." He showed me a Polaroid that didn't look like people, just shapes. "It will be called *Landscapes*," he explained.

I said to myself, "This is unbelievable, this guy is turning asses into rolling hills."

"The idea," he went on, "is to get people talking about and writing about how we got that effect."

Listening to Warhol, I had the feeling that if I'd asked in advance to watch him work he'd have said no. With artists, you never know what reaction you'll get. Sometimes being spontaneous and jumping on an opportunity is the only way you can see art being made.

Jamie Wyeth and I became good friends, and months later, when the weather warmed up, he invited me to the family farm in Pennsylvania, near the Brandywine River Museum, where some of his father's best paintings are displayed. I met Jamie's wife, Phyllis, and then he brought me next door to an old farmhouse to meet his dad.

Andrew Wyeth, then sixty, was fencing when we walked in. No one else was there, but it definitely looked like he was facing an opponent because he even had on the mask. "Dad!" Jamie called, waving to get his attention. They talked for a moment, and then Wyeth turned toward me and took off the mask. Jamie said, "Dad, this is Arnold Schwarzenegger, and he's in *Pumping Iron*, and I'm painting him."

After we chatted for a while, Andrew asked, "Do you want to drive up with me to see the field where I'm painting right now?"

"Sure!" I said. I was curious to see how he worked. Wyeth led me out back to a beautiful, gleaming vintage sports car from the Roaring Twenties called a Stutz Bearcat: a two-seater convertible with huge exposed wheels, big, swooping fenders and running boards, exposed chrome exhaust pipes, and big headlights separate from the hood. It was a beautiful pimp car. I knew about the expensive, rare Stutz Bearcat because Frank Sinatra, Dean Martin, and Sammy Davis Jr. each owned one. We started driving up a dirt road, with Wyeth explaining that he'd gotten the car from a vodka company in exchange for working on an ad. Meanwhile, I was noticing that we weren't driving on a road but on a farm track with ruts for the wheels and with weeds growing up on both sides and in the middle—clearly not meant for cars like this. Then even the track ended and yet Wyeth kept driving up a hill, bumping through knee-high grass.

Finally, we arrived at the top, where I noticed an easel and a woman who was sitting on the ground wrapped in a blanket. She wasn't beautiful, exactly, but sensuous, strong looking, and captivating—there was something unique about her. "Take it off," Wyeth said. She dropped the blanket and sat with her breasts exposed, beautiful breasts, and I heard him mutter, "Oh, yeah." Then he said to me, "I'm painting her now," and he showed me the beginnings of a painting on the easel. "Anyway, I wanted you to meet because she speaks German."

This was Helga Testorf, who worked at a neighboring farm and who was Wyeth's obsession. He drew and painted her hundreds of times over many years, in sessions they kept secret from everyone. A decade later the story of the paintings and the obsession ended up on the covers of *Time* and *Newsweek*. But in 1977 I just happened to be there, and he let me in.

Running around promoting *Pumping Iron* ate up a lot of time, but I enjoyed the work. At the Boston premiere, George Butler introduced me to his longtime friend John Kerry, then a first assistant county district attorney. He was there with Caroline Kennedy, JFK and Jackie's nineteen-year-old daughter who was an undergraduate at Harvard. She seemed reserved at first, but after the movie we all went to dinner and she warmed up. Caroline told me she wrote for the *Harvard Crimson*, the university's daily student newspaper, and asked if I would come speak the next day. Of course I agreed happily. She and other *Crimson* staff members interviewed me about government and my sport. Someone asked who was my favorite president. I said, "John F. Kennedy!"

All of this was fun, and it was also a good investment in my future. By promoting *Pumping Iron* and bodybuilding, I was also promoting myself. Every time I was on the radio or TV, people became a little more familiar with my accent, the Arnold way of talking, and a little more comfortable and at ease with *me*. The effect was the opposite of what the Hollywood agents had warned. I was making my size, accent, and funny name into assets instead of peculiarities that put people off. Before long people were able to recognize me without seeing me, just by name or by the sound of my voice.

The biggest promotion opportunity on the horizon was France's Cannes Film Festival, in May. In preparation, I decided to do something about my clothes. Up until now, my uniform had pretty much been double-knit pants, a Lacoste shirt, and cowboy boots. One reason for this was lack of money. I couldn't afford to have a wardrobe custom made, and the only off-the-rack clothes that could be made to fit came from big men's stores, where the waist had to be taken in by a foot and a half. Another reason was that up to now, clothes were just not part of the plan. Every dollar should be invested to turn into two or three dollars and make me financially secure. With clothes, the money was gone. George told me the best tailor in New York was Morty Sills. So I went to him and asked, "If I had to pick one suit to own, what would it be?"

"Where are you wearing it?" he asked.

"First of all, a month from now, I'm going to the Cannes Film Festival."

"Well, that's a beige linen suit. There is no debate about that."

So Morty made me a light beige linen suit and picked the tie and the shirt so that I would look really snappy.

Without question, the clothes were important when I got to Cannes. Decked out in the suit I was so proud of, with the right shirt, the right tie, the right shoes, I circulated among the thousands of journalists there and drummed up a lot of press for *Pumping Iron*. But the biggest splash I made there was on the beach, where George had the idea of staging a photo op featuring a dozen girls from Crazy Horse, the Parisian strip club and cabaret. They were outfitted in frilly summer dresses, bonnets, and bouquets—and I was just in my posing trunks. Pictures of that scene appeared in newspapers around the world, and the *Pumping Iron* screening was packed to overflowing.

So many famous stars were at Cannes—like Mick and Bianca

Jagger!—and I was part of it. I kicked around a ball with the great Brazilian soccer star Pelé. I went scuba diving with French military frogmen. I met Charles Bronson for the first time. The woman who headed European distribution for his movies hosted an evening for him at the hotel on the beach. She sat next to him at the head table, and I was close enough to hear their conversation. It turned out that Bronson wasn't an easy guy to talk to. "You're contributing so much to our success," she said to him. "We're so lucky to have you here. Isn't the weather wonderful? We're so lucky to have sunshine every day." He waited a beat or two and then answered, "I hate small talk." She was so shocked that she turned to her other dinner partner. I was stunned. That's the way he was, though: rough around the edges. It never seemed to hurt his movies, but I decided I'd stay with a friendlier style.

Now that I was interested in clothes, my agent Larry Kubik was happy to take me shopping after I got back to LA. "You can find those same pants in this other store that's *not* on Rodeo Drive for fifty percent less," he'd say. Or, "Your brown socks won't go with that shirt. I think you should have blue socks." He had a good eye, and for both of us, shopping was a welcome diversion from turning down terrible parts. The most recent offers were for me to play a muscleman in *Sextette*, starring eighty-five-year-old Mae West, and, for $200,000, to be in commercials about automobile tires.

For months it seemed like the only action for me in LA was in real estate. Partly because of inflation and partly because of growth, Santa Monica property values were going through the roof. My apartment building wasn't even on the market, but around the time that *Pumping Iron* came out, a buyer offered me almost double what I'd paid for it in 1974. The profit on my $37,000 investment was $150,000—I'd quadrupled my money in three years. I rolled the whole amount into a building twice the size, with twelve apartments rather than six, with the help of my friend Olga, who, as always, had found just the place to buy.

My secretary, Ronda Columb, who had been running the Arnold mail-order business and organizing my crazy schedule for years, was tickled to see me turning into a real estate minimogul. She was a transplanted New Yorker, four times divorced and ten or twelve years older than me. Her first husband had been a bodybuilding champ in the 1950s. I'd met her through Gold's Gym. Ronda was like an older sister. Her latest boyfriend was a real estate developer named Al Ehringer.

Out of the blue one day she said, "You know, Al loves you."

"He gets to go home with my secretary; of course he loves me!" I said.

That got a laugh. "No, really, he loves you and wants to be in business with you. Would you think about doing business with him?"

"Well, find out what he has in mind, because there's a building for sale down on Main Street, and if he wants to get involved . . ." Al had a reputation as a shrewd real estate brain, very good at sensing which areas to develop. He'd played a major role in reviving the historic district of Pasadena, California, with shops and lofts. I thought Santa Monica might be ripe for the same treatment. Main Street, which ran parallel to the ocean a few blocks in from the beach, was run down and full of drunks and drifters, and there was a lot of property for sale. I was looking to invest $70,000 I'd saved up from *Pumping Iron* and other work.

Al was already familiar with the building that had caught my eye. "That property and three others are for sale now," he said. "Pick which one you like, and I'll go in with you." So Al and I bought the building and started organizing the turnaround of Main Street.

Our building started to pay for itself almost immediately. It came with three small houses out back, facing onto the next street, and we sold those off for enough money to reimburse our entire down payment. That made it easy to get a big loan and do a total renovation. And because the building was more than fifty years old, it qualified for historic status and a big tax advantage. This was yet another reason to love America: back in Austria, if you tried to get a building declared historic, they'd laugh at you unless it was five hundred years old.

Making money this way doubled my confidence. I adjusted my life plan: I still wanted to own a gymnasium chain eventually, but instead of making money from movies, like Reg Park and Steve Reeves did, I would make it from real estate.

Ronda always put public appearance requests in a pile for me to consider. The one that grabbed my attention that spring was an invitation from the Special Olympics signed by "Jacquie Kennedy." It asked if I would fly to the University of Wisconsin to help with research on whether or not weight training made sense for mentally handicapped kids.

If I'd stopped to think, I would have realized that this wasn't *the* Jackie Kennedy whom I'd met—that woman's last name was now Onassis, she didn't spell her name *Jacquie*, and she lived in New York. But I thought that maybe she was the honorary chair or something. So I said impulsively to Ronda, "I'll accept." I was already doing seminars on weight training and on how to be a winner, and I thought that consulting at a university would be a nice credential that would elevate bodybuilding as a sport, even though they weren't offering to pay. I wasn't sure if weight training could help intellectually challenged kids, but it fascinated me that they wanted to try, and for me this would open up a whole new world.

There was still snow on the ground in April when I arrived: this was the university's northern branch, way up in Superior, Wisconsin, near Duluth. The two women who picked me up were both research scientists with PhDs. They introduced me to Jacquie, a slim, lively person from the Special Olympics, and showed me to the weight room in the gymnasium where the kids would be the next morning.

"What exercises can we have them do?" Jacquie asked.

"I don't know how handicapped those kids are," I said, "but a safe thing to do is bench press. Another safe thing is dead lift, another safe thing is the curls, another safe thing is . . ."

"Okay," Jacquie said. "The first day, let's just keep it at that."

So we set up the equipment and the camera, checking to make

sure there would be enough light to film, and made a plan for the next day. That night I lay in bed wondering how I would deal with the kids. Rather than worry, I decided just to improvise.

There were about ten boys in their early teens, and the minute I walked in the room, it was clear what to do. They milled around me and wanted to touch my muscles, and when I flexed for them, they exclaimed, "Wow! Wow!" I realized that they were putty in my hands. Authority for them was much more visual than intellectual—they would listen to me not because I'd studied physical therapy or anything like that but because of the biceps.

I started with the bench press, just the bar with one ten-pound plate on each side, and had the boys take turns doing ten reps each, with me there to position the bar and lower it down to their chest. The first couple of kids were fine, but the third boy panicked when he felt the weight and started to scream because he thought it would crush him. I lifted the bar off his chest, and he jumped up.

"That's okay," I said to him. "Don't worry. Just breathe, relax, stay here, and watch your buddies."

So he stood and watched the others taking their turns and lifting the weight up and down ten times. After a while I could see that he was interested again. I suggested, "Why don't you try now?" and he agreed. He had a little bit more confidence when I put the empty bar on him, and he did ten reps. "Hold the bar," I said. "You're really strong; I think you can handle the plates now." I added the plates, twenty pounds total, and he not only did ten more reps easily but also asked me to put on more. I realized I was witnessing something unique. This kid had been completely intimidated twenty minutes before, and now he had all this confidence. I did sessions with other groups of kids over the next couple of days, trying different things until the researchers had gotten all the data they needed. One observation that emerged was that weight training was a better confidence builder than, say, soccer. In soccer, sometimes you make a good kick and sometimes not, but in weight training, you know when you lift four plates that the next time you will be able to lift four plates. This predictability helped the kids gain confidence quickly.

Out of this work came the power-lifting events at the Special Olympics, which now draw more competitors than any other sport. We looked for the lifts that would be safe; sometimes because of their handicap, the kids don't balance well, for instance, so we left out squats. We narrowed it down to the dead lift, where nothing can go wrong because you're simply lifting the bar until you stand straight up, and the bench press, where you can have spotters present to steady the bar if needed.

One of the researchers had a dinner for me at her house, and in the course of conversation, Jacquie asked about my education. "Well, I've taken five thousand courses but never went for a degree because they're at a mishmash of three colleges," I said.

And she said, "We have the biggest off-campus learning program in the country, so maybe you can finish your degree here. Why don't you mail us your transcripts?"

I followed up after I went home, and after analyzing my records, they wrote back that I was missing only two courses for a degree: basic science and physical education. I had to laugh about the second one. But we made a plan to fill in both gaps.

When Bobby Zarem called in early August with a real Kennedy invitation, I almost said no. It was to play in the Robert F. Kennedy Celebrity Tennis Tournament in Forest Hills, New York.

"I don't know how to play tennis," I told him. What sense did it make to show up if you couldn't really contribute to the occasion? I'd turned down celebrity golf tournaments for the same reason.

"You should go," Bobby said. "This is a tough invitation to get." He explained that he'd been able to grab a last-minute spot for me because actor James Caan had dropped out. "Think about it at least, okay?"

This was just the sort of dilemma Larry loved, so I called him. "Take it," he said, almost before the words were out of my mouth. "You just need to get a coach. Why don't you use the guy Bruce Jenner used? He got invited there, and he'd been taking lessons from this guy for only a year, and he won."

Bobby called again and had Ethel Kennedy, Robert Kennedy's widow, on the phone with him. That convinced me.

I said to myself, "Don't be stupid. You can't turn down Ethel Kennedy! And don't you like to jump into things?" Plus, it was for a great cause. So I told them yes and started driving up to Malibu three times a week to hit with Olympic star Bruce Jenner's tennis pro.

The tournament was scheduled for August 27, so we had only three weeks. At first balls were flying all over the place, but I practiced enough to be able to hit the ball back and forth. Also, I was good at running around, which helped. Larry and Craig would take time off from work and volley with me when I didn't have the pro. They wanted to make sure I looked as good as possible among all the celebs out there on the court.

It was a new experience, training for something I had no hope of winning. I didn't even mind if people laughed—I expected it. But I hoped to make a good showing, and it was good for the cause.

CHAPTER 12

Dream Girl

ON FRIDAY, AUGUST 26, 1977, I flew to New York for the Robert F. Kennedy Celebrity Tennis Tournament. The pretournament party was at the Rainbow Room on top of the NBC building in Rockefeller Center. Tom Brokaw was standing there with a drink when I walked in. I knew him from Los Angeles, where he'd been NBC's late-night news anchor before getting sent to cover the White House. He was a friend of the Kennedys and was becoming a major figure in network news.

"Hi, Arnold," he said. "How are you? Here, meet Ethel, she's the host today."

Ethel Kennedy gave me a big smile. "How wonderful to have you here! How nice to meet you. I've read so much about you, and thank you for helping us out. We're raising money for . . ." and she talked about the tournament's charities. Then she said, "Here, meet Teddy."

Teddy Kennedy, the senator from Massachusetts, was also standing there with a drink. He came over and shook hands. Then Tom asked, "Are you here by yourself?"

"Yeah."

"Well, I have the right girl for you. You've got to meet Maria. Where's Maria? Guys, get me Maria!" Maria Shriver came over. She had on an attractive outfit that was both evening-y and casual. She looked like this was her moment. She was funny, and she liked to laugh. A little later, I was also introduced to Eunice Kennedy Shriver, Maria's mother. The first words I blurted out were "Your daughter has a great ass." I always loved to say outrageous things to people, but Eunice didn't even blink. "That's very nice," she replied.

Maria invited me to sit at her table for dinner. Afterward, we danced. "Wow," I thought, "this girl is totally my style." Not that I fell in love, because I didn't know her. But I could see that Maria was full of joy, she had a good personality, she had this long black hair, and she was a bundle of positive energy that I wanted to be around.

The next morning our instructions were "Leave your belongings and valuables in your room. Dress in your tennis clothes and be downstairs at nine o'clock." A bus took us to the West Side Tennis Club in Forest Hills. There we hung out in the area that served as the green room, we had fun, we schmoozed, we ate. I met everybody, including Vice President Walter Mondale, comedian Bill Cosby, singers Diana Ross and Andy Williams, tennis stars Ilie Năstase and Renée Richards, former *Tonight Show* host Jack Paar, and Pelé. All the while, the tennis games were being played out on the club's two central courts. It was not a real tournament: it just moved along, and whenever they called you to play, you did, because it was all about charity and not about trying to win. The whole time, Caroline Kennedy and Maria were circulating, each with a camera, photographing everybody and taking many pictures of me.

Whoever matched up the doubles partners definitely had a sense of humor. Mine was Rosey Grier, the six-foot-five-inch, three-hundred-pound ex-football star. He played tennis only a little better than me, fortunately. Our opponents were a couple of ten-year-olds. We managed to get the ball back and forth with them, and when Rosey and I lost a point, we ripped off our shirts and threatened the kids—that made the crowd laugh, which is what Ethel wanted. People were donating a lot of money and paying to sit there and watch the whole day, so they deserved a good show. At one point, I introduced Pelé to receive an award, and he introduced me, and Bobby Kennedy Jr. came onstage and praised all the participants and handed out more awards. As the tournament was wrapping up in the late afternoon, Caroline and Maria came up to me in the staging area and asked, "What are you doing after this?"

"I don't know; going home to Los Angeles."

"You should think about coming to Hyannis Port."

I knew that was someplace north of New York, but I didn't know exactly where. "How do we get there?"

"By plane."

"How long is that flight?"

"Maybe an hour and a half. But we have our own plane, so don't worry about that."

Afterward, we moved on to a restaurant for an early dinner, and here the push from Caroline and Maria continued. "You've got to come to Hyannis Port."

Looking back, I think I know what happened. Maria and Caroline decided, "Wouldn't it be funny to have Arnold come to Hyannis Port?" That was their sense of humor. "Hercules at Hyannis Port! What a show that would be." Caroline knew me from my visit to Harvard earlier that year, and I don't know how much she egged Maria on. But for sure they'd told their cousins about the plan. So now they were on a mission.

I wasn't sure if I should go. It seemed too complicated. Plus, I had no money with me and only the tennis outfit and the racket they'd given me.

"Don't worry about your clothes being back at the hotel," Maria said. "The room's paid for anyway by the foundation until tomorrow night. By that time, you'll be back, and you can pick up your stuff and fly home. In the meantime, come with us. What we do, so you know—are you into waterskiing?"

"Yeah, I know how to water ski. I can't get up on one ski, but I can get up on two."

"Do you swim?"

"Yeah, yeah. I feel very comfortable swimming."

"Well, because we go out sailing and taking turns getting dragged behind the sailboat, and we go out to the Egg Island. And we have a great time! All we do is water stuff. So you really don't need to bring anything. You already have tennis shorts, and Bobby, my brother, can give you other shorts, or a shirt, whatever you need."

"I have no money with me, nothing."

"You're staying at our house! You don't need any money."

First a planeload of the "grown-ups" flew up: Ethel, Teddy, and that generation. Then at nine o'clock I went up with the cousins. I remember landing at ten thirty or so at night, and we were now at the big house in Hyannis Port, and Maria was really showing off. "Let's go for a swim!" she said.

"What do you mean, go for a swim?"

"It's a beautiful night! Let's go for a swim."

So we went out. We swam to a boat quite a long way out. She was a regular water rat, climbed on board to catch our breath, then swam back in.

All of this was part of the test. The cousins drag people up to the Kennedy compound all the time, and they test them. And play tricks. Of course, I had no idea.

Finally we went to sleep. Bobby gave me his room, right next door to Maria's. The next morning I woke up to this big commotion. "Everybody get dressed! Everybody get dressed! We're meeting at church; Grandma is coming to church. The Mass is for her!" Everyone was racing around taking clothes from everybody else.

Suddenly I realized: I had only a tennis outfit. I said, "I have nothing to put on."

"Well, here, take one of Bobby's shirts," said a cousin. The shirt didn't look so promising: Bobby weighed 170 pounds, and I weighed 230. It was bursting at the seams; buttons were ready to pop. I had no clothes, and we were going to church *with Rose Kennedy meeting us there*. Bobby tried to lend me pants, but they were *way* too small. I couldn't get them past my thighs. So I had to go to church wearing shorts, like a little kid. It was highly embarrassing—which, of course, was the purpose. All the cousins were laughing. "This is hilarious! Look at his pants! Look at his shirt!"

Then we went back to the house for breakfast. I had a little bit of a chance to regain my bearings. The Kennedy compound was a cluster of white two-story houses on big lawns along the water; very picturesque. Rose had her own house, and so did each of her kids. I was at the Shrivers' house because Maria and Caroline had agreed that I would be mainly Maria's guest.

Over the course of the day, the grown-ups were gathering at this or that house for breakfast, lunch, cocktails, and so forth. The idea that I wouldn't need any dressy clothes was absolutely bogus because the men were all were decked out in their white pants and blazers for the cocktails—and there I was in my shorts. But I made the best of it, as Maria and Caroline introduced me.

Rose came over to meet me. She was very curious about this guy from the muscle world and started asking about exercising. "Our kids don't get enough exercise, and I'm concerned. Can you show us some exercises now? I need something myself, for my stomach." Rose was almost ninety at the time. Soon I had the younger grandkids plus some of the parents doing crunches and leg raises, and it was hilarious.

But there was a lot here to figure out. Why was there a family compound? Why have all these houses bunched all together? It was fascinating how the Kennedys circulated among themselves: "Today we'll have cocktails at Teddy's, and then we'll have dinner at Pat's, and tomorrow we'll have breakfast over with Eunice and Sarge," and so on.

The cousins were supercompetitive and wanted to test me to see if I was a good sport: they dragged me on a line behind the sailboat, for instance. But under the leadership of Joe Kennedy II, the oldest, they were also gracious. When they were getting ready for their usual game of touch football on their grandmother's lawn, he asked me, "Do you play?"

"I've never touched a football," I said.

"I noticed yesterday that you introduced Pelé like you really knew him, so you must come from a soccer background."

"Yeah."

So he made them all play soccer that day. It was one of those little gestures that you never forget. Joe, Robert F. Kennedy's firstborn son, had a reputation as a rough guy who would have fits of anger and shout. But that day, I saw how classy he was and how understanding. He wanted to know what I was doing, what my training was about, and the world I came from, Austria. It helped that he was closest to me in age—five years younger—he related to me more than some of the others did. When a person shows me that kind of consideration, I will do anything for him for the rest of my life.

Toward sunset, Maria and I took her grandmother for a walk. Rose quizzed Maria about grammar, as if to make sure her college education was up to par: "Is it so-and-so and *me*, or so-and-so and *I*?" Then she switched into German to talk to me, explaining that she'd gone to convent school in Holland as a girl. Rose conversed fluently about Beethoven, Bach, and Mozart, and told us how she loved the opera and the symphony, and how she had played piano her whole life. It was very interesting to be that close to the Kennedy matriarch I'd read and heard so much about—to be that close to history.

Later that night, I had to leave. Maria took me to the airport, and we were talking by the ticket counter when I remembered I had no money. Maria had to write a check for my airfare. Having to ask a twenty-one-year-old girl to lend me money sent my temperature up about a hundred degrees from embarrassment. The reason I always wanted to earn was that I never wanted to ask for a handout or loan. The first thing I did when I came back to Los Angeles was tell Ronda, "Write out a check right away, and we have to send it to Maria because she loaned me sixty dollars. I have to get that money back as quick as possible." I sent it along with a thank-you note.

Maria and I weren't in touch again until close to Halloween. By then I was on a promotional tour for my new book, *Arnold: The Education of a Bodybuilder*, a combination memoir and introduction to weight training that I did with a writer-photographer named Douglas Kent Hall after retiring from competition. The publisher, Dan Green at

Simon & Schuster, was fascinated by bodybuilding and masterminded the project. When I went to meet with him about the marketing plan for the book, he was enthusiastic. "This is going to do really well," he said. "It'll be as big a bestseller as *Pumping Iron*."

"Not if we stay with this publicity plan," I said. The proposal he was showing me involved visiting only a half dozen of the biggest cities.

"People won't buy this book unless we tell them it exists," I pointed out. "Otherwise, how do they know? If you want to see it to go through the roof, then don't just send me to six cities. We're going to go to thirty cities, and we're going to do it in thirty days."

"Thirty cities in thirty days! That's crazy!"

"Be happy," I said. "We're going to cities where normally celebrities don't ever go, and we can get more time on the morning shows that way."

"Yeah, that's true," he said. I reminded him that *Pumping Iron* had succeeded because we'd promoted it more broadly than usual and sold it in unconventional places, like sporting goods stores.

Promotion tours for sports books often skipped Washington, DC. But I had promoted *Pumping Iron* there, so it made sense to go back and get the same journalists involved. And since Maria lived in DC, it seemed natural to get in touch. I called ahead of time, and she enthusiastically offered to show me around the city. I didn't arrive until late, eight or nine in the evening on Halloween. Maria picked me up dressed in a gypsy costume and took me out and showed me the bars and restaurants where she had worked while she was in college—she'd just graduated from Georgetown University. She really looked the part, with her colorful dress, bracelets, big earrings, and her mass of beautiful black hair. We had a wonderful time until one in the morning or so, when she went home. The next morning, I had my interviews with the press and then traveled on.

I sent flowers for her birthday a week later, November 6, which I'd never done before for a girl. I had a crush on Maria, and I'd discovered recently that you could order flowers by phone—it was a new way of showing appreciation, like learning the American custom of writing thank-you notes. In any case, Maria was pleased.

As soon as I came back from Europe, I continued the book tour. It took me to Detroit to do a shopping mall appearance. I called Maria and said, "Hey, if you want to come join me, I have some wonderful friends there, and we can go out." My friends, the Zurkowskis, were part owners of Health & Tennis Corporation, the country's biggest fitness chain, with more than a hundred gyms all over America. Maria agreed to come, and we all got together. To me this was a clear indication that she was interested in starting a relationship. She'd been seeing a guy from college, but that candle seemed to be sputtering out, and I thought she was ready to move on.

For my part, I didn't know what I had in mind when I called her. I had such a good time with her on Halloween that I wanted to see her again. And she was on the East Coast, and I thought of Detroit as being in the neighborhood. I wasn't at the point of wanting a serious relationship, especially not an East Coast–West Coast thing. She was talking about going to TV production training in Philadelphia, and I thought, "No way. Philadelphia and Los Angeles would be tough."

But it developed into exactly that: an East Coast–West Coast relationship. There was no talk about whether we were now officially going out or whether we were seeing anyone else. It was more like, "Let's see each other when we can." But I liked it that she was so ambitious and wanted to become a force in TV news. I told her my ambitions too. "One day I'm going to make a million dollars for a movie," I said, because that was what the highest-paid actors, like Charles Bronson, Warren Beatty, and Marlon Brando, were making. I had to be one of them. I told her my goal was to be a leading man and to be as successful in movies as I was in bodybuilding.

The Hollywood community was very much aware of me after *Stay Hungry*, *Pumping Iron*, and *The Streets of San Francisco*. But nobody knew what to do with me. Studio executives are always overwhelmed with projects, and none of them was going to sit down and say, "Jeez, what about this guy? He has the body and the looks. He has a personality. He can act. But he doesn't fit into any ordinary role, so what can we do?"

I needed to connect with an independent producer. Fortunately, one came looking for me: Ed Pressman, who'd made *Badlands* with writer-director Terrence Malick and was working on *Paradise Alley* with Stallone. He was a short, professorial-looking guy from New York, elegant and very well dressed, whose father had founded a toy company, and who had a philosophy degree from Stanford University. Ed's pet project was to bring to the screen a 1930s pulp fiction barbarian warrior named Conan. He and his partner spent a couple of years negotiating for the movie rights and had just locked them up when they saw a rough cut of *Pumping Iron*. Right away they decided I would be perfect for Conan.

Ed didn't even have a script. He gave me a pile of comic books to look at while I made up my mind. I'd never heard of Conan, but it turned out that there was this whole cult of young guys who were really into it. There had been a big Conan revival since the sixties, with fantasy paperbacks, and Marvel Comics picked up the character too. To me this meant there would be plenty of ready-made fans if Conan came to the screen.

What Ed envisioned was not just one movie but a whole Conan franchise, like Tarzan or James Bond, with a new installment every couple of years. I don't remember exactly how he put it, because Ed was extremely low-key, but he was very persuasive. To get studio backing, he explained, he needed to lock me up. I couldn't accept other he-man roles—like another Hercules, say—and I'd have to commit to being available to make sequels. Just looking at the covers of the paperbacks, I knew I wanted the part. They were these fantastic illustrations by the artist Frank Frazetta showing Conan raising his battle-axes in triumph as he stands on a pile of slain enemies, a beautiful princess at his feet, and Conan charging on a warhorse through an army of terrified foes. In the fall of 1977 we agreed on a deal for me to star in *Conan the Warrior* and four sequels. The money was all laid out: $250,000 for the first film, $1 million for the next, $2 million for the next, and so on, plus 5 percent of the profits. All five movies would be worth $10 million over ten years. I thought, "This is fantastic! I'm way beyond my goal."

Word of the deal traveled fast in Hollywood. The trade press picked it up, so when I walked down Rodeo Drive, shopkeepers would come out of their stores and invite me in. Even though there were still a lot of ifs, signing that contract made me confident that I would be among the million-dollar players in the movie business. So when I told Maria that was my vision, I knew that it could become real.

I didn't realize it would take several more years, but I was in no rush. Having tied up the rights and tied up the actor, now Ed had to find a director and money to make the first film. John Milius wanted the project because he loved the mixture of macho and mythology in the Conan books. But he was busy shooting a coming-of-age surfer movie with Gary Busey, *Big Wednesday*. So Ed was still looking for a director. He had better luck with financing. Paramount Pictures agreed to put up $2.5 million for initial development as long as Ed attached a name screenwriter to the project.

That was how I met Oliver Stone. He was known at that point as a rising star and had finished the screenplay for *Midnight Express*, based on the true story of a young American in Turkey who gets busted for trying to smuggle hashish out of the country and is sentenced to life in a brutal Turkish prison. That script would win Oliver his first Oscar. *Conan* attracted him because it was epic and mythical and had franchise potential—and because Paramount was willing to pay.

Often when I was in town over the next year, Oliver and I would meet. He was a crazy guy, very smart and very entertaining. He thought of himself as a great writer, and I got a kick out of the fact that he was so confident, like me. We hung out together and had mutual respect, even though politically he was left and I was right. He'd enlisted in the army and fought in Vietnam, and now was very antiestablishment, always railing against the government, against Hollywood, and against the war.

Oliver made me read a lot of comic books and fantasy novels out loud, wanting to get a sense of how I handled dialogue and what did and didn't sound good in my voice. He'd sit on the couch and close his eyes while I read passages like "Hither came Conan, the Cimmerian, black-haired, sullen-eyed, sword in hand, a thief, a reaver, a slayer, with gigantic melancholies and gigantic mirth, to tread the jeweled thrones of the Earth under his sandaled feet."

Ed had encouraged Oliver to think big—he was budgeting up to $15 million for the film, almost double the cost of an average movie—and Oliver did. He transformed the story into what Milius later described as "a feverish dream on acid." He changed the setting from the remote past to the future after the downfall of civilization. He imagined a four-hour-long saga in which the forces of darkness are threatening the earth, and Conan must raise an army to restore the kingdom of a princess in an epic battle against ten thousand mutants. Oliver dreamed up the most extraordinary images, like the Tree of Woe, a huge, predatory plant that seizes Conan's comrades as they hack at it and imprisons them in a world below—the tree's hell. His script also called for a multiheaded dog, a harpy, small bat-like creatures, and much more.

By the time the script began circulating the following summer, though, it still wasn't clear whether the project would go anywhere. Oliver's vision would cost a fortune to shoot: not $15 million but *$70 million*. Even though 1977's *Star Wars* was setting records at the box office and the studios were looking for epics, that was too much, and Paramount got cold feet. Ed had been developing Conan for four years, and now he and his partner were in debt.

I'd decided to take a zen approach. I had my contract, and I knew that major productions can take a long time to develop. I was not in any hurry, I told myself. These delays were meant to be. I just wanted to be sure to use the time wisely so that when the day of shooting came, I would be ready.

Ed lined up projects to give me more experience in front of the camera. I played a supporting part in *The Villain*, a Western spoof starring Kirk Douglas and Ann-Margret. The name of my character was Handsome Stranger, and the rest of the movie was just as lame. It flopped totally at the box office when it came out in 1979, and the best thing I can say about it is that I improved my horse-riding skills. I also costarred with Loni Anderson in a made-for-TV movie, *The Jayne Mansfield Story*, in which I played Mansfield's second husband, the 1950s bodybuilding champ Mickey Hargitay. These were not starring roles, and they didn't involve much pressure, but they did help prepare me for the real deal: Conan, the big international movie that would get worldwide promotion and had $20 million behind it.

At the same time, I tended to my businesses. I was still running my bodybuilding enterprises and coproducing the championship in Columbus, Ohio, that would eventually become the Arnold Classic. Each year Jim Lorimer and I were able to raise the cash prize, and the event grew in popularity and prestige. Meanwhile, there were real estate opportunities that were too good to pass up. In Southern California, the value of property was rising at almost twice the rate of inflation. You could put down $100,000 to buy something for $1 million, and the next year it would be worth $1.2 million, so you'd made 200 percent on your investment. It was crazy. Al Ehringer and I flipped our building on Main Street and bought a city block for redevelopment in Santa Monica and another in Denver. I traded up my twelve-unit apartment building for a thirty-unit one. By the time Ronald Reagan came into office in 1981 and the economy slowed, I'd achieved another piece of the immigrant dream. I'd made my first million.

Conan the Barbarian might still be stuck in the comic books today if John Milius hadn't reentered the picture in 1979. He took Oliver Stone's script, chopped it in half, and rewrote it to cost much less, but still $17 million. Even better for Ed Pressman, Milius had a path to money. He was under contract to do his next movie for Dino De Laurentiis, who loved fantasy. Late that fall, Dino and Ed worked out a deal in which Dino effectively bought the project from Ed. With Dino's connections came big-league distribution, as Universal Pictures agreed to handle *Conan* in the United States.

All of a sudden—*bang!*—the project really started rolling.

What was good for Conan the Warrior wasn't automatically good for me, however. De Laurentiis still despised me from our first encounter. Even though I was under contract, he wanted to get rid of me.

"I don't like the Schwarzenegger," he told Milius. "He's a Nazi."

Luckily John had already decided that I was perfectly cast. "No, Dino," he said. "There is only one Nazi on this team. And that is me. *I am the Nazi!*" Milius wasn't a Nazi, of course. He just wanted to shock Dino, and he loved saying outrageous things. For the rest of the production, he would go to odd antique stores and buy these little lead figurines of Mussolini and Hitler and Stalin and Francisco Franco and put them on Dino's desk.

Dino's next move was to send his company lawyer to renegotiate with me. The guy's name was Sidewater, and my agent Larry nicknamed him Sidewinder. The lawyer announced, "Dino doesn't want to give you five points, like it says in the contract. He wants to give you no points."

I said, "Take the points. I'm in no position to negotiate."

He gaped. "All five?" It astounded him to hear me simply say that, because he'd expected a fight. Each of those little digits can add up to many thousands of dollars when a film hits big.

"All the points," I repeated, "take it. Take it all." I was thinking, "You can take it and shove it because that's not what I'm doing the movie for." I understood the reality. The situation was lopsided. Dino had the money, and I needed the career, so it made no sense to argue. It was just supply and demand. But, I also thought, the day will come when the tables will turn, and Dino will have to pay.

With John Milius, everything was drama, I learned as we got to be friends. He was a cigar-smoking, bearlike, Harley-Davidson-riding guy, with black, curly hair and a beard. History obsessed him, especially war, and he had an encyclopedic knowledge of battles and weapons from the time of the Egyptians, Greeks, and Romans all the way up to the present day. John could talk authoritatively about the Vikings, the Mongols, pirates of every period, the samurai, medieval knights, and longbowmen. He knew every size of bullet used in the Second World War and what kind of pistol Hitler wore. He didn't need to do research, it was already in his head.

John liked to call himself a Zen fascist, and he'd brag that he was so far to the right that he wasn't even a Republican. Some people in town thought he was sick. But he was such a fantastic writer that even the liberals would call him for help on their scripts, like Warren Beatty with *Reds*. Nobody was better at writing macho lines. A great example of his work is the soliloquy in *Jaws*, when Robert Shaw's character, Captain Quint, recalls the sinking of the USS *Indianapolis* in World War II after it had delivered the atomic bomb to be dropped on Hiroshima. It took five days for rescuers to arrive, too late for most of the crew. Quint's speech ends: "So, eleven hundred men went into the water. Three hundred sixteen men come out, the sharks took the rest, June the 29th, 1945. Anyway, we delivered the bomb."

Milius also wrote Robert Duvall's iconic line in *Apocalypse Now*, "I love the smell of napalm in the morning . . . It smells like . . . victory." And of course the line that was already my favorite in *Conan*, when the barbarian is asked, "What is best in life?" and he says, "Crush your enemies, see them driven before you, and hear the lamentation of their women."

It was fun hanging out with a guy who was so totally committed to the macho fantasy, the Teddy Roosevelt ideal. I liked to step in and out of it. I could be an actor one minute, the next minute a beach bum, the next minute a businessman, the next minute a bodybuilding champion, the next minute a Romeo—whatever it was—but Milius was locked in. It was part of his charm. At his office, there were always guns, swords, and knives lying on his desk. He would show off his Purdeys: British shotguns, custom fitted and specially engraved, each of which took months to make and cost tens of thousands of dollars. He treated himself to a new one after every movie. The shotgun was always part of the deal. If John brought the movie in on time, he'd automatically get a Purdey.

He knew so much about the world, and he loved to share his knowledge with anyone who'd listen. He'd grab a sword and say, "Feel this sword. Feel the weight of it. That was the difference between the British sword and the French sword. The French was always lighter . . ." And off he'd go. Or he'd look at an actress and say, "Yeah, she's beautiful, but she is not erotic for the age of Conan. I don't think they had those oversized breasts. And see how wide-set her eyes are, and the shape of her nose and lips? Those are not Egyptian lips."

Right away Milius had me start watching movies he thought were important for my preparation. He'd put on the 1954 Japanese classic *Seven Samurai* and say, "You've got to see Toshiro Mifune. Notice the way he wipes his mouth, the way he talks, the way he grabs the women? Everything has style, everything's a little bit larger than life and done with mischief. That's the way Conan is." He also made me pay attention to the swordsmanship, because *kenjutsu* was part of a whole range of combat styles that Milius was weaving into the Conan universe; the script called for an entire museum's worth of swords, battle-axes, lances, knives, and armor from throughout history.

He started sending experts to train me: masters in martial arts, armorers, stunt people who were horse-riding specialists. For three months I was tutored in broadsword combat two hours a day. Unlike the samurai sword, which is very light and very sharp—designed for lopping off heads and limbs and slicing bodies in half—the broadsword is massive and double edged. It's meant to deliver big blows that eventually hack through armor and flesh. I had to learn which parts of the body are vulnerable to attack and how to swing the sword, not to mention what happens if you miss. The momentum of an eleven-pound sword can pull a fighter out of position, like a gun with tremendous recoil, so you have to anticipate and channel the momentum in order to come back right away with another chop.

A *kenjutsu* trainer came next, and then an expert in a style of Brazilian fighting that combined punching and wrestling, with all kinds of throws, elbow blows, and body slams. A stuntman taught me climbing techniques, how to fall and roll, and how to jump fifteen feet onto a mat. Milius was busy with postproduction on *Big Wednesday,* but he always took time to come by to check my progress and videotape me.

The training was as intense and time consuming as getting ready for a bodybuilding competition, and I took to it completely. I felt like my movie career had suddenly come into sharp focus. The vision had always been there, but hazy: I never knew which direction it would go or how I was going to get the big break. But being chosen for *Conan* was like winning my first international bodybuilding title. Until then I could see my progress in the mirror, I could see my muscles slowly grow, but I really never knew where I stood. Then, after winning Mr. Universe, I thought, "Jesus, that was international judging, and I was competing against guys I see in the magazines, and I won. I'm going to succeed."

Some of Hollywood's biggest players now had a stake in my career. Dino was giving me an opportunity to prove myself in movies, a little like Joe Weider had in bodybuilding. And I now had a connection with Universal Pictures, a major international studio that was doing giant hits like *The Deer Hunter* and *Jaws.* Now the studio was making a movie about a lovable extraterrestrial stranded here on Earth: *E.T.* The guys who ran Universal, Lew Wasserman and Sid Sheinberg, were legendary characters, people who manufactured stars.

My stunt trainer, a Hollywood veteran who was a shrewd observer of the scene, wasted no time pointing this out. "Man, you are so lucky," he said. "Do you realize that you're now part of the Hollywood machine? Do you know how much money will be spent on you? Just on you? Twenty million on the movie—*twenty million!*—and you're playing the title role. All that machinery is going to work for you. You are going to be huge."

I thought about the people who had come to Hollywood and were struggling to make ends meet, working as waiters and waitresses while they auditioned for parts. I'd met some of them in acting class and heard them say things like "I was turned down again, I don't know what to do." The rejections in Hollywood go on and on, and the psychological beating can be relentless. Then you have to go home embarrassed after having failed. It's why so many actors and actresses turn to drugs. I'd been able to avoid that kind of despair, and now I was the one getting the shot. They'd picked me. Of course, now I had to show I was worthy, but I didn't feel at all concerned. I would do whatever it took to get there. I didn't share my feelings of pride with anybody. My style was to keep moving and not reflect too much. But it felt great.

By far the wildest trainer Milius found for me was a Conan fanatic who actually lived outdoors in the mountains. He was so into the Conan stories that he wanted to experience the Conan life, and he'd become an expert at sleeping in the snow, climbing trees, living off the land. He even called himself Conan. Dirt and freezing cold didn't seem to bother him: I went skiing with him in Aspen, Colorado, and he skied in shorts. I wondered if he'd resent me for being cast as Conan instead of him, but instead he loved that I'd gotten the job. The news had gone out among the Conan fans that I was training heavily for the part and that I was going to do the horseback riding and the sword fighting myself. So the die-hard fans decided that I was a great choice, especially since my body looked so much like Conan's in the comics. I felt happy to be accepted, and it was a promising sign for the film, because the core audience who would go back to see the movie again and again and recommend it to all their friends was supposed to be guys like this. As a reward for taking the time to help, we brought "Conan" to Europe when we did the shoot. He got to play an enemy warrior in a fight scene, where he was hacked to pieces—by me.

CHAPTER 13

Maria and Me

ALTHOUGH MARIA AND I were on opposite sides of the fence politically, it was politics that brought us together geographically, when she moved to California to work on Teddy Kennedy's 1980 presidential campaign. In American politics, it was almost unheard of for an incumbent president running for reelection to be challenged from within his own party. But Jimmy Carter's first term had been so disappointing, and America was in such a depressed state, that Teddy decided to run. Of course, when any Kennedy ran for office, it was all hands on deck. If you were a family member, you were supposed to put your life on hold and campaign.

The first thing that Maria and her friend Bonnie Reiss did was plaster Kennedy '80 posters and bumper stickers all over my Jeep. I had a brown Cherokee Chief that I was really proud of. It was massive compared to ordinary cars—the first-ever sport-utility vehicle—and I'd gone all the way up to Oregon to take delivery so that I could get $1,000 off the price. I'd had my Jeep outfitted with a loudspeaker and siren for showing off or scaring other drivers out of my way. But now when we drove around town, I'd sink a little lower in the seat, hoping that no one would see me. It was weird pulling up at the gym every day: like most of the people there, I was known as a Republican, and now here I was with the Teddy stickers.

Personally, I was hoping that Ronald Reagan would be elected president, but no one was asking my opinion; it was Maria they wanted to see. Hollywood, of course, is a big liberal town, and her family connections went deep. Her grandfather Joe Kennedy had been heavily involved in movies, running no fewer than three studios in the 1920s, and the Kennedys were famous for involving entertainers in political campaigns. So everyone in the family was very much aware of Hollywood, and they turned to actors, directors, and executives for help in fund-raising. Maria's uncle Peter Lawford was a big star, and buddies with Frank Sinatra and Dean Martin. She'd heard about those guys in the "Rat Pack" growing up, had seen them at her parents' house, and had been to their places in Palm Springs, California. No sooner did she arrive in 1980 than she got to know their wives.

The Kennedy campaign center would call the studios and talent agencies and line up appointments for Maria with big shots and celebrities. "Maria would like to visit you and talk about an event we have coming up," they'd say, and almost invariably the reaction would be "Omigod, a Kennedy is coming!" and doors would open. Usually Maria would go with other campaign staff, but sometimes I'd tag along or even drive her. Teddy's candidacy was so controversial that winning endorsements wasn't easy. Often I'd listen to people like producer Norman Lear explaining to Maria why they didn't support Teddy and were either backing the independent candidate, Illinois congressman John Anderson, or sticking with Carter.

Maria wasn't even twenty-five, but already she was a force to reckon with. That had been clear to me early on. In 1978, about six months after we first met, I posed for a photo essay in *Playgirl* magazine. Ara Gallant, my trendy New York photographer friend, had the assignment, and I came up with the idea that we should do a beer hall scene. It would be a traditional beer hall, but instead of hefty German women serving the beer steins and pretzels and sausages around me, it would be young sexy girls with bare tits. It was one of my crazy ideas and Ara loved it. But when I described this to Maria and said, "We're just now working on the layout," she told me instantly that the whole thing was a mistake.

"I thought you wanted to go into movies," she said. "So if you pose with those girls with their tits hanging out, is that going make producers say, 'Hey, wow! I want this guy'? I doubt it. What's your goal in doing this?"

I had to admit I had no answer to that. I'd just been in a silly mood and said to Ara, "Let's do something funny." I wasn't trying to get anything out of it.

"Well, since there's no goal and it's not going to lead anywhere, kill it. You don't need it. You had your fun, now move on." She was relentless and so convincing that I ended up talking *Playgirl* into killing the story and paying $7,000 to reimburse the magazine for the shoot.

She was wise about public perception because that was the world in which she'd grown up. Maria was the first girlfriend I ever had who didn't treat my ambitions as an annoyance, some kind of madness that interfered with her vision of the future: namely, marriage, kids, and a cozy little house somewhere—and the stereotypical all-American life. Maria's world wasn't small like that. It was gigantic, because of what her grandfather did, what her father did, what her mother did, what her uncles did. I'd finally met a girl whose world was as big as mine. I'd reached some of my goals but a lot of my world was still a dream. And when I'd talk about even bigger dreams, she never said, "Come on, this can't be done."

She'd seen it happen in her family. She came from a world where her great-grandfather was an immigrant and her grandfather made a vast fortune in Hollywood and the liquor business, real estate, and other investments. It was a world in which seeing a relative run for president or senator was not out of the ordinary. She'd heard her uncle John F. Kennedy pledge in 1961 that by the end of the decade the United States would land a man on the moon. Her mother had created the Special Olympics. Her dad was the founding director of the Peace Corps and had created the Job Corps, VISTA (Volunteers in Service to America), and Legal Services for the poor, all under the Kennedy and Johnson administrations. And Sargent Shriver had been Lyndon Johnson's and Richard Nixon's ambassador to France. So if I said, "I want to make a million per picture," it didn't automatically strike Maria as absurd. It just made her curious. "How are you going to do that?" she'd ask. "I admire how driven you are. I don't understand how anyone can have this discipline." What's more, by watching me, she got to see something she'd never actually witnessed firsthand: how you make one dollar into two, and how you build businesses and become a millionaire.

The way she was raised gave her huge advantages such as an exceptional education and her parents' extensive knowledge and wisdom. She got to meet the influential people and hear their conversations. She got to live in Paris when her father was ambassador, and was able to travel the world. She grew up playing tennis, skiing, and competing in horse shows.

But there were drawbacks too. Eunice and Sarge were so forceful that the kids never got to develop their own opinions about things. The two of them made a point of letting the kids know that they were smart. "This is a very good idea, Anthony," I'd hear Eunice tell her youngest son, who was only starting high school. "The way I would approach it is thus and so, but it's a very good point you have. I didn't think about that." But the household was a strict hierarchy in which the parents, usually Eunice, made the choices. She was a very dominating personality, but Sarge didn't mind.

When you grow up that way, it's hard to make your own decisions, and eventually you feel like you can't function without your parents' input. Eunice and Sarge decided which colleges to consider, for example. Yes, there was some participation on the kids' part, but overall, the parents ran the show. Then again, many times not even *they* ran the show, the Kennedy family did. The degree of conformity among the Kennedys was extreme. Not a single one of the thirty cousins was a Republican, for example. If you gather thirty members of any extended family, it's almost impossible that all of them are the same. That's why I always used to tease Maria, "Your family's like a bunch of clones. If you ask your brother to name his favorite color, he doesn't know. He'll say, 'We like blue.' "

She would laugh and say, "That's not really true! Look how diverse they are."

I'd say, "They are all environmentalists, they are all athletic, they all are Democrats, they all endorsed the same candidates, and they all *do* like blue."

The other big disadvantage involved public perception. No matter what you did as a Kennedy or a Shriver, no one gave you credit for your accomplishment. Instead, people would say, "Well, if *I* were a Kennedy, I could do that too." For all these reasons, Maria had to fight harder than most people to carve out her own identity.

Sarge and Eunice welcomed me. The first time that Maria brought me to their town house in Washington, Sarge came downstairs holding a book. "I'm just reading about these great accomplishments of yours," he said. He'd found a mention of me in a book about American immigrants who had arrived with nothing and made a success. That was a nice surprise because I wasn't expecting to be in books yet. Bodybuilding was such an odd thing. I thought they'd be writing about immigrants like former US secretary of state Henry Kissinger, not me. It was so gracious and generous of Maria's dad to notice that passage and show it to me.

Eunice put me right to work. She was thrilled to hear that I'd been involved with Special Olympics research at the University of Wisconsin. Before I knew it, I was helping her push the idea of adding power lifting to the Special Olympics and conducting workshops on weight training for the mentally handicapped wherever I traveled.

If the Shrivers hadn't been so gracious, the first dinner I had at their house could have been difficult. Maria's four brothers, Anthony, Bobby, Timothy, and Mark, ranged in age from twenty-three to twelve, and right away one of the younger ones piped up, "Daddy, Arnold loves Nixon!" Sarge was a great friend of Hubert Humphrey's; in fact, when

Humphrey ran against Nixon in 1968, he'd wanted Sarge as his running mate, but the Kennedy family torpedoed the idea.

So I felt really awkward sitting there at the table. But Sarge, always the diplomat, said evenly, "Well, everyone thinks differently about these things." Later on we discussed it, and I explained why I admired Nixon. It was my reaction against having grown up in Europe, where government was totally in charge of everything, and 70 percent of people worked for the government, and the highest aspiration was to get a government job. That was one of the reasons why I left for the United States. Sargent happened to be a scholar of German, because he was of German descent. He had spent student summers in Germany in the mid-1930s wearing lederhosen, exploring the German and Austrian countryside, pedaling from village to village on his bicycle. During his first summer there, 1934, Adolf Hitler's recent rise to power as German chancellor didn't make much of an impression on Sarge. But in his second summer, 1936, he learned to recognize the brown-shirted "storm troopers" of the Nazi paramilitary, the Sturmabteilung (SA), and the black-uniformed members of Hitler's elite guard, the Schutzstaffel (SS). He read about political prisoners being sent to concentration camps. Sarge actually heard Hitler speak.

He came home convinced that America should try to keep its distance from the growing crisis in Europe—so much so that in 1940 at Yale University he cofounded the antiwar America First Committee with classmates Gerald Ford, the future thirty-eighth president, and future Supreme Court justice Potter Stewart, among others. Nevertheless, Sarge enlisted in the navy before Pearl Harbor and served throughout the war. We spoke German together many times. He wasn't fluent, exactly, but he could sing in German.

Family meals in the Shriver household were about as far from my upbringing as you could get. Sarge would ask me at the dinner table, "What would your parents have done if you'd talked to them the way my kids are talking to me here?"

"My dad would have smacked me right away."

"Did you hear that, guys? Arnold, repeat that. Repeat that. His father would have smacked him. That's what I should do with you kids."

The boys would say, "Oh, Daddy," and then throw a piece of bread at him.

They had that kind of humor at the table, and I was amazed. The first time I was there for dinner, the meal ended with one of the boys farting, another one burping, and another one leaning so far back in his chair that it toppled to the floor. Then he just lay there groaning, "Oh, man, I am fucking full."

Eunice snapped, "Don't ever say that again in this house, do you hear me?"

"Sorry, Mom, but I am so full. Your cooking is unbelievable." Of course that was a wisecrack too. Eunice did not even know how to soft-boil an egg.

"Be happy that you were fed," she said.

Maria's parents certainly had a much more casual approach to childrearing than Meinhard and I had experienced. We were always told to shut up, whereas the Shriver kids were encouraged to join in the conversation. If, let's say, the subject came up of Independence Day and what a great celebration it was, Sargent would ask, "Bobby, what does the Fourth of July mean to you?" They would talk about policy issues and social ills and things that the president had said. Everyone was expected to come up with something and take part.

Although Maria and I lived on opposite coasts, our lives became intertwined. She came to my graduation up in Wisconsin—after a decade of course work, I was awarded a degree in business, with a major in international fitness marketing. She was just starting her TV career, producing local news shows in Philadelphia and Baltimore. I'd visit her there, and once or twice I went on a show with her buddy Oprah Winfrey, who was also just starting out and had a talk show in Baltimore. Maria always picked interesting friends, but Oprah really stood out. She was talented and aggressive, and you could tell she believed in herself. For one of her shows, she came to the gym and worked out with me to demonstrate how important it is to stay fit. Another time we talked about the importance of teaching kids to read and getting them interested in books.

I was proud of Maria. For the first time I saw how determined she was to make her own niche. There were no other journalists in the family. When she went for her job interview, they asked, "Are you willing to work fourteen hours a day, or do you expect to be pampered as a Shriver?" She said she was willing to work hard, and she did.

We traveled together to Hawaii, LA, Europe. Our ski trip to Austria in 1978 was her first Christmas away from her family. I would also accompany Maria to family get-togethers, of which there were many. An aspect of being a Kennedy cousin, I quickly learned, was that you were never completely free. Maria was expected to go to Hyannis Port in the summer, accompany the family on winter vacation, and be home at Thanksgiving and Christmas. If someone had a birthday or a wedding, she had better be there. Since there were so many cousins, the number of command performances was high.

When Maria could get away from work, she visited me in California. She warmed up really well to some of my friends, especially Franco, and also to some of the actors and directors I knew. Others she didn't like: guys she felt were hangers-on or were trying to use me. She and my mom got to know each other too, during my mom's annual Eastertime visits.

The more serious we became, the more Maria talked about moving to California. So for us, Teddy's 1980 presidential campaign was well timed. I was ready to buy a house, and our first major decision as a couple was to look for it together and to call it our place. In late summer we found a 1920s Spanish-style house in a nice section of Santa Monica off San Vincente Avenue. We called it our house, but it wasn't really. It was mine. It had a curved stairway to the left as you entered, lots of nice vintage tile, a big living room with a beamed ceiling, and beautiful fireplaces in the living room, the TV room, and the master bedroom upstairs. There was a long lap pool and a guesthouse for my mom to stay in when she visited.

The fact that it was our house was just between Maria and me, because she didn't want her parents to know we were living together—especially Sarge, who was very conservative. She told them she lived a few blocks away, on Montana Avenue, and we actually rented and furnished an apartment so that when Sarge and Eunice visited, Maria could invite them over for lunch there. I'm pretty sure that Eunice knew what was going on, but the separate apartment was important for the family image.

Of course, total anonymity is almost impossible in Hollywood, especially for a Kennedy cousin. One of the real estate agents who knew of Maria's Kennedy connection said to us while we were house hunting, "I have a fascinating house to show you in Beverly Hills. I'm not going to tell you what makes it so interesting; you just have to see." We went, and she showed us around. Then she said, "Do you know who lived here? Gloria Swanson!" And she took us to the basement and showed us a tunnel that led to another house nearby. Joe Kennedy had used that tunnel during his and the actress Gloria Swanson's long-running affair in the late 1920s. Afterward, Maria asked me, "Why did she show us this?" She was partly fascinated and partly mad and embarrassed.

Teddy's campaign gave me an amazing opportunity to see what it is like to jump into a presidential race. I went to New Hampshire with Maria in February to experience the primary. The campaign staff was staying in a little hotel that buzzed like a beehive with media and campaign staff and volunteers and people with newspapers under their arm scurrying off to read the latest coverage. Organizers would send Maria out to some local factory to shake hands.

The operation seemed Mickey Mouse to me, because I didn't understand the way campaigns work. Teddy Kennedy was a big-shot politician who made the cover of *Time* magazine when he decided to run. So I imagined that he would be addressing huge rallies. I'd already been to several rallies for Republican candidate Ronald Reagan that year, and he always drew one thousand to two thousand people, sometimes more. Even if Reagan was just stopping off at a factory somewhere to talk to the workers, it still looked like a rally, with flags, banners, patriotic music.

But there we were in this rinky-dink hotel. Shaking hands, going to shops, going to restaurants. "This is so odd," I thought. "Why stay at this awful little hotel? Why not a grand hotel?" I didn't know that when you start out, it is all about one-to-one contact. I didn't know you can't have campaign staff staying in grand hotels because somebody will inevitably write a story about how you are wasting the campaign money that hardworking people had donated. I didn't understand that some events are big and some are smaller and more intimate, depending on the circumstances.

The 1980 Democratic race developed into something especially brutal. Before he jumped in, Teddy was ahead of President Carter in opinion polls by a margin of more than two to one. Everyone was egging on Teddy to run. Journalists were writing about how fantastic and powerful he was and how he would win easily against Jimmy Carter and save the day for the Democrats. He could do no wrong. But as soon as he announced his candidacy in November 1979, everything turned. The attacks were relentless. I couldn't believe the difference. It didn't help that in a national interview on CBS, Teddy couldn't give a convincing answer when asked why he wanted to be president. People challenged his character because of the 1969 car crash on Chappaquiddick Island, Massachusetts, that killed his passenger, Mary Jo Kopechne, a former campaign worker for RFK. They also claimed that Teddy was just living off his brothers' reputation, even though he'd been a senator for eighteen years.

I was shocked. It was amazing to be in the front row and watch it all play out in front of my eyes.

Teddy lost the crucial early primaries in Iowa and New Hampshire, and that caused some of his funding to dry up—which meant that the campaign had to downsize even before the primaries in the larger states. But then he fought his way back enough to win several major states, including New York in March, Pennsylvania in April, and—thanks in part to Maria's efforts—California in June. However, he lost in dozens of other states, and in the national opinion polls, he never caught President Carter again. Teddy ended up winning only ten primaries out of thirty-four. On the first day of the Democratic National Convention in August, it was clear that President Carter had enough delegates to lock up the nomination, and Teddy was forced to drop out.

All of a sudden, after months of intense effort, it was over, and Maria was sad and depressed. The family had experienced so much devastation just in her lifetime, starting with President John F. Kennedy's assassination when she was eight, and Bobby Kennedy's when she was twelve, and the Chappaquiddick incident the following summer. Then on top of those, she saw her father lose in a landslide as George McGovern's vice presidential running mate in 1972, and lose when he tried to get the Democratic presidential nomination in 1976. And now Teddy had run, and they'd been handed another loss.

She'd put her heart into the campaign. I could see how overwhelming politics can become and how totally out of control. When you run for president, you feel the public pressure every day. The national and local media track everything you say and do, and everyone is analyzing you. Seeing her uncle go through that and lose was really, really tough. I was happy to play a supportive role in these difficult circumstances. "You did a fantastic job," I told her, "the way you spoke to the media, the way you busted your butt for Teddy." The experience confirmed Maria's dim view of politics as a career choice.

I used all the skills I had to cheer up Maria. I whisked her away to a vacation in Europe, where we had a great time visiting London and Paris and going all around France. Soon Maria stopped feeling like a beaten-down campaign worker, and her enthusiasm and sense of humor returned.

Before Maria had left the East Coast, she'd made a gutsy career change. She'd started with the goal of being the producer, the person in the control room. Now she decided to go on camera and compete for one of those scarce top jobs in network news. I'd always advanced by starting with a clear vision and working as hard as possible to achieve it, and I could see that same determination unfolding in Maria. I thought it was great.

No one in the Kennedy family had ever been an on-camera journalist. It was a totally new thing, and it was *hers*. I'd watched some of her cousins carve out their niches, but it almost always involved specializing in a cause or issue within the framework of the family beliefs. For Maria to go out and be in front of the camera was a real declaration of independence.

As soon as we got back to Santa Monica, she set to work making connections and getting the necessary training, much as I had done with my acting. What did it take to succeed in front of the camera? She had to figure that out. What did she need to change about her looks, her voice, her style? What should she keep the same? Her teachers would say, "Your hair's too big, you have to cut it down. Or can you pull it back? Let's try that. Your eyes are too strong; maybe let's tone down the eyes." There was all this shaping and molding going on. She had to learn what makes you easy to look at and listen to day after day on TV, and not be overly dramatic and divert attention from the news, which should be the focus.

During my *Conan* shoot in Madrid the following winter, we couldn't see each other for five months. She mailed me photos showing that she'd lost ten pounds and shortened her hair and put a little wave in it. *Conan*, meanwhile, had been scheduled and postponed several times. We were supposed to go on location in Yugoslavia in the summer of 1980, but Yugoslavia became unstable due to the death of its dictator, Marshal Tito, in May. The producers decided it would be cheaper and simpler to move the production to Spain in the fall. Then when Maria and I got back from Europe, I learned that the project had been delayed again until after New Year's.

—

This opened the way for a crazy plan that I'd only been toying with up to now: to make a surprise comeback and reclaim the world bodybuilding championship and the title of Mr. Olympia. Bodybuilding had grown tremendously in the four years since *Pumping Iron.* Health clubs were sprouting up all over the country, and strength training was a key part of what they offered. Joe Gold sold his original gym to franchisers and built a big, new establishment near the beach called the World Gym, which welcomed women as well as men.

The Mr. Olympia competition was thriving. In one of Joe Weider's periodic pushes to expand worldwide, the International Federation of Body Building (IFBB) was holding this year's contest in Sydney, Australia. In fact, I was due to work the event as a color commentator for CBS-TV. This would pay very well, but the appeal of doing it melted away once I felt the fire to compete again. The vision became irresistible as it crystallized in my mind. Reconquering the sport was the perfect preparation for *Conan*. It would show everyone who was the real king—and the real barbarian. Frank Zane had held the title for three years, and at least a dozen contenders were jockeying to win, including guys I saw at the gym every day. One was Mike Mentzer, a five-foot-eight Pennsylvanian with a dark, droopy mustache who'd finished a close second the previous year. He was promoting himself as the up-and-coming guru of weight training and spokesman for the sport and was always quoting the philosophy of the novelist Ayn Rand. Often there were rumors that I would return to competition, and I knew that if I denied everything and waited until the last minute to jump in, the uncertainty would gnaw at people like him.

Maria thought all this was unwise. "You *run* competitions now," she pointed out. "You left bodybuilding as the champion and this could turn people against you. Besides, you might not win." I knew she was right, but the desire to compete wouldn't go away. "If you have so much extra energy, why don't you learn Spanish before you go to Spain for the movie shoot?" she said. Having just seen Teddy lose the Democratic presidential nomination, she didn't want another risk in her life. The night before, she'd freaked when Muhammad Ali, who was coming out of retirement to try to become the first four-time World Heavyweight Champion, was beaten convincingly by the current champ Larry Holmes. It was like that was symbolic.

But I just couldn't let it go. The more I thought about it, the more I dug in on the idea.

Then one night, to my surprise, Maria turned around. She said that if I was still determined to compete, she'd support me. She became an extraordinary partner.

Maria was the only person I told. Of course Franco guessed. My longtime friend was a chiropractor now and was working as my training partner in preparation for *Conan*. He'd been saying things like "Arnold, the Olympia is coming up. You must go into it and shock everybody." Some of the guys in the gym were really uneasy. When they saw me start blasting two-hour workouts twice a day, they couldn't figure it out. They knew that I was supposed to play Conan, and I'd told them that being ripped was required for the part. Yes, I was going to Sydney, but that was to do TV commentary, wasn't it? Besides, Mr. Olympia was only five weeks away: *nobody* could start heavy training this late and get ready! Still, they weren't sure, and I fed the uncertainty. As weeks passed and the competition drew near, I would drive Mentzer crazy just by smiling at him across the gym.

It was the hardest training I'd ever done, which made it fun. I was amazed by how deeply Maria involved herself in every step, even though she was focused on her own goal. She'd grown up around sports, of course: not bodybuilding, but baseball, football, tennis, and golf, but it is all the same thing. She understood why I had to get up at six in the morning to train for two hours, and she'd come with me to the gym. At dinner she'd see me about to dig into some ice cream, and she'd literally take it away. All the enthusiasm she'd focused on Teddy's run for president was now transferred to me.

The Mr. Olympia contest was staged in the Sydney Opera House, the spectacular architectural masterpiece shaped like a row of sails on the edge of Sydney Harbour. Frank Sinatra had performed there just before us. It was an honor to appear in such a place—and a sign of how bodybuilding was moving up in prestige. The prize money was $50,000, the most ever offered in a bodybuilding competition, and fifteen champions registered in advance, making it the largest field ever.

An opera house turned out to be the perfect setting because from the day we arrived, the contest was full of drama, emotion, and intrigue. It caused an uproar when I announced that I was there not to observe but to compete. The federation officials had to debate: could a contestant jump in without registering beforehand? They realized there was no rule against it, so I was allowed to participate. Next came a rebellion against certain rules of the competition itself, in the form of a petition signed by all of the bodybuilders except me. The organizers had to negotiate to avoid chaos. After much commotion, they agreed not only to adopt the changes but also asked the contestants to approve the judges.

All this backstage maneuvering brought out a side of Maria that made me think of Eunice in action. Even though Maria tried to separate herself, she had her mother's political instincts and was wise beyond her years. In politics, when disputes arise and camps form, you have to grasp what's happening and move very quickly. She was right there with lightning-fast perceptions and really good advice. She talked to the right people and helped me avoid getting isolated or blindsided. She was a total animal. I wondered how someone who had never been involved in the bodybuilding world and who had barely even met the players could step in so quickly and be so effective.

In the end I won my seventh crown as Mr. Olympia. But that victory remains controversial to this day. The judges awarded a split decision, voting 5–2 for me against the closest competitor, Chris Dickerson of the United States. It was the first nonunanimous decision in Mr. Olympia history. When my name was announced, only half the two thousand people in the opera house cheered, and for the first time in my life, I heard boos. Right afterward, one of the top five finishers threw around chairs backstage, while another smashed his trophy to smithereens in the parking lot and yet another announced he was quitting bodybuilding for good.

Training for competition and winning again gave me pleasure, but in hindsight, I have to admit that the episode was not beneficial for the sport. It created a lot of divisiveness, and I could have handled it differently. The old camaraderie of bodybuilding was gone. Eventually I reconciled with all those guys, but with some it took years to patch up.

Conan wasn't due to start filming in earnest for a couple more months, but I had to fly to London in late October to shoot a preliminary scene. When I arrived, John Milius took one look at me and shook his head. "I've got to ask you to retrain," he said. "I can't have Conan looking like a bodybuilder. This is not a *Hercules* movie. I want you to be chunkier. You need to gain a little weight. You have to look like someone who's been a pit fighter and a warrior and a slave chained for years to the Wheel of Pain. That's the kind of body I want." Milius wanted everything to look as consistent as possible. That was logical, even though Conan was entirely a fantasy world. In the scene we shot in England, I was made up to look like Conan the king in his old age, giving a soliloquy meant as the introduction of the film:

"Know, O Prince; that between the years when the oceans drank Atlantis and the rise of the sons of Aryas, there was an age undreamed of . . . Hither came I, Conan, a thief, a reaver, a slayer, to tread jeweled thrones of the earth beneath my feet. But now my eyes are dim. Sit on the ground with me, for you are but the leavings of my age. Let me tell you of the days of high adventure."

I was draped in robes and furs, so the Mr. Olympia physique didn't show. But before we went on location in December 1980, I would have to reshape my body again.

—

Heading back to LA from Sydney, I thought about how the tribulations of recent months had united Maria and me. I was so glad I'd tolerated those Teddy Kennedy posters on my Jeep and that I hadn't make an issue about my own political opinions. Because for the first time, I felt that I really, truly had a partner. Throughout that spring and summer, I'd succeeded in helping her with the ups and downs of the campaign, and I felt that taking her to Europe afterward had been exactly the right impulse. And now I saw how she'd gotten involved and been able to help with *my* thing, which was as foreign to her world as it could be.

I could imagine the pressure she must be under from the Kennedy friends in Hollywood to move on to a more suitable boyfriend. Older women especially—friends of her mother or of Pat Kennedy Lawford, Peter's ex-wife—used to say to Maria, "Why are you going out with that bodybuilder? Let me introduce you to this wonderful producer," or "this young, very attractive businessman," or "Do I have the man for you! He's a little older, but he's a billionaire. Let me set you up with him."

The outside world looked at our relationship in a simpleminded way, as a juicy success story. "Isn't it amazing that he wins Mr. Olympia and all these bodybuilding championships, and then he gets this big movie contract, and then he gets a Kennedy as his girlfriend?" According to this way of thinking, Maria becomes part of my trophy collection.

But the reality is that she was not a trophy. It made no difference what the name was. If I hadn't been her style and she hadn't been mine, we never would have ended up together. Her personality, her look, her intelligence, her wit, what she brought to the table, and how much she was able to participate without missing a beat were what mattered to me. Maria meshed with everything that I was, what I stood for, and what I was doing. That was a very important reason why I was considering that this woman could be my life partner. I got addicted to her. When I reached Spain, it was hard to be without her.

I understood what Maria wanted to accomplish. She wanted to

become the next Barbara Walters. And I wanted to become the biggest movie star, so we were both very driven. I understood the world that she wanted to get into, and she understood the world that I was trying to explore and where I wanted to go, and we could be part of each other's journey.

I also understood why I appealed to her. Maria was such a forceful personality that she would just run over guys. They would become immediate slaves. So here was me, whom you can't run over. I was confident, I'd accomplished things, I was somebody. She admired the fact that I was an immigrant who had come over here and built a life. She could see from my personality that I'd figure out her family and feel comfortable around them.

Maria wanted to get away from home as much as I did—and what better way than to fall in love with an ambitious Austrian bodybuilder who wanted an acting career? She liked being away from Washington and the lawyers and politicians and Beltway talk. She wanted to be unique and different.

If there was anything in her family for Maria to compare us to as a couple, it was her grandparents. Joe was a self-made man, and I was a self-made man. He was very aggressive in making money, and so was I. Rose had chosen him when he was penniless and she was the daughter of the mayor of Boston, John Francis "Honey Fitz" Fitzgerald, because she had absolute faith in Joe's ability to succeed. I was relentless, disciplined, hands-on, and street-smart enough to get there too. That was what made Maria want to be with me.

What I represented physically was also a factor. She liked guys who were athletic and strong. Maria told me that when she was a kid and JFK was president, she would hang out with the Secret Service men in Hyannis. At night, when they were on duty and trying to stay awake, sometimes they'd read muscle magazines—with me on the cover! She was too young to pay much attention, but she did notice that those bodyguards were all working out. It stuck in her mind enough that when the book *Pumping Iron* came out, she bought it as a gift for her oldest brother, Bobby.

We started decorating our house before I had to leave in December for preproduction on *Conan*. Maria was into floral curtains and a conservative look, which I liked; it was very East Coast and also a little European. She'd inherited a lot of it from her family. They'd all grown up with floral patterns and certain couches and chairs, some with wooden backs and others that were stuffed. All of their houses, all of their apartments, had a piano in the living room, dozens of framed pictures of family members on all the sideboards and surfaces, and on and on.

My style was more rustic, so when we needed a dining room set, I went to an antique fair in downtown LA and bought a heavy oak table and chairs. Maria took charge of the living room. She ordered big, overstuffed couches and had them upholstered with those floral prints, and then easy chairs to be covered in solids so they complemented the couches. One of Eunice's friends was a great decorator, and she helped with suggestions.

What Maria and I shared was the idea that our home had to be comfortable. Neither of us wanted a place that was so decorated that you couldn't put your feet up and kick back. I saw that she had taste, so I let her do her thing, and she saw that I had taste. It was great to have someone who also had strong opinions and yet be able to work together, rather than work in a vacuum where I'd have to do everything myself and always be guessing, Does she like this? Does she like that? Is this house just a reflection of me? She brought a great foundation of knowledge and was a great partner to work with because we both grew.

Maria loved it when I took her to the antique shows and we looked at the old stuff. My taste had developed over the years, partly from watching Joe Weider collect his antiques, but it was still not refined, and I did not buy above a certain level. It always depended on how much money I had and how much I wanted to spend. I'd never had a piece of furniture custom upholstered; I would just buy what was on the floor or look for a deal. But now that I was on a roll with *Conan*, I felt I could open my wallet a little more and get pieces covered with the materials Maria liked.

All of this developed without arguments. It became clear that we were good mates and could live together, which was something we'd wanted to test. I had a taste for art, once again in part due to Joe Weider's influence. To develop my own taste, I went to a lot of museums, auctions, and galleries, and Maria and I enjoyed going to see art together. I started collecting. In the beginning, less expensive works were all I could afford, such as lithographs by Marc Chagall, Joan Miró, and Salvador Dalí. But I quickly moved up to paintings and sculptures.

The idea of getting married came up shortly before I was scheduled to leave for Spain. I wanted Maria to be with me there and be part of my career. Especially after we'd gone through so much together during that summer and fall, it was obvious that she was the ideal woman for me.

I invited Maria to come to the set and hang out with me, or at least come visit for a month at a time. She said that she couldn't because her mother and dad would disapprove. It would bother them knowing that she was with me on location and spending nights together, because we weren't married.

"Well, then why don't we get married?" I said.

But that was even worse. She kind of flipped out about how Eunice would react. "No, no, no," she said, shaking her head, "I could never go to her with that."

Eunice had gotten married late—so late that it was part of the family lore. There were a lot of other things she'd wanted to do first. After she graduated from Stanford with a sociology degree during the Second World War, she worked for the State Department helping returned former prisoners of war readjust to civilian life. Then after the war, she worked on juvenile delinquency for the Justice Department as a social worker at a West Virginia federal prison camp for women and at a women's shelter in Chicago. Sarge, who was movie-star handsome and managed the Chicago Merchandise Mart for Joe Kennedy, fell in love with her in 1946 and courted her for seven years. He had pretty much given up hope when one day she took him into a side chapel after morning Mass and said, "Sarge, I think I'd like to marry you."

The bottom line was that she didn't marry until her early thirties and after she'd accomplished a lot. So Maria felt quite comfortable not marrying now when she was twenty-five but rather waiting until thirty at least. There was a lot she wanted to do first.

I was glad to hear that the problem wasn't with me, it was just that marriage wasn't in her plans for the time being. Marriage wasn't necessarily in my plans either at that point, although I wanted to be with her so much that I would have done it. I knew I would miss Maria greatly on the set. On the other hand, this was actually perfect. We could now continue for years without me hearing "Where is this heading? We've been going out for four years now, and you still can't make up your mind . . ." Or "Am I not good enough? Are you looking for someone else?" Instead, the subject just faded away.

I could go on for hours about what draws me to Maria but still never fully explain the magic. Ronald Reagan famously would sit and write ten-page love letters to his wife, Nancy, while she was sitting just across the room. I used to think, "Why wouldn't he just tell her?" But then I realized that writing something is different from saying it—and that love stories are built around people's idiosyncrasies.

CHAPTER 14

What Doesn't Kill Us Makes Us Stronger

CONAN THE BARBARIAN IS set in primitive Europe during the fictional Hyborian Age, after the sinking of Atlantis but thousands of years before the dawn of recorded history. I arrived in Madrid in early December to witness it taking shape in modern-day Spain. John Milius had been telling people we were out to make "good pagan entertainment, first and foremost a romance, an adventure, a movie where something big happens"—and also full of action and gore. "It'll be barbaric," he promised. "I'm not holding myself back."

To bring his vision to the screen, he'd recruited the A team: masters like Terry Leonard, the stunt director who'd just worked on *Raiders of the Lost Ark*; Ron Cobb, the production designer responsible for *Alien*; and Colin Arthur, formerly of Madame Tussauds, to supervise the making of human dummies and body parts. By the time I got there, *Conan* was already its own little industry. The movie's headquarters was in a swanky hotel in central Madrid where most of the actors and senior crew would stay, but the real action took place in locations all across Spain. Two hundred workers were busy building sets in a large warehouse twenty-five miles outside of the city. Outdoor sequences were scheduled for the mountains near Segovia, as well as the spectacular dunes and salt marshes of Almería, a province on the Mediterranean coast. A Moroccan bazaar in the provincial capital was to be dressed as a Hyborian city, and we were also due to film at an ancient fortress nearby and at other historical sites.

The $20 million production budget was lavish: the equivalent of $100 million today. Milius used the money to put together an amazing roster of people and special effects. He brought in artisans, trainers, and stunt experts from Italy, England, and the States, as well as the dozens of Spaniards the film employed. The script called for an animal population of horses, camels, goats, vultures, snakes, dogs, a hawk, and a leopard. More than 1,500 extras were hired. The score was to be performed by a ninety-piece orchestra and a twenty-four-member choir, singing in a mock Latin language.

Milius was fanatical that every bit of clothing and gear be true to the fantasy. Anything made of leather or cloth had to be aged by having cars drag it through the dirt until it looked dirty and worn. Saddles had to be hidden under blankets and furs because John said in those prehistoric times, there would have been no saddle makers stitching leather. The weapons came in for an endless amount of attention. The two broadswords for Conan himself were custom forged to Ron Cobb's drawings and inscribed with a pretend language. Four copies were made of each sword at $10,000 each. Naturally John insisted that these swords and all the other weapons had to be weathered looking, not gleaming. They were meant to kill, not shine, he said. Killing was the bottom line.

I busied myself during December studying lines, helping block out action scenes, and getting to know the other people on the *Conan* team.

Milius had unorthodox ideas about choosing a cast: he picked athletes instead of actors for other big parts. As my sidekick, the archer Subotai, he hired Gerry Lopez, a champion surfer from Hawaii who had starred as himself in Milius's previous movie, *Big Wednesday*. And as Conan's love, the thief and warrior Valeria, he chose Sandahl Bergman, a professional dancer recommended by director-choreographer Bob Fosse. John believed that the rigors of weight training, dancing, or being out seven hours a day surfing waves that could kill you built strength of character, and he was sure that this would show through on the screen. "Look at the faces of people who went through horrible times; people from Yugoslavia or Russia," he would say. "Look at the lines, the character in their faces. You can't fake that. These people have principles that they will stand and die for. They are tough because of the resistance they've fought through."

Even a fanatic like John realized that our lack of experience in front of the camera might be a problem. To inspire us and help offset the risk, he cast some veterans too. James Earl Jones was just finishing a run on Broadway as the star of Athol Fugard's *A Lesson from Aloes*, and he signed on to play Thulsa Doom, the evil sorcerer and king who slaughters Conan's parents and sells the young hero into slavery. Max von Sydow, the star of many Ingmar Bergman films, joined as a king who wants to reclaim his daughter who has run off to join Thulsa Doom's snake cult.

One of Milius's concerns was finding guys bigger than me to play Conan's enemies, so it didn't look like Conan was just going to run over everybody. He was very particular about that: they had to be taller and more muscular than me. On the bodybuilding circuit, I'd met a Dane named Sven-Ole Thorsen, who was six foot five and weighed over three hundred pounds. Sven also had a black belt in karate. I contacted him on Milius's behalf and put him in charge of looking for other big guys. At the beginning of December they all came to Madrid, a half dozen big, really threatening-looking Danes: power lifters, hammer throwers, shot-putters, martial-arts experts. Among them I felt like the little guy, and I'd never felt that before. We worked together, training with the battle-axes and swords and the horseback riding. I had a big head start, of course, but by the time we started shooting in January, the Danes were getting pretty good, and they made a major contribution to the battle scenes.

I was thrilled to see all of this unfold around me. Just as my stunt teacher predicted back in LA, the movie machinery was working on my behalf. I was Conan, and millions of dollars were being spent to make me shine. The movie had other important characters, of course, but in the end it was all geared to making me look like a real warrior. The sets were built for that purpose too. For the first time, I felt like the star.

It was different from being a bodybuilding champion. Millions of people were going to watch this movie, whereas in bodybuilding the biggest live audience was five thousand and the biggest TV audience was one million to two million. This was *big*. Movie magazines were going to write about *Conan*, the Calendar section in the *LA Times* was going to write about it, and magazines and newspapers around the world were going to review it and analyze it—and debate about it, no doubt, because what Milius envisioned was so violent.

Maria came to visit for a few days at the end of December after spending Christmas with her parents. This gave me a chance to introduce her to the crew and the cast, so she wouldn't think I'd dropped off the face of the earth. She got a laugh out of how I'd already assembled a whole posse of friends from the muscle world: not just the Danes but also Franco, because I'd arranged a small part for him.

I was glad that Maria wasn't still there when we started filming a week later. In the first scene we were scheduled to shoot, an unarmed Conan, newly released from slavery, is being chased by wolves across a rocky plain. He escapes by scrambling up an outcropping, where he will stumble upon the mouth of a tomb containing a sword. In preparation for this sequence, I'd been working every morning with the wolves, just to conquer my fear. The wolves were actually four German shepherds, but without telling me, Milius had ordered the stunt coordinator to rent animals that had some wolf in them. He thought that would heighten the realism. "We'll time it all out," he promised me. "You'll already be running when we release the dogs, and they won't have enough time to cross the field and get you before you're up the rocks."

On the morning we shot the scene, they sewed raw meat into the bearskin on my back to attract the dogs. The cameras rolled, and I sprinted across the field. But the trainer let the dogs loose too soon, and

I didn't have enough of a head start. The wolf pack caught me before I could get all the way up the rocks. They bit at my pants and dragged me down off the rock, and I fell ten feet onto my back. I tried to stand and rip off the bearskin but fell over into a thornbush. The trainer called out a command, and the dogs froze and stood near me, drooling.

I'm lying there full of thorns and bleeding from a gash where I'd landed on a rock. Milius was not sympathetic. "Now you know what the film is going to be like," he said. "This is what Conan went through!" I went off to get stitches, and when I saw him later at lunch, the director was in a great mood. "We got the shot. We're off to a great start," he said. The next day I ended up needing more stitches after I cut my forehead leaping into a rocky pool. When Milius saw the blood running, he said, "Who did that makeup? It's terrific. Looks like real blood." He refused to think about what would have happened to the production if I'd been crippled or killed. But of course there was no stunt double because it would have been very difficult to find anyone who had a body like mine.

The rest of the week was devoted to an elaborate action sequence from much later in the plot. In our warehouse outside Madrid, the crews had constructed the Orgy Chamber of Thulsa Doom's mountain temple. From the outside, the warehouse was a big, drab two-story building made of corrugated steel and surrounded by a dusty parking lot, tents, and a crude sign that said "Conan" in red paint. But inside, after you wended your way through the makeup, costume, and prop departments, you were transported into the debauched splendor of the sorcerer's cannibalistic snake cult. The Orgy Chamber was a high-ceilinged hall with marble terraces and staircases lit by torchlight and draped in beautiful satin and silk, with a dozen naked women and their consorts sprawled on thick cushions in a central pit, dozing and reveling. In the center of the pit rose a pink and gray twelve-foot marble pillar with four giant snake heads carved on top. The feast was being served by attendants from a bubbling cauldron in which you could see severed hands and other body parts.

The script called for Conan, Valeria, and Subotai to burst in on this orgy, slay the guards, and seize the wayward princess who had fallen under Thulsa Doom's spell. The guards, of course, were supposed to be subhuman thugs, some of them wearing reptile masks, and I was stripped to the waist with my face and torso painted in fearsome black camouflage stripes that looked like lightning bolts. Sandahl and Jerry were painted in stripes too. It felt fantastic putting our weapons training into action, and Milius was pleased as we worked our way through dozens of shots.

Movie sets are noisy places between takes, with people talking, equipment clattering, and crews bustling around. On the fourth morning, we were getting ready for a shot in Thulsa Doom's private alcove, carved high in the wall of the Orgy Chamber, when somebody said, "Dino is here," and I heard the commotion suddenly stop. I looked down the broad sweep of stairs, and there, in the pit, amid all the naked girls, was our legendary producer making his first appearance on the set. De Laurentiis was immaculately groomed, wearing the most elegant suit with a beautiful cashmere overcoat, which, being Italian, he draped over his shoulders like a cape.

He stood surveying the whole scene and then climbed up the steps to where we stood. Maybe there were twenty steps, but to me it seemed like a hundred, because it took a long time. I just watched him come closer and closer, with those naked women in the background. Finally he reached the top and walked right to me.

"Schwarzenegger," he said, "*you are Conan.*" And he made a snappy turn and walked back down and off the set.

Milius had been near the camera, and the microphones were on. He came over to me. "I heard that," he said. "You realize that's the greatest compliment you're ever gonna get from this guy? This morning he watched the three days of film we've shot, and now he's a believer."

I felt this was Dino's way of telling me I was off the hook for calling him short four years ago. From that point on, he would come to Spain once a month or so and invite me to his hotel for coffee. Slowly, we warmed to each other.

Dino delegated the actual nuts and bolts of producing *Conan* to his daughter Raffaella and to Buzz Feitshans, who'd worked with Milius on earlier films. Raffaella was a pistol: she was his middle daughter with the Italian actress Silvana Mangano, and she'd known she wanted to be a producer from the time she was a kid. Even though Raffaella was only Maria's age, Dino had been teaching her the ropes for ten years, and this was already her second major feature.

I'd learned enough about movie production by now to be impressed with the job that she and Buzz did. They really had to scramble to find a country to shoot in after the Yugoslavia plan fell through. Every country has a film commission, and typically, when you produce a film, you start by calling and saying, "We want to make this movie in your country. What can you do for us?" In the case of *Conan*, Spain jumped at the chance. The commission told Raffaella and Buzz, "First, we have a great warehouse you can make into a studio. There's running water, flush toilets, and showers. There's room for the generators you're going to need. We have an extra warehouse you can also rent, plus an empty hangar on an air force base. We have a luxury apartment complex in Madrid that's perfect for the actors and senior crew. It's attached to a five-star hotel, so you'll have restaurants and room service always available. There's room for your production offices too, right around the corner."

All that carried a certain price tag. *Conan* was a complicated project, so Buzz, Raffaella, the designer, the location scout, and others on the production team had to factor in a thousand other items. How many horses would we need, and how many stunt riders? Were they available in Spain, or would they have to be brought in from Italy or other places? Did Spain have the right kinds of desert, mountain, and seaside locations? Could we get permission to shoot there? What about historic ruins? And, of course, Raffaella and Buzz wanted to stay within the budget, so they were constantly looking for deals.

They sized up other countries too, and within a remarkably short time, they were able to come back to the studio with a rundown. "In Spain, we can shoot the movie for eighteen million," they said. "In Italy, it will cost us thirty-two million. Or we can do it in Las Vegas and build the sets in the Nevada desert, and it will cost even more. Or we can do it on soundstages in LA, and it will cost even more."

The choice was the same as always in modern movie production: between countries with an established moviemaking industry and labor unions, like Italy, and entrepreneurial, nonunionized countries like Spain. Unions or not, Dino had a reputation for getting things done. When he wanted to shoot sixteen hours a day, he shot sixteen hours a day. He was very powerful in that way, and people in Hollywood knew it and didn't mess with him. If the studios wanted a movie done for a certain price, they worked with him. In this case, he backed Raffaella and Buzz when they picked Spain. "We'll have to build the whole thing in a warehouse," they told the studio, "but it's still much cheaper than using real soundstages where labor can hold us up." We definitely had no labor problems on *Conan*. Everyone worked together. If a shot needed to be changed quickly, everyone lifted lights and moved things around.

In fact, Spain was a great place to shoot in every way, with one little exception: the stunt guys took too long to die. Milius would tell them over and over, "When he cuts you, just drop." Instead, they would fall theatrically, get partway back up, fall down again, gasp—this was their moment, and they were going to play it to the hilt. I'd be busy slaying my next opponent when I'd hear Milius shout to the guy behind me, "You're dead! Stay down! He cut you, don't move!" But they were like zombies. Finally Milius offered to pay them extra if they died immediately and *stayed* dead.

These were the kinds of things they don't teach you no matter how many years you go to acting class. For all the talk about sense memory and getting into character, no one prepares you for what to do when the wind machine is blowing snow in your face and you're freezing your ass off. Or when somebody's holding a measuring tape up to your nose to mark the focus on a shot. Then how do you do all this sense-memory shit? All that stuff about being in the moment goes out the window.

There's a whole production going on while you're trying to act. You have to deal with the distractions of 150 people on the set working and talking. The lighting guy is putting up ladders in front of you and saying, "Can you move? I don't want to drop a lamp on you." The soundman is fooling around with your waistband to put on a battery pack. The boom guy is shouting at the camera guy to get out of the way. The set designer is saying, "I need more plants in the background, guys." The director is trying to coordinate. The producer is screaming, "In five minutes we have to get lunch! If you want the shot, get it now!"

Then the director says, "Arnold, look your opponent in the eye. Head straight up. Dominate this scene." This sounds good: we've worked on that in acting class. Except what if he has put you on a horse that's very lively? The horse is spinning and rearing up. How do you look dominant when you're scared that the horse will go nuts and throw you off? So you have to stop and rehearse with the horse. Under those circumstances, how do you act real?

I'd never done a love scene on camera and found it really strange. A closed set means that you can't bring guests, but you still have endless people looking on: the script supervisor, the lighting techs, the camera assists. And you're naked. No one in acting class ever talks about what to do in a nude scene when you really get excited. In sex, one thing leads naturally to another. It can be embarrassing. They say you should stay in character, but that's not really what they want, trust me. All you can do is try to think about something else.

Even though the set was supposedly closed, the sex scenes seemed to have a magnetic effect. After Conan escapes from the wolves, he is seduced by a witch who puts him on the trail of Thulsa Doom. Cassandra Gava, who was playing the witch, and I were rolling around naked in front of a roaring fire in the witch's stone hut. Out of the corner of my eye, I noticed the walls of the hut move. A little gap opened in the corner, and I could see a pair of eyes glinting in the firelight.

"Cut!" Milius called. "Arnold, where you looking at?"

"Well, actually," I said, "it's the funniest thing. I saw that corner of the room move apart, and I think I saw eyes peeking through." A guy ran behind the set, and we heard voices. Then Raffaella came out looking totally sheepish. She said, "I'm sorry, but I just had to peek!"

Conan's true love in the film is Valeria. Sandahl Bergman had never done love scenes either and felt just as awkward as I did. I was somehow supposed to be this weird combination of a barbarian and a gentleman, but not too much of either. It was hard to get in the mood because you don't have a chance to practice with your costar; you just have to start mechanical and cold. On top of all that, Sandahl and Terry Leonard the stunt chief had fallen in love, and I was intensely aware that he was standing by probably ready to rip off my head. Meanwhile, Milius was working hard to avoid the censors, saying things like, "Arnold, can you move your behind so it's in that shadow there? And make sure you hide her breasts with your arm, because we can't have nipples in the shot."

The action scenes had perils of their own. Conan lives in a world of constant danger. You never know what's going to attack you in the fantasy world. It could be a snake one day and a wolf-witch the next. When shooting such scenes, I had to be on my toes.

Doing battle with a giant mechanical snake left me sore for a week. The sequence was in the middle of the movie, where Conan and his allies sneak into the Tower of the Serpent and steal some of the cult's precious jewels. We were supposed to climb the tower (actually a forty-foot-high set built in the abandoned air force hangar) and then lower ourselves into a dungeon ankle deep in garbage and the bones of sacrificial virgins. The snake, thirty-six feet long and two and a half feet wide, was a replica of some kind of boa constrictor, operated remotely and animated with steel cables and hydraulic pumps capable of exerting nine tons of force. It turned out to be pretty hard to control, and the operator hadn't practiced enough. One time it coiled around me and started slamming me against the dungeon wall. I was yelling to him to ease up. In the script, Conan kills the snake, of course: Subotai crawls out of a tunnel to find his buddy in danger and tosses him a broadsword, which Conan, in a single, swift motion, catches by the hilt and chops into the snake. I had to grab the heavy sword and strike a precise point behind the snake's head to trigger the exploding blood pack. Conan, of course, has to be totally confident as he does all this. But part of me was thinking "I hope this goes well." I'm proud to say that two and a half years of training paid off, and I nailed it in the first take.

James Earl Jones was late joining the production because he had to wrap up his commitment on Broadway, but after he arrived, we quickly became friends. By mid-March, when the production moved from Madrid to Almería to film the battle scenes and the climactic confrontation at Doom's mountain citadel, I spent days hanging out in his trailer. He wanted to keep in shape, so I helped him with his training, and in return, he coached me on my acting. With his powerful bass voice, James was a wonderful Shakespearean actor, and he'd won both a Tony Award and an Oscar nomination for his performances in *The Great White Hope,* a drama about racism and boxing. (His character was based on Jack Johnson, the World Heavyweight Champion from 1908 to 1915.) Lately he'd become internationally known as the *Star Wars* villain Darth Vader. He told me the amazing story of how he'd gotten into acting. As a kid in Mississippi, James had such a serious stutter that from the time he started school at age five until he was fourteen, he refused to talk. The schools classified him as functionally mute. Then in high school he fell in love with literature and felt a desire to read great works aloud. His English teacher encouraged him, "If you like the words, you've got to be able to learn to say them."

Milius wanted me to add a half page of dialogue that he'd written during the shooting. It was in the quiet before the climactic battle at the Mounds, a Stonehenge-like ancient burial ground of warriors and kings by the sea. Conan and his allies have fortified the monument and are waiting to be attacked by Thulsa Doom and a large troop of savage henchmen on horseback. Thulsa Doom has already killed Valeria, and Conan and his friends are greatly outnumbered and expect to die. So before the battle, Conan is sitting on a hillside with his chin on his fist, looking at the sea and the beautiful blue sky and thinking melancholy thoughts. "I remember days like this when my father took me to the forest and we ate wild blueberries," he says to Subotai. "More than twenty years ago. I was just a boy of four or five. The leaves were so dark and green then. The grass smelled sweet with the spring wind.

"Almost twenty years of pitiless cumber! No rest, no sleep like other men. And yet the spring wind blows, Subotai. Have you ever felt such a wind?" (*Cumber* means "burdens.")

"They blow where I live too," says Subotai. "In the north of every man's heart."

Conan offers his friend the chance to leave and go home. "It's never too late, Subotai."

"No. It would only lead me back here another day. In even worse company."

"For us, there is no spring," Conan says grimly. "Just the wind that smells fresh before the storm."

I'd practiced these lines dozens of times, as I always did before a shoot. But I told Milius, "It doesn't feel natural to me. It doesn't feel like I'm really, you know, searching and seeing it." You can't just recite a monologue like that. It truly has to seem like you are thinking about an earlier time, the memories are coming to you, ideas are popping into your head. In some moments you say things in a rush, and in other moments you just stare. The question was how to create that naturalness.

Milius said, "Why don't you ask Earl? He does this onstage where the pressure's even higher because you can't edit out the mistakes."

So I went to James Earl's trailer and asked if he would mind taking a look at the dialogue.

"No, no, absolutely. Sit down," he said. "Let's look at that." He read it and asked me to deliver the lines.

When I finished, he nodded and said, "Well, what I would do is have this retyped two ways. Do it once so the lines are really narrow and go down the entire length of the page. And the second time do it with the paper turned sideways, so that you have the widest lines possible." He explained that I'd practiced so much that I'd unconsciously memorized the line breaks. So each time I hit one, it came across as a break in thought. "You need to throw off that rhythm," he explained.

Seeing the lines retyped made me hear them in a different way, which helped tremendously. I came back later in the day, and we dissected and rehearsed the dialogue line by line. "Well, normally after a sentence like this you would pause, because that's a pretty heavy thought," he'd say. And, "Here maybe you want to shift position a little bit. Whatever comes to mind, whether it's a stretch or a shake of the head or just a pause. But you shouldn't program yourself," he stressed, "because it could be different from one take to the next, unless John tells you that'll cause a problem with editing. But usually they only keep a shot until the thought changes, and then they'll go to another angle."

Max Von Sydow was generous and helpful too. It was great being able to watch two great stage actors rehearse and fine-tune until they got it right. Working with professionals, you learn a lot of nuances. I realized, for example, that actors often shift gears when the director moves from a master shot, to a medium shot, to a close-up shot, to a micro-shot (which captures, say, the eyes wincing). Some actors pay very little attention to the master shot because they know this is just to establish where they are physically in the scene. Therefore, they don't overexert themselves. But the closer the shot, the more they perform. You realize how important it is to pace yourself: don't go all out on the first takes; give just 80 percent. Eventually your close-up will come, and that's when you really need to act. I figured out that this was also a way to get more close-ups of yourself into the film, because the editing will often pick the shot with the best performance.

Making *Conan* brought back memories of the wild summers with my Austrian buddies pretending that we were gladiators on the shores of the Thalersee. Here it was Milius's fantasy that set the pace. Before we shot a scene, he'd tell endless stories from history, about how barbarians ate, how they fought, how they rode, their religions, and their cruelties.

For the orgy sequence, he talked about the decadence of ancient Rome, the women, the nudity, the sex, the violence, the intrigues, the feasts. Around us he had the best weapons experts, the best horse people, the best designers, wardrobe, and makeup people, all to draw us into the *Conan* world.

I loved the immersion of being on location: sharing the Apartamentos Villa Magna with the other actors, driving from there to the warehouse, learning a whole new way of functioning for six months. I'd never filmed in a foreign country before. I picked up a lot of Spanish because very few people on the set spoke English. At first the work was too intense for me to allow myself to do anything but train, rehearse, and shoot. But after a month or two, I started to relax. I realized, "Wait a minute. I'm in Madrid! Let's go see some museums, let's go see interesting architecture, buildings, and streets. Let's try some of the restaurants everyone talks about and have dinner at eleven at night like the Spaniards." We discovered boot makers, leather makers, and tailors, and started buying uniquely Spanish things like ornate silver ashtrays and beautifully tooled leather belts.

Working for Milius was a constant adventure. I had to tear apart a vulture with my teeth, for example. This was in the scene where Conan's enemies crucify him in the desert upon the Tree of Woe. The tree was a huge outdoor prop built on a rotating base so that the angles of the sun and shadows would stay constant. As Conan nears death in the boiling heat, vultures circle and gather on the branches, and when one lands to try to feed on his face, I bite its neck and rip it apart with my teeth. Naturally, with Milius the birds on the branches were real—they were trained, yes, but still vultures, with lice all over them. During the three days we needed to shoot the scene, the vultures were taken into a tent every hour to rest while I stayed out on the hot tree with five new vultures. The bird I tore apart was an animated prop made of dead vulture parts. I had to rinse out my mouth and wash my skin with an antibiotic afterward.

We also had to contend with camels. I'd never been around a camel, much less ridden one, but the script demanded exactly that. A week before we were due to shoot the scene, I told myself, "You'd better make friends with the camel and figure this out." I discovered quickly that they're very different from horses. They get up on their back feet first and throw you forward. And you can't just tug on the reins as you would with a horse, because if you do, the camel will turn its head 180 degrees until it's face to face with you. It might spit in your eye, and if it does, the saliva is so caustic that you need a doctor. And camels bite—usually the back of your head, just when you've forgotten they're around.

In addition to the mechanical snake that had its way with me, I had to contend with real snakes too. They were some sort of water snake, and their handler worried that they were getting dehydrated. So he put them in the apartment house swimming pool. In the United States, the department of health or animal welfare would have been there in two seconds, and also the water would have been full of chlorine, which wouldn't have been good for the snakes' skin. But in Spain and around Milius, these kinds of things happened all the time.

Milius always pushed the envelope. Environmentalists complained that our sets disrupted the salt marshes, and the producers had to promise to restore the sites. Animal-protection advocates complained because *Conan* included scenes in which a dog gets kicked, a camel gets punched (by me, but it was just a fake punch), and horses get tripped. None of that would have been allowed in the United States. The production had excellent stunt riders who knew how to turn the horse during a fall so that it would roll and not break its neck, but even so, those stunts were dangerous for both the horses and the people; I saw many bruises and cuts and split heads. Such stunts have since been outlawed from movies.

Even so, the bloodshed in *Conan* seems tame by today's standards. At the time, however, the film introduced a whole new dimension of violence on screen. Up until then, swordfights had always been a little too tidy: characters would crumple to the ground, and maybe you'd see a little blood. But Milius was strapping five-quart blood packs on actors' chests. Five quarts is about as much blood as you have in your entire body. When a battle-axe struck one of those packs, blood flew everywhere. And anytime blood was being spilled, he was insistent about making sure it was against a light background so that you could really see the carnage.

Milius didn't think he needed to apologize for this. "It's Conan *the barbarian*. What do you expect?" he told reporters. But after the shooting wrapped in May and we came home, the issue continued to percolate. The decision makers at Universal were worried that advance word of excessive violence would drive away viewers.

At that point, they were considering *Conan* for a November or December holiday release. That was until Sid Sheinberg, the president of Universal, who was famous for discovering director Steven Spielberg, saw a rough cut in August. He watched me hacking people apart, blood everywhere, and halfway through the screening, he stood up and said to the other executives sarcastically, "Merry Christmas, guys," and walked out. So *Conan* was pushed back: Universal's Christmas 1981 releases were *On Golden Pond*, the family drama starring Henry Fonda, Jane Fonda, and Katharine Hepburn, and a horror flick.

We all knew that *Conan* would be controversial, and the puzzle was how to market it and present it to the media. I watched Milius give some of the early interviews, drawing reporters into the macho fantasy. One of his big talking points was Friedrich Nietzsche; the epigraph at the beginning of *Conan,* "That which does not kill us makes us stronger," is paraphrased from the German philosopher's 1889 book *Twilight of the Idols*. The other big talking point was steel. "Steel gets harder and more durable the more you pound it," John would tell the reporters. "It's no different than the character of a human being. It needs to be tempered. It needs to overcome resistance. The more a man struggles, the stronger he is. Look at people who come from war-torn countries or tough city neighborhoods. You can see the struggle in their faces. A makeup artist can't do that. And that's what makes Conan the fiercest and most powerful warrior, what he went through as a child. Luxuries and comforts are evil for humans." For Milius, *Conan* was making a statement that went way beyond action movies and comic books. It all tied back to Nietzsche.

He'd show the reporters one of his samurai swords and say, "You know, a samurai sword is heated and pounded on an anvil seven times so that it has the necessary strength. The samurai warriors would practice on criminals. They'd take them out and make them stand and cut off the head with a single swing." He would act out this whole drama as the reporters took notes. And I would be thinking, "How does he come up with this shit?" My approach was much more direct. I sold the entertainment aspect, the joy of *Conan* as a fun ride and epic adventure, like a *Star Wars* set on earth.

To promote the movie, it was important to work every possible angle. We used special-interest magazines to build an audience—stories on sword fighting for the martial-arts magazines. Stories for horse magazines. Stories for fantasy magazines that were into swords and sorcery. Stories for bodybuilding magazines on how you needed top conditioning to be Conan.

The movie, of course, needed a rating before it could be released. I was really annoyed by the way that powerful studio executives kowtowed to the members of the ratings board. The board was made up of Motion Picture Association of America appointees whose names were never even publicly announced. Most were middle-aged people with grown kids, but they reacted to *Conan* like a bunch of old ladies: "Oh, ah, ah, the blood! I've got to close my eyes!" The word came down that we had to edit out some of the gore.

I said to myself, "Where did they get these squeamish idiots? Let's have some young, hip people rate it." I asked one of the studio guys, "Who is in charge of this? There must be someone in charge. Why don't you go and get them fired?"

"No, no, no, no," he said. "You don't want to rock that boat."

No one was willing to fight back on anything.

I didn't understand there was a chess game being played. Universal had in the works Spielberg's *E.T.*, which the studio was counting on as its summer blockbuster of 1982. It didn't want to do anything to antagonize the raters. It wanted to be loved, it wanted Spielberg to be loved, it wanted *E.T.* to be loved. So then here come Milius and Schwarzenegger, slaughtering all these people on the screen. Milius is already Hollywood's bad boy, with his right-wing Republicanism and his reputation for saying outrageous things. And, of course, the studio is ready to say, "Let's cut those *Conan* scenes right now, so that when we bring *E.T.* to the rating board next week, we don't get crucified," even though there was no harm in *E.T.* at all.

I was mad as hell because I felt that every one of the killings in *Conan* was well shot and extraordinary. So what if the first thing you see is Thulsa Doom raiding Conan's boyhood village and that his mother's head goes flying through the air? You could say we needed that scene to make Thulsa Doom the ultimate villain, so that when Conan hunts him down, it's justified. But you fall in love with your own work. In hindsight, I think that making us tone down the violence helped bring more people to the film.

This was my first experience with large-scale studio marketing. A media tour was being planned to promote Conan internationally. In the first meeting I went to, the marketers said, "We're going to Italy and France."

"Okaaay," I said, "but if you look at the globe, there are more countries than Italy and France." Being European, I was very conscious that there was a whole world out there besides the United States. In the early 1980s, movie grosses were two thirds domestic and one third international, but you could see it starting to shift. If you didn't promote internationally, who knew how much money you left lying on the table?

I said, "Guys, why don't we be more systematic? Spend two days in Paris, two days in London, two days in Madrid, two days in Rome, and then go up north. Then say that we go to Copenhagen, and then to Stockholm, and then down to Berlin. What's wrong with that?"

When people come to me with a movie concept or a script, I always ask, "What is the poster? What is the image? What are we trying to sell here?"

Michael Ochs Archives / Getty Images

I starred in *Hercules in New York* in 1969, but the producer went broke before the movie could be released. Seven years later I got a supporting part in director Bob Rafelson's *Stay Hungry*, for which I won a Golden Globe (that's Raquel Welch I'm hoisting in celebration). Jeff Bridges, who starred, was generous with acting tips.

Frank Edwards / Getty Images

Courtesy of MGM Media Licensing

When we promoted *Pumping Iron* at the Cannes Film Festival in 1977, George Butler had the idea of dressing cabaret girls from the Crazy Horse in Paris in frilly dresses and bonnets to pose with me on the beach. *Keystone / Getty Images*

I jumped at the chance to work with Kirk Douglas and Ann-Margret in the Western spoof *The Villain*. The name of my character was "Handsome Stranger."

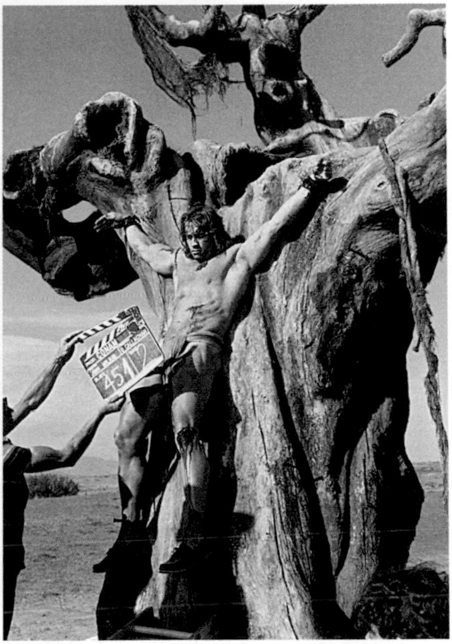

On the set of *Conan the Barbarian* in Spain we created a vivid and violent prehistoric world. Above left, the fighting pit in which young Conan slaughters his way out of slavery. Above right, I broiled in the hot sun while I was crucified on the Tree of Woe. Right, director John Milius, who loved stogies as much as me, was fanatical that the fantasy be accurate in every detail.

Courtesy of Universal Studios Licensing, LLC

In 1983, before heading to Mexico to shoot *Conan the Destroyer*, I celebrated becoming a U.S. citizen. *Michael Montfort / interTOPICS*

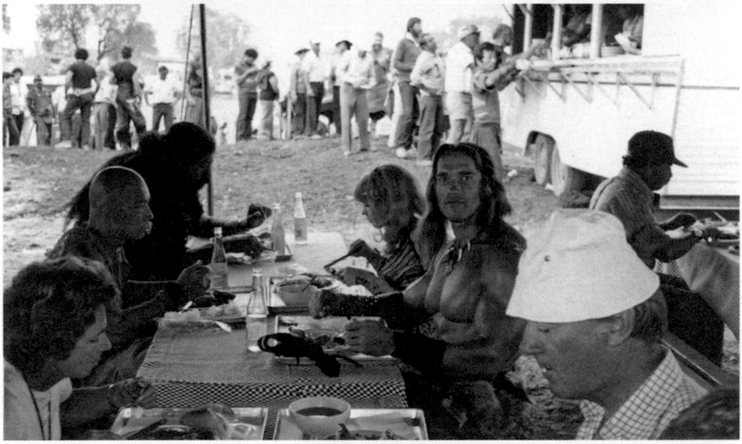

Why eat all alone in your personal trailer when you can hang out with the crew and cast? Above, it's chowtime on location in Mexico for *Conan the Destroyer*. Right, Wilt Chamberlain, who played the treacherous Bombaata, and André the Giant, who played the evil beast god Dagoth, give me the unusual sensation of being the little guy. *Courtesy of Universal Studios Licensing, LLC*

As the Terminator, I worked on selling the idea that I was a machine that can't be bargained with, can't be reasoned with, doesn't feel pity, remorse, or fear, and will not stop, ever, until its target is dead.
Courtesy of MGM Media Licensing

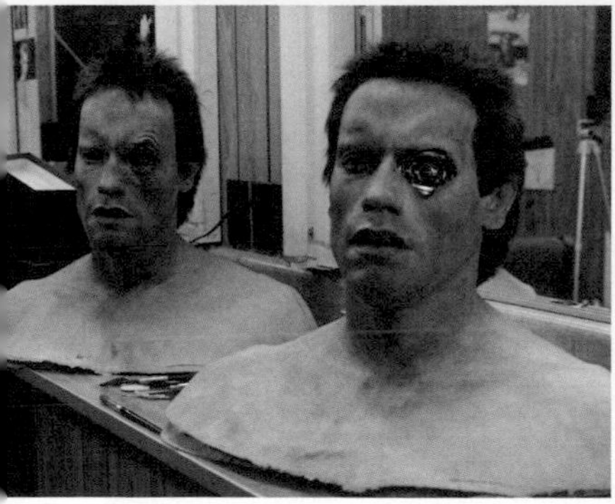

The scene in the makeup trailer is sometimes even weirder than what shows up onscreen. Here, preparations for the Terminator's do-it-yourself forearm and eyeball repairs.
Schwarzenegger Archive

I visited the Vatican with Maria and her parents in 1983 for a private audience with Pope John Paul II. To him, besides religion, life was about taking care of both your mind and your body. So we talked about his workouts. *Schwarzenegger Archive*

Right: After the sacrifices she'd made to raise my brother and me, I wanted my mother to have a rich life. Here I've brought her to meet President Reagan at a state dinner at the White House in 1986. *Official White House photo*

Below: Milton Berle became my comedy mentor. He'd encourage me by saying, "You being funny with your accent is twice as big a deal as me being funny. They *expect* me to be funny!" *Schwarzenegger Archive*

The great Nazi hunter Simon Wiesenthal himself helped me force a retraction when a London tabloid called me a neo-Nazi in 1988.
Art Waldinger / Tru-Dimension Co.

I helped Vice President George Herbert Walker Bush in his successful bid for the presidency in 1988. Here we prepare speeches between campaign stops aboard Air Force Two.
Official White House photo

Economist Milton Friedman, whom I got to know in his retirement, had a profound influence on my political philosophy.
George T. Kruse

It took just five years after the premiere of *Conan the Barbarian* for me to earn the ultimate Hollywood validation, a star on the Walk of Fame.
Michael Montfort / interTOPICS

My political mentor, Fredi Gerstl, is a Jew who joined the resistance in World War II and ended up president of the Austrian parliament.
Schwarzenegger Archive

Less than forty-eight hours before Maria and I were due to be married in Hyannis Port, Massachusetts, I was covered with mud in a Mexican jungle shooting *Predator*.
© 1987 Twentieth Century Fox. All rights reserved.

Danny DeVito is a master of comedy, loves stogies, and cooks pasta on the set—no wonder he made such a great twin.
Schwarzenegger Archive

Paul Verhoeven directs Sharon Stone and me for the scene in *Total Recall* in which my character loses his illusions about his marriage.
StudioCanal

Director Ivan Reitman took a chance on me as a comic hero. Here we clown around with cotton candy on the set of *Kindergarten Cop*.
Courtesy of Universal Studios Licensing, LLC

Arnold - Turn, damn it, Turn !!
All Best
Camp David
Jan 13, 1991
Geo Bush

Tobogganing at Camp David, President George H. W. Bush and I are about to crash into the First Lady. His inscription on the photo reads in part, "Turn, damn it, turn!!"
Official White House photo

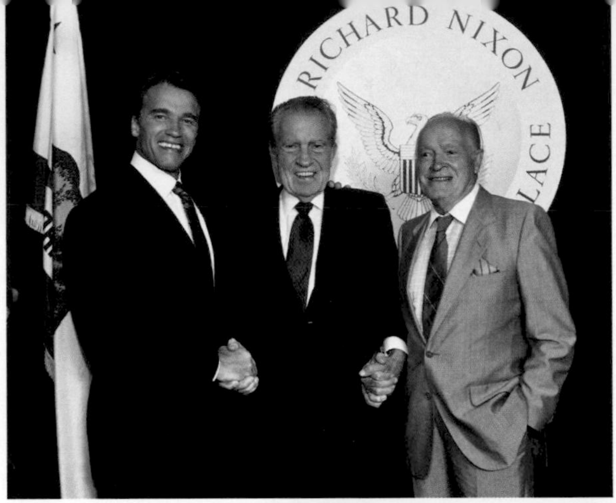

President Nixon put me on the spot to speak at a holiday exhibit opening at his presidential library—afterward, with him and comedian Bob Hope, I was feeling relieved. *Ron P. Jaffe / The Nixon Foundation*

Sly Stallone, Bruce Willis, and I had great fun opening Planet Hollywood restaurants around the world. This opening was in London. *Dave Benett / Getty Images*

My character and his stolen Harley were a perfect combination of cyborg and machine in *Terminator 2: Judgment Day*. StudioCanal

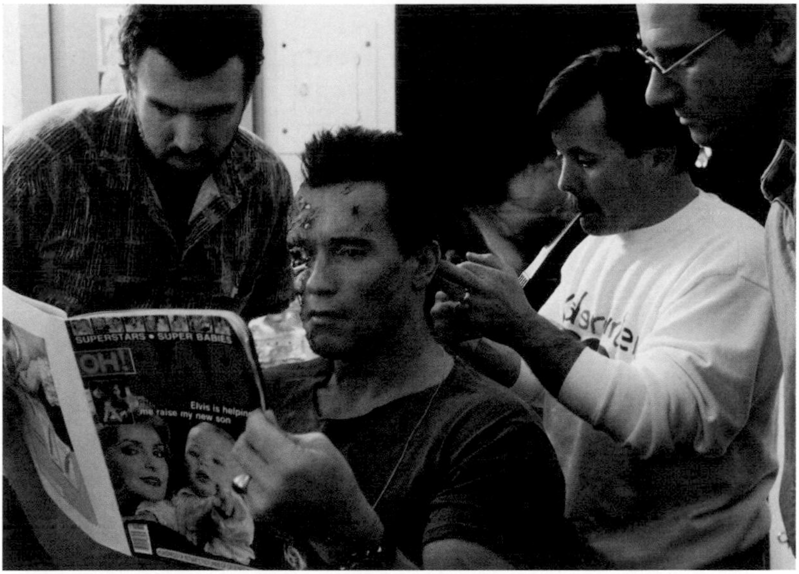

In the makeup trailer on the set of *Terminator 2*, I'm boning up on real life—our daughter Katherine was turning one and another baby was on the way. *StudioCanal*

Sometimes it's hard to explain to your toddler what you do at the office. Katherine was freaked out by the Terminator mannequin at the studio of special effects wizard Stan Winston. *Schwarzenegger Archive*

Clint Eastwood, one of my heroes, described a shot to me when I visited the set of *In the Line of Fire* in 1993.

Maria and I turned the making of *True Lies* in 1993 into a family adventure. Patrick was a newborn, Christina was two, and Katherine almost four.

Jim Cameron shows how he wants my character Harry Tasker to fight his way out of a terrorist camp, on location in the Florida Keys. Jamie Lee Curtis (below) was Helen, my onscreen wife.

I've been retired from bodybuilding since 1980 but I'll always stay involved. Here I'm celebrating the winners of the 1994 Arnold Classic, Kevin Levrone and Laura Creavalle.

Schwarzenegger Archive

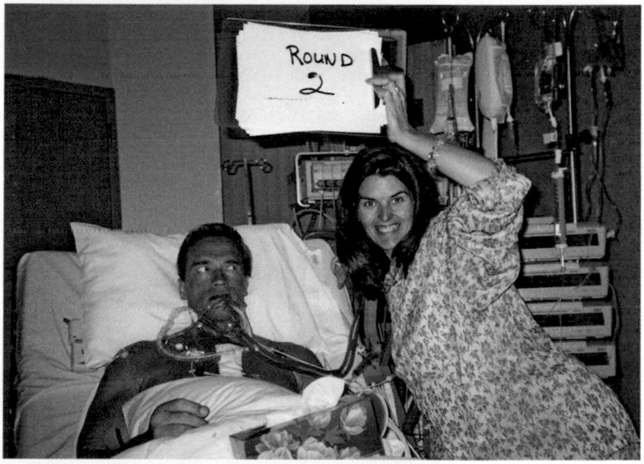

Maria puts a brave face on a scary situation. Open-heart surgery in 1997 to replace a defective valve failed on the first try; the next day the doctors had to open me up again.

Schwarzenegger Archive

Muhammad Ali and I had been friends for over twenty years when we teamed up in 2000 to raise funds for the Inner City Games Foundation and the Muhammad Ali Center.

Herb Ritts / trunkarchive.com

Christina, six, climbed up for a friendly Daddy-daughter chat while I was crucified for *End of Days*, a turn-of-the-millennium thriller. Below, Christopher, one, and Patrick, four, also visited the set. *Courtesy of Universal Licensing, LLC*

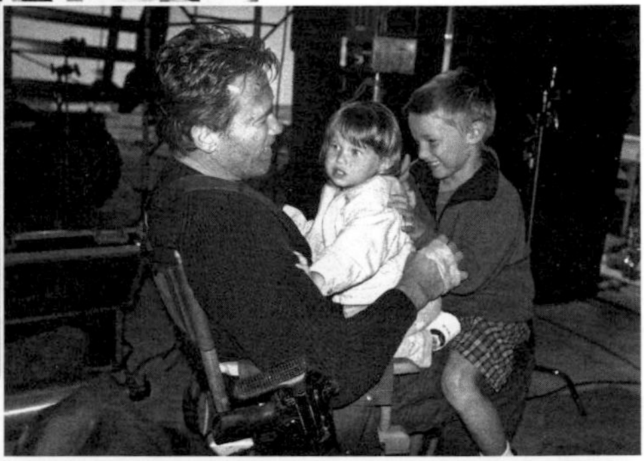

I loved working with Danny Hernandez, on my left, the ex-Marine who masterminded the Hollenbeck Youth Center in East LA. It provides kids in a poor, gang-infested neighborhood with a place to go and gives problem kids a second chance. *Schwarzenegger Archive*

I get goose bumps when Nelson Mandela talks about inclusion, tolerance, and forgiveness. In 2001 we met at Robben Island, where he spent twenty-seven years in prison, to light the Flame of Hope for the Special Olympics African Hope Games. *Christian Jauschowetz*

My first political campaign was crusading in 2002 to pass a ballot initiative to set up after-school programs at every elementary and middle school in California. *Frazer Harrison / Getty Images*

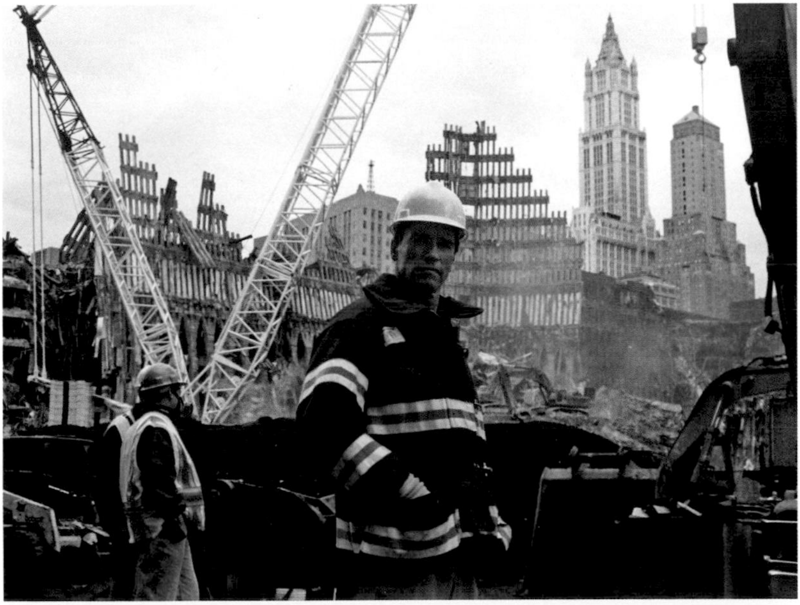

At the request of New York City mayor Rudy Giuliani, I toured Ground Zero three days after 9/11 to thank the first responders and help boost morale. *FDNY Photo Unit*

Former President Bill Clinton loved visiting movie sets. On his way to a speech in 2003, he stopped by the set of *Terminator 3*. *Robert Zuckerman*

In 2010, during my last year as governor, the state partnered with environmentalists and preservationists to set aside the land around the iconic Hollywood sign. *California State Archives / Peter Grigsby*

As soon as I left the statehouse, I went back to work on the movie set. Right, I'm on location with Sly and Bruce in Bulgaria, where we filmed *Expendables 2*. *Frank Masi / Millennium Films*

Below, I'm duking it out on top of a truck in *The Last Stand*. *Courtesy of Lionsgate*

"Well, that's not the way we do things. You know the movie is released on different dates in different countries, and we don't want to give interviews too far in advance."

"So what about working out a deal with the magazines and newspapers in those countries to hold their stories until the release date?"

"We'd have to check that out."

I knew another reason for their reluctance to send me on a PR tour was that very few actors like to sell. I'd seen the same thing with authors in the book business. The typical attitude seemed to be, "I don't want to be a whore. I create; I don't want to shill. I'm not into the money thing at all."

It was a real change when I showed up saying, "Let's go everywhere, because this is good not only for me financially but also good for the public; they get to see a good movie!" Eventually the studio agreed to have me promote Conan in five or six countries. I felt that was a big stcp forward.

It was the same debate I'd had with my publisher when my book *Arnold: The Education of a Bodybuilder* came out. The United States accounts for only 5 percent of the world's population, so why would you ignore the other 95 percent? Both industries were shortchanging themselves. I'd learned from Joe Weider always to think of the global market.

I saw myself as a businessman first. Too many actors, writers, and artists think that marketing is beneath them. But no matter what you do in life, selling is part of it. You can't make movies without money. Even if I had no publicity obligation in my contract, it was still in my interest to promote the movie and make sure it made as much money as possible. I wanted to be involved in the meetings. I wanted everyone to see that I was working very hard to create a return on the studio's investment. I felt it was my responsibility to pump up the grosses.

Conan's breakthrough came just after Valentine's Day 1982. The first test screening, in Houston, was such a success that Universal couldn't believe the data: viewers rated the movie a 93 on a scale of 1 to 100, which almost always signals a major hit. The studio telephoned that night and said, "This is huge. We want to try it again in Las Vegas tomorrow. If we do that, can you come?" Driving past the cineplex the next afternoon, we could see this was no ordinary screening. A line stretched around the block, and besides the comic book fans that Universal had expected, there were bodybuilders with tight shirts and bulging muscles, gays, freaks with weird hair and glasses, people wearing Conan outfits. There were some women but the crowd seemed to be mostly men, including a major contingent of bikers in full leather. Some of those guys looked ready to riot if they didn't get in. Universal simply kept opening auditoriums until everybody was seated—it took three to accommodate them all.

The studio had been banking on die-hard fans of *Conan* in the comics and fantasy novels to make the movie a success. They were supposed to become the core audience; the people who, if they like a movie, will see it several times and tell all their friends. What Universal didn't count on was my guys: the bodybuilders. They made up probably a third of the audience that night—and you can imagine the test scores they gave Conan. Without them, the film might have gotten maybe an 88, but with them, it was again 93, just like in Houston. The studio was very excited. And Dino De Laurentiis was flipping. He came over to me that night and said, "I make you a star." With his accent, I wasn't sure whether he meant that he intended to make me a star or that he already had. But this time I didn't tease him about it.

After that night, *Conan* was unstoppable. A month later, sneak previews in sixteen cities across the country drew overflow crowds. The cops had to be called in Manhattan because people on line were literally fighting to get in; in Washington, DC, the line went for blocks and caused a major traffic jam; in LA, they did three showings back to back instead of the one they had planned—some people waited in line eight hours.

News write-ups in the trade press after the screenings helped us get placement in hundreds of theaters. When *Conan* opened nationwide on May 14, it became the first blockbuster of what is still talked about as the best movie summer ever. That summer also brought us *The Road Warrior, Rocky III, Star Trek II: The Wrath of Khan, Blade Runner, Fast Times at Ridgemont High, The World According to Garp, Poltergeist, An Officer and a Gentleman, Tron, The Thing,* and, of course, *E.T. Conan the Barbarian* held its own among them all.

CHAPTER 15

Becoming American

BACK IN SANTA MONICA, Maria welcomed me home from Madrid and the Hyborian Age by giving me a little Labrador puppy she had named Conan.

"You know why she gave you the dog, don't you?" one of her friends teased me.

"Because her family is always into dogs?" I said.

"It's an audition! She wants to see how you'd handle children."

I didn't know about that, but Conan and I—that is, Conan the Canine and Conan the Barbarian—got along very well. I was happy to be back in our house, too, which was totally transformed by the décor that Maria and I had started on together.

The other big change during my absence was the January inauguration of Ronald Reagan. Nobody in Hollywood seemed to know what to make of the fact that he was president, not even the conservatives. Just after his election, Maria and I had dinner with friends of mine from the entertainment business who had worked on his campaign.

"Why did you push this guy?" she asked. "He's not presidential material. Jeez, guys, he's an actor!"

Instead of defending Reagan, they said things like, "We know, but people like listening to him." They didn't talk about what he'd done for California while he was governor or about his vision or his ideas. Probably they were just being polite. They didn't want to come right out and say in front of Maria that the time for Democrats was over.

I was amazed to see how negative most of the people in Hollywood remained toward Reagan during his presidency. Never mind that he was bringing the economy back; all I heard was criticism of how he'd cut the parks, or cut public employees' salaries, or thrown out the air traffic controllers, or not done the right thing by the environment, or kissed up to the oil companies, or gotten rid of Jimmy Carter's synthetic fuel, wind, and solar energy projects. It was always some complaint. There was no sense of the big picture and of what was being accomplished.

What mattered to me was that he represented the values that had brought me to America. I came because the United States was the greatest country with the best opportunities, and now that it was my home, I wanted to keep it that way and make it even better. After the turmoil and gloom of the 1970s, Americans voted for Reagan because he reminded them of their strength. Maria would say, "I don't know why you are for this guy." But that was why.

That spring, I met one of the great thinkers of the twentieth century: economist Milton Friedman. The Nobel Prize winner had shaped Reagan's ideas about free markets and also had a big influence on me. Friedman's 1980 public television series *Free to Choose* was a big hit, and I'd watched every installment, soaking up his ideas like a thirsty sponge. He and his wife, Rose, had written a bestselling book, also called *Free to Choose*, and I'd sent copies to all my friends as a Christmas present. The producer of the TV series, Bob Chitester, somehow heard about that and tracked me down to ask if I'd like to meet the Friedmans, both of whom had retired from their professorships at the University of Chicago. They lived in San Francisco, where Milton was now a fellow at the Hoover Institution think tank on the Stanford University campus.

Getting ready for the evening, I was like a kid going on an exciting field trip. "Where's my camera?" I asked Maria. "Do I have on a nice enough tie?" Friedman had become one of my heroes. His concept of the roles of governments and markets in human progress was a giant leap beyond the economics I'd studied in school; it explained so much about what I'd seen in the world and experienced for myself as an American entrepreneur. His core argument, of course, was that markets perform more efficiently when government intervention is reduced. Like Reagan, he was wonderful at painting ideas in ways that everyone could understand. He used a pencil, for instance, to argue for the free market:

"The wood came from Washington State, the graphite came from South America, and the rubber came from Malaya—literally thousands of people on three different continents each contributed a few seconds of time to make this pencil. What brought them together and induced them to cooperate? There was no commissar sending out orders from some central office. Because there was demand. When there's demand for something, markets find a way."

I used Friedman's ideas when debating with Sargent Shriver about the price of milk. Sarge was saying, "I remember we campaigned in Wisconsin, and they had so much milk that the price was dropping. And then we went to Illinois, where milk was scarce and the price was going up, so I got on the phone and complained to the regulators . . ."

I said to him, "Don't you think the market could have sorted that out? If there was that much need for milk in Illinois, eventually someone would've brought it in from Wisconsin or some other state. I think they wanted to keep milk tight so they could jack up the price. They made that conscious decision in the private sector. But you used government power to interfere with supply and demand, and I don't feel government should do that."

Much later I learned that when you get in the trenches, pure laissez-faire principles fall short. There's a gap between the theory and the reality. Just from a public investment standpoint, it makes sense to put taxpayer money into after-school programs if you want to save many dollars down the line on crime and prisons. You can't put the burden of a disabled child all on the family if the family is poor. There has to be a social safety net. There has to be investment in the public good.

The Friedmans were short, lively people who seemed perfectly in sync. Someone had told me, "Make sure that you talk to Rose. They see each other as equal partners, but too many people talk to him and ignore her because he's the Nobel Prize winner." So I was careful to ask Rose as many questions as I asked Milton. That unlocked the conversation. We spent a wonderful evening talking about economics, their lives, the books they'd written together, and their involvement in the TV series. One of the fascinating things Friedman told me was that he'd worked for the government during the New Deal, President Franklin D. Roosevelt's program in the 1930s for economic recovery and social reform. "There were no other jobs," he said. "It was a lifesaver." Even though he was against most regulation, I was impressed to hear that he favored government relief and government jobs during mass unemployment because this could inspire the economy to grow.

As good as Reagan's administration was for returning coherence to the US economy, I'd have made more money if Jimmy Carter still occupied the White House. Under Carter, real estate was going nuts, with properties appreciating by 10 percent to 20 percent every year. My partner Al Ehringer and I were about to make a killing on our investment in Denver: a whole city block in a blighted area of town down by the railroad tracks. Thanks to President Carter's programs for dealing with the oil crisis, the energy business in Denver was booming, and a real estate consortium was planning to build a thirty-story tower on our land. We were ready to sign papers when Reagan came in and put the squeeze on inflation. Suddenly people started looking at energy and real estate in a different light. The project fell apart. The developers told us something like, "Economic growth is slowing down, money's not as available as we thought. Shale oil exploration has stopped. This whole thing's not going to happen." Ultimately Coors Field, home of baseball's Colorado Rockies, was built a block away, and our big payday came. But for many years that Denver property felt a little like the supersonic airport that Franco and I had bet on years back. This kind of volatility was normal in real estate, where you accept higher risks in hopes of higher returns. Reagan did the right thing to tighten credit, but the tightening hit us the wrong way.

The real estate opportunities I found under Reagan were closer to home. Santa Monica's Main Street had begun to change just as Al and I had hoped, with the alcoholics and vagabonds slowly giving way to pedestrians and little restaurants and shops. Now you'd actually hear people say, "Let's go to Main Street." The revitalization hadn't reached all the way south to the Santa Monica–Venice border, though, where Al and I were sitting on an entire city block of empty lots. It was land from the old Red Car trolley system that in the 1940s used to connect downtown LA, Santa Monica, and Venice Beach. Now it was no-man's-land. The last building at that end of Main was a bar called the Oar House. Next door stood a health food store run by guys who wore turbans. And across the street were a little synagogue and a boarded-up building that belonged to a famous comedian. The nearby storefronts were all cheap to rent, and several were occupied by odd little religions and sects. There was a Scientology location. It was all really, really run down, with no foot traffic and very few shops. Our plan was to build a beautiful block-long low-rise red-brick building featuring shops at street level and a couple of floors of office space above. We wanted other investors and businesses to say, "Wow, they're building that far south; maybe we should also."

It was a big roll of the dice for us: a $7 million, thirty-nine-thousand-square-foot project capitalized with our profits from the office building we'd redeveloped farther up Main Street. In the last year of the Carter administration, we'd sold it for a $1.5 million profit. Al and I figured that we would control the risk by making sure the building was fully leased the day it opened. To do that, we put together a slide show selling the bright future of the neighborhood. We made the presentations ourselves and accomplished our goal.

I had a good feel for the neighborhood because my office was still right there. Oak Productions—a reference to my nickname in bodybuilding, the Austrian Oak—had moved to a corner loft in an old gas company building in Venice, just a block away from Main. It had a big bank of windows, white-painted brick walls, and a high open ceiling with skylights. I had the idea of leaving the ductwork exposed and painting the pipes bright red and blue. My inspiration was the Centre Pompidou, a postmodern cultural center in Paris, and everyone loved it. The office was also decorated in old oak furniture, red carpet, and a blue L-shaped sofa across from my desk, which gave it a very patriotic feel. The partitions were made of glass so that we could all see each other, and a separate area had little wall-mounted cubicles to store T-shirts and booklets for the Arnold mail-order business.

With my business and movie careers expanding, I'd finally broken down and hired more assistants. Ronda was still my mainstay. She'd worked for me since 1974, and now she was in charge of investments and keeping the books. Although she had run a toy store, she had no formal training as a businesswoman, so she took business classes at Santa Monica College and UCLA. I remember a few years later, the first time we got a million-dollar check as part of a real estate deal. She came running into my office holding it and said, "Oh my God, I've never held this much money. What am I supposed to do with it? I'm so nervous."

Anita Lerner, a thirty-year-old assistant who had to learn about travel, took over scheduling and trip planning, while the mail-order business went to an artist in her twenties named Lynn Marks. We'd bring in a fourth assistant to handle special projects such as books, photo permissions, seminars, and bodybuilding events in Columbus in partnership with Jim Lorimer. Mail order still provided a lucrative income stream because of those Ohio events and because stories about me were still a key element of Joe Weider's magazines. Scarcely an issue of *Muscle & Fitness* or *Flex* appeared without at least one picture of me, attached to an Arnold retrospective, or an essay under my byline about training or nutrition, or a report on my adventures in the movie world. Every mention helped sell more Arnold courses and T-shirts.

Sales of my books, meanwhile, were going great guns; I had a mainstream publisher and a literary agent taking care of those. We were just putting the finishing touches on the *Encyclopedia of Modern Bodybuilding*, a huge project I'd been working on for three years with photographer Bill Dobbins. To cash in on the fitness craze touched off by Jane Fonda's exercise videos, I also did my own video, *Shape Up with Arnold Schwarzenegger*, as well as updated editions of my books *Arnold's Bodyshaping for Women* and *Arnold's Bodybuilding for Men*. All this involved my going out on more promotional tours, which I didn't mind a bit.

We all had new things coming our way. Lynn might point out, for example, "We're getting an enormous amount of mail from people who want a lifting belt like you wore in *Pumping Iron*."

"Let's add that," I'd say. So then we'd all team up to create the product. You couldn't buy the belts ready-made, or there would be no profit. So where would we get the leather? We'd need to commission a manufacturer. And what about the buckle? How would we make the belt look aged and spotted with sweat so that it seemed authentic? We all started calling our contacts and calling companies and found all the elements. Within a couple of days, we'd have it figured out. Then the next question would be, How do we package the belts? How do we deliver them fast and cheap?

I was pushing all the time, and from the perspectives of Ronda, Anita, and Lynn, the work could be incredibly hectic. We were juggling projects in movies, in real estate, in bodybuilding. I was flying around constantly, schmoozing with people from all walks of life. Everything just nonstop. But they were not average workers with a punch-the-clock mentality. They became like members of my family. They looked out for one another and saw me as a challenge. They would accelerate to my speed, and when I sped up, they sped up.

Fostering this atmosphere didn't require extraordinary effort or management genius. For starters, all three were warm, wonderful people. I paid them fairly and drew on my Austrian upbringing to make myself a good employer. A pension plan and great medical insurance were automatic—nobody had to ask for that. And I paid fourteen months of salary per year rather than twelve—the thirteenth month was your summer vacation pay, and the fourteenth was your holiday bonus so that you could take care of your family at Christmas. That was the tradition in Austria, and my office was not on a tight budget, so I could afford it.

My other technique was to make them feel included. They were learning on the job just like I was. When I was in the office, we would analyze all the stuff that was happening to me. The women would sit around, and each would give her point of view. Even if I didn't agree, I'd take it in. The funny thing was, they were all liberal Democrats. Even as we added more people, it was rare to find another Republican besides me in the office for many years.

To me the work didn't feel intense at all—just normal. You do a movie or a book, you promote the hell out of it, you travel around the world because the world is your marketplace, and in the meantime, you work out and take care of business and explore even more. It was all a joyride, which is why I never thought, "Oh my God, look how much work there is. It's so much pressure."

When I had to work at night, it might mean going to a meeting to talk about movies. How bad was that? I was talking about movies! Or some business guys would ask me to fly to Washington. That was great too—always the laughs and the stogies. I'd get to see Ronald Reagan give a speech. Then at midnight, we'd all go to adult shops and look at the latest of the latest. Seeing the other side of some of these straitlaced conservative guys was pretty funny.

So for me work just meant discovery and fun. If I heard somebody complaining, "Oh, I work so hard, I put in ten- and twelve-hour days," I would crucify him. "What the fuck are you talking about, when the day is twenty-four hours? What else did you do?"

I loved the variety in my life. One day I'd be in a meeting about developing an office building or a shopping center, trying to maximize the space. What would we need to get the permits? What were the politics of the project?

The next day I'd be talking to the publisher of my latest book about what photos needed to be in it. Next I'd be working with Joe Weider on a cover story. Then I'd be in meetings about a movie. Or I'd be in Austria talking politics with Fredi Gerstl and his friends.

Everything I did could have been my hobby. It *was* my hobby, in a way. I was passionate about all of it. My definition of living is to have excitement always; that's the difference between living and existing. Later, when I learned about the Terminator, I loved the idea that he was a machine that never had to sleep. I said to myself, "Imagine what an advantage that would be to have those extra six hours every day for something else? Imagine, you could study a whole new profession. You could learn an instrument." That would be unbelievable, because for me the question was always how to fit in all the stuff I want to do.

Therefore, I seldom saw my life as hectic. The thought rarely even crossed my mind. Only later, as Maria and I went from being boyfriend and girlfriend to being engaged and then married, did I pay any attention to balancing my work and my home life.

When I wanted to know more about business and politics, I used the same approach I did when I wanted to learn about acting: I got to know as many people as I could who were really good at it. One place to find them was the Regency Club, a newly opened retreat for LA's business elite. It occupied the top floor and penthouse of a new high-rise on Wilshire Boulevard, with sweeping views of the whole LA Basin. Both the building and the club belonged to David Murdock, one of the city's richest men. His life was another of those great American rags-to-riches stories. David was an Ohio-born high school dropout who, after serving in World War II, turned a $1,200 loan into a fortune in Arizona and California real estate. Now he owned huge stakes in International Mining, and Occidental Petroleum, as well as real estate and hotels, and was a collector of animals, orchids, fine furniture, and chandeliers. His wife, Gabrielle, an interior designer who was born and raised in Munich, decorated the new club in a formal, elegant, Old World style. That reinforced the tone: very proper, very genteel. You couldn't go there without a tie.

Pete Wilson, who won his US Senate seat during the months that I was promoting *Conan the Barbarian*, later hung out there with his whole team. So did George Deukmejian, who'd won the governorship by edging out Democrat Tom Bradley in the same 1982 election. Heavy hitters from the Reagan administration who were passing through town would stop to have dinner and spend time at the Regency. A lot of conservative businesspeople were regulars, and so were some liberal Hollywood agents and show business executives. I started going there to attend events for Wilson, supporting his successful bid to succeed Deukmejian in 1990. Gradually I expanded my circle of friends.

Guido's restaurant on Santa Monica Boulevard was another good place to make business connections and soak up ideas. Likewise, if you wanted to hang out with actors, there was the 72 Market Street eatery in Venice, or the Rock Store in Malibu Canyon if you wanted bikers. I took Maria to the Regency several times; even though she liked Gabrielle's décor, the conservative crowd and the gentility put her off. I was not really into the formality either, but you just had to be disciplined and embrace it. I felt like there was no reason I shouldn't be able to play both sides: my very outrageous side, wearing motorcycle boots and leather, and my conservative side, with the elegant suit and tie and British wing-tip shoes. I wanted to feel comfortable in both worlds.

Maria and I circulated in the liberal community too. In fact, it was at Jane Fonda's invitation that I first connected with the Simon Wiesenthal Center, at a benefit where Jane had agreed to appear as a celebrity and recruit guests. Maria and I were friendly with her and her then husband, activist and California assemblyman Tom Hayden. They invited us to their house several times to meet political or religious leaders, including Bishop Desmond Tutu. On the night of the benefit, Jane introduced me to Marvin Hier, a rabbi from New York who had moved to LA to found the Simon Wiesenthal Center there in 1978. His goal was to combat anti-Semitism and promote religious and racial tolerance. You'd think that in a town with as many powerful Jewish people as Hollywood, he'd have had an easy time. But he was struggling, he told me. "If you're at all into this, I would appreciate your help," he said. "You're a rising star; people will pay attention to you in the future. We've had a difficult time getting Hollywood people involved, beyond just buying a seat or a table at a benefit. We need people coming in and joining our board and donating a million dollars, or three million, and holding fund-raisers. That's where the big money is, and we need it because we're trying to build a Museum of Tolerance, which will cost fifty-seven million dollars."

"I'm not at that level," I warned. But the idea of building a museum made sense to me. If you want to promote fitness and fight obesity, you need gyms; if you want to feed people, you need grocery stores. So if you want to fight prejudice, you have to have tolerance centers everywhere, places where kids can go and learn the history of what happens when people are prejudiced and hate one another.

The more I learned of his mission, the more I felt it was my responsibility to get involved. I'm not a religious person, but I said to myself, "This can only be God's doing." Jewish people had played such key roles in my life: Fredi Gerstl, Artie Zeller, Joe and Ben Weider, Joe Gold, my new film agent Lou Pitt. And yet, I wasn't even sure that *I* was free from prejudice myself. I'd made prejudiced comments, I'd said stupid things. This was almost like God telling me, "If that's the way you want to be, then I'm going to put you right here, where the dialogue of tolerance begins, and you're going to raise funds for them, and you're going to fight for them, and you're going to battle against that side of yourself that may or may not be there." I donated regularly to the center after that and took part in many fund-raising events. The museum, housed in a magnificent building, opened in 1993.

Though I made no secret of my support for Reagan and gave what I could to Republican candidates and causes, I stayed off the political stage. My movie career was my focus. When you promote a movie, you want to win over everybody, and if you give political speeches, you are bound to turn off some percentage of viewers no matter what you say. Why do that?

Besides, I wasn't famous enough yet for very many people to be interested in my views or for politicians to seek my endorsement. I wasn't even an American citizen yet! I had my green card, paid my taxes, and considered the United States my permanent home, but I couldn't vote. I put stickers on my car for the candidates I supported, but I gave no speeches.

I kept quiet about politics when I visited Austria, too. The media there lionized me as a native son made good, and I never wanted to be perceived as some wise guy coming back and telling people what to do. Once or twice a year, when I visited, I'd hang out with my friends and catch up on the latest political debates and developments. My political mentor Fredi Gerstl had become a member of the Graz city council and was an increasingly influential voice in the conservative People's Party nationally. I found it enlightening to talk with him about how the American and Austrian systems compared: private ownership versus public ownership of industries; representative democracy versus parliamentary government; private funding versus public finance. Fredi gave me an inside view of the political maneuvering in Austria on key issues, such as the push to privatize the transportation systems, as well as the tobacco, steel, and insurance industries, and the fight against the resurgent extreme right wing.

Fredi also introduced me to Josef Krainer Jr., who won the governorship of the state of Styria in 1980. He was a little younger than Fredi, and his whole life had been in politics. His father, Josef Sr., had been the governor of Styria throughout my boyhood—a national figure who'd won election after spending all of World War II in prison because of his opposition to the *Anschluss*: the occupation and annexation of Austria by Nazi Germany in 1938. Josef Jr. had studied in Italy and America, and his beliefs were an interesting blend of economic conservatism and environmental advocacy that I found very appealing.

Another good friend of mine was Thomas Klestil, a fast-rising diplomat who'd been the consul general in LA when I first arrived. He was now Austria's ambassador to the US and was destined within a few years to become Austria's president, succeeding Kurt Waldheim.

Ties like these made me reluctant to renounce my Austrian citizenship in 1979, when I became eligible to apply in the United States. (I'd had my green card for the required minimum of five years.) I never like to cut things from my life, I only add. So dual citizenship would be ideal. But while it was permitted in America, Austrian law said I had to choose—I couldn't have it both ways. The rare exceptions were typically for distinguished diplomats, and the decision had to be made by the governor of an Austrian state. I asked Fredi what I should do. He told me that with Josef Krainer Jr. about to run for governor, I'd be wise just to wait. Three years later, I was deeply honored when Josef granted me the exception. I celebrated by taking Maria to dinner at 72 Market Street and applied for my American citizenship immediately.

After another year, it was granted. On September 16, 1983, I stood proudly among two thousand other immigrants in the Shrine Auditorium across from the University of Southern California campus and swore my allegiance to the United States. I'd felt like an American from the time I was ten years old, but now it was becoming real. Raising my hand and repeating the oath gave me a chill, and I felt goose bumps all over my body. Afterward, photographers tracked me down and took pictures of me showing off my naturalization certificate, with Maria beside me, both of us grinning. I told the reporters, "I always believed in shooting for the top, and to become an American is like becoming a member of the winning team."

At home we had a party for our friends. I put on an American flag shirt and an American flag hat and I couldn't stop smiling with the joy of being officially an American at last. It meant that I could vote, and I could travel with an American passport. I could even run for office someday.

CHAPTER 16

The Terminator

WHEN I FIRST SAW the mock-up for *The Terminator* movie poster, the killer robot pictured was O. J. Simpson, not me. A few weeks earlier, I'd run into Mike Medavoy, the head of Orion Pictures, which was financing the project, at a screening of a picture about a police helicopter.

"I have the perfect movie for you," he said. "It's called *The Terminator*." I was instantly suspicious because there'd been a schlock action movie called *The Exterminator* a few years before.

"Strange name," I said.

"Well," he said, "we can change it. Anyway, it's a great role, a leading role, very heroic." He described a sci-fi action movie where I would be playing a brave soldier named Kyle Reese, who battles to save a girl and protect the future of the world. "We've pretty much got O. J. Simpson signed up to be the terminator, which is like a killing machine.

"Why don't we get together?" Medavoy suggested. "The director lives down in Venice near your office."

This was in the spring of 1983. I'd been reading lots of scripts with the idea of doing a new project in addition to the *Conan* sequel, which was supposed to start shooting near the end of the year. I was being offered war movies, cop movies, and even a couple of romances. A script about Paul Bunyan, the mythical lumberjack and he-man, was tempting. I liked it that he went around righting wrongs, and I thought that having a blue ox for a sidekick would be funny. There was also a folk hero script called *Big Bad John*, based on country singer Jimmy Dean's 1961 hit song. It was about the legend of a hulking, mysterious coal miner who uses his strength to save the lives of fellow miners during a mine collapse but doesn't make it out himself. Now that I'd done a big movie connected with names like Dino De Laurentiis and Universal Pictures, studios and directors were courting me and the projects I was being offered were getting better and better all the time. Shortly before *Conan* came out, I changed agents, signing with Lou Pitt, the powerful head of motion picture talent at International Creative Management. I felt bad leaving Larry Kubik, who'd helped me so much when I was nowhere in my movie career. But I thought I had to have a major agency like ICM behind me because it handled all the big directors and big projects and had the connections. And it was satisfying, of course, to come in at the top of one of the giant agencies that had turned me down just a few years earlier.

My mind quickly adjusted to the new world I was in. I'd always told Maria that my goal was to make $1 million for a movie, and with the second *Conan* movie, the money was locked in. But I no longer wanted to be just Conan. The whole idea of making a few Hercules-type movies and then taking the money and going into the gym business like Reg Park went right out the window. I felt I had to aim higher.

"Now that studios are coming to me," I said to myself, "what if I go all out? Really work on the acting, really work on the stunts, really work on whatever else I need to be onscreen. Also market myself really well, market the movies well, promote them well, publicize them well. What if I shoot to become one of Hollywood's top five leading men?"

People were always talking about how few performers there are at the top of the ladder, but I was always convinced there was room for one more. I felt that, because there was so little room, people got intimidated and felt more comfortable staying on the bottom of the ladder. But, in fact, the more people that think that, the more crowded the bottom of the ladder becomes! Don't go where it's crowded. Go where it's empty. Even though it's harder to get there, that's where you belong and where there's less competition.

It was very clear, of course, that I would never be an actor like Dustin Hoffman or Marlon Brando, or a comedian like Steve Martin, but that was okay. I was being sought out as a larger-than-life character in action movies, like Clint Eastwood and Charles Bronson, and John Wayne before them. Those were my guys. I went to see all their movies. So there would be plenty of work—and plenty of opportunity to become as big a star as any of them. I wanted to be in the same league and on the same pay scale. As soon as I realized this, I felt a great sense of calm. Because I could see it. Just as I had in bodybuilding, I believed 100 percent that I'd achieve my goal. I had a new vision in front of me, and I always feel that if I can see it and believe it, then I can achieve it.

Lou Pitt and I were already looking at war movies and heroic movies as a fallback in case *Conan* ever lost steam. Otherwise, it was more of a speculative exercise, because under the terms of my current contract, Dino De Laurentiis owned me for ten years. It called for me to make one *Conan* movie every two years for as long as Dino chose, up to five movies, and to take no other roles. So if *Conan* became the success we all wanted, we would do a third movie in 1986, a fourth in 1988, and so on, and we'd make a lot of money. As to being tied up, Lou told me, "Don't worry about that. If we need to, we can renegotiate." So I put that worry aside as the idea of going from muscles to mainstream action movies gained stronger and stronger appeal.

Mike Medavoy arranged for me to have lunch with the director of *The Terminator*, as well as the producers, John Daly and Gale Anne Hurd. I read the script before I went. It was really well written, exciting and action packed, but the story was strange. A woman, Sarah Connor, is an ordinary waitress in a diner who suddenly finds herself being hunted down by a ruthless killer. It is actually the Terminator, a robot encased in human flesh. It has been sent back in time from the year 2029, an age of horror where the world's computers have run amok and set off a nuclear holocaust. The computers are now using terminators to wipe out what's left of the human race. But human resistance fighters have begun turning back the machines, and they have a charismatic leader named John Connor: Sarah's future son. The machines decide to eliminate the rebellion by keeping Connor from ever being born. So they use a time portal to send a terminator to hunt down Sarah in the present day. Her only hope is Reese, a young soldier loyal to John Connor, who slips through the time portal before it is destroyed. He is on a mission to stop the terminator.

James Cameron, the director, turned out to be a skinny, intense guy. This whole weird plot had come out of his head. At lunch that day, we hit it off. Cameron lived in Venice, and like a lot of the artists there, he seemed much more real to me than the people I met from, say, Hollywood Hills. He'd made only one movie, an Italian horror flick called *Piranha II: The Spawning*, which I'd never heard of, but I got a kick out of that. He told me how he'd learned moviemaking from Roger Corman, the low-budget producing and directing genius. Just from Cameron's vocabulary, I could tell he was technically advanced. He seemed to know everything about cameras and lenses, about the way you set up shots, about lights and lighting, about set design. And he knew the kinds of money-saving shortcuts that let you bring in a movie for $4 million instead of $20 million. Four million was the amount they were budgeting for *The Terminator.*

When I talked about the movie, I found myself focused more on the Terminator character than on Reese, the hero. I had a very clear vision of the terminator. I told Cameron, "One thing that concerns me is that whoever is playing the terminator, if it's O. J. Simpson or whoever, it's very important that he gets trained the right way. Because if you think about it, if this guy is really a machine, he won't blink when he shoots. When he loads a new magazine into his gun, he won't have to look because a machine will be doing it, a computer. When he kills, there will be absolutely no expression on the face, not joy, not victory, not anything." No thinking, no blinking, no thought, just action.

I told him how the actor would have to prepare for that. In the army, we'd learned to field strip and reassemble our weapons by feel. They'd blindfold you and make you take apart a muddy machine gun, clean it, and put it back together. "That's the kind of training he should do," I said. "Not too different from what I was doing in Conan." I described how I'd practiced for hours and hours learning to wield a broadsword and cut off people's heads like it was second nature. When coffee came, Cameron said suddenly, "Why don't *you* play the Terminator?"

"No, no, I don't want to go backward." The Terminator had even fewer lines than Conan—it ended up with eighteen—and I was afraid people would think I was trying to avoid speaking roles, or, worse, that a lot of my dialogue had been edited out of the final film because it wasn't working.

"I believe that you'd be great playing the Terminator," he insisted. "Listening to you, I mean, you could just start on the part tomorrow! I wouldn't even have to talk to you again. There's no one who understands that character better." And, he pointed out, "You haven't said a single thing about Kyle Reese."

He really put on the hard sell. "You know, very few actors have ever gotten across the idea of a machine." One of the few to succeed, he said, was Yul Brynner, who played a killer robot in the 1973 sci-fi thriller *Westworld*. "It's a very difficult, very challenging thing to pull off, from an acting point of view. And Arnold, it's the title role! You are the Terminator. Imagine the poster: *Terminator: Schwarzenegger*."

I told him that being cast as an evil villain wasn't going to help my career. It was something I could do later on, but right now I should keep playing heroes so that people would get used to me being a heroic character and wouldn't get confused. Cameron disagreed. He took out a pencil and paper and began to sketch. "It's up to you what you do with it," he argued. "The Terminator is a machine. It's not good, it's not evil. If you play it in an interesting way, you can turn it into a heroic figure that people admire because of what it's capable of. And a lot has to do with us: how we shoot it, how we edit . . ."

He showed me his drawing of me as the Terminator. It captured the coldness exactly. I could have acted from it.

"I am absolutely convinced," Cameron said, "that if you play it, it will be one of the most memorable characters ever. I can see that you are the character, and that you are a machine, and you totally understand this. You're passionate about this character."

I promised to read the script one more time and think about it. By now the check for lunch had arrived. In Hollywood the actor never pays. But John Daly couldn't find his wallet, Gale Anne Hurd didn't have a purse, and Cameron discovered that *he* didn't have any money either. It was like a comedy routine, with them standing up and searching their pockets.

Finally I said, "I have money." After having to borrow plane fare from Maria, I never left the house without $1,000 in cash and a no-limit credit card. So I paid, and they were very embarrassed.

My agent was skeptical. The conventional wisdom in Hollywood is that playing a villain is career suicide. Besides, once I've locked in on a vision for myself, I always resist changing the plan. But for a lot of reasons, *The Terminator* felt right. Here was a project that would get me out of a loincloth and into real clothes! The selling point would be the acting and the action, not just me ripping off my shirt. The Terminator was the ultimate tough character, with cool outfits and cool shades. I knew it would make me shine. I might not have a lot of dialogue, but at least I'd expand my skills to handling modern weapons. The script was great, the director was smart and passionate, and the money was good: $750,000 for six weeks of shooting right in LA. Yet the project was also low-profile enough that I wouldn't be risking my entire reputation by trying something new.

I thought if I did a great job with *The Terminator*, it would open more doors. The key thing was that the next role after that could not be a villain. As a matter of fact, I shouldn't do another villain for quite some time. I didn't want to tempt the movie gods by playing a villain more than once.

It took me just a day to call back Jim Cameron to say I'd play the machine. He was as happy as he could be, although he knew that before anything could proceed, we needed to get Dino De Laurentiis's release.

When I went to see Dino at his office, he wasn't the hot-tempered little man I'd insulted a few years before. His attitude toward me seemed benevolent and almost fatherly; I'd felt the same thing from Joe Weider many times. I pushed to the back of my mind the way that Dino had clawed back my 5 percent of *Conan* at the beginning of our relationship. It wasn't important, I decided, and I always prefer to be driven by what's positive. Standing in his office, I didn't focus on the big desk anymore but on the statues and awards from all over the world: Oscars and Golden Globes, Italian awards, German awards, French awards, Japanese awards. I admired Dino tremendously for what he'd achieved. He'd been involved in more than 500 movies since 1942 and had officially produced something like 130. Learning from him was much more important than making back that stupid 5 percent. Besides, he'd stuck to the deal to pay me $1 million for *Conan II*, enabling me to achieve my goal. I was grateful for that.

I didn't have to say anything for him to figure out why I was there. He knew I was getting other offers, and I think other people in Hollywood wanting me made him appreciate me more. He'd also realized that I think more like a businessman than like a typical actor, and that I could understand his problems. "I'm seeing tremendous opportunities, and I want to be free enough to do some of these other things in between the *Conan* movies," I told him. I reminded him that we could only do a Conan every two years because the marketers needed two years to reap each installment's potential. "So there's time for other projects," I argued. I told him about *The Terminator* and a couple of other movies that interested me.

Dino could easily have kept me tied up for ten years. Instead, he was flexible. He nodded when I finished my pitch and said "I want to work with you and do many movies with you. Of course I understand your thinking." The agreement we worked out was to keep making *Conan* installments as long as they were profitable. And if I would commit also to make a contemporary action movie for him, to be specified later, then he would free me to pursue other projects. "Go and do your movies," he said. "When I have a script ready, I call you."

The only other caveat was that he didn't want me distracted from

Conan II, so I wasn't released until that movie had been filmed. I had to go back to Cameron and Daly and ask if they'd be willing to postpone the *Terminator* shoot until the following spring. They agreed. I also cleared it with Mike Medavoy.

Compared to *Conan the Barbarian, Conan the Destroyer* felt like a trip to Club Med. We were shooting in Mexico, on a budget about equal to the first *Conan*'s, so there were great settings and plenty of money to work with. What was missing was John Milius, who wasn't available to write or direct the sequel. Instead, the studio took a much more active role, leading to what I thought were big mistakes.

Universal had *E.T.* on the brain. The company had made so much money on Spielberg's blockbuster that the executives decided that *Conan*, too, should be made into family entertainment. Somebody actually calculated that if *Conan the Barbarian* had been rated PG instead of R, it would have sold 50 percent more tickets. Their idea was that the more mainstream and generally acceptable the movie, the better it would succeed.

But you couldn't make Conan the Barbarian into Conan the Babysitter. He was not a PG character. He was a violent guy who lived for conquest and revenge. What made him heroic was his physique, his skill as a warrior, his ability to endure pain, and his sense of loyalty and honor, with a little humor thrown in. Toning him down to PG might broaden the audience at first, but it would undermine the franchise because the hard-core *Conan* fans would be upset. You have to satisfy your best customers first. Who were the people who read *Conan* stories? Who were the *Conan* comic-book fanatics? They'd made it clear that they loved *Conan the Barbarian.* So if you wanted to make them love the sequel even more, you should improve the plot, make the story spicier, and make the action scenes even more amazing. Focusing on ratings was the wrong approach.

I made my opinion clear to Dino, Raffaella, and the studio, and we had our discussions. "You are wimping out," I told them. "You are not being true to what *Conan* is about. Maybe you should get out of the business of doing a *Conan* franchise if you are embarrassed about the violence or what the character represents. Just drop it or sell it to someone else! But don't go and make it something that it is not." It was no use. In the end I was stuck with their decision because I was bound by a contract.

This time Richard Fleischer was the director. He'd been making movies in Hollywood for forty years, including some very memorable ones like *Tora! Tora! Tora!* and *20,000 Leagues Under the Sea*. It wasn't his idea to make Conan PG, but at age sixty-six he was happy to have a job and was not about to argue with the studio or Dino. They told him to make the tone more comic-book-like, more fantasy and adventure, and use magic castles instead of the Nietzsche and the gore. On *Conan the Destroyer*, Richard was a terrific director in every other way, but he was adamant that we stick to those guidelines.

What made the film fun in spite of all this was the chance to work with Wilt Chamberlain and Grace Jones. Raffaella had picked up Milius's trick of casting interesting nonactors. In the plot of the movie, a sorceress queen promises to resurrect Conan's lost love, Valeria, if he will retrieve some jewels and a magical tusk. To help on this quest, she lends him her beautiful young niece, who is the only human who can handle the jewels, and the captain of her palace guard, the giant Bombaata, who is supposed to kill Conan once they recover the goods.

Bombaata was Chamberlain's first movie role. Not only was he one of basketball's all-time greats, but seven-foot-one Wilt the Stilt was also living proof that weight training does not make you muscle bound. He took a whole stack of weights on the Universal Gym and did triceps extensions with 240 pounds like it was nothing. On the court, from 1959 to 1973, he was so powerful and competitive that no one could push him out of the way, and I saw his athleticism in his sword fighting.

But the most interesting fighting took place between him and Grace Jones. She played a bandit warrior named Zula whose weapon is a fighting stick—with which Grace put two stunt men in the hospital by accident in fight scenes. I knew her from the Andy Warhol crowd in

New York: a six-foot-tall model, performance artist, and music star who could be really fierce. She spent eighteen months training for this shoot. She and Chamberlain kept getting into arguments in the makeup trailer about who was really black. He would refer to her as an African-American, and Grace, born and raised in Jamaica, would just explode. "I'm not African-American, so don't you call me that!" she'd yell.

The makeup trailer is a place on the set where everyone talks. If anybody's worried about anything, that's where you see it. Sometimes people come to the trailer and are comfortable, entertaining, and funny; other times they come in looking for an argument. Maybe they're feeling insecure. Or maybe they have a lot of dialogue in the next scene and they're scared, and then anything sets them off.

Some big celebrities have their makeup done in their own trailer. I don't like to do that. Why would I want to sit by myself and not be with the other cast members? I always went to the makeup trailer.

There you hear every conversation that you can think of: concerns about the next scene, complaints about the movie, things that people have to work through.

It's the mother of all beauty salons, because actresses, of course, have many more problems than the average housewife does. "Now I have to do this scene, and the scene is not clicking, and what does it mean?" Or "I got a pimple today, and how can you get rid of it?" The director of photography may have already told her, "I'm not a surgeon. I cannot get rid of a pimple." So now she has a hang-up about that and comes back to the makeup trailer.

All this stuff comes out about personal relationships. You're always torn when you go on location for two months or three months or five months, away from home, from your family. So guys complain about kids who are left behind, they complain about the wife who may be cheating.

Everyone schmoozes, and everyone chimes in: the actors, the makeup guy. Then the director comes, and he's concerned about some actor's frame of mind. Sometimes you see people naked, getting tattoos put on for the scene. It's great for comedy and drama. But even for a makeup trailer, Wilt's and Grace's arguments were wild. I couldn't figure out their hostility, but it was there.

"I'm not like you," she would tell him. "I don't come from uneducated slaves. I'm from Jamaica, I speak French, my ancestors were never slaves."

The N-word was thrown around, which shocked me. Wilt would be saying, "There's nothing black about me. Don't give me this crap! I live in Beverly Hills with the white guys, I fuck only white women, I drive the same cars as the white guys, I have money like white guys. So fuck you, you're the nigger."

At one point I intervened. "Whoa, whoa, whoa, whoa, guys! Guys, please, this is a makeup trailer; let's not have those arguments. See, the makeup trailer is supposed to be all about a soothing atmosphere, because you're getting ready for the scene. So let's not get agitated here.

"Furthermore, have you looked at yourselves in the mirror lately? Because how could you argue you're not black? I mean, both of you are black!"

And they said, "No, no, you don't understand, it's got nothing to do with the color. It's the attitude, it's the background."

The points they made got very, very complicated. They were not really talking about color, they were talking about how different ethnic groups came to America. There was something comical about seeing two black people *accusing* each other of being black. We laughed about it later, at the wrap party, and Grace and Wilt got along really well in the end. They're both very talented, entertaining people. This was just an argument they had to have.

Mexico quickly became one of my favorite places to film. The crews were hardworking, and their craftsmanship on the sets was unbelievable. It was to the old European standard. And if you needed something right away—let's say a hillside as a background for a shot—within two hours that hillside would be there, with all the palm trees or pine trees or whatever the shot called for.

Conan the Destroyer involved so much riding that it felt like the horses belonged to us even when we weren't shooting. Maria would come to visit, and I would take her out on the horses up into the mountains. She is an extraordinary rider who'd grown up doing English-style riding and show jumping. We'd strap our picnic baskets to the horses, and we'd take out the food, the bottle of wine, and just relax on the mountainside, dreaming. We had nothing to worry about, no responsibility.

When I came back from Mexico in February 1984, I was ready to start preparing for *The Terminator*. I had just a month before we started shooting. The challenge was to lock into the cyborg's cold, no-emotion behavior.

I worked with guns every day before we filmed, and for the first two weeks of filming I practiced stripping and reassembling them blindfolded until the motions were automatic. I spent endless hours at the shooting range, learning techniques for a whole arsenal of different weapons, getting used to their noise so that I wouldn't blink. As the Terminator, when you cock or load a gun, you don't look down any more than Conan would look down to sheath his sword. And, of course, you are ambidextrous. All of that is reps. You have to practice each move thirty, forty, fifty times until you get it. From the bodybuilding days on, I learned that everything is reps and mileage. The more miles you ski, the better a skier you become; the more reps you do, the better your body. I'm a big believer in hard work, grinding it out, and not stopping until it's done, so the challenge appealed to me.

Why I understood the Terminator is a mystery to me. While I was learning the part, my mantra was the speech Reese makes to Sarah Connor: "Listen, and understand. That terminator is out there. It can't be bargained with. It can't be reasoned with. It doesn't feel pity, or remorse, or fear. And it absolutely will not stop, ever, until you are dead." I worked on selling the idea that I had no humanity, no expressiveness, no wasted motion, only will. So when the Terminator shows up at the police station where Sarah has taken refuge, and he tells the night sergeant, "I'm a friend of Sarah Connor. I was told she is here. Can I see her, please?" and the sergeant responds, "It'll be awhile. You wanna wait, there's a bench," you just know it won't be pleasant.

Cameron had promised to make the Terminator a heroic figure. We talked a lot about how to do that. How do you make people admire a cyborg that lays waste to a police station and massacres thirty cops? It was a combination of how I played the part, how he shot the character, and subtle things Jim did to make the cops look like schmucks. Instead of being competent guardians of public safety, they're always off base, always a step behind. So the viewer thinks, "They're stupid, they don't get it, and they're arrogant and condescending." And the Terminator wipes them out.

Control freaks like Jim are big fans of night shooting. It gives you total command over the lighting because you create it. You don't have to compete with the sun. You start with the dark and then build. If you want to create a lonely street scene where the viewer can sense at a glance that this is no place to hang, it's easier to do it at night. So most of *The Terminator* was shot after dark. Of course, for the actors, night shooting means a tortuous schedule, and it's not as comfortable or as fun as shooting in the day.

Cameron reminded me of John Milius. He loved moviemaking passionately and knew the history, the movies, the directors, the scripts. He would go on and on about technology. I didn't have much patience when he talked about technical things that couldn't be done. I thought, "Why don't you just direct the movie well? I mean, the cameras are good enough for Spielberg and Coppola. Alfred Hitchcock did his movies and wasn't complaining about the equipment. So who the fuck are you?" It took me awhile to figure out that Jim was the real deal.

He choreographed everything precisely, especially the action scenes. He hired expert stunt guys and met with them beforehand to explain what he wanted in each shot, like a coach charting a play. Two cars in a chase would burst onto a boulevard out of an alley, say, almost hitting the oncoming traffic, which would be swerving just so, and one of the cars would skid and clip the rear fender of a pickup truck going the other way. Jim would be shooting this as the master shot, and then he would pick up the shots from other angles. He was so knowledgeable that the stunt guys felt like they could really talk shop with him. And then they'd go and take the risks, whatever was necessary, to do those scenes.

I'd probably be asleep in the trailer at three in the morning when they shot; they wouldn't need me for two hours, so I'd grab a little sleep. But watching the footage the following day, I'd be in awe. It was amazing that a second-time director would have the skill and confidence to pull this off.

On the set, Cameron knew every detail and was constantly on his feet adjusting things. He had eyes in the back of his head. Without even looking up at the ceiling, he'd say, "Daniel, dammit, get me that spotlight, and I told you already to put that flag on it! Or do I have to climb up there and do the fucking job myself?" Daniel, ninety feet up, would just about fall off his scaffold. How did Cameron know? He knew everyone's name and made it very clear that you couldn't fuck with him or cheat. Don't ever think you'll get away with it. He'd scream at you and punish you publicly and make a scene, all the while using precise terminology that made the lighting guy feel, "This guy knows more about lights than I do. I'd better do exactly as he says." It was an education for someone like me, who does not pay attention to such details.

I realized, though, that Cameron wasn't just a detail man—he was a visionary when it came to the storytelling and the bigger picture, especially the way women are shown on screen. In the two months before we made *The Terminator*, he wrote the screenplays for both *Aliens* and *Rambo: First Blood Part II. Rambo* shows he could do macho, but the most powerful action figure in *Aliens* is a woman: the character Ripley, played by Sigourney Weaver. Sarah Connor in *The Terminator* becomes heroic and powerful too.

This wasn't just true of Jim's movies. The women he married, even though it turned out to be a long list, were all women you didn't want to mess with. *The Terminator's* producer, Gale Anne Hurd, married him later during the making of *Aliens*. It was her job to bring in our project on budget—which ultimately got stretched to $6.5 million. But even that figure was extremely tight for a movie this ambitious. Gale, who was in her late twenties, had gotten into production after graduating from Stanford and starting out as Roger Corman's secretary. She was passionate about movies and devoted to the project. Early on, she and her pal Lisa Sonne, one of the production designers, came by our house at three in the morning to wake me up and talk about the film.

"So where are you guys coming from?" I asked.

"Yeah, we just came from a party," they said. They were a little high. All of a sudden I found myself deep in conversation about *The Terminator*, what needed to be done, how they needed my help. Who comes to do this at three in the morning? I thought it was fantastic.

Gale would seek me out to talk about the script, the shooting, and the challenges. She was professional, and she was tough, but she could turn on the sweetness if she thought it would help. She'd be sitting on my lap in my trailer on the set at six in the morning, saying, "You've worked really hard this whole night, and do you mind if we have you another three hours and keep shooting? Otherwise we're not going to make it." I always think the world of people who make a project their own and are on it twenty-four hours a day. She needed all the help she could get, too, because it wasn't like she had produced five thousand movies before. So whereas a lot of actors would have been on the phone complaining to their agent, I gladly gave her the overtime.

Coming from a huge, expensive Universal Studios shoot abroad to the nighttime penny-pinching world of *The Terminator* was a whole different experience. You weren't part of this giant machine; you didn't feel like just the actor. I was together with the moviemakers. Gale was right next door in her trailer producing, and Jim was always there and would include me in a lot of the decision making. John Daly, who'd put up the money, was around a lot as well. There was no one else beyond that. It was us four slugging it out. We were all in the beginning stages of our careers, and we all wanted to make something successful.

The same was true of key people on the crew. They were not really known and hadn't made much money yet. Stan Winston was getting his big break by creating the terminator special effects, including all the moving parts for the scary close-ups; the same was true for makeup artist Jeff Dawn and for Peter Tothpal, the hairstylist who invented ways to make the Terminator's hair look spiky and burned. It was a wonderful moment that got us all worldwide recognition for our work.

I didn't try to build chemistry with Linda Hamilton and Michael Biehn, who play Sarah Connor and Kyle Reese. Just the opposite. They get a lot of screen time, but they were irrelevant as far as my character was concerned. The Terminator was a machine. He didn't care what they did. He was just there to kill them and move on. They would tell me of scenes they shot when I was not there. That was all good, as long as the acting was good and they sold their stuff. But it was not a situation where we had a relationship. The less chemistry, the better. I mean, God forbid there's chemistry between a machine and a human being! So I kept my mind off them. It was almost like they were making their own drama that had nothing to do with mine.

The Terminator was not what I'd call a happy set. How can you be happy in the middle of the night blowing things up, when everybody is exhausted and the pressure is intense to get complicated action sequences and visual effects just right? It was a productive set where the fun was in doing really wild stuff. I'd be thinking, "This is great. It's a horror movie with action. Or, actually, I really don't know what it is, it's so over the top."

Much of the time, I had glue all over my face to attach the special-effects appliances. I have strong skin, luckily, so the chemicals never ruined it much, but they were horrible all the same. Wearing the Terminator's red eye over my own, I'd feel the wire that made it glow getting hot until it burned. I had to practice operating with a special-effects arm that was not mine, while for hours my real arm was tied behind my back.

Cameron was full of surprises. One morning, as soon as I was made up as the Terminator, he said, "Get in the van. We're going to go shoot a scene." We drove to a nearby residential street, and he said, "See that station wagon over there? It's all rigged. When I give the signal, walk up to the driver's side door, look around, punch in the window, open the door and get in, start the engine, and drive off." We didn't have the money to get permission from the city and to properly set up the scene of the Terminator jacking a car, so that's how we did it instead. It made me feel like I was part of Jim's creativity, sneaking around the permit process to bring in the movie on budget.

Lame ideas really irritated him, especially if they involved the script. I decided one day that *The Terminator* didn't have enough funny moments. There's a scene where the cyborg goes into a house and walks past a refrigerator. So I thought maybe the fridge door could be open, or maybe he could open it. He sees beer inside, wonders what that is, drinks it, gets a little buzz, and acts silly for a second. Jim cut me off before I could even finish. "It's a machine, Arnold," he said. "It's not a human being. It's not E.T. It can't get drunk."

Our biggest disagreement was about "I'll be back." That of course is the line you hear the Terminator say before it destroys the police station. The scene took a long time to shoot because I was arguing for "I will be back." I felt that the line would sound more machinelike and menacing without the contraction.

"It's feminine when I say the *I'll*," I complained, repeating it for Jim so he could hear the problem. "I'll. I'll. I'll. It doesn't feel rugged to me."

He looked at me like I'd lost my mind. "Let's stick with *I'll*," he said. But I wasn't ready to let it go, and we went back and forth. Finally Jim yelled, "Look, just trust me, okay? I don't tell you how to act, and you don't tell me how to write." And we shot it as written in the script. The truth was that, even after all these years of speaking English, I still didn't understand contractions. But the lesson I took away was that writers never change anything. This was not somebody else's script that Jim was shooting, it was his own. He was even worse than Milius. He was unwilling to change a single apostrophe.

When *Conan the Destroyer* hit the theaters that summer, I went all out to sell it. I went on as many national and local talk shows as would book me, starting with *Late Night with David Letterman*, and gave interviews to reporters from the biggest to the smallest magazines and newspapers. I had to lean on the publicists to line up appearances abroad, despite the fact that $50 million, or more than half, of the first *Conan* movie's box office had come from outside the United States. I was determined to do everything in my power to make my first million-dollar role a success.

The second Conan outearned *Conan the Barbarian* in the end, breaking the $100 million mark in worldwide receipts. But what was good for my reputation was not such great news for the franchise. In the United States, *Conan the Destroyer* made it onto fewer screens than the original and grossed $31 million, or 23 percent less money. Our fears had come true. By repackaging Conan as what film critic Roger Ebert cheerfully called "your friendly family barbarian," the studio alienated some of our core audience.

I felt like I was finished with Conan; it was going nowhere. When I got back from my publicity tours, I sat down again with Dino De Laurentiis and told him definitively that I didn't want to do any more prehistoric movies, only contemporary movies. It turned out he had cooled off on Conan too. Rather than pay me millions for more sequels, he'd rather I make an action movie for him, although he still didn't have a script. So for now I was free to do more projects like *The Terminator*.

It was very agreeable and just as we had talked about the previous fall—except that, being Dino, he had a favor to ask. Before I hung up my broadsword for good, he said, "Why don't you just do, you know, a cameo?" He handed me a script called *Red Sonja*.

Red Sonja was Conan's female counterpart in the *Conan* comics and fantasy novels: a woman warrior, out to avenge the murder of her parents, who steals treasure and magic talismans and battles evil sorcerers and beasts. The part that Dino had in mind for me wasn't Conan but Lord Kalidor, Red Sonja's ally. A big part of the plot has to do with his lust for Sonja and her virginity. "No man may have me unless he's beaten me in a fair fight," she declares.

Maria read the script and said, "Don't do it. It's trash." I agreed, but I felt I owed Dino a favor. So at the end of October, just before *The Terminator* was due for release, I found myself on an airplane to Rome, where *Red Sonja* was already filming.

Dino had searched for more than year to find an actress Amazonian enough to play Sonja. He finally found Brigitte Nielsen on the cover of a magazine: a six-foot twenty-one-year-old Danish fashion model with blazing red hair and a reputation for being a hard partyer. She had never acted, but Dino just flew her to Rome, gave her a screen test, and cast her as the star. Then to make the movie happen, he brought in veterans from the *Conan* team: Raffaella as producer, Richard Fleischer as director, and Sandahl Bergman as the treacherous Queen Gedren of Berkubane.

My so-called cameo turned out to involve four whole weeks on the set. They shot all the Lord Kalidor scenes with three cameras, and then used the extra footage in the editing room to stretch Kalidor's time onscreen. So instead of making a minor appearance, I ended up as one of the film's dominant characters. The *Red Sonja* poster gave twice as much space to my image as to Brigitte's. I felt tricked. This was Dino's way of using my image to sell his movie, and I refused to do any promotion the following July when *Red Sonja* appeared.

Red Sonja was so bad that it was nominated for three Golden Raspberry awards, a kind of Oscar in reverse for bad movies: Worst Actress, Worst Supporting Actress, and Worst New Star. Brigitte ended up "winning" as Worst New Star. Terrible movies can sometimes be hits at the box office, but *Red Sonja* was too awful even to be campy, and it bombed. I tried to keep my distance and joked that I was relieved to have survived.

The biggest complication of *Red Sonja* for me was Red Sonja. I got involved with Brigitte Nielsen, and we had a hot affair on the set. Gitte, as everyone called her, had a personality filled with laughter and fun mixed with a great hunger for attention. After the shoot, we traveled in Europe for a couple of weeks before parting ways. I went home assuming our fling was over.

In January, however, Gitte came to LA to do the looping of the movie—the rerecording of dialogue to make it clearer on the soundtrack—and announced that she wanted a continuing relationship. We had to have a serious talk.

"Gitte, this was on the set," I told her. "It was fun over there, but it wasn't serious. I'm already involved with the woman I want to marry. I hope you understand.

"If you're looking for a serious relationship with a Hollywood star," I added, "there are guys around who are available, and they will flip over you. Especially with your personality." She wasn't thrilled, but she accepted it. Sure enough, later that year, she met Sylvester Stallone and it was love at first sight. I was happy for her that she'd found a good partner.

The Terminator had become a sensation in my absence. Released just a week before Halloween 1984, it was the number one movie in America for six weeks, on its way to grossing close to $100 million. I didn't quite realize how successful it was until I got back to the United States and some people stopped me walking down the street in New York.

"Oh man, we just saw *The Terminator*. Say it! Say it! You've got to say it!"

"What?"

"You know, 'I'll be back!' " None of us involved in making the movie had any idea that this was going to be the line people remembered. When you make a movie, you can never really predict what will turn out to be the most repeated line.

Despite *The Terminator*'s success, Orion did a terrible job of marketing it. Jim Cameron was bitter. The company was focused instead on promoting its big hit *Amadeus*, the story of the eighteenth-century composer Wolfgang Amadeus Mozart, which went on to win eight Oscars that year. So without giving *The Terminator* much thought, the marketers positioned it as an ordinary B movie even though there were signs from the start that it was much more. Critics wrote about it as a major breakthrough, as if to say, "Wow, where did that come from?" People were amazed at what they saw and how it was shot. And it wasn't just guys who liked it. *The Terminator* was surprisingly appealing to women, partly because of the powerful love story between Sarah Connor and Kyle Reese.

But Orion's advertising campaign was pitched to action fanatics, and featured me shooting and blowing everything up. The TV commercial and the movie-house trailer would make most people say, "Ugh, crazy, violent science fiction. That's not for me. My fourteen-year-old might like it. Oh, but maybe he shouldn't go. It's rated R." What Orion telegraphed to the industry was "This is a bread-and-butter movie to help pay the bills. Our classy movie is about Mozart."

Cameron went nuts. He begged the studio to expand the promotion and raise the tone before the movie came out. The ads should have been broader, with more focus on the story and on Sarah Connor, so the message would be: "Even though you may think it's crazy science fiction, you'll be quite surprised. This is one of our classy movies."

They treated him like a child. One of the executives told Jim beforehand that "down-and-dirty action thrillers" like this usually had a two-week life. By the second weekend, attendance drops by half, and by the third week, it's over. It didn't matter that *The Terminator* opened at number one and stayed there. Orion was not going to increase the promotional budget. If its executives had listened to Jim, our box office could have been twice as big.

Nevertheless, from an investment point of view, *The Terminator* was a big success, because it made $40 million domestic and $50 million abroad, and cost only $6.5 million. But our profits weren't in *E.T.*'s league. For me, in a weird way, it was lucky that the movie *wasn't* bigger. Because if it had earned, say, $100 million right off the top in US theaters alone, I would have had a tough time getting cast as anything but a villain. Instead, it fell into the category of "that was a great surprise." It made *Time* magazine's list of the year's ten best movies. For me personally, the fact that both *Conan* and *The Terminator* each took in $40 million at home demonstrated that the American public accepted me as both a hero and a villain. Sure enough, before the year was out, Joel Silver, the producer of the Nick Nolte–Eddie Murphy hit *48 Hrs.*, came to my office and pitched me on playing Colonel John Matrix, the larger-than-life hero in an action thriller called *Commando*. The pay was $1.5 million.

The fling with Brigitte Nielsen underlined what I already knew: I wanted Maria to be my wife. In December she acknowledged that she was thinking more and more about marriage. Her career was taking off—she was now an on-air correspondent for CBS News—but she would be turning thirty soon and wanted to start a family.

Since Maria had been quiet about our marrying for so long, I didn't need for her to signal twice. "This is it," I told myself, "the end of dating, the end of telling people 'I believe in long escrows,' and all this bull. Let's take this seriously and move forward." Literally the next day, I asked friends in the diamond business to help design a ring. And when I wrote down my list of goals for 1985, at the very top I put, "This is the year I will propose to Maria."

I liked having the diamond in the middle, bookended by smaller diamonds on the left and right sides. I asked my friends in the jewelry business to come up with ideas along those lines and sketched for them what I envisioned. I wanted the main diamond to be a minimum of five carats and the others to be maybe a carat or two each. We worked on that idea, and then within a few weeks, we had designs. And in another few weeks, I had the ring.

From that day on, I kept it wrapped up and ready in my pocket. Everywhere we went, I was just looking for the right moment to propose.

I almost asked Maria at various points in Europe and Hyannis Port that spring, but it didn't feel quite right. I was actually planning to propose when I took her to Hawaii in April. But the minute we got there, we met three other couples who all said, "We're here to get engaged," or "We're here to get married."

I thought, "Arnold, don't propose here, because every schmuck's coming over here to do the same thing."

I had to be more creative. I knew my wife would be telling the story to my kids someday, and my kids would be telling their kids, so I had to come up with something unique. There were many options. It could have been on an African safari or on the Eiffel Tower, except that going to Paris would be a dead giveaway. The challenge was to make it truly a surprise.

"Maybe I should take her to Ireland," I thought, "where she actually traces her ancestry—maybe some castle in Ireland."

In the end I just proposed spontaneously. We were in Austria in July visiting my mom, and I took Maria out rowing on the Thalersee. This lake was where I'd grown up, where I'd played as a kid, where I'd learned to swim and won trophies for swimming, where I'd started bodybuilding, where I'd had my first date. The lake meant all of those things to me. Maria wanted to see it, since she'd heard me talk about it. It felt right to propose to her there. She started crying and hugging and was totally surprised. So it was exactly the way I envisioned it; the way it ought to play out.

After we got back to shore, of course, all kinds of questions came into her mind: "When do you think we should get married?" "When should we have an engagement party?" "When should we make the announcement?"

And she asked, "Have you talked to my dad?"

"No," I said.

"It's a tradition in America that you have to talk to the father and ask him."

"Maria," I said "do you think I'm stupid? Ask your father and he will tell your mother and your mother will blabber it to you immediately. What do you think, their loyalty is to me? You are their daughter. Or she will tell Ethel, and she will tell Bobby, and she will tell everybody in the family before you even find out. I had to have my chance to actually propose. So of course I didn't talk to them, nobody."

I did call her father that evening. "Normally I know I'm supposed to ask you first," I said, "but I was not about to ask you anything because I know that you would tell Eunice and Eunice would tell Maria."

"You're goddam right. That's exactly what she would have done," said Sarge.

"So I'm just asking you now."

He said, "Arnold, it is a great pleasure to have you as a son-in-law." He was very, very gracious, Sargent, always.

Then I talked to Eunice and told her, and she acted very excited. But I'm sure that Maria had called her before I ever did.

We spent a lot of time with my mom. We hung out, we took her to Salzburg, and traveled around and had a great time. Then we went home to Hyannis Port. We had a little party to celebrate, with everyone sitting around the dinner table: the Shriver family, Eunice and her sister Pat, Teddy and his then wife, Joan, and many Kennedy cousins as well. They always had those long extended tables and a lot of people for dinner.

I had to tell in minute detail exactly how it came about. That was fun. They were hanging on every word and there were all these sounds: "Oh! Ahh! Fantastic!" And bursts of applause.

"You went on a rowboat! Jesus, where'd you find a damn rowboat?"

Teddy was boisterous and very loud and having a good time. "That's amazing! Did you hear that, Pat? What would you have done if Peter had asked you to marry him in a rowboat? I know Eunice would have preferred the sailboat. She'd say, 'A rowboat? That's no good! I want action!' "

"Teddy, let Arnold finish the story."

Everyone was asking questions.

"Tell me, Arnold, what did Maria do then?"

"What was the expression on her face?"

"What would you have done if she'd said no?"

Before I could answer, someone else said, "What do you mean, said no? Maria couldn't *wait* for him to propose!"

It was this very Irish way of relishing the smallest details and turning everything into great fun.

Eventually Maria got a chance to speak. "It was so romantic," she said. And she held up the ring for everyone to see.

CHAPTER 17

Marriage and Movies

WHEN YOU SET THE date and say, "Okay, April 26 next year will be our wedding," you have no idea whether you'll be shooting a movie then or not. As 1986 rolled around, I tried to get the production of *Predator* put off for a few weeks, but Joel Silver, the producer, was worried that we'd run into the rainy season if we waited. That's how I found myself deep in the Mexican jungle near the ruined Mayan city of Palenque less than forty-eight hours before I was due at the altar. I had to charter a jet for the first time in my life to make sure I got to the rehearsal dinner in Hyannis Port on time.

The day I was scheduled to leave, pro wrestler Jesse Ventura shadowed me on the set. We were shooting an action sequence in the jungle, and he'd be hiding in the bushes, not involved in the scene. While I was supposed to be screaming to the other guys, "Get down! Get down!" we'd hear Jesse chanting in that deep voice, "I do, I do, I do." We were all laughing like hell and blowing take after take. The director kept asking, "Why are you not concentrating?"

Maria was not happy that I missed the final preparations. She wanted my mind to be on the wedding, but my mind was on the movie when I arrived. *Predator* had big problems, and—rightly or wrongly—in the mind of the public, the star is responsible for a movie's success. There was talk of having to stop production, and when that happens to a movie, there is always the chance that it might never restart. It was a risky moment in my career. I refocused, of course, so that my mind was on the wedding, but not 100 percent. Meanwhile, some of our guests were wondering why the groom had showed up with a military crew cut. I made the best of it. Even if the situation wasn't ideal, doing it this way was adventurous and fun.

I'd closed my ears to my friends' horror stories about married life. "Ha! Now you get to argue about who should change the diapers." Or "What kind of food makes a woman stop giving blow jobs? Wedding cake!" Or "Oh boy, wait until she hits menopause." I paid no attention to any of that. "Just let me stumble into it," I told them. "I don't want to be forewarned."

You can overthink anything. There are always negatives. The more you know, the less you tend to do something. If I had known everything about real estate, movies, and bodybuilding, I wouldn't have gone into them. I felt the same about marriage; I might not have done it if I'd known everything I'd have to go through. The hell with that! I knew Maria was the best woman for me, and that's all that counted.

I'm always comparing life to a climb, not just because there's struggle but also because I find at least as much joy in the climbing as in reaching the top. I pictured marriage as a whole mountain range of fantastic challenges, ridgeline after ridgeline: planning the wedding, going to the wedding, deciding where we'd live, when we'd have kids, how many kids we'd have, what preschools and schools we'd choose for them, how we would get them to school, and on and on and on. I'd conquered the first mountain already, planning the wedding, by realizing that it was a process I couldn't stop or change. It didn't matter what I thought the tablecloths would look like or what we'd eat or how many guests there should be. You simply accept that you have no control. Everything was in good hands, and I knew I didn't have to be concerned.

Maria and I had both been cautious about getting married and had waited a long time: she was thirty, and I was thirty-seven. We now were like rockets in our careers. Just after we got engaged, she'd been named coanchor of the *CBS Morning News*, and soon she would be switching to a similarly high-paying, high-profile job at NBC. These assignments were in New York, but I'd made it clear that I would never stand in her way. If our marriage had to be bicoastal, we would work it out, I said, so we should not even debate that now.

I always felt that you should wait to marry until you are set financially and the toughest struggles of your career are behind you. I'd heard too many athletes, entertainers, and businesspeople say, "The main problem is that my wife wants me to be home, and I need to spend more time at my job." I hated that idea. It's not fair to put your wife in a position where she has to ask, "What about me?" because you are working fourteen or eighteen hours a day to build your career. I always wanted to be financially secure before getting married, because most marriages break up over financial issues.

Most women go into a marriage with certain expectations of attention; usually based on the marriage their parents had, but not always. In Hollywood, the gold standard for husbandly devotion was Marvin Davis, the billionaire oilman who owned 20th Century Fox, Pebble Beach Resorts, and the Beverly Hills Hotel. He was married to Barbara, the mother of his five children, for fifty-three years. All the women were melting over Marvin Davis. We'd be at a dinner party at their house, and Barbara would boast, "Marvin's never, ever been gone a single night without me. Every time he goes on a business trip, he comes home that same day. He's never gone overnight. And when he is, he takes me with him." And the wives would say to their husbands, "Why can't you be like that?" Or if your wife was within range, you'd receive jabs or kicks under the table. Of course, not long after Marvin died in 2004, *Vanity Fair* magazine published a story revealing that he'd been broke and Barbara was left trying to continue their philanthropic causes and cope with a bunch of debts. *Then* a lot of Hollywood wives were really pissed at his example.

I'd promised myself that we would never have to use Maria's money—neither the money she earned nor any from her family. I wasn't marrying her because she came from wealth. At that point, I was making $3 million for *Predator*, and if it did well at the box office, I'd earn $5 million for the next project and $10 million for the next, because we'd been able to nearly double my "ask" with every film. I didn't know whether or not I'd end up richer than her grandfather Joseph P. Kennedy, but I felt very strongly that we would never have to rely on Shriver or Kennedy money. What was Maria's was hers. I never asked how much she had. I never asked how much her parents were worth. I hoped that it was as much as they dreamed of having, but I had no interest in it.

I also knew that Maria wouldn't want a two-bedroom rental apartment lifestyle. I had to provide her with a lifestyle similar to the way she'd grown up.

My new wife and I were extremely proud of what we'd already achieved. She picked a house for me to buy for us after we got engaged, much more lavish and luxurious than the one we'd started in. The new place was a five-bedroom, four-bath, 12,000-square-foot Spanish-style mansion on two acres of a ridge in Pacific Palisades. Wherever you looked, there were beautiful sycamore trees, and we had views of the entire LA Basin. Our street, Evans Road, led up the canyon to Will Rogers State Historic Park, with its fabulous horse and hiking trails and polo grounds. The park was so close that Maria and I would ride our horses up there; it was like a big playground we could use day and night.

In the months before the wedding, I was busy promoting *Commando* and shooting *Raw Deal*—the action movie I'd promised to make for Dino De Laurentiis—and getting ready to start *Predator*. Maria was even busier in New York. But we carved out time for renovating and decorating. We expanded the swimming pool, put in a Jacuzzi, built the fireplace we wanted, and fixed the tiles, the lighting, and the trees. Under the house, where the land sloped down to the tennis court, we excavated and finished a level, which then served as a tennis house, entertainment area, and extra space for guests.

Maria had chosen curtains and fabrics, but when I came back in late

May after shooting *Predator*, they hadn't yet been installed. She wasn't due home from New York for another three weeks. I wanted to make sure that the renovation was finished exactly as she'd envisioned it so that Maria and I could move in and have the perfect house to live in as husband and wife. So I leaned on the decorator to finish the job, and there was a frenzy of painting and furnishing and hanging art. I'd been working with the contractors long distance while I was on the *Predator* set and flying home on weekends to check on the renovation. I also had a Porsche 928 waiting for her at the house.

On the living room wall, the best spot was reserved for my wedding gift to Maria: a silk screen portrait of her I'd commissioned from Andy Warhol. I liked the famous prints he'd made of Marilyn Monroe, Elvis Presley, and Jackie Onassis in the sixties. He'd done these by shooting Polaroid portraits and then picking one to enlarge as the basis for a silk screen. I called him and said, "Andy, you have to do me a favor. I have this crazy idea. You know how you always do the paintings of stars? Well, when Maria marries me, she will be a star! You'll be painting a star! You'll be painting Maria!" This made Andy laugh. "So I would like to send her down to your studio, and she will sit for you, and you will photograph her and then paint her." The image he created of Maria was a dramatic forty-two-inch square painting that captured her wild beauty and intensity. He ended up doing seven copies in different colors: one for my office, one for Maria's parents, one for himself, and four for this wall, where they were clustered in a giant eight-foot square. Lithographs and paintings by Pablo Picasso, Miró, Chagall, and other artists we'd collected hung elsewhere in the room. But among all of those beautiful images, Maria's was the gem.

I played a big role in decorating our house, but the wedding itself was out of my hands. The Kennedys have a whole system worked out for weddings in Hyannis Port. They hire the right planners, they handle the limos and buses, they make sure the guest list isn't so big that people are spilling out the back of the church. For the reception, they know just where in the family compound to put up the heated tents for the cocktails, dinner, and dancing. They manage public and media access so that well-wishers can glimpse the comings and goings and reporters can get the photos and video clips they need without disrupting the event. Not a single detail of food, or entertainment, or accommodations gets missed. And people have a really great time.

Franco was my best man, and I'd invited a few dozen family and friends, and people who had helped me the most in my life: like Fredi Gerstl, Albert Busek, Jim Lorimer, Bill Drake, and Sven Thorsen, the Danish strongman I'd become buddies with during *Conan*. Maria's list numbered almost one hundred just in relatives. Then there were her longtime friends like Oprah Winfrey and Bonnie Reiss, and close colleagues from work like her coanchor Forrest Sawyer. There were also friends we knew as a couple, and beyond that an entire galaxy of amazing people who knew Rose Kennedy, Eunice, or Sarge: Tom Brokaw, Diane Sawyer, Barbara Walters, Art Buchwald, Andy Williams, Arthur Ashe, Quincy Jones, Annie Leibovitz, Abigail "Dear Abby" Van Buren, 50 people or more connected to the Special Olympics—and on and on. In all, we had 450 guests, and I probably knew only a third of them.

Seeing so many new faces didn't detract from the wedding; it made the event even more colorful for me. It was an opportunity to meet a lot of people, full of fun, full of life, full of toasts. Everyone was upbeat. Maria's family and relatives were extremely gracious. My friends kept coming up and saying, "This is amazing, Arnold." They had a really good time.

My mother already knew Eunice and Sarge—she'd met them during her annual spring visits. Sarge was always joking with her. He loved Germany and Austria, spoke German to her, and knew just how to make her feel good. He would sing beer-hall songs to her and invite her to waltz. They'd spin through the living room. He always pointed out what a great job she'd done raising me. He would talk about details of Austria, different towns he'd traveled through on his bicycle, and about *The Sound of Music*, the history of Austria, when the Russians left and

Austria became independent, and what a great job of rebuilding the Austrians had done, how he loved the wines, how he loved the opera. My mom would say afterward, "Such a nice man. So educated. How little I know about America compared to how much he knows about Austria!" Sarge was a charmer. He was a professional.

At the wedding, she met Teddy and Jackie too. They were incredibly gracious. Teddy offered his arm and walked her out of the church after the ceremony. He was very good at important little gestures like that; taking care of the family this way was his specialty. Jackie made a fuss over my mom when we went to her house the afternoon before the wedding. Her daughter, Caroline, as maid of honor, was hosting a lunch there for the bridesmaids, groomsmen, and close family—thirty people in all. Not just my mom, but everyone meeting Jackie for the first time walked away impressed, just as I had been when we'd first been introduced at Elaine's. She talked to everybody, really sat down and engaged in conversation. Having watched her through the years, I could see why she'd been such a popular First Lady. She had an amazing ability to ask questions that would make you wonder, "How did she know that?" She always made my friends feel welcome when I brought them to Hyannis. My mother fell in love with her too.

My mom gave the rehearsal dinner that night at the Hyannisport Club, a golf club overlooking the Shrivers' house. We billed the evening as an Austrian clambake, and mixing the American and Austrian cultures was the theme. We put out red-and-white-checked tablecloths from an Austrian beer hall, and I showed up wearing a traditional Tyrolean outfit and hat. The menu was a combination of Austrian and American food, with a main course of Wiener schnitzel and lobsters, and a dessert of Sacher torte and strawberry shortcake.

There were great toasts that evening. The toasts on Maria's side were about her and how great she is and how I'd benefit from being her husband. From my side it was the opposite: what a great guy and perfect human being I am, and how she'd benefit from that. Together we'd make a perfect couple. The Kennedys really know how to celebrate these moments. They all jump in and have a great time. That was very entertaining for the outsiders. And for my friends, it was the first time being exposed to that world. They'd never seen that many toasts and such a lively audience. I took the occasion to give Eunice and Sarge their copy of Warhol's portrait of Maria. "I'm not really taking her away, because I am giving this to you so you will always have her," I told them. And then I promised all the guests, "I love her, and I will always take care of her. Nobody should worry." Sargent put in his two cents: he had this rap about being the luckiest man in the world. "You're the luckiest guy in the world to marry Maria, but I'm the luckiest son of a bitch alive to be with Eunice. We're both lucky!"

The wedding was held at St. Francis Xavier, a white clapboard church in the middle of Hyannis, a couple of miles away. It was a Saturday morning, and literally thousands of well-wishers were waiting outside as we arrived. I rolled down the window of the limo and waved to the crowds behind the barricades. There were dozens of reporters and cameras and video crews on hand too.

I loved watching Maria coming up the aisle. She looked so regal with her beautiful lace dress and long train and ten bridesmaids, but at the same time, she was radiating happiness and warmth. Everyone settled down for the formality of the nuptial Mass, during which the exchange of vows takes place about one third of the way through. When the moment came, Maria and I stood before the priest. We were about to say "I do," when all of a sudden the back door of the church went *bang!*

Everyone turned around to see what was going on. The priest was staring past us and we looked over our shoulders too. There, silhouetted against the daylight in the entrance of the church, I saw a skinny guy with spiky hair and a tall black woman wearing a dyed-green mink hat: Andy Warhol and Grace Jones.

They were like gunslingers coming in through the swinging doors of a saloon in a Western movie, or at least that's how it seemed to me because I was seeing it larger than life. I thought, "This fucking guy, I can't believe it. Stealing the show at my wedding." It was wonderful in a way. Andy was outrageous. Grace Jones could not do anything low-key. Maria and I were delighted that they made it, and when the priest in his sermon counseled us as a couple to have at least ten good laughs a day, we were already on our way.

There aren't many guys who would describe their wedding reception as enriching and educational, but that's how ours was for me. As my new father-in-law took me around to introduce me, I was again in awe of how many different worlds Sarge and Eunice had touched. "This guy ran my Peace Corps operation in Zimbabwe, which then was called Rhodesia . . ." "You'll love this guy; he's the one who took charge when there were riots in Oakland, and we put in VISTA and Head Start."

I was in my element because I was always eager to meet as many people as possible from different fields and backgrounds. Sarge accounted for the lion's share of the guests from politics and journalism and the business and nonprofit worlds. It was a collection of people he had worked with in the Peace Corps and the Kennedy administration, in politics over the years, in Moscow on his trade mission there, in Paris during his ambassadorship, and on and on. Another guy he wanted me to meet was from Chicago: "Unbelievable, Arnold, an extraordinary human being. He single-handedly managed the entire legal aid program I started, and now people who have no money can get legal advice and representation." This went on all day long. "Arnold, come over here! Let me introduce you to this friend from Hamburg. Ha ha, you'll love talking to him—he cut this deal with the Russians . . ."

When it came time to dance, Maria ditched her pumps and switched to white sneakers to protect a toe she'd broken the previous week. Then as Peter Duchin and his orchestra struck up a waltz, she wound the train of her dress five or six times around her wrist, and we showed off the steps we'd been practicing, to much applause. My friend Jim Lorimer from Columbus had arranged for us to take ballroom dancing lessons. Those helped us a lot.

The cake was a copy of the legendary one at Eunice and Sarge's wedding: a carrot cake with white icing and eight tiers, standing more than four feet tall and weighing 625 pounds. Its appearance started another round of toasts.

I made one remark at the reception that seemed like a minor thing at the time but would dog me for years. It involved Kurt Waldheim, the former secretary general of the United Nations, who was running for president of Austria. We'd invited him and other leaders, including President Reagan, the president of Ireland—even the Pope. We didn't think they'd come, but it would be great to get back letters from them for the wedding album. I'd endorsed Waldheim as a leader of the conservative People's Party with which I'd been associated since my weightlifting days in Graz.

A few weeks before the wedding, the World Jewish Congress accused Waldheim of concealing his past as a Nazi officer in Greece and Yugoslavia while Jews there were being sent to the death camps and partisans were being shot. This was hard for me to take in. Like most Austrians, I saw him as one of the greats—as secretary general, he'd been not just a national leader but also a world leader. How could he have any kind of Nazi secrets? He'd have been investigated long before this. Many Austrians thought it was an election-year smear tactic by the rival Social Democrats—a stupid move that embarrassed Austria in the eyes of the world. I said to myself, "I will continue supporting him."

Although Waldheim did not attend our wedding, the People's Party sent two representatives to the reception who unveiled an attention-grabbing present: a life-size papier-mâché caricature of Maria and me wearing Austrian folk outfits. In a toast I gave thanking people for all the letters and gifts, I wove that in. "I want to thank also the representatives from the Austrian People's Party for coming here, for giving us this gift, and I know that this is also with the blessing of Kurt Waldheim. I want to thank him also for it, and it's too bad he's going through all these attacks right now, but that's what political campaigns are all about."

Someone gave this to *USA Today*, which mentioned it in a story about the wedding, drawing me into an international controversy that dragged on for years. When it was finally proven that Waldheim had lied about his military record, he came to symbolize Austria's refusal to face its Nazi past. I was still struggling to understand the horrors of Naziism myself, and if I'd known the truth about Waldheim, I would not have mentioned his name.

That regret was still to come, however. Maria and I jumped in the limo and headed for the airport feeling like this was the best wedding we'd ever been to. It was a very special day. Everyone was happy. Everything was a straight ten.

Maria had told her fans on the *CBS Morning News* that she was taking off only a few days. I didn't have much time to honeymoon either. We went to Antigua for three days, and then she came with me to Mexico to spend a couple of days on the *Predator* set. When we arrived, I had everything prepared: the flowers were ready in the room, and I took Maria to a romantic dinner with mariachi music. When we came back to the room, I opened a bottle of great California wine, which I figured would lead to some good action. Everything was perfect the whole evening—until she went to take a shower. Then I heard loud screams coming from the bathroom, like in a horror movie.

I should have known. Joel Kramer and his stunt crew had decided play a joke on us newlyweds. Actually, it was payback, because some of the stunt guys and I had put spiders in Joel's shirt and snakes in his bag. The set was like a summer camp in that way. So when Maria opened the shower curtain, there were frogs hanging off it. You'd think she'd understand the mentality, because her cousins in Hyannis were playing practical jokes all the time. But she has a quirk: although she's physically daring—Maria wouldn't think twice about jumping off a thirty-foot cliff into the ocean—if she sees an ant, or a spider, or there's a bee in the bedroom, she freaks. You'd think that a bomb had gone off. Same thing with her brothers. So the frogs really triggered some drama. There was no way Joel could have known this, but even so his joke was highly successful. Fucking Joel screwed up my entire night.

Then Maria headed home, and it was time for me to get back to work as Major Dutch Schaefer, the hero of *Predator*. It's a sci-fi action movie, of course, in which I'm leading my team in the jungles of Guatemala as guys are getting picked off and skinned alive by an enemy we don't understand. (It turns out to be an alien, equipped with high-tech weapons and invisibility gear, that has come to earth to hunt humans for sport.) Producers Joel Silver, Larry Gordon, John Davis, and I took a big risk in picking John McTiernan to direct. He had done only one movie, a low-budget horror film called *Nomads* about some people who drive around in a van and create mayhem. What set it apart was the tension McTiernan maintained in a film that cost less than $1 million to make. We felt that if he could create that kind of atmosphere with so little money, he must be very talented. *Predator* would need suspense from the moment the characters arrive in the jungle—we wanted the viewer to feel scared even without the predator around, just from the mists, the camera movements, the way things came toward you. So we gambled that McTiernan could handle a production more than ten times as expensive.

Like any action movie, *Predator* was more of an ordeal than a pleasure to make. There were all the hardships you'd expect in a jungle: leeches, sucking mud, poisonous snakes, and stifling humidity and heat. The terrain McTiernan picked to shoot on was so rough that there was hardly an inch of level ground. The biggest headache, though, turned out to be the predator itself. Most of the time it keeps itself invisible, but when it appears onscreen it is supposed to look alien and fearsome enough to terrify and wipe out big, macho guys. The predator we had wasn't up to the job. It had been designed by a special-effects company that the movie studio chose to save money: Stan Winston, who created the Terminator, would've cost them $1.5 million, and this other shop charged half that. But the creature came across as ridiculous, not menacing; it looked like a guy in a lizard suit with the head of a duck.

We started to worry as soon as we started test shooting, and after a few scenes, the worry crystallized. The creature didn't work, it was hokey, it didn't look believable. Also, Jean-Claude Van Damme, who was playing the predator, was a relentless complainer. We kept trying to work around the problem. Nobody realized that the creature footage couldn't be fixed until we were all back from Mexico and the film was in the editing room. Finally the producers decided to hire Stan Winston to do a redesign and arranged to send us back down to Palenque to reshoot the climactic confrontation. That's a night sequence where the predator is revealed fully and goes mano a mano with Dutch in the swamp.

By now it was November, and the jungle was freezing cold at night. Stan's predator was much bigger and creepier than the one it replaced: a green extraterrestrial, eight and a half feet tall, with beady sunken eyes and insect-like mandibles for a mouth. In the dark it uses thermal vision technology to find its prey, and Dutch, who by this time in the movie has lost all his clothes, covers himself with mud to hide. To shoot that, I had to put cold, wet mud on my body. But instead of actual mud, the makeup artist used pottery clay—the same clay they use to make the bottle-holders that keep your wine chilled at the table in restaurants. He warned me, "This will make the body cool down a few degrees. You may be shivering." I was shivering nonstop. They had to use heat lamps to warm me, but that made the clay dry out, so they didn't use them much. I drank jägertee, or hunter's tea, a schnapps mixture you drink while ice curling. It helped a little, but then you got so drunk it was hard to do the scene. You try to control your shivering while the camera is on, hold onto something really hard to stop the shaking, because as soon as you let go, it starts again. I remembered putting mud all over myself as a kid on the Thalersee and thought, "How did I ever enjoy *that*?"

Kevin Peter Hall, the seven-foot-two-inch actor who had taken over in the predator suit, was facing his own challenges. He had to look agile, but the costume was heavy and off balance, and with the mask on, he couldn't see. He was supposed to rehearse without the mask and then remember where everything was. That worked most of the time. But in one fight, Kevin was supposed to slap me around but avoid my head; all of a sudden there was a "whap!" and there was this hand right in my face, claws and all.

The hassle paid off at the box office the following summer. *Predator* had the second-biggest opening weekend of any 1987 film (after *Beverly Hills Cop II*) and ended up grossing $100 million. McTiernan turned out to have been a great choice, and you could see from *Die Hard* the next year that his success with *Predator* was no fluke. In fact, if a director of his caliber had done the sequel to *Predator*, the movie could have become a major franchise on a par with *Terminator* or *Die Hard.*

I had a parting of the ways with the studio executives about that. What happened with *Predator* happens to a lot of successful movies with first-time directors. The director goes on making hits, and his fee goes up: after *Die Hard*, McTiernan's was $2 million. And, of course, costs had risen in the years since *Predator*, but the studio executives wanted to do a sequel that would cost no more than the first movie. That ruled out McTiernan. Instead, they hired another relatively inexperienced and inexpensive director; in this case, the guy who'd made *A Nightmare on Elm Street 5.* Joel Silver wanted me to do *Predator 2*, but I told him that the movie would take a major dive. Not only was the director wrong, but the script was wrong too. The story was set in Los Angeles, and I told him, "Nobody wants to see predators running around downtown LA. We already *have* predators. Gang warfare is killing people all the time. You don't need extraterrestrials to make the town dangerous." I felt that unless they paid to bring in a good director and a good script, hiring me wasn't going to do anything. He wouldn't budge, so I walked away. *Predator 2* and all the other *Predators* that followed flopped, and Joel and I never worked together again.

The studios have the hang of it better today. They do pay for the sequel of a successful picture. They pay the actors more money, and the writers more money, and they bring back the director. It doesn't matter if the sequel costs $160 million to make. Franchises such as *Batman* and *Ironman* are going to gross $350 million per movie at the box office. The *Predator* movies could have been like that. But with a cheaper director, and cheaper writers and actors, *Predator 2* became one of the biggest bombs of 1990. They didn't learn and made the same mistake with the third *Predator* movie twenty years after that. Of course it's always easy to be smart in hindsight.

I was riding the great wave of action movies, a whole new genre that was exploding during this time. Stallone started it with the *Rocky* movies. In the original *Rocky*, in 1976, he'd looked like just a regular fighter. But in *Rocky II*, he had a much better body. His *Rambo* movies, the first two especially, also had a giant impact. My 1985 movie *Commando* continued that trend, coming out in the same year as the second *Rambo* and *Rocky IV*. Then *The Terminator* and *Predator* expanded the genre by adding sci-fi dimensions. Some of these movies were critically acclaimed, and all of them made so much money that the studios could no longer write them off as just B movies. They became as important to the 1980s as Westerns were in the 1950s.

The studios couldn't wait to cook up new scripts, dust off old scripts, and have writers tailor scripts to me. Stallone and I were the leading forces in the genre—although Sly was really ahead of me and got paid more. There was more work for action stars than either of us could do, and others emerged in response to the demand: Chuck Norris, Jean-Claude Van Damme, Dolph Lundgren, Bruce Willis. Even guys like Clint Eastwood, who were doing action movies all along, started bulking up and ripping off their shirts and showing off muscles.

In all this, the body was key. The era had arrived where muscular men were viewed as attractive. Looking physically heroic became the aesthetic. They looked powerful. It was inspiring: just looking at them made you feel that they could take care of the job. No matter how outlandish the stunt, you would think, "Yeah, he could do that." *Predator* was a hit partly because the guys who go into the jungle with me were impressively muscular and big. The movie was Jesse Ventura's acting debut. I was at Fox Studios when he came to interview for the job, and after he walked out, I said, "Guys, I don't think there's even a question that we should get this guy. I mean, he is a navy frogman, he's a professional wrestler, and he looks the part. He's big and has a great deep voice; very manly." I'd always felt we lacked real men in movies, and to me Jesse was the real deal.

My plan was always to double my salary with each new film. Not that it always worked, but most of the time it did. Starting from $250,000 for *Conan the Barbarian*, by the end of the 1980s, I'd hit the $10 million mark in pay. The progression went like this:

The Terminator (1984)	$750,000
Conan the Destroyer (1984)	$1 million
Commando (1985)	$1.5 million
Red Sonja "cameo" (1985)	$1 million
Predator (1987)	$3 million
The Running Man (1987)	$5 million
Red Heat (1988)	$5 million
Total Recall (1990)	$10 million

From there I went on to $14 million for *Terminator 2* and $15 million for *True Lies*. Bang, bang, bang, bang; the rise was very fast.

In Hollywood, you get paid for how much you can bring in. What is the return on investment? The reason I could double my ask was the worldwide grosses. I nurtured the foreign markets. I was always asking, "Is this movie appealing to an international audience? For example, the Asian market is negative on facial hair, so why would I wear a beard in this role? Do I really want to forgo all that money?"

Humor was what made me stand out from other action leads like Stallone, Eastwood, and Norris. My characters were always a little tongue in cheek, and I always threw in funny one-liners. In *Commando*, after breaking the neck of one of my daughter's kidnappers, I prop him up next to me in an airline seat and tell the flight attendant, "Don't disturb my friend, he's dead tired." In *The Running Man,* after strangling one of the evil stalkers with barbed wire, I deadpan, "What a pain in the neck!" and run off.

Using one-liners to relax the viewer after an intense moment started accidentally with *The Terminator.* There's a scene where the Terminator has holed up in a flophouse to repair itself. A paunchy janitor pushing a garbage cart down the hall thumps on the door of the Terminator's room and says, "Hey, buddy, you got a dead cat in there or what?" You see from the Terminator's viewpoint as it selects from a diagram listing "possible appropriate responses":

YES/NO

OR WHAT

GO AWAY

PLEASE COMF BACK LATER

FUCK YOU

FUCK YOU, ASSHOLE

Then you hear the one it chooses: "Fuck you, asshole." People in the theaters were howling at that. Was the guy going to be the next victim? Would I blow him away? Would I crush him? Would I send him to hell? Instead, the Terminator just tells him to fuck off, and the guy goes away. It's the opposite of what you expect, and it's funny because it breaks the tension.

I recognized that such moments could be extremely important and added wisecracks in the next action film, *Commando*. Near the end of the movie, the archvillain Bennett nearly kills me, but I finally win and impale him on a broken steam pipe. "Let off some steam," I joke. The screening audience loved it. People said things like "What I like about this movie is there was something to laugh about. Sometimes action movies are so intense you get numb. But when you break it up and put in some humor, it's so refreshing."

From then on, in all my action movies, we would ask the writers to add humor, even if it was just two or three lines. Sometimes a writer would be hired specifically for that purpose. Those one-liners became my trademark, and the corny humor deflected some of the criticism that action films were too violent and one-dimensional. It opened up the movie and made it appealing to more people.

I'd visualize an inventory of all the different countries in my mind's eye—a little like the Terminator's list of "possible appropriate responses" in that flophouse scene. "How will this play in Germany?" I'd ask myself. "Will they get it in Japan? How will this play in Canada? How will this play in Spain? How about the Middle East?" In most cases, my movies sold even better abroad than in the United States. That was partly because I traveled all over promoting them like mad. But it was also because the movies themselves were so straightforward. They made sense no matter where you lived. *The Terminator, Commando, Predator, Raw Deal, Total Recall*—they all focused on universal themes such as good versus evil, or getting revenge, or a vision of the future that anyone would fear.

Red Heat was the only movie that was even slightly political—it was the first American production ever allowed to film in Moscow's Red Square. This was during the détente period of the mid-1980s, when the USSR and the US were trying to figure out how to work together and end the Cold War. But my intentions were mainly to make a buddy movie, with me as a Moscow cop and Jim Belushi as a Chicago cop teaming up to stop Russian cocaine dealers from sending the stuff to America. Walter Hill, our director, wrote and directed *48 Hrs.*, and the idea here was to combine action and comedy.

All Walter had in the beginning was an opening scene, which is often how movies get made: you have one idea and then sit down and cook up the rest of the roughly one hundred pages for the script. I play a Soviet detective named Ivan Danko, and in this scene I'm chasing a guy down. I find him in a Moscow pub, and when he resists arrest, we fight. After I have him subdued and helpless on the floor, to the horror of the bystanders, I lift his right leg and brutally break it. Moviegoers would be grossed out by that. Why would you break a guy's leg? Well, in the next instant, you see that the limb is artificial, and it's filled with white powder: cocaine. That was Walter's idea, and as soon as I heard it, I said, "I love it, I'm in."

We talked back and forth as he wrote the script, and we decided that it would be good to have the buddy relationship reflect the working relationship between East and West. Which is to say that there is a lot of friction between Danko and Belushi's character, Detective Sergeant Art Ridzik. We're supposed to be working together, but we're constantly on each other's case. He makes fun of my green uniform and my accent. We argue about which is the most powerful handgun in the world. I say it's the Soviet Patparine. "Oh, come on!" he says. "Everybody knows the .44 Magnum is the big boy on the block. Why do you think Dirty Harry uses it?" And I ask, "Who is Dirty Harry?" But our working together is the only way to stop the cocaine smugglers.

Walter had me watch Greta Garbo in the 1939 film *Ninotchka* to get a handle on how Danko should react as a loyal Soviet in the West. I got to learn a little Russian, and it was a role for which my own accent was a plus. I loved filming in Moscow and also loved doing the fight scene in the sauna where a gangster challenges Danko by handing him a burning coal. He's amazed when Danko doesn't flinch; the cop simply takes the coal and squeezes it in his fist. Then he punches the guy through a window and leaps after him to continue the fight in the snow. We shot the first half of that scene in Budapest's Rudas Thermal Bath and the second half in Austria because Budapest had no snow.

Red Heat was a success, grossing $35 million in the States, but it wasn't the smash I'd expected. Why is hard to guess. It could be that audiences were not ready for Russia, or that my and Jim Belushi's performances were not funny enough, or that the director didn't do a good enough job. For whatever reason, it just didn't quite close the deal.

Whenever I finished filming a movie, I felt my job was only half done. Every film had to be nurtured in the marketplace. You can have the greatest movie in the world, but if you don't get it out there, if people don't know about it, you have nothing. It's the same with poetry, with painting, with writing, with inventions. It always blew my mind that some of the greatest artists, from Michelangelo to van Gogh, never sold much because they didn't know how. They had to rely on some schmuck—some agent or manager or gallery owner—to do it for them. Picasso would go into a restaurant and do a drawing or paint a plate for a meal. Now you go to these restaurants in Madrid, and the Picassos are hanging on the walls, worth millions of dollars. That wasn't going to happen to my movies. Same with bodybuilding, same with politics—no matter what I did in life, I was aware that you had to sell it.

As Ted Turner said, "Early to bed, early to rise, work like hell, and advertise." So I made it my business to be there for test screenings. A theater full of people would fill out questionnaires rating the film, and afterward twenty or thirty would be asked to stay and discuss their reactions. The experts from the studio were concerned primarily with two things. One was to see if the movie needed to be changed. If the questionnaires indicated that people didn't like the ending, the marketers would ask the focus group to elaborate so we could consider changing it. "I thought it was fake for the hero to survive after all that shooting," they might say, or "I wish you'd shown his daughter one more time so we could see what happened to her." Sometimes they would point out issues you hadn't thought about while filming.

The marketers were also looking for cues on how to position the film. If they saw that a majority loved the action, they'd promote it as an action movie. If people loved the little boy who appeared at the beginning, they'd use him in the trailer. If the people responded to a particular theme—say, the star's relationship with her mother—then they'd play that up.

I was there for personal feedback. I wanted to hear what the test audience thought about the character I played, about the quality of the performance, and about what they'd like to see me do more or less of. That way I knew what I needed to work on and what kinds of parts I should play next. Many actors get their cues from the marketing department, but I wanted it directly from the viewers, without the interpretation. Listening also made me a more effective promoter. If someone said, "This movie isn't just about payback. It's about overcoming tough obstacles," I would write down those lines and use them in the media interviews.

You have to cultivate your audience and expand it with each film. With each movie, it was crucial to have a certain percentage of viewers say, "I would go see another movie of his anytime." Those are the people who'll tell their friends, "You've got to see this guy." Nurturing a movie means paying attention to the distributors also: the middlemen who talk theater owners into putting your movie on their screens rather than somebody else's. The distributors need to know you're not going to let them hang out there by themselves. Instead, you'll appear at ShoWest, the National Association of Theatre Owners convention in Las Vegas, and take pictures with the theater owners, and accept an award, and give a talk about your movie, and go to the press conference. You do the things that the distributors feel are important because then they go all out in pushing the theaters. Later that week, one of them might call you and say, "You gave that speech the other day, and I just want you to know how helpful it was. The guys who own these multiplex theaters agreed to give us two screens at each multiplex rather than one screen, because they felt like you are really pushing the movie, that you believe in it, and because you promised to come through their town promoting the movie."

Early in my movie career, the hardest thing was giving up control. In bodybuilding everything had been up to me. Even though I relied on Joe Weider and my training partners for help, I was in total control of my body, whereas in movies, you depend on others right from the start. When the producer approaches you with the project, you're relying on him to pick the right director. And when you go on a movie set, you're relying on the director totally, and a lot of other people besides. I learned that when I had a good director, like a John Milius or a James

Cameron, my movies went through the roof because I was directed well. But if I had a director who was confused or did not have a compelling vision for the movie, it would fizzle. I was the same Arnold either way, so the director was the one. After realizing this, I couldn't take myself too seriously even when I got heaped with praise. I didn't make *The Terminator* the success that it was; it was Jim Cameron's vision, he wrote the script, he directed it, he made the movie great.

I did become part of the decision-making in a lot of films, with power to approve the script, approve the cast, and even to choose the director. But I still made it my rule that once you pick a director, you have to have total faith in him. If you question everything he does, then you will have nothing but struggles and fights. Many actors work that way, but not me. I will do everything I can to make sure that we check out the director beforehand. I'll call other actors to ask, "Does he handle stress well? Is the guy a screamer?" But after you pick him, you've got to go with his judgment. You may have picked the wrong guy, but still you cannot fight throughout the movie.

In 1987, just one week into filming *The Running Man,* director Andy Davis was fired. The producers and studio executives staged a coup on the set while I was away for a few days promoting the springtime bodybuilding championships in Columbus. By the time I came back, they'd replaced Andy with Paul Michael Glaser, who had gotten into directing TV shows after being an actor on TV. (He played Detective David Starsky on the 1970s series *Starsky and Hutch.*) He'd never directed a movie, but he was available, and so he was hired.

It was a terrible decision. Glaser was from the TV world, and he shot the movie like it was a television show, losing all the deeper themes. *The Running Man* is a sci-fi action story based on a novel by Stephen King, built around a nightmare vision of America in 2017—thirty years from when we were shooting. The economy is in a depression, and the United States has become a fascist state where the government uses TV and giant screens in the neighborhoods to distract people from the fact that nobody has a job. This public entertainment goes way beyond comedy or drama or sports. The number one show is *The Running Man*, a live contest in which convicted criminals are given a chance to run for freedom but are hunted down and slaughtered onscreen like animals. The story follows the hero, Ben Richards, a cop who has been wrongly convicted and winds up as a "runner" fighting to survive.

In fairness, Glaser just didn't have time to research or think through what the movie had to say about where entertainment and government were heading and what it meant to get to the point where we actually kill people onscreen. In TV they hire you and the next week you shoot, and that's all he was able to do. As a result, *The Running Man* didn't turn out as well as it should have. With such a terrific concept, it should have been a $150 million movie. Instead, the film was totally screwed up by hiring a first-time director and not giving him time to prepare.

Scripts for *Total Recall* had been kicking around Hollywood for so long that people were saying the project was jinxed. Dino De Laurentiis owned the rights for much of the 1980s and tried to produce the movie twice—once in Rome and again in Australia. It was a different kind of movie from what it ultimately became: less violent and more about the fantasy of taking a virtual trip to Mars.

I was pissed that Dino didn't offer it to me, because I told him that I would like the part. But he had a different vision. He hired Richard Dreyfuss for the Rome attempt and Patrick Swayze from *Dirty Dancing* for the Australian attempt. Meanwhile, he gave me *Raw Deal*. They finally got as far as building sound stages in Australia and were about to start shooting *Total Recall* when Dino ran into money trouble. This had happened several times during his career. It meant he had to get rid of some of the projects.

I called Mario Kassar and Andy Vajna at Carolco, which was then the fastest-growing independent film production company, riding high from doing the *Rambo* movies. They'd bankrolled *Red Heat*, and I thought they'd be perfect for *Total Recall*. I said, "Dino is wiping out.

He has a lot of great projects, and there's one specifically that I want to do." They moved fast, launched an all-out assault, and bought it from him within days. I was the driving force through all these years.

So now the question was who should direct. It was still unresolved a few months later when I ran into Paul Verhoeven in a restaurant. We'd never met, but I recognized him: a skinny, intense-looking Dutch guy about ten years older than me. He had a good reputation in Europe, and I'd been impressed by his first two English-language movies, 1985's *Flesh+Blood* and, two years later, *RoboCop*. I went over and said, "I would love to work with you someday. I saw your *RoboCop*. It's fantastic. I remember *Flesh+Blood*, and it was also fantastic."

"I'd love to work with you too," he said. "Maybe we can find a project."

I called him the next day. "I have the project," I said and described *Total Recall*. Next I called Carolco and said, "Send Paul Verhoeven the script immediately."

A day later Verhoeven told me that he loved the script, even though there were a few changes he wanted to make. That was normal: every director wants to pee on the script and make his mark. His suggestions were smart and made the story much better. He immediately dug into the research on Mars: How would you free the oxygen that's bottled up in the rocks there? There had to be a scientific basis for it. Paul added a dimension of realism and scientific fact. Control of Mars in the story now hinged on controlling the oxygen. So many things he said were brilliant. He had a vision. He had enthusiasm. We got together with Carolco and discussed what he wanted to change, and Paul signed on to direct the movie.

That was in the fall of 1988. We went into full swing in rewriting, and then into full swing on where to shoot it, and then into full swing on preproduction, and we started filming in late March at the Churubusco Studios in Mexico City. We shot all the way through the summer.

We chose Mexico City in part for the architecture: some of its buildings had just the futuristic look the movie needed. Computer-graphics imagery was not yet very capable, so you had to do a lot of work in the real world, either by finding the perfect location or by building full-scale sets or miniatures. The *Total Recall* production was so complex that it made *Conan the Barbarian* seem small-scale. The crew, which numbered more than five hundred people, built forty-five sets that tied up eight sound stages for six months. Even with the savings that came from working in Mexico, the movie cost more than $50 million, making it the second most expensive production in history at that point, after *Rambo III*. I was glad that *Rambo III* had been a Carolco production, so Mario and Andy weren't allergic to the risk.

What drew me to the story was the idea of virtual travel. I play this construction worker named Doug Quaid who sees an advertisement from a company called Rekall and goes there to book a virtual vacation to Mars. "For the memory of a lifetime," the ad says, "Rekall, Rekall, Rekall."

"Have a seat, make yourself comfortable," the salesman says. Quaid is trying to save money, but right away the salesman, who's a little slippery, tries to get him to upgrade from the basic trip. He asks, "What is it that is exactly the same about every vacation you've ever taken?"

Quaid can't think of anything.

"*You!* You're the same," says the salesman. "No matter where you go, there you are. Always the same old you." Then he offers alternate identities as an add-on for the trip. "Why go to Mars as a tourist when you can go as a playboy, or a famous jock, or a . . ."

Now Quaid is curious in spite of himself. He asks about going as a secret agent.

"Aaaah," says the salesman, "let me tantalize you. You're a top operative, back under deep cover on your most important mission. People are trying to kill you left and right. You meet a beautiful, exotic woman . . . I don't wanna spoil it for you, Doug. Just rest assured, by the time the trip is over, you get the girl, you kill the bad guys, and you save the entire planet."

I loved that scene of a guy selling me a trip that, in reality, I never would actually take—it was all virtual. And, of course, when the Rekall surgeons go to implant the chip containing the Mars memories into Quaid's brain, they find another chip already there, and all hell breaks loose. Because he isn't Doug Quaid: he's a government agent who was once assigned to the rebellious mining colonies on Mars and whose identity has been wiped and replaced with Quaid's.

The story twists and turns. You never know until the very end: did I take this trip? Was I really the hero? Or was it all inside my head, and I'm just a blue-collar jackhammer operator who may be schizophrenic? Even at the end, you aren't necessarily sure. For me, it connected with the sense I had sometimes that my life was too good to be true. Verhoeven knew how to balance the mind games with action. There's a scene in *Total Recall* where Quaid, now on Mars, stands in front of his enemies as they start shooting at him from close range. Thousands of bullets are flying, and you're grabbed by the suspense. Suddenly he vanishes, and you hear him calling out from nearby, "Ha ha ha, I'm over here!" They were shooting at a hologram he'd projected of himself. In science fiction you can get away with such stuff, and no one even questions it. That's great, great storytelling; the kind that has international appeal and staying power. It wouldn't matter if you watched *Total Recall* twenty years from now, you could still enjoy it, just as you can still enjoy *Westworld* today. There's just something very appealing about futuristic movies if they have great action and believable characters.

It was a tough movie to make, with lots of stunts and injuries and craziness and night shooting and day shooting and dust. But when the set is the tunnels of Mars, it's interesting work. Verhoeven did a great job directing me and the other leads, Rachel Ticotin, Ronny Cox, Michael Ironside, and Sharon Stone. Sharon, who plays Quaid's wife, Lori, is actually a government agent sent to keep an eye on him. She follows him to Mars, breaks into his room, and kicks him in the stomach.

"That's for making me come to Mars," she says. By the end of the next scene, she's saying, "Doug . . . you wouldn't hurt me, would you, honey? Sweetheart, be reasonable . . . We're married," while she's pulling out a gun to kill him. He shoots her between the eyes. "Consider that a divorce," he says. Where else in movies do you get away with that: a guy shoots his beautiful wife in the head and then makes a wisecrack? No such thing. Forget about it. That's what makes science fiction wonderful. And what makes acting wonderful.

Working with Sharon will always be a challenge. She is a sweetheart of a person when not on the set, but there are some actors who just need more attention. One violent scene was hard to film because I was supposed to grab her by the neck, and she freaked. "Don't touch me! Don't touch me!" At first I figured that she hadn't been brought up like a tomboy and tried to sympathize, but it was more than that. We found out that she'd had a serious neck trauma early in her life. I think she even had a scar.

"Sharon," I said, "we all rehearsed this in the hotel room on Sunset. Paul was there, we all were there, going through scene by scene. Why did you never say, 'By the way, when we get into the fight scene, it says here that you're strangling me, I have a little hang-up about my neck'? Then we could have worked around it step-by-step. I would gently put my hand on your neck, and then you let me know when I can squeeze tighter and when we can get a little rough. Because I'm the first one to understand." Paul calmed her down, and Sharon was willing to work through the scene. She wanted it to be a success; we just had to go through the difficult step first. That's the way it was.

When you're an actor and when you're a director, you deal with all of those problems. No one gets up in the morning and says, "I'm going to be difficult today," or "I'm going to derail the movie," or "I'm going to be a bitch." People just have their hang-ups and insecurities, and acting definitely brings them out. Because it's *you* who is being judged, it's *your* facial expressions, *your* voice, *your* personality, *your* talent—it's everything about you so it makes you vulnerable. It's not some product you've made or job you've done. If someone tells the makeup guy, "Can you tone this down a little bit? I have too much powder there," he says, "Oh, sorry," and just wipes it off. But if someone says, "Can you get rid of that self-conscious smile while you're doing the scene? You have something weird going on in your face," you feel like "Jesus!" Now you don't know what to do with your face. Now you're self-conscious. In acting you take criticism so much more personally. You get upset. But every job has its downside.

In spite of Verhoeven's amazing work, *Total Recall* almost got lost on the way to the screen. The trailer we had playing in movie theaters in anticipation of the movie's release was really bad. It was too narrow; it didn't convey the film's scope and weirdness. As always, I was looking at the marketing data from the studio: the "tracking studies" as they're called, which measure a movie's buzz.

Marketing departments generate hundreds of statistics, and the trick is to find, right away, the numbers that are really important. The ones I lock in on are "awareness" and "want to see," which measure how people answer the questions "On this list of movies that are coming out, which have you heard about and which do you want to see?" If people respond, "I know about *Total Recall* and *Die Hard 2*, and I'm dying to see them," then you know your movie will be up there. An awareness figure in the low to mid-90s means that your movie will probably open at number one and make at least $100 million at the box office. For every percentage point below that, you might gross $10 million less, which is why studios and directors often tweak their movies at the last minute.

Another useful measure, "unaided awareness," shows whether people spontaneously name your movie among the films they know are coming up. A score of 40 percent or more means you have a winner. Two other numbers also matter a lot: "first choice," which has to hit 25 percent to 30 percent to guarantee success; and "definite interest," which has to be between 40 percent and 50 percent.

With some hits, like *Conan the Barbarian*, the numbers are promising right from the start. With other films, they signal that it could go south. That was the case with *Total Recall.* Even after weeks of trailers and advertisements, its awareness was in the 40s, not the 90s, first choice was only 10 percent, and it wasn't being named as a "want to see."

I knew pretty much all there was to know about the marketing of movies by then, but it wasn't doing me much good. The source of the problem wasn't *Total Recall* itself but TriStar Pictures, the distributor, which was responsible for cutting the trailers and handling the publicity. Its marketers didn't know what to do with the film, and the studio itself was in upheaval. TriStar and its sister studio, Columbia Pictures, were being taken over by Sony and merged in one of those 1980s megadeals. New leadership had arrived—Peter Guber and Jon Peters—to oversee the whole thing, which meant that many TriStar executives were about to lose their jobs.

In most cases, a change in studio management can sink a movie. Not only do the new guys have their own projects, but also they want to make the previous administration look bad. That wasn't a problem with Guber and Peters, both of them highly successful producers, because they were animals. They just wanted success, no matter who started the project. Over the years, I'd gotten to know Guber well enough to be able to get him on the phone and raise the alarm about *Total Recall.*

"Peter, we are three weeks away from opening, and there's only a forty percent awareness of the movie," I said. "That, to me, is disastrous."

"What's the problem?" he asked.

"The problem is that your studio is screwing up the publicity campaign and the trailers that are in the movie houses. But don't take my word for it. I want you and Jon to have a screening of the movie and the trailer. I'm going to sit there with you. Let's look, and you tell me what you think."

So we sat down and watched *Total Recall* and the trailer. "This is incredible," Peter said. "The movie looks like a hundred-million-dollar movie, but the trailer makes it look like a twenty-million-dollar movie." He was all set to call in the TriStar marketers and say, "I want to see size, guys! I want to see the big action that we have here!"

But I stopped him. "I think we've got to hire outside help," I said. "Don't let the studio make those decisions anymore, because they're not capable until you clean house. You haven't done that. The old guard is still there. Give the movie to an outside company to do the marketing. Let's go to the top three and have a bidding war to see which firm comes up with the best idea."

They listened, and we held meetings with three promotion firms. Cimarron/Bacon/O'Brien, which was number one in the business, articulated the failings of the *Total Recall* trailer even better than I had. It won the contract, and by the following weekend, we were out there in the marketplace with new trailers and a totally different campaign. It sold the movie using taglines like, "They stole his mind. Now he wants it back. Get ready for the ride of your life," and "How would you know if someone stole your mind?" The trailers highlighted the amazing action and special effects. They got the message across: in fourteen days, we went from a 40 percent awareness to 92 percent awareness. It was the talk of the town. Joel Silver called, in spite of our falling-out over *Predator*, and said, "Fantastic. Fantastic. It's going to blow everyone away."

Sure enough, *Total Recall* had not only the number one spot at the box office in its opening weekend, it was the number one opening weekend of all time for a nonsequel movie. We pulled in $28 million in the first three days, on the way to $120 million that year in the States alone. The equivalent today would be more than $200 million, because the ticket prices have doubled. The film was a huge success abroad as well, earning over $300 million worldwide. It won a Special Achievement Oscar for its visual effects. (A Special Achievement Oscar is how the Motion Picture Academy honors an accomplishment for which there is no set category.) Paul Verhoeven had a masterful vision and did a great job. I was proud that my interest and passion helped to bring about the movie. But the experience also proves how important marketing is—how important it is to tell the people what this is about; really blow up their skirt and make them say, "I have to go see this movie."

CHAPTER 18

Comic Timing

I LOVED BEING AN action hero, and with my body and background, it was a natural for me. But you can't spend your whole life running around blowing things up. I'd dreamed of doing comedy for years.

I've always believed that everything in life has a funny side. It was funny to be posing all oiled up in little skinny briefs in front of all these people, trying to be the world's most muscular man. It was funny getting paid millions of dollars to fight a predator from outer space. It was funny going through Lamaze classes trying to pretend that pregnancy is a team effort. I saw great humor in Maria and me coming from totally opposite upbringings. I laughed about my accent, and I loved *Saturday Night Live*'s Hans and Franz characters takeoff on me. I'd always been the perfect target for jokes; there was so much material to work with. Being Austrian, marrying Maria, being Republican, the accent. With all this going for you, you need a sense of humor so you can join the fun.

In 1985, the year after *The Terminator* became a hit, I was at a dinner in Denver on the eve of the Carousel Ball, a famous charity extravaganza organized by Marvin and Barbara Davis. Marvin, who was then the owner of Fox Studios, where I was making *Commando*, was known for his sense of humor. He and Barbara were seated with a bunch of comedians who were due to perform at the gala, including Lucille Ball and her husband, Gary Morton. I was at the next table with the Davises' son, John, and the younger crowd. There was a lot of laughing at Marvin's and Barbara's table, and the jokes were starting to fly thick and fast. I heard Marvin call out, "Hey, Arnold, come over here. Why don't you tell us a joke?" That was typical Marvin, I later learned. But I was speechless. I didn't have a joke prepared. I didn't even know what kind of jokes to make at such an event.

All I could say was, "Give me a little bit of warm-up time here. Maybe tomorrow I tell you," or something like that.

But Lucille Ball jumped right in. "He's very funny. You don't have to worry about him," she said. "I worked with him." So she covered for me, and then Gary Morton interrupted with a joke, and then Milton Berle went off on a routine about what would Gary Morton be without Lucille Ball. I was saved, but it was a perfect example of how important it is to be prepared for such moments.

I'd met Milton Berle at the West Coast engagement party for Maria and me in 1985. Berle's wife, Ruth, and Maria knew each other from the Share Girls, a charity group that Maria joined when she moved to LA; it included Johnny Carson's wife, Dean Martin's wife, Sammy Davis Jr.'s wife, and so on, and we called it the rich broads' foundation. There was a great history between the Berles and the Kennedys because Milton had been a big fan of JFK. They'd hung out together, and Milton had given JFK a humidor that eventually sold at the Kennedy auction for $520,000 to Marvin Shanken, the publisher-editor of *Cigar Aficionado* magazine. Milton gave me one just like it, one of only three he ever gave away.

So Maria and Ruth became good friends, and Ruth brought Milton to our engagement party. The first thing he did was walk up to some guy I didn't know and shake his hand. He said, "It's so nice to be here today at this engagement party. Maria is marrying Arnold Schwarzenegger, and Arnold, this is great, thank you so much for inviting me."

I totally fell for it. I said, "I am over *here*!" What a stupid trick, but people were laughing, and that broke the ice, and then he did a whole routine. "Ruthie, my wife," he said. "Look at her lips. The last time I saw lips like that, it had a hook through it."

Ruthie, who was sitting next to Maria, said to her, "Oh God, that joke. I've heard it a thousand times."

Berle sat down with us afterward, and we had a great time. Finally, he said, "Let's get together."

"Absolutely!" I said.

We met at Caffé Roma in Beverly Hills, and it became our place. We always had lunch there, and I'd hang out with him and his friends like Sid Caesar and Rodney Dangerfield, and Milt Rosen, who wrote a lot of the jokes. Or I would go to his house, where we'd smoke stogies while I asked him a thousand questions about comedy.

Berle was the president of the Friars Club of Beverly Hills, which he founded in 1947 with other comedians like Jimmy Durante and George Jessel. It was on a side street between Wilshire and Santa Monica Boulevards, in a white building that resembled a bunker from the outside but inside was a private restaurant and nightclub. I would go every month or two for a lunch or a dinner or some event. The Friars had good boxing matches and was famous for celebrity roasts. But Milton was almost eighty, and it was very clear that the club was outdated.

He and his buddies had such a strong lock on it that new comedians weren't joining. Guys like Eddie Murphy, Steve Martin, Danny DeVito, and Robin Williams would visit, and you would see them getting frustrated and thinking, "Who are these old farts? I can make jokes that will blow everyone away."

But I was not a comedian, so I was not putting myself on that level. What's more, I grew up in a culture where you respect the elders. To me, someone as accomplished as Berle ought to be honored and complimented and pumped up because maybe he didn't have much going on anymore. It must have been weird to be Milton Berle, and, after becoming a legend as "Mr. Television" and then being a big star in Las Vegas and on Broadway, all of a sudden your only identity is the Friars Club. No matter where he was, Milton tried to steal the show because he still had that craving for attention, which was why he'd become a comedian.

I discovered that all these comedy legends could have a normal conversation, but not often. They would talk about everyday stuff if we were hanging out at Caffé Roma, but then Robin Williams would come by, or Rodney Dangerfield in his Bermuda shorts, and that would stir things up. If you went with that same bunch to an event where there was any kind of audience, the madness never stopped: joke upon joke and attack upon attack, with everyone going after everybody else. But the funniest thing was that a lot of the comedians brought their wives, who were normal-looking hausfraus. They would roll their eyes at the jokes. You could almost hear them say, "Here we go again. Oh God." In fact, sometimes you *did* hear one of them say, "Aw, come on, how many more times are you going to use that one?" That was the worst. The old comedians just hated it.

The Friars Club guys didn't see me as a comedian. They liked me as a person and liked my movies, and they felt that I had some talent for jokes with certain safe material that was not too complicated. They also knew I respected them and admired their talent. That was fine. You have to figure out your potential. So let's say on a scale of 1 to 10, with Milton Berle a 10, my potential is a 5. In comedy his potential was much greater than mine, obviously, but maybe not in something else. It's hard to imagine Milton Berle as an action hero.

But the trick is how do you reach 100 percent of your potential? It was the right time in my career to expand into comedy and throw everything off a little bit. But I also knew comedy was a tricky thing to get involved with. Particularly for me as a European, because I didn't have an American sense of humor, and my timing and delivery of lines tended to be a little cockeyed. So meeting these guys and being included in their world gave me a chance to understand it better. I discovered that I really like being around people who are funny and who

Maria was full of personality and joy, a bundle of positive energy that I wanted to be around. At the beach in 1980. *Albert Busek*

Above: We weren't looking for an East Coast–West Coast relationship, but before we knew it, Maria and I were going out. Here on a river-rafting trip near Sacramento in 1979.
Douglas Kent Hall

Left: When Maria decided she'd stay in California after the 1980 presidential campaign, I bought my first house, on 21st Street in Santa Monica, for us to live in together. *Schwarzenegger Archive*

Maria and Conan the dog and I dressed up as bikers for Halloween in the early eighties.
Schwarzenegger Archive

When in Austria, I often put on traditional clothes and do as the Austrians do: above, hiking in the Alps; below left, ice curling; below right, dancing in a beer-hall version of a conga line. *Schwarzenegger Archive*

Tom Eitzinger/Fototom.at

Schwarzenegger Archive

Maria and I saw each other for eight years before this happy day in spring 1986. I was thirty-eight and she was thirty. *Denis Reggie*

Franco was best man, and among my twelve other groomsmen were my nephew Patrick Knapp, my friends from the bodybuilding world Albert Busek and Jim Lorimer, and Sven-Ole Thorsen, who played a thug in many of my movies. *Schwarzenegger Archive*

I escort my mom and my new American mother-in-law across the Kennedy compound to the reception tent. Fortunately, Aurelia and Eunice got along well. *Schwarzenegger Archive*

Andy Warhol was outrageous and Grace Jones could not do anything low-key. Warhol's version of a tuxedo at the reception was a motorcycle jacket. *Schwarzenegger Archive*

Traveling with Maria and Eunice and Sarge in Europe was fun. Here we are on a ferry crossing the Chiemsee, a big Bavarian lake. *Albert Busek*

Hiking in the Alps I'd sometimes wear loud obnoxious Hawaiian shorts just to get a rise out of the lederhosen traditionalists. Here I have charmed a dairy cow. *Schwarzenegger Archive*

In Santa Monica, Maria and I lived so close to a state park that we kept horses and rode there every day. My horse was named Campy. *Schwarzenegger Archive*

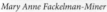

Mary Anne Fackelman-Miner

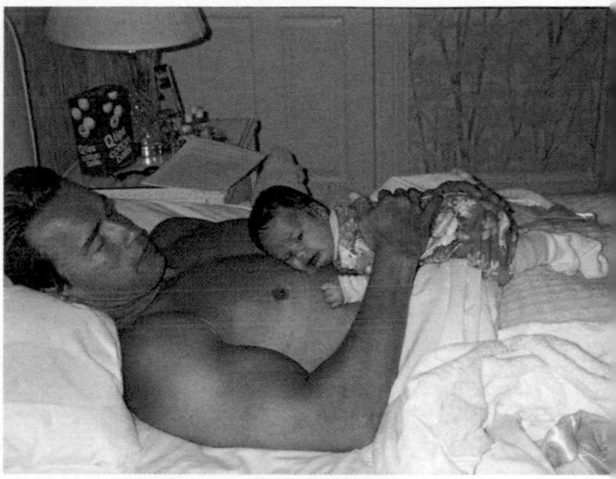

Left: Katherine had just been born when the first President Bush named me fitness czar and we staged the Great American Workout on the South Lawn of the White House. *Above:* With Christina, our second child, I perfected the art of letting the baby sleep on my chest. *Schwarzenegger Archive*

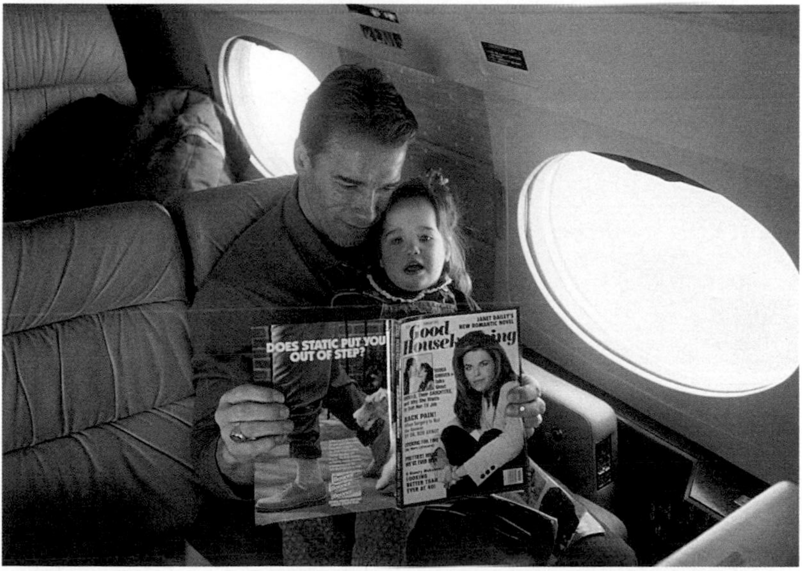

On the way to vacation in Sun Valley in early 1993, I'm showing Christina a magazine story about how Maria balances family and career.

Schwarzenegger Archive

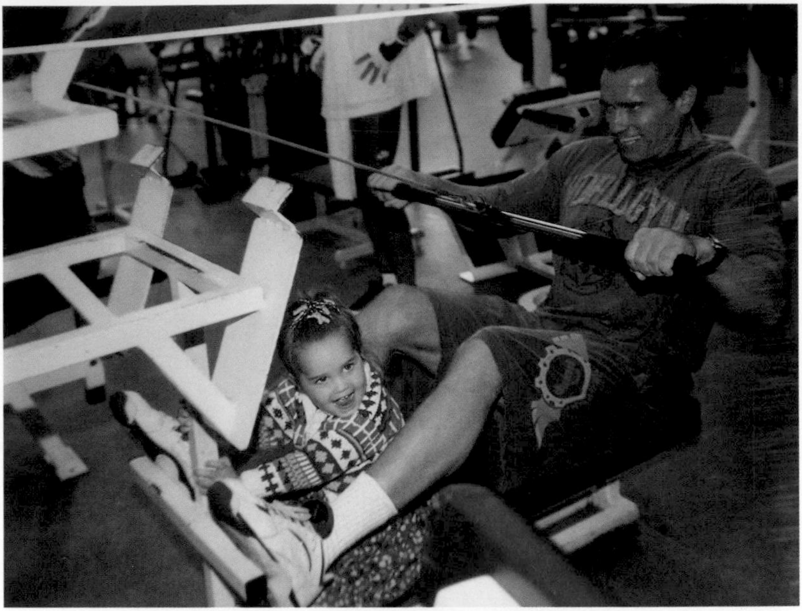

Most days I would bring Christina with me to the gym. *Schwarzenegger Archive*

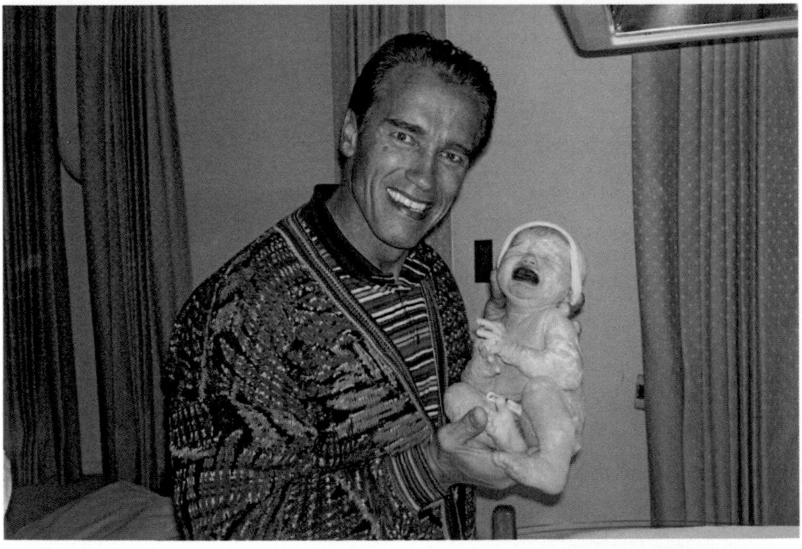

Patrick, our older son, was born in September 1993. *Schwarzenegger Archive*

By this time, I had the nurturing thing down. Above, Katherine snuggles while Patrick snoozes on my chest. Left, I was also adept at his diapers and bottles. Below, I celebrated my forty-eighth birthday in Sun Valley with the guys: my old friend Adi Erber, a ski pro, my nephew Patrick Knapp, my brother-in-law Bobby Shriver, financial advisor Paul Wachter, and *Godfather* producer Al Ruddy.
Schwarzenegger Archive

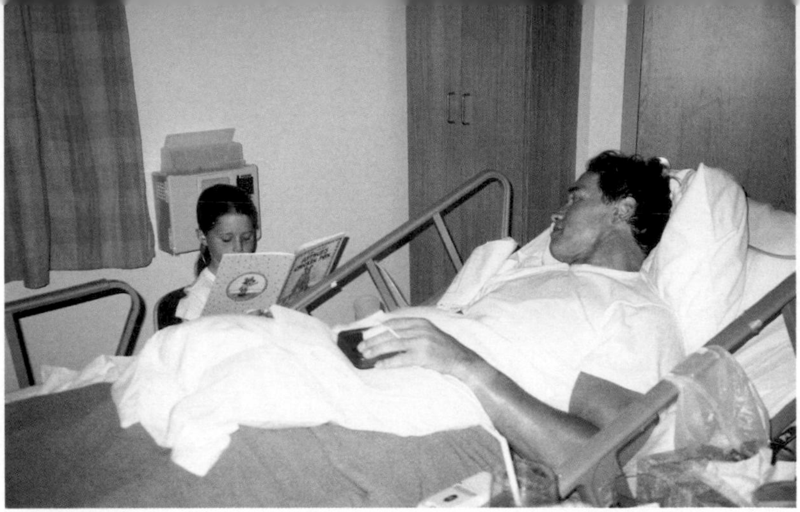

Katherine read *Arthur's Chicken Pox* to me while I was recuperating from the heart-valve replacement surgeries, 1997. *Schwarzenegger Archive*

We Schwarzeneggers clown around at a hotel in Hawaii, 2000. Our youngest, Christopher, is three. *Schwarzenegger Archive*

After fishing at a pond near our house in Sun Valley. *Schwarzenegger Archive*

Katherine and I horse around in the Santa Monica Mountains.
Schwarzenegger Archive

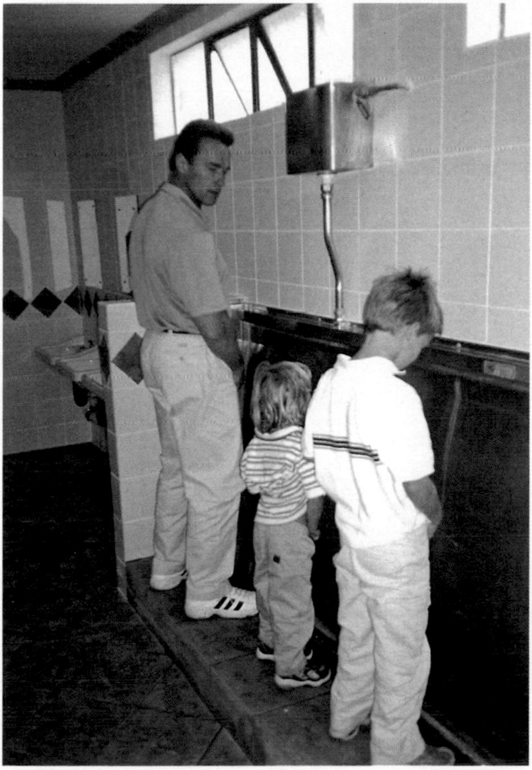

I supervise Christopher and Patrick at a cricket stadium during a trip to South Africa for the Special Olympics, 2001.
Schwarzenegger Archive

Tranquilized lioness, park ranger, and us on safari in Tanzania. I was at least as excited as the kids because big cats have always fascinated me. *Schwarzenegger Archive*

We're a skiing family, here in Sun Valley—snow and skis and pine forests and mountains have always been part of my life. Christopher isn't in the photo because he was only four and was busy that day skiing on the bunny slope. *Schwarzenegger Archive*

This is me kissing me on Halloween, 2001, except that the right-hand Arnold is Maria wearing a Terminator mask. As you can tell from the photo below, Halloween is a big deal in the Schwarzenegger house.
Schwarzenegger Archive

Patrick and Christopher with me behind the governor's desk in Sacramento.
California State Archives / Steven Hellon

Trips like this one to Maui during spring break 2007 were a happy change from all the time our family spent apart because of the governorship. *Schwarzenegger Archive*

I still love driving my M47 tank from the Austrian army, which now resides at a studio lot outside Los Angeles and appears occasionally in World War II movies. On board with me are Patrick, Christopher (in the tanker's helmet), and my assistant Greg Dunn. *Schwarzenegger Archive*

Katherine draping her long hair over my head for laughs. *Schwarzenegger Archive*

In winter 2011, my nephew Patrick and I went to the grave of Meinhard, my brother and his father, in Kitzbühel, Austria, during an unusually heavy snow. *Schwarzenegger Archive*

Cindy Gold

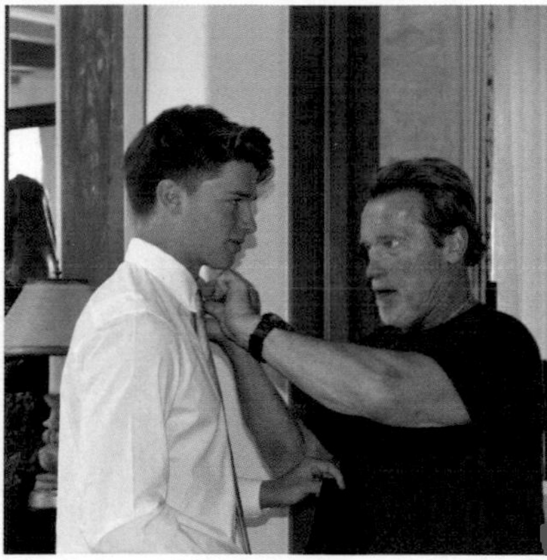

Schwarzenegger Archive

Schwarzenegger Archive

June 2012 was graduation month for Patrick, who finished high school, and Katherine, who completed her bachelor's degree at the University of Southern California. I'd grown the goatee for my role in *The Tomb*, a prison movie with Sylvester Stallone. Above, suiting up with Christopher and Patrick. Left, Katherine and Christina.

Cindy Gold

For my fiftieth birthday, July 30, 1997, Maria surprised me with this poster. It's a still life of tchotchkes and hobbies showing what I was all about: hiking, Hummers, fine pipes and watches, drawing in pen and ink, stogies and schnapps, being a dad, chess and pool, tennis and golf, movie scripts, motorcycles and leather, the history of weightlifting, and the future of bodybuilding. My list of interests has only grown since then. *Schwarzenegger Archive*

write comedy and who are always looking to say things in a unique way—though I had to get used to Milton wisecracking that I had bigger tits than my girlfriend.

He became my comedy mentor. He used to encourage me by saying, "You being funny with your accent is twice as big a deal as me being funny. They *expect* me to be funny!" He taught me a lot about how to deliver jokes, how to play down the humor and not stress the punch line too much. I would ask how to pick jokes to lighten up a serious situation and tie them in so the humor seems organic. I learned how if you're doing standup, nothing has to tie together at all. First, you make a few jokes about whatever's in the news, like Jay Leno does. Then you pick some people in the audience and work them over, and you make sure to throw in some jokes on yourself to take the curse off the fact that you're making fun of other people.

Often Milton would coach me on timing. "You get a lot of awards when you're a star, and lots of them are irrelevant," he said. "But you still have to give an acceptance speech. So here's what you do. You say, 'I've gotten many awards, but this one . . . for me . . .' —and you have to get emotional here and make like you're choking up—'this one . . . for me . . . is the most . . . *recent!*' See? You show the emotion so you get the audience going the other way."

Berle wrote his own jokes—*The Milton Berle Show* was the biggest and longest-running program on TV in the early days—but he was also famous for stealing from everybody else. Jack Benny once got accused of stealing a joke from Berle, and he said, "When you take a joke away from Milton Berle, it's not stealing, it's repossessing."

His biggest frustration with me was the way I always went over the top. He was helping me get ready once for a roast that he couldn't attend. On that occasion, I was the person to be roasted, and Milton was giving me jokes to use when my turn came to respond to the other speakers. "Don't burn, just singe," he said, reminding me of this old rule about roasts. I didn't pay much attention. One of the jokes he gave me was about comedian Henny ("Take my wife—please!") Youngman:

"Henny has a weight problem. But it's not really a weight problem, it's just water retention. He is retaining Lake Mead."

On the night of the roast, during my turn to speak, I gestured toward Henny and said, "Look at this fat pig. But he's not really fat. He has a water retention problem . . ."

Milton's friends from the Friars Club knew he'd been coaching me, and the next day they called him up yelling, "How could you tell Arnold to call Henny a fat pig!" Milton said I should call the club members who were offended and apologize. "I thought by going beyond what was written on the card, it would be funnier," I told them. "But I know it was against the rules, and I'm sorry."

When I see a great performer, I always start to dream. Wouldn't it be cool to be a rock 'n' roll star like Bruce Springsteen? Wouldn't it be cool to give a speech to the applause of one hundred thousand people like Ronald Reagan? Wouldn't it be cool to do a hilarious half-hour standup routine like Eddie Murphy? Maybe it's the Leo in me, the perpetual performer who always wants to be the center of attention.

So with Milton Berle, I was saying to myself, "Maybe I will never get to his level, but if I can learn just a little bit of what he knows . . ." How many times in life do you have to give a toast? How many times do you have to give a speech for some worthy cause like physical fitness? Or appear at a press conference at some movie festival?

With action movies, the problem is compounded. Fifty percent of the critics will automatically say, "I hate action movies. I like love stories. I like movies you can take the family to see. This guy just kills people, and kids watch it, and then they go out on the street and kill people." Starting with something disarming and funny is a good way to stand out. You become more likable, and people receive your information much better.

Whenever I watched a comedy, whether it was *Animal House* or *Ghostbusters* or *Blazing Saddles*, I always thought, "I could have done that!" But nobody was going to hire me for that kind of part, and it made no sense to dig in my heels and insist, "My next movie has to be a comedy." I hadn't gone all the way with action movies. If I was going to branch into comedies anytime soon, I would need someone to be my cheerleader.

That problem resolved itself at a ski lodge in Snowmass Village, Colorado, outside of Aspen, in late 1986. Maria and I found ourselves hanging out by the fireplace one evening with Ivan Reitman and Robin Williams and their wives. Robin and I were having a good time trading funny stories about skiing and who in Aspen was sleeping with whom. Ivan was the master. He had produced *Animal House* and produced and directed *Ghostbusters* and *Legal Eagles,* and I wanted to work with him really badly, so I was using all the joke-telling skills I'd learned from Milton Berle. It worked. By the end of the evening, Ivan was looking at me thoughtfully.

"You know," he said, "there's a certain innocence about you that I've never seen come through on the screen, and a certain sense of humor. I think Hollywood wants to keep you pigeonholed as the action hero, but it could be quite attractive to see you play a strong guy with that innocence."

After we came back from Aspen, I called Ivan and suggested that we develop something together. He agreed. He asked some writers to come up with five ideas for me and gave me all five: two-page memos that each sketched a character and a story. We eliminated four very quickly, but the fifth—about mismatched twins who are the product of a scientific experiment to breed the ideal human—seemed great. Julius Benedict, the Arnold character, who gets all the good genes, is virtually perfect but naïve. He goes in search of his brother, Vincent, a smalltime crook, with comical results. We agreed that the title, *The Experiment*, didn't work, given my Germanic background, so the project was renamed *Twins*. From that point, everyone fell in love with the concept.

I cooked up the idea of casting Danny DeVito as Vincent, because I'd run into Danny's agent and thought it would be very funny to have the twins look so different physically. Everyone liked that idea. They talked to Danny. *He* loved the idea, although right away he had reservations. "Okay, it's a great sight gag, Arnold and me as twins," he said. "Now how do we sustain that?" Danny liked to have things nailed down. And that is how the project began.

Ivan, Danny, and I made an interesting team. Ivan's mother was a survivor of the Nazi death camp at Auschwitz, and his dad had been a resistance fighter; they emigrated from Czechoslovakia after the war. Like many children of Holocaust survivors, Ivan has incredible drive, and he's combined this with his wonderful talent for directing and producing comedy. Danny turned out to be hilarious to work with, and in spite of his huge successes on TV and in movies, he's the opposite of a crazy Hollywood personality. He drives normal cars and has a great family and lives a normal life. And he's extremely well organized financially.

Being realistic and levelheaded about business enabled the three of us to add a little chapter to Hollywood business history. We knew that selling *Twins* in the usual way would be difficult. In theory, the studios would love the idea: you just had to picture me and Danny DeVito next to each other on a movie poster. But in reality, what we were proposing was an offbeat picture by three expensive guys. If each of us got paid his going rate, the budget would be so top-heavy that we thought no studio would touch it. And yet none of us wanted to take a pay cut because working for less can hurt your negotiating power in future deals.

So when we pitched Tom Pollock, the head of Universal, we proposed to make *Twins* for no salary at all. Zero. "I can guarantee it will be a hit, because of Ivan and Danny here," I told him. "But I understand that you see me as an action guy. I've never done comedy, and I'm an unknown quantity. Why should you have to take the risk? So don't pay us anything until we prove we're worthy." What we wanted in exchange was a piece of the movie: a percentage of the box-office receipts, video sales and rentals, airline showings, and so on. Hollywood calls this the back end.

Tom was so convinced that the movie was going to be a hit that he said, "I'd rather give you the cash." But by this time, Ivan, Danny, and I had really gotten attached to our idea. "We don't want cash," we said. "None of us is short of cash. Let's all share the risk here."

The deal we ended up with guaranteed the three of us 37.5 percent of all the income for the movie. And that 37.5 percent was real, not subject to all the watering-down and bullshit tricks that movie accounting is famous for. We divvied up the 37.5 percent among ourselves proportionally based on what each of us had earned on his previous movie. Because I'd been paid a lot for *The Running Man,* I ended up with the biggest slice, almost 20 percent. It made the math simple: if *Twins* was a decent-sized success and made, say, $50 million, it would put almost $10 million in my pocket.

Tom Pollock knew full well how rich these terms could turn out to be. But he didn't want us to go to another studio and get offered more. Besides, if *we* made money, Universal would make plenty of money too. He had a great sense of humor about it. We were in his office, and after we agreed, he stood up and theatrically turned his pants pockets inside out. "Okay," he said. "Now I'm going to bend over. Go ahead. You can steal everything from me and fuck me!" It became one of those legendary lines from a studio executive. We all laughed. Then he said, "I think it's a good deal. Let's do it."

I'd never realized that moviemaking could be so much fun when you're not covered in freezing jungle mud or getting beaten around by mechanical snakes. We shot *Twins* in Los Angeles, New Mexico, and Oregon in the early months of 1988. I got to do things on camera that I'd never done before. I got to waltz. I got to sing. I got to play a thirty-five-year-old virgin getting seduced by a beautiful girl (played by Kelly Preston, John Travolta's wife, who was a joy to work with). I got in touch with what Ivan called the innocent side of me.

Danny DeVito was the Milton Berle of comic acting. He never tried to throw in funny lines, never depended on a joke to create humor—that doesn't work on camera. Instead, he depended on the circumstances to create the humor. He was so smart in the way that he used his voice and eyes, and the way he threw his body around. He knew exactly what worked for him, what people love about him, what would sell. He knew exactly how far he could take the dialogue, and for all of us, there was a constant back-and-forth with the writers as we fine-tuned scenes and lines. And as a partner on the set, Danny was great! He smoked stogies. He made pasta for us once and sometimes twice a week. He made the good espresso, and he was always ready with the Sambuca and the good after-dinner or after-lunch drinks.

The chemistry between us worked really well right from the start. As shady Vincent, he was always trying to play me like putty. He'd conned a lot of people, and now he was going to con me. And I, as Julius, was an easy mark but at the same time smart enough to figure out the situation and do something about it. I just had to play my character exactly the way it was written: naïve, strong, smart, educated, sensitive, able to speak a dozen languages.

Compared to being an action hero, it was a lot easier to be a comic star. The rehearsals were all about changing the rhythm of my persona. I had to get rid of the stern looks, the hard lines, the commanding, machinelike talk. No more of that Terminator slow monotone. I had to throw out everything I'd learned in action films to telegraph leadership and command. Instead, I had to soften everything. I had to say the words more gently, roll them together, and combine them with gentler looks and smoother turns of the head. There's a scene early in the movie where a bad guy on a motorcycle zooms up from behind Julius and tries to snatch his suitcase. But Julius doesn't let go, and the guy wipes out. I had to do that scene without any show of anger or effort—to Julius, it's just common sense to hold on to his suitcase, and he's born with such tremendous strength that it's no effort at all. I'm not *trying* to make the guy crash. As a matter of fact, I'm worried that he's hurt and try to help him!

The comedy was there. We knew we had a winner. The idea of opposite twins worked perfectly, and there was always laughter on the set.

Every evening when we watched the dailies, cast and crew who had seen us do four, five, or six takes of a scene would still laugh when they saw it on the screen. At first we shot in LA, and then we moved to the desert near Santa Fe, New Mexico.

No matter where we went, people would visit because word spread that it was a happy set. Clint Eastwood dropped by on the day we shot the scene where I sing. Julius is on an airliner listening to rock 'n' roll on headphones for the first time in his life. He starts singing along to a 1950s hit by the Coasters, "Yakety Yak," without realizing that all the other passengers can hear. It was my movie singing debut, and let's just say that I'm no Frank Sinatra. Afterward, Clint said, tongue in cheek, "I didn't realize you had such talent." The only time I sing in real life is at the end of a party when I want the guests to leave.

One of the running jokes on the set was, "Never ask Arnold about politics." Not that I'd get upset, but if you asked me, I'd fill your ear with sales talk about Vice President George H. W. Bush. It was presidential primary season, and he was battling Senator Bob Dole of Kansas and evangelist Pat Robertson for the Republican nomination to succeed Ronald Reagan. The other cast members of *Twins* were all Democrats, and the joke was that if I started talking, *they'd* get upset with *me*, which would threaten the sunny mood.

Something did happen during the time we were filming *Twins* that dampened my sunny mood, although it had nothing to do with either the movie or US politics. In February the *News of the World*, a London tabloid, ran a front-page story about me headlined "Hollywood Star's Nazi Secret."

The story attacked me, but the focus was my father. It claimed that he'd been a Nazi and a member of the SS, and that he'd rounded up homosexuals and Jews for the concentration camps. It called me "a secret admirer" of Hitler and claimed that I took part in the neo-Nazi movement and held "fervent Nazi and anti-Semitic views."

Normally I would just blow off criticisms, but I'd never been libeled about something so serious. I knew I would have to respond. My first move after talking to lawyers and publicists was to call the paper's owner, Rupert Murdoch, whom I'd met before in Aspen. He listened as I explained that the story was false. "I would appreciate it if you don't print it in America," I said. "And I would appreciate it if the paper would publish an apology and say that it was a mistake, they got the wrong information. That'll be the end of it. Mistakes can be made."

"Well," said Murdoch, "my guys over there tell me that they did a very thorough investigation. And if it is true, then I don't think anyone should apologize. But in the meantime, I can promise you that I won't print it here."

"I'm not blaming you for every story in all your papers and outlets," I emphasized. "But I want to bring to your attention that this is an injustice. Please look into it." Rupert was as good as his word; he never did publish the story in his US publications or report it on his new Fox TV network. But nothing else happened. And while my lawyers sent a formal letter demanding a retraction and prepared to sue, other journalists started asking for my response.

I was in a very uncomfortable position. I knew that what the story said about me was false, but what about the accusations against my father? I thought they must be wrong, but what did I really know? There had been so little conversation at home about the Second World War. I truly had no idea.

So I decided to call my friend Rabbi Marvin Hier at the Simon Wiesenthal Center. "I need your help," I told him. "I know you have a system for tracking down war crimes. Could you check out my father's war record? I want to know, Was he a Nazi? And second, did he belong to the SS? What was he in charge of during the war? Did he commit any war crimes—actively or passively? Did he do any of those things?"

"Arnold," the rabbi said, "within a week or two I'll have everything, because we have access to all the papers." He called his people in Germany and maybe even the great Nazi hunter Simon Wiesenthal himself in Vienna, whom I met later. After three or four weeks, he came back with the information. He said, "Your father had the Nazi party membership card, but there is no evidence of any killing or war crimes on your father's part, against homosexuals or Jews or anyone else.

"He was a sergeant, not in a position to order such acts without the authority of an officer. There is no indication that there was such an order given."

The Simon Wiesenthal Center sent that information officially so that it could be used in court.

As for the *News of the World*'s allegations against me, Simon Wiesenthal himself wrote a letter to the court stating that there was no evidence whatsoever to back them up. Having those statements, together with the tabloid's inability to produce facts to support its story, made it clear that its sources were unreliable. It took many months in court, but the tabloid eventually published a total retraction and paid substantial damages in an out-of-court settlement. The money went to the Special Olympics in Great Britain.

The *Twins* shoot wrapped just before Easter 1988, in the middle of the presidential primary season. Vice President Bush had been fighting hard battles. Even though he had Reagan's endorsement, he lost some of the early primaries to Bob Dole. That's because many people regarded Bush as Reagan's shadow: what Austrians would call his *Waschlappen*, or dishrag. I knew the vice president from my visits to the White House. He was always very gracious, a real mensch, and he had his act together because of the important positions he had held previously, such as UN ambassador and director of the Central Intelligence Agency. Contrary to the Democrats' spin on him, he had tremendous strength of character and will. But of course political campaigns are unfair. You look for vulnerability in your opponent; some flaw that you can make stick. The Democrats knew very well that Bush was fulfilling his office just as the Constitution meant the vice president to do: by supporting the president and standing ready to step in and lead if necessary. But they gained ground at the start by calling him weak. Bush battled back, and by the time we finished shooting, he'd dominated the primaries on Super Tuesday and had the nomination sewed up.

I followed the presidential campaigns that year with great interest and accepted happily when I was invited to take part in the Republican National Convention in New Orleans in August. My assignment was to add celebrity power to one of the "caucus teams" of Reagan administration officials and Bush supporters whose job it was to glad-hand the state delegations and chat them up on key issues.

I'd been to Republican conventions before, but this was the first since I'd married a Shriver. Maria and I believed that we should continue as we always had: she would go to the Democratic convention and to gatherings for all the things she believed in, and she would cover Republicans as a journalist, and I would keep going to the Republican convention. But we needed to be careful to avoid unnecessary controversy. Everything went well in New Orleans until my friend and trapshooting buddy Tony Makris, the PR guru of the National Rifle Association, mentioned that the NRA was holding a brunch in honor of Texas Senator Phil Gramm—would I like to stop by? I'd gotten to know Gramm well by then. When I showed up the next morning, other celebrities were there also, but the reporters converged on me. The Kennedys, having endured two tragic political assassinations, were very antigun, so what was I doing at an NRA reception? I hadn't even thought about it. If I had, I would have been sensitive enough not to attend this NRA event. They also asked, as a Kennedy by marriage, was I supporting the NRA? What was my position on automatic weapons? Saturday night specials? Sniper rifles? Cop-killing bullets? I didn't know how to respond. I belonged to the NRA because I believed in the constitutional right to bear arms, but I hadn't thought through all those issues and details. There was even a question about my very presence at the 1988 Republican National Convention: was it some kind of statement in defiance of the Kennedy family? The truth was that none of the Kennedys cared, particularly not Sargent or Eunice, who depended on support from both parties for their programs and had Republican lawmakers over to their house. But I realized that the NRA was a bigger issue, and I left the brunch before the speakers even began. I was just dropping by, and I didn't want my presence there to become the story. I'd come to the convention to support George Bush, and I wanted them to write about that rather than guns.

I needed to regroup. The swarm of attention and publicity surrounding Maria's family was something I was still getting used to. This was the first time I'd really felt its sting. It was a blessing and a distraction, much more intense than what usually comes with stardom. I attended the rest of the Republican convention but skipped the meetings of my caucus group with the individual state delegations.

The contest that autumn between George Bush and the Democratic nominee, Massachusetts governor Michael Dukakis, boiled down to the whether or not Americans approved of the course that Reagan had set. Just before the election, the vice president himself invited me to campaign with him and introduce him at some rallies. By now Bush had a decisive lead over Dukakis in the polls—something like 55 percent to 38 percent, with 4 percent undecided—so my job was just to help attract crowds and maintain the momentum. But I leaped at the chance; I wasn't going to turn down a trip in Air Force Two!

We hit Ohio, Illinois, and New Jersey a few days before the election. Peggy Noonan was on the plane to help out during the closing days of the campaign. She was the brilliant speechwriter who'd written many of Reagan's great speeches. She'd also written the powerful acceptance speech Bush delivered in New Orleans. I loved the passage where Bush talked about who should succeed President Reagan: "In 1940, when I was barely more than a boy, Franklin Roosevelt said we shouldn't change horses in midstream. My friends, these days the world moves even more quickly, and now, after two great terms, a switch will be made. But when you have to change horses in midstream, doesn't it make sense to switch to one who's going the same way?" That was also the speech where Bush told voters, "Read my lips. No new taxes"—a promise that hurt him later, but still a very powerful line. The day after that speech, he shot up in the polls. He'd shown leadership. He appeared determined. It was clear in America that this was our next president.

Our starting point was Columbus, where my friend and business partner Jim Lorimer organized a rally of five thousand people in the big plaza next to the headquarters of his company, Nationwide Insurance. It was a perfect day for speeches, sunny and cool, and the company let out its employees to help make sure that the plaza was full. Peggy Noonan had scripted me, as well as the vice president. You could tell she had fun playing off my action-hero persona. I introduced him as "the *real* American hero." I told the crowd, "I am a patriotic American. I saw Ronald Reagan and George Bush take an economy that looked like Pee-wee Herman and make it look like Superman." And I dissed Governor Dukakis with a line that got picked up in all the media: "I only play the Terminator in my movies. But let me tell you, when it comes to the American future, Michael Dukakis will be the real terminator." Bush loved my speech and christened me Conan the Republican.

Aboard Air Force Two, we relaxed and kicked back as we flew from stop to stop. We talked about the campaign, about his speeches, about whether he ever lost track of what city he was going to, and how he liked campaigning. Bush had a very casual approach to the campaign trail; not everything had to be set up perfectly.

Our conversation also came around to a specific interest of mine. Back in 1980, at the start of the Reagan administration, I'd turned down an offer to join the President's Council on Physical Fitness and Sports. This was a twenty-four-member advisory panel that, in spite of its imposing title, was no longer part of the White House at all. It dated back to a fitness initiative by President Eisenhower, which, at the height of the Cold War, had been a really big deal—both he and his successor, John F. Kennedy, championed fitness as a way for America to stand strong against the Soviet threat. I especially loved the stories about what Kennedy did to promote fitness and sports. He started out as president-elect by publishing an essay in *Sports Illustrated* magazine called "The Soft American," which got a lot of attention. Once he was in the White House, he dug up an executive order from Teddy Roosevelt challenging the US Marines to complete a fifty-mile hike in twenty hours. JFK turned around and issued that same challenge to his White House staff. Being a typically competitive Kennedy brother, Bobby took him up on it and received national attention by hiking fifty miles in his leather oxford shoes. That stunt touched off a national fad of fifty-mile hikes and helped launch many fitness programs on the state and local levels—often promoted and coordinated through the President's Council.

During Vietnam, however, physical fitness fell out of the spotlight. The President's Council became an appendage of the US Department of Health, Education, and Welfare bureaucracy and stayed that way for twenty years. The Council was still prestigious enough: astronaut Jim Lovell chaired it for a long time, and so did George Allen, the legendary NFL coach. But it never got much done. For instance, when the president would invite the US Olympic team or the World Series champs to the White House, the President's Council was no longer even in the loop. That was why I turned down the invitation in 1980: I didn't want to be part of a moribund organization. Now, almost ten years later, I felt it could be turned around.

"There's a huge opportunity there," I told Bush. I described how great it would be for the White House to reassert leadership on health and fitness—especially by shifting the focus back to the idea that fitness is important for all Americans, not just athletes. "What about the other 99.9 percent of the people who never go out for sports?" I pointed out. "Who is paying attention to the overweight kid? He will never be drafted for a football game or a tennis team or a swimming team or a volleyball team or a water polo team. And what about the scrawny kid with the Coke-bottle glasses? Who is paying attention to that kid?

"A lot of schools have great athletic programs but not great *fitness* programs," I continued. "What can we do for the majority of kids who didn't go out for sports? And what about all the adults who have gotten out of shape or maybe never been in shape? It was good for JFK to highlight competitive sports to inspire people. It was good that Lyndon Johnson had made it the President's Council on Physical Fitness *and Sports*. But now we should shift the emphasis from competitive athletics to fitness for all, and make sure that everyone participates."

I knew that George Bush liked sports and kept himself in very good shape. "That's a brilliant idea if you want to put the time aside," he said. "It would take some time. If you do something, you want to do it well."

From Columbus we traveled on to Chicago, where we held a rally at a high school. On the way back to the airport, the vice president noticed this place called the Three Brothers Coffee Shop and said, "Hey, there's a Greek diner. Let's stop." So the cars all pulled over, and we went in. He did it so casually, the way he went into that restaurant and tried all the food and schmoozed with the customers, the waiters, and the kitchen help, I thought it was wonderful. Then as I thought about it afterward, I realized, "Arnold, you schmuck, he's campaigning against a guy named Dukakis. *Of course* he's going to stop at a Greek diner!"

It was a privilege to get such an inside view of a presidential campaign, especially just two weeks before the election. I'd never been involved in even a mayoral election, but now here I was seeing what the candidate does on the plane, how long he sleeps, how he preps for the next speech, how he studies the issues, how he communicates, and how relaxed he makes it all look. I was impressed with how easy Bush was with the people, how he posed for photos and talked to everybody and always knew the right thing to say. And how he kept his energy level up. He took a forty-five-minute nap on the plane. As Jimmy Carter once said, politicians are experts at naps. Then you have to wake up and absorb your briefing quickly. His staff would prep him so that he knew a little bit about the area. His daughter Doro was always along with him to lend moral support.

It was a whole different level of intensity from a movie set because everywhere you go, the media are there. You have no room for mistakes. Every wrong word, every gesture you make that's a little odd, they will pick up and amplify into some huge thing. Bush dealt with it casually.

By Thanksgiving, as the Republicans were savoring Bush's victory, we were getting ready to launch *Twins*. I'd never seen a director fine-tune a movie as methodically as Ivan Reitman. He'd sit in a test screening, talk to the audience, and then go back and change the music or shorten a certain scene and test the movie again. And the crucial "want to see" statistic would now be two points higher. Then he'd make another change, and it would go up another point. We literally drove *Twins* from 88 to 93, which Ivan said was even higher than *Ghostbusters*.

The premiere of the movie was a much happier combination of my worlds than the Republican convention had been. Eunice and Sarge engineered a huge benefit event at the John F. Kennedy Center for the Performing Arts, where the showing of *Twins* capped a daylong festival of entertainment in Washington, DC, promoting the Special Olympics. President-elect Bush came with his wife, Barbara, and Teddy Kennedy, Massachusetts congressman Joe Kennedy II, and other members of the Kennedy and Shriver clans all came. Barbara Walters and TV news anchorwoman Connie Chung were there, and even business tycoons Armand Hammer and Donald Trump. Out front there was a traffic jam of stretch limos, along with dozens of cameras crews and hundreds of fans.

A demo of gymnastics and weight lifting by Special Olympics athletes opened the show. Then the president elect got up onstage and praised the athletes for their courage before turning to me. "There are all kinds of courage," he joked. "There is the courage of my friend Arnold Schwarzenegger, who more than once campaigned with me across this country—then returned home each time to take the heat from his own in-laws." That got a laugh.

In fact, Eunice and Sarge always went to see my movies, and they would call me the next day to tell me what they thought. But not everyone in the Kennedy family was as enthusiastic about my films, because of the weapons and violence. So Eunice was only half joking when she said, "At last, the family can go see one of your movies." *Twins* was the comedy hit of the season, which of course I loved because this was my first Christmastime movie, and it went over the top. The movie had a big opening weekend in mid-December and just kept going and going. Every day between Christmas and New Year's, our US box office receipts topped $3 million—or more than a half million tickets sold per day. It was a happy ending for everybody who had taken a chance. Ivan went on producing and directing hit comedies, including *Kindergarten Cop* and *Junior* with me. Danny kept expanding his amazing talent into directing films like *The War of the Roses* and producing films like *Pulp Fiction* and *Get Shorty*. For Universal, *Twins* capped a year of five or six successes with a huge hit—and after Tom Pollock retired, he became chief executive of Ivan Reitman's production company.

Hollywood is the town of copying. Now that I'd added a comedy dimension to my career, everybody started sending me comedy scripts in addition to scripts for action movies. More important, thanks to our unprecedented deal with Universal, I ended up making more money with *Twins* than I have with any of my *Terminator* movies. It didn't take studios long to draw the line. Today nobody can come close to a deal as open ended as the one we had on *Twins*.

Counting international sales, video rights, and so on, *Twins* has been worth more than $35 million to me alone—and counting, because the DVDs keep selling and it keeps being shown on TV. For twenty-five years I've been trying to convince Universal to do a sequel. It would be called *Triplets*, and Eddie Murphy, whom I love and admire, would play our unknown other brother. Just recently at the Polo Lounge at the Beverly Hills Hotel we agreed to fast-track the project, and now *Triplets* is on the way.

As my success grew, Sarge was always challenging me to do more for the public good. "Arnold," he would say, "your movies and your acting are great. Now tell me: how many times do you want to do another car chase?" He didn't know anything about the entertainment business.

In 1978, for the premiere of the first *Superman* movie, he and Eunice hosted a Special Olympics fund-raiser in a big tent at their house. Seated next to Sarge at the head table was none other than Superman himself, Christopher Reeve.

"What do you do?" Sarge asked him.

"I'm in the movie. I play Superman."

"That's fantastic! Superman!" exclaimed Sarge. "But you know, I think it's more interesting that we have supermen in real life." There was a side of him that wanted to be diplomatic and respectful but also another side that couldn't understand how anyone could waste all those hours wearing costumes and makeup. Sarge never read the entertainment pages.

"How many people do you save when you look good on the set?" he'd ask me. He'd tease me about how I'd been awed by James Earl Jones during the making of *Conan*. "You told me James Earl Jones was in the middle of a speech and forgot his line and how professional he was, how he held his gesture and his pose and said, 'Give me the line, guys, give me the line.' And the next line was 'I am the wellspring, from which you flow,' and then he said, 'Oh, yeah . . . I am the wellspring, from which you flow.'

"So is *that* what's important to you? To be able to freeze in the middle of a scene and to have somebody give you your line? Wouldn't it be much better to go through Africa and show them how to dig wells and how to make vegetables grow and inspire them to plant?"

It was a collision of worlds, but I didn't disagree entirely. Acting went only so far in terms of real accomplishment. Still, I felt Sarge was hitting below the belt. I was only trying to explain why I admired James Earl Jones. I got him back a year later. He was telling me about traveling with Armand Hammer to make oil deals in Russia after Sarge went back to the private practice of law. He described hanging out at night with Russian oil experts. "You have no idea what great vodka they have," Sarge said.

"Is that what you really admire?" I asked. "Is that what your life is all about? That you have the best vodka?"

"No, no, no! We made a huge deal."

"I'm just joking. Remember when you said to me about acting, 'Is that all you care about, being able to freeze in the middle of a scene and ask for a line?' "

"I get it, I get it," Sarge admitted.

Public service accounted for a lot of the conversation in his and Eunice's house. "Arnold, you have such an unbelievable personality," they'd tell me. "Imagine using all of what God gave you to reach out and pump up other people: the Special Olympians, the homeless, the sick, the returning military. It almost makes no difference which cause you pick. You would bring such a spotlight because of your energy and your stardom."

I was already on a crusade around the world to promote health and fitness to young people. I'd stepped up my commitment to the Special Olympics so that now I was the US national coach of power lifting, regularly conducting seminars and making appearances all over the country. And with my growing popularity as a movie star, I was ready to take on more.

"What else can I do?" I asked Sarge and Eunice. They had plenty of ideas. Eunice was a constant inspiration. What she'd accomplished, to my mind, was larger than the work of most mayors, governors, senators, and even presidents. Not only did she expand the Special Olympics to encompass more than 175 countries, but she also changed people's thinking around the world. Many nations viewed the mentally challenged as a drag on society or a danger to themselves, to be treated as outcasts or warehoused in mental institutions. Eunice used her name and her influence to free those people to have regular lives and the same social benefits as other citizens. It was a tough challenge, because governments didn't want to be told they were doing something wrong. They felt embarrassed when Eunice Kennedy Shriver would show up and put the spotlight on the institutions where the mentally disabled were locked up. But one by one, the nations came around—even China, which eventually overcame centuries of social prejudice to host the

International Special Olympics Games in 2007. Those were the biggest games in the history of the movement. There were eighty thousand people in the stadium, and the president of China came. I was there too, leading the American team in the opening ceremony.

After the 1988 election, I'd sent word to the president-elect reiterating my interest in the President's Council on Physical Fitness and Sports. I said that I hoped he would consider me when he turned to other appointments after building his cabinet. If he needed help on the fitness council, I'd be more than happy to come in and share my vision. Bush's staff, of course, was aware of my passion for promoting health and fitness for youngsters. Eunice sent a letter recommending me for the job and pointing out that I was "the number one star" in the United States. The president responded, thanking her for "recommending our man Conan."

At present, though, she was much more focused on the production of grandchildren. Eunice had become very concerned when Maria and I didn't have kids right away. We'd been married now for almost three years. She kept saying to Maria, "Why don't you have kids?" and Maria kept saying, "I have my job; it doesn't fit in yet. And Arnold is too busy; he's always on sets." And so on. Those obstacles were real. Maria had become one of the top personalities of NBC News. Not only was she coanchor of the *Sunday Today* show and *Main Street,* NBC's award-winning monthly newsmagazine for young people, but also she anchored the weekend news and was a regular stand-in for Tom Brokaw on the *NBC Nightly News* and other news programs. All of these shows were based in New York. In summer 1988 Maria had won an Emmy as coanchor of NBC's coverage of the Olympics in Seoul, South Korea. She was making well over $1 million a year and traveling all the time—hardly the right circumstances for becoming a mom.

But her mother felt, "No, there has to be another reason. Maybe they're having problems getting pregnant." So Eunice started looking into the effects of steroids on male reproduction. She never talked to me about it, but she sent Maria a five-page scientific briefing by one of the doctors connected to the Special Olympics. I could visualize exactly how it had come about. Eunice had done what she always did, which was to go to her office and say, "Get me an expert to help with this issue" or "Get me someone to write this speech" or "Get me the White House on the phone."

It was a very thorough report, custom written for Maria. It explained that if you have sex regularly and you're trying to get pregnant but you don't, there are many possible reasons, but one might be if your husband has used or abused steroids. Then it went into explaining everything medically.

I just happened to see the report on Maria's desk, so I read it, and I was laughing my head off. I said, "Your mother is out of control."

"I know, I know," Maria said. She was laughing too. "Can you believe that? I have to calm her down."

It was typical for Eunice to try to plant herself in the middle of the action. I used to joke that she wanted to sleep between us in bed on our honeymoon in order to supervise. In the Kennedy family, this wasn't completely far fetched: the legend was that when Eunice and Sarge went on their honeymoon to France, they arrived at the hotel to discover Teddy in the lobby. Joe had sent him as a chaperone.

Apart from all this, however, Maria did hear the ticking of the biological clock. She had just turned thirty-three, a year older than Eunice had been when she and Sarge had their first baby. So in 1989, we decided to get going, and Maria became pregnant with Katherine.

I was back in action-hero mode that spring, making *Total Recall,* but fatherhood was never far from my mind. One day in my trailer, wading through scripts, I came across a draft of *Kindergarten Cop.* I couldn't put it down; the idea of a tough detective who has to go undercover teaching a bunch of preschoolers made me laugh. People in Hollywood always said, "Never act with kids or animals. They're impossible to work with, and then they look so cute onscreen that they steal the show." I'd already had experience with animals as Conan, and they'd been fine. But I'd been interested in doing a movie with kids for years, and the prospect of becoming a dad inspired me. I thought, "Great! Let the kids steal the show. As long as the movie succeeds." I called to make sure the script was available. Then I asked Ivan Reitman if he'd direct me again. We both wanted changes in the script to add social relevance: I wanted to add a physical fitness theme, and he wanted it to touch on broken homes, child abuse, and family life. But we agreed to go ahead. Since Ivan already had *Ghostbusters II* in the works for the 1989 holidays, we started planning *Kindergarten Cop* for Christmas 1990.

CHAPTER 19

The Real Life of a Terminator

WHEN OUR FIRST BABY arrived in December 1989, I was right there in the delivery room with the video camera.

"Hold it right there!"

"No, we have to pull the baby out."

"No, no, wait. Just let me make sure I got the shot." Those people in the delivery room probably have seen it all.

Maria and I had made all the preparations that first-time parents make. As her due date neared, we had a Lamaze teacher come to the house. Of course, I did all that; as the father, you have to. You have to show extraordinary interest in the pregnancy and the childbirth and the afterbirth and cutting the cord and all that, unlike in my father's world, where the guy was totally out of the picture. (Somebody made a video of me imitating our Lamaze class, and seeing that helped convince Ivan Reitman to do the movie *Junior*, in which I play a scientist who becomes pregnant as part of a scientific experiment.)

The whole Lamaze thing was horrifying to both our mothers.

"You're down there helping pull out the baby?" my mother asked. "You're videotaping her vagina? I'm sorry, this is too much for me."

Eunice's reaction was more or less the same. "Good for you if it makes Maria happy. For myself, I wanted them to give me a shot and put me out. Sarge wasn't allowed to come in for three days. And when he did come, I looked like a picture postcard, and the only thing different was the baby."

Seeing Katherine's birth, I felt the most unbelievable joy. I said to myself, "Fuck! This is my first baby!" That's the interesting thing about the human mind, that you can be so overwhelmed by something that billions of people in history have done. Of course, I took charge of the situation right away: working with the nurse to clean up the baby, bringing her over to get weighed, putting the little hat on her so she didn't get cold, and putting on the little outfit and the diaper—and, naturally, taking endless photos and videos. Maria was crying for joy, and I stayed with her while she rested, and after awhile the nurse came in and showed us how to breast-feed. Whenever I heard guys say that they cried after their baby was born, I always thought, "That is such bullshit." But sure enough, when I went home and called my friends about Katherine's birth, I cried.

Maria's parents were in Washington, and my mom was in Austria. "We are not going to come until you invite us. This should be your moment together," Sarge and Eunice had said. Maybe Maria told them to say that, I don't know. But while childbirth was definitely not Eunice's thing, Maria was her only daughter, and the next day, she was there. I didn't mind; we'd had our private moment. Maria felt it was the first thing we'd done in a big way alone, without her mother interfering. She loved just the two of us going to the hospital.

A dozen paparazzi were shooting from across the parking lot when we left the hospital the next night, but we got Katherine home, and then the whole drama of the adjustment began. Because from that moment on, your life as a couple has changed. Even after your kids leave home, you will still feel responsible. I had others to look after now: Maria and me, my mom, Katherine, and more children would follow. Maria always wanted to have five kids because she came from a family of five, while I preferred two because I came from a family of two. I thought we would settle somewhere in the middle.

When Maria came home, and Sarge and Eunice arrived from Washington a day later, we tried to work out the rhythm of the breast-feeding and the diaper changing and the question of how the baby room should be decorated. Pretty quickly a nanny came into the picture, and I felt my importance kind of slipping away. Baby care became a dialogue between her and Maria. At first I didn't pay much attention to this, but then I read something and also saw something on TV about "gatekeeping." I said to myself, "Yes! That's exactly what's happening to me! I'm getting aced out, I can't make a move that is right, everyone is always worried that I'm holding the baby the wrong way." I decided I had to break through all that and have more fun with it.

It must have been in some magazine I picked up in a doctor's office, because normally I wasn't into reading about how to take care of the baby. I felt that there were no magazines or books around in the Stone Age, and yet every schmuck took care of babies back then, so how wrong could you go? As long as you love the baby, you figure it out, just like with everything you love doing. Caring for babies is hardwired into the brain. I've sat on an airplane many times and felt startled by even the tiniest peep from a baby twenty rows back.

In fact, I felt lucky, because Maria was a fabulous mother, which is not something you can necessarily tell about a person in advance. In spite of the gatekeeping, I admired how totally in control of the situation she was. I didn't have to worry at all. She had the instincts, she had the knowledge, she'd studied enough books, and she worked closely with the nanny—there was no shortcoming there whatsoever, which I could see even as I was being pushed aside.

Even so, I was determined that gatekeeping would not happen again. So a couple of years later, in July 1991, when we had Christina, I put my foot down from Day One. Not that I said, "No, you can't tell me to leave the room anymore." Instead, at night when we went to bed and when Maria finished breast-feeding Christina, I would take the baby from her immediately and put her on my chest. Christina would be kind of spread-eagled, with her hands and feet hanging off the sides. I don't know who'd told me to do this; it was some guy who said, "I always put my baby on my chest."

"How can you sleep like that?" I asked him.

"I don't know. Somehow it works. I have no idea. Maybe I never slept that deeply, but it was okay because it was for the baby."

I said to myself, "Yes! That's what I'm going to do." I found that with Christina on my chest, I would sleep, but not so soundly that I would turn and roll over on top of her. Nature had built in that safeguard. I'd be lying there asleep, and all of a sudden I'd hear the baby making little stirring noises. I'd look over at the clock and see that four hours had passed. It was just like the nurse in the hospital had said: "You'll need to breast-feed every four or five hours." So I'd hand the baby to Maria, she'd breast-feed her again, and I'd take the baby back for a couple more hours of sleep.

I was much more on top of the diaper situation too. I started changing them right away and said to the women, "Now, girls, I totally failed with the first baby because for every hundred diapers Maria did, I did maybe one. That's not fair. Not fair to the baby, not fair to you, not fair to me. I want to participate more this time." I would just close the door, and lock it if they tried to hover.

So I just moved right in there, boom, boom, boom, and did it. Within a week or two, I graduated to the level that when we heard the baby, I was allowed to go upstairs and change her diaper without anyone following me.

"This is an enormous breakthrough," I said to myself. It felt like heaven, being in the room alone, just looking at this little girl, with no one hanging over my shoulder, and changing the diaper. It calmed down Christina, and all of sudden she went back to sleep, and I felt like, "I did that!" It was such a great sense of accomplishment and great joy of participating.

But then with our third baby, it was a battle again, because Patrick was the first boy. He had to be treated differently, "like a boy," whatever that meant. We both were ecstatic, and I had not expected Maria to be that over-the-top ecstatic about the idea that it was a boy. She was really into being *the* force in his growing up. So, again, it was very hard at first to share parenting, but we did. And by the time Christopher, our second son, arrived in 1997, we were very good at the balancing act. When the boys come, instead of buying Barbie dolls, all of a sudden you're into trucks and remote controls, cars and tanks. You buy building blocks and build castles and locomotives. You get into knives and later take them shooting with pistols, shotguns, and rifles. All of which made me very happy.

The birth of our daughters came just as I reached the stratosphere with my movie career. By Christmas 1990, a few weeks after Katherine's first birthday, *Time* magazine put me on the cover as Hollywood's top star and called me "at forty-three, the most potent symbol of worldwide dominance of the US entertainment industry." *Kindergarten Cop* was in the theaters that holiday and was already a major hit.

But I had an even bigger project in the works: *Terminator 2: Judgment Day.*

Seven years had passed since *The Terminator* lifted both our careers, and Jim Cameron and I had always felt committed to a sequel. He'd directed a couple of huge pictures since then—*Aliens* and *The Abyss*—and, finally, in 1990 he got the rights and preliminary financing in place for *Terminator 2*. Still, I was a little thrown when Jim sat me down at a restaurant and told me his concept for my character in the film.

"How can the Terminator not kill anyone?" I asked. "He's a terminator! That's what people want to see, me kicking in doors and machine-gunning everybody." I was suspicious that the studio was pulling back and trying to make the Terminator into something rated PG. That had destroyed Conan and I didn't want to see it happen to the Terminator.

"No, no," said Jim. "You're still really dangerous and violent. But this time the Terminator comes back when John Connor is a kid, and he's programmed to protect him. He's not the villain anymore. The villain is a new, smaller, even scarier terminator—the T-1000—that is programmed to kill Connor. Your terminator has to stop it." The killing was still there, but it was done by the T-1000. As soon as I understood that the movie was going to stay R-rated, I relaxed.

As *T2* began taking shape, my other businesses were booming. I'd used some of the money I'd earned in films as capital to expand in real estate. Now I owned three good-sized apartment buildings in LA with a total of more than two hundred units, plus the Denver property, which Al Ehringer and I were developing into offices, restaurants, and shops. Our gamble on the run-down side of Santa Monica had paid off too: 3110 Main was now a thriving complex of offices and shops, and the neighborhood had become hip. Our first set of tenants—boring corporate tenants like a bank, an insurance agency, and a real estate office—had given way to producers, directors, and entertainers. Johnny Carson had his office on the second floor, and I split the third floor with Oliver Stone. "Why don't I take the space to the left of the elevators," he suggested, "and you take the space to the right? That fits with our politics." I laughed and agreed, which is why my office is where it is today. A little later, LA Lakers basketball star Shaquille O'Neal moved into the building, and then other producers and sports managers followed.

I was also launching a huge public service project. Very soon after Katherine's birth, I got the call from the White House that I'd been hoping for. "The president would like you to chair the President's Council on Physical Fitness and Sports," the representative told me formally, adding, "He says he wants you to do just what you proposed during the campaign: to put fitness for everybody back on the national agenda." Being named "the president's fitness czar," as the media called it, was the most satisfying development in my work life. I saw this as part of the crusade I'd started decades ago, promoting bodybuilding as a means to fitness and health. Also, by working with the Special Olympics, I was selling the idea of sports and fitness for everyone, not just athletes. This was why I'd been so emphatic with President Bush about wanting the job. So much could be done with it. The White House always made the mistake of appointing big sports names, but not people who had a record of getting the job done or had the ability to follow through. You needed an athlete or idol, yes, but someone who would do the work, not just sit on the throne. I had a clear vision of what had to be done. And by this time, I was addicted to public service, especially doing things for kids. It had nothing to do with fame anymore.

This news was almost as gratifying to my mother-in-law as it was to me. Eunice had written personally to President Bush to recommend me—she felt passionately about fitness not only because of her leadership of the Special Olympics but also because the strongest presidential champion for fitness since Teddy Roosevelt had been her brother Jack. When I called to thank her, she asked immediately, "How are they planning to announce it?"

"I don't know," I said. "What would you suggest?"

"First of all, I'd have you meet with the president in the Oval Office. Have them take a picture of that meeting and release it to the public. After the meeting, I'd have you and the president come out of the White House together and talk to the press. You should be ready to make a statement about what you bring to the table and what your mission as chairman is going to be. You always have to have a mission and a reason why you're the right choice."

Eunice had the Kennedy political genius. She knew that a job appointment at this level was not normally considered big enough to justify a press conference. The president has all kinds of councils: the Council of Economic Advisers, the health council, the drug council, the job creation council, and on and on. Ordinarily, for an appointment like mine, the White House press office would simply put out a statement along the lines of: "Today President Bush announced that he has chosen Arnold Schwarzenegger to be the chairman of the President's Council on Fitness." After that, it would be an uphill battle to get anybody's attention. But if the press sees you coming out of the Oval Office with the president, you'll win respect.

The president, it turned out, was totally on board—he had his guys orchestrate the announcement to make me look like a big shot. It was very close to what Eunice had envisioned. I went outside the White

House to where the journalists were. I talked about my appointment, my meeting in the Oval Office, my enthusiasm, my vision, my mission statement.

The challenge of being fitness czar really excited me, and by the time I met with the president again, up at Camp David in Maryland a few weeks later, I'd done my homework. I wanted to bring back and expand all the sports and fitness events that JFK had held. I'd asked Sarge and Eunice what they thought I could do with this appointment. They'd been around when Jack was in charge; what was his vision? Why did he hold fitness events in front of the White House on the South Lawn? I wrote down everything. I met with the Department of Health and Human Services, the Department of Agriculture, and White House officials. That's how I started building an agenda. I also sought out experts like John Cates of the University of California, San Diego, implementer of the country's first Youth Fitness Camps. So I was ready with a detailed proposal.

"The council has been thinking small," I told President Bush. "We need to change that." I described how we would bang the drum in DC and get the departments in charge of health, education, and nutrition to coordinate on a national fitness campaign. We'd also make fitness much more visible at the White House. "Let's do a public fitness demo on the White House lawn this spring," I suggested.

I sketched how this would work: we'd set up stations for golf, tennis, aerobics, weight training, baseball, rope climbing, and other activities that the average person could undertake. We'd invite trainers, athletes, parents, grandparents, and kids, and the national media, especially the morning shows. "We'll get everyone involved," I said. "Then you and Barbara can come out of the White House and take the lead and try things. It'll be a celebration, like Fourth of July, and it will show that fitness is fun."

The president became very enthusiastic. "When we get back to Washington on Monday," he said, "I want you to meet with the White House staff and get this under way." I also proposed restoring the presidential awards program, the fitness certificates and medals that JFK had handed out. "People were very proud of those certificates and medals," I said. "They lead to challenges in schools, and that's how you get the kids involved in the movement." He liked that idea too.

My own mission, I explained, should be to get out and promote. Digging into the realities of fitness in United States, I'd realized that I would have to address it both state by state and locally. Some states had a governor's council on fitness, some didn't. Some had statewide programs, others left it up to local governments and the schools. Only one state actually required daily physical education in schools from kindergarten through twelfth grade. I felt very strongly that I had to carry to all fifty states the message that fitness was a national priority.

"You're going to all fifty states?" he asked.

"You'll see," I told him. "I love being on the road and meeting people and selling. That's what I do best."

At the first meeting at the White House to plan the Great American Workout, about fifteen government officials were present. And they all said no. The guy from the parks department said no because so many people would ruin the lawn. The guy responsible for public safety said, "The weather in Washington can get very hot in May. People will be fainting, and they'll need water and food, and we don't have a budget for that." The guy from the Secret Service said, "We can't cover that many people if the president is moving from station to station. Too much risk."

Afterward, I told Jim Pinkerton, the White House policy advisor I'd been working with, that it was the worst meeting I'd ever had. "Let me explain this to the president, and you should talk to him too," he said. I saw President Bush a couple of days later and described the official reaction I'd gotten.

"Oh, that's typical government." He laughed. "It always starts out like that. But don't be discouraged. Let me talk to them."

At the next planning meeting, they all sat down and said, "It's a great idea. We found a way around the problems. It's very complicated, but the president wants to do this."

So on Tuesday, May 1, 1990, at precisely 7:19 a.m., President and

Mrs. Bush emerged from the White House to join what he declared was the first annual Great American Workout. Two thousand visitors were already on the South Lawn doing the activities we'd set up across four or five acres: aerobic dancing, exercise machines, horseshoe pitching, hoop shooting, soccer, and ball playing. The cameras followed as the president and Barbara went from activity to activity. We'd put together a spectacle that would have impressed even JFK. It put across both the importance and the joy of physical activity.

We'd done a walk-through the day before. I didn't think about it at the time, but watching the preparations, I learned things that I would put to use later in my own campaigns. I saw firsthand how to plan and stage the event for the media: figuring out where you want them to be part of it, where you *don't* want them to be part of it, and when and how they would be invited. The Great American Workout was officially open from seven to nine o'clock in the morning. The reason the president joined at 7:19, I learned, was that 7:19 was the moment of peak viewership on the *Today* show and *Good Morning America.* Until then, I'd made dozens of appearances on morning TV and never paid any attention to what time I was scheduled to be on the air. But from then on, I would always insist on appearing sometime right around 7:30.

Not long after the Great American Workout, I took time out from being fitness czar to fly to Cannes. I went primarily to promote *Total Recall,* which was scheduled for release that June. But the ride over, on the Carolco jet, was all about *Terminator 2.* Jim Cameron had just finished the script with his coauthor and had promised to bring it along for everyone to see. He handed it out after we took off. By the time we landed, we'd read it and were jumping all over the airplane in excitement about how big and technologically sophisticated the story was. I never expected *T2* to be just an ordinary sequel: Cameron is a big believer in surprising the audience, and I felt confident that *Terminator 2* would be as amazing and unexpected as the original. But this script blew me away. I asked a lot of questions about the shape-shifting

Terminator 1000 that my character would be fighting against—it was a challenge even to imagine a machine made of liquid metal alloy. That's when I realized that Cameron's knowledge of science and the world of the future went way beyond the ordinary. After we reached Cannes, the foreign distributors flipped over the script and couldn't wait to sign up. No one batted an eye that *Terminator 2* would cost $70 million to produce—more than ten times as much as the original. They knew it was going to be a huge success.

T2 was always meant to be much bigger than *The Terminator*. Not only did it have a giant budget, but also it took eight months to shoot rather than six weeks. We were in a race against the clock: the movie had to be ready for summer 1991 to meet its financial commitments. The preproduction was so complicated that filming couldn't start until October 1990, and by the time production finished in May 1991, *T2* had become the most expensive film project in history, at $94 million.

Cameron told a reporter, "Every time I start a film, I have a fantasy that it will be like a big family, and we'll have a good time, and we'll have all of these wonderful, creative moments together. But that's not what filmmaking is; it's a battle." What made my character challenging is that this time the Terminator is adopting human behavior patterns as the plot unfolds. It was typical Cameron genius to have character development in a machine. The kid says to the Terminator, "No more killing; promise," and orders me to talk less like a dork and more like a person. So the part has me transforming from being a killing machine to something that's attempting to be human but not always getting there. I'm not very convincing the first time the kid gets me to say "Hasta la vista, baby." Gradually the Terminator becomes humanized, but only to a certain extent. It's still very dangerous and causes a lot of mayhem. Still, compared to the T-1000, I am definitely the good guy.

We were shooting the scenes out of sequence, so we were always having to figure out the right degree of humanity for the Terminator to show for that stage in the plot. For the first several weeks, I was constantly asking Jim, "Is he too human now, or not human enough?"

T2 opened whole new possibilities in visual effects. The T-1000 is made of liquid metal and can morph before your eyes to mimic any person or object it touches. The computer-graphics guys handled that challenge. But the movie also required grueling work from the actors and stunt doubles. Cameron would push his brother Mike, who was creating props and stunts, and Mike would push the envelope and us.

We started rehearsing the stunts months in advance. In the spectacular chase scene in the dry Los Angeles drainage canal, the Terminator is supposed to blast away one-handed with a sawed off ten-gauge lever-action shotgun while driving a Harley: pull out the gun, aim, fire, spin it to recock it, fire again, and so on. It all sounded great in the script, and it was doable—just a matter of reps, reps, reps. But the preparation was pure pain and discomfort. I couldn't wear a glove because it would get stuck in the gun mechanism, and I tore the skin off my hand and fingers practicing a hundred times until I mastered the skill. Then I had to learn to do it while riding the Harley. Then I needed to put the riding and the gun skill together with the acting. It's hard to watch where you're driving and look where the director wants you to look at the same time. In one shot, I had to bring the front wheel of the moving bike almost to the lens of the camera on a truck in front of me. Simultaneously I was supposed to be shooting out, not looking down. And it would ruin the shot to have my eyes darting around.

I also had to ride the Harley toward a chained gate and shoot open the padlock before crashing through it. That took weeks of practice, first with gun alone, then on the bike, and then to do it all with cool. I did the takeoff of a spectacular jump with the bike into the canal bed. The other adult leads, Linda Hamilton as Sarah Connor and Robert Patrick as the T-1000, had it just as tough. Linda put herself through months of three-times-a-day physical conditioning to make herself convincing as a survivalist warrior. All of the stunts were so big that they took a lot more perspiration than in *T1*.

Every few weeks, when there was a break in the shooting, I'd morph from being the Terminator to being President Bush's fitness czar. The job and my friendship with the president quickly became a very big part of my life. My compensation for the movie included a Gulfstream III jet, the perfect vehicle for visiting the states. My plan was to cover all fifty during President Bush's first term in office. That gave me three years. I put the map of the United States in front of me and looked to see which states were close together. My idea was to group them and, whenever I had a few days free from shooting or other business, hit four or six at a time—leaving room for improvisation, of course, because the governors wouldn't always be available when I was. Many times if I had other business—a seminar, say, or a contest in Columbus, or a vacation in Hawaii—I'd organize the surrounding states.

When I visited the governors, I assured them that politics wouldn't come into play. This was pure fitness and sports. For many governors, that was hard to understand. "The Terminator is coming from the Republican White House to expose me as not paying enough attention to children," they would think, worrying that I would steamroll in and embarrass them. But we made it clear in advance that this was not our agenda. I wasn't preaching a Republican philosophy but a fitness philosophy. Word got around, and suddenly the governors were at ease. We started to be welcomed. Everyone joined the fitness crusade.

It was a great, great learning experience to see firsthand the way state and local governments work. I'd never seen so many instant advocates for physical fitness. I figured out that we could do two states a day. Usually we'd start with breakfast with the governor, and I'd talk to him or her about improving fitness in the state. Every state was different, so I had to study up. Then we'd head to a school and join the kids in a fitness class. Next would come a press conference. In some states they were huge: a whole gymnasium packed with parents and kids would welcome us, with the school band playing. I'd always present the governor with a Tony Nowak jacket with the President's Council logo, and help him put it on, and there would be a photo op of him surrounded by kids.

The final step was always a "fitness summit," where we invited people from the Departments of Education and Health and Human Services, the governor's staff, education officials, health club owners, the YMCA, the American Alliance for Health, Physical Education, Recreation and Dance, and so on. Usually it would be a crowded meeting room with fifty to one hundred people. We'd talk about the importance of fitness for kids and the health risks of not exercising. And they would make recommendations about how to work together. Then we'd get back on the plane, go to the next state, and do exactly the same thing in the afternoon.

Later on, I realized that it had a lot in common with a campaign trip. You're on a tight schedule, you have to be there at a certain time, do the speech, pump everyone up. The school bands welcome you, and the local politicians come out and drum up a storm of support. After being the fitness czar, running for governor of California felt like déjà vu.

Interestingly, nobody ever objected to my using my own plane. If people asked, "Is the government paying for this?" it was good to be able to tell them, "No. I'm paying for everything myself. Including the stationery. I'm not doing this for money. I'm doing it to give something back. My talent is fitness and, therefore, this is something I can give back." It felt great to be echoing Sarge.

Those fitness summits were like a crash course in politics. In California, when I urged the attendees to step up the physical education in the schools, they jumped on me.

"Well, tell our governor to put more money into education, so we can hire phys-ed teachers."

"But there's a recession," I said, "and from what I've read, our state is getting less revenue, so our governor doesn't have the funds."

"He should reallocate funds from other programs. This is for the kids."

"But if there's no money, why don't you look somewhere like the YMCA or one of the local sports clubs, and see if they can provide trainers to help out?"

"Oh! So the schools should use volunteers instead of teachers? That's a good one. In fact, if you read our state law, Arnold, you'd know it's illegal to fill an existing teaching slot with a volunteer."

I was running into a teachers' union taboo against volunteers in the schools. Encountering that attitude was a real eye-opener. It was not about the kids, as they claimed. It was about getting more teachers jobs. Of course, I understood that's what unions do: fight for their own.

Of all the governors, the one who made the deepest impression on me was Mario Cuomo. New York was about the tenth state I visited. From a distance, I'd never liked Governor Cuomo because of the way he'd attacked Reagan in his 1984 Democratic convention keynote address: "Mr. President," he said, "you ought to know that this nation is more a 'Tale of Two Cities' than it is just a 'Shining City on a Hill.' " But when I met him and we talked about fitness, he was responsive and complimentary. He gave very valuable pointers. For example, he advised, "You have to mention more about kids' health, and you've got to talk about the costs. That is big, big, big. Talk about the health disaster that will develop and what it will cost the taxpayer if kids don't get fit." He was very supportive of what I'd done. I could see why Cuomo was so well liked in his state and why he was a great leader.

Then we went before the media, and he did a whole spiel about how great it is for me to travel around the United States and to use my own money and do all this voluntarily. "This is what service is about," he said. I thought, "He knows that I'm a Republican and that I represent a Republican president; it's really gracious and generous of him to make this much of an effort." More than that, I thought he was right. I still had forty states to go, and I was able to incorporate his suggestions in my message.

My friendship with President Bush was warm from the time we first met during the Reagan years. I felt honored when he asked me to attend the inauguration and to introduce him at some of the surrounding events—although introducing him was also somewhat uncomfortable at times, I have to admit. There were so many people who perhaps would have been more worthy. In particular, I remember a Martin Luther King Day celebration where there were a lot of African-Americans in the audience and many black speakers. If I'd been sitting there, I'd have wondered, "Why is *he* the one introducing the president?" But that's the way Bush was. He didn't care about any of that. If you had talent and did him a favor or he liked you, he would push you forward whether it made sense or not. He was a different breed, a sweetheart of a guy. Both he and Barbara were really courteous and kind. Every single thing I did for them, he would drop me a handwritten note or call to say thanks.

We grew quite close after he chose me for the fitness job. I could go over to the White House and see him anytime I was in Washington. We had that kind of relationship. Anytime. John Sununu was his chief of staff in the beginning, and he also was welcoming to me. It was never "The boss is busy now, come back tomorrow."

We felt honored to be invited many times to join the president and Barbara at Camp David. The White House can be very confining, and they loved to get away there on the weekend, even though the president always brought along work. I would fly up with them on the helicopter or meet them there. We'd go out to local restaurants and go to church on Sunday. And, of course, President Bush loved physical activity and games.

One time, when a journalist asked him, "Mr. President, did Arnold show you some exercises?" he laughed and said, "Oh, when he comes up to Camp David, we work out together all the time. He teaches me weight training and I teach him about wallyball."

"Wallyball? You mean volleyball."

"No, no, wallyball."

"What's wallyball?"

"We have this indoor arena where we play volleyball, and we have special rules that let you play the ball off the wall. Arnold has played several times already, and he's getting better."

I bowled up there with the president. We threw horseshoes. We swam. We lifted weights. I went trap shooting with him! (When does the Secret Service ever let you carry a gun around the president?) On a snowy weekend in early 1991, just as Katherine was learning to walk, the three of us visited the Bushes and went tobogganing. Unfortunately, I did not know the toboggan. It's different from a sled, which you can steer with your feet; the toboggan is flat, and it slides differently. The president and I came down the hill too fast and crashed into Barbara, and she ended up in the hospital with a broken leg. I still have the photo President Bush sent me afterward. It shows him and me on the toboggan and is inscribed, "Turn, dammit, turn!"

Heavy meetings went down at Camp David after Iraq's August 1990 invasion of Kuwait. It was so strange to shuttle back and forth between a real-world crisis and the make-believe threat to the future on the *Terminator 2* set in LA. Defense Secretary Dick Cheney and General Colin Powell, the chairman of the Joint Chiefs of Staff, would come up to Camp David to brief the president and hold decision making sessions. By fall, President Bush had launched Operation Desert Shield, the massive buildup of US and coalition forces along the Saudi Arabian border with Iraq and Kuwait. I made my own small contribution to the military effort after reading a newspaper report that American troops in the desert were doing their weight training using pails of sand. Of course, a person's muscles don't care where the resistance comes from. Still, I thought we could do much better for the troops. I remembered how I'd carried weights and a training bench on my tank in the Austrian army. So I went to General Powell and asked him what he thought of sending over proper weight-training equipment. He loved the idea, and within a few days, I was able to enlist manufacturers to donate forty tons of weight machines, benches, barbells, and other gear for Operation Desert Shield. Sending it aboard a cargo ship would have taken many weeks, so instead Powell and Cheney worked out a way to have it airlifted from Oklahoma along with private contractors' shipments. Within two weeks, the gear was delivered to the troops, and I started receiving extraordinary letters and photos thanking me and describing how soldiers were training in shifts to maximize access to the new equipment.

I've always felt appreciative of the armed forces because I've benefited from the American dream, and their courage and dedication is what safeguards it. From my early days as a bodybuilding champion, I made a point of visiting military bases and warships whenever I had the opportunity. As I got into movies, it was natural to add USO appearances to my promotional tours abroad. I often visited marine detachments at American embassies too, in Japan, Germany, South Korea, Russia, and many other countries. There's no school to teach you how to entertain the troops, but I traded notes with other celebrities like Jay Leno and developed a shtick. I'd talk about my movies, do a little standup (the grosser the better), bring along a new movie for the troops to watch, and maybe hand out some stogies. It was all about pumping them up—and saying thank you. Much later, when I was governor, people in the state capital of Sacramento always asked, "Why do you spend so much time on the armed forces? Why are you fighting for them to get a free education? Why are you helping with their student loans? Why are you fighting for them to get jobs? Why are you fighting to speed up the construction of veterans' homes and build more veterans' housing than any governor in California history? Why are you battling to get the establishment to acknowledge post-traumatic stress syndrome and help these young men and women when they come back?" The answer was simple: America wouldn't be the land of the free if it wasn't the home of the brave. When you see the work they do and the risks they take, you realize what we owe our military.

Only once at Camp David did I personally witness serious business. The conference room that served as the president's command center was normally off-limits to guests, of course. But one afternoon in February 1991, while I was visiting and sitting in my room reading a script, the president called. "Come on over, meet the guys," he said.

They were relaxing around the big conference table taking a sandwich break. He introduced me and said, "You know, we're making some important decisions about the Middle East war." The air-attack part of Operation Desert Storm was already under way, and for months the United States and its coalition partners had been massing their armored forces. "Look at these pictures," the president said, showing me aerial reconnaissance photos. Then he played a video taken with a tanker's helmet camera, showing how close to the border they were. The tank divisions were maneuvering, feinting attacks on the border and then pulling back, and he explained that one day soon they would just keep going into Iraq and Kuwait. "So they'll get hit by surprise, and at the same time, they'll get nailed with—" and he showed me the ship positions in the Persian Gulf where the navy was ready to launch cruise missiles plus an amphibious landing by US Marines. "They're going to get hit with so much, they won't believe it," he said.

The war planning picked up informally around the table where it had left off. The conversation had a kind of intensity and focus that made me think of doctors in an operating room. Yes, they were dealing with life and death, but they'd made decisions like this before and knew what they needed to do. There was no panic. The informal tone was just a reflection of Camp David—it was less fraught than the White House, which was why they loved meeting up there.

When they finished eating, the president said, "Okay, I'm going to take Arnold over and show him this horse, and I'll be back in twenty minutes."

I left the next day knowing that the ground war was going to start in forty-eight hours. It was a Thursday, and two days later, on February 23, they were going to attack. I walked around thinking, "I know something no one else knows except in that circle. Not the press, nobody." The fact that President Bush put such trust in me had a powerful effect. I felt there would never, ever be a time, no matter what happened, when I would violate that trust or let the man down.

The rest of 1991 was golden for me: at home, in my public service work, and in my movies. *Terminator 2: Judgment Day* opened in theaters on the Fourth of July weekend and quickly became the biggest box-office hit of my career. Just three weeks later, Christina was born. I also became the proud owner of the world's first civilian Hummer, whose military counterpart, the HMMWV or Humvee, had played a big role in the Gulf War. I'd noticed the Humvee just the summer before, up in Oregon, while we were shooting scenes for *Kindergarten Cop.* A convoy of US Army Humvees drove by, and I fell in love. It was the best-looking, most rugged SUV I'd ever seen. The Humvee had as standard equipment features that guys would spend thousands and thousands of dollars adding to their Jeeps or Chevy Blazers: oversize wheels and mirrors, high ground clearance, extra lights, including infrared, a brush bar in front, and a winch for hauling yourself out of trouble. The Humvee looked ballsy without having to add anything!

Not only did I want one for myself, but also I knew there would be a ready-made market if I could talk the manufacturer into building a version for the public. That was my sales pitch when I went to see the CEO and other executives at AM General in Lafayette, Indiana, which made Humvees for the military. I finagled permission to buy one, and then turned it over to a company to make it street-legal and civilize the interior, and then sent it back to AM General, saying "Now, copy this." That's what it did, and that's why the Hummer became so closely identified with me when it went on the market.

There was an interesting business adventure that year too. I joined Sylvester Stallone and Bruce Willis in New York that October for the official launch of a glitzy new moneymaking machine: a celebrity restaurant and merchandising chain called Planet Hollywood. Every celebrity you can think of was there. It was not just an event, it was the beginning of an empire.

The idea was to put Planet Hollywoods all over the world and make them a magnet for people who loved American movie stars. Movie memorabilia and props would be the décor—like Tom Cruise's flight suit from *Top Gun*, Jayne Mansfield's swimsuit from *The Girl Can't Help It*, and a motorcycle from *The Terminator.* The restaurants would host premieres and visits by the stars and sell specially designed jackets, T-shirts, and other souvenirs. It was the brainchild of Keith Barish, a movie producer, and Robert Earl, who had built up the global restaurant business based on music memorabilia, the Hard Rock Café. Keith had convinced Robert that Hollywood-themed restaurants could be even bigger than music-themes ones—especially now that the Iron Curtain had fallen and the whole world was wide open to American culture. The two brought the idea to me. "We want you to be our business partner," they said. "We don't want a crazy celebrity who doesn't understand. You have a business mind. And you're the number one star. If you do this, others will follow."

I thought the idea made sense, and word got around fast. Pretty soon my lawyer, Jake Bloom, who also represented Sly and Bruce, said they were asking to sign on. "Would you mind if they're in on it?" he asked.

"Absolutely not," I said. I was especially happy about Sly. Jake knew that Stallone and I had been feuding for years. This went back to the early *Rocky* and *Rambo* days, when he was the number one action hero, and I was always trying to catch up. I remember saying to Maria when I made *Conan the Destroyer,* "I'm finally getting paid a million dollars for a movie, but now Stallone's making three million. I feel like I'm standing still." To energize myself, I'd envisioned Stallone as my archenemy, just like I had demonized Sergio Oliva when I was trying to take the Mr. Olympia crown. I got so into hating Sly that I started criticizing him in public—his body, the way he dressed—and I was quoted as badmouthing him in the press.

I couldn't blame him for hitting back. In fact, he'd escalated the fight by secretly feeding negative stories about me to the media. For a while he even paid the legal bills for a British journalist whom I'd sued for libel. But time had passed, I was a lot more confident about being a star, and I wanted to make peace. I said to Jake, "Tell him that he is welcome to be in it, and it's my way of being gracious and making up."

So Sly, Bruce, and I became a team. We'd fly to the latest Planet Hollywood opening, greet the local celebrities, wave at the cameras, talk to the press, and do everything we could to reward the loyalty of the fans. On the airplane, Sly and I were smoking stogies and constantly trading jokes. We never talked about the feud. We were typical guys, totally in denial, as if there had never been any problem and nothing had ever happened. That's how we moved forward.

Even with all this going on, I could feel myself starting to get restless. It reminded me of the restlessness I'd felt after winning my third or fourth Mr. Olympia. All of a sudden the idea of having the most muscular body didn't mean that much to me anymore. It was a phase I'd gone through and a means to an end: bodybuilding had brought me to America and launched me into the movies. But I grew out of that phase as much as I'd grown out of playing with little wooden trains as a kid. Of course, I always wanted to promote the sport of bodybuilding, and I wanted to promote fitness. But being the most muscular man didn't mean anything to me anymore.

Becoming the biggest action star had been the next challenge. Eventually I'd accomplished that as well. Then I'd gone another step, into comedies. But I'd always known I'd grow out of that too.

In the seven years between the two *Terminator* movies, my feelings about the business had changed. Throughout the 1980s, I was enthusiastically grinding out the films. I was gunning for the top, trying to double my salary with every project and have the number one movie at the box office and be the biggest star. I literally hated having to sleep. When I did *The Terminator,* I dreamed of being able to operate nonstop like a machine. Then I could shoot all night on the set with Jim Cameron, and in the morning just change wardrobe and drive over and do a daytime movie on a daytime set with a daytime director. "Wouldn't that be cool?" I thought. "I could do four movies a year!"

But now, after *Terminator 2: Judgment Day,* I saw things completely differently. I had a growing family. I wanted to have a nice life. I wanted to enjoy my wife and kids. I wanted to see Katherine and Christina grow up. I wanted to be able to go to events with them and take them on vacation. I wanted to be home when they came home from school.

So I tried to figure out how to balance my time. I thought that doing one movie a year might be the perfect pace. People now accepted the fact that I was one of the biggest stars, so I didn't have to prove anything. But they were expecting more movies, so I had to make sure I came back and gave them good ones. If I heard an idea or saw a script that was exceptionally good and triggered something in me, I wanted to be able to make that movie. But there were other opportunities out there as well, and movie acting was no longer enough.

I thought that maybe the way to keep myself interested was to do what Clint Eastwood does and spice up the movie career with directing and producing every so often—sometimes appearing in the movie and sometimes not. And so on. I loved the idea of new challenges, along with new dangers of failure. Clint was one of the very few Hollywood personalities who had his head screwed on straight. He was good in business. He never lost money. He was wise in the ways he invested. He was always getting involved in ventures he felt passionate about, like his restaurant business and his golf businesses in Northern California. From the time I came to America, he was always someone I'd idolized. I didn't know if I had that kind of talent, but maybe I could try to be like Clint when acting was no longer enough for me and I was looking for the next challenge.

Then there was a completely different path I could see myself taking. Clint had been elected mayor of Carmel, California, his hometown. That too appealed to me, although I did not know at that point *which* office I might seek one day. Still, I couldn't help but feel influenced by being around the Shrivers and the Kennedy family, even though we were on different sides of the fence politically.

In November 1991 a surprise push in the direction of running for office came from Richard Nixon. He invited me to stop by his office before a fund-raiser and the opening of a holiday exhibit at his presidential library, scheduled a few hours after the opening of the Reagan library. I knew how Nixon was hated by many people, and I was aware of the Watergate scandal and the hardship it put the country through. Taking that out of the equation, however, I admired him and thought he was a terrific president. I suspect he knew I was a fan, because I'd praised him in the media even at the height of his unpopularity. I *especially* loved talking about him then because of the side of me that likes to be rebellious and shock people.

He'd told me on the phone when he invited me to his event, "I want you to *enjoy* it, Arnold." In fact, he was setting me up to make a speech without telling me. So I agreed unsuspectingly and brought along my nephew Patrick, the son of my late brother and his fiancée, Erika Knapp. Patrick, now in his midtwenties, had graduated from the University of Southern California Law School and had been hired as an associate by my entertainment lawyer, Jake Bloom. I loved hanging out with him and teaching him the ropes. We went down and greeted President Nixon at the holiday opening, which drew about thirteen hundred people.

Nixon was very good at paying attention to you. He would get into your head, and I was impressed. He said, "Arnold, I want you to come into my office."

"Can my nephew come in with us?"

"Oh, absolutely." We walked into his office, and he closed the door and pumped me for information about all kinds of things: what was I doing, how was it going with the movies, what made me a Republican, why was I involved in politics. After answering, I told him what was in my gut: "I came to America because it's the greatest place in the world, and I'm going to do everything I can to keep it the greatest place. For that to happen, we can't have schmucks running for president or hanging out at the White House. We need good leaders, and we need to move the agenda forward and have it be the same in the states and the same in the cities. So I always want to make sure that I vote for the right person and that I campaign for the right person. I need to know what they stand for, how they've voted in the past, how did they represent their state, were they great leaders, and all those kinds of things." I told him about the challenges facing California in the areas of health and education, based on what I'd learned as the fitness chairman. And I talked about the challenge of making the state more business friendly.

Then someone came in and said, "Mr. President, they're almost ready for you." So we stood up. He turned to me just before we went and said, "You must run for governor of California. If you run for governor, I'll help you all the way." That caught me by surprise because we hadn't been talking about that at all. He was the first ever to mention it to me in a serious way.

He sent Patrick to take a seat but told me, "Stay up here; stand over near the podium." There were others standing there as well, including Bob Hope and other celebrities, and I joined the group.

He then got in front of the microphone and started talking. The speech was good, relaxed, and I was impressed because he had no notes. He spoke eloquently about the library and its mission, certain things that he had accomplished in his life, certain policies that must continue, and so on. "And, of course, I have a great following here. You people are responsible for making this all happen, and I am very grateful for your support," he said. "But now I want to bring someone up who is the future of this state and . . ."

I didn't hear what he said after this because my heart was racing.

"Maybe he just wants to mention me," I thought. But I knew he was about to ask me to speak. The two sides of my mind immediately started a debate. One was saying, "What the fuck? Jeez, I'm not ready for this," and the other side was saying, "Man, President Nixon is talking about you. Be happy!"

I heard the president say, "Arnold, come on up here." And there was huge applause.

So I stepped out in front of all those people and stood there shaking his hand. Then he whispered to me, but so that you could still hear it clearly over the microphone, "I think you should say a few words."

Luckily, when you feel good about someone and you know specifically why, it is not difficult at all to speak from the heart. I didn't miss a beat. I even made a joke of it. "Well, I always like to be called up for a speech without any prior notice, but thank you very much." That got a little bit of a laugh. I went on and spoke for a few minutes about how I became a Republican. I told the story of seeing Nixon on television for the first time during the 1968 presidential campaign "when he was talking about *supporting law enforcement*!" A few people applauded. I said, "He was supporting the military, the Pentagon, military expansion, and America can be powerful only if you have *a strong military*." More applause.

"And he was talking about building an economy that is a global economy. He was talking about eliminating tariffs and barriers to trade, and ultimately it is *our prosperity* we have to protect, not labor!" Still more applause. "I loved hearing all those lines from him. And coming from a socialist country, I especially liked hearing someone say *get government off our back*." Applause and cheers.

"Therefore, I became a big fan of this man. I was a big supporter of his, and I'm here today because I'm still a big supporter of his. We need more leaders like him!" Now everyone was applauding and cheering. It was heaven.

Afterward, President Nixon took me back to his office and said, "Remember what I told you about running for governor."

I figured that the idea of eventually ending up in politics was not that far fetched when someone like Nixon suggested it. But my sense of it was never so intense that I felt "this is definitely going to happen." It was never one of those "I'll do it this year" items. I didn't dwell on it, didn't put a timeline on it. I was very relaxed.

CHAPTER 20

The Last Action Hero

NOBODY IN HOLLYWOOD WINS all the time. At some point, you're bound to get a beating. The next summer, it was my turn, with *Last Action Hero*. We'd promised the world a blockbuster hit: "the big ticket of '93" and the "biggest movie of the summer" was how we promoted the movie. *Terminator 2: Judgment Day* had been the biggest movie of 1991, and the expectation was that *Last Action Hero* should top it.

Instead, Steven Spielberg's *Jurassic Park* became the summer hit everybody had to see; it ended up outdoing even *E.T.* as the biggest success in movie history. Meanwhile, we delivered a film that didn't have the snappiness it needed to be great entertainment, and we had the bad luck to have scheduled the movie's release for the weekend after *Jurassic Park*'s opening. From the moment *Last Action Hero* hit the theaters, it got stomped. The front-page banner headline of *Variety* said, "Lizards Eat Arnold's Lunch."

But in fact, *Last Action Hero* made money and was a failure only in comparison to what had been anticipated. If I hadn't been such a big star, no one would have noticed. It was too bad, because I loved the idea of the movie. It was a combination action movie and comedy, the two kinds of roles I did best. To appeal to the broadest audience, we were making it PG-13—a big summer fun ride, essentially; a spoof, without too much graphic violence, crude language, or sex. I starred as the action hero, Jack Slater, a maverick Los Angeles Police Department detective. I was also the movie's executive producer, which meant that I had to approve every facet of the project: developing the script, picking the director and the cast, lining up the studio for financing, distribution, and marketing, setting the budget, getting a PR firm on board, planning the foreign release, and on and on. The added responsibility was a pleasure. In the past, I'd often taken an active hand in my movies, bringing together the deal or lining up the director, and, of course, planning the marketing. But sometimes when I said, "Let me see the poster" or "Let's figure out a better photo to use," I felt like I was butting in. Now I could be involved in everything, from dreaming up promotional stunts to approving the prototypes for Jack Slater toys.

The plot is built around a kid named Danny Madigan, an eleven-year-old who is the ultimate fan. He's obsessed with action movies and knows everything there is to know about them. Danny gets a magic ticket that lets him cross into the latest film featuring the action hero Jack Slater, his all-time favorite.

For director, I was happy to land John McTiernan, who had made *Predator*, as well as *Die Hard* and *The Hunt for Red October*. John always has great clarity of vision, and on *Last Action Hero* that gave me my first hint of trouble. We were having a drink after shooting until three in the morning one night in New York, and John said, "What we're really making here is *E.T.*" When I heard that, I had a sinking feeling that maybe the whole PG-13 thing was a mistake. Even though we had a kid costar in the movie, people might not buy me doing a family-friendly action film. That was okay for Harrison Ford in *Raiders of the Lost Ark* but not me. I'd made the comedies, of course, but those were different because no one expects you to blow people up in a comedy. When you're selling a movie with the word *action* in the title, you'd better deliver some. *Conan II* had fizzled because we'd made it PG. Now we were betting we could pack in enough amazing stunts and energy to make *Last Action Hero* live up to its name.

The idea of a warmer, more cuddly action movie did seem right for the times. Arkansas governor Bill Clinton had just beaten George Bush in the 1992 presidential election, and the media were full of stories about baby boomers taking over from the WWII generation and about how America was now going in an antiviolence direction. Entertainment journalists were saying, "I wonder what this means for the conservative hard-core action heroes like Sylvester Stallone, Bruce Willis, and Arnold Schwarzenegger. Are the audiences now more into peace and love?" That's the trend I wanted to connect with. So when the toy people showed up with their prototypes of a Jack Slater doll, I vetoed the combat weapons they proposed. I said, "This is the nineties, not the eighties." Instead of wielding a flamethrower, the toy Jack Slater threw a punch and said, "Big mistake!"—which was Slater's tagline against the bad guys. On the toy package it said, "Play it smart. Never play with real guns."

We went all out on merchandising and promotion. Besides the action toys, we licensed seven kinds of video games, a $20 million promotion with Burger King, a $36 million "ride film" to go into amusement parks, and—this was my favorite—NASA picked us to be the first-ever paid advertisement in outer space. We painted "Last Action Hero" and "Arnold Schwarzenegger" on the sides of a rocket and then held a national sweepstakes whose winners would get to push the launch button. We put up a four-story-tall inflatable statue of Jack Slater on a raft just off the beach at Cannes during the film festival in May, and I set a personal record there by giving forty TV interviews and fifty-four print interviews in a single twenty-four-hour period.

Meanwhile, the production was running late. At our only test screening, on May 1, the movie was still so unfinished that it ran for two hours and twenty minutes, and you couldn't make out most of the dialogue. By the end, the audience was bored. After that, the schedule was so tight that we ran out of time for more tests. Instead, we were forced to fly blind without the feedback you need to fine-tune a movie. Still, nobody at the studio wanted to postpone the opening, because that might create the perception that the movie was in trouble, and I agreed.

A lot of people liked *Last Action Hero*, as it turned out. But in the movie business, that's not enough. You can't have people just *like* your movie, you need them to be passionate. Word of mouth is what makes movies big, because while you can put in $25 million or $30 million to promote the movie on the first weekend, you can't afford to keep doing that every week.

We had terrific awareness and anticipation going in. Yet maybe because of *Jurassic Park*, ticket sales were below expectations the first weekend: $15 million instead of the $20 million we'd predicted. And when I realized that people were coming out of the theaters warm but not hot, saying things like "It was actually pretty good," I knew we were dead. Sure enough, the second weekend, our box office dropped by 42 percent.

The criticism went way beyond *Last Action Hero*. My career was over, history. Writers attacked everything I'd ever done in movies, as if to say, "What do you expect from a guy who works with John Milius and talks about crushing his enemies? That's the world that they want to live in. We want to live in a compassionate world."

Politics came into it. As long as I'd been on a roll, I'd never been attacked for being Republican, even though Hollywood and the entertainment press are generally liberal. Now that I was down, they could unload. Reagan and Bush were out, Republicans were out, and so were mindless action movies and all the macho shit. Now was the time for Bill Clinton and Tom Hanks and movies that had meaning.

I framed the criticism philosophically and tried to minimize the whole thing. I had all kinds of movie projects lined up—*True Lies*, *Eraser*, and *Jingle All the Way*—enough to feel confident that one movie going in the toilet would have no impact on my career or on the money I made or on anything real. I said to myself it didn't matter, because at one point or another, you're going to get the beating. It could have been for another movie. It could have been three years later. It could have been five years later.

No matter what you tell yourself or what you know, at the time you're going through it, it *is* bad. It's embarrassing to fail at the box office and have your movie not open well. It's embarrassing to have terrible stories written about you. It's embarrassing to have people start calling this your year to fail. As always, I had the two voices battling inside my head. The one was saying, "Goddammit, oh my God, this is terrible." And the other was saying, "Now let's see what you are made of, Arnold. Let's see how ballsy you are. How strong are your nerves? How thick is your skin? Let's see if you can drive around in your convertible with the top down and smile at people, knowing that they know that you just came out with a fucking stinker. Let's see if you can do that."

I had all this stuff going on in my mind, beating myself up and trying to encourage myself at the same time, wondering how to go through this. It was kind of a repeat of the night after I lost Mr. Universe against Frank Zane back in 1968.

Maria was a great support. "Look, the movie was good," she said. "Maybe it was not what we expected, but it was good, and you should be proud. Now let's move on. Let's go to the next project." We went to our vacation house in Sun Valley, Idaho, and played with the kids. "Don't take this so seriously," she said. "Look what we have here. You should think about that, not about the stupid movie. Those things come and go. Plus, on top of it, out of your twenty or so movies, at least two-thirds were successful, so you have nothing to complain about."

But I think she too was disappointed and probably embarrassed when friends called. That's what they do in Hollywood. They say, "I'm so sorry about the box-office grosses," when they are really trying to see how you respond. So Maria was getting calls from friends saying things like, "Oh my God, I saw the *LA Times* story. God, I'm so sorry! Is there anything we can do?" That kind of dialogue.

We all do it. It's human nature to empathize with someone else's troubles. I would call Tom Arnold if one of his movies went down. I would call Stallone. I'd say, "Fuck the *LA Times*, fuck the trades, those stupid motherfuckers. You're a great, talented actor." That's what you do. But at the same time, there is still a side of you that wonders, "What is he going to say?" So why wouldn't people call me and do the same thing?

And when you feel embarrassed like I did, you tend to assume that the whole world is focused on your failure. I'd go into a restaurant, and somebody would say, "Oh, hey, how are you doing? I see the new movie's out, that's great!" And I'd feel like, "That's *great*? You motherfucker. Didn't you read the *LA Times*?" But, in fact, not everybody reads the *LA Times* or *Variety* or goes to see every movie. The poor guy probably knows nothing about it and just wants to say something nice.

These woes were nothing another big hit wouldn't fix. Before summer ended, I was back in front of Jim Cameron's cameras, galloping a black horse across downtown Washington, DC, chasing a terrorist on a motorbike. *True Lies* was a large-scale action comedy that had over-the-top special effects, including a shoot-out between terrorists holed up in a Miami skyscraper and me in a Harrier jet, and a nuclear explosion that takes out one of the Florida Keys. And it had funny, complicated relationships, especially between me and my onscreen wife, played by Jamie Lee Curtis. My character, Harry Tasker, is a James Bond–style superspy whose wife, Helen, initially thinks that he's a computer salesman. Jamie Lee played the part so well that she got nominated for a comedy Golden Globe.

I'd learned about *True Lies* the previous year, when Bobby Shriver called and said he'd seen a French movie that I might like to remake for the American screen. "It's called *La Totale!*," he said, "and it's about this 007-type ass-kicking guy whose wife doesn't know what he does for a living. Sometimes he comes home all banged up and has to make excuses. He'll be arresting these international criminals, and, meanwhile, he can't figure out how to deal with his teenage daughter, who's doing crazy things."

"Sounds funny," I said.

"Yeah, yeah, it's comedy and action. You laugh, but there's a lot of suspense." I called the movie's agent and asked him to send it over, and I fell in love with it. Bobby was right, though: it was too static for an American movie and needed action and energy. "Jim Cameron!" I thought. "He's been planning to shoot *Spider-Man*, but that just fell through." So I called Cameron and said, "Let's do this together, the way you envision things: *big*."

Soon we had a deal with Fox, and Jim was writing the script. All his movies feature strong female characters, and he transformed Helen Tasker from an ordinary hausfrau to the character Jamie Lee plays: smart and sexy, with her *own* secret life. He'd call me in to consult while the script was taking shape. At one point, we holed up for two days in Las Vegas, exploring how I would talk to my wife, how I'd confront her if I suspected her of having an affair, what I would say to a terrorist before I killed him, how I would handle it if I found out my daughter was stealing from my friend. In those conversations, we tailored the rhythm of the dialogue to me. The timing of the project worked out perfectly: just a few weeks after the disappointment of *Last Action Hero*, we went into preproduction and were shooting by September 1.

Maria and I turned the making of *True Lies* into a family adventure. She was eight months' pregnant when the filming started, and when she announced her maternity leave on her show *First Person with Maria Shriver*, she told the viewers, "Arnold will be here in Los Angeles when I give birth. Then I'll pack up my family and go with him, and see how long I last as a set wife." Cameron arranged it so that we would shoot in LA for three weeks until Patrick was born. Then the production moved to Washington, DC, and sure enough, a few days later, Maria, Katherine, Christina, the baby, and the nanny joined me.

We lived in Washington for a month, and it was an extremely happy time. Cameron, as usual, preferred shooting at night. So I'd work until daybreak, then come home and sleep, and in the afternoon, I'd get up and play with the kids. Katherine was now four and Christina, two and a half, and besides just tickling and horsing around, one of the things we liked to do was paint. My assistant, Ronda, the artist, had gotten me back into painting, something I'd loved as a kid. I'd always talked about going back to it, but I never had the patience to assemble all the materials and sit down to try. So one Saturday morning she came over to the house with a selection of acrylic paints and canvas and said, "For the next three hours, we're going to paint."

"Okay," I said.

We sat, and I picked out a Matisse from an art book and set about copying it: a room with a rug, a piano, and a flower in a vase, with French doors opening to a balcony overlooking the sea. That got me back into art. So now I would draw castles in pen and ink and paint Christmas and birthday cards for Maria and the kids. The girls and I got into this delightful rhythm of making drawings and playing together, and I crayoned a beautiful Halloween pumpkin for Patrick and a birthday cake with candles for Maria.

We were like gypsies for the next several months. We moved with the *True Lies* production to Miami, where I took Maria and the girls jet skiing. Then we moved to Key West, and then Rhode Island, and, finally, back out west. I did much better than my secret agent character at integrating family and work. Cameron ran an incredibly organized set, and each day there was always time for work and for play. Even so, making *True Lies* was challenging, and I don't just mean the many hours I spent doggedly practicing the tango for the ballroom scenes. Cameron was pushing the envelope with the stunts and special effects, and in addition to employing forty-eight stunt people, he had the actors do many stunts ourselves. Jamie Lee dangled from a helicopter that lowered her onto a speeding car on the bridge that joins the Florida Keys. I swam in the ocean to escape a wall of flames. I trusted Cameron not to lead us down the path of death, but those stunts were inherently risky, and if you screwed up, nobody could protect you 100 percent.

My closest call was riding that black horse. In the movie, Harry Tasker chases the terrorist on a motorcycle across a Washington, DC, park, into a luxury hotel, through a ballroom and a fountain, and into a bank of elevators with people wearing tuxedoes and ball gowns until he finally corners the bad guy on the roof. But incredibly, the terrorist revs his bike and does a spectacular jump off the building and into the rooftop pool of an adjacent building. In the heat of the chase, Harry spurs his horse and charges the edge of the roof to make the leap. But at the last instant, the horse puts on the brakes and comes to a skidding stop—so suddenly that Harry flips out of the saddle in a big arc over the horse's neck and ends up dangling by the reins over the street many stories below. Now his life depends on the horse, which he's trying to coax to step back from the edge. The rooftop was actually a studio set built ninety feet up in the air. The movie crew was nervous that the horse might not stop in time and we'd skid over the edge, so they'd extended a safety platform, like a heavy-duty gangplank, out from the edge of the roof. That way, if the horse took an extra step or two, we wouldn't fall. The image of the platform would be edited out of the final print.

Doing a stunt like that, you need a really feisty horse, because you have to do a lot of takes. An ordinary horse will figure out that you are not really going to let it jump, so after the first few tries, it won't charge all the way to the edge of the roof. Instead, it will slow down halfway across and come to an easy stop. But a feisty horse loves the idea of jumping so much that he'll charge the edge of the roof all day, hoping that this time you'll let him go. So I was on a feisty horse, well trained but very aggressive. I loved it because I knew how to handle the animal from my training as Conan.

Before we could start, they had to check the camera angles and measure the focus. So I had to walk the horse to the edge of the roof and onto the gangplank above the studio floor. Suddenly, by accident, one of the cameras on a long boom dropped down into the horse's face. It actually hit the horse—not hard, but enough to spook him. He tried to back up, but his hooves started slipping on the gangplank. I slid off him as fast as I could, but there was no place to go: I was on the gangplank, ninety feet up, and under the horse. All I could think was "Stay alive, stay on this platform, watch those hooves." He was dancing around, and if he stepped on me or slipped again, he could take us both down. I realized that people have survived much larger falls. But I knew that in this case, the horse and I would land on the cement floor, and it would be over.

The last thing anybody thought was that just taking measurements would be dangerous. But our stunt director, Joel Kramer, knew that this stunt had never been tried before, and he was alert. I saw him jump out onto the platform and hold on to the horse, calming it and gently easing it back so that I could escape.

My brain worked the way it always does when I have a close call: I immediately dismissed the episode as if it didn't exist. Once the horse settled down, we came back and shot the scene just as we'd planned. But I gave Joel a box of Montecristo cigars. Everybody realized that if he hadn't looked out for us, the horse and I would probably be dead.

Maria was too much of a force to stay on the mommy track completely for very long. By the time we were in Florida, she was already back at work, lining up future stories, and when shooting broke for the production to move to Rhode Island, she and I went to Cuba for a day. Cuba, of course, was still off-limits to Americans, but Maria could go as a journalist. She'd already conducted a couple of interviews with President Fidel Castro, including one in which she asked him point-blank if he'd had anything to do with killing JFK. Now she was laying the groundwork for another interview, and I went along as the spouse.

The high point for me, of course, was cigars. While Maria was busy with her meetings, I visited the Partagas factory, where they make Cohibas, Punches, Montecristos, and other legendary brands. I love factories, and whenever I'm passionate about a product, I want to see it being made. I love to watch cars being produced, shoes crafted, and glass blown. I love going to the Audemars Piguet watch factory in Switzerland to see the technicians at work in their white coats, gloves, glasses, and headgear so that no dust gets in the mechanism. And I also enjoy stopping at the wood-carving shops in Germany's Black Forest, where they hand carve religious figures and masks. This Cuban factory was cigar heaven. Imagine a very large grade school classroom for a hundred students, with benches and wooden desks like in the old days. That's exactly what it looked like. Men and women sat at the desks rolling cigars, and in the middle of the room was a platform, just like we had when I was in middle school, where the teacher was always elevated above the class. Here there was a guy sitting and reading the news out loud. My Spanish isn't good enough that I understood everything, but it was news interwoven with propaganda. To sit there and read the news like that, you have to be colorful, almost an entertainer, like Robin Williams as the deejay in *Good Morning, Vietnam.* This guy was like that, talking and exclaiming a mile a minute and waving his hands. I'm sure it helped the workers pass the time.

I was amazed to see how they treat that extraordinary tobacco like gold. I'd seen security measures like this in the diamond and gold mines of South Africa but never anywhere else. When the workers arrive, they file into a huge room that was humidified perfectly and where the leaves are hanging—big, long leaves, perfectly groomed and cured. Each worker got an allotment of leaves and with it, three cigars for himself or herself. Those cigars were not at all as high quality as the leaves, though, and the rule was "Don't ever roll a cigar for yourself." From that point on, the workers would be checked so that all the tobacco was accounted for.

That's how precious the tobacco is. It has to be grown a certain way. It has to be treated a certain way. It has to be groomed. It has to be carefully dried until it turns brown and is ready to be rolled. Everything has to be perfect, and the Cubans are geniuses at this. They have the best climate, they have the best soil, and they have the tradition: generations of people who are passionate about rolling cigars and who are always looking for ways to make the cigar ever more perfect.

You see them make the cigar: first the core, which has a particular quality of tobacco; and then the binder leaf, which has a different quality of tobacco; and then the wrapper, which has to be a leaf with absolutely no veins. When you look at a cigar and it has those thick veins in it, then it's a cheaper cigar or someone wasn't paying attention. You can buy a cigar like that for $8, and it will smoke well, but it's not a pretty cigar like Davidoffs usually are, or Montecristos, or Cohibas. I watched the workers putting on the cigar bands. As with everything, it's important to have a great-looking label. When you're a cigar smoker, the interest increases with the band—especially if it looks international, if it looks Cuban, bright and Latino and loud, with the reds and yellows and sometimes a beautifully painted female figure.

Cuban cigars truly are as good as people say. There are plenty of fake Cubans around, but if you're an expert, you can sniff out the fake ones from the real ones within seconds because the real Cuban cigar smells strongly like fertilizer. I know that sounds weird, but that's how they smell. It tastes delicious to smoke, but when you open up the box and inhale—someone who doesn't know about cigars wouldn't like it.

Now that Bill Clinton was in the White House, my name was no longer quite so golden around Washington anymore. Even before Inauguration Day, Donna Shalala, the new secretary of Health and Human Services, asked me to resign as fitness czar. She said simply, "You campaigned for Bush, and we cannot have you be the chairman of the President's Council." And when we started shooting *True Lies* and asked Bruce Babbitt, the new secretary of the interior, for permission to ride the black horse through the reflecting pool at the Washington Monument, he turned us down flat even though they'd done it with other movies.

Maria was not a bit surprised. "Welcome to politics. That's just the way it is," she said. Of course, she was sorry to see me forced to give up the position as chairman. I was good at it, and I loved it. On the other hand, even though she liked George Bush personally, she couldn't wait for Bill Clinton to get in. Deep down, what the balance of her feelings was, I don't know. There may have been a little bit of a smirk mixed in there, because I'd been riding the Republican wave for so long, telling her Ronald Reagan this and George Bush that and how conservatives were going to straighten out the country. She couldn't wait for a change.

I'd learned so much as presidential fitness czar that I knew exactly what I wanted to focus on next. Three years of travel around the United

States had made me increasingly concerned about a major issue involving kids: too many of them were rattling around after school and in the summer with nothing to do and too little adult supervision. No matter what state I visited, I'd see the kids being let out of school at three o'clock. Half of them were getting picked up, or had a school bus, and half of them were just milling around.

As I got interested in this, I became friends with Danny Hernandez, an ex-marine who ran the Hollenbeck Youth Center in a poor, gang-infested part of LA. In Danny's experience, summer vacations were always the toughest time for the kids; the time when they were most prone to become involved in crime, drugs and alcohol, and gangs. So in 1991 he developed the Inner-City Games—kind of like the Olympics—to give meaning and structure to the summer months. From June through August, kids from the different schools would train, and then on the last day of vacation they would compete.

Danny took me to see the center, which was the product of an unusual collaboration in the 1970s between local businesses and the LAPD. It had basketball courts, a weight room, and physical education classes, plus a computer room and computer classes and a place for doing homework. There was a beautiful boxing ring too, because this was East Los Angeles, a Latino area, and boxing is a big part of the culture. The idea, Danny explained, was to provide kids with a place to go and to give problem kids a second chance. Police stations in Hollenbeck and other East LA neighborhoods would often send kids to the center instead of to court. They'd tell the kid, "Just get off the street, go work out there after you're through with school, do your homework there, there are computers there, there is a gym there, there's boxing, so go!"

The Los Angeles riots in the spring of 1992 brought the need to keep kids out of trouble painfully to the fore. What triggered the violence was the acquittal of the LAPD officers who'd beaten an African-American motorist named Rodney King after he eluded a traffic stop. A video made at the scene indicated that police beat him severely despite the fact that he'd surrendered. Parts of LA went up in flames, dozens of people were killed, and there was rioting in other cities too. During the rioting, the Hollenbeck Youth Center served as a safe haven. I made a public service music video with Arsenio Hall, the actor and talk-show host, called "Chill," which begged people to calm down.

In the aftermath, Danny and I stepped up our efforts to expand the Inner-City Games to involve more schools and more kids and to extend the program so it would be available year-round. By the time *True Lies* hit the theaters and topped the summer box office for action movies in 1994, the Inner-City Games were really catching on. We were now reaching thousands of kids, climaxing in nine days of finals for five thousand kids at the University of Southern California. We were expanding beyond sports, into art and essay contests, theater programs, dance competitions, and even programs for young entrepreneurs. Atlanta had launched its own Inner-City Games, and plans were in the works for Orlando, Miami, Chicago, and five other cities.

Working with these kids taught me a lot about myself. Until then I thought I was the poster boy for the American dream. I came to the United States virtually broke, worked hard, kept focused on my goal, and made it. This really was the land of opportunity, I thought. If a kid like me could do it, anybody could. Well, that wasn't so.

Traveling to schools, I saw that it wasn't enough to grow up with the United States as your address. In the inner cities, kids didn't even dare to dream. The message they got was "Don't bother. You'll never make it. You're a loser."

I thought about what I had that those kids didn't. I grew up poor too. But I had a fire inside of me to succeed and two parents who pushed me and taught me discipline. I had a strong public school education. I had after-school sports with coaches and training partners who were role models. I had mentors who told me, "You can do it, Arnold," and then made me believe it. They were around me twenty-four hours a day, supporting me and making me grow.

But how many inner-city kids had those tools? How many learned the discipline and determination? How many got the encouragement that would let them even glimpse their self-worth?

Instead, they were told they were trapped. They could see that most of the adults around them were trapped. The schools were short of resources, the teachers were worn out and not always the best, and mentors were scarce. There were families in poverty and gangs all around.

I wanted them to feel their own drive, ambition, and hope, and get up to the same starting line. So it was never hard to work for these kids or to think of the right thing to say. "We love you," I would tell them. "We care for you. You are great. You can make it. We believe in you, but the most important thing is that you believe in yourself. All these opportunities are out there waiting for you as long as you make the right decisions and have a dream. You can be anything you want to be. A teacher, a police officer, a doctor, you can do that. Or a basketball star or an actor. Or even the president. Anything is possible, but you have to do your end of the work. And we as grownups have to do ours."

CHAPTER 21

Heart Trouble

MAKING MONEY WAS NEVER my only goal. But I always kept an eye on my earning power as a gauge of success, and money opened the door to interesting investments. *True Lies* and *Junior* were both hits in 1994, and that put my movie career back on track. I had plenty of work, and the money poured in: during the rest of the 1990s, almost $100 million from movie paychecks alone. Each year, I was collecting additional millions from videos, cable distribution, and broadcasts of my old films. Even my first film, *Hercules in New York*, was making money as a cult movie, although I didn't get a cut. Tens of millions more came in from real estate, Planet Hollywood, books, and other business ventures.

Like many Hollywood stars, I also made money doing commercials in Asia and Europe. Making commercials in the United States would have undermined the Arnold image and the Arnold brand, but commercials by American celebrities had cachet abroad, especially in the Far East. The makers of products such as instant noodles, canned coffee, beer, and Vffuy, a Japanese vitamin drink, were willing to pay me as much as $5 million per ad. And the commercial was usually shot in one day. The deal always included a "secrecy clause" holding the advertiser responsible for not letting the commercial reach the West. That possibility no longer exists—shoot a commercial today, and it's all over YouTube—but in the mid-1990s the internet was just an odd new idea.

As my business interests expanded, I knew that we'd eventually get into territory where I no longer had time to tend them all and where Ronda would be overwhelmed. She'd been taking business classes, true, but at heart she was an artist. That's exactly what happened in 1996. She came to me and said, "This is so much money now, it's beyond me. I don't feel comfortable anymore." I loved Ronda and was determined never to make her feel like she was being replaced. I promised that she could keep the work she was comfortable with and that, meanwhile, I'd get help with the bigger projects, where more and more money was at stake.

I always felt that the most important thing was not how much you make, but how much you invest, how much you keep. I never wanted to join the long list of famous entertainers and athletes who wiped out financially. It's a staggering list, including Willie Nelson, Billy Joel, Zsa Zsa Gabor, Bjorn Borg, Dorothy Hamill, Michael Vick, and Mike Tyson. All those people had business managers; I remember Burt Reynolds and his manager showing up in Palm Springs each driving a Rolls-Royce. Then the money was gone. No matter what you do in life, you have to have a business mind and educate yourself about money. You can't just delegate it to a manager and tell him, "Half has to stay locked in investments so that we can pay the taxes, and I'll keep the other half." My goal was to get rich and stay rich. I never wanted to have the phone call where the manager says, "Something went wrong with the investment. We can't pay our taxes." I wanted to know the details.

My interests were so diverse that I could have ended up with a whole grab-bag of specialist advisors. Instead, I worked closely with an extremely smart investment banker named Paul Wachter, whom I'd known for years. Paul was a longtime friend of my brother-in-law Bobby Shriver's—they became pals after law school in the 1970s while clerking for judges in Los Angeles—and we'd gotten quite close. You wouldn't think I had much in common with a Jewish lawyer and banker from Manhattan's Upper East Side who'd never been near a weight room or a movie set in his life. It seemed strange to other people how well Paul and I got along. But he had a strong Austrian heritage: his father was a Holocaust survivor from Vienna, and his mother was from a German-speaking part of Romania. German had been Paul's primary language at home growing up. And his father, unlike many post–World War II immigrants, had maintained strong connections with the Old World. In fact, his business was importing and exporting ham and other meat products between the United States and places like Poland and Bavaria. Paul had spent his summers in Europe as a kid and later worked as a ski instructor in the Austrian Alps.

Compared to most Americans, he thought a lot like me. We both had alpine scenery in our blood: the snowy landscapes, the pine forests, the big fireplaces and chalets. For example, when I told Paul that I dreamed of building a large chalet overlooking LA for my family, he understood. We were both extremely competitive, and I would challenge him at tennis and skiing. From his father, whom I really liked also, Paul understood the immigrant mentality of coming to America and starting a business and making good.

So here was someone I trusted who was funny and athletic—a guy I could hang and schmooze with; ski, play tennis, and go golfing with; travel with; and shop with. Those things are important to me. I never like business relationships that are purely work. Maria and I are very different in that way. She grew up in a world where a sharp line was drawn between friends and the help. With me, there is almost no line. I find it valuable to work with people I can also be friends with, go river rafting with, go to Austria with and hike in the mountains. And I'm like a little kid who loves to show off and share things that I have experienced. If I go to the top of the Eiffel Tower for lunch and have an extraordinary meal, and someone comes with the cart with five thousand stogies in it, and I like the way they present the cigar and light it, I want all my buddies to experience that. So the next time I'm promoting a movie overseas, I'll figure out how to arrange for some of them to come along. I want them to see the Sydney Opera House. I want them to see Rome. I want them to experience World Cup soccer games.

—

When I was doing the Planet Hollywood deal, Paul was my unofficial rabbi. He'd encouraged me to bring in my own lawyer when everybody else was using the company's man. He'd also insisted that we take the time to do the deal right. We spent almost two years negotiating my ownership stake, and while the other stars focused mainly on including freebies and perks in their contracts, the arrangement I ended up with was more lucrative and had more safeguards built in in case the business went south. Over time Paul and the investment bank he worked for, Wertheim Schroder & Co., helped me on other deals. His official specialty at Wertheim was gaming and hotels; he'd sold golf courses, tennis clubs, and ski resorts. But I saw him in action enough to know that he had much greater range. No matter what was thrown at him—a production studio, a winery in Napa, California, a shopping mall development—he always cut to the heart of the deal. He was the quickest study I knew.

He and I had been working together informally for years when Ronda reached her limit. Common sense had been telling me that I needed to diversify beyond real estate, which was the only sector I really knew. The economy was booming, new companies and industries were starting up, and the stock market was expanding like crazy. I wasn't interested in buying and selling stocks per se or spending my time researching companies. But I knew that the overall market had appreciated in real terms more than sixfold since Jimmy Carter was elected. I wanted to tap into that growth. Paul arranged for me to buy an ownership interest in a privately held mutual fund company called Dimensional Fund Advisers, which had offices right in Santa Monica. I met the founder, David Booth, a student of my hero Milton Friedman, and Paul couldn't say enough good things about the business.

"I've seen hundreds of companies, but never a group of people like this," he told me. "They are extremely ethical, they are brilliantly intellectual, and they are good businesspeople." Though still small and under the radar, DFA was poised to dominate a part of the index mutual fund business that the industry giant, Vanguard, didn't serve. I jumped at the opportunity, and Dimensional quickly became one of my most valuable assets.

I'd been pushing Paul to go out on his own, and in 1997 he set up shop in my building as an independent wealth manager with exactly one initial client: me. We understood each other so well by then that I gave him just a few instructions. The first was my old motto: "Take one dollar and turn it into two." I wanted big investments that were interesting, creative, and different. Conservative bets—the kind that would generate 4 percent a year, say—didn't interest me. Offshore corporations and other gimmicks didn't interest me; I was proud to pay taxes on the money I earned. The more we paid the better, in fact, because it showed I was making more money. I also wasn't interested in the investments that often attracted Hollywood business managers, such as trendy hotels and clubs. I could tolerate big risks in exchange for big returns, and I would want to know as much as possible about what was going on. My openness to new ideas and my involvement, plus the amount of money coming in, attracted Paul. He knew there would be plenty to do.

The idea of buying a Boeing 747 snuck up on us slowly. We had an acquaintance in San Francisco, David Crane, whose investment firm had gotten into the aircraft leasing trade. Aircraft leasing is a whole industry that exists because airlines often don't like to own their airplanes. Owning ties up a lot of capital and can be a big distraction when your real business is flying around passengers and freight. So the airlines often lease the planes from somebody else. In a lease arrangement, the airline operates and maintains the plane for, say, eight years, and then returns it to the owner, who is free to sell it or lease it out again.

David's firm was working with Singapore Airlines, which I knew had the best reputation in the airline business. It planned to expand its route system aggressively, and to free up capital, it was selling planes and leasing them back through contracts backed by Singapore government guarantees. I did some reading about airlines and leases and let it all simmer in my mind. Then one day I woke up, and the vision was crystal clear: "I've got to own one of those 747s!"

As far as I could tell, the opportunity was solid. I also felt a little of the same impulse that came over me when I saw my first Humvee. The 747 was the ballsiest airliner, and the price was as big as the plane. A new one cost anywhere between $130 million and $150 million, depending on the model and on options like the cabin and seating, cargo capacity, instrumentation, and so on. Of course, you wouldn't pay the entire amount because buying a jet for lease is a little like buying a commercial building for lease. You invest, say, $10 million, and take out bank loans to cover the rest.

We got in touch with David Crane. He was skeptical. Aircraft leasing deals are the realm of huge financial institutions like GE Capital. Individuals had never done it. "I doubt it, but I'll check," he said, promising to ask his clients in Singapore.

A week later, he came back to me. "It's impossible. You can't do it. They don't want any individuals, only institutions."

"Well, I can understand why," I said. "They probably think this is some Hollywood schmuck who's made some money overnight, and all of a sudden he thinks that he can buy a 747. But by the time they put together the deal, his movie falls through or something, and he backs out. They don't want to deal with these Hollywood drug addicts and weirdos. I understand that. So can we get them to meet? Do they ever come to Los Angeles on business?

"Let me check it out."

The next day, we learned that his clients had a West Coast trip planned in two weeks and were willing to come to my office. "Ah," I thought. "As is so often the case, something that is impossible slowly becomes possible." By the time the Singapore Airlines executives arrived, we'd done our homework, and it was easy to sell them on the idea. I spent the beginning of the meeting reviewing the deal, mainly just to show them that I understood how it worked. You could see them relax right away. After thirty minutes, we were taking pictures together and the deal in principle was done. I gave them *Terminator 2* jackets as souvenirs, plus *Predator* gimme caps and bodybuilding T-shirts. I knew that deep down they were fans.

Now came the hard part—for Paul. Sometimes when you look at a deal and you don't have all the knowledge or are not overly smart about what's involved, you see less danger and you're too willing to take the plunge. I saw just what was in front of me, and it all seemed good. Sure, it also looked and smelled risky. But the more risky things are, the more upside there is.

It was my job ultimately to say, "I like this thing." It was Paul's job to make sure it was really okay and that we understood the risks. The idea of owning this giant thing . . . You are signing documents and you think you have no liability because maintenance and safety are the responsibility of the airline—but was that totally true? Paul uncovered wrinkles that were bizarre. For example, if the plane crashed, you'd certainly have trouble sleeping at night, but at the same time, there was ample insurance to cover the loss. On the other hand, if *other* Singapore Airlines planes crashed and the reputation of the airline was ruined, then the value of your investment would be hurt. Other airlines might not want your plane after the lease was up and Singapore Airlines gave it back.

"That's one way this whole thing could go south," David Crane explained. "You'd be sitting there with a 747 nobody wants and you'd still have to make your payments to the bank." It was true that the profitability of the investment depended heavily on this so-called residual value. And residual value could be affected by everything from the reputation of the airline, to the state of the world economy, to oil prices, to technological innovation ten years from now. But when I heard David's worst-case scenario, I had to laugh. "Right!" I said. "That's exactly what's going to happen to me." I just had faith that it wouldn't.

Finally, we were comfortable with the deal. I was excited. "You should talk to other people in Hollywood," I told Paul. "They might like the idea too, and you can do a little business." He actually went and pitched it to five or six top executives and stars but came back empty-handed. "They looked at me like I had three heads," he told me. "Mostly what I saw in their eyes was fear. Like the whole thing was just too big and too weird for them."

The plane we ended up with cost $147 million. Before signing the papers, we went to the airport to see it. There's a picture somewhere of me literally kicking the tires of my 747. We signed all kinds of confidentiality agreements, of course, but the banks couldn't help themselves, and the news leaked the first day. I loved it because everybody thought I had bought the 747 to fly around in, like the sheik of Dubai. It didn't dawn on anyone that we'd do such an outlandish deal as an investment. It paid off very handsomely in profits, in tax benefits, and in pride of ownership. I'd hear guys bragging about their new Gulfstream IV or IV-SP, and then I'd get to say, "That's great, guys. Let me talk about my 747 . . ." It was a great conversation stopper.

Buying the plane was a happy adventure in an otherwise difficult time. During the filming of *Batman and Robin*, late the previous year, I'd learned at my annual physical that I would have to make room on my calendar for a major heart operation.

The timing had been a surprise, but the problem itself wasn't—for twenty years I'd known I had a hereditary defect that would someday need to be repaired. Way back in the 1970s, during one of my mother's springtime visits, I'd brought her to the hospital because she was feeling dizzy and nauseous. They discovered that she had a heart murmur due to a faulty aortic valve, the main valve leading out of the heart. Eventually it would need to be replaced. Middle age is often when you detect those things, the doctor said, and she was then in her fifties. I was only thirty-one, but they checked me too and found out that I shared the defect.

The doctor had told me, "Your valve won't need treatment for a long time. We'll just keep an eye on it." So every year I would get my heart checked. He would listen to the murmur and say, "There's nothing to worry about, just stay in shape and keep your cholesterol low" and blah, blah, blah. And I'd push the problem out of my mind for another year.

Eventually, when they told my mother that it was time for surgery, she refused. "When God wants to take me, I'm ready to go," she declared.

"That's funny, you didn't say that when you had your hysterectomy," I pointed out. "And you've fixed every other health problem all along. So why all of a sudden now with the heart are you are talking about God? God is the one who made the science possible. God trained the doctors. It's all in God's hands. You can extend your life."

"No, no, no." It was one of those Old World things. Still, even without the repair, she seemed healthy enough and was now seventy-five.

But I wasn't fine. The first sign of real trouble came after making *True Lies*. I was home swimming laps in the pool and felt this weird burning in my chest. It was a signal that the valve was beginning to fail. The doctor said, "This is now going to deteriorate slowly and then eventually it's going to deteriorate very fast. We want to catch it just at the beginning of that rapid slide—that's the best and safest moment to do the repair. If you wait beyond that, the aorta gets affected and the heart gets enlarged, and you don't want that. But I can't tell you when that moment will be. It could be next year, it could be five years from now. Everyone is different."

I didn't feel any more symptoms and continued doing my thing. I skied, I made movies, I went to Planet Hollywood openings, I did my public service. But at my annual checkup in 1996, the doctor said, "The moment has come. You need heart surgery. It doesn't have to be tomorrow, but do it this year."

I visited three hospitals to talk to the surgeons. I believe you should get three opinions when facing a big medical decision. The doctor I chose was Vaughn Starnes at the USC University Hospital. He was a trim guy with rimless glasses who was totally matter-of-fact about the problem and the risks. He also could understand where I was coming from.

"I love your action movies, and I want to see you keep making them," he said. "So I don't want you running around with an artificial valve." The better course was to put in a replacement valve made of living tissue, he explained. With a mechanical valve, I would have to take blood thinners and limit my activity for the rest of my life. But with an organic valve, "You can continue doing stunts, you can continue doing sports, you can go skiing, you can go motorcycle riding, horseback riding—whatever you want to do."

That was the upside. The downside was risk. The particular procedure he recommended worked only six times out of ten. "I want you to understand that in sixty percent to seventy percent of cases the surgery works, but in thirty percent to forty percent of the cases, the replacement valve fails," he said. "Then we have to go back in and try again."

Big risk, big reward. That made sense to me. "It's fine," I said. "I'll take the risk."

We scheduled the surgery for immediately after I finished *Batman and Robin,* so that I could come back without missing a beat. After the operation in April, I wanted to promote *Batman and Robin* that summer and then shoot my next picture, whatever it might be, in late 1997.

I didn't tell anybody about my heart surgery. No one knew. Not my mother, my nephew, my kids or anybody. Because I didn't want to talk about it. To ease my anxiety, I pretended that it wasn't really heart surgery; it would be more like getting a wisdom tooth removed. I would go in, get it done, and then go home.

I didn't even want to tell my wife. Maria was in the middle of a difficult fourth pregnancy, and I did not want her to be upset. She had a tendency to blow things up into high drama, even things that were not life and death, whereas I would play everything down. For instance, I would never tell her, "Three months from now, I'm going to Norway for a speech," because from that point on, she'd fret that I would be gone that week and she would be by herself. She'd be relentless: "What flight are you going to take? Why leave on Saturday rather than Sunday? Do you really have to go for that long? What are those two extra meetings?" By the time I got on the plane, I couldn't enjoy it because I'd talked too much about it. So I always told Ronda and Lynn, "Never share my calendar with anybody," and I would tell Maria only a few days in advance. I'm a person who does not like to talk about things over and over. I make decisions very quickly, I don't ask many people for opinions, and I don't want to think too many times about the same thing. I want to move on. That's why Maria always said I was just like her mother.

Maria is the opposite. She's a genius with medicine, and her method is to flesh everything out by talking to a lot of people. She's an outward processor, while I keep things bottled up. I was afraid that if she did that, word would get around before I had surgery. I also was concerned that she would second-guess me so that every night there would be a discussion. I needed to be in denial. I'd made my decision in the doctor's office, and I never wanted to deal with it again. If she were to bring it up all the time, then my denial trick wouldn't work. It would disrupt my way of coping with life and death. So I felt it was better never to let Maria know until just before the trip, or in this case, just before I went to the hospital.

As the surgery approached, I let Dr. Starnes in on my plan. "I will tell my family that I'm going to go to Mexico," I said. "I'll say I need a little vacation for a week. And then we do the heart surgery. You said I will be out of the hospital after five days. So after five days, I'll go to a hotel. I will lie in the sun and get tanned, I will look healthy, and then I'll go home, and no one will even know I had heart surgery. How about that?"

The doctor seemed a little surprised. He looked at me and then said in his straightforward manner, "Won't work. You'll have pain, you'll need help, you'll never be able to fake it. I strongly recommend that you tell your wife. She's pregnant. She should be included. I would tell her now."

That night I said casually to Maria, "Interestingly enough, do you remember I said one time that someday down the line I will need to have the valve replaced? The doctor has a slot available for me in two weeks, and I said to myself that's actually a good idea because if I do it right now, I'm in between movies, and I don't have to go to Europe for the *Batman* promotion for another six or seven weeks. So I can squeeze it in. This is a good time to do it, so I just want you to know."

Maria said, "Wait! Whoa, whoa, whoa, whoa. Wait a minute, are you telling me you need heart surgery?"

It was as if I'd never talked about it before. From that point on, she did talk about it continuously, but she also helped me keep it secret. My mother was staying with us for her annual spring visit, and we didn't even tell her.

The night before I was due at the hospital, I shot pool until one in the morning with Franco and a bunch of friends. We drank schnapps and had a great time, and I didn't tell any of them where I was going the next day. Then at four in the morning, Maria got up and drove me to the hospital. We used the family van, not the fancy Mercedes. At Maria's suggestion, I'd arranged to be admitted under a different name. The parking attendant was expecting us, and we got whisked into the garage. By five I was being prepped and hooked up to the machines, and by seven o'clock the surgery was in full swing. I loved that. Go in at five, start the surgery at seven, and by noon it's over. Bang, bang, bang. At six o'clock that evening, I woke up ready to shoot some more pool.

Well, that was the idea. They agreed to dress me in my Hawaiian shirt after the surgery so that when I woke up, I'd feel like I wasn't actually in the hospital. That was the whole theme. Sure enough, it worked. I woke up, saw Maria sitting there, felt fine, and went back to sleep. When I woke up again the next morning, Maria was still there, and I glanced over and saw a Lifecycle stationary bike that had been ordered for me to use later in the week. Within two hours, I was out of bed and on the bike. The doctor came in and was stunned. He said, "Please, you've got to take this Lifecycle out of here."

"There is no resistance on it," I said. "It's just for me, for my head, that I am sitting on the Lifecycle right after surgery."

He examined me and was pleased with my progress. But that evening, I started coughing. Fluid was building up in my lungs. The doctor came back at nine o'clock and ordered a bunch of tests. A little later, after Maria went home to see the kids, I tried to sleep. But the coughing got worse, and soon I was having trouble getting air. At three in the morning, the doctor came back in. He sat down on the bed and held my hand. "I'm terribly sorry," he said, "but this didn't work. We have to take you back into surgery. I'm putting together the best team. We are not going to lose you."

"Lose me?" I said.

"We are not going to lose you. Just hang in there tonight; maybe we'll give you some medication so you sleep. Where's Maria?"

"She's home."

"Well, I have to call her."

"Look, she will freak out. Don't even tell her."

"No, she has to be here."

There's a moment going into surgery that I really hate. It's the moment when the anesthesia starts to take hold, when you know you're going out, when you're losing consciousness and don't know if you'll ever wake up. The oxygen mask felt like it was suffocating me—I was gasping for air, short of breath.

This was a much bigger version of the claustrophobia I fought when I was having face and body masks made to play the Terminator or Mr. Freeze in *Batman and Robin.* For me, Stan Winston's special-effects studio was torture. To make the masks, they need a mold, and to make the mold, they place these huge, heavy casts on your head. A lot of actors hate it, so Stan and his helpers have a whole routine.

When you first arrive, the music is on, everyone is happy and welcoming, "Yay, it's good to have you here!" Then they sit you down and say, "This is going to be a little challenging. Are you claustrophobic?"

"Nah," I'd always answer, trying to play ballsy.

So they start wrapping you with strips of fabric dipped in cement. Soon your eyes are covered, and you can't see anything. Then your ears are closed, and you can no longer hear. One by one, all your senses are shut off. Now your mouth is sealed, so you can no longer talk. Finally, they cover your nose, except for two little straws poking out of your nostrils to let you breathe.

You have to wait maybe a half hour for the cast to set. The mind starts to play tricks. What if you can't get enough air? What if a little bit of cement gets in one of the straws and blocks off a nostril? Because they've had so many actors freak out, they try to keep things light with the music and casual conversation. After you can't hear anymore, you still feel them moving around you as they're applying the wrap. They tell you ahead of time that if you feel you are really flipping out, "I'm right here. Just signal with your hand or tap me on the arm."

After awhile the real fear sets in. You feel the cast getting hard, which means it's no longer possible to just rip it off your head. Now it will have to be cut. You noticed the tools when you sat down—the little electric circular saw they use to cut off casts—but you didn't ask enough questions when you had the chance.

So now you're thinking, "Wait a minute. *How do they know how deep to cut?* What if that saw slices into my face?"

The first time I went through this, I worried so much about the saw that I started hyperventilating. I couldn't get enough air through my straws, and I started feeling really freaked. I tried to calm down. "Stop thinking about that, stop visualizing that saw," I ordered myself. "Push it out of your mind . . . Yeah, okay, I've got it out of my mind now. Okay, now let's think about something else. Maybe I should think about the ocean. Maybe I should think about a great forest, something pleasant; maybe birds chirping and leaves rustling in the wind and in the distance people working and the sound of a . . . chainsaw!" And I'd be anxious again. Of course, by this time, the attendants had disappeared. Maybe not out of the room, but I didn't know where they were. Maybe they'd told me, "Okay, just ten more minutes," but I couldn't hear. I was locked in. There was no one around. And so I was just kind of hoping for the best.

Surgery reminded me of that.

Maria was so frightened to get a call from Dr. Starnes at four o'clock in the morning that she telephoned her friend Roberta and asked her to come with her to the hospital. Roberta Hollander, a CBS news producer, had been like a sister to Maria when she first got in front of the camera—a strong leader and tough broad who really knew how to deal with people. A few hours later, she and Maria sat in Dr. Starnes's office as I went back under the knife. He had a huge monitor in his office that let him see and hear what was going on in the operating room because there were parts of the procedure, like taking the patient off the heart-lung machine, that he didn't perform. He'd go back to his office, see other patients and hold his meetings, keeping track in case he was needed. Maria told me later that she looked away many times. She couldn't watch when they cut open my chest, used surgical pliers to undo the wires holding together my rib cage from the first operation, and exposed the heart. But Roberta pulled her chair right up to the screen. "Did you see that?" she said. "They just cut the aorta, and they're stitching in the new valve!"

So I got a second or third lease on life, depending on how you count it. I woke up from the surgery and discovered Roberta there with Maria, giving moral support. Again I felt good. The painful coughing was gone. I could breathe. "Amazing!" I said. "This is great! When did the doctor say I could go home?"

We'd found an Austrian guy in the hospital kitchen who knew how to fix Wiener schnitzel, and the first two days I had that. It tasted delicious. But on the third day, when the attendant came in with the food, I said, "Can you please take that away? I cannot stand the smell." It smelled like rotting garbage.

From that point on, I could only stomach ice cream and fruit. Everything smelled bad. I lost my sense of taste. I hated everything they put in front of me and began to feel really low.

The doctor had warned that open-heart surgery often leaves people depressed. But after what we'd just been through, Maria was very concerned. "This isn't like you," she said. When a couple of days passed, and I didn't bounce back emotionally, she thought that the doctors were being too blasé. "You've got to do something," she told them. "We can't have him like that. When I come back tomorrow, you'd better have him cheery."

The residents had the idea of sneaking me a cigar, because they knew I love stogies. They thought that would really do it. There was an area on the roof where they could shoot baskets to unwind, and they brought me up there to smoke. Little did they realize that I had no sense of taste and that I hated everything. I put the cigar in my mouth and almost threw up. "No, thank you, I just can't," I said. I ended up sitting in the wheelchair watching them play basketball, like a character in *One Flew Over the Cuckoo's Nest*. I was just staring. I didn't even know what I saw, just bodies jumping around. There was nothing in it for me, that was for sure. Eventually they wheeled me back down to the room. I did feel a little bit better, I guess, to be outdoors a bit.

Eventually I came around, especially after I got home. I played with the kids and little by little started working out in the gym. Not bench presses, of course, but riding the Lifecycle a little and afterward walking up the hill to Will Rogers Park with Conan and Strudel, our black Lab that Franco gave me on one of my birthdays. A little later I could go back to weights, but heavy training was out of the question from now on because it would put pressure on the valve. No forcing, no struggling, the doctor said. Not ever again.

I never realized how badly the news of my surgery was going to hurt me in Hollywood. We announced it because word had started to circulate anyway, and it would have seemed suspicious not to tell the public. Immediately I got phone calls from executives at the studios I'd been working with. "Don't worry about the script," they said. "We are going to hold it for you. Just take care of yourself and feel better. And as soon as you're ready, let us know."

I should have known it was not that simple. The more you promote yourself as the ultimate action hero, and the more you advertise how fit you are and how you do the riding, jumping, and fighting yourself, people form a larger-than-life perception of you. They see you as an *actual* action figure, not just some guy in a costume on the screen. And the heart symbolizes it all. It's the center of the body, the physicality. It's the foundation of courage and will. The heart is emotion too—it's love and passion and compassion. Heart, heart, heart, heart, it's the center of everything.

Now all of a sudden people hear that you've had surgery. This thing that has driven you for decades is being operated on. And they talk: "What happened? Did he have a heart attack? Oh, a valve change; I don't know what that is, really. But Jesus Christ, open-heart surgery. They had to stop his heart and open it up and change parts in there. And having to do two surgeries must mean there's something really wrong. Sounds like terrible news. Poor guy. I mean, fuck, it's over!"

People reacted totally differently to David Letterman's coronary bypass surgery ten years later. Within two weeks, he was back on the show, and life went on. But no one expected him to lift up the set or run through flames or swing from the ceiling. Commonly after heart surgery, you can go back to your normal everyday life. But my everyday life was anything but normal. My stunts were not normal, and my movies were not normal, so I was seen differently. It was more like when a theoretical physicist has brain surgery. Everyone goes off the deep end and says, "Well, they said one-third of his brain was affected, and this is a disaster."

Access Hollywood and other celebrity-gossip shows went to town on the situation. So-called medical experts who had never even met me and didn't know of my hereditary condition or the specifics of my treatment were interviewed on TV. They'd say things like, "Under normal circumstances, when you have a surgery like that, it means you'll have an artificial valve, and you'll be taking blood thinners, and you would have to avoid strenuous activity that might cause injury, like a movie stunt, which might cause severe internal bleeding, and you could die immediately." We could clarify that I hadn't received a mechanical valve and didn't need blood thinners, of course, but the damage was done. The studios were making decisions based on inaccurate information. People thought, "We won't be seeing Arnold in any action movies anymore."

In spite of all this, I did experience the wonderful physical rebound that often results from a heart repair. I felt as vigorous as Hercules, ready to leap back into work. In July, I was already traveling around the world promoting *Batman and Robin.* And, as usual, I had projects at various stages of development, with roles that interested me. *With Wings as Eagles* was a film in which I would have played a German army officer in the closing months of World War II who ignores orders to kill Allied POWs and saves them instead. *Minority Report* was envisioned as a sequel to *Total Recall,* with a script by the same writer. I would have played the detective role that eventually went to Tom Cruise. In *Noble Father* I would have played a widowed cop trying to raise three daughters and fight crime. There was a proposed movie version of *S.W.A.T.*, a 1970s TV action series; a movie called *Crossbow*, based on the legend of William Tell; and *Pathfinder*, about a Viking orphan raised by Native Americans at the time of the first European explorations of North America.

I didn't even notice at first that the studios were holding back. But when I started submitting stories and scripts I wanted to do, people were slow responding. I became aware that the studios seemed reluctant to commit really big money. Fox was backing away from the idea of *Terminator 3.* Warner put the brakes on *I Am Legend,* a postapocalyptic vampire script that I was supposed to shoot that fall with Ridley Scott directing. He wanted a budget of $100 million, while Warner wanted to spend only $80 million. That was the reason the studio gave for pulling back, anyway—the real reason was my heart surgery.

In the midst of all this, I was also trying to keep Planet Hollywood from going up in smoke. Was it a fad, or was it a real business? The startup had become, to put it mildly, a crazy adventure. In the past eighteen months, I'd taken part in restaurant openings in Moscow, Sydney, Helsinki, Paris, and more than a dozen other cities all over the world. Often these openings were more like national events. Ten thousand people turned out in Moscow, and forty thousand in London. Our opening in San Antonio, Texas, turned into a citywide celebration where more than one hundred thousand people were partying in the streets. It was a huge sensation. There was no press that didn't cover it. Planet Hollywood was like the Beatles: a genius idea with sophisticated promotion and the best marketing.

An impressive number of stars signed up as owners and participants as the company grew: Whoopi Goldberg, Wesley Snipes, Antonio Banderas, Cindy Crawford, George Clooney, Will Smith, Jackie Chan, and on and on. We had a lineup of athletes that was just as fantastic, including Shaquille O'Neal, Tiger Woods, Wayne Gretzky, Sugar Ray Leonard, Monica Seles, and Andre Agassi. The athletes were associated with the Official All Star Cafe, Planet Hollywood's chain for sports celebrities. When Planet Hollywood went public in 1996, it had the busiest first day of trading on the Nasdaq stock exchange ever, and the total value of the company stood at $2.8 billion.

It was clear that Planet Hollywood was a great venue for a party. When we held the premiere celebration for *Eraser* at the Official All Star Cafe in Times Square, traffic was gridlocked for blocks. Inside, for $15, you could get a burger and a beer and watch George Clooney, Vanessa Williams, me, and the rest of the cast and our guests hanging out on the main floor below. There were interesting nostalgia displays, like part of Charlie Sheen's collection of baseball memorabilia and a preserved slice of wedding cake from Joe DiMaggio's wedding to Marilyn Monroe. There were counters where you could buy specially designed clothing and souvenirs.

The Planet Hollywood trips, openings, and events were all fun. Sometimes I would bring Maria and the kids, and we'd make the trip a minivacation. Sly, Bruce, and I got together and hung out. It was always interesting to meet the local celebrities, too, who were an essential part of the business. Every city has celebrities, whether it's a football star or an opera singer or whatever. When we opened in Munich or Toronto or Cape Town or Cancún, we always involved both the international stars and the locals, and that's what made the celebration. Local celebrities would join in because they could mingle with the international stars, and often they would have financial participation in that particular restaurant. After the grand opening, the international celebrities would draw back, and the locals would support the restaurant as a regular hangout, throw parties there, have screenings there—almost every Planet Hollywood was built with a screening room.

Going public gave the company capital to expand. But we saw very quickly the drawbacks of being publicly owned, too. Compared to regular restaurant chains such as Ponderosa or Applebee's, Planet Hollywood had high expenses, and if you weren't on the inside, or out there promoting the business, it was hard to see why certain big-ticket items made sense.

For instance, corporate jets: Planet Hollywood spent lots of money flying celebrities around. Actually, this was the best way to cement the loyalty of the stars; even more effective than the stock options they also received. Big-time celebrities don't like flying commercial, and yet very few have their own planes. For this reason, the Warner Bros. studio operated its own little air force for twenty or thirty years, keeping a set of planes to fly Clint Eastwood and other major actors and directors around. Warner also had houses in Acapulco, Mexico, and Aspen and apartments in New York. These were like candies for celebrities. If you were part of the Warner family, you could use all of that for free. And those actors and directors stayed with the studio, signing contract after contract, because they knew if they went to, say, Universal, there would be no more corporate jet. We had that same magic working for us, and yet shareholders would say, "Wait a minute, why are you wasting all this money on celebrities? I don't want to pay for that."

They complained about the design expenses also. The restaurants all sold merchandise, from cool-looking bomber jackets to caps to key chains, and these were being refreshed and updated constantly. Fans would try to see how many Planet Hollywood T-shirts from different cities they could collect. Sometimes a customer would show up at an opening with thirty T-shirts for me to sign because he or she had been to thirty cities all over the world. It was a good, good spin. But stockholders would still want to know, "Why are you designing jackets and merchandise all the time? Why don't you keep the same ones?"

The biggest pressure from the public markets was to expand. Wall Street was in the heat of the internet boom, and investors demanded fast growth. The founders, Robert Earl and Keith Barish, were each now worth about $500 million on paper because they still owned 60 percent of the stock. They promised to increase both total sales and the number of locations by 30 percent to 40 percent a year. This meant building restaurants in lots of second- and third-tier US cities like Indianapolis, Saint Louis, and Columbus, as well as in dozens more cities abroad. In April 1997, the month I had my heart operation, the company made a deal with Saudi billionaire Prince Alwaleed bin Talal to open almost three dozen Planet Hollywoods across the Middle East and Europe, starting with Brussels, Athens, Cairo, Lisbon, Istanbul, and Budapest. And it made a deal with a tycoon in Singapore, Ong Beng Seng, to build almost two dozen restaurants in Asia.

I kept telling Robert and Keith that this was a mistake. They were losing their grip on the central concept. If you went to the Planet Hollywood in Beverly Hills, you really *might* see Arnold. If you went to the one in Paris, you really might see beloved French film star Gerard Depardieu. If you went to the All Star Cafe in Tokyo, you really might see Ichiro Suzuki, the great baseball player. And in Orlando, you really might see Shaq during the years that he played there. But if you went to the Planet Hollywood in Indianapolis, would you see Bruce Willis having lunch? It started to feel like bullshit. We couldn't deliver on that promise. By October, I was worried enough to ask Robert and Keith to come to my office and talk. We sat around the big conference table, just the three of us and Paul Wachter, and I made my pitch to them about fixing the strategy. We now had restaurants all over the world in great locations, I told them, and those held enormous potential that was still untapped. I had a whole presentation prepared on how to do that. For instance, we had a big opportunity to work with the studios on movie premieres. "Hollywood is turning out fifty movies a year," I said. "Every one of those movies is going to open up across the United States and the world. So where do they hold the party?"

I wanted to bring studio executives into the business, fly them to the premieres, offer them perks, and treat them like kings so they would sit in their marketing meetings and say, "We're going to open this movie with Planet Hollywood in Moscow, Madrid, London, Paris, and Helsinki—ten cities. In each city, we'll have a screening at the restaurant, and then a huge screening at a local theater, and Planet Hollywood will host a big after-party. And here's the good thing, guys: Planet Hollywood will fly the celebrities over and pay for the party. We'll take care of the hotel rooms and all the other stuff involved in the premiere itself. By splitting the costs, we'll save, and we'll still get a ton of attention."

Pulling off those kinds of deals meant that we would need a point person to schmooze with the studio. My first choice would have been Jack Valenti, the longtime head of the Motion Picture Association of America and Hollywood's top lobbyist in Washington. Jack was a good friend and had been one of my closest advisors when I was chairman of the President's Council on Physical Fitness and Sports. I thought we should go to him and say, "Jack, you're seventy-five. You have done a terrific job for the movie business, but what are they paying you? A million dollars a year? Here's two million a year. Relax. And here's a pension, and here are benefits for your grandchildren." All of a sudden we'd have Jack Valenti schmoozing all the studios and making the deals.

Another vital matter that I raised: our hamburgers and pizzas were good, but I wanted to serve more interesting food. And I saw huge potential in the merchandise. Rather than cut back our spending on design, I believed that we should do more. I was fascinated by the way fashion designer Tom Ford had gone into Gucci and transformed it from an old-fuddy-duddy company into a source for hip jackets and hip shoes. Before Ford's arrival, I never bought from Gucci; all of a sudden, I was in their store.

"You've got to get a guy like that to design for Planet Hollywood," I told Robert and Keith. "You need actual Planet Hollywood fashion shows that you can take to Japan, Europe, and the Middle East, so that people will want to have the latest Planet Hollywood stuff. Rather than always selling the same old bomber jacket, the bomber jacket should change all the time, with different kinds of buckles and with different kinds of chains hanging off it. If you make the merchandise snappy and hip and the newest of the new, you'll sell tons of it."

Throughout my pitch, Robert and Keith kept saying, "Yes, yes, great idea." At the end, they promised to get back to me on the points I'd raised. But Paul had been the only person taking notes. "I don't think they got it," he said after they left. I'd hoped this would be a game-changing meeting, because promotion and merchandising were realms I truly understood. But I had the sense that Robert and Keith were overwhelmed. The pressure from the market was getting to them. While Robert was supposedly focused on operations and Keith on the strategic vision, mostly they talked about investor deals. And Planet Hollywood had reached a scale where it was no longer possible for two entrepreneurs to do it all. The company needed structure, and it needed people who were expert in managing a global operation. I'm a loyal person, and I stayed committed to the business for several more years. But its popularity declined steadily, and the stock fell and fell until eventually the company went bankrupt. Financially I did fine, thanks to the protections we had negotiated into my deal, although I made nowhere near the $120 million or so my stock had once been worth on paper. I was better off than the many shareholders who lost money, however, and better off than many of the other actors and athletes.

Even so, I'd love to do it again, only have it managed better. Whoopi, Bruce, Sly, and all the other big-name participants would tell you that Planet Hollywood was fun. With the huge parties, openings, and premieres, we met people all over the world and had the time of our lives.

CHAPTER 22

Family Guy

MARIA HAD A TERRIBLE time with morning sickness while she was pregnant with Christopher in 1997. It got so severe that she had to check into our local hospital because she couldn't keep anything down. I was worried even though she had good medical attention, and the kids were upset because Maria was gone. Katherine was only seven years old, Christina was five, and Patrick was three. To help them get through it, I put off commitments and spent a lot of extra hours at home trying to be both mom and dad.

I figured that what would reassure them most was making sure they saw Maria every day and otherwise keeping up the daily routine. Every morning on the way to school for the girls, we'd stop off at the hospital, and again in the afternoon. I explained to them that Mommy would want to have a part of home with her, so each morning before we left, we'd go into our garden and pick the most elegant flower to bring her.

Maria and I had been raised in wildly different ways, which meant we could draw on the best of each style for our parenting routine. Meals, for example, were definitely in the Shriver tradition. Both sets of parents insisted that we all sit down as a family every night, but that's where the similarity ended. In my parents' house when I was a kid, no one discussed anything at the dinner table. The rule was, when you eat, you eat. Each of us was very private, and if you had a problem, you worked it out yourself. But in Maria's family growing up, they all shared what they'd done that day. Everybody told a story. I'm good at communicating, but Maria was so much better at creating fun at dinner, explaining everything to the kids. She brought her family's atmosphere to our table. It was something that I tried to pick up on for myself, to learn and become the same way. It's very helpful to have at least one parent with those skills.

When our kids had homework, we each went with our strengths. Maria would help with anything involving language, and I would help with anything involving numbers. She is a very good writer, with an unbelievable vocabulary and grace with words. In fact, motherhood inspired her to author books of insight for young people. Her first, *Ten Things I Wish I'd Known Before I Went Out into the Real World,* tore down the myth of the superparent who can barrel on unchanged at work while raising kids. "Children Do Change Your Career (Not to Mention Your Entire Life)," one chapter was titled, and its takeaway was "At work, you're replaceable . . . But as a parent, you're irreplaceable." We both strongly believed that.

I've always been comfortable with numbers. As a kid, as I learned about math, it all made sense. The decimals made immediate sense. The fractions made immediate sense. I knew all the roman numerals. You could throw problems at me, and I'd solve them. You could show me statistics, and instead of glazing over the way a lot of people do, I'd make out facts and trends that the figures were pointing to and read them like a story.

I taught our kids math drills that my father had used on Meinhard and me. He always made us start them a month before school, and we had to do them every day because he felt that the brain has to be trained and warmed up like the body of an athlete. Not only did my brother and I have to do the math drills but so did anybody who came over to play. Pretty soon a lot of kids avoided our house. I hated all this, of course. But here I was thirty-five years later drilling my own kids. I always gave them the bill in restaurants to figure out the 20 percent tip.

They'd add it up and sign my signature. I always checked to make sure they did the math right. It was a whole routine, and they loved it.

When it came to chores, we used the Schwarzenegger tradition. In Europe, you grow up helping to keep the house clean. You take off your shoes when you come in, otherwise all hell breaks loose. You turn off the lights when you leave the room because there is a limited amount of power. You conserve water because somebody has to fetch it from the well. You are much more involved in the basics. I remember my shock when I first got to know Maria, who had grown up with people to pick up after her. She'd come into the house and take off her sweater—it was a cashmere sweater—and if it fell on the floor, that's where it stayed. To me, even today, I can't treat a cashmere sweater that way. I'd have to pick it up and hang it on a chair. And even though I can afford it, I would never wear cashmere to go skiing or play sports. It has to be cotton or wool or something cheaper, like a $10 sweatshirt, before I feel comfortable getting it sweaty.

Although Maria eventually became a neat freak like me, I was still the one who brought European discipline to the house—with tolerance added, of course, because I knew I couldn't go crazy. You have to tone it down, unlike some of my friends in Austria. The way they discipline their kids may work for them there, but it doesn't work here. Otherwise, when your kids compare notes with their friends at school, they will think that their father is a weirdo. I'd also promised myself, this is the generation where the physical punishment stops. I wasn't going to carry on that Old World tradition.

Maria and I settled on our own approach, where we pamper the kids a little, but also have rules. From the time they were little, for instance, they had to do their own wash—learn how to use the washing machine, put the detergent in, put the clothes in and choose a medium or large load. Then how to put the clothes in the dryer and fold them and put them away. Also how to time yourself so your siblings have a chance to do their laundry too.

Every day before taking the kids to school, I would inspect to make sure that the lights were off, the beds made, and drawers and closets closed. There could be stuff lying around and a little bit of mess; I was much more lenient than my dad. Nevertheless, those beds were made. I wasn't looking for perfection, like in the military. But I didn't want the kids to think that someone else was going to pick up after them. The epic struggle, though, was teaching the kids to turn off the lights when they left a room or went to sleep. It was me against the entire Maria clan, because the kids inherited keeping the lights on from her. When we first got together, she never went to sleep without the lights on. It made her feel secure. Then when we'd visit Washington or Hyannis Port, and I'd arrive late and they would all be asleep, I would walk into a house with the door unlocked and all the lights on. I could never understand it. It was the wildest thing. The next day the excuse would be, "Oh, we knew you were coming in late and wanted you to feel welcome, so we left the lights on." But even if I was already there, and I went downstairs in the middle of the night, the lights would be on. Everywhere it was like Times Square. I'd explain to my kids, we have a shortage of energy, and there is only so much water in this state. You can't stand under the shower for fifteen minutes. Five minutes is the limit. I'll time it from now on. And be sure to turn off lights because when you're not in the room, you don't need them anymore.

To this day, my daughters won't go to sleep without the hallway light on. I finally had to get used to the fact that they feel more comfortable that way. As for leaving the lights on when they're not in a room, my father would have solved that with a smack, but we don't hit our kids. When communication fails, our method is to take away privileges: canceling a playdate or a sleepover, grounding, not letting them use their car. But punishments like that seemed over the top for the light-switch problem. One of the boys was the worst offender, so I finally unscrewed one bulb in his room each time I found the lights left on. I pointed out that there were twelve bulbs in his room, and if he kept it up, soon he'd be in the dark. And that is what happened. Eventually my crusade was effective. Now when we're home, I only have to turn off the lights after the kids maybe two days a week.

Among the joys that kids bring are the holidays that have been mostly missing from your life since your own childhood. Holidays become much more meaningful when you have a family, because now you see them in two ways. I remembered Christmas vividly from when I was a kid: my mother and father lighting the candles on the tree with the toys underneath, holding hands, singing "Heil'ge Nacht," and my father playing the trumpet. Now I also saw Christmas through a parent's eye.

I considered myself a tree-decorating expert. It was in my blood. In Austria, my father and the other men from the village would go out into the forest three days before Christmas and bring back trees. Kids were not supposed to know about it because the tree officially came from Christkindl: a female angel like the Christ child who was the Austrian version of Santa Claus. One time my brother mistakenly blurted out, "I saw Dad leaving with an axe," and my father went nuts because my mother had not kept us away from the window. But normally it was the most fun thing. They decorated our tree with all kinds of candies, wrappings, and ornaments, so that the branches would droop down, with the presents underneath. The tree was always so tall that the highest ornament touched the ceiling. There were real candles mounted with clips on the outer branches, which meant that you could light the tree only for a few minutes each time.

At six o'clock on Christmas Eve, my father would turn down the radio, and there would be total silence. My mother would say, "Let's listen, because remember Christkindl always comes around six o'clock." Soon we would hear a little bell ring: one of the ornaments that decorated the tree. Obviously the neighbor girl had crept up the rear stairs and in the back door of our bedroom, but we never caught on to that until later. For years, Meinhard and I would race to our room, skidding on the throw rug on the hardwood floor and wiping out before we even got to the door, and the next thing, pushing and shoving, we would storm in. There was great, great joy.

Maria and I didn't do the secret tree because that's not the American tradition. The tradition here is to set up the tree three or four weeks before Christmas, and I didn't want to insist on waiting and have the kids constantly ask, "How come we don't have a tree yet?" Instead, we'd have friends over American style, where each friend hangs an ornament. As the kids got older, they did more and more until they were in charge of putting up the angel, or the star, or Jesus or Mary, or whatever the highest ornament would be, and deciding on the look of the tree.

We made a big deal of the other holidays too. Easter always came during my mom's annual visit. She'd arrive as early as mid-February and live with us for two or three months, depending on the cold and snow in Austria. Besides wanting to spend time together, part of her motivation was to escape the harshest part of the winter. For Easter she was the perfect grandparent to have on hand, because the big traditions all trace back to that part of Europe: the bunny, the baskets, the eggs, the chocolates. She always colored eggs with the kids; she was an expert, and they'd have their little aprons on. My mother would take over the kitchen and make pastry, covering all the counters with dough rolled so thin that no one could figure out how she did it. Then she'd lay out the apple slices and fold up the dough and bake the most delicious apple strudel in America. On Easter the festivities would go on all day: first big Easter baskets and an exchange of small gifts, then Mass, and then an Easter egg hunt and a feast, followed by visits from relatives and friends.

Maria made a big effort with my mother, and they really got along. And of course I was in heaven when Eunice or Sarge would come stay with us. So we never had in-law problems. The kids called my mother Omi, and she spoiled them, and they loved her. She'd picked up English over the years and had even taken some classes, so by now she was fluent enough to have conversations with the kids, even though talking to kids in your second language is never easy to do. She and Christina especially sought each other out—Christina whose middle name is Aurelia.

My mother spoiled our dogs as well. Conan and Strudel were not allowed upstairs, but after we went to sleep, my mother would sneak them into her room, and in the morning the dogs would be curled up on the rug by her bed. She was in LA enough that she established her own life and her own circle of friends—other Austrians and European journalists—to shop with, have lunch with, and hang out. I'll never forget seeing her at an awards banquet once, deep in conversation with the mothers of Sophia Loren and Sylvester Stallone. They were probably all claiming credit for our success.

Mom was seventy-six when she died in 1998. It was my father's birthday, August 2, and as my mother always did, she walked to the cemetery on a hill outside town to spend time at his grave. She would hold imaginary conversations with him for an hour, telling him everything she'd been doing, asking questions, as if he were right there but on the other side.

The weather that day was humid and stiflingly hot, and the cemetery was a steep climb up. People who saw her said that when she reached the grave, she sat down suddenly as if she felt faint, and then slumped to the ground. The medics tried to revive her, but by the time they got her to the hospital, she was brain-dead from oxygen deprivation. She'd never had her heart repaired, and it had failed.

Maria and I flew to Graz for the funeral. My nephew Patrick and Maria's brother Timmy and Franco came along. I'd missed the funerals of my father and my brother, but for my mom's we got there a day in advance and helped organize. We saw her in the casket, wearing a traditional Austrian dirndl dress.

She had been fine and cheerful as always during her annual spring visit, staying all through May, so of course this came as a terrible shock. But later, looking back on her life, I felt that by the time she passed away, I had no regrets. None, because of the relationship that I'd nurtured with her after I came to America, as I learned to think a little bit more about my family rather than just myself. Now that I had kids, I realized how my leaving must have upset her. I'd appreciated her earlier as a devoted mother, but I'd never thought about the pain my leaving caused. That maturing happened too late for me to reconnect with my brother or dad, but with my mother I built a good relationship where she and I really communicated.

I offered many times to buy her a house in Los Angeles, but she didn't want to leave Austria. In addition to Easter and Mother's Day, she came for all of our kids' christenings. She saw every movie I made and came to a lot of the premieres. Starting with *Conan the Barbarian*, I brought her to the set of every one of my movies. She hung out on the set, hung out in my trailer, watched me film. When I was on location, in Mexico or Italy or Spain, she came and stayed sometimes for a week or two at the hotel. No one else brought their mom to the set, but mine was a natural tourist and this was something she happened to enjoy. It was partly because she got so much attention from everyone. We'd have breakfast together, and then my driver would take her wherever she wanted to explore, so she always came home with photos to show her friends: a marketplace in Mexico, the Vatican while in Rome, museums in Madrid. I brought her to the White House to meet Ronald Reagan in the 1980s, and she attended the Great American Workout at the White House with George Bush. He was really, really nice to her, talking up a storm and complimenting her by telling her what a great job she'd done raising me.

I loved doing things for my mother not only because I wanted to make her feel that she'd done a good job as a parent, but also because it was kind of a reward for the hardships of her earlier life. When I look at the photographs of her at twenty-three or twenty-four, when my brother and I were born, she looked haggard and skinny. It was after the war. She was begging for food. She had a husband who got crazy and drunk every so often. She was in this little village. The weather was shitty a lot of times, with rain, snow, and gloom, except in the summer. She never had enough money. It was a struggle all along.

So I felt that in her remaining years, she should have the best time possible. She would be rewarded for carrying us kids at midnight over the mountain to the hospital when we got sick, for being there when I needed her. Also, she should be rewarded for the pain that I caused her by leaving. She deserved to be treated like a queen.

We buried my mother at the gravesite where she died, next to my dad, which was very sad but also romantic. She was so connected to him.

If Easter belonged to my mom, Thanksgiving was a special Sarge and Eunice holiday from long before we got married. Shriver children, spouses, and grandchildren would always converge on their beautiful white Georgian mansion outside Washington. It was like a three-day family festival. Many couples have to negotiate about whether to spend a holiday with the in-laws, but this arrangement just fell into place naturally. I said to Maria, "Let's stay with this because we have a great time at Thanksgiving with your parents and then we can always have Christmas at home. It doesn't mean your parents can't come, but we'll have Christmas on our turf." She liked that as well. I was always sensitive that our marriage had taken her far from her family and that she often missed them and wanted to hang out even though she also wanted her independence. So I always told her, "Remember that any of your family you want to invite is automatically a guest of mine too." Welcoming my in-laws was easy because I liked them a great deal, and they always brought laughter and fun.

Thanksgiving at the Shriver house started out with church—Sarge and Eunice went to Mass every day—followed by breakfast and then lots of sports. In Georgetown, there were great clothes stores and gift shops that offered different merchandise than shops in California, so I'd grab the opportunity to get a start on Christmas shopping. We'd meet again at night, and many times Teddy would come over with his wife for dinner or drinks, or Robert Kennedy Jr., the environmentalist, would come with his son, or his sister Courtney and her little girl, Saoirse (her name is pronounced *Seer*-sha, which means "freedom" in Gaelic). In Hyannis Port every August, the cousin scene was really wild because the Kennedys and Lawfords, as well as the Shrivers, would come. You'd see thirty cousins swimming, sailing, and waterskiing, and going to the snack bar to get fried shrimps and clams. Morning to night, it was a big sports camp.

I always believed that Eunice and Sarge would have a big influence on our children. They certainly did on me. I worked with them on the Special Olympics, serving as a torchbearer to help the organization expand. The summer when Katherine was twelve and the other kids ranged in age down to four, Maria and I brought them all along on a mission to South Africa.

This was my first visit there in twenty-six years, since I'd won Mr. Olympia in Pretoria during the days of apartheid. It was breathtaking to see how the country had changed. Back then, Mr. Olympia had been the first racially integrated athletic competition there. During my visits to South Africa in those early days, I'd become friends with Piet Koornhof, the minister of sports and culture and a strong progressive voice against apartheid. He opened the way for me to do bodybuilding exhibitions in the townships and said, "Every time you do something for whites, I'd like to see you do something for blacks." He'd also taken the lead in getting South Africa to bid for the Mr. Olympia competition, and I'd been part of the delegation from the International Federation of Body Building that worked with him. Now apartheid was long gone, and Nelson Mandela was the nation's distinguished former president.

Since leaving office, Mandela had committed himself to raising the profile of the Special Olympics across the entire continent, where millions of people with intellectual disabilities were stigmatized, ignored, or worse. Sarge and Eunice had planned to come with us, but Eunice, who'd just turned eighty, broke her leg in a car crash a day before we left. So when we got to Cape Town, it was up to us, the younger generation: Maria, me, and her brother Tim, who'd succeeded Sarge as Special Olympics president. Tim brought his wife, Linda, and their five kids as well.

Mandela was a hero to me. I got goose bumps when he talked in his speeches about inclusion, tolerance, and forgiveness—the opposite of what you might expect from a black man in a white racist nation who'd rotted in prison for twenty-seven years. Such virtue doesn't just happen, especially not in prison, so to me it was like God had put him among us.

We were there to launch a torch run involving athletes from across southern Africa. It was for the dual purpose of raising the profile of the Special Olympics and supporting the cause of law enforcement within South Africa itself. Mandela lit the flame in the grimmest possible setting: his old cell at the Robben Island prison. Standing there, we had a chance to talk before we began, and I asked how he'd achieved insight in such a place. I'm sure he'd been asked this a thousand times, but he said the most remarkable thing. Mandela said it was good that he'd been in prison. It had given him time to think—time to decide that his approach as a violent young man had been wrong, and to be ready to emerge as the person he is. I admired him, but I didn't know what to make of that. Was it real or just something he'd talked himself into? Could Mandela really believe that twenty-seven years in a cell was necessary? Or was he looking at the bigger picture: what those lost years meant to South Africa, not to him? You're just one person, and the country is much bigger, and it's what will live forever. That was a powerful thought. Afterward, I said to Maria, "I don't know if I can buy it or not, but it was amazing for him to say—that he felt totally content with what he went through and with losing whole decades."

The kids were with Maria and me throughout the day. Of course Christopher, who was just four, wasn't taking in as much as his brother and his sisters, who were eight, ten, and twelve. But I knew that seeing all this would have an impact, even if they didn't understand everything right away. At some point they would write papers at school about meeting Mandela, and lighting the torch, and hearing him compare the prejudice that Special Olympians face with the injustice of apartheid. They'd be able to look back and ask Maria and me about what we'd all seen, and then write about the beauties of Cape Town and the contrast with the townships and the poverty of families who live there. The experience would take time to sink in. Before leaving Africa, we spent a few days on safari, which for everybody was an instant 10. I was just as amazed as the kids were watching what seemed like the entire animal kingdom roaming round before our eyes: lions, monkeys, elephants, giraffes. And then at night to lie in a tent and hear the calls and the cries all around. The ranger was on the lookout for a particular lioness that had a special tag on its ear. It was time to replace a tracking device the lion wore. Finally, he spotted the lioness and said, "I have to tranquilize her." He took careful aim and shot her with a dart, and suddenly the lioness was roaring, pissed off, and running away. "She'll make it about two hundred yards," the ranger said. Sure enough, all of a sudden the lioness was walking, and then she was looking back at us, and, finally, she rolled onto her side.

We drove to him and got out, and the kids had a chance to take pictures and to see how big the paws were; bigger than their faces. Big cats have always fascinated me. When we were filming *Total Recall* in Mexico, we had all kinds of animals on the set, including a panther kitten and a cougar kitten. I loved playing with them. The trainer would bring them to my RV every Saturday when we had a two-hour break. They were maybe five months old at the beginning, and they were growing fast. By the last month of filming, they were seven months old. One day the cougar was lounging at the back of the RV when I stood up and walked toward the front. With no warning, he leaped all the way across the length of the vehicle and onto the back of my neck: one hundred pounds of cougar knocking me forward into the steering wheel. He could have killed me with a quick bite to the spine, but he just wanted to play.

A full-grown lioness can easily weigh three times as much. But I couldn't resist resting my chin on top of the lioness's head to show the kids how big it was; compared to hers, mine looked like a little pin. We laughed and took pictures, and I was *really* glad that she was totally knocked out.

I was always thankful for the opportunity to spend more time with my family and take them on holidays and adventures. But I also wanted to get my movie career moving again, and that took some real doing. I had to mount a whole campaign to convince people that I could still do the job. Sitting down with Barbara Walters on national TV nine months after my heart surgery was a first step. "You could have died," she said. "Were you scared?"

"I was very scared," I told her, especially when the valve repair went wrong and they had to do it again. I thought the best approach was to let people see me and to lay out the facts. She asked about my family, teased me about gray hairs, and gave me the platform I needed to say that I felt totally energetic and raring to go.

The next step was photos: making sure that images of me running on the beach, skiing, and weight lifting made it into newspapers so people would know I was back. Even so, the studios still were slow returning calls. I was amazed to discover that insurance was an issue. Not only were they telling my agent "We don't know how people feel about him now," but also, "We just don't know if we can insure him." There seemed to be endless questions and uncertainties that they didn't want to deal with.

A whole year passed without a new movie. Finally, I had a visit from Army Bernstein, a producer whose daughter had gone to the same preschool as our kids. He'd heard the talk from the studios and knew I was looking for work. "I'll do a movie with you anytime," he said. "And I've got a fantastic movie being written." Independent producers like Army are the saviors in Hollywood because they'll take risks that the big studios won't. He had his own company with a string of successes and was well financed.

The film he had in mind for me was *End of Days*, an action-horror-thriller that was being timed to reach theaters in late 1999 and cash in on all the buzz around the world about Y2K, the turn of the millennium. I play Jericho Cane, an ex-cop who has to stop Satan from coming to New York and taking a bride in the closing hours of 1999. If Jericho fails, then the woman will give birth to the Antichrist, and the entire next thousand years will be a millennium of evil.

The director, Peter Hyams, came recommended by Jim Cameron, and like Cameron, he preferred to shoot at night. So when we went into production near the end of 1998, we were on a nighttime schedule in a studio in Los Angeles. To my amazement, there were insurance people and studio executives sitting on the set—the executives were from Universal, which had signed on to distribute the film. They were watching to see whether I'd faint or die or have to take a lot of breaks.

As it happened, the first scene we shot called for Jericho to get attacked by ten Satanists who beat him to a bloody pulp. The fight is at night, in a dark alley during a pouring rain. So we went to work, and we would fight until I ended up flat on my back staring up into sheets of man-made, backlit rain falling down on me as I lose consciousness. After the take, I'd come off the set and sit by the monitor, dripping with a towel around my shoulders, ready to go out and do the next one.

Around three in the morning, one of the insurance guys said, "Gee, isn't it exhausting to do this over and over and get soaking wet and beaten to a pulp?"

"Actually not," I said. "I love shooting at night because I have a lot of energy at night. I get a lot of inspiration. It's really terrific."

Then I would go out for another beating, and come back again and sit down and say, "Can I see a playback?" And I would study the playback as the technicians ran it on the monitor.

"I don't know how you do it," the insurance guy said.

"This is nothing. You should see on some of the other movies, like the *Terminator* movies, where we went really wild."

"But don't you get tired?"

"No, no. I don't get tired. Especially not after the heart surgery. It gave me energy beyond belief. I feel like a totally new person." Then the guy from the studio would ask the same question.

After that first week, the insurance guys and studio guys never came back. Meanwhile, word went out from the stunt guys and makeup and wardrobe people that I was feeling great, doing well, and so forth. From then on, offers started to come in again, and I no longer had to convince people that I still had a pulse.

CHAPTER 23

A Political Proposition

PEOPLE LOVED TO JOKE about the possibility of me entering politics. At a governor's council dinner in Sacramento in 1994, Governor Pete Wilson greeted me from the podium, saying, "I'd like to see you run for governor, Arnold. Someone who has played *Kindergarten Cop* already has the requisite experience to deal with the legislature." That got a laugh. But it was not far-fetched that someone from Hollywood would run for governor. Ronald Reagan had already blazed the trail.

The year before, in Sylvester Stallone's sci-fi movie *Demolition Man,* his character suddenly lands in the year 2032. He does a double take when he hears somebody talking about the Arnold Schwarzenegger Presidential Library. Running for president was off the table for me, of course, because I wasn't a natural-born US citizen, as the Constitution requires. But I'd fantasize sometimes: what if my mother had gotten frisky at the end of the war, and my father wasn't really Gustav Schwarzenegger but, in fact, an American GI? That could explain why I always had this powerful feeling that America is my true home. Or what if the hospital where she gave birth to me was actually in an American-occupied zone? Wouldn't that count as being born on US soil?

I thought I was better suited temperamentally for being a governor than a senator or a congressman, because as a governor I'd be the captain of the ship—the chief executive—rather than be one of 100 senators or 435 representatives making decisions. Of course, no governor calls the shots all by himself. But he can bring a vision to the state and at least feel like the buck stops at his desk. It is very much like being leading man in a movie. You get blamed for everything, and you get credit for everything. It's high risk, high reward.

I felt tremendous loyalty and pride about California. My adopted state is bigger than a lot of countries. It has thirty-eight million people, or four times as many as Austria. It is 800 miles long and 250 miles wide. You can easily bicycle through some of the smaller states in the US, but if you want to tour California, you should think about riding a Harley and getting your exercise in some more moderate way. California has spectacular mountains, 840 miles of coast, redwood forests, deserts, farmlands, and vineyards. The people speak over a hundred languages. And California has a $1.9 trillion economy—bigger than that of Mexico, India, Canada, or Russia. When the G20 sit down for a summit of the world's twenty major economies, California should be right there at the table.

The state had gone through fast and slow phases during the years I'd lived in LA, but mainly it had thrived, and I saw myself as a happy beneficiary of that. In my political beliefs, I was conservative in the way that a lot of successful immigrants are: I wanted America to stay the bastion of free enterprise, and I wanted to do whatever I could to protect it from following Europe in the direction of bureaucracy and stagnation. That's how Europe had been when I lived there.

The 1990s were prosperous years, and California now had its first Democratic governor since the mid-1980s, Gray Davis. He got off to a strong start when he took office in 1999, expanding public education and also improving relations with Mexico. He was a skinny, reserved guy, not much of a showman, yet his programs were popular, and he had a big budget surplus to work with, thanks mainly to the Silicon Valley boom of the eighties and nineties. His approval rating among voters was high: around 60 percent.

The trouble began with the dot-com crash. In March 2000, just before I finished shooting *The 6th Day*, a sci-fi action film about cloning humans, the internet bubble burst, and the stock market entered its worst decline in twenty years. A big slump in Silicon Valley was bad news for the state, because tax revenues would fall and a lot of hard choices would have to be made regarding government services and jobs. California gets a huge amount of revenue from Silicon Valley. When those businesses drop 20 percent, that ends up as a 40 percent hit on the state's coffers. That is why I recommended using excess revenues in boom years for infrastructure, paying down debt, or setting aside a rainy-day fund to cover the wobbly economic years. You make a big mistake to lock in programs that require you to keep spending at boom-time levels.

On top of that came the 2000 and 2001 electricity crisis: first, a tripling of electricity rates in San Diego, and then power shortages and blackouts around San Francisco that threatened to engulf the entire state. The government seemed paralyzed, with state and federal regulators pointing fingers at each other instead of taking action, while middlemen—mainly the now-infamous Houston energy company Enron—curtailed supplies to drive prices through the roof. In December 2000, Gray Davis made a point of turning off the Christmas tree lights in the capital right after he lit them, to remind people to conserve electricity and to be ready for power shortages in the coming year. I hated the way this made California look: like some developing country rather than America's Golden State. It made me angry. Was that our answer to the energy shortage in California? Turning off the Christmas tree lights? It was stupid. I understood it was meant as symbolic, but I wasn't interested in symbols. I was interested in action.

A lot of this was not Gray Davis's fault; the economy was just on a slide. But at the halfway mark of his term, people began to think that he would be vulnerable when he came up for reelection in 2002, and soon his approval ratings showed a huge decline. I felt as frustrated as the next guy. The more I read up on California, the more it was like bad news piled on top of bad news. I found myself thinking, "We can't continue this way. We need change."

All this played into that long-running debate in my brain about what should be the next mountain to climb. Should I produce movies? Or produce, direct, and star, like Clint? Should I become an artist, now that I'd gotten back in touch with how much I love to paint? I was in no rush to resolve these questions; I knew they'd crystallize into a vision in their own good time. But I still had my old discipline of setting concrete goals each New Year's Day. Most years, whatever movie I had in the works would be at the top of the list. But while I was committed to a few films in development, including *Terminator 3*, nothing was actually scripted or scheduled. Instead, on January 1, 2001, I put at the very top of my list "explore running for governor in 2002."

The very next morning, I made an appointment with one of California's top political consultants, Bob White, Pete Wilson's chief of staff for almost three decades, including Wilson's eight years as governor. Bob had been the guy who made the trains run on time, and he was seen as one of the key Republican power brokers in Sacramento. I knew him from years of fund-raisers and dinners, and when he'd left the statehouse, I'd asked if we could stay in touch.

Of course, hiring Bob and his team of strategists and analysts didn't mean that I had the support of the Republican Party. I was too much in the political center for the party higher-ups. Yes, I was fiscally conservative, pro-business, and against raising taxes, but everybody knew I was also pro-choice, pro-gay, pro-lesbian, pro-environment, pro–reasonable gun control, pro–reasonable social safety net. My connection to the Kennedys made many conservative Republicans nervous too, including my admiration for my father-in-law, whom they viewed as a big-government tax-and-spend type. You could almost hear them thinking, "Yeah, right, that's all we need: Arnold and his liberal wife, and then in comes his mother-in-law and father-in-law, and then Teddy Kennedy, and then they'll all come. It's the goddamn Trojan horse." The party leaders were very appreciative that I helped raise funds and talked about their candidates and Republican philosophy on the campaign trail. But it was always, "This was very nice, thank you so much for helping." I don't think they had ever really warmed to me.

That wasn't why I went to Bob and his associates, though. I wanted a thorough, professional assessment of my potential to run and win, along with the polling and research to back it up. Even though I'd been part of campaigns, I also wanted to know what it *really* took to run for office, given that I wasn't a typical candidate. How many hours would I have to spend on a campaign? How much money would I need to raise? What would be the theme of a campaign? How do you keep your kids out of the spotlight? Was Maria's coming from a Democratic family an asset or a liability?

My wife didn't know about my inquiry to Bob. She read about my possible candidacy in the papers and saw me flirting with the idea, but she assumed that I'd never want the schedule, keeping twenty appointments a day, and the general crap you have to take when you're in politics. I'm sure she was thinking, "He loves life too much. He's into the pleasure principle, not the suffering principle." I didn't tell her I was seriously considering a run, because I didn't want endless conversation about it at home.

The consultants identified pluses and minuses right away. The Ronald Reagan factor was my biggest plus. He'd proven that entertainment cuts across party lines: not only do people know your name but also they'll pay attention to what you say no matter whether they're Democratic, Republican, or independent—as long as you're not a flake. Governor Pat Brown and his political handlers totally misjudged the power of celebrity when Reagan beat him in 1966, and I think that power is still hard for politicos to believe. When George Gorton, who had been Pete Wilson's top strategist, came with me to an after-school event at the Hollenbeck Youth Center, he was stunned to find nineteen TV crews waiting to record my visit for the evening news. That was at least a dozen more cameras than he'd ever seen show up for the governor himself at this kind of event.

The first poll they took, of eight hundred California voters, gave the kind of mixed picture that you would expect. All the voters knew who I was, and 60 percent had a positive image of me. That was a plus. But when they were asked to choose today between Gray Davis and me as governor, they picked Davis by more than two to one. I wasn't even running, of course, but I was very, very far from being a favorite. The consultants listed other obvious minuses: although I had a strong philosophy and lot of opinions, my knowledge of issues like jobs, education, immigration, and the environment wasn't so deep. And, of course, I had no fund-raising organization, no political staff, no experience dealing with political reporters, and no track record in getting elected to anything.

One question that came up was whether to campaign for the governorship in 2002 or wait until 2006. Waiting would give me more time to establish myself in Californians' eyes as a contender. George Gorton suggested that whenever I ran, a good way to lay the groundwork would be to campaign for a ballot initiative. Among all the states, California is famed for its tradition of "direct democracy." Under the state constitution, legislators aren't the only ones who can create laws; the people can too, directly, by placing propositions on the ballot in state elections. The ballot-initiative system dates back to Hiram Johnson, California's legendary governor from 1911 to 1917. He used it to break the power of a corrupt legislature controlled by the giant railroads. Its most famous modern-day application was in the California tax revolt of 1978. That was when voters passed Proposition 13, a constitutional amendment officially titled "People's Initiative to Limit Property Taxation." I'd been in America only ten years at that point, and I remember marveling at how ordinary citizens could limit the state's power.

If I sponsored a ballot initiative, Gorton pointed out, I could get out in front of the people without having to announce right away for governor. I'd have a reason to build an organization, hold fund-raisers, form alliances with important groups, talk to the media, and do TV ads. And if the initiative passed, it would prove that I could win votes across the state.

But before I tackled any of that, Bob and his colleagues felt they ought to impress upon me what I might be getting into. I was paying them, but they were ambitious guys who wanted to make sure they weren't wasting time on some Hollywood vanity campaign. In fact, they got ex-governor Wilson himself to deliver the message personally. He took charge of a four-hour strategy session at my office in March 2001. Wilson told me that he hoped I would run and that I had the beginnings of a good team to get it done. But, he added, "You need to be realistic about how this will affect your life, your family, your finances, and your career." Then he went around the table, and each advisor laid out ways in which my life would change. Don Sipple, a political strategist, talked about how Eisenhower and Reagan had made the transition to political life successfully, while Ross Perot and Jesse Ventura had failed. Perot, a Texas businessman, came from out of nowhere in 1992 to run for president as an independent, and won an astounding 19.7 million votes, or almost one in five votes cast that November. Ventura, my former castmate in *Predator* and *The Running Man*, and a former pro wrestler, was midway through a shaky term as governor of Minnesota, after which he would not seek reelection.

The difference between those who adapted and those who didn't, Gorton said, was a willingness to totally commit. Others talked about how I'd need to put up with media criticism like I'd never imagined; how I'd need to become expert in wonky topics; how I'd need to ask for campaign contributions. I took such obvious pride in my financial independence that they realized the last item would be hard for me.

But what surprised me was the level of enthusiasm in the room. I thought they were going to tell me that this wasn't right for me and maybe I should try for an ambassadorship or something. That was the way people in Austria had reacted when I said I wanted to be a bodybuilding champ. "In Austria we become ski champs," they'd said. And it was the way that Hollywood agents had reacted when I said that I wanted to become an actor. "Why don't you open a gym?" they'd said. But I could tell that these political pros weren't just stringing me along. These guys knew me from the campaigning I had done for Wilson.

They knew I was funny. They knew I spoke well. They saw me as a serious possibility.

Over the next several weeks, I spent a lot of time out of the state: at an Inner-City Games event in Las Vegas, a Hummer promotion in New York, a visit to Guam, a premiere in Osaka, Japan, and Easter in Maui, Hawaii, with Maria and the kids. But along the way, I started sounding out close friends. Fredi Gerstl, my mentor from Austria, was very supportive. As far as he was concerned, nothing was harder than being a good political leader—so many interests, so many constituents, so many built-in obstacles. It's like captaining the *Titanic* as opposed to driving a speedboat. "If you like challenges, this is the best," he said. "Go for it."

Paul Wachter, my financial advisor, told me he wasn't surprised—he'd sensed me getting restless over the past year—but he felt obliged to remind me of the money I'd have to pass up if I switched careers. He really liked seeing those $25 million movie paychecks coming in. He pointed out that if I got elected, I'd have to forgo two movies a year at $20 million or more each, plus spend millions of my own money on personal expenses that would not be tax deductible. It wasn't a stretch to say that the total cost to me over two terms could be more than $200 million.

Another close friend I wanted to touch base with was Andy Vajna, who with his business partner, Mario Kassar, had produced *Total Recall* and *Terminator 2* and owned the rights to make *Terminator 3*. Andy is Hungarian-American, an immigrant like me, and besides his success in Hollywood, he owns casinos in Hungary and other businesses here. Also, Andy had worked in government in Hungary and was close to Victor Orbán, who became prime minister. I saw Andy and Mario as part of my Hollywood kitchen cabinet for kicking around ideas. So I wanted to sound them out on my running for governor. If they were enthusiastic, I meant to hit them up for a lot of money for the campaign and then have them go out and ask other producers to contribute.

When I went to their office to talk about the governorship in April,

2001, I didn't expect them to bring up *Terminator 3*. I'd signed a "deal memo" to star in it if it ever got made, but the project had been in development limbo for years. Andy and Mario had even lost the rights at one point and had to buy them back in bankruptcy court. Jim Cameron had moved on to other projects, and as far as I knew, they didn't have a director or a script. But as I made my pitch about politics, I saw them looking at me as if to say, "What the fuck are you talking about, running for governor?"

Terminator 3, it turned out, was a lot farther along than I'd thought. A script was almost ready, and, not only that, they'd entered into merchandise and international distribution deals worth tens of millions of dollars. They were planning to start production within a year. Andy was reasonable and friendly but firm. "If you back out, I will get sued, because we sold the rights based on you as the star," he said. "I'm the last person interested in suing you, but if I get sued, I will have to sue you because I can't afford to pay all these guys back. With damages! The numbers will be huge."

"Okay, I got it," I said.

I pride myself on being able to juggle many tasks, but I could see that running for governor and making a *Terminator* movie at the same time was a nonstarter even for me. People would think it was totally half-assed.

So now what? I still wanted to do something political. In fact, I was pumped. So when I went back to my political team and broke the news that I couldn't run, I told them not to stop. I told them that we'd do a ballot initiative instead. They were skeptical about this; it was hard for them to imagine how a person could do justice to a movie and an initiative campaign at the same time. To me, it was no different from what I'd done all my life. I'd gotten a college education while I was a bodybuilding champ. I'd married Maria in the middle of filming *Predator*. I'd made *Kindergarten Cop* and *Terminator 2* and launched Planet Hollywood while I was the president's fitness czar. And I had a clear vision of the issue I wanted to pursue.

Working on the President's Council on Physical Fitness and Sports had made me aware of the problem of millions of kids left after school with nothing to do. Most juvenile crime is committed between three and six o'clock in the afternoon. That's when kids get exposed to mischief, hustling, gangs, and drugs. Experts contended that we were losing our kids not because they were bad but because they were unsupervised. There had long been cops and educators who campaigned for after-school programs, which provided an alternative to gangs and a place for kids to get help with homework. But the legislators never listened. So the cops and educators became my first allies.

As part of expanding the Inner-City Games, I'd created a foundation to make them a nationwide movement and recruited a close friend of Maria's and mine, Bonnie Reiss, to lead it. Bonnie is a high-powered New Yorker with curly black hair who is funny and fast-talking and almost as fierce an organizer as Eunice. She and Maria met while Maria was in college and Bonnie was in law school and clerking for Teddy Kennedy; the two of them had moved to LA together to work on Teddy's 1980 presidential campaign. Later Bonnie founded an influential nonprofit called the Earth Communications Office, which focused on raising money for environmental issues. Essentially she became Hollywood's go-to person on the environment. She was a big fan of the Inner-City Games as well and welcomed the chance to spread the idea.

Los Angeles still stood out not only because it was the home of the Inner-City Games but also because it was the only big city that had after-school programs in every one of its ninety elementary schools. I went to consult the woman who'd accomplished this, a dynamic educator named Carla Sanger. After I'd asked a million questions, she suggested, "Why don't you carve out the middle schools and high schools and do programs there?" So Bonnie and I started raising funds to do just that. Our plan was to bring Inner-City Games after-school programs into four schools in 2002 and expand from there.

Pretty quickly, though, I realized that the task was too big. We would never be able to raise enough money to put a program into every middle school and high school that needed it. Even worse, Los Angeles was just one city in a state that had roughly six thousand schools and six million students.

When you run up against a problem that gigantic, sometimes government has to help. But Carla told me that she'd tried many times to lobby for funds in Sacramento, and it was hopeless. State officials and lawmakers just did not see after-school programs as important. I checked with a few state senators and assembly people I knew, and they said she was right.

That left only one possible avenue: putting the issue directly before the California voters as a ballot initiative. I saw in this idea the chance to improve the lives of millions of kids and at the same time to get my feet wet in state politics. This wasn't the right time for me to run for governor, but I committed myself to spend the next year campaigning for what came to be known as Proposition 49, the After School Education and Safety Program Act of 2002.

I signed up George Gorton as the campaign manager, along with other members of the Pete Wilson brain trust, and they set up a headquarters downstairs from my office, a space we had previously leased to actor Pierce Brosnan and his production company. Soon they were surveying voters, researching the issues, preparing lists of donors and media contacts, networking with other organizations, planning for signature gathering and public events, and so on. I was like a sponge soaking it all in.

In my movie career, I'd always paid close attention to focus groups and surveys, and, of course, in politics opinion research plays an even bigger role. I felt right at home with that. Don Sipple, who was expert in political messaging, sat me down in front of a camera and had me talk at length. Those tapes got edited into three-minute segments to be shown to focus groups of voters. The purpose was to pick out what themes and traits of mine appealed to people and what might put them off. I learned, for example, that people were impressed with my success as a businessman, but when I mentioned on the tape that Maria and I lived in a relatively modest house, the people in the focus groups felt that I must be out of touch.

That fall I'd blocked out two weeks to promote my latest action movie, *Collateral Damage,* which was scheduled to be released on October 5. This was just one of hundreds of millions of plans that had to change in the aftermath of September 11, 2001. Any other year, *Collateral Damage* would have been exciting big-budget action entertainment, but after 9/11, it just didn't work. I play a veteran Los Angeles firefighter named Gordy Brewer whose wife and son are bystanders killed in a narco-terrorist bombing at the Colombian consulate downtown. When Brewer sets out to avenge their deaths, he uncovers and thwarts a much larger narco-terror plot involving a hijacked airliner and a major attack on Washington, DC. After 9/11, Warner Bros. canceled the premiere and reedited the movie to delete the hijacking. Even so, when *Collateral Damage* debuted the following February, it felt both irrelevant and painful to watch in light of the actual events. The irony was that in making the film, the producers had this big debate about whether firefighting was a macho enough profession for an action hero. That was one question that the real-life heroism at ground zero laid to rest.

I learned there is a whole art to shaping a proposition so that it doesn't put people off or cause unnecessary fights or resistance. For instance, to keep after-school from crowding out existing programs that people liked, we designed it to take effect no earlier than 2004, and only if the California economy was growing again and annual state revenues had gone up by $10 billion. To hold down the overall cost, we made it a grant program to which schools had to apply. And we made it so that wealthy districts that already had after-school programs would be expected to wait in line behind districts that couldn't afford them.

All the same, when education experts estimated the annual cost—$1.5 billion—we were all in sticker shock. Even in a state with $70 billion in revenue, that was much more than voters would approve. So before we even started campaigning, we scaled down our proposal to cover just middle schools, not high schools. This decision was painful, but something had to go, and the younger kids were more vulnerable and needed the programs more. Narrowing the program cut the price tag by more than $1 billion.

But before we filed it in late 2001, we circulated drafts and went around making presentations to unions and civic groups: teachers, principals, school superintendents, chambers of commerce, law-enforcement officials, judges and mayors and other public officials. We wanted the broadest possible coalition—and the smallest possible number of enemies. Just as Pete Wilson's guys had predicted, I found the fund-raising part hard at first. The reason I wanted to be wealthy was that I never wanted to ask anyone for money. It was so against my grain. When I made the first solicitation, I was literally sweating. I told myself it wasn't really me asking, it was the cause.

That first call was to Paul Folino, a technology entrepreneur and a friend of the Wilson campaign, and after a short and gracious conversation, he committed $1 million. My second call was to Jerry Perenchio, a producer and mover and shaker who ended up owning the Spanish-language television network Univision and then selling it for $11 billion. I knew Jerry personally. He promised to raise another $1 million. Those were heavenly calls; I felt so relieved when I hung up the phone. Then I made smaller calls for $250,000. I ended the day flying high.

The next day I went to hit up Marvin Davis in his office in the Fox Studios tower. He weighed about four hundred pounds. "What can I do for you?" he asked. I'd made movies for Fox, and his son had produced *Predator*. I gave him the whole rap, putting a lot of enthusiasm into explaining what I could do for California. But when I looked up from my notes I realized he'd fallen asleep! I waited until he opened his eyes again, and then said, "I totally agree, Marvin, we have to be fiscally responsible." He could sleep all he wanted as long as he gave us the check. But instead, he said, "Let me talk to my guys. We'll be in touch with you. It's a very courageous thing to do." Of course I never heard back.

Soon Paul Folino hit on a solution to make me feel more comfortable asking for money. He suggested that we make my fund-raisers low-key: dinner parties and small receptions. We found that as soon as I was in a relatively informal setting where I could schmooze, I was able to pass the hat very effectively.

I loved finding new allies. In November I took our draft of Prop 49 to John Hein, the political chief of the California Teachers Association, the most powerful union in the state. John was used to people asking for favors. I didn't expect him to be very receptive because Republicans and unions usually don't mix. So when I made my pitch, I told him right off the top, "We need no money from you. If you endorse this, you don't have to put a million dollars into the funding or anything like that. I'll go out and raise the money. But we want to go into this together." I also made the point that after-school programs not only help the kids but also reduce the strain on their teachers.

To my delight, he approved of our idea. In fact, he recommended only two changes in the proposal, the main one being that we add some language about hiring retired teachers. This wasn't something I wanted to encourage too much, because young kids relate better to young people, especially after a whole day of teachers and school. They want counselors in jeans and with spiky hair, who can serve as parent figures but who don't look like them. Still, it wasn't a lot to ask, and we made the deal. And ultimately it worked out fine because not that many retired teachers wanted to go back to work anyway.

By normal standards, the start of an election year is way too early to put a ballot initiative before the public, since the vote isn't until November. But I had to juggle Prop 49 and *Terminator 3*, which was ready to start filming. So we had our kickoff in late February, just before the California state primaries. Instead of some boring press conference, I did a two-day fly-around of cities up and down the state, with rallies and kids and hoopla to get us on TV and pump up support.

Then we went back to the slow, painstaking work of building alliances and raising funds. Just like bodybuilding, campaigning is all about reps, reps, reps. I met with Parent-Teacher Associations, city councils, taxpayer groups, and the California Medical Association. This is when I discovered that raising cash from the set of a movie was a huge advantage, and *Terminator 3* was the greatest set of all. People loved coming to see the special effects, the loading of the weapons, the explosions. Sometimes I'd meet them with my makeup still on: an *LA Times* columnist interviewed me one day when the Terminator had been through a fight. About a quarter of my face and scalp were bloody and torn off, exposing my titanium skull. It was a funny way to be talking about middle school.

The California attorney general, Bill Lockyer, also came to visit, and he was a Democrat! I knew him from *T2*, when he was a state senator who helped get us permission to film the scene in San José where the T-1000 rides a motorcycle out of a second-story window into a helicopter. I talked to him about the initiative. We needed him because it's the attorney general's office that issues an opinion on the cost and legal propriety of every initiative. He was on the set the day I was hanging from the hook of a giant crane. This was like heaven for him. No wonder he went for the initiative.

In September, after *Terminator 3* moved into postproduction, I went to Sacramento to ask for endorsements from state senate and state assembly leaders. I was curious to see what they'd say, although I wasn't holding my breath. The legislature was two-thirds Democrats, for one thing. And elected officials usually hate ballot initiatives because they reduce their power and make the state harder to govern. In fact, our loudest opponent was the League of Women Voters, which was adamantly against what it called "ballot box budgeting" for any program. Still, I had in my pocket a three-page, single-spaced list of all the organizations that endorsed us; we'd built the widest coalition that anybody could remember for a ballot initiative. That was going to be hard for the politicians to ignore.

One of my first stops was Bob Hertzberg, the speaker of the assembly. Bob is a smart, ebullient Democrat from the San Fernando

Valley, about the same age as Maria. He's so friendly that his nickname is Huggy. Within two minutes, we were swapping jokes. "What's not to like?" he said about our ballot proposition. But he warned me not to expect support from the Democratic Party itself. "God forbid we should endorse a Republican initiative," he wisecracked.

I got into heated debates with some labor leaders. The head of one of the big state employees unions asked, "What is your funding mechanism?" Other interest groups would claim that we were crowding out their programs. But two years earlier, legislators had approved a pension deal that could potentially involve $500 billion in unfunded liabilities. To the same people who were now asking me about my funding mechanism, I said, "You just committed the state for hundreds of billions of dollars. What's *your* funding mechanism? We're just talking about four hundred million a year for the kids."

"We take it out of the taxes."

"Well, you're crowding out plenty."

The support of the Republicans was no slam dunk, either. They would normally oppose any additional spending. But assembly minority leader Dave Cox, an older guy who was very gruff on the surface but sweet underneath, became our unexpected ally. He not only endorsed Prop 49 but also invited me to San Diego while the Republican lawmakers were holding a regular powwow. Standing before them, I could see as much skepticism as enthusiasm on their faces as they listened to my pitch. Then Dave got up and turned to the group. "You know why this is a Republican issue?" he asked "Because it is a *fiscal* issue. You may see this as asking the taxpayer to spend four hundred twenty-eight million more dollars. But, in fact, we are saving almost 1.3 billion."

Then he described a new study I hadn't even heard about, by this very prestigious institute at Claremont McKenna College. "For every dollar we spend in an after-school program," Dave said, "we save three dollars down the line because of fewer arrests and less teenage pregnancy and less trouble in the neighborhood." You could feel the mood in the room shift. All the Republicans really needed was that fiscal rationale— they voted unanimously to endorse Prop 49.

As November approached, I felt confident we would win, but I wasn't taking it for granted. California had been in recession, and since the dot-com crash in 2000, household incomes were down and the state was running billions of dollars in the red. Voters were worried about spending more money. Meanwhile, the governor's race had turned ugly between Gray Davis and his main challenger, a conservative pro-life Republican businessman named Bill Simon. The governor still had low approval ratings, but voters in surveys said they disliked Simon even more.

We wanted to make sure that Proposition 49 didn't get swept away in some big tsunami of gloom. So in the closing weeks, we added more rallies and poured an extra $1 million into TV ads.

On election night, my advisers thought we should gather at a fancy LA hotel, which was the custom in California races. I insisted we go to the Hollenbeck Youth Center, which was much more relevant to what we were trying to achieve. We ordered food for the neighborhood kids, well-wishers, and people who'd worked on the campaign, and waited around for results. Just before midnight, enough polling data were in for us to declare victory and start a big party on the basketball court. Proposition 49 ended up passing with 56.7 percent of the vote, while Republican candidates lost every election in the state.

Gray Davis won that night too. But it wasn't much of a reelection to celebrate. After the most expensive campaign in California history, most voters simply stayed home—it was the lowest turnout for a governor's election in the history of the state. Davis won with only 47 percent of the vote against Simon and the minor candidates. That was a much narrower margin than in 1998, when he'd won by a sizable majority.

To the amazement of the rest of the country, a grassroots movement to unelect Gray Davis started almost the minute his new term began. Outside the state, people thought this was just more evidence that Californians are crazy. But the same direct-democracy provisions of the state constitution that allowed for ballot initiatives also provided a process for recalling state officials through special election. Like ballot initiatives, gubernatorial recalls had a long and colorful history. Pat

Brown, Ronald Reagan, Jerry Brown, and Pete Wilson had all faced attempts, but none of their challengers had ever collected enough signatures to get anywhere.

The Recall Gray Campaign started among a handful of activists. It tapped into the widespread feeling that the state was heading in the wrong direction and he wasn't doing enough to fix California's problems. There was an uproar in December, for example, when Davis announced that the state budget deficit might be 50 percent more than had been estimated just a month earlier, or $35 billion total—as much as all the other state deficits in America combined. People were still angry about the electricity crisis too. You could see those and other concerns reflected in the recall petition, which accused the governor of "gross mismanagement of California Finances by overspending taxpayers' money, threatening public safety by cutting funds to local governments, failing to account for the exorbitant cost of the energy fiasco, and failing in general to deal with the state's major problems until they get to the crisis stage."

I didn't pay much attention to the recall campaign at first, because it seemed like a total long shot. Besides, the after-school movement was having a crisis of its own. In February Bonnie Reiss and I were flying around the country promoting the Inner-City Games. We'd just landed in Texas when her cell phone rang. It was a friend calling to alert us that President George W. Bush had just submitted a budget proposal that wiped out the federal dollars for after-school: more than $400 million of annual funding that programs all over the country depended on. Of course, the Texas media couldn't wait to ask my reaction. Wasn't this a direct insult to my favorite cause? Was the White House declaring war on Arnold?

"I'm sure the president believes in after-school," I told them. "The budget isn't done yet." As soon as I could, I called Rod Paige, Bush's secretary of education, to ask what was going on. He explained that the reason Bush gave for zeroing out the money was a new scholarly study claiming that after-school programs really weren't as effective as we'd thought in steering kids away from crime, drugs, and such.

"You know what?" I said. "That doesn't mean we should zero it out. It means let's learn from this study and fix the problem. Why don't we have a 'Best of After-School' summit?" I didn't think this was a crazy idea. I knew the experts, I had experience making people from the public and private sectors and from both parties work together, and I had a track record of organizing summits across fifty states. How difficult could it be? Secretary Paige liked that idea and said his department might be willing to sponsor it. I'd suggested the summit instinctively, so I laughed when Bonnie interpreted it as a clever political tactic. "I see what we're doing," she said after the call. "If the administration holds a summit about how to improve after-school programs, that gives the president cover to reverse his position and put back the funds."

"Hey," I said, "we're just trying to fix the problem."

We immediately planned a trip to Washington to lobby key lawmakers on the budget. When my political guru Bob White got wind of this plan, he sent me a memo strongly advising me not to do it. Essentially it said, "Let it go. Never second-guess a president from your own party. If you succeed in getting back the money, you seem disrespectful. If you fail to get it back, you look bad as a leader. Either way, you hurt your future chances of running for governor."

I could see the political wisdom of this, but my own feeling was that protecting after-school was worth the risk. Losing federal funding would do great damage to a lot of kids. I said to myself, "Let's not pay attention to politics in this case."

So we went to Washington in early March to make our case. Our first stop was to see Congressman Bill Young, the powerful Florida Republican who chaired the Appropriations Committee. I'd become good friends with him and his wife, Beverly, because their passion was helping wounded veterans at places like Walter Reed Army Medical Center and Bethesda Naval Hospital. They'd gotten me involved in visiting the hospitals regularly. There were never any cameras or press for these occasions; I went because I loved seeing the young veterans and entertaining them and thanking them for their great work.

When Bonnie and I got to Bill's office, he was laughing. "Before you say anything, let me tell you a story," he said. Beverly had come to him the minute she heard about the president's budget proposal. "What's the story with the four hundred million that Bush cut out for after-school?" she asked.

Bill said to her, "Well, we're going to have a debate."

"Hell no! You are not going to have a debate about this. I'm telling you right now, that money's back in, do you hear me?"

So Bill assured us that he would do everything he could on our behalf.

Our next stop was Bill Thomas, the Republican congressman from Bakersfield, California, who was the chairman of the House Committee on Ways and Means. He was legendary in Congress for his brains and hot temper. Bonnie and I sat down with him and his top aide and had just begun to chat when he said, "You know, this is our first time meeting, and I don't know if you want to bullshit for a little while or just get down to it."

I smiled and said, "Let's get down to it."

"I know you're here to get the money back for after-school," he said. "That's done, in. Let's talk about the recall."

Then he launched into an analysis about why the Gray Davis recall movement was a phenomenal opportunity for me. "In a normal election, you have to raise at least sixty million dollars," he said. "Then you have to run in the primary, and since you are such a moderate, you might not even get the nomination, because in Republican primaries it's mostly the hard-core conservatives who come out to vote.

"But in a recall situation, *there is no primary!* Any number of candidates can get their names on the ballot, and whoever gets the most votes wins."

I'd assumed that a recall would be just like a normal election. "Let's back up," he said and then proceeded to explain how the process worked under California law. If enough voters petition for a recall, the state is required to hold an election within eighty days. The ballot consists of two questions. First, should the governor be recalled? That is a simple yes-or-no choice. Second, if the governor does get recalled, who should replace him? To answer that, the voter chooses one name from a list of citizens who have qualified as candidates. Getting on the list was easy, Thomas explained. Instead of spending millions on a primary, you need to collect only sixty-five signatures and pay a $3,500 fee to enter your name as a candidate. "Of course, that means it'll be a crowded race," he said. "It'll be a madhouse! But the more crowded it gets, the more you have the advantage. Everybody knows you."

He said he would back me if I ran. But the thing I had to do right now was to step in and be willing to put up a couple of million dollars to collect the necessary signatures to qualify the recall petition. Almost nine hundred thousand signatures were needed under the law, and right now the recall petition was circulating on much too small a scale.

Running for governor of California was not on my list of goals for 2003, of course, but I was fascinated and promised the chairman I'd give it careful thought. Instinctively, though, I knew the strategy he was recommending was wrong for me. If I were to lead the recall, it would seem brazen and disrespectful. After all, we'd just had an election, and Gray Davis had won it fair and square. I could have tried to run against him, but I had to make *Terminator 3* instead. It wouldn't be right for me to suddenly turn around and say, "Okay! Now that the movie's done, I'm going to take him out; now it's convenient for me, so please can we have another election?" Instead, I had to keep my distance. If a recall came about, it had to be organic, the will of the people, not something paid for by me. Even so, I followed the recall movement much more closely over the next couple of months.

Just as the congressmen had promised Bonnie and me, after-school funding was restored as the budget made its way through Congress. And the After-School Summit, held in Washington in early June, produced an important breakthrough. When organizers from around the country pooled their experience, we discovered that after-school programs that included academic as well as physical activities were by far the most effective. From then on, homework help became a key element in the after-school world.

The White House was my final stop while I was in Washington for the summit. Like many of the people who'd worked for the first President Bush, I wasn't close to his son, but the governor situation in California made me want to touch base with his senior domestic advisor, Karl Rove. I did this because, to everybody's amazement, the prospect of a recall election that fall suddenly seemed very real. The Gray Davis recall campaign had been energized by Congressman Darrell Issa, a wealthy San Diego Republican who had his eye on becoming governor himself. In May he'd decided to pump almost $2 million of his own money into advertising and signature gathering, which pushed the campaign into high gear. Now it had more than three hundred thousand signatures, while the governor's popularity continued to sink.

Rove greeted me in the reception area on the second floor of the West Wing and led me to his office, just above the president's study. We talked for a half hour about the California economy, the Special Olympics, and helping with President Bush's reelection in 2004. Then I said, "Let me ask you, what do you think will happen with the recall? Issa just put in two million dollars, and the signature gathering is gaining momentum." I pretended to be innocent. "You're the master behind getting Bush elected. What is your take on the whole thing?"

"It will never happen," Rove said. "There will be no recall election. Plus, if there were to be one, I don't think anyone can unseat Gray Davis." Before I could ask a question or express my surprise, he went on. "As a matter of fact, we're already focused on 2006." Then he stood and said, "Come with me." He led me down the stairs to the first floor, where, almost like they had choreographed it, Condoleezza Rice came walking toward us from down the hall.

"I have someone here who is interested in running for governor," Rove said to me, "and I wanted you to meet her because this is our candidate for 2006. You should get to know each other." He said it smilingly, but it was the kind of smile that meant "Arnold, shit in your pants because this woman is going to trample all over you. There won't be a recall, the governorship will be up for grabs in 2006, and when 2006 comes, *I* have already planned it, I have it all laid out, and this is going to be the Republican candidate."

How could Rove have been so wrong? He was a political genius, and he dismissed me! And he dismissed the recall! I understood why Condi was getting the nod. She's intellectual, she's Stanford, she's the National Security Advisor. I'd heard that story before about 2006. At a Rod Paige education dinner, Maria and I were sitting with a group of Republicans, and a woman turned to me and said, "We've gotten the signal from the White House to go with Condi." So I was aware.

By the time I got home, I told this as a funny story, but at the moment it happened, it stung. "What an asshole," I thought. But I reminded myself right away, "Actually, this is good! This is one of those situations where someone dismisses you, and you come from behind and surprise the shit out of them." I never argued with people who underestimated me. If the accent and the muscles and the movies made people think I was stupid, it worked to my advantage.

I didn't sign any movie contracts that summer. If the governorship really became a possibility, this time I wanted to keep my options open. As the recall movement continued to gain momentum, I kept in touch with my advisors and broadcast to the public that I shared the sentiment behind it. "Our elected leaders will either act decisively, or we will act in their place," I told the audience at a celebration of the twenty-fifth anniversary of Proposition 13.

I didn't exactly say I wanted to be governor, but I couldn't resist leading off my remarks that night with a joke about Gray Davis. "This is really embarrassing," I said. "I just forgot the name of our state governor. But I know that you will help me recall him." It got a good laugh. I sent another smoke signal about running by telling the *New York Post*, "If the party needs me, I would without any doubt be interested in doing that rather than doing another movie. I would give up my movie career for that."

Meanwhile, in trying to reduce the budget deficit, Governor Davis found a sure way to commit political suicide: he tripled the "car tax." This was a fee Californians have to pay when they register their vehicles. Technically, he wasn't raising the fee, just canceling an abatement, put in place by his predecessor, that was costing the state $4 billion a year in lost revenue. But Californians love their cars, and none of that mattered. The number of signatures being collected each week for the recall petition went through the roof.

Each time Gray Davis made another mistake, I was boiling. What was he doing giving driver's licenses to illegal immigrants? Why was he increasing fees rather than pushing back on pensions? Why had he taken campaign money from Indian tribes that owned casinos? Why were we running out of electricity? Why would he sponsor job-killing legislation that would force businesses to flee the state?

I thought about what I'd do: cut taxes, end driver's licenses for illegal immigrants, cut the vehicle license fee. Spend no more than the state is taking in. Rebuild California. Find alternatives to fossil fuels. Make the Indian gaming tribes pay their fair share of taxes. Stop the whole system of money in, favors out. And bring business back to California.

I also had a personal beef with the guy. I'd asked him five times what he wanted from the Governor's Council on Fitness. He never replied.

I began to despise everything about Gray Davis. When I saw his picture in the newspaper, I didn't see the picture, I saw a monster. I had a plan. I visualized myself taking him down. (Oddly enough, later, when we met after I became governor, we became friends. I realized it was hard for any governor to make the changes that were needed. Gray Davis couldn't do it by himself. No one could.)

But I had to ask myself, Why did I want to step into this mess? Why not just stay an actor? The state was staring at a deficit that had grown to $37.5 billion, businesses were moving away, the lights couldn't stay on, the courts were ordering prisons to release inmates due to overcrowding, the political system was rigged for the incumbents, the spending was locked in by formulas, and no one ever seemed to fix the schools.

But I love it when people say that something can't be done. That's when I really get motivated; I like to prove them wrong. And I liked the idea of working on something bigger than me. My father-in-law always talked about how it gives you extra power and energy, but you don't really feel it until you're in the middle of it. Plus, I was going to be the governor of California! It is the place where everyone in the world wants to go. You never hear anyone from abroad say, "Oh, I love America! I can't wait to get to Iowa!" Or "Gosh, can you tell me about Utah?" Or "I hear Delaware is a great place." California was wrapped in problems, but it was also heaven.

It wasn't too early to be thinking about a campaign strategy, and I'd begun to envision one that made sense. This was the subject of long, private discussions with Don Sipple, the top media consultant for our after-school campaign. It was essential, we agreed, not to jump in too soon; better to wait until a recall election was formally qualified and scheduled. Don crystallized our approach in a fax called "Some Thoughts," which he sent me at the end of June 2003.

If I did jump in, my campaign would have to be truly unique, because I was a nonpolitician responding to a populist revolt. We needed to avoid trying to win over the press and instead play to the people. When I went on TV, I'd go on entertaining national shows like Jay Leno, Oprah, David Letterman, Larry King, and Chris Matthews rather than wonky local broadcasts. And then, just as the media decided my candidacy was lightweight, we'd surprise them with speeches that went deep on key issues like education, health care, and public safety. Above all, the campaign had to be *big*. I was all about leadership and major projects and reforms that could attract massive public support.

I especially liked the way Don channeled my message: "There is a disconnect between the people of California and the politicians of California. We the people are doing our job: work hard, pay taxes, raise our families. The politicians are not doing their job. They fiddle, they fumble, and they fail. Governor Davis has failed the people of California, and it is time to replace him." These words resonated more strongly than any movie script I'd ever read. I memorized them and made them a kind of mantra.

I shifted gears to promote *Terminator 3.* It opened across the country on Wednesday, July 2, and became America's top movie for the Fourth of July weekend. But by then I was half a world away. After the premiere in LA, I flew to Tokyo for the Japanese premiere, and then on to Kuwait. And on July 4, three months after US-led coalition forces had seized Baghdad, I was in the Iraqi capital showing *Terminator 3* and entertaining the troops at a former palace of the toppled dictator Saddam Hussein.

I opened, as I always do, with a joke. "It is really wild driving around here," I told them. "I mean, the poverty, and you see there is no money, it is disastrous financially, and there is the leadership vacuum—pretty much like in California right now."

From Baghdad, I flew from one Iraqi city to the next and then worked my way back west making appearances across Europe. Then I made promotional trips to Canada and Mexico. During all this, I didn't even think about running for governor; I stored it in the back of my mind but wasn't consciously making plans.

On July 23, the last day of my trip, I was in Mexico City when it was announced that the California recall election would go forward. Over 1.3 million voters had signed the petition, almost 500,000 more than were needed. The following day, the special election was scheduled for the first Tuesday in October 2003, less than three months away. Candidates had barely two weeks—until Saturday, August 9—to declare.

The quick deadline didn't deter people from jumping into the race. Because of the low entry barrier, the recall was a magnet for dozens of fringe candidates, attention seekers, and people who just wanted an interesting item for their résumé. Eventually the ballot listed 135 candidates. We had a porn queen and a porn publisher. We had a bounty hunter, an American Communist, an actress whose main claim to fame was advertising herself on billboards around LA, and a female swing dancer who had also run several times for president. Gary Coleman, the former child star, jumped in. So did author and political pundit Arianna Huffington, who would become my foil in the debate before dropping out. There was an antismoking crusader and a sumo wrestler.

Serious candidates who had political capital and financial backing faced a tough choice about whether to risk getting lost in the circus atmosphere. US senator Dianne Feinstein, a hugely popular Democrat, said she didn't like the whole idea of recalls—she'd faced a recall attempt at an earlier point in her career when she was mayor of San Francisco. Congressman Issa, who had been a real visionary in bankrolling the signature gathering, stepped away too, saying tearfully at a press conference that he could go back to his job in Washington now that others were prepared to lead.

As soon as the election was confirmed, I knew I had to run. I saw myself in Sacramento, solving problems. I was not the least bit intimidated by the thought of a campaign. It was like every other major decision I'd ever faced. I thought about winning. I knew it would happen. I was locked in automatic pilot.

It was time to talk to Maria.

CHAPTER 24

Total Recall

AS EVERY SPOUSE KNOWS, you have to pick the right moment to bring up a loaded subject. The recall of Gray Davis was just a maybe when I flew off to promote *Terminator 3* at the beginning of July, and Maria and I hadn't talked about it or what it might mean for me during the three weeks I'd been away. At home, after the kids were in bed, we often took a Jacuzzi to relax, and that was the moment I chose.

"This recall election is coming up," I said.

"Yeah, people are saying that you are running, and I tell them they're crazy," she said. "You would never do that."

"Well, actually, I want to talk to you about that idea. What would you think about me jumping in?" Maria gave me a look, but before she could say anything, I said, "Look what's happening to the state! We're becoming a laughingstock. When I came here, California was a beacon. I know I could go there and straighten it out."

"Are you serious?"

"Yeah, I'm serious."

And she said, "No, no, come on, please tell me that you're not serious."

Then she added, "Don't do this to me."

I said, "Look, I was just . . . I haven't made a commitment. I'm just thinking about it. Obviously if you say no, I'm not going to run. But

I was just thinking it's a perfect opportunity. It's a recall, and there is only a two-month campaign; it wouldn't be that much. I think we can work our way through these two months. And then I'm governor! And, Maria, I can see it. I can feel it. This can really be done!" I felt a surge of enthusiasm just talking about it.

"I'm tired of this acting stuff," I went on. "I need a new challenge. I've had that urge to do something different for some time. This is a chance to do the kind of public service your father talks about. And I think I could do a much, much better job than Gray Davis."

As I rattled on, I was astonished to see my wife start to tremble and cry. I just couldn't believe it. I guess instead I expected a Eunice to emerge and say, "All right, now, if *that's* what you want to do, let's sit down right away and make some decisions. Let's get the experts and start the briefings." I expected that kind of Kennedy-esque response. I wanted her to say, "This is unbelievable. We inspired you, and now you're joining the family business. You've grown so much since I've known you. Here you're willing to give up millions to become a public servant. I'm so proud of you!"

But I was dreaming.

"Why are you crying?" I asked. Maria began to talk about the pain of growing up in a political family. I knew that she hated being dragged around to events, always being part of the photo op, and then on Sunday nights having the house invaded by advisors and operatives, and having to get dressed up for that. She'd hated her father's campaigns, having to be out there at five in the morning in front of the factory, telling people, "Vote for my daddy, vote for my daddy."

But the part that never registered with me was the trauma she'd felt as a kid. We had been together twenty-six years and married for seventeen, and it was a shock to me that her childhood as a Kennedy—with its intrusions, its humiliations, and its two assassinations—had shaken her to the core. Sure, her father lost his campaigns for vice president and president. I put those in the category of experiences that make you stronger. I didn't understand the *public* embarrassment she felt. In politics, everybody knows everything. You're totally exposed. All your girlfriends in school talk about your stuff. Maria had suffered tremendously: not only her father's losing two campaigns but also the tragic deaths of her uncles Jack and Bobby. Then there was her uncle Teddy's accident at Chappaquiddick, with horrible stories in the press. And then tauntings in school and on the sports field and anywhere she went in public. Kids would make cruel remarks: "Your dad lost. What does it feel like to be a loser?" Every time it was like being stabbed.

Given all that, my telling her that I wanted to be governor was like an accident where she saw her whole life flashing before her. All of those upsets and fears came flooding back, which was why she was trembling and crying.

I held her and tried to calm her down. All kinds of thoughts were racing through my mind. Total shock, first of all, to see her in such pain. I knew she had been through a lot of drama, but I thought it was in the past. When I met Maria, she was full of life, excitement, and hunger for the world. She wanted to be a rebel, not have a job on Capitol Hill. That was why she wanted to be a news producer and be in front of the camera and be really good at it. She didn't want to be lumped in with the Kennedys; she wanted to be Maria Shriver—the woman who interviewed Castro, Gorbachev, Ted Turner, Richard Branson. At the time, I thought, "That's just the way I am; we really have this in common! We both want to be really good and unique and stand out." Later on, as we got more serious, I felt like whatever I wanted to do, whatever the goal was, she was a woman who could help me achieve it. And I felt like whatever *she* wanted to do, I would help her get there.

But, to be fair, politics had never been part of the deal. Just the opposite. When Maria met me, she was twenty-one years old and she felt very strongly that she wanted a man who had absolutely nothing to do with politics. There I was, this Austrian country boy with big muscles who was a bodybuilding champion and wanted to go to Hollywood and be a movie star and get rich in real estate. She thought, "Great! That will take us as far away from politics and Washington as possible." But now, almost thirty years later, the whole thing was coming full circle, and I was saying, "What do you think about the idea of me running for governor?" No wonder she was upset. I realized she'd shared some of this with me before, but it had gone right over my head.

Later that night, I lay in bed thinking, "Man, this is not going to work. If Maria doesn't buy into the idea, then it is impossible to go out and campaign." I never intended to cause her that kind of pain.

What I hadn't told Maria was that I'd already committed to appear on Jay Leno. The day the recall election was confirmed, I'd bumped into *The Tonight Show*'s producer at the hairstylist. "Whether you're running or not running, I'd like to be the first show where you talk about it," he said. I thought, "If I really run, this would be a cool way to announce it." So I'd said yes, and we'd agreed on a date of Wednesday, August 6, three days before the filing deadline.

It was not a pretty night. All the tears, all the questions, very little sleep. "If she doesn't want me to do it, then we just don't do it," I thought. This meant I would have to unwind my vision, which would be very difficult because it was now fixed in my mind. I'd have to turn off the automatic pilot and manually fly the plane back to the airport.

The next morning I told Maria, "Running is not the most important thing to me. The family is the most important thing. You are the most important thing, and if this is a tremendous burden for you, then we don't do it. I just want to tell you that there's a great opportunity here, and I think that if you want California to do better—"

"No," she said. "It would be terrible. I don't want you to do it."

"Okay, it's over. I'm not going to do it."

That evening at the dinner table, she announced to the kids, "You should all thank Daddy because he made a decision that was good for our family: not to run for governor. Because Daddy wanted to run for governor." Of course, the kids all started talking and having their reactions. "Thank you, Daddy," said one. And then another one said, "That would be really cool, running for governor, wow."

Several things unfolded over the next few days. First, Jay Leno called to check in, and I felt obliged to tell him that I was likely not to run. He said, "No problem." There had been so much speculation about me running that he knew he would get a big audience either way. "You'll be the first guest," he said.

Meanwhile, Maria talked to her mother, and Eunice wasn't happy. She and Sarge were big believers in me and were always encouraging me to serve the public. In fact, after I'd told reporters in June that I was thinking about joining the race, Sarge had sent me a note that read, "You're making me very happy. I can't think of any person today that I would rather have in office. If I were a resident of California, I hope you realize that I'd be voting Republican for the first time ever!" As for Eunice, she'd always had the drive to be in public life and the will to move past defeats and tragedies. Maria always joked, "I married my mother." So now, when Maria told her mother that she didn't want me to run, Eunice told her to snap out of it. "What happened to you?" she said. "We women in our family always support the men when they want to do something!" I wasn't there for the conversation, of course, but Maria told me later on. "And by the way," her mother added, "when a man gets that ambition to run, you can't put it out. And if you stop him, he'll be angry for the rest of his life. So don't complain. Get out there and help him."

During that time, we were having almost daily talks with my friend Dick Riordan, the former mayor of Los Angeles. He and his wife, Nancy, lived just a mile away. Dick was a moderate Republican like me, who had lost the gubernatorial primary the previous year. Most people expected him to run in the recall, and he had a very good chance to win. He had a terrific campaign manager named Mike Murphy, whom he had already called back in. But then word went around that Dick had taken to skipping political meetings and playing golf instead.

I called to find out what was going on. "I'm not likely to run," I told him, "and if I'm not running, I want to say I'm endorsing you."

He thanked me and later invited us to join him and Nancy for dinner at their new beach house in Malibu. We spent the whole meal talking about the Riordans running and us not running. That's when I noticed a little softening in Maria's stance.

"Arnold almost decided to run, and then he decided not to because we really didn't like the idea," she told them.

"These are the decisions you make," I added. "I feel good that I made the decision not to run."

Maria turned to me. "Well, I know this must be really hard on you. But in the end you make the decision that you want to make, and you should do whatever you want to do."

This threw me. Was she now saying, "I freaked out when I heard about you running, but now I feel a little better about it?"

After dinner, Dick casually took me outside to the terrace. He punched me lightly in the stomach and said bluntly, "You should run."

"What do you mean?"

"To be honest with you, I don't have that fire in the belly like you have." Dick was seventy-three years old. He said, "You should run. Why don't *I* endorse *you*?"

While driving home, I said to Maria, "You won't believe what just happened," and I told her about the conversation.

"I *thought* that there was something off about him during dinner!" she said. "Well, what did you tell him?"

"I told him the story about you, that you are totally against—"

"Look," she interrupted, "I don't want to be a spoiler here. I don't want that responsibility. Maybe you *should* run."

And then I said, "Maria, we've got to make up our mind by next week."

It went back and forth like that for days. I could now see her dilemma. One side of Maria was ballsy and brave and wanted to be a strong partner, and the other side was telling her, "This is the same roller coaster you've ridden before. Chances are he'll lose, and that'll make you a loser too. You'll be a fifty-fifty partner in an embarrassing mess you didn't cause." She would tell me to make my own decision, but every time I sounded like I was getting serious about running, she would get upset again.

I was off my stride too. Up to now, making a career decision had always been an incredible high. Like when I went into acting, and I said I wasn't going to compete as a bodybuilder anymore. The vision became clear, I made the leap, and that was that. But making a career decision as a husband and a father was a whole different deal.

Normally, I would have called my friends to talk this through. But declaring a candidacy was so loaded that I couldn't go to anybody. I emphasized to Maria, "This is just between us. We will figure it out."

In the middle of all this, Danny DeVito asked me over to his house. He had three movie projects he wanted to pitch, including *Twins II* and one that he'd written himself that he wanted to direct. I said, "That's a great idea, Danny, I'd love to work with you again."

Then I added, "But, Danny, you know, California is in terrible shape."

"Well, yes, probably. But what's that got to do with my movies?"

"Well it could be that if my wife agrees, I may run for governor."

"What! Are you crazy? Let's do a movie together!"

"Danny, this is more important. California is more important than your career, my career, everyone's career. I've got to run if my wife lets me." He said okay, figuring that it wasn't going to happen anyway.

Suddenly it was Wednesday, August 6, the day I was supposed to go on TV. I still didn't know what I would announce. I was in the bathroom that morning, and I heard Maria call from outside the door, "I'm leaving now. I'm going over to NBC. I wrote up something for you that will help you at *The Tonight Show*." And she pushed two pieces of paper under the door.

One was a set of talking points that essentially said, "Yes, Jay, you're absolutely correct, California is in a disastrous situation, and we need new leadership. There are no two ways about it. That's why I'm here to announce that I'm going to endorse Dick Riordan to be governor, and

I'm going to work with him, but I'm not going to run." Dick still hadn't jumped in, but she was figuring he would.

The other piece of paper said essentially, "Yes, Jay, you're absolutely correct, California is in a disastrous situation, and we need new leadership. This is why I'm announcing today that I am going to run for governor of the state of California. I will make sure that we are going to terminate the problems." And so on.

By the time I finished reading, Maria was already out the door. "Okay," I said to myself, "she is leaving this to me. We've had this conversation for a week. I am not going to think about it again until I'm on the show. Whatever comes out of my mouth, that is how it will be." Of course I was leaning toward declaring I would run.

No political advisor would ever tell you to announce a serious candidacy on *The Tonight Show*, but I'd been a guest dozens of times and felt comfortable there. Jay was a good friend. I knew he'd cover me and ask interesting questions and get the audience involved. You don't hear the roar of the crowd at a press conference.

Leno had announced countless times that I'd be there to make a very important announcement. Everyone from my close friends to the driver taking me to the studio was asking, "What are you going to say?" In the green room, Leno came in and asked the same question. But everything leaks in the political world, where everybody owes a journalist and every journalist wants a scoop. The only way I could truly make news was to answer no one. I never said anything until we were on camera.

By sunset it was done: I was in the race. *The Tonight Show* airs at eleven but tapes at five thirty in the afternoon California time. After I made my announcement, I answered questions for a hundred reporters and TV crews gathered outside.

The crazy California recall suddenly had a face! Within days, I was on the cover of *Time*, wearing a big smile over a one-word headline: "Ahhnold!?"

The next day, my Santa Monica office became Schwarzenegger for

Governor central. When you launch a campaign, you're supposed to already have a thousand ingredients in place: themes, messages, a fund-raising plan, a staff, a website. But because I'd kept everybody in the dark, there was none of that. Even a fund-raising team would have been a giveaway. So all I had was my Prop 49 team. We were organizing on the fly.

This was bound to result in ragged moments. On Friday, I got up at three in the morning for interviews with the *Today* show, *Good Morning America*, and *CBS This Morning*. We started with Matt Lauer from *Today*. As he pressed me for specifics on how I would bring back the California economy and when I would release my tax returns, I realized I was unprepared. Unable to answer, I finally had to resort to the old Groucho Marx stunt of pretending the connection was bad. "Say again?" I put a hand to my earpiece. "I didn't hear you."

Lauer ended the interview by remarking sarcastically, "Apparently we are losing audio with Arnold Schwarzenegger in Los Angeles." It was my lamest performance ever.

Maria had kept her distance up to now, adjusting to this new drama in our lives. But seeing me stumble on TV roused the sleeping Kennedy lioness. Later that morning, she joined a meeting of the consultants who were scrambling to put together the campaign.

"What is your plan?" Maria asked quietly. "Where is the staff? What is the message? What was the point of these TV appearances? What direction is the campaign going in?" Without raising her voice, she was bringing generations of authority and expertise to bear.

Afterward, she decided, "We need more people and soon. And we need someone to come in on top and stabilize this thing." She called Bob White in Sacramento, who had helped launch the after-school campaign and who had recommended most of the guys I was working with. "You've got to come down here," she told him. "You've got to help." So Bob opened his Rolodex and guided us to a campaign manager, a strategist, a policy director, and a communications chief. He also stayed on himself, informally overseeing it all. Ex-governor

Pete Wilson pitched in as well. Not only did he endorse me but he also volunteered to hold a fund-raiser at the Regency Club and joined me in lining up big donors over the phone.

One of my very first moves as a candidate was to seek out Teddy Kennedy. There was no chance of getting an endorsement; in fact, Teddy put out a written statement that said, "I like and respect Arnold . . . but I'm a Democrat. And I don't support the recall effort." Still, on Eunice's advice, I went to see him. When she heard that I had to fly to New York for an After-School All-Stars event in Harlem right after I announced—a commitment I'd agreed to months before—she urged me to stop at Hyannis Port and talk to her brother. "You're not up his alley politically," Eunice said, "but he has run many campaigns and won all of them except the presidential election, so I would pay close attention to what he says."

Teddy and I talked for several hours, and he gave me one piece of advice that had a profound effect: "Arnold, never get into specifics." He told me a little story to explain. "There is no one who knows more about health care than me, right? Well, I once held a four-hour public hearing in which we talked about health care in minute detail. Then I came out of the hearing chamber and went to my office, where the same reporters who'd been at the hearing caught up with me: 'Senator Kennedy, Senator Kennedy, can we talk to you about health care?'

" 'Yes, what do you want to know?'

" 'When do we finally get to hear the specifics?' " Teddy laughed. "That just shows that you can never provide enough details that they won't ask for more. It's because what they really want is for you to trip up and say something newsworthy. Covering a four-hour congressional hearing is one thing, but journalists are trying to break news. That's what makes them shine."

Teddy continued, "Right away, from the top, all you say is, 'I'm here to fix the problem.' Make that your approach. In California, you need to say, 'I know we have major problems—we have blackouts, we have unemployment, we have companies leaving the state, we have people who need help—and I will fix it.' " Hearing this made a big impression on me. Without Teddy's advice, I would probably always have felt intimidated when a reporter asked, "When are we hearing the specifics?" It was Matt Lauer demanding specifics that had embarrassed me on *Today*. But Teddy showed me that instead of responding to that question, I could say confidently, "Let me give you a clear vision for California."

It was my financial advisor Paul who pointed out that my first campaign challenge was credibility. He, Maria, and Bonnie Reiss were my closest advisors, and Paul had flown back from a family vacation the minute he heard that I'd announced. As the campaign headed into its second week, he reported that he was getting calls about me from friends in business and finance, saying, "C'mon, he's not serious." Sure, everybody knew who I was, and at least some people knew of my long track record in public service, but in this recall circus, as the reporters liked to call it, I had to show that running for governor was not just some celebrity vanity project. How could I convince them that I wasn't just another clown in the clown car?

My campaign team urged me to call George Shultz. He was like the godfather. Secretary of state under Reagan and secretary of the treasury under Nixon, Shultz was now at the Hoover Institution at Stanford and was perhaps America's most distinguished Republican senior statesman. He was expecting to hear from me, but even so, when I reached him, he growled, "You've got two minutes to tell me why I should endorse you."

I said essentially, "The state shouldn't spend more money than it has, and it needs a leader to get it into that position. I want to be that leader, and I would appreciate your help."

That was the right answer.

"I'm in," he said. I told him I'd like to do a press conference with him.

"Let me call you back," he said. On our next call, he told me, "I have an idea. Warren Buffett has said positive things about you, and he's a Democrat. It might be wise for you to call him and have him be in the press conference too. It sends the message that you're not partisan, you just want to fix the problems. We'll talk about goals that set you above the political stuff."

I'd met Buffett, the legendary investor, at a private conference, and we'd hit it off. To my delight, even though he was a Democrat, he'd offered to back me if I decided to run. But, of course, as soon as you actually jump in, people can back away. So I asked Paul, who knew Warren well, to check whether he was still willing to commit. Warren agreed immediately.

With the election barely two months away, the campaign staff was urging me to get out and make public appearances. But while I had passion, vision, and money, I knew that I needed a deeper understanding of the complicated issues the state faced before I could venture out very much as a candidate. Shultz sent a Hoover Institution colleague to give me an intensive five-hour tutorial on California's debt and deficits. The tutorial was a combination of charts, talk, and readings, and it was so useful and enjoyable that I immediately asked to arrange similar lessons on other big issues. "I want to meet with the best briefers in the world," I said. "It doesn't matter what party." For the next few weeks, I was basically in sponge mode. The staff called it Schwarzenegger University, and the house was like a train station, with experts coming and going constantly. They included Ed Leamer, a liberal economist and head of the Anderson School of Management at the University of California at Los Angeles, and Pete Wilson. Republican politicians who had almost jumped into the race themselves graciously took time to help educate me, including Dick Riordan, Darrell Issa, and Dave Dreier. I was learning about everything from energy, to workers compensation, to college tuition fees. The staff kept trying to cut these sessions short so I could get out and campaign, but I resisted the pressure. I needed the knowledge not just for the campaign but also for running the state—because in part of my mind, I'd already won.

It turns out that the governor of California has more authority to name appointees than any elected official in America except the president of the United States and the mayor of Chicago. The governor can also suspend any state law or regulation by declaring an emergency, and he can also call a special election if he wants to put a proposal directly to the voters—levers of power that might be important.

As Schwarzenegger University wound down, my staff assembled a white binder with the most important content of the briefings. I carried that binder everywhere on the campaign trail. In it were the actions I wanted to take as governor. And at the back, I kept a running list of every promise that I made.

Buffett and Shultz weren't the types to just to sit back when they endorsed somebody. With our joint press conference approaching, they jumped at the idea of calling a bipartisan summit of business and economic leaders to explore ways to get the economy back on track. We named this the California Economic Recovery Council.

They agreed to cochair this meeting, which would be a two-hour closed-door session preceding the press conference, and they came up with a list of almost two dozen names. Paul and I invited these people to the summit ourselves, phoning them one by one from my kitchen. They included heavy hitters such as Michael Boskin, former economic advisor to the first President Bush; Arthur Rock, a cofounder of Intel Corp. and a pioneering Silicon Valley venture capitalist; Bill Jones, a former California secretary of state; and UCLA's Ed Leamer. Of course, these were not names that would be familiar to the typical *Terminator 3* or *Twins* fan, but their involvement would signal to the political media and policy establishment that my candidacy was for real.

The meeting, on August 20, generated useful ideas, and the press conference that followed was a smash. We'd taken over the ballroom of the Westin Hotel near Los Angeles International Airport, and it was packed with reporters and video crews from all over the world and was buzzing with excitement. I'd just done a *Terminator 3* press conference in Cannes in May, and this one was much bigger.

"Perfect!" I thought. Buffett the Democrat and Shultz the Republican flanked me, dramatizing the fact that I was a candidate for all of California. After they made a few opening remarks, I took questions for forty-five minutes and outlined what I'd do if the voters chose me to replace Gray Davis. Restoring California's economic health was priority one, I emphasized, and taking fast action toward balancing the budget would be key to that plan: "Does that mean we are going to make cuts in state spending? Yes. Does this mean education is on the table? No. Does this mean I am willing to raise taxes? No. Additional taxes are the last burden we need to put on the backs of the citizens and businesses of California."

I'd been nervous about this event, because this was the serious media, not the entertainment media. So I was wondering, "Should I change the tone? Should I sound more governor-ly?" But Mike Murphy, who had just signed on as my campaign manager, said, "Show that you're having a good time. That you love what you're doing. Be likeable, be yourself, be humorous, have fun. Don't worry about saying something wrong, just be ready to make a joke about it right away. People don't remember what you say, only whether they like you or not." So it was all right to be me. I went out and had a great time. One of the first questions was about Warren Buffett and Proposition 13. A week before, he'd told the *Wall Street Journal* that a good way for California to generate more revenue would be to rethink that law, which kept property taxes unrealistically low. "It makes no sense," he said. So now a reporter asked, "Warren Buffett says that you should change Prop 13 and raise property taxes. What do you say about that?"

"First of all, I told Warren if he mentions Prop 13 one more time, he has to do five hundred sit-ups." That got a big laugh, and Warren, who is a good sport, smiled. Then I said unequivocally that I would not raise property taxes.

There were questions about everything from immigration to how I would get along with the Democrats who controlled the legislature. "I'm trained to deal with Democrats," I said, pointing out that I was married to one.

Inevitably, a reporter asked when I would provide specifics about my economic and budget plans. I said, "The public doesn't care about facts and figures. They've heard figures for the past five years. What the people want to know is if you are tough enough to clean house. The thing the citizens of California can count on is, I will take action." It didn't make sense, I added, to come up with exact positions on complex questions before I was in a position to know the facts.

A reporter asked if I would have to come up with specifics before October 7, Election Day. Silently thanking Teddy, I said simply, "No."

My advisors were thrilled, and the coverage of my remarks in the following hours and days was overwhelmingly positive. I had to laugh, though, when I saw the headline in the *San Francisco Chronicle* the next morning:

Tough Talk by Actor to Tame Deficit;
But Schwarzenegger Provides Few Details

Maria, who was just back from a vacation in Hyannis with the kids, told me I'd handled myself well. She was also pleased to find much more order and coherence in the campaign—thanks in large part to the changes she'd set in motion during those first few days. And there was something else as well. I think that for the first time she smelled victory; that it was actually possible for me to win.

From that day on, the campaign picked up steam. We chose a theme a week: the economy, education, jobs, the environment. We also held a press conference at the Sacramento train station, where the legendary Governor Hiram Johnson had given a historic speech denouncing the rail barons and advocating the ballot initiative process as a way for voters to take back the state. I chose the location to emphasize that I would tackle systemic political problems like gerrymandering, which let elected officials decide the shape of their own districts so that they could keep their lock on them forever.

Maria put aside her reluctance and really dove in. When she came into campaign headquarters, you could see she was in her element. She joined in meetings on everything from strategy to slogans. She offered insights and suggestions, sometimes to the staff and sometimes to me privately.

She made one basic suggestion that somehow we'd managed to overlook: she advised us to open a campaign office on street level, so people could actually stop in. "You can't just stay up here on the third floor," she said. "People like to be able to walk by and see things are happening. They like to talk and drink coffee and get leaflets that they can go hand out." We found a large vacant storefront nearby, and the landlord was willing to lend it to us for the campaign. We decorated it with flags, posters, and balloons. Then we held a grand opening party, which was packed. I'd seen movie crowds and bodybuilding crowds and after-school crowds—but there was a different kind of excitement in this scene. This was a real political campaign.

In September Maria and I flew to Chicago to go on the season premiere of *The Oprah Winfrey Show*. I was delighted to appear because Republicans had stupidly been alienating women, and it was crucial to get them on board. I especially needed to court women because my movie audiences had always skewed heavily male. I had progressive views on issues that are particularly important to female voters—education reform, health care reform, the environment, raising the minimum wage—and *Oprah* was the perfect vehicle for making my case.

Meanwhile, big-time Democrats were campaigning for Gray Davis. Bill Clinton spent a whole day with him in Watts and South Central LA. Senator John Kerry, Jesse Jackson, and Al Sharpton all showed up. The only key Democrat who didn't appear was Teddy.

Both President Bush and his father offered to campaign with me, but I declined graciously. I wanted to be the little guy taking on the Gray Davis machine.

Maria followed the polls like a pro. She tracked very closely, for example, how the ultraconservative Tom McClintock, a California state senator, kept chipping away at my support among Republicans. We had staff members constantly slicing and dicing the data too, of course. But Maria picked up on factors that didn't show up in the numbers. She startled me at one point by saying, "There's nobody major attacking you. That's a good sign."

"What do you mean?" I asked. How could the *absence* of attacks mean anything?

She explained that if people thought I was crazy, or so bogus that my getting elected would hurt the state, the opposition would be much broader and fiercer. "You're only getting attacked by the far left and far right," she pointed out. "That means you're accepted as a viable candidate."

What the polls did show by mid-September was that Gray Davis was toast; voters were leaning almost two to one in favor of booting him out.

But the number one contender to replace him wasn't me, it was Lieutenant Governor Cruz Bustamante. He was the choice of 32 percent of the voters surveyed. I was at 28 percent, Tom McClintock was at 18 percent, and the remaining 22 percent of voters surveyed were either undecided or splintered among our 132 rivals in the circus.

Bustamante was a tricky opponent for me—not because he had great charisma but because he appealed to Democrats who didn't like Gray Davis. He promoted himself as the safest, most experienced alternative, with the not-very-catchy campaign slogan "No on the recall, Yes on Bustamante." In other words, I'm not here to undermine my fellow Democrat Gray Davis, but in case you kick him out, pick me!

By now our campaign was in full swing. With my private jet, I could cover a lot of ground in one day. We would travel from airport to airport, and sometimes the rally would be right there, with a thousand people in a hangar. We'd fly in, park the plane, I'd walk to the hangar, pump up the crowd, and then fly to the next city. We also did crazy stunts, like driving around in a campaign bus named "Running Man" and dropping a wrecking ball onto a car to symbolize what I would do to Gray Davis's vehicle registration fee if I were elected.

Every day, I learned more about policy and government. My press conferences went better: I learned how to compress my preparation for big speeches from a week to one night, and I was faster on my feet, too. Our TV ads were playing really well. My favorite one started with a slot machine labeled "California Indian Casinos," where you see the number 120,000,000 come up on the slots—$120 million was the amount the tribes had contributed to political campaigns in the Gray Davis administration. Then I come on camera and say, "All the other major candidates take their money and pander to them. I don't play that game. Give me your vote, and I guarantee you things will change." People were shocked that I was taking on the gaming tribes. They thought, "He's the real Terminator."

Rather than try to sway Bustamante's partisans, we wanted to attract the millions of independents and undecided voters. The best opportunity to do that was the September 24 debate, just two weeks before the election. For the first and only time, all five of the major candidates to replace Gray Davis were going to mix it up on stage: me, Cruz Bustamante, State Senator Tom McClintock, Peter Camejo of the Green Party, and the TV pundit Arianna Huffington.

The prep for the debate was funny. We cast people from our staff to play my opponents. All the candidates were given the questions in advance, but the debate itself would be open, with participants allowed to speak up when they wished. We worked on policy, every possible attack or rebuttal:

"How can you be for the environment if you fly a private plane?"

"You make thirty million dollars for a movie. How can you be in touch with the poor?"

"Your movies are violent. How can you say you support law enforcement?"

I also had to be ready to attack. I knew I couldn't beat McClintock at policy—he was a wonk—and I couldn't outjabber Arianna. Humor was my chance to eliminate them. So we made up one-liners and commissioned jokes from John Max, who writes for Leno, and rehearsed so they'd be at my fingertips. I had a line ready if Arianna challenged me on taxes. If she got overly dramatic, I could say, "I know you're Greek" or "Switch to decaf."

We rented a studio and practiced, sitting in a V formation facing where the audience would be. It was reps, reps, reps for three days. I reminded myself: don't get caught up on detail. Be likable, be humorous. Let the others hang themselves. Lure them into saying stupid things.

The event attracted a huge amount of media. When I arrived, the entire parking lot was full. It looked like a Lakers game. There was a sea of media vans and trailers, and satellite dishes from Japanese, French, and British TV, as well as from all the US networks. It was scary and wild to have so much attention focused on one event.

We were not allowed to bring notes as we took our places onstage. Sixty seconds before we started, I did a mental spot check. "Health care: what would you change?" I quizzed myself. But all of a sudden I could remember absolutely nothing about health care! "Okay," I thought, "let's go with the pension issue." But my mind was a blank. Totally frozen. Once or twice in movies I'd experienced a brain lock like this, but it was very rare. And in movies, you can always ask for your lines. Luckily, I still had my sense of humor. "This will be interesting," I thought.

The debate started with each candidate addressing the question of whether the recall should be held in the first place. We all agreed that it should, except for Bustamante, who called it "a terrible idea," which emphasized his awkward position of opposing the recall while promoting his own "just in case" campaign.

Very quickly the exchanges became "feisty" and "spirited," as reporters described it later. Bustamante wasted no time attacking my lack of experience, prefacing just about every remark he made to me with "I know you may not know this, but . . ." Being condescending backfired because it made people dislike him and gave me a chance to show people that I did know the issues. That made an impression, and so did my humor. When things got especially intense, with everyone shouting over everyone else, I'd say something outrageous that would make the audience laugh.

Arianna and I got into it a couple of times. At one point, she was blaming the state's budget crisis on tax loopholes and the immorality of Republicans and corporations. I said, "What are you talking about, Arianna? You are using tax loopholes so big that I could drive my Hummer through." The next day's polls put me on top. My numbers jumped from 28 to 38, while Bustamante's fell from 32 to 26.

But even though Bustamante and I had been the main contenders, the media coverage afterward focused on the sparring between Arianna and me. At one point during the debate, as the candidates discussed the state budget, she complained that I was interrupting her and accused me of being sexist. "This is the way you treat women," she said. "We know that. But not now."

I responded jokingly, "I just realized that I have a perfect part for you in *Terminator 4*." I meant that she could play the part of the ferocious female Terminator. But she took it as an insult and told a reporter the next day that women were outraged by my remark. "I thought it really hurt him with women, which was already his vulnerability," she said.

She was drawing attention to the allegations of bad behavior on my part, which had surfaced at various times over the years. The following week, with just five days left before the election, such accusations were the focus of an exposé in the *Los Angeles Times*: "Women Say Schwarzenegger Groped, Humiliated Them." My staff went nuts: apparently there is some unwritten rule in politics that you don't run exposés on candidates in the final week of a campaign. But I hadn't jumped into this race without expecting to face some heat. As I'd told Jay Leno on TV the night I announced, "They're going to say that I have no experience and that I'm a womanizer and that I'm a terrible guy, and all these kinds of things are going to come my way . . . but I want to clean up Sacramento." I wasn't campaigning as a social conservative with a values agenda. As soon as I declared, the *LA Times* had assigned a team of reporters to produce a series of investigative pieces on me. Several articles had run already, including a story on my father's Nazi past and one on my use of steroids as a bodybuilder. My rule of thumb about damaging accusations was that if the accusation was false, fight vigorously to have it withdrawn; if the accusation was true, acknowledge it and, when appropriate, apologize. So as the earlier stories appeared, I'd acknowledged my early steroid use, just as I had in the past, and I'd worked with the Simon Wiesenthal Center to track down newly available documents about my father's war record.

None of the groping accusations was true. Even so, I had sometimes acted inappropriately and did have reason to apologize for my past behavior. In my first speech the next day, I told a crowd in San Diego, "A lot of those stories are not true. But at the same time, I always say wherever there is smoke, there is fire. And so, yes, I have behaved badly sometimes. Yes, it is true that I was on rowdy movie sets, and I have done things that were not right, which I thought then was playful, but now I recognize that I have offended people. And those people that I have offended, I want to say to them, I am deeply sorry about that, and I apologize."

Now, as in the past, many people came to my defense, and my most important ally was Maria. Speaking to a Republican women's organization that day, she said she deplored gutter politics and gutter journalism. "You can listen to all the negativity, and you can listen to people who have never met Arnold, or who met him for five seconds thirty years ago. Or you can listen to me," she said, and she praised me for having the guts to apologize.

As our polling had suggested all along, California voters were far more concerned about other issues, like the economy. My speech in San Diego was to kick off a final bus tour to rallies across the state. Three thousand people showed up that morning, and we had six thousand people at the next event in the Inland Empire area east of LA, and then eight thousand people in Fresno Saturday morning. When we finally pulled into Sacramento on Sunday, almost twenty thousand people were massed in front of the capitol to cheer, celebrate, and enjoy the hoopla. I stood on the steps and gave a five-minute speech. Then the band played—a hip band, one that the kids could relate to—and I took out a broom, and that was the photo op: Schwarzenegger is here to clean house. You could feel the momentum. This was it! We were ready to clinch the deal.

The night of the election, I was getting dressed to go to the party. I didn't know the outcome yet because it was too early, but I felt my chance of winning was really high. As I walked into the bedroom to put on my shoes, I heard an announcer on CNN say, "We can call the election now. The new governor will be Arnold Schwarzenegger." I had tears streaming down my face. I couldn't believe it. I'd been counting on it, but actually hearing the news on CNN—the official acknowledgment from an international cable network—was overwhelming. I never thought I'd walk by a TV set and hear "Schwarzenegger is the new governor of California."

I sat there a little while. Katherine walked in and said, "Daddy, what do you think of this dress?" I wiped away the tears. I didn't want her to see. Maria, who had been dressing in a separate bathroom, joined me upon hearing the news, and she too was overjoyed: not only did she like the idea of becoming California's First Lady, but here was a political victory that could help her forget past family defeats.

The people had voted to recall Gray Davis by a margin of 55 percent to 45 percent, and a large plurality had chosen me over Cruz Bustamante and the other contenders. The breakdown of the vote was 49 percent for me, 31 percent for Cruz, 13 percent for McClintock, 3 percent for Camejo, and 4 percent spread among the rest of the pack.

One of the sweet moments of victory came a week later, when President George W. Bush stopped off to see me on his way to a diplomatic mission in Asia. We met at the Mission Inn, a historic hotel in Riverside, California, where ten presidents have stayed. Karl Rove was there with the president when I was shown into the suite, and after we all exchanged greetings, Rove said, "I'm going to leave so the two of you can talk alone."

President Bush, who knew that his political architect had told me not to run, tried to mend fences. "Don't be mad at Rove for what he said to you in Washington. Karl is Karl. He's a good guy. We have to work together."

I said I'd never let personality conflicts get in the way of what we needed to achieve for America and California. "It will be a pleasure to work with him in the future," I added. "I know he's doing a good job."

Bush then called Rove back in and said, "He likes you." Karl shook my hand and smiled. "I'm looking forward to working with you," I said.

They probably guessed what I would say next. After the debate, I'd complained to the media about how much in taxes Californians pay the federal government and how little California gets back compared to other states like Texas. I'd told CNN, "I am not only the Terminator but the Collectinator," and vowed to get our fair share out of Washington as governor.

So I said, "We can have a good relationship, but I need your help. As you know, for every dollar of taxes we pay, we are getting only seventy-nine cents back. I want to get more money back for the state of California because we are having problems."

"Well, I don't have any money either," the president said. But we had a good dialogue in which he promised to find ways to be helpful, especially on infrastructure programs.

Three weeks later, I was back in Sacramento, on the same steps of the capitol where I'd raised the broom, being sworn in as the thirty-eighth governor of the state. Vanessa Williams, my costar in *Eraser*, sang "The Star-Spangled Banner" at the swearing in. Maria held an antique leather-bound Bible on which I put my hand as I took the oath.

In my speech, I reflected on the lessons I'd learned studying to become a citizen: how sovereignty rests with the people, not with the government, and how the United States emerged in a time of turmoil by a coming together of contending factions. That had been called the miracle of Philadelphia, I said, and "now the members of the legislature and I must bring about the miracle of Sacramento. A miracle based on cooperation, good will, new ideas, and devotion to the long-term good of California." Emphasizing that I was a newcomer, I said that I would need a lot of help. But I let the crowd see how eager I was for this giant challenge. I wanted our state to be a beacon for the world just as it had been for an immigrant like me. The crowd cheered, and a choir sang songs from *The Sound of Music* as the congratulations began. Gray Davis, who had conceded very graciously, and his three predecessors, George Deukmejian, Jerry Brown, and Pete Wilson, all had come to see me sworn in. They drew me off to the side as we headed toward a reception. They were in a jovial mood.

"Enjoy this day," said Deukmejian, the oldest of the three. "There is only one other day when you will feel this good."

"When is that?"

"The day you leave." The others smiled and nodded. Seeing I was skeptical, they started to explain. "Soon you're going to be attending funerals of firefighters and law enforcement officers, and you'll have tears in your eyes. You'll be devastated that you have to shake the hand of some three-year-old who just lost his dad," they told me. "And then you will be stuck here in Sacramento for three months every summer not being able to go on vacation with your kids, because those assholes in the legislature won't pass a budget. You will be sitting here with frustration and anger."

They bopped me on the shoulder and said, "So have a good time! Let's go have a drink."

CHAPTER 25

The Governator

I WAS THE SECOND person in American history to be elected governor in a recall election, and I came into office after the shortest election campaign in the modern history of California. My transition period was three weeks shorter than a normal transfer of power between governors. I took office, with no previous experience as an elected official, at a time of crisis, with the state facing massive budget deficits and an economic slump.

I'd been a student of politics for a long time, and I'd done my homework at Schwarzenegger University, but there's only so much you can absorb by cramming, even if it's twelve hours a day. I wasn't familiar with the cast of characters in Sacramento: not only the lawmakers themselves but also the thousands of lobbyists, policy experts, and influence peddlers who do much of the work—and write much of the legislation.

I didn't even know most of my own staff. Everyone wanted to meet with me, but still, it was hard to hire people so quickly. Our scramble was especially tight: we had just five weeks after the election to fill the 180 staff positions in the governor's office, including 40 or so high-level ones. Our pool was small because few political professionals had expected me to win, and some of the best candidates had already found new jobs after the 2002 election. I tried to hit the ground running, by looking for people with experience in California politics, Republicans or Democrats. But few of those political veterans had experience with me, and even those who had worked on my campaign had known me for only a few months.

We ended up drawing heavily on veterans of the Pete Wilson administration. For my chief of staff, I brought in Patricia Clarey, who had been Governor Wilson's deputy chief of staff. She was an organized, hard-driving fiscal conservative who had gone to the John F. Kennedy School of Government at Harvard, and had worked in the insurance and oil industries. Rob Stutzman, my communications director, was another tough Wilson veteran who had been through a thousand fights.

I did bring with me a handful of key aides who'd known me for years: Bonnie Reiss, my right-hand person in the after-school movement; David Crane, the San Francisco financier who was my closest advisor on economics and finance; and Terry Tamminen, an environmental innovator whom I chose to head California's Environmental Protection Agency. They were Democrats, but that didn't matter—at least not to me. When Republican Party stalwarts objected, I explained respectfully that I wanted the best, regardless of their party affiliation, if they shared my vision in a particular area. These new appointees were all smart, thoughtful, open-minded people, but, like me, they didn't know Sacramento or its strange ways.

The only way to understand Sacramento, we learned, was to throw away your civics books. It didn't help to know how Washington works or how other state capitals work, because Sacramento runs by completely different principles. Common sense is not one of them. Nothing adds up.

For example, the biggest single thing Sacramento does is allocate money for K–14 education. Because of Proposition 98, passed by the voters in 1988, K–14 education claims nearly half the state budget. This doesn't count the money for building schools or for funding the pensions of retired teachers or the billions of dollars from the state lottery dedicated to education. Prop 98, the Classroom Instructional Improvement and Accountability Act, ensures that education funding increases every year regardless of whether or not the state takes in more money. The formula that governs this is so arcane that only the guy who wrote it knows exactly how it works. His name is John Mockler. He likes to joke that he wrote it that way on purpose and put his kid through Stanford advising people about the formula. The nonpartisan Legislative Analyst's Office had to produce a twenty-minute video explaining to state lawmakers how the law works, and even it needed to hire Mockler for advice.

Multiply the education funding formula a thousand times, and you get a picture of the absurdity of Sacramento. Its full-time legislature passes so many new laws each year—more than a thousand—that legislators don't have time to even read the bills before they vote on most of them. Voters get so frustrated that they pass major legislation by initiative, like Prop 98, to force Sacramento to focus on real problems like education funding. Absurd.

Sacramento grew up as a boomtown: it was the main trading post in the great California Gold Rush of 1849. When Californians made it the state capital, they built a grandiose capitol building to rival the US Capitol in Washington, DC. But they didn't get around to building a White House, so there's no separate place where the governor can work. Instead, he and his staff share the capitol building with the legislature, and each governor makes his own living arrangements. The governors before me had all moved their families to Sacramento, but Maria and I decided we didn't want to uproot the kids. So she stayed in Los Angeles with them while I rented the top-floor suite of a hotel near the capitol. My idea was to shuttle back and forth every week to spend time at home.

The governor's offices are called the Horseshoe, as they occupy three sides of an open-air atrium on the ground floor of the capitol. The legislators' offices are on the five floors above. Protocol called for the governor to stay put and for lawmakers who wanted to see him to make the trip downstairs. That wasn't my way. I often left my office and took the elevator to the upper floors to call on the legislators myself. Being in movies actually provided a great opening: a lawmaker might not know what to make of me as governor, but his staff would want to take pictures with me and would ask for autographs to bring home to their kids. If a lawmaker felt intimidated that I really might be the Terminator—it's funny how literally people take these movie roles—I wanted him to think of me more as the open-minded Julius in *Twins*.

I'd promised the voters that I would deliver results fast. Within an hour of being sworn in, I canceled the tripling of the vehicle registration fee and, soon after, with the help of the legislators upstairs, got rid of the law allowing drivers' licenses for illegal immigrants. "Now, that's what you call action," I told the cameras. Within two weeks of taking office, I put before the legislature the financial-rescue package on which I'd based my campaign—including a refinancing of California's debt, a sweeping budget reform, and a reform of the workers' compensation system that was driving employers out of the state. We were pushing for a "hard spending cap" as the anchor of my budget reform proposal. That was where the Democrats drew the line, and soon we were headed for war. When talks with the Democrats broke off, I got lots of advice from across the political spectrum, most of it contradictory.

The Republican veterans of Pete Wilson's administration who were on my team urged me to take a hard line: put all my reforms on the ballot for the voters to consider next year. Republican legislators were gleefully putting on war paint and suggested we let the state government run out of money and shut down until the Democrats caved. I was feeling pretty bullish myself. But at a dinner that week (ironically, in celebration of bipartisanship), I put the idea to George Shultz and to Leon Panetta, the beloved California statesman who had served Republicans and Democrats and had most recently been Bill Clinton's White House chief of staff. They raised their eyebrows.

"Is that the way you start your term, with a showdown?" George asked. "Your guys are right that you have momentum with the voters and you'll probably win. But it will be a long, bloody fight, and what will happen in the meantime? There will be chaos, and everyone will get depressed that nothing has changed in Sacramento. California will suffer because businesses won't have confidence to invest or create more jobs."

Panetta agreed, saying, "It's more important to cut a deal. Even if you only postpone the budget problems, it's a way to show the public that you can work with both parties and make progress. You can come back later on for a fuller reform of the budget."

I took that advice to heart. After assuming office and winning some immediate big victories using the momentum of my election, it was important to show the people that Sacramento can work together to solve California's fiscal problems. So I went back to the capital, called the legislative leaders from both parties, and said, "Let's sit down and try one more time."

My fellow Republicans acted like they'd been punched in the stomach. "You have them on the ropes, *go in for the kill!*" they said. This was my first real taste of the new Republican ideology that any compromise is a sign of weakness. The Democrats were relieved to avoid a huge fight, but some interpreted my willingness to negotiate as a sign that I'd rather back down from a fight than risk my popularity with voters. That made negotiations more difficult. After so many years of ugly, pointless fighting in Sacramento, both sides had lost touch with the art of negotiation. In fact, the legislative districts were drawn to elect the most partisan, uncompromising members of each party; legislators who were bred to fight, like roosters bred for cockfighting.

After many days of negotiations, we agreed on a compromise in which I got a balanced budget amendment, a ban on using bond debt to pay for operating expenses, and a weak version of my rainy-day fund. The legislators got their economic recovery money. The proposal was on the ballot in the March election and passed with two-to-one support from the voters. We completed major workers' compensation reform just a few weeks later. That showed leadership and got us off to a great start. Refinancing the debt lifted California's credit rating dramatically and saved the state over $20 billion in bond interest over ten years. And when the business community saw that I was able to deal with both parties, some of the gloom on the economy started to lift.

My relationship with lawmakers was now complicated, however. Part of that complication was due to the huge mismatch in popularity between me and them. As I proved that I could get things done, my public approval rating shot up into the seventies while the legislature's was down in the twenties. I was being lionized as the "Governator," not only in California but also in the national and international media. In a presidential election year, journalists speculated about me as a future contender, although that would require a change in the Constitution that nobody really expected. My numbers stayed high all year, right through the November 2004 election, when California's voters backed me on every ballot initiative on which I took a position. The most dramatic of these were measures to stop "shakedown" lawsuits against businesses and the landmark stem cell initiative, in which we put up $3 billion for groundbreaking scientific research after the Bush administration restricted federal funds. We also shot down two initiatives that would have increased the already outrageous privileges of the Indian gaming tribes.

I was making such a splash that Republican leaders asked me to help in the push to get President Bush reelected. They invited me to give the prime-time keynote address at the Republican National Convention. Never mind that I was much more of a centrist on most issues than the Bush administration, which had shifted more and more to the right. They knew I could attract attention.

So on the night of August 31, I stood at the podium at Madison Square Garden—my first time in the spotlight there since my victory as Mr. Olympia thirty years before. Except that back then, it had been in front of four thousand fans in the Felt Forum. Tonight it was fifteen thousand cheering delegates in the main arena, in prime time on national TV. Maria, who in years past would have been an NBC correspondent covering the convention, sat with the kids next to the elder

George Bush. Every time the cameras looked for his reaction, she was captured smiling in the shot. I was touched by what a team player she was that night.

My heart was pounding, but the cheering crowd reminded me of winning Mr. Olympia, which had a calming effect. As I began to speak and heard them respond, I felt like it was no different than posing. I had them in the palm of my hand.

I'd prepped for this appearance more intensively than any in my life. The speech had been revised and revised, and I'd practiced it dozens of times, doing my reps. It was a pinnacle of my life.

"To think that a once scrawny boy from Austria could grow up to become governor of the state of California and then stand here in Madison Square Garden and speak on behalf of the president of the United States—that is an immigrant's dream," I told the crowd.

My favorite part of the speech was an incantation on "how you know if you are Republican." If you believe that government should be accountable to the people, if you believe that a person should be treated as an individual, if you believe that our educational system should be held accountable for the progress of our children—those were some of my criteria. I wrapped up with an appeal to return George W. Bush to the White House for another term and led the convention chanting, "Four more years! Four more years." The speech brought wild applause.

Eunice and Sarge, who had watched it on TV, joined Maria and me for breakfast at the hotel the next morning. Eunice had really gotten a kick out of my inclusiveness theme. "The way you made it sound, *I'm* a Republican!" she wisecracked.

Back in California, my political opponents tried to portray me as a bully in part because of my popularity. But I went to great lengths to charm the legislators during that first year and encourage them to work with me. I'd call their mothers on their birthdays. I'd invite them to schmooze in my smoking tent in the atrium outside my office. The tent was the size of a cozy living room, furnished with comfortable rattan chairs, a glass-topped conference table with a beautiful humidor, lamps, and an Astroturf floor. Photographs hung along the walls, suspended by wires from the metal framework. I'd set up the tent so that I would have a place to smoke my stogies (since smoking is forbidden in California's public buildings), but people nicknamed it my deal-making tent.

I paid special attention to leaders like John Burton, the president pro tempore of the state senate, and Herb Wesson, the assembly speaker. John was a crusty San Francisco Democrat who had actually boycotted my inauguration. He wore round wire-rim glasses and had a bushy white moustache. The first time we met, he was barely willing to shake hands. So I sent flowers. Once we got to know each other a bit, it turned out that we had things in common. He knew a little German because he'd been stationed in Europe in the army. (He was fascinated by the great nineteenth-century Austrian diplomat Metternich.) Often we disagreed, especially in the beginning. But eventually we found that our views were similar on major social issues like health insurance and foster care, and we got to a place where we could say, "Forget the big fighting in public; let's find things we can work on." We became effective collaborators and even friends; he'd drop by the tent sometimes just to bring me apple strudel and *Schlag* for my espresso.

Herb Wesson, the assembly speaker, was an easygoing five-foot-five guy from LA who would tease me about whether I was actually six foot two, like my bio says. I teased him back by calling him my Danny De-Vito and sending him a pillow so he could sit taller in a chair. I didn't get to know him as well as I got to know John, because he was nearing his term limit. His successor, a smart ex-union leader named Fabian Núñez, also from LA, would in time become one of my closest allies among the Democrats.

I also formed a solid relationship with the new minority leader of the assembly, Kevin McCarthy. He was a high-energy thirty-nine-year-old from Bakersfield whose district included Antelope Valley, where my supersonic airport would have been. Kevin got his start as an entrepreneur who opened his first business, a sandwich shop, at age nineteen to help pay for college, and we clicked as fellow businessmen. He's now the majority whip of the US House of Representatives.

Turning on the charm with the lawmakers helped get my reform ideas into the legislative debate and produced some agreements that were an important start. But after trying a bunch of different maneuvers, I found that what gave me by far the greatest leverage was the ballot-initiative process. Because of my big approval ratings, I could threaten to go directly to the voters and thus pressure the legislature to do things they wouldn't do otherwise.

That was how we ended the abuse of workers' comp. I'd made it one of the top issues in my campaign, because it was poisoning our economy and driving businesses out of state. As in every state, employers in California are required to carry insurance that pays medical expenses and lost wages for workers who are injured on the job. But in California, premiums had doubled to twice the national average. How did that happen? Mainly because the laws had been written so loosely by the Democrats that it was easy for people to abuse the system. I knew a guy who'd hurt his leg skiing one weekend. He waited to go to the doctor until after work on Monday and said, "I hurt my leg working." When businesses challenged bogus claims like these, the worker always won. I also knew a guy at the gym who was squatting four hundred pounds. He told me, "I'm on workers' comp leave."

"What do you mean?" I asked. "You're squatting more weight than me!"

"I needed to take care of my family," he said.

Unions, lawyers, and doctors had prevailed on the legislature to relax the rules so much that an employee could play the system and get treatment for just about any ailment—not only work-related injuries—and be fully reimbursed with no cap or even a copay. This amounted to free, unlimited health care and sick leave with pay, all paid for by the private sector. It was a backdoor way for the Democrats to get what they wanted. John Burton once came straight out and told me, "Workers' comp is our version of universal health care." Which is another way of saying that the law was written to be abused.

I became something of an expert on the subject because Warren Buffett was in insurance, and he told me long before I ran for governor how screwed up California was. I had allies in the business community draft a ballot initiative that would put an end to this. The initiative was much tougher than parallel legislation that I supported in the legislature—it took more away from workers. But that was the strategy. If workers, attorneys, and doctors feared the initiative, they might be willing to give more ground in a legislative deal.

I sold the initiative hard. Whenever negotiations with the legislature bogged down, I'd leave Sacramento and travel the state to help gather signatures on the initiative in Costco stores.

The public found this very entertaining, and it succeeded. The Democrats and workers' groups did get scared, and they struck a deal on legislation that would save employers big money on their premiums. The Democrats hated being threatened with an initiative, though, and they dragged out negotiations, offering a few more reforms each time I showed them a new stack of signatures we'd collected. We reached the agreement just as the number of signatures on the initiative hit the one million mark—which would have been enough to qualify it for the ballot. Applying leverage had worked. Because of our reform, within the next few years, premiums dropped by 66 percent, and a total of $70 billion went back to California businesses in the first four years.

Still, the budget itself remained badly broken. And when I sent the legislature a $103 billion proposal for the fiscal year beginning on July 1, 2004, they stalled for more than a month of pointless negotiations so that the budget was late. July 1 came and went, and then a week, and then another week. This was exactly what I'd promised the voters we'd avoid, and I suddenly remembered what those previous governors had warned me about the day I was inaugurated: you're going to spend a lot of summers solo and sweating in Sacramento. That didn't seem to have worked too well for them, so I took my great poll numbers and went out to the people. Speaking to hundreds of shoppers in a Southern California megamall, I made the case that our lawmakers were part of a political system that was "out of shape, that is out of date, that is out of touch, and that is definitely out of control. They cannot have the guts to come out there in front of you and say, 'I don't want to represent you. I want to represent those special interests: the unions, the trial lawyers.' "

I don't regret having said any of that. But in the next breath, I went over the top: "I call them 'girlie men.' They should get back to the table, and they should finish the budget."

Needless to say, the girlie-men line was unscripted. It was the kind of outrageous improvisation that my team always worried I was going to come up with in front of a crowd. The joke got big laughs. The crowd knew that I was alluding to the *Saturday Night Live* spoof of me featuring the characters Hans and Franz. I also urged the crowd to "be terminators" on Election Day and throw out the legislators who voted against my budget.

My playful joke caused an uproar, with headlines nationwide. I got blasted for being sexist, antigay, a name caller, and a bully. The most damning criticism came from Assembly Speaker Núñez, who said, "Those are the kinds of statements that ought not to come out of the mouth of a governor." He added that his thirteen-year-old daughter, whom I'd met and who liked me, was upset by what I'd said.

On one level, he was right. The voters had elected Arnold, and talking movie talk and saying outrageous things had helped me win. But once I got to Sacramento, I was representing the people, and I couldn't just be Arnold anymore. I was supposed to work with legislators who are constitutionally part of the system, so I shouldn't belittle them.

Besides, it was stupid to antagonize the legislators. When you are governor, you cannot pass legislation; you can only sign or veto legislation. *They* have to pass it. That's the way the political system is set up. So if you need the legislators to make your vision of the state a reality, why insult them? Yes, you can put the squeeze on them, embarrass them, let the public see that they are not doing their jobs. But there are other ways to do that than to call them girlie men.

I decided I had to acquire new diplomatic skills if I wanted to accomplish big things. I would have to be more cautious in giving speeches—not just the written ones but also the statements I would deliver without notes. Of course, then I went right out and opened my big mouth again.

One of Maria's inspirations upon becoming First Lady was to take a California women's conference that dated back to the 1980s and transform it into a major national event. In December 2004, ten thousand women gathered at the Long Beach Convention Center for a one-day agenda on "Women as Architects of Change." The program featured prominent women from California's business and social-services worlds, as well as high-profile speakers such as Queen Noor of Jordan and Oprah Winfrey.

Because it was officially the California Governor's Conference on Women and Families, it was natural for me to kick off the event. I joked that for once I got to be Maria's "opening act." As I began this carefully prepared speech celebrating women's contributions to California, a group of protestors jumped up and created a commotion on the floor. They unfurled a banner, waved signs, and started chanting, "Safe staffing saves lives!"

The protestors were from the nurses' union, and they were angry because I'd suspended a Gray Davis mandate that would have cut the standard workload for hospital nurses from six patients per nurse to five. Most of the audience in the giant hall barely seemed to notice, but the news cameras zoomed in on the fifteen chanting women being escorted away. I found their behavior really irritating. If their beef was with me, why screw up Maria's event? Turning to the audience, I said, "Pay no attention to those voices over there. They are the special interests. Special interests don't like me in Sacramento because I kick their butt." Then I added, "But I love them anyway."

Big mistake. Ridiculing the protestors embarrassed Maria, for one thing. And the nurses' union took my words as cause for war. For months afterward, I was greeted by nurses picketing and chanting at every public appearance.

In the top drawer of my desk, I kept a list of the ten major reforms I'd promised to bring about when I ran for governor. I knew a certain amount of confrontation was inevitable because I was challenging the powerful unions that controlled the Democrats and were exploiting the state. High on that list were abuses like tenure for mediocre teachers, gold-plated pensions for state employees, and gerrymandering of political districts to protect the elected class.

Above all was the crying need for budget reform. Even though we'd finally passed a balanced budget for 2004, and the state economy was starting to revive, the system was dysfunctional. While revenues in 2005 were projected to go up by $5 billion, expenses were set to go up by *$10 billion* because of those weird budget formulas that mandated increases no matter what. These included big program expansions and generous pension benefits that the Democrats had locked in for the public-employee unions at the height of the tech boom. Maddeningly, California was headed right back into the red. We were facing another multibillion-dollar deficit for 2005. Unless we made fundamental changes, this same imbalance was going to cripple us year after year.

I saw our workers' comp victory as a model. I'd used the threat of a ballot initiative to force the other side to negotiate and make a deal. So why not apply the same strategy to achieve reform on a much larger scale? I was pumped about that success, and the one we'd had on the economic recovery money. With that sense of accomplishment, during the last months of 2004, my staff and I set out to draft a whole new arsenal of ballot initiatives.

In education policy, we wanted to make it harder for inferior teachers to get tenure. (Instead of being retrained or fired, bad teachers would often be shuffled from school to school in what was known as "the dance of the lemons.") In budget policy, we wanted to prevent the state from spending money it didn't have, and to get out from under the automatic increases for education. We wanted to change public-employee pensions, making them more like modern 401(k) plans in the private sector. And we wanted to weaken the unions' grip on the legislature by requiring them to obtain permission from their members before using dues to fund political contributions. It might have been naïve to think we could do so much, but my natural instinct after that first year was to just keep punching through my to-do list.

These initiatives eventually became known as my reform agenda. When I unveiled them that January, I told the legislature, "My friends, this is a time for choosing . . . I get up every morning wanting to fix things here in Sacramento. I ask you today: help me fix them." I proclaimed grandly that 2005 would be California's year of reform. What I didn't realize at the time was that my rhetoric came across as way over the top. In essence, I had declared war on the three most powerful public-employee unions in the state: the prison guards, the teachers, and the state employees. People who heard the speech told me afterward that it was either a crazy-brilliant strategy to empty the entire war chest of the labor unions going into the next election year, or it was just crazy—political suicide.

I didn't grasp how big a mistake I'd made. The way I presented my plans made everybody in the labor movement say, "Uh-oh. This is a whole different Arnold. We'd better mobilize." The public-employee unions weren't looking to do battle until then. They could have been persuaded to come to the table and reach a reasonable agreement. Instead, I'd given them Pearl Harbor—a motivation to band together and fight.

Teachers, firefighters, and cops quickly joined the nurses protesting at my public appearances. Every time I arrived at an event, they'd be out there, waving signs, booing, chanting, and ringing cowbells. The unions formed coalitions with names like the Alliance for a Better California and started pouring millions of dollars into TV and radio ads. One commercial featured a firefighter who was convinced that my pension reforms would take away benefits to widows and orphans. Another showed teachers and PTA members saying how disappointed they were with me for trying to put California's budget troubles on the backs of the kids.

The heat of the protests surprised me, but the reforms were too important to give up. My spokesman told the press, "Our door will be open twenty-four hours a day to any Democrat who is serious about negotiating. But they haven't been serious before, and we can't wait forever." I started running counteradvertisements to dispel the worst of the unions' distortions and to remind voters that California needed to change. A commercial showed me on a cafeteria line talking to people and asking them to "help me reform California so we can rebuild it."

But if you're perceived to be attacking teachers, firefighters, and cops, your popularity is going to take a beating. My approval ratings dropped like they'd been tasered, from 60 percent in December to 40 percent in the spring. The surveys showed that a lot of voters were also frustrated that I seemed to be turning into just another Sacramento politician, picking partisan fights that would just lead to more paralysis.

My Year of Reform campaign was extremely uncomfortable for Maria. The Kennedys and Shrivers had always been close to labor, and here I was making antilabor moves. She pulled back. I could feel the change: I no longer had a partner who was taking my side but all of a sudden a kind of a neutral partner. "I'm not going to talk about these issues in public," she said.

Despite our different views, politics had never been an issue in our marriage up until then. In my mind, I wasn't antilabor, I was just straightening out California's mess. When Teddy had been campaigning for his seventh US Senate term in 2000, Maria and I had helped by hosting a party for five hundred people at our house. Every important union leader in America was there to support Teddy and lobby him for deals, and afterward they wrote the most gracious thank-you letters to Maria and me. I remembered walking around greeting people on the lawn and deciding, "I feel okay hosting these labor leaders at my house." There were a lot of trade unions—plumbers, butchers, pipe benders, carpenters, bricklayers, and cement workers—and I always had a good relationship with them. It was the excesses of the public-employee unions that I found intolerable.

As summer arrived, I made good on my threat that if the Democrats and their backers wouldn't come to the table, we would let the voters decide. Exercising my prerogative as governor, I called a special election on my reform initiatives for November. This intensified the pressure on Maria. She started getting calls and letters from labor leaders around the country saying, "You'd better talk to Arnold about this issue." She always informed me about these contacts but never argued their case.

She also found herself having to defend me to Eunice and Sarge. They would ask questions like, "Does he really have to go after labor this way? Does he really have to be so harsh? Why doesn't he try being harsh on businesses too?"

"Arnold is trying to deal with a fifteen-billion-dollar deficit, and labor wants more money," Maria would explain. "And he promised reform in his campaign, and now he's trying to deliver. Of course, that doesn't go over very well with labor! I understand your position, but I also understand his concerns." Being caught in the middle made her feel awkward and weird.

My phone was ringing too. Business leaders and conservatives were saying to me, "I know those Kennedys are trying to convince you to back off, but just remember, we've got to continue this battle." The idea of me living and sleeping with the enemy had always driven them nuts. You could almost hear the extreme ones thinking, "Holy shit, this could very well be when Teddy takes over California."

Behind the scenes, negotiations moved by fits and starts. I was having a hard time not only because the unions were so fierce but also because many on my own staff disagreed with me. Pat Clarey and other veteran Republicans were cynical about our chances of ever getting the unions to negotiate in good faith, and took a hard line. They seemed to want a big political fight more than I did.

Rather than argue with them, I went around them. I reached out personally on my own. I met quietly with the teachers' union, which had been my ally during the campaign for my after-school initiative, although that now seemed like centuries ago. I sought out leaders of the police and firefighters' unions with whom I'd worked successfully. And I enlisted my friend Bob "Huggy" Hertzberg, the Democratic former assembly speaker, to set up secret meetings with Assembly Speaker Fabian Núñez.

I made progress in these talks, particularly the talks with Núñez, which took place not in Sacramento but on my home patio. My goal was to work out compromise measures to replace the ballot initiatives. Then I would either take the initiatives off the ballot one by one and work with the legislature to make the reforms, or replace the initiatives on the ballot with compromise versions agreed to by all sides.

We were told by Secretary of State Bruce McPherson, a Republican, that the deadline for revising the ballots was mid-August. As it drew near, Fabian and I were close to a deal. But two things stood in the way. Some of the unions were reluctant, even though I was willing to meet them more than halfway. I'm sure their political advisors were pointing to the public-opinion surveys and asking, "Why compromise now when you can crush him in the special election?" They were on their way to spending $160 million in a campaign against me, and they tasted blood. All of a sudden, the lions saw they could eat the lion tamer. The crack of the whip wasn't scary anymore.

The other problem was my staff, which still did not believe that the unions would ever agree. They also thought my agenda was so big that it couldn't be accomplished on my timetable. That's not how government works, I kept being told; they just don't move that fast upstairs. Fabian and I raced against the clock to complete a deal in time to cancel the special election. After around-the-clock negotiations, we came to an agreement—only to be told by the secretary of state that it was too late to cancel; that there wasn't enough time to draft and vote on the bills in the legislature before the overseas absentee ballots had to be mailed. The special election was on; there was no turning back.

The special election became a cause célèbre for public-employee labor unions nationwide. Before I knew it the *New York Times, Washington Post,* and *Wall Street Journal* were all writing about it, and the story was even being picked up in the international press. It was the biggest political news to come out of California since the recall of Gray Davis, only now it was *my* governorship that was being tested. I hadn't bargained on this tough a fight, but in a way I was glad. We were making Americans aware how far labor will go protecting its interests even when the deal is unfair.

I saw Teddy Kennedy when I joined Maria and the kids in Hyannis in August. "If you want me to talk to the national union chiefs or get involved," he volunteered, "let me know."

"Tell them I know they are sending money to California to beat me and my initiatives," I said. "Try to calm them down and explain that an adjustment is inevitable. It's not just California, it's every state. We can't afford to keep paying these rich contracts when we have less money."

I ran the best campaign I could for the initiatives. But we were overwhelmed by the ad campaign. The California Teachers Association mortgaged its headquarters in the Bay Area suburb of Burlingame to raise extra tens of millions for its attack. It blanketed the airwaves with commercials complaining that California was worse off and turning the election into a referendum on me: Arnold is not keeping his promises. Arnold is failing the children. Arnold is failing the elderly. Arnold is failing the poor. The association put up billboards around the state that read, "Arnold Schwarzenegger: Not Who We Thought." They even enlisted Hollywood stars like Warren Beatty and his wife, Annette Bening, and director Rob Reiner to campaign against me.

We raised money aggressively too. We spent from the war chest for my possible reelection campaign in 2006, and I even donated $8 million of my own. But while we raised $80 million, we couldn't compete with the labor money. The two sides ended up spending more than

$250 million, making the election the most expensive in California history.

I've had good defeats, and I've had bad defeats. A good defeat is a loss that nevertheless brings you a step closer to your ultimate goal. Losing my first Mr. Olympia competition to Sergio Oliva in 1969 was like that, because in preparing for that contest, I could honestly say I'd left no stone unturned. I'd eaten the right foods, I'd taken the right supplements, I'd trained five hours a day, I'd practiced my posing, I'd gotten properly psyched, and I was in the best condition I'd ever been. I even had my best-ever tan. When Sergio won, I knew I'd done my utmost and that I would come back even stronger the following year.

This defeat, however, did not feel that way. It really hurt. It was like losing to Frank Zane in Miami when I first came to America, when I'd gone into a major competition overconfident and underprepared. That time when I lost, I had only myself to blame. This time I had told voters I would fix their problems, and instead I had exhausted their patience by forcing them, just twenty-four months after a trying recall election, to go back to the polls and digest all kinds of big ideas. I had put the burden of solving problems on them, when they wanted *me* to take care of it. Even Maria complained that she couldn't possibly do all the reading necessary to make informed decisions on the initiatives. The voters thought they were getting a diet pill when they elected me. Instead, I had turned around and asked them to meet me at the gym at five in the morning for five hundred push-ups.

I didn't wait until the actual election to analyze what I'd done wrong. One night in late October, I sat in the Jacuzzi on our patio, smoking a stogie, staring into the fire, and thinking. I remembered back to the transition, and meeting the father of a firefighter who had died in the line of duty. I told him, "This is a terrible tragedy. If there is anything I can do, let me know." And his answer was, "If you want to do something for me, do it in honor of my son. Please, when you go to Sacramento, stop the fighting. Get along." Those words came back to me now.

I forced myself to face the fact that the failure of the initiatives was not simply a matter of the unions digging in their heels. I'd taken too confrontational an approach, I'd been in too much of a hurry, and I hadn't really listened to the people. We overreached. And it had backfired.

What's more, I'd allowed my reform crusade to threaten the other major commitment I'd made in becoming governor: to revitalize California's economy and rebuild our state. I'd led my staff into a losing battle, and you could see the effects on them. They were a good team, especially considering that we'd pulled them together in the mad scramble of the recall. They'd helped me rack up the important successes of our first year. But with the impending defeat of the reform agenda, there was growing dysfunction and dissent. Morale was low. People were insecure about their jobs. There were leaks to the press. They were working at cross-purposes with one another and sometimes at cross-purposes with me.

We'd been making mistakes not only behind the scenes but also in public. At a press conference called to promote redistricting reform, the staff had me stand in the wrong location. The event was supposed to be at the border of two gerrymandered districts, which we tried to dramatize by laying down bright orange tape right through the middle of a neighborhood—except that the real border turned out to be blocks away.

All this put a strain on Pat. She was tired of the fighting. "When the time comes, I'll move on," she said. "I want to go back to the private sector, and you should get someone else to come in."

Now I said to her, "Whatever happens in this vote happens. We'll wait a little while for people to catch their breath, but then it's time. I have to bring in new people." She agreed.

The opinion polls weren't wrong: November 8, 2005, was a total disaster. All four of my ballot measures lost, with the voters rejecting the most important one, the budget reform, by a huge margin of 24 percentage points. At a gathering that night, Maria stood by my side as I struck a conciliatory note. I thanked the voters for coming to the polls, including those who had voted against my reforms. I promised to meet with the Democratic leaders and find common ground. Soon afterward, I told a televised news conference at the capitol that I did not want the staff to be blamed for my mistakes: "The buck stops with me. I take full responsibility for this election. I take full responsibility for its failure."

I promised that the fighting was over. Next year would begin with a different tone.

CHAPTER 26

Comeback

AT THE END OF 2005, I was happy to leave Sacramento thousands of miles behind by climbing on an airplane and embarking on a long-planned trade mission to China. I led a delegation of seventy-five California employers—including high-tech entrepreneurs, strawberry growers, construction engineers, and merchants—and for six days, we traversed the world's fastest-growing economy promoting the strengths of our state. For me, it was an important trip, not just because it provided a welcome change of scenery after having lost the special election but also because seeing China transforming itself helped put things back into perspective. The Chinese were building on such a vast scale. I felt I was witnessing a modern power taking shape before my eyes and felt the challenge and opportunity this posed for Americans. And, of course, for a pitchman like me, it was also a thrill to be out in the world again, selling California products in Asia. That trade mission brought California a nice little symbolic success. For the first time, we were able to export California strawberries legally to Beijing, just in time for the 2008 Summer Olympics there.

When I got back to California, my staffing issues took center stage. It was a hard time to make big changes, with the 2006 gubernatorial election less than a year away. But it was right to make them. I now knew far more about California politics, and I knew more of the players. I needed not just smart, experienced people but also a cohesive team. After the special election, only 27 percent of voters in public-opinion surveys thought that California was headed in the right direction, and my own approval rating was only 38 percent. I also needed ballsy people who weren't going to be paralyzed by that, and who could even see the black humor in the fact that my approval rating was almost as low as the legislature's.

I already knew who I wanted as my new chief of staff: Susan P. Kennedy. She was, as the press quickly began to describe her, a small, tough, blonde, cigar-smoking lesbian—and the least conventional choice I could have made. Not only was she a lifelong Democrat and a former abortion-rights activist, but also she had served as cabinet secretary and deputy chief of staff for Gray Davis. She'd quit that job out of disgust with the paralysis in the capitol building.

I had come to respect Susan when she was a Public Utilities Commissioner, because even though she was a Democrat, she was always pushing to eliminate regulations that got in the way of business growth. She would occasionally send memos with dead-on, crystal-clear commentaries about the challenges my administration faced. She was frustrated because she thought we were in danger of squandering a historic opportunity for change.

We had some preliminary discussions, and I offered Susan the job. Before accepting, she came down to talk to Maria and me at our house as soon as I got back from China. The discussion covered a lot of issues, including what Susan would be up against in dealing with the Republicans on the staff. "I'll do everything possible to avoid a bloodbath, which would just slow us down and damage your image even further," she said. "But you have to give me the ability to recommend whatever changes need to be made. And if there's a fight, you have to back me one hundred percent."

"I'll back you up; we'll work on this together," I promised.

Finally I asked her the question you always ask at the end of a job interview: "Do you have any questions for me?"

"Yeah," she said. "What do you want your legacy to be as governor?"

I looked at her for a few seconds before I said anything. When you're a governor, you get that question all the time. And I knew she was already aware of what my administration had achieved and what we were trying to do. But I thought this short, feisty woman might really want to know what I cared most about. "I want to build," I said. "I want to see cranes everywhere." We were soon going to have fifty million people in our population, and we didn't have the roads, bridges, schools, water systems, communication systems, rail, or energy projects to be ready for that.

I got pretty animated talking about building, and then she got animated, and next the thing you knew, we were both hyperventilating about cranes, trains, highways, and steel. "I saw you on TV talking about that while you were in China!" she said. "You said we should be talking about a fifty-billion-dollar or one-hundred-billion-dollar bond measure—not Mickey Mouse stuff—and then your staff tried to walk that back down to something smaller. Well, that's bullshit, and you were absolutely right!"

That's when I knew we were going to click. Susan didn't roll her eyes like so many people did when I started talking about infrastructure. She shared my view that the state had not scaled up its roads, bridges, dams, levees, and rails to match the growing population: it was living off the visionary investments of governors in the 1950s and 1960s who'd built highways and water projects and had helped nurture the state's economy. As a result, we had a system built for a population of eighteen million rather than the fifty million who would be living in California by 2025. Susan didn't balk at investing in projects that wouldn't be completed until many years after we were out of office.

Instead of wrapping up the interview, I relit my cigar.

"No way California can go on like this," Susan agreed.

"We need to rebuild in a big way," I said.

"But in Sacramento, nobody thinks like that."

That was true. I'd learned that for the politicians, it was all incremental. The rule of thumb in Sacramento was that you can't have a bond issue over $10 billion because the voters will never approve double digits. That's why the Democrats were talking about asking for $9.9 billion this year. And then they'd divvy it up among all the interest groups and say, "Two billion dollars for schools, two billion for highways, two billion for prisons," and so on. Never mind that you couldn't build anything with that!

Susan said that it bugged her to see my staff undermining me when I talked about big plans. In China, one of my aides had told reporters, "No, no, no. The governor didn't really mean fifty billion or a hundred billion. He was just thinking out loud."

She'd put her finger on something that had been eating at me: when I talked about my vision, I often felt like I was being humored. Not being taken seriously had been a big problem. I would say, "I want a million solar roofs," and the staff would react like I was exaggerating for effect—as if maybe I meant only one hundred thousand solar roofs. But I did mean a million! California is a giant state; there was every reason to shoot for a million solar roofs.

I was often coming up with ideas only to be advised that they were too much, as well as the wrong thing politically. And up until now, I'd had nobody to bounce those big ideas off professionally, to shape and refine them and not simply dial them down. Susan likes to say that she thinks of me as the biggest engine in the world, and her job is to build a chassis that can hold together with the engine running at top speed. Now I had a partner.

Before I hired Susan, I made enough phone calls to know what the reaction was going to be. Not pretty. My choice blew a lot of minds, especially among my fellow Republicans. All they knew was that she was a Democrat and a former activist. They didn't know she was a seriously pissed-off Democrat who wanted to see change.

Their standard reaction to my choosing Susan was "You can't do that!" and I would reply, "I can. Of course I can. I can and I will." A couple of times, I had to explain that even though her last name was

Kennedy, she wasn't a member of the Kennedy clan, and Teddy really wasn't taking over the state. A few people even talked about drafting actor Mel Gibson, whose controversial movie *The Passion of the Christ* had been a big hit among religious conservatives, to run against me in the 2006 Republican primary.

The directors of the California Republican Party asked for a private meeting with me at the Hyatt Regency hotel across the street from the capitol. They demanded that I reconsider my choice. One of the party leaders insisted that Republicans wouldn't work with me if I didn't pick someone else. "We don't trust her, and we won't let her in our strategy meetings," was the message. "So you'll end up completely isolated."

I told him he had to make decisions as a leader of the party, but I had to make decisions as a governor. It was my responsibility, not theirs, to select a staff. And I said I was confident that Republican legislators would cooperate with Susan because she was terrific.

She started unofficially just before Thanksgiving 2005. The first move that Susan made was really shrewd. Instead of starting by making personnel changes, she focused on the big goal of rebuilding the state. She called together the senior staff and told them to collect all the information they could find on expanding highways, water, housing, prisons, and classrooms. She asked them, What kind of California did we envision twenty years from now? And how much would it cost? Some objected to the idea as too ambitious, but Susan said, "I hear what you're saying. But let's suspend disbelief and just plan."

The answers came back and added up to $500 billion. That was how much federal, state, local, public-private partnership, and private money we would need to build the California of 2025. Half a *trillion* dollars. The figure was so mind boggling, even for us, that we couldn't work with it. So we cut the time frame to ten years and asked the staff to repeat the exercise. Now the number became $222 billion, of which the state contribution would be $68 billion in general obligation bonds. Those figures were still enormous. If California tried to borrow that much for construction, it would be by far the biggest bet on itself that the state had ever made. But we came up with a plan to spread the borrowing over the whole ten years. Then it became a manageable amount of debt. California leaders had abdicated responsibility for planning major investments, leaving big infrastructure projects to the whims of a handful of special-interest groups that would collect signatures and "sell" pots of bond money to those willing to help fund the campaign for the initiative. The result was that voters approved tens of billions of dollars in general obligation bonds over the years, most of which got spent on special-interest projects, and nothing valuable got built.

I'm a tightwad when it comes to spending taxpayers' money, but I'm an equally strong believer in investing for the future. I had to educate the legislators about that, especially Republicans, who thought that building was the same as spending. When you spend money, it's gone. It's like building a house versus buying a new couch. Build a house, and your investment returns value. Buy a couch, and the minute you take it out of the furniture store, it loses value. That's why I always say a house, you invest in; furniture, you spend money on.

In fact, building infrastructure is one of only three ways to lock in a benefit from a dollar one hundred years in the future. Number one is to build public works that will last for that long. Number two is to use your dollar to invent something that will still be used in a century. And number three is to educate your children and grandchildren so that they see the benefits of knowledge and educate their own children and grandchildren in turn. Do any of these successfully, and you've invested wisely. You may even be remembered for it.

The vision of all the schools, roads, transit systems, bridges, ports, networks, and waterworks that $68 billion would finance was like heaven to me. I told Susan and the staff to go ahead and develop a formal plan. I thought Californians would love the idea of building for the coming generations, and I knew I could sell it.

Our decision to focus on a major project right away dispelled fears among the staff and did a lot to restore morale. People perked up and got back to work. And as it turned out, not as many people needed to be replaced as we thought. The staff shakeup proceeded more gradually, and in the end we brought in just six new senior people. As my spokesman, I hired Adam Mendelsohn, a brilliant, imaginative Republican who'd worked with Matt Fong, California's previous treasurer. For the key operating position of cabinet secretary, I brought in Dan Dunmoyer, a conservative Republican insurance executive with a lot of Sacramento experience. We also brought in a few aides who had a history of working successfully with Susan, led by Daniel Zingale, a Democratic health care expert and a onetime advisor to Gray Davis. He was also Maria's chief of staff. The team jelled almost instantly and became the only truly bipartisan administration in California history. And they had one vision: mine.

With the gubernatorial election coming up, I also needed new political consultants. I turned to Maria for help. Finding talented people is one of her great skills—she inherited it from her father. And even though she was not as familiar with the talent on the Republican side, she worked behind the scenes to recruit high-powered Republicans who were comfortable with my often-unconventional views. We signed up Steve Schmidt, who had helped shape George W. Bush's campaign for a second term, and Matthew Dowd, formerly the chief campaign strategist of George W. Bush. Schmidt was pretty blunt about my dismal reelection prospects. At one of the first meetings that we held to discuss them with the senior staff and Maria, he told me the polls showed the voters were mad. They didn't think they had elected a partisan guy, and they certainly didn't think they should be doing the deciding for me. But there was a bright spot to his message: people liked me. His advice was: "Be humble. Apologize for making a mistake and stop pulling political stunts like the thing with the wrecking ball." When Schmidt finished talking, I took a few puffs on my cigar. I think in images, and I needed thirty seconds to visualize who that governor would be. Finally, I told him, "I can play that role perfectly."

When I stepped to the podium in the statehouse on January 5, 2006, to deliver my State of the State speech, I was a better governor. I wasn't the bullying, belligerent conservative I'd been portrayed as in the special election. I appeared pragmatic and earnest, and I wanted to make progress.

It made sense to start with an apology: "I've thought a lot about the last year and the mistakes I made and the lessons I've learned," I said. "I was in too much of a hurry. I didn't hear the majority of Californians when they were telling me they didn't like the special election.

"I have absorbed my defeat, and I have learned my lesson. And the people, who always have the last word, sent a clear message: cut the warfare, cool the rhetoric, find common ground, and fix the problems together. So to my fellow Californians, I say: message received."

I joked about my approval rating, which by now had sunk further, to the low thirties, and the fact that people had started asking, "Don't you wish you were back in the movie business?" But I said that I still thought this was the best job I ever had, and that I now stood before them happy, hopeful—and wiser.

I bragged about things for which we all deserved credit, from balancing the budget without raising taxes, to banning soda and junk food in schools. I reminded them of the big things we had accomplished—the workers' comp reform, the funding of stem-cell research, the refinancing of state debt, new laws to make government more transparent and accessible.

And then I laid out the big numbers: the hundreds of billions of dollars of investment that we would need in order to support California's growth in the future. As a first step, I presented the ten-year plan my team had scrambled to refine. We'd named it the Strategic Growth Plan. I asked the legislature to put before the voters the $68 billion in bonds we would need.

The headlines in the newspapers the next day were perfect: the governor saying "Build It." I'd taken a lot of lawmakers by surprise by proposing something so politically inclusive and big. Of course, there was skepticism on both sides, with Democrats saying, basically, "Yeah, sounds good, but show me," and Republicans saying, "How are you going to pay for this?" Still, so many people from both parties and from labor came to me and said, "Okay, let's get a fresh start," I knew I was on the right track.

With the election approaching, we had three messages we wanted to send voters: Arnold is a public servant, not a party hack. He is not afraid to tackle big problems. You are better off today than you were under Gray Davis. We drove home those messages using one strategy: every time we get something passed, we go out and declare victory.

Behind the scenes, we were also doing an incredible amount of fence mending. We needed to make nice with the important groups that my special election had managed to alienate and that had just spent $160 million beating me. In her office, Susan put up a white board that listed all the groups, and Schmidt titled it "The Coalition of the Pissed Off." It included all public-employee groups, of course: the teachers' union, firefighters, nurses, and prison guards, as well as all the major Indian gaming tribes, and on and on. Also on the list were groups that usually lean Republican, such as police chiefs, sheriffs, manufacturers' associations, and small business associations.

In fact, with the single exception of the California Chamber of Commerce, every important political interest group in California was planning to either not support me or work actively to defeat me. And, as I'd learned the hard way, they had the power to block initiatives and stop change. We needed to choose our battles and our opponents if we were to get anything done.

One by one, we set out to work with our friends and neutralize our opposition. It helped enormously that California's economy was finally growing again, so billions in tax revenues were unexpectedly swelling the treasury. We settled an old lawsuit with the teachers, and we met repeatedly with the fire chiefs, police chiefs, and sheriffs to ease their concerns about pensions. In some cases, the fence mending took months. Key unions had contracts coming due, so we took our time with negotiations, knowing that the unions would watch my growing strength in the opinion polls and decide that there was a good chance I'd be reelected, and that they might have to deal with me for four more years.

As always, the biggest challenge was winning the cooperation of the Democratic majority in the statehouse. We did that by taking on the issues that Democrats couldn't oppose, such as infrastructure investment and the environment. The approach gave them a bitingly clear choice: they could fight me and be seen as obstructionist while I tried to move the state forward. Or they could work with me and make progress on issues dear to the hearts of their constituents. They realized that having a Republican governor lead on big issues was a "Nixon goes to China" moment they couldn't afford to pass up.

After months of hard negotiations, the Democrats chose the path of cooperation. In May we achieved the two-thirds majority required to put through the bond package. My $68 billion proposal had gotten reworked and resized and came out as $42 billion. It took us two more years to negotiate funding for the prison and water proposals, but we got it all eventually. By far, this was the most ambitious infrastructure package of its kind in California history. The press called it "historic." Now the package would have to go before the voters for approval in November, but its passage in the legislature alone—the fact that California had gotten its act together on a major issue confronting every state—made national news.

I knew exactly how to sell something that sounds as boring as "infrastructure" to the voters. We presented it on the personal level. We didn't just harp on infrastructure and bond amounts. Instead, I talked to voters up and down the state about how angry they were at always being stuck in traffic, about how they were missing their kids' soccer games or dinner with the family. I talked to them about how frustrated they were with the crowded and temporary classrooms where many of their kids went to school.

After Hurricane Katrina in 2005, it was easier for me to make people aware of how vulnerable California's old levees were. In prehistoric times, the whole middle part of the state had been a vast inland sea, and now it was a little like Holland. Except for the levees and flood control, the waters could come back and turn us into the Louisiana of the West Coast. One bad earthquake could destroy the system and flood the interior valley, wiping out the source of drinking water for tens of millions of people in the southern part of the state.

I also had big plans to complete the state's plumbing: a canal to ensure the flow of water from the North, where it is abundant, to the South, where it is not. In the early 1960s, Governor Pat Brown, Jerry's father, had begun the project with ambitions to make the system so monumental that water would never be fought over again. But Ronald Reagan had put a stop to the construction when he came into office in 1967, and the issue continued to cause battles between Californians, as it had through most of their history.

To sell the package to voters, I invited legislative leaders of both parties to travel with me around the state. It was the weirdest thing: Democrats and Republicans had done something together! The fact that Democratic legislators were campaigning with a Republican governor who was running for reelection made it all the more stunning to see us together on the trail. And it drove my Democratic opponent, Phil Angelides, crazy. But the legislators were able to declare victory, and they saw how positively the people responded. They were so used to hearing "Your poll numbers are in the toilet, no one likes you, you're wasting money, you're a self-serving bastard, you're in cahoots with labor, you're in cahoots with business . . ." Now all of a sudden they felt like winners. They'd passed these bonds, and the public was saying, "Wow that is really great, Republicans and Democrats working together—finally!"

So the logjam broke. The momentum from the bond package propelled us into a very productive year. That summer, we passed a $128 billion budget for 2006–07 that included a big increase in funding for schools plus $2 billion in debt repayment. We did so without the perennial delays and fights, making it the first on-time budget in years. After some wrangling, we negotiated a long-overdue increase in the minimum wage. My Million Solar Roofs Initiative became law in September, creating $2.9 billion of incentives for Californians to equip houses with solar power. The idea was to stimulate innovation, create jobs, and get 3,000 megawatts of solar up and running in ten years—enough to replace six coal-fired power plants.

In 2006 we took our boldest policy leap: landmark legislation on climate change, one of the most divisive issues in modern American politics. The California Global Warming Solutions Act committed California to cap and then drastically reduce carbon emissions in the next fifteen years: 30 percent by 2020, and 80 percent by 2050. It was the first such legislation in the nation, and political and environmental leaders predicted it would have ramifications worldwide. British prime minister Tony Blair, who'd helped sell the Democrats on cap and trade, attended the signing ceremony via satellite hookup. He was from the Labor Party, and he convinced Fabian and other Democrats that cap and trade was okay. We received a formal commendation from Japan.

For California to meet such aggressive goals, we would have to attack greenhouse gases from every angle. The law would affect not only dozens of industries but also our cars, homes, freeways, cities, and farms. As the *San Francisco Chronicle* pointed out, it could lead to more public transportation, more densely built housing, the planting of a million new trees, and major investments in alternative energy.

The global warming act was news not only because California was America's second-biggest emitter of greenhouse gases after Texas but also because we were taking such a radically different course than the Congress and President Bush. California and Washington, DC, had been at odds over climate change well before I came to Sacramento. Gray Davis had signed a law requiring automakers who wanted to sell cars in California to reduce passenger car emissions by nearly a third by 2016, and boost average fuel efficiency from twenty-seven miles per gallon to thirty-five miles per gallon. Passenger car emissions accounted for 40 percent of the greenhouse gases in our state. But the Environmental Protection Agency under President Bush blocked us from enforcing this so-called tailpipe law. The auto companies were fighting our environmental vision so hard that they banded together and sued California—and me! They went all out to try to stop our progress, but in the end we won. When President Barack Obama came into office in 2009, he basically adopted California's standard, and the automaker coalition agreed to a compromise that would require them to build cars for the entire nation that improved fuel efficiency to thirty-five miles per gallon by 2016, a 40 percent improvement over today's twenty-five-miles-per-gallon standard.

I'd never made a secret of my impatience with President Bush's foot-dragging on climate change, and we had talked directly about it. He was a Texan who thought he was a great environmentalist for setting aside acres of forests and sea. But even though his administration proposed ways to reduce greenhouse-gas emissions, his EPA administrator tried to derail our efforts at every turn. For me, action meant bringing in people and making them part of the movement. A lot of environmentalists who talk about global warming want only to expose the problems. That's a good way to make people feel guilty and hopeless—and nobody likes to feel like that. Besides, it's hard to relate to a polar bear on an ice floe when you're out of a job, or worried about your health insurance or about educating your kids. I promoted the California Global Warming Solutions Act as good for business—not only large and established businesses but also entrepreneurial businesses. In fact we wanted to create a whole new clean-tech industry that would create jobs, develop cutting-edge technology, and become a model for the rest of the country and the world.

Building a consensus was very hard, and the Global Warming Act was far from perfect. There were fierce disagreements internally and with legislators and interest groups. But we dealt with those disagreements by listening to one another and debating the merits. We talked to leading activists and top academics. We talked to carmakers, energy giants, utilities, growers, and transportation companies. While we were working on the climate change act, I went to the heads of Chevron, Occidental, and BP because I wanted to assure them that this was not an attack on them. This was an attack on a problem we never foresaw one hundred years ago, when the industrialized world shifted to oil and gas.

I wanted *them* to endorse our idea and to attend the bill signing, and I wanted them to start working toward that goal of a 30 percent reduction of greenhouse gas emissions by the year 2020. I said, "The way to do that is by starting to invest in biofuels and in solar and in other means that don't cause the pollution and the side effects."

I worked hard to convince the members of my own party too. There is no contradiction in being both a Republican and an environmentalist. After all, it was Teddy Roosevelt who established the national parks, and Richard Nixon who created the Environmental Protection Agency and championed the Clean Air Act. Ronald Reagan signed environmental laws both as governor and as president, including the historic Montreal Protocol to protect the earth's ozone layer. And the first president Bush put in place a pioneering cap-and-trade system to curb acid rain. We were continuing that tradition.

We were so focused on the California Global Warming Act and other big changes that there was scarcely any time to campaign for reelection in the usual way. It didn't matter. Making real progress on major issues that both Democrats and Republicans cared about was more effective than any slogan or campaign ad—that was a big part of our reelection strategy.

I had formed a reelection committee as early as 2005 for a simple reason: the people who supported my agenda wanted to make sure they weren't wasting their money or time on someone who wouldn't stick around. They were asking, "Why should I invest in Arnold if he leaves next year and a Democrat comes in and punishes me?" Eunice sent me $23,600, the most her household could contribute under the law. In her note, she said, "Please don't tell Teddy. I've never given him this much even when he ran for president."

Not everyone in my family was delighted by my decision to seek

Celebrity helped me get elected governor and boost California into the spotlight, especially on global issues like the environment.

I love it when people say something can't be done—I jumped into the California recall election of 2003. Above, a sea of supporters in Riverside. Right, a carpet of signs at my office in Santa Monica.

Ron Murray

Warren Buffett the Democrat and George Shultz the Republican flanked me at my first press conference, dramatizing that I was a candidate for all of California.

David McNew / Getty Images

On the eve of the election, I raised a broom on the steps of the capitol in Sacramento and vowed to clean house.

Justin Sullivan / Getty Images

Maria and I celebrated my victory on election night, October 7, 2003, at the Beverly Hilton Hotel.

Hector Mata / AFP / Getty Images

Eunice and Sarge, who always encouraged me to do public service, joined the victory celebration.

Ron Murray

Six weeks later, on November 17, we all walked the corridor of the state capitol to take the stage for my first inauguration.

Wally Skalij / Los Angeles Times

Maria held the Bible as I was sworn in as the thirty-eighth governor of the state of California.

Silvia Mautner

I took office with no previous experience as an elected official, at a time of crisis, with the state facing massive budget deficits and an economic slump.

California State Archives / John Decker

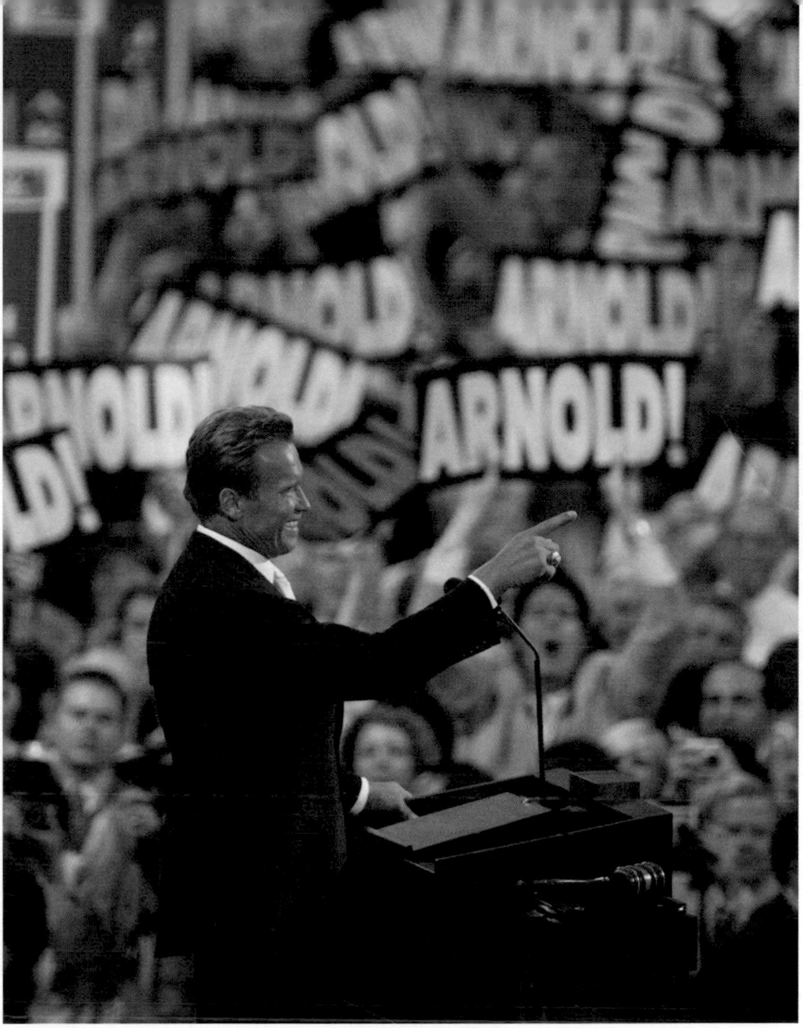

Never mind that I was a centrist—I was making such a splash that the party leaders asked me to help get George W. Bush reelected. Addressing the Republican National Convention at Madison Square Garden, August 30, 2004. *© 2004 Rick T. Wilking*

I set up a tent on the patio outside my office so I'd have a place to smoke stogies. It became known as the deal-making tent. Democratic assemblymen Fabián Núñez and Darrell Steinberg have come to horse-trade in June 2004. *California State Archives / Steven Hellon*

Democrat Herb Wesson, left, the state assembly leader when I took office, would tease me about my height; here we chat with Reverend Jesse Jackson at an Urban League party in 2005. *California State Archives / Duncan McIntosh*

Each December, a few days after officially lighting the Christmas tree, we would celebrate Chanukah on the steps of the capitol. *California State Archives / John Decker*

Overly generous public-employee pensions are now a nationwide issue, but in 2005 we were already campaigning to stop California from spending more than it was taking in. *California State Archives / Duncan McIntosh*

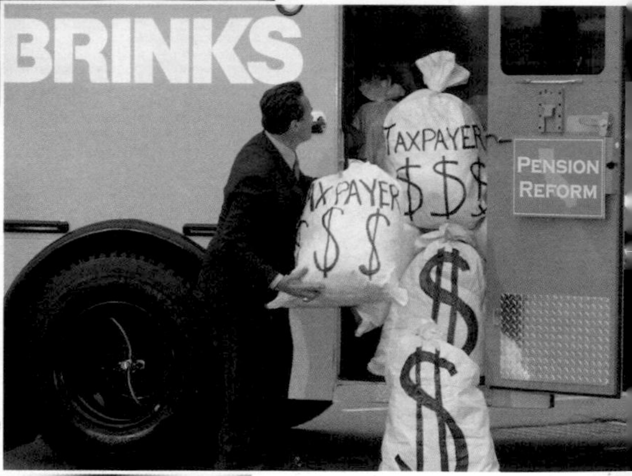

The issues were serious, yet we still had a good time—here I'm discussing water resources at a May 2005 staff session with (from left) my cabinet secretary Terry Tamminen, chief of staff Pat Clarey, and state and consumer services secretary Fred Aguiar. *California State Archives / Steven Hellon*

Senator Dianne Feinstein, a hugely popular Democrat, advised us on how to deal with Washington and with members of her party on behalf of our state. At this media conference we're joking that it will take muscle to solve California's water problems. *California State Archives / William Foster*

My mother-in-law was a font of wisdom and insight. Notice that she has chosen the seat at the head of the table in the cabinet room when she dropped by to chat in March 2004. *California State Archives / Steven Hellon*

Paul Wachter had no official position but remained an important advisor—and regular chess partner—while I was governor. *California State Archives / Peter Grigsby*

California agriculture secretary A. G. Kawamura and I hyped our local produce—those are plums on the tray I'm holding—during this 2005 trade mission to Hong Kong.
California State Archives / John Decker

California is prone to floods, droughts, and other natural disasters, and I put huge emphasis on readiness and response. Right: comforting residents who have lost everything in the Humboldt wildfire of June 2008, which burned 23,000 acres and destroyed 87 homes. Below: in the wake of a January 2005 mudslide in La Conchita that claimed ten lives.

California State Archives / William Foster

California State Archives / Duncan McIntosh

A few days before his reelection, I welcomed President Bush and introduced him to an enthusiastic crowd at a rally in Columbus, Ohio.
California State Archives / Steven Hellon

Arizona Senator John McCain rode the bus with me to help campaign for my ill-fated "Reform and Rebuild" initiatives in 2005.
California State Archives / John Decker

I liked to call California a nation-state; it was a magnet for foreign leaders. Mexican president Vicente Fox was a great partner in cross-border initiatives; he and his wife Marta visited during the busy months leading to my reelection in 2006.
California State Archives / John Decker

I was eager to meet the Dalai Lama when he spoke at the Governor's Women's Conference in Long Beach in 2006. We chatted about his travels and his long exile from Tibet; at right is California's chief of protocol, Charlotte Shultz.
California State Archives / Duncan McIntosh

Strategist Steve Schmidt, chief of staff Susan Kennedy, and communications director Adam Mendelsohn helped me mend fences with the "coalition of the pissed off" and get reelected in 2006.
California State Archives / John Decker

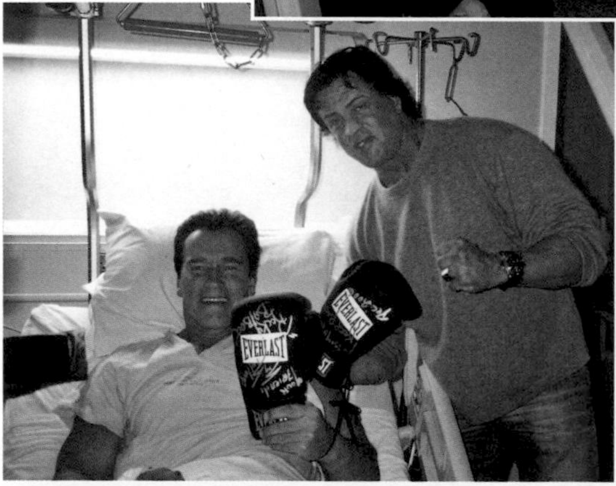

Sly encouraged me to keep fighting when I felt sorry for myself after breaking my leg in December 2006 . . .
Schwarzenegger Archive

. . . and I decided not to wimp out, instead showing up on crutches for my second inauguration.
Ron Murray

Just as Ronald Reagan often went across the aisle to work with Democrats, Teddy came to speak at the Reagan Library in 2007. *California State Archives / Duncan McIntosh*

British Prime Minister Tony Blair was a key ally of our 2006 climate initiative. I visited him at 10 Downing Street the following year.
California State Archives / Duncan McIntosh

"California is moving the United States beyond debate and doubt to action," I told the United Nations in 2007. Secretary General Ban Ki-moon invited me to speak about our pioneering new laws combating climate change.
Don Emmert / Getty Images

In January 2008, Senator John McCain and New York City mayor Rudy Giuliani came to tour one of California's energy start-ups.
California State Archives / William Foster

President Obama knew about my bipartisan record and that we shared goals on the environment, immigration, and health care reform. When I visited Washington in 2010 he picked my brain about making huge public investments in infrastructure.
Official White House photo / Pete Souza

I allied with New York City mayor Michael Bloomberg, an independent, and Pennsylvania governor Ed Rendell, a Democrat, to do something about the fact that the US is falling behind in infrastructure investment. We're on our way to meet with Obama in the White House in 2009.
AP Images

Visiting Iraq in 2009, I shared lunch with a National Guard military police brigade in Baghdad (above and bottom right). A memorable experience during that trip was whacking golf balls off the patio at Saddam Hussein's former palace (left). I met with Prime Minister Nouri al-Maliki, who quizzed me about economic rebuilding. (Thanks to California's global importance and Hollywood star power, when I traveled I was often welcomed as a head of state.)

California State Archives / Justin Short

Bill Clinton and I crossed paths again at an energy and environment forum in Jerusalem in 2009. We are both passionate about building a green energy future for America and the world. *California State Archives / Justin Short*

I had huge ambitions for California as a leader in renewable energy and the environment—here US interior secretary Salazar (in the white hat) joined me in the Mojave Desert at the world's largest solar power plant. *California State Archives / Peter Grigsby*

Just before my governorship ended I journeyed to the Shanghai Zhenhua Port Machinery Company in China to thank the workers building parts of the new San Francisco Bay Bridge. *California State Archives / Peter Grigsby*

Susan Kennedy and I hug in relief after winning a hard-fought budget victory.
California State Archives / Justin Short

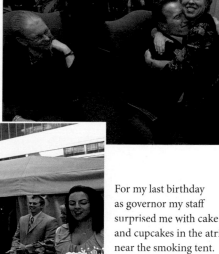

For my last birthday as governor my staff surprised me with cake and cupcakes in the atrium near the smoking tent.
California State Archives / Justin Short

Rula Manikas, my Sacramento assistant, was the only one authorized to touch my necktie and pick the color.
California State Archives / John Decker

In the dead of August 2008 as we wait for a legislative vote, I crack jokes with staffers Mona Mohammadi (seated), Daniel Ketchell, Greg Dunn, Karen Baker and guest, Daniel Zingale, and Gary Delsohn.
California State Archives / Peter Grigsby

I've benefited from the American dream, and the courage and dedication of the US military safeguards it. From my early days as a bodybuilding champion, wherever I traveled, I would visit bases and warships to pump up the troops—and say thank you. Here I'm with the US Army garrison in Seoul, South Korea, in 2010. *California State Archives / Peter Grigsby*

a second term. Maria again had to read about it in the papers, and she was upset. And with her biting sense of humor, she found a way to get her message across: she sent me a lovely framed photograph of her, with a handwritten question at the bottom. "Why would you run again when you can come home to this?" Having watched American politics up close, she was a big believer in how it could destroy relationships. She was thinking, "He's gotten a taste of power—it's typical, he's hooked. Maybe he'll run for Senate next." I smiled when I got the picture, but I wanted to finish what I had started. My original plan was to go for one term, fix the problems, and walk away. But by now I had realized that you can't do that in three years.

Luckily, I benefited from having a weak opponent. To run against me, the Democrats nominated Phil Angelides, the state controller. He was a very smart man and a caring public servant, but he was a poor candidate. He ran on the single-minded notion of raising taxes. That set me up for my best ad lib in our one televised debate: "I can tell from the joy I see in your eyes when you talk about taxes, you just love to increase taxes. Look out there to the audience right now and just say, 'I love increasing your taxes.' " It left him speechless, just as he reacted when I asked him in the same debate what had been the most fun moment in the campaign so far.

Of course, ad libbing can backfire when you're running for governor. I got in trouble by referring to my friend Bonnie Garcia, a Latina legislator from near Indio, as "very hot" because of her "Black and Latino blood." I said it during a two-hour private yack session with my staff which ended up on the internet—unedited. We were brainstorming in preparation for a big speech and the speechwriter was taping so he wouldn't miss any pearls of wisdom. Bonnie is a Latina who can be passionate and blunt when she locks in on an issue, like me. I declared that this passion was genetic. "Cuban, Puerto-Rican, they are all very hot," I said. She reminded me of Sergio Oliva, the Cuban weight-lifting champion I battled for the Mr. Olympia title back in the 1970s. He was a fierce competitor, a hot-blooded, passionate guy.

Adam, my communications director, was used to hearing me say wild things. But this time his shop accidentally put the unedited transcript on the server that held our public press releases. It didn't take long for Phil Angelides's people to find it and release the politically incorrect part to the *Los Angeles Times.*

My campaign staff scrambled to do damage control. They found Bonnie, who was not only gracious and helpful but also really funny in accepting my apology. (The papers reported her wisecracking later, "I wouldn't kick him out of bed.") I called every Latino and Black leader I knew, starting with Fabian Núñez and Alice Huffman, president of the California NAACP, both of whom dismissed my comments as Arnold being Arnold and not the least bit offensive. Rather than let Angelides leak out sections at a time to keep the negative stories going, Adam simply released the entire two hours of unedited transcript to the public. In the end the media credited us with handling "Tapegate" very effectively, and we went back to campaigning.

To my mind Angelides was too negative. He criticized me, but never offered a clear alternative vision of what California's future should be. Without that, he just didn't catch fire with the voters. For me, talking convincingly about the future was easy: all I had to do was point to what we'd achieved since I came into office.

On November 7, 2006, the people of California chose me in a landslide: a 17-percentage point margin of victory. And they passed all of the bond propositions too—the Strategic Growth Plan provided $42 billion we could use to start building the twenty-first-century Golden State.

CHAPTER 27

Who Needs Washington?

I WAS IN A fantastic mood when I headed off to Sun Valley in late December with Maria and the kids. After working really hard in Sacramento and on my reelection campaign, I was eager for a break. Two days before Christmas, we were at the ski area near our house, where we ski so much that there is even a trail called Arnold's Run. I'm a good skier, and Arnold's Run is a black diamond, or expert, trail full of moguls. But when I broke my leg that afternoon, I have to admit it was on a bunny slope—and I simply tripped over one of my poles. I was going too slowly for my skis even to pop off. As I went down on the pole, it applied so much leverage to my leg that the thigh bone broke. I felt a snap.

We had a makeshift Christmas in Sun Valley, and then I flew back for surgery in LA. Maria came with me, but she flew right back to host a big party we gave up there every year. Being laid up in a hospital, missing my family and the party—not to mention the excruciating pain—made me miserable. The surgeons had to insert a metal rod with a wire around the bone. According to the doctors, I'd need eight weeks to recover. Late one night, Sylvester Stallone dropped by to cheer me up. He gave me a pair of boxing gloves to remind me to fight. Others like Tom Arnold and our pastor Reverend Monsignor Lloyd Torgerson, came to the hospital, and during one visit, I burst into tears. "This must be the medications talking," I told my friends. "I'm really not the crying type."

I was depressed not only because the injury put a damper on the holidays but also because it threatened to wreck the inauguration and keep me from starting my second term with a bang. I was scheduled to deliver the inaugural address on January 5, 2007, and my State of the State address four days later. I had prepared landmark statements of what I wanted to accomplish in the next four years. But if I was distracted by pain or doped up on painkillers, it was hard to see how I'd deliver them. Teddy Roosevelt, of course, once got shot by a would-be assassin while making a speech and calmly finished his remarks before seeing a doctor. I wondered how he'd pulled that off.

I was preparing for my speech as best as I could, but as the date drew closer, Maria assessed the severity of my condition. Finally she said, "This is not going to happen." I was still recovering from complex surgery, wearing a brace on my thigh, and in no condition for an inaugural event. We agreed to postpone it.

The next morning I was fuming at myself. I had visions of my visits with injured soldiers at Walter Reed Army Medical Center, veterans who'd been operated on the day before. They wanted to heal, get back to the battlefield, and continue the fight. I thought to myself, "Those guys want to go back into battle, but I want to cancel a speech?" I felt like a total wimp.

I had to go forward with the inaugural, even if I had to crawl on all fours up the steps of the capitol. I called Maria and told her we had to resume our original plans. She recognized that I was in machine mode and that no one was going to stop me, and she went all out to make the inauguration a success. Besides boosting my morale, she personally supervised the construction and arrangement of the inaugural stage in Sacramento so that I could get on and off easily with crutches.

The gathering in Sacramento was packed and festive, with members of both parties, leaders from business and labor, press, friends, and family. Willie Brown, one of the longest-serving Democrats and the former speaker of the state assembly, was the emcee of the event, a gesture to sell the idea of postpartisanship. I felt proud to be there.

I had big ambitions heading into my second term. I was determined to keep my reelection promises and take on big, tough issues that would position California as a leader in health care, the environment, and political reform. We'd already launched major programs on climate change and infrastructure. The recession was past, the economy was growing again, and thanks to that and a lot of discipline, we'd narrowed the budget deficit from $16 billion in 2004 to $4 billion in the current fiscal year. In the budget for the year starting July 2007, which I was about to submit to the legislature, the deficit would be zero for the first time in years. So the stage was set for dramatic action.

I planned to use my inaugural speech to challenge partisanship itself. I was dismayed by the crazy polarization of our political system and the waste, paralysis, and damage it caused. Despite bipartisan deals in 2006 on infrastructure, the environment, and the budget, California had become deeply divided. Republicans and Democrats could no longer meet in the middle and compromise on shared interests as they had during the great boom of the postwar years. Now California politics was this big centrifuge that forced voters, policies, and parties away from the center. Election districts had been drawn to eliminate competition; conservative Republicans ran some, liberal Democrats ran others. The late congressman Phil Burton was so proud of the gerrymandering he did for California's Democrats in drawing the congressional lines in 1981 that he called it his contribution to modern art. I said in my 2007 State of the State speech that because of gerrymandering, the California legislature had less turnover than in Austria's Hapsburg monarchy.

There had been a really appalling example of this in the two days after 9/11. While the nation was reeling from the terrorist attacks on New York and Washington, DC, the legislature pushed through a redistricting bill that further entrenched incumbents and hard-liners of both parties. This was a worldview that put parties ahead of people, and I thought it needed to change.

So when I got out of bed, picked up my crutches, and went to give my inaugural speech, I challenged Californians to stop yielding to the far left and the far right and return to the center. To the politicians, I said, "Centrist does not mean weak. It does not mean watered down or warmed over. It means well balanced and well grounded. The American people are instinctively centrist. So should be our government. America's political parties should return to the center, where the people are."

And I reminded the voters, "The left and the right don't have a monopoly on conscience. We should not let them get way with that. You can be centrist and be principled. You can seek a consensus and retain your convictions. What is more principled than giving up some part of your position to advance the greater good? That is how we arrived at a Constitution in this country. Our Founding Fathers would still be meeting at the Holiday Inn in Philadelphia if they hadn't compromised."

Four days later, I delivered the State of the State speech to the legislature. I was able to compliment them despite the ways we'd often tortured each other during my first term. I didn't even have to lie; all I had to do was contrast them with the politicians in Washington. "Last year the federal government was paralyzed by gridlock and games," I said. "But you here in this chamber acted on infrastructure, the minimum wage, prescription drug costs, and the reduction of greenhouse gases in our atmosphere. What this said to the people is that we are not waiting for politics. We are not waiting for our problems to get worse. We are not waiting for the federal government. Because the future does not wait."

Then I painted a vision for the state. "Not only can we lead California into the future, we can show the nation and the world how to get there. We can do this because we have the economic strength, the population, and the technological force of a nation-state. We are the modern equivalent of the ancient city-states of Athens and Sparta. California has the ideas of Athens and the power of Sparta." And I laid out a half dozen ambitious ways for California to set national and international examples, from building classrooms to combating global warming.

The average politician doesn't give a shit about Athens or Sparta, of course, or any kind of vision. But I'd just won an election, so for the moment, they had to listen to me. I was willing to bet that at least some would rise to the challenge of doing even more than we'd achieved in 2006.

Before I was off my crutches, my staff and I were back in high gear. Between the goals I'd laid out in my speeches and the budget initiatives that year, we launched the most ambitious reform agenda of any state administration in modern history: the most sweeping health care reform legislation in America; carrying out the most comprehensive climate change regulations in the country, including the world's first low-carbon fuel standard; parole reform and new prison construction; and the massive, most controversial project in California's legendary water wars: the canal to finish what Governor Pat Brown had started thirty years earlier.

We continued pushing budget reform and political reform: strengthening the rainy-day fund and banning fund-raising during the budget approval process. We launched the second attempt at a redistricting ballot measure aimed at forming an independent, nonpartisan committee. And I spent long hours trying to help ordinary people deal with extraordinary problems. We met for weeks with mortgage companies like Countrywide, GMAC, Litton, and HomEq to fast-track help to keep subprime borrowers who were underwater from losing their homes. We met with local law enforcement leaders in the Central Valley and the Salinas Valley to help them come up with a better approach to fight gang violence.

The workdays often ran to sixteen hours, and most nights I simply stayed in Sacramento. I liked the weight and the complexity of the challenges and being constantly on the move. But I missed Maria and the kids, and I still made sure to try to spend Friday plus every weekend in LA.

This schedule had worked in my first term, mainly, I thought, because of Maria's skill as a mom. But one evening in spring when I came back from Sacramento, and we were all sitting around the kitchen table, Christina started to cry. "Daddy, you're never home," she said. "You're always in Sacramento. You didn't show up at school when I had my recital." Another one said, "You didn't show up for parents' day. It was just Mommy there." The next one started crying and said, "Yeah, me too. You missed my soccer game." All of a sudden, there was this chain reaction. All of them were crying, and they all had a complaint.

Christina must have seen the shock on my face. I was having such a great time being governor that I'd completely missed what was boiling at home. She said, "Sorry, Daddy, but I had to say it."

"No, Christina," said Maria. "That's okay. I think it's important that you tell your daddy what you think and what you feel. So just tell him everything." She was unhappy too that I was away so much, and encouraged them all to speak up.

I can be such a locomotive sometimes. Now I worried about how long they'd felt this way and how long it had taken them to have the courage to say it. I'd always told them that in a family everyone has to make sacrifices. Whenever you have six people together, no one can go off and do everything he or she wants 100 percent of the time. Well, now it was my turn. I promised that from that moment, I would spend only one night a week in Sacramento. "I might have to leave some mornings before you get up, and I might get home just as you're going to sleep," I said. "But from now on, I'll be here."

They always say that politics erodes marriages. You get so immersed in the job that there are side effects on the people you love. Even if you succeed in partly protecting your wife and kids from the public spotlight, they feel they're sharing you and losing you. Maria, of course, was strong and had her own career. When she saw that my passion for being governor was causing us to drift apart, she did the best she could do under the circumstances: took great care of the kids, stepped up to the opportunities and responsibilities of being First Lady, was there for me when I needed her. And waited.

Just before a press conference the previous spring while we starting the reelection campaign, my top staff had begged me not to take on health care reform. Susan Kennedy and Daniel Zingale brought it up specifically: "Please don't say you're going to do it." Daniel was our health care guru. Before becoming Maria's chief of staff, he'd founded California's Department of Managed Health Care for Governor Davis.

But I was feeling my oats, and I went out and told the media, "I'm going to do health care reform in my second term." Afterward, Susan and Daniel were saying, "Oh, shit, he just grabbed the third rail." They begged me not to promise we'd have a plan ready in time for the State of the State address; they said it couldn't be done. So the next time I saw a reporter, I said, "and I will have a plan by the State of the State address." Susan joked later that she had to hold a paper bag over Daniel's mouth to stop him hyperventilating when he heard. He couldn't believe we were going to have to develop a comprehensive health care reform plan in eight months for the state of California; they said it took two years in Massachusetts, a state smaller than Los Angeles County. I had to calm everyone down.

Their fear was easy to understand. Trying to reform health care had almost destroyed Bill Clinton's presidency. And the same health care demons that confronted America also confronted us as a state: soaring costs, inefficiency, fraud, rising burdens for employers and policyholders, and millions of people uninsured. But I'd always thought it was a disgrace that the greatest country in the world did not provide a health care system for all of its people, as many European countries do. That said, I believe in the private sector and was opposed to any government-run system like single payer. We framed the idea differently than anybody before or since.

I didn't try to guilt-trip businesses and people who already had health insurance into taking on the huge extra costs of the uninsured and the underinsured. Instead, I argued that they were already paying these bills through a big hidden tax: their own rising health care costs. So by covering the uninsured directly, they would be paying no more than they were now, and health care could be managed more efficiently. I also spotlighted that most Californians without health insurance—three-quarters of them, in fact—had jobs. This was the core of California: young working families who weren't adequately covered.

Daniel Zingale led a team that did a brilliant job of creating our plan. Universal coverage was going to require sacrifice from all the players—

hospitals, insurers, employers, doctors—and he brought them all to the table and got them involved. The plan had three components. Coverage for all. A requirement that every Californian buy insurance. And a requirement that insurers guarantee coverage for everyone, regardless of age and including those with pre-existing conditions. There were also subsidies for people who couldn't afford insurance on their own, as well as aggressive measures to control costs and to focus on prevention.

So instead of avoiding health care, I made it a top priority in 2007, which I talked up as the year of health care. Public events and private meetings on the issue were on my schedule every day. I traveled the state meeting patients, doctors, nurses, and hospital CEOs. I went to roundtables mostly just to sit and listen. In May I actually got Jay Leno to let me talk about health care finance on *The Tonight Show*; Jay gave an example of a relative who had spent three months in a hospital in England and paid only $4,500.

Assembly Speaker Fabian Núñez worked his tail off corralling the big labor unions to support health care reform, while I worked the major business groups. Together we negotiated every major detail with hospitals, doctors' groups, and patient advocates on a comprehensive plan that would pay for itself, require everyone to have health insurance, and reduce the cost shift to taxpayers. By December, the California Health Care Security and Cost Reduction Act had won the support of the assembly, despite opposition from the nurses' union and liberal Democrats who were holding out for a government-run single-payer plan to cover everybody.

But in January 2008, after a year of intense work, health care reform wasn't even taken up for a vote in the state senate. The plan simply died in a senate committee. Word was that the senate leader, Democrat Don Perata, couldn't stomach that this young upstart Democratic speaker, working with a Republican governor, would deliver two of the biggest reform measures in modern California history: climate change and health care reform. Some Democrats complained openly that it was political malpractice to give a Republican governor such a huge victory on "Democratic" issues. (In the early seventies, Teddy Kennedy followed a similar line in blocking President Nixon's national health care reform.) I couldn't believe that a major issue for the people of California could be derailed because of what amounted to a political snit between two Democratic leaders in the legislature.

It was a major defeat. But I don't regret the effort, because it wasn't a defeat for the cause of health care. Our legislation was studied closely in Washington and was one of the models for national health care reform in 2010. Our plan addressed some of the perceived weaknesses in Mitt Romney's pioneering health care reform in Massachusetts by strengthening the individual mandate and focusing on prevention—key cost containment measures. In effect, our health care reform became America's, and California led the way.

The world certainly noticed the contrast between the action in California and the gridlock in DC. *Time* magazine put a picture of New York mayor Michael Bloomberg and me on the cover in June over the headline "Who Needs Washington?" The point of the story was that Bloomberg's city and my state were doing the big things that Washington failed to do. Washington had rejected the Kyoto Protocol to combat global warming, but in California we passed America's first cap on greenhouse gases. The administration had rejected stem cell research, but in California we'd invested $3 billion to promote it. The administration turned down our request for money to repair our water system's levees, but we'd pushed through billions of dollars in bonds to protect the levees and start rebuilding our infrastructure. I told *Time*, "All the great ideas are coming from local governments. We're not going to wait for Big Daddy to take care of us."

Bloomberg and I both understood the power of reaching across borders. In May he chaired the second climate summit of mayors of more than thirty of the world's largest cities, with the aim of slashing carbon emissions. That summer he and I allied with Pennsylvania governor Ed Rendell, a Democrat, to form Building America's Future Educational Fund, a nonprofit to promote a new era of US investment in infrastructure. And I was already making a series of pacts with other countries and states in the areas of trade and climate change. After our state passed the greenhouse gas cap in the fall of 2006, which included the toughest-ever fuel-efficiency standards for passenger cars registered in our state, we signed a climate alliance with the province of Ontario, Canada, just across the river from Detroit. This infuriated some of the automakers' groups, and a Republican congressman in Detroit even put up a billboard that said: "Arnold to Detroit: Drop Dead." I told the media my response: "Arnold to Detroit: Get off your butt!"

My willingness to work across party lines alienated conservative Republicans. If they thought I wasn't really a Republican for taking on climate change, they really lost it when I took on health care reform. In September I opened a party conference near Palm Springs by taking another shot at narrow partisanship.

"We are dying at the box office," I told my fellow Republicans. "We are not filling the seats. Our party has lost the middle, and we will not regain true political power in California until we get it back. I am of the Reagan view that we should not go off the cliff with flags flying." I noted that I had learned this the hard way in 2005, when the unions rallied voters to crush my ballot initiatives.

"The road to our comeback is clear," I said. "The California Republican Party should be a right-of-center party that occupies the broad middle of California. That is lush, green, abandoned political space that can be ours." I closed with a pledge to work hard to help the party achieve this. But the speech went over with a thud. Polite applause, nothing more. They didn't like the lush, green center; they wanted to be out on the cold, mean fringe.

The next speaker was Governor Rick Perry of Texas, a right-winger. He pooh-poohed climate change, condemned infrastructure projects as runaway government spending, and declared that the Republican Party was on a roll. The audience went wild. With the 2008 presidential election just a year away, I wondered if Ronald Reagan was prophetic: "rolling off the cliff with flags flying" was just where the Republicans were headed.

CHAPTER 28

The Real Life of a Governator

BESIDES BEING GOLDEN AND prosperous, California is disaster prone. Our geography and climate make us unusually vulnerable to fires, floods, mudslides, droughts, and, of course, earthquakes.

Given the frequency of such events, I had to assume that some kind of natural disaster would happen on my watch. Our firefighters, police forces, and other first responders were among the best in the world, but for me it wasn't enough just to meet their commanders or read the disaster plans. I drove our excellent secretary for Health and Human Services, Kim Belshé, crazy with my questions.

What if we had a pandemic in LA, and ten thousand people needed to be hospitalized? How would the hospitals respond? What was their ability to set up tents, with beds, oxygen tanks, and a clean environment? Where *were* the tents? Where were the beds? Where would they get doctors and nurses? Did they have lists of retired doctors and nurses who could be called back in? Had we tested these lists ourselves?

After the Hurricane Katrina disaster in 2005, everyone was painfully aware of the failure of the government's response, and I was determined that no such thing would happen here. I knew that the action-hero governor would not get away with failure on this front. This meant that we had to step up our drills and exercises. Even when acting in a movie, I would not shoot a stunt if I hadn't rehearsed it a minimum of ten times. So how could I expect an emergency response to succeed if we haven't rehearsed the scenarios of fires, floods, and earthquakes? And what if you have an earthquake that triggers a major fire? Now you're in a situation where people can't get around, *and* you have the fires, *and* the fire station is hit too, *and* the doors are jammed so the truck can't come out. The communication systems are disrupted. What now?

This was so ingrained in me that even before Katrina, in 2004, I started a statewide exercise we called Golden Guardian. It was a massive preparedness test for every possible disaster and terrorist attack. We tested everything: planning, procedures, communications, evacuation routes, hospital readiness, and federal, state, and local cooperation. Each year we planned for a different type of emergency. The first year, it was a terrorist attack using "dirty" bombs designed to contaminate multiple ports and airports up and down the state with radioactivity. Other years, we tested for massive earthquakes, floods, and more terrorist attacks. These were the largest, most comprehensive emergency response exercises in the country, involving literally thousands of participants statewide. Each took years to plan. Matt Bettenhausen, our emergency services chief, appreciated this fixation of mine. "How great is it to have a boss who says practice, practice, practice?" he said.

One year, I was getting briefed on the next Golden Guardian, which was to focus on a massive 7.8 magnitude earthquake in Southern California. The briefer explained that a California Highway Patrol helicopter was supposed to pick me up and take me to a situation room down in Orange County, where the senior people would converge. "The earthquake will happen at five forty-five, and we'll pick you up at six," he said. This got me thinking. I asked, "How do you know that the earthquake is going to happen at five forty-five?"

"That's the schedule. They want everyone together down south."

I didn't say anything more. I thought, "This is bogus. How do I know we're really prepared, when we 'prepare' for a preparedness drill?"

So that morning I got up at four o'clock and called the Highway Patrol. "The earthquake just happened," I said. "The clock is running on this exercise."

You have no idea what an explosion this caused. The CHP and the US Department of Homeland Security freaked out. Everybody had to scramble. They ended up doing a great job, and the exercise exposed some ways the system could break down, but the senior Homeland Security guy was pretty irritated. "I can't believe you didn't give me a heads-up," he told me later when we had a chance to talk.

"We're not out to embarrass anybody," I said. "But we've got to know where we fall short when we have no notice." We agreed in the future to gradually tighten the lead time on exercises and to tell participants, "Last time we gave you twelve hours' notice; this time we'll give you six."

All our preparation paid off in late 2007, when particularly severe wildfires broke out up and down the state. The worst were in the south, near San Diego, where despite the firefighters' best efforts, the blazes were spreading, and there were predictions of hurricane-force winds. On the third day of the fires, Monday, October 22, I called my staff for a briefing, as I usually did at six in the morning. They told me that large areas of San Diego were now in danger, and the order had gone out to evacuate a half million people. A half million people! That's a population the size of New Orleans before Katrina and probably the largest one ever forced out of their homes in California history. Already, thousands were headed toward Qualcomm Stadium, which we'd designated as the main gathering point for evacuees with no place else to stay.

"We're going down there," I said. Instead of leaving that morning for Sacramento, I used my office in Santa Monica as a jumping-off point and started making phone calls while my team assembled there. I called San Diego mayor Jerry Sanders, a former police chief, and made plans to meet at the stadium later in the day. Bettenhausen, talking to commanders on the ground, reported that residents were responding to our evacuation message as we'd hoped. The order was designed to convey the two things you needed to know most if your home was in a fire's path: first, when the police tell you to leave, grab your stuff and go, because a wildfire can spread faster than a person can run; second, not only would we fight to protect your home from the fires, but also the police would patrol your neighborhoods to keep looters away.

We expected ten thousand or more people at Qualcomm Stadium. I figured that under the circumstances, no one would be thinking about things such as diapers and baby formula and dog food. So I made a list and called the head of the California Grocers Association to ask if stores in the region could deliver those items to Qualcomm immediately. He was eager to pitch in.

Then I called the White House and briefed President Bush. Up until this point, we'd had a professional but guarded relationship. President Bush was always available to talk, and while we did not always agree on what the federal government could do for California, I learned quickly that if I raised only one issue at a time, I would get a fair hearing. It wasn't surprising that I had a warmer relationship with his father. With George H. W. Bush, I was more of an admiring protégé, soaking up everything I could learn. George W. and I were almost exactly the same age, and we both had to represent interests that were sometimes at odds.

But when the fires raged, President Bush was incredibly impressive. He'd learned lessons about emergency responsiveness the hard way during Katrina, and he asked the kinds of questions that only someone who'd been through a disaster would know to ask. He understood that the federal government might not initially move quickly enough, out of a natural need to save responders for other emergencies throughout the country. President Bush told me that his chief of staff would get us everything we needed and that I should call him, the president, directly if there was anything I wanted him to know. I was skeptical, so I called him back forty-five minutes later to ask a question, and he picked up the phone again.

Within three days, President Bush was on the scene. He shook hands with firefighters, visited homes, held press conferences, and peppered me and the fire chiefs with questions. He showed real leadership.

My own chief of staff, meanwhile, reported that the National Guard was on its way. Susan was staying in Sacramento to coordinate the governor's office response with Dan Dunmoyer, the cabinet secretary, and I'd directed her to have one thousand National Guard troops pulled off a border-security operation and sent to Qualcomm Stadium. She called the adjutant general to say we needed the troops. The guy had obviously never encountered Susan in commando mode before, and he made the mistake of insisting on paperwork. "Okay," he told her. "We need a mission order."

"The mission order is to get one thousand men off the border and get them to Qualcomm stat," she repeated.

"But I need a mission order. It has to say—"

"Here's your fucking mission order!" she exploded. "Get a thousand troops to Qualcomm. I want them on the move within the hour." The general got us the troops.

Then she turned to the cots that people would obviously need that night. Thousands of cots, pillows, and blankets had been stockpiled in the region for emergencies. "They're on their way," officials kept saying. But she and Dan kept calling and discovered the supplies hadn't arrived.

"That's not good enough," she said, "We need to *know* they are on the trucks. I want to know exactly where they are en route right now. Give me the cell phone numbers for the drivers." Hours went by, and the cots couldn't be found. Rather than wait, we called Walmart and other giant retailers in the state. Later that day, a California National Guard C-130 cargo plane crammed with thousands of donated cots flew out of Moffett Field in Mountain View to San Diego.

Moves like these are not in any disaster response manuals. I saw what happened during Katrina when officials at every level waited for someone else to take action—because that's what the manuals say you're supposed to do. "Every disaster is local," the experts told me. State officials are supposed to wait until local officials ask for assistance; federal officials wait until state officials ask for help, and so on. "Bullshit," I said. "That's how thousands of people were left stranded on rooftops in New Orleans. That is *not* going to happen here." My rule was simple: "I want *action*. If you need to do something that's not in the manual, throw the manual out. Do whatever you have to do. Just get it done."

Once my team was assembled, we headed for San Diego. We could see the gray haze from the fires over one hundred miles away as soon as the plane took off. That afternoon, I would fly in a helicopter to visit the fire bases and see the blazes firsthand. But communicating with the public was the first concern. I met Mayor Sanders and other local leaders outside Qualcomm, and we went around as a team: first, walking through the hallways and the parking lot to greet the evacuees, emergency workers, and volunteers streaming in, and then talking to the media.

Fortunately, I'd been well prepared on how to communicate during a fire emergency by my predecessor. During the transition period, Gray Davis had graciously contacted me in the midst of a significant but much smaller fire. He asked if I wanted to accompany him while he met firefighters, visited homes, talked to families, and addressed the media. I saw how he absorbed a briefing, and the way he thanked firefighters for their service, while trying not to distract them from their mission. He even served them breakfast as they were coming off the night shift. He would go from home to home, comforting victims, asking them if there was anything the state needed to do. He was a source of strength.

That time we spent together smoothed the transition and proved that we could work together, even though we had battled during the campaign. More importantly, Gray showed me how a governor takes action rather than just phoning in from Sacramento.

In San Diego we started holding regular press conferences so that people would understand that there were no secrets. We spelled out everything step-by-step, saying things like, "We have sixty-mile-per-hour winds, and the flames can jump a mile and a half at a time. But we are going to get this under control." We sent a clear signal that federal, state, and local responders were all working together, but we were also quick to admit mistakes. Our rule was, "Never bullshit." When cots got lost, we acknowledged it. It was great to have a guy with Bettenhausen's experience and sense of humor on hand. He stayed glued by my side, keeping us in touch with the fire chiefs and commanders at the fires. Although the news often wasn't good, their voices were never frantic, only disciplined and firm: "Governor, we have a major problem. We just lost fifty more homes. We've got three firefighters injured, and we're repositioning our men. We're evacuating this other area, and CHP and the sheriff are involved, to close off the roads and protect people's homes . . ."

We kept open communications with the commanders and always asked what more they needed, and we used their information to give regular public updates.

We heard that the winds had shifted and that the residents of a nursing home in the fire's path were being evacuated to a makeshift shelter at the Del Mar racetrack. Del Mar was set up as a shelter for horses, not people. It was already evening, but my instincts told me to see it for myself; that it could be a particularly dangerous situation for the elderly residents.

It was sunset by the time we arrived. Close to three hundred patients had been evacuated. I hated what we found there: old folks parked in wheelchairs with IV bags, propped up against walls, lying on mats on cold cement. A few people were crying, but most were silent and still. I felt like I was walking through a morgue. I put a blanket on one old fellow and folded up a jacket to use as a pillow under a lady's head. None of these people had their medication; some needed kidney dialysis. A nurse-practitioner and Navy Reserve commander named Paul Russo had bravely taken charge of the scene and, with the help of fellow volunteers, was struggling to find hospital beds. It was clear we had to get help or some of the elderly people weren't going to make it. Immediately, Daniel Zingale and I and a couple of others got on the phone and started calling ambulance companies and hospitals to move the sickest people right away. We stayed a few hours until we were sure progress was being made, and that night we came back twice to check on Paul and his volunteers and the patients who remained. By the next day, we were able to get the National Guard to set up a military field hospital nearby.

Fortunately, failures like the one at Del Mar were rare. The wildfires in San Diego burned for another three weeks, but those first few days set the tone for our disaster response. We evacuated more than a half million people, the largest evacuation in the history of the state. Nine people died and eighty-five, mostly firefighters, were injured. A half million acres burned, and the property damage was widespread, including more than 1,500 homes and hundreds of businesses, at an estimated cost of $2.5 billion. The statistics in the wake of a disaster are always tragic. But we avoided another Katrina, and I was satisfied that our emphasis on preparedness had paid off.

There was a much larger disaster brewing that would disrupt many more households and change many more lives than the wildfires. America was on the brink of the worst economic collapse since the Great Depression. In Sacramento, our first whiff of trouble came even before the fires, as we started developing a budget for 2008–09. In the spring, we saw effects of a serious slowdown in the state housing market, despite more optimistic economic forecasts nationwide and internationally.

The economists who consulted for the state were saying, "We're facing some headwinds in housing, but the economy will pick up again in the next couple of years. The fundamentals are strong, and you can expect continuing healthy growth in 2009–10." Yet only two months later, our monthly revenues from taxes began falling alarmingly short: $300 million below expectations in August, $400 million in November,

$600 million in December. The prediction was that we would have a $6 billion shortfall in our budget by the time the next fiscal year began in July 2008. I thought, "*What is that about?*"

While the beginning of the Great Recession is often dated to the financial market meltdown in September 2008, the crisis came earlier and harder to California than to the rest of the country. This was because of the scale of our housing market and the impact of the mortgage meltdown. California's already legendary property values skyrocketed during the 1980s and 1990s, and homeowners started using the ever-increasing equity in their homes to fund retirement plans, finance college costs, or buy vacation homes. But now people were falling behind on mortgages and losing their homes at double the national rate. By some estimates, more than $630 billion in value was gone, lost, disappeared, and with it went tens of billions of dollars in tax revenue.

Part of the blame belonged to the federal government, which allowed fast and loose subprime mortgage deals. In the past, a 25 percent down payment had been required. What's more, quasi-government entities Fannie Mae and Freddie Mac were encouraged to increase loans to low-income borrowers in order to stimulate the economy and expand the culture of home ownership. This helped fuel the housing bubble. Just as I'd learned from Milton Friedman, when the federal government meddles in markets, the states pay the price. Californians suffered in part because of a federal fuckup, and as governor, I was caught short.

I didn't have much money to work with, but I used every bit of cash I could get my hands on to respond. We desperately tried to accelerate infrastructure bond spending to build highways and rail lines, build new roads, and repair old bridges. We found money for job programs to retrain construction workers losing their jobs. We persuaded big lenders to freeze interest rates for more than one hundred thousand home owners most at risk. We hired more than one thousand people to staff state call centers to advise mortgage holders in trouble and help people with unemployment benefits.

Just before Christmas, US treasury secretary Hank Paulson visited to discuss the subprime mortgage crisis. He and I held a "town hall" meeting in Stockton, and I listened to him talk about "minimizing the spillage" of the housing downturn into the overall economy. At that point, I was still willing to describe the problem as a "hiccup" in my comments to the audience. But I had a bad feeling about it. I flew to Washington not long afterward for a governors' conference where Alphonso Jackson, President Bush's housing secretary, gave a speech about how the American Dream of owning a home was alive and well. I knew Alphonso slightly and cornered him during the break to ask what was really going on. "It doesn't look good," is all he would say. The expression on his face alarmed me. He showed more concern than he'd shown onstage.

I decided that we should throw out the economic forecasts for fiscal year 2008 and budget for zero revenue growth. In our boom-addicted state, zero growth in the Sacramento budget would be much more painful than it sounds. We were facing $10 billion worth of automatic increases in pensions, education, health care, and other programs that were protected by law or federal funding mandates. So if state revenues stayed flat, the only place to come up with the funding was cuts in other programs that weren't so protected. The choices were really tough. If we reduced spending on prisons, we had to let prisoners out and maybe make neighborhoods less safe. If we cut education, what did that say about our concern for our children, the most vulnerable of our citizens? If we cut health, were we saying we really didn't care about old people, or the disabled, or the blind?

In the end I decided to cut all programs 10 percent across the board. It's painful to have just endorsed things that you now have no money for. For example, I had supported a bill to strengthen foster care so kids would not wind up on the street. I believed such bills would ultimately reduce state expenses in health care and law enforcement because some foster care children get in trouble once they're out on their own. But after passionately advocating this plan, I had to withdraw it when the financial crisis hit. I felt terrible, and I looked like a schmuck, backing out on a commitment we wanted to make but could no longer afford.

The final working days of December 2007 were devoted to a procession of interest-group advocates and community leaders whom I'd invited to the cabinet room near my office. I felt I had to look in their eyes and tell them myself what we were up against financially. The consequences of cuts are not just dollars, but people. Talking about fiscal responsibility sounds so cold when you have a representative for AIDS patients or poor children or the elderly sitting across from you. "Democrats are getting screwed, Republicans are getting screwed, we're all getting screwed," I told them. When I asked for their input, to my surprise, they thanked me for leveling with them. Many offered helpful advice.

It galled me that some of this pain could have been avoided. Even before I was elected in 2003 I'd insisted that the boom-and-bust nature of California's dynamic economy created a huge downside risk in the event of a bust—and that California desperately needed a cushion. I'd tried to put in place a rainy-day fund that would have accumulated $10 billion by now, but I'd failed to convince the legislators or the voters to adopt one with rules stringent enough to keep the money locked up until there was a major emergency. Well, it was starting to rain, and I was forced to make unpopular decisions that nobody, least of all me, was happy about.

By spring 2008, state revenues were in a steep plunge. The budget deficit widened by $6 billion between January and April alone. And that was still months before the financial crisis went global.

I endorsed John McCain for president that January, even before the primaries ended. The senator from our neighboring state had helped me for years, particularly in the hard days of 2005, when John spent an entire day riding around Southern California with me on my bus campaigning for my doomed reform initiatives.

At the same time, as the presidential campaigns unfolded, I did not criticize Hillary Clinton or Barack Obama. The truth was that on the biggest issues, particularly the environment and building a new energy economy, I thought any of the candidates would be better than the current administration. I told an audience at Yale: "President McCain, President Obama, or President Clinton will all shift this country into a much higher gear on climate change. All three candidates will be great for the environment. So things will immediately pick up speed after inauguration day."

I skipped the Republican National Convention that August for the first time in twenty years. I was stuck in California wrestling with the budget, but indirectly my absence reflected a much larger concern. The growing conservatism of the party didn't appeal to me or to the vast majority of California voters. This tilt toward the far right became obvious when McCain chose Sarah Palin as his running mate. At the time of her nomination, I praised her as a smart, courageous leader and reformer. But ultimately I decided that I didn't like the polarizing effect she had on the country.

If you visited the Schwarzenegger household that fall, you got a real blast of political diversity. I had a big John McCain poster on the front door. And in the living room stood a life-sized Obama cutout. The kids, for the first time, seemed politically engaged; the drama of the presidential election interested them much more than my job. I'd always teased Maria about coming from a family of political clones, but that was no problem in our household. One of our kids was a Democrat, one was a Republican, and two were independent/decline to state.

When it hit in late 2008, the Great Recession more than wiped out the progress we had made through years of discipline and cuts. Looking ahead to the next budget year, 2009–10, which began in July, we faced a combined gap for the current year and the coming year of $45 billion. In percentage terms and dollar amount, that was the biggest shortfall California had ever faced—in fact, it was the biggest shortfall any state had ever faced. The deficit was so huge that you could close all the schools and all the prisons and fire every state employee and still be in the hole.

Even when I took actions to save money, the budget got worse. With the collapse of the financial markets, we had to kick in billions of dollars to cover shortfalls in the public-employee pension system. I pushed hard for changes that removed the worst pension abuses, but it wasn't enough. Meanwhile, prison spending soared, thanks to sweetheart contracts signed years before by previous governors as well as increases ordered by federal judges who actually took over parts of the system. I'd worked to save more than $1 billion by making controversial changes, including cutting out automatic pay raises for guards and reforming our parole policies. I had to fight the fiercest labor union in the state—the prison guards—at the same time I had to push hard against my strongest supporters in law enforcement, like the sheriffs and police chiefs. We proposed treating more nonviolent felonies as misdemeanors, shipping more prisoners out of state, and creating alternatives to prison for lower-risk offenders, like GPS monitoring and house arrest. We won major battles on those fronts, but prison costs still rose. In fact, we were now spending more on prisons than on universities.

The budget battles became like the movie *Groundhog Day*. No sooner would we finish doing all the negotiating and cutting for one budget than the revenue numbers would come in even lower than forecasted, and we'd have to start again.

Early 2009 was the worst. Budgets are normally negotiated in June (and often into the summer, on and on). But California's financial picture deteriorated so quickly during the global meltdown that I called the legislature into special session and held budget talks over Christmas. It wasn't just the deficit. We had a cash problem. The state was running low on money and in danger of having to issue IOUs to pay bills.

I always wanted to cut fast. Part of this was my philosophy: when you're spending more money than you're taking in, you cut spending. Simple. Part of this was math. In budgeting, the sooner you make cuts, the less deep they have to be. But for the legislature, the scary numbers had the opposite effect: they were paralyzed. The talks dragged into January and then February. I pressed them to act. Outside my office, I put up a display that said "Legislature's Failure to Act" and counted the number of days and the additional debt being racked up for every day they didn't move on the budget.

In mid-February, when we were in late-night negotiations, sometimes I would remind myself that this was nothing compared to being up to my neck in freezing jungle mud in *Predator* or driving a Cadillac down stairs in *The 6th Day*. And I'd think how budget negotiations are no different than grueling five-hour weight-lifting sessions in the gym. The joy in working out is that with each painful rep you get a step closer to achieving your goal.

Still, the weight of the crisis put even my optimism to the test. The hardest moment for me came after a conversation with Warren Buffett. I'd call him periodically to ask what he was seeing out there in the world beyond California, where he had a much better vantage than I did. The Obama administration was adding to the emergency stabilization measures launched under President Bush, and I wanted his advice on when all this would have an effect. He said, "The economy this time is like a deflated ball. It won't bounce back. When you drop it, it just goes splat and lies there until you pick it up and pump some air back in."

This was the big picture, and it didn't look good. He explained what he meant. Not only had the United States taken a beating. So had Germany, England, France, India, and even China. This wasn't just another American recession as usual. He said, "If assets have lost twenty percent of their value, the income from those assets will be less. Before you can really start to grow again, the whole world has to adjust to that fact. Propping up values artificially isn't going to work. Everyone has to get used to living with less and building from a lower base."

"How long will all that take?" I said.

"Years. It could easily be 2013 or 2015."

What, 2013? I was counting in my head: 2009, 2010, 2011, 2012. My term ran out on December 31, 2010, and if Warren was right, I'd be back on my patio reading movie scripts long before any real growth returned.

Maria and Susan both noticed me moping around. What Buffett said meant hard times and diminished expectations for billions of people, not just Californians. I spread the word; Susan heard me describe the conversation many times to members of our staff and key lawmakers. It was a valuable reality check that helped us make hard and unpopular choices in the time that followed.

In fact, the financial crisis made necessary the biggest and most difficult deal of my political career. After months of grueling negotiations, late one night in February 2009, we finally agreed on a budget. It involved $42 billion in budget adjustments and costly compromises on all sides. Democrats had had to make big concessions on things important to them like welfare reform and union furloughs. Now I was asking Republicans to commit heresy—the equivalent of asking a pro-choice Democrat to become pro-life. In running for office I'd promised never to raise taxes except under the most dire circumstances. But I'd also taken an oath to do what was best for the state, and not for me or any ideology. So I gritted my teeth and actually signed a budget that raised income taxes, sales taxes, and even the car tax for the next two years. This was the very same car tax that had cost Gray Davis his governorship and that I cut as my first official act.

I dropped in the opinion polls like Warren Buffett's deflated ball, as I knew I would. And I wasn't the only one who took a beating. I coaxed legislative leaders of both parties to go along with me, and they all paid a price. The Democrats, senate leader Darrell Steinberg and assembly speaker Karen Bass, made themselves wildly unpopular with the liberals by agreeing to support open primary elections as well as even more welfare reforms—removing things like automatic cost of living increases. They enraged the public-employee unions by agreeing both to pension reform and to another condition I insisted on: the creation (at last!) of a strict rainy-day fund that could be used only in a true emergency. The Republican leaders paid an even higher price. The party stripped State Senator Dave Cogdill of his leadership position the night of the vote and forced Mike Villines, the assembly Republican leader, out of his post a few weeks later—all because they had accepted a compromise that included a tax increase.

That February budget compromise wasn't the end of the story. California has so many budget formulas that are baked into the constitution or dictated by previous ballot initiatives that you can do very little fiscally without going back to the voters for approval. To complete the deal, I had to call a special election that May.

This election became a contest of the extremes—left and right—against the middle, those who were inclined to support the deal. Democrats battled Democrats against the spending cuts, and Republicans battled Republicans against the tax increases. The deal itself was messy—nobody really loved it, including me—and that made it politically vulnerable. I was deeply frustrated with party leaders and the press for not making plain the budget history, and the inescapable realities, that had led us to this point. Unions campaigned especially hard against the rainy-day fund because of the limits on spending it would impose.

I was disappointed at the lack of support for elected officials, including me, who had gone out on a limb. Democrats and unions had demanded more revenues for years. Now I, a Republican, had given them tax increases, and what were they doing? They were opposing these tax increases!

My salesmanship failed me. I found that after six years of trying to get citizens to reckon with the state's budget problems, they were not with me. When it looked like we were going to lose, I even tried scare tactics. I put forward an apocalyptic "budget alternative" to show voters how all hell could break loose if they turned us down. The proposal warned of the release of fifty thousand prisoners, the firing of thousands of teachers and other public workers, and the forced sale of state landmarks such as San Quentin State Prison and the Los Angeles Memorial Coliseum.

We still lost. The voters rejected every key measure, and in the next few months, the legislature had to go back to the drawing board and grapple with the 2008–2009 budget yet again. Sadly, my apocalyptic vision wasn't far off. In June I had to announce $24 billion of spending cuts. Thousands of teachers and public servants were laid off. The state had to hand out $2.6 billion of IOUs to pay bills, since we were again about to run out of cash. (We didn't sell the coliseum or San Quentin, though.)

In our household, that summer was a time of terrible loss. Eunice and Sarge went as usual to Hyannis Port for vacation, even though they were now very frail and old: he was ninety-three, and she was eighty-seven. Sarge was in such an advanced stage of Alzheimer's that he no longer recognized anybody, even Eunice. They'd been in Hyannis for only two weeks when on August 9 Eunice was rushed to Cape Cod Hospital; two days later she died.

Eunice had touched so many lives that there was a global outpouring of grief. The Kennedys mourned her at a requiem Mass in the same church where Maria and I had gotten married more than twenty years before. And while Sarge was able to attend the requiem, Teddy couldn't come because he was in the end stage of brain cancer. Two weeks later, in Boston, he too died.

It was hard for me to let Eunice go. She'd been my mentor and cheerleader and the best mother-in-law in the world. But my loss was nothing compared to my wife's. Maria was in more pain than I'd ever seen her experience. We had long conversations about her mom, but she wouldn't talk publicly about her grief until after two months, when she went to speak at her women's conference. She told thousands of attendees who had gathered at the Long Beach Arena, "When people ask, I say I'm fine, I'm holding up well. But the real truth is that I'm not fine. The real truth is that my mother's death has brought me to my knees. She was my hero, my role model, my very best friend. I spoke to her every single day of my life. I tried really hard when I grew up to make her proud of me."

I traveled to Denmark later that fall on a mission that I knew would have made my mother-in-law proud. Eunice and Sarge never hesitated to step across borders or to break bureaucratic barriers when there was important work to do for other people. That was how Eunice built the Special Olympics and how Sarge built the Peace Corps.

The United Nations secretary-general Ban Ki-moon and I had been working on an ambitious response to global warming. Two years earlier, in 2007, he'd been so impressed by California's climate change initiative that he'd invited me to speak at the opening session of the United Nations. When I stepped to the podium that fall, I was almost overwhelmed to realize that I was standing where John F. Kennedy, Nelson Mandela, and Mikhail Gorbachev had all addressed the UN before me. The occasion gave California a world stage—and an opportunity to contribute to a crucial international conversation.

Now, two years later, the United Nations Climate Change Conference in Copenhagen was meant to be the most important meeting on global warming since the completion of the Kyoto Protocol in 1997. After years of environmental conferences and programs and debates, leaders from more than 110 nations were coming to Copenhagen to hammer out an action plan. But Secretary-General Ban was concerned that the prospects for agreement between industrialized nations and developing ones were poor. The United States had failed to ratify the Kyoto accords, while China and India had made it plain that they didn't want Europe or America dictating their climate policies. The problems went on and on.

Since his visit to San Francisco in 2007, Ban had watched with great interest as California built broader and broader coalitions with other US states and "subnational" players abroad. The Western Climate Initiative, our regional cap-and-trade program for carbon emissions, had expanded to include seven US states and five Canadian provinces. And our second Governors' Global Climate Summit in late 2009 drew governors and provincial leaders from six continents in spite of the world recession.

This subnational climate change movement had built bridges to the developing world. Washington and Beijing on a national level were still in a stalemate over climate issues, but they were willing for us to form region-to-region connections. California had already made agreements with the city of Shanghai and several of China's most industrialized provinces aimed at reducing greenhouse gases and cooperating on projects in solar and wind power and electric buses and high-speed rail.

As news got around about these developments, people in the environmental community began to sense a giant opportunity here. Ban Ki-moon was receptive when I pitched California's approach as plan B for Copenhagen, to supplement the main UN effort to address climate change. "Even if the negotiations hit an impasse," I argued, "the conference doesn't have to look like a failure. You can say that although the national governments are stuck, we have great successes over here on the subnational front, and we're going to continue the fight."

All great movements in history—civil rights, women's suffrage, the campaign against apartheid, worker safety—start out on a grassroots level, not in places like Washington or Paris or Moscow or Beijing. That was my inspiration in trying to cope with climate change. For instance, when we cut our pollution by 70 percent at the Port of Long Beach, the second-busiest seaport in America, Washington didn't tell us to do it. We did it ourselves. We passed laws that forbid trucks from idling, and gave truckers tax incentives to switch over to electric engines and clean diesel and hybrids. In the same way, California built the Hydrogen Highway (a chain of refueling stations for hydrogen-powered vehicles), launched the Million Solar Roofs program, and committed to cut its greenhouse gas emissions radically, all without waiting for Washington. So if we could create a groundswell of such projects around the world, getting people involved, getting companies involved, getting cities involved, getting states involved, national governments could then respond.

That was the idea I took to the national leaders assembled in Copenhagen. We held a press conference after the speech, but at a separate hotel from the conference, to dramatize the message: "While the national governments are meeting over there, we are here. You should pay close attention to us as well as to them. Not to us *instead* of them, because we are supporting players and they are the stars. But without the supporting players, they are not going to get it done."

As the pessimists had predicted, no binding agreements were reached at the Copenhagen summit. President Obama dominated the headlines, with his dramatic personal intervention and his effort to hammer out an eleventh-hour accord with China, India, South Africa, and Brazil. Our initiative was not enough to change the course of events, but it did add a crucial new dimension to the debate. Ban Ki-moon and I became good friends, and in the following year, we teamed up to seek new ways for subnational governments to take climate change policy forward.

President Obama and I became friends too. Shortly after his 2008 election night victory, I congratulated him in a speech before a Republican audience, saying that I hoped he would be a successful president because Californians would benefit from effective national leadership. Knowing that I wanted to cooperate with him, President Obama invited me to the White House, and we developed a strong working relationship. He knew about my bipartisan record and the goals we shared on the environment, immigration, health care reform, and infrastructure, and that I could be trusted not to take potshots at him once I left his side. He greeted me with a hug. Our conversations were relaxed and full of humor, even though we were both facing dreadful economic challenges: a recession, high unemployment rates, huge deficits.

In the public opinion polls, my approval rating was down to 28 percent, reflecting the widespread unhappiness and misery about the economy. At least it wasn't as low as the legislature's approval rating of 17 percent. I had a choice. I could go along to get along and try to improve my poll numbers, or I could continue fighting hard to fix what was broken in Sacramento and watch my approval ratings kiss the floor. I chose to fight. Unlike regular politicians, I had nothing to lose. I had only a year left in my governorship, and I was barred by term-limit laws and the Constitution from seeking another term or the presidency.

Six years of ups and downs forged me as a governor the way Conan was forged by pit fighting and the Wheel of Pain. I now understood politics and government, and in spite of all the struggles and the recession and low approval ratings, I had more forward momentum than ever before. I felt more like a hungry eagle rather than a lame duck.

In 2010 I managed to achieve some important goals. I persuaded the legislature to once again adopt a sweeping budget reform measure establishing spending limits and a rainy-day fund. This was my final chance to fix a broken budget system. The measures passed in 2004 were good for starters but weren't big enough to fix the system. The most carefully crafted, bipartisan measure passed by the legislature in 2009 got killed by the voters because it was tied to the "grand compromise" that included temporary tax increases. This time—the last, best chance we had to stop the crazy deficit spending once and for all in Sacramento—I convinced a worn-down legislature to put the measure back on the ballot (without the hated tax increases), even though it wouldn't be voted on until after I left office. I vowed to raise the money to get it passed by the voters come hell or high water. I was disappointed when I learned that my successor, Governor Jerry Brown, signed a bill to remove those reforms from the 2012 ballot at the behest of Democrats and labor unions. The polls had shown it headed for a landslide victory this time, with 84 percent planning to vote yes, according to the reform group the Think Long Committee for California. In the end, politics as usual produced a tax increase with no real safeguards to restrict further spending. And now the budget reform initiative will not be voted on until 2014.

In the fall, I signed a historic pension reform that rolled back some of the worst excesses threatening to bankrupt the state. By cutting a lot of red tape, we issued permits for so many solar power plants in California—more than 5,000 megawatts in 2009 alone (one hundred times all the solar permitted in the United States a year earlier)—that California was being called the Saudi Arabia of Solar. California is now on track to build not just the most but also the largest solar projects in the world. I clinched agreement with the federal government and the state of Oregon to remove dams on and near the Klamath River, the largest dam removal and river restoration in US history. We adopted the nation's first Green Building Standards requiring all new buildings in California to meet strict energy efficiency and sustainable development standards.

In 2010 I also teamed up with the NAACP and President Obama's education secretary, Arne Duncan, to win a huge victory on education reform, giving parents the right to move their children out of failing schools. The teachers' unions and school administrators fought vehemently against these reforms, but the bipartisan force of a Republican governor teaming up with a Democratic president and the premier civil rights group in the country was too much even for the most powerful labor union in the state.

But the real measure of success in 2010 came from the voters. I was more aware than ever that the key to real, permanent reform is being in sync with the hearts and minds of the people. In June, despite my low approval ratings, the voters passed the second piece of our political reform package: the open primary. The first piece, a landmark reform that broke a 200-year-old American tradition of rigging the boundaries of election districts, had passed in 2008. Combined with that reform, the open primary system would once and for all end the dominance of the far left and the far right special interests in our election system. The top two vote getters in each primary would square off in the general election regardless of political party. Independents and moderates of either party would be able to vote for any candidate they chose, ending the stranglehold that extremists had over both parties in a closed primary system. It passed with 54 percent of the vote.

The final test came in November. We had rattled so many cages on the left and the right with our reforms that we faced three ballot measures designed to repeal our victories. First was an effort to repeal the redistricting measure passed in 2008. Both parties funded the campaign to repeal the measure and return the districts safely into the hands of incumbents. They were also trying to defeat a new measure to expand fair districts to congressional races. Democratic House Speaker Nancy Pelosi made her California members pony up millions of dollars to defeat this measure and repeal ours. The fight was on.

The second was a referendum placed on the ballot by labor unions to punish business for supporting my spending cuts and political reforms. The referendum would have repealed the business tax reforms we fought so hard to win in 2009 as part of the compromise. Unfortunately, this was a typical move: get historic bipartisan agreement on tax increases and tax reforms that lower costs for business, and then the labor unions try to repeal the business reforms after the tax increases are in place.

The third measure was the centerpiece. Proposition 23 was put on the ballot and funded mainly by Texas oil companies to repeal our historic global warming act. Their campaign preyed upon peoples' fears about the economy and claimed that our climate change efforts would push unemployment even higher. They plastered the state with TV ads that said. "Jobs First—Yes on 23." We answered with a stunningly powerful campaign cochaired by George Shultz, Jim Cameron, and venture fund leader Tom Steyer which raised $25 million. One of our most effective ads showed a kid reaching for an inhaler and struggling to catch his breath. We didn't just beat Proposition 23. We pulverized it by 20 points. We terminated any hope the Texas oil industry had of rolling back California's leadership on climate change.

In fact, the voters backed every one of our initiatives that year, over the passionate opposition of political parties, labor unions, and Texas oil companies. Historic political reform, business tax reform, the strongest possible endorsement of our climate change efforts: it felt good to be in the powerful center again, with the people standing behind us.

We were turning a corner. All across California, you could see a new energy economy taking hold. A decade that had begun with blackouts and despair ended with the state approving more renewable energy projects than the entire United States combined and leading with resolve. A state in love with freeways and automobiles was now leading the nation in the development of alternative fuels. A state mired in gridlock was now blowing up the partisan boxes that shielded political parties from the voters they are supposed to represent.

My schedule got busier as my term neared the end. On the final leg of a trade mission to Asia in September, I'm proud to say I found a way to cram thirty-six hours of work into a single day. On Wednesday, September 15, I started at eight in the morning in Seoul by meeting the American Chamber of Commerce at the Grand Hilton. Then I spent time with Special Olympics athletes, met the chairmen of Korean Air and Hyundai Motor, chatted up the mayor of Seoul, signed a business cooperation agreement between Korea and California, rode a high-speed train, visited a department store, and rallied the US troops based in Korea. When I learned about a massive gas-pipeline explosion in San Bruno, I cut my schedule short and flew directly to the Bay Area instead of going home, crossing the international date line so that it was again Wednesday afternoon when I arrived. In San Bruno, I visited the scene of the explosion, was briefed by emergency officials and talked with victims who were still in shock. I spoke to families who lost their homes, their loved ones, their community. Of all the things I've done in my life, nothing is seared in my memory more than looking into the eyes of a person who has just lost everything he loved in the world.

In December, after the voters chose Jerry Brown to succeed me and plans for the transfer of power were well under way, a reporter asked why I didn't quietly coast out the door like most governors would after two hectic terms. I told him I believe in sprinting through to the finish line. "There's a lot of work that still can be done," I said. "So why would I stop in November or December? It wouldn't make any sense."

The state was still in the grip of the deepest national financial crisis in modern history, and regardless of all our efforts, the next governor would be staring down the barrel of a continued budget deficit, probably for the next two years. I could have just ignored the numbers through the fall, leaving the task to Jerry Brown. Democratic legislative leaders certainly wanted me to do that; they were sick and tired of me pushing them for more spending cuts. But it would have been irresponsible to let months go by without action. So I called yet another special session of the legislature. This time I knew in advance that the legislature would fail to act. They were out of gas, and they prayed that the new Democratic governor would come in on a white horse and raise taxes, saving them from having to make more cuts. There was no way in hell they were going to make more cuts no matter how hard I pushed them. The media wrote the obvious: "He started with budget problems, and he ended with budget problems."

Yes, I did. But we made a hell of a lot of progress, and we made a lot of history: workers' comp reforms, parole reforms, pension reforms, education reforms, welfare reforms, and budget reforms not once, not twice, but four times. (And I will be there campaigning in 2014 to make sure the budget reforms pass the voters.) We made our state an international leader in climate change and renewable energy; a national leader in health care reform and the fight against obesity; we launched the biggest infrastructure investment effort in generations; and tackled water, the thorniest issue in California politics. We put in place the most significant political reforms since Hiram Johnson was governor—and in June 2012, the first election in which California's new open primary system was in effect, the upsurge in the number of moderate, pragmatic candidates drew national attention. And we accomplished all this while dealing with the greatest economic disaster since the Great Depression.

I do not deny that being governor was more complex and challenging than I had imagined. One incident, in particular, stands out for the gap it shows between what people think you can do for them and the reality you face as governor. During the terrible drought of 2009, I went to talk to the farmers in Mendota in the Central Valley. I was with Alan

Autry, the mayor of Fresno and a onetime pro football quarterback who did more than anyone to call my attention to the farmers. Mendota was one of the communities that had been hardest hit by the double wave of the economic crisis and devastating drought. Agricultural production was at a standstill, the fields had turned to dust, and there was 42 percent unemployment. We needed more water from the Sacramento–San Joaquin Delta. But environmentalists argued that diverting the water would threaten a little fish called the delta smelt, and a federal judge ordered the water kept off. The federal government thought that the delta smelt needed to be protected more than the farmers.

The farmers were demonstrating with signs that said "Turn On the Pumps" and showed me their dusty fields. They were saying things to the media like, "I'll be damned if I'll let a little fish take all my water away. We will fight the government to the end."

I told them that we were negotiating with Secretary of the Interior Ken Salazar. "Those things take time and patience," I said.

A farmer stood up and asked, "How can you say that? Why can't you go there and turn the valve? You go there and turn it on."

I realized people had the vision that I'd push aside the federal judge, push aside whoever was guarding the pumping station, go up to this huge chained valve, break the chain, and turn the wheel, releasing a torrent of water into the land, turning it a lush green and returning the farmers to work. But I couldn't do that in real life! That's the problem of presenting yourself as the Governator. You can do miracles but not the kind that require wearing a cape and being able to fly. Instead, it took months of pushing and cajoling the Department of the Interior and some dedicated negotiations with the Obama administration to get the water turned on.

As governor, you're neither a solitary champion nor a star. You have to work with the legislature, the courts, the bureaucracy, and the federal government, not to mention with the voters themselves.

Politics can be a lot like crowd surfing in a mosh pit. All these hands reach out and carry you along, and sometimes you end up where you want to go, and sometimes you don't. But compared to making a movie, when you do accomplish something in government, the satisfaction is so much larger and long lasting. In a movie, you are entertaining people for a few hours in a dark theater. In government, you are affecting entire lives; generations, even.

It was always the most extraordinary feeling when we would reach an agreement, and some measure would pass the legislature or win ballot approval. I would pull out a cigar and light it up, pull out my list of things I wanted to accomplish, and take a pen and mark that item off. Although I certainly wish I had been able to cross more items off the list, I feel good about what we did get done.

Even Maria agreed that the challenge had been worth it. Speaking at a wellness conference in 2010, she said, "I'd like to admit today that I was wrong to try to talk Arnold out of running for governor seven years ago, and he was right not to listen to me. The fact is, I didn't want Arnold to run because I myself didn't like growing up in a political family. I was afraid something bad would happen. I was afraid of the unknown. It turns out Arnold was right to follow his dream and run. He's loved this governor's job more than anything he's ever done in his life. It ended up being a perfect match for his intellect, his love of people, his passion for public policy, and his competitive streak. I've never seen him happier or more fulfilled. Even with all the ups and downs of the last seven years, he says if he had to do it over again, he would in a heartbeat, and I believe him. I never thought I'd say this, but I thank him for not listening to me."

I was luckier than I deserved to have such a wife.

CHAPTER 29

The Secret

DURING MY HECTIC LAST few months as governor, Maria and I went to see a marriage counselor. Maria wanted to talk about the end of my term of office, and we focused on issues that a lot of couples face in middle age—like the fact that our kids were starting to go out on their own. Katherine was already twenty-one, a junior at USC, and Christina was a sophomore at Georgetown University. In a few years Patrick and Christopher would also be gone. What would our lives be like?

But when Maria made the appointment for the very morning after I left office and became a private citizen again (it was a Tuesday), I sensed that this time was different. This time she had something very specific in mind.

The marriage counselor's office was dimly lit, with neutral colors and minimalist décor—not the kind of room I'd want to hang out in. It had a sofa, a coffee table, and the therapist's chair. The minute we sat down, the therapist turned to me and said, "Maria wanted to come here today to ask about a child—whether you've fathered a child with your housekeeper Mildred. That's why she wanted to meet. So let's talk about it."

In the initial instant, when time seemed to stand still, I said to myself, "Well, Arnold, you wanted to tell her. Surprise! This is it. Here's your moment. Maybe it's the only way you'd ever have the nerve."

I told the therapist, "It's true." Then I turned to Maria. "It's my child," I said. "It happened fourteen years ago. I didn't know about him at first, but I've known it now for several years." I told her how sorry I felt about it, how wrong it was, that it was my fault. I just unloaded everything.

It was one of those stupid things that I promised myself never to do. My whole life I never had anything going with anyone who worked for me. This happened in 1996 when Maria and the kids were away on holiday and I was in town finishing *Batman and Robin.* Mildred had been working in our household for five years, and all of sudden we were alone in the guest house. When Mildred gave birth the following August, she named the baby Joseph and listed her husband as the father. That is what I wanted to believe and what I did believe for years.

Joseph came to our house and played with our kids many times. But the resemblance hit me only when he was school-age, when I was governor and Mildred was showing her latest photos of him and her other kids. The resemblance was so strong that I realized there was little doubt that he was my son. While Mildred and I barely discussed it, from then on I paid for his schooling and helped financially with him and her other kids. Her husband had left a few years after Joseph was born, but her boyfriend Alex had stepped in as their dad.

Maria had asked me many years before if Joseph was my child. At the time I didn't know that I was his father, and I'd denied it. My impression now was that she and Mildred, who by this time had worked in our home for almost twenty years, had talked it out. In any case, very little of what I had to say seemed to be news to Maria. The issue was out on the table, and she wanted answers.

"Why didn't you tell me earlier?" she asked.

"Three reasons," I said. "One is that I didn't know how to tell you. I was so embarrassed and didn't want to hurt your feelings and didn't want us to blow up. Two is that I didn't know how to tell you and still keep it private, because you share everything with your family and then too many people would know.

"Three is that secrecy is just part of me. I keep things to myself no matter what. I'm not a person who was brought up to talk." I said this for the benefit of the therapist, who didn't know me well.

I could have come up with ten more reasons, and they all would have sounded just as lame. The fact was that I'd damaged the lives of everybody involved and I should have told Maria long ago. But instead of doing the right thing, I'd just put the truth in a mental compartment and locked it up where I didn't deal with it every day.

Normally I try to defend myself. But now there was none of that. I tried to be as cooperative as possible. I explained that it was my screw-up, that she should not feel it had anything to do with her. "I fucked up. You're the perfect wife. It's not because anything is wrong, or you left home for a week, or any of that. Forget all that. You look fantastic, you're sexy, I'm turned on by you today as much as I was on the first date."

Maria made up her mind that we needed to separate. I couldn't blame her. Not only had I deceived her about the child, but also Mildred had stayed working at our house all these years. It was Maria's choice to move out of our house. We agreed to work out an arrangement that wouldn't totally disrupt the kids. Even though our future as husband and wife was uncertain, we both felt strongly that we were still parents and we would continue to make all the decisions about our family together.

The crisis in our marriage made a difficult year for Maria even worse. She was still grieving for her mother, who had died fifteen months before. And she and her brothers had made the difficult decision to move Sarge, who was now ninety-five, to a memory-care facility.

We'd only begun to sort out our separation and to talk about it to the kids when Sarge died. It was a terrible loss. Sarge was the last of that generation of great public figures from the Shriver and Kennedy clan. The requiem, in Washington on January 22, 2011, was almost fifty years to the day after Sarge had founded the Peace Corps. Joe Biden, First Lady Michelle Obama, Bill Clinton, and many other leaders came to the Mass and Maria honored her dad with an eloquent and moving remembrance, during which she talked about how Sarge had taught her brothers to respect women. That may have been partly directed at me, but I'd heard Maria praise her father in similar words many times.

After the funeral, Maria flew back to LA with me and the kids, except for Christina, who stayed at Georgetown. We kept our separation very quiet. In April she moved to a condo attached to a hotel near our house, where there was plenty of room for the kids to stay as they shuttled back and forth between her place and our house.

I asked myself what had motivated me to be unfaithful, and how I could have failed to tell Maria about Joseph for so many years. A lot of people, no matter how successful or unsuccessful they are in life, make stupid choices involving sex. You feel you'll get away with ignoring the rules, but in reality your actions can have lasting consequences. Probably my background, and having left home at an early age, also had an effect. It hardened me emotionally and shaped my behavior so that I was less careful about intimate things.

As I told the therapist, secrecy is part of me. Much as I love and seek company, part of me feels that I am going to ride out life's big waves by myself. At key moments in my life I've played it close to the vest—like when I left my decision to run for governor until the afternoon I walked onstage with Jay Leno. I've used secrecy—and denial—to cope with difficult challenges, like when I wanted to keep my heart surgery to myself and pretend it was just a kind of vacation. Here I was using secrecy to avoid confessing something that I knew would hurt Maria, even though the cover-up ultimately made the problem worse. At the time I found out for sure that Joseph was my son, I didn't want the situation to affect my ability to govern effectively. I decided to keep it secret, not only from Maria but also from my closest friends and advisors. Politically, I didn't feel it was anybody's business because I hadn't campaigned on family values. I blocked out the fact that as a husband and father, as a man with a family and a wife, I was letting people down. I let them all down. Joseph too—I wasn't there for him as the father a boy needs. I had wanted Mildred to continue working in our home because I thought I could control the situation better that way, but that was wrong, too.

The world didn't find out Maria and I had separated until May, when the *Los Angeles Times* called asking questions. We responded with a statement that we had "amicably separated" and that we were working on the future of our relationship. Predictably, the news set off a media frenzy, amplified by the fact that we hadn't explained why.

The therapist thought we should include the truth, "so that it's clear who is the victim and who is the wrongdoer." I was opposed, on the grounds that I wasn't a public official anymore and wasn't obliged to share my private life with anybody. Yet I also had to admit to myself, "I've let the public know everything else about me, so why hide the negative side?" But if I was going to talk about bad behavior, I wanted to do it on my own timetable.

It was silly to think I would have any choice. People talked, people wrote e-mails, and within a few days, the Movie Channel started asking questions about a son born out of wedlock. Then the *LA Times* picked up on the story.

The day before it published the news, a reporter called to let us know and to ask for a comment. I gave a response that said, in essence, "I understand and deserve the feelings of anger and disappointment among my friends and family. There are no excuses and I take full responsibility for the hurt I have caused. I have apologized to Maria, my children and my family. I am truly sorry. I ask that the media respect my wife and children through this extremely difficult time. While I deserve your questions and criticism, my family does not." I wanted to protect my family's privacy, which remains a priority of mine today.

And then, knowing that the story would break the next morning, I had to tell my kids. I told Katherine and Christina over the phone, because they were in Chicago with Maria for Oprah Winfrey's farewell show. Patrick and Christopher were home with me, so I asked them to sit down and told them face to face. In each conversation I explained that I'd made a mistake. I said, "I am sorry about it. This happened with Mildred fourteen years ago and she got pregnant and now there's a child by the name of Joseph. It doesn't change my love for you and I hope it doesn't change your love for me. But that is what happened. I'm terribly sorry about it. Your mother is very upset and disappointed. I'll work very hard to bring everyone together again. This is going to be a challenging time, and I hope it won't be too awful with the response of other kids at school, or the parents when you go to your friends' houses, or when you turn on TV or pick up the paper."

I should have added "or go on the internet," because one of the first things that Katherine and Patrick each did was tweet how they felt. Patrick quoted from the rock song "Where'd You Go": "some days you feel like shit, some days you want to quit and just be normal for a bit," and added, "yet I love my family till death do us part." Katherine wrote, "This is definitely not easy but I appreciate your love and support as I begin to heal and move forward in life. I will always love my family!"

It took weeks for them to begin to trust the fact that our family hadn't totally blown up. Our kids saw Maria and me communicating almost daily. They saw us go out for lunch or dinner. Patrick and Christopher developed a certain rhythm going back and forth between the house and the condo. All of this helped restore a little bit of stability.

I regretted also the impact on Mildred and Joseph. They weren't used to living in the public eye, and all of a sudden they found themselves besieged by publicity-hungry lawyers and by reporters from gossip shows and tabloids. I stayed in touch with Mildred and helped arrange a more private place for them to stay. Mildred was never adversarial and handled the situation honestly, and when she left our household she told the media we'd been fair with her.

Although Maria and I remain separated as of this writing, I still try to treat everyone as if we are together. Maria has a right to be bitterly disappointed and never look at me the same way again. The public nature of our separation makes it doubly hard for us to work through it. The divorce is going forward, but I still have the hope that Maria and I can come back together as husband and wife and as a family with our children. You can call this denial, but it's the way my mind works. I'm still in love with Maria. And I am an optimist. All my life I have focused on the positives. I am optimistic that we will come together again.

During this past year, Maria has sometimes asked, "How can you go forward with your life when I feel like everything has fallen apart? How come you don't feel lost?" Of course she already knows the answer because she understands me better than anybody else. I have to keep moving forward. And she has kept moving forward too, becoming more and more involved in causes associated with her parents. She has traveled all over the country promoting the fight against Alzheimer's, and is very active on the Special Olympics board, helping prepare for the 2015 International Special Olympics Games in Los Angeles.

I was glad to have a busy schedule after we separated because otherwise I *would* have felt lost. I kept working and stayed on the move. By the summer, I'd appeared at a series of post-governorship speaking engagements across the northern United States and Canada. I went to the Xingu River in Brazil with Jim Cameron; to London for Mikhail Gorbachev's eightieth birthday party; to Washington, DC, for a summit on immigration; and to Cannes to receive the Legion d'Honneur medal and promote new projects. Yet while I was as busy as ever, none of it felt the way it should. What had made my career fun for more than thirty years was sharing it with Maria. We'd done everything together and now my life felt out of kilter. There was no one to come home to.

When the scandal broke in the spring of 2011, I was scheduled to give the keynote speech at an international energy forum in Vienna organized in conjunction with the United Nations Development Program. I worried that the media frenzy would hamper my effectiveness as an environmental champion, and half expected the invitation to be withdrawn. But the organizers in Vienna wanted to proceed. "This is a personal matter," they said. "We don't think it will affect the great example you set in environmental policy. The million solar roofs are not going to be dismantled . . ." In that speech, I promised that I would make it my mission to convince the world that a green global economy is desirable, necessary, and within reach.

When I left Sacramento, I knew I would want to pick up my entertainment career. I had taken no salary during my seven years as governor and it was time to get back to paid work. But the media onslaught of April and May made it temporarily impossible. To my embarrassment and regret, painful consequences of the scandal rippled out beyond my family to many of the people I worked with.

I announced that I was suspending my career to work on personal matters. We postponed *The Governator,* an animated-cartoon and comic-book series I'd been collaborating on with Stan Lee, the legendary creator of Spiderman. Another project that got derailed was *Cry Macho,* a movie I'd looked forward to making the entire time I was governor. Al Ruddy, the producer of *The Godfather* and *Million Dollar Baby*, had been holding this movie for me for years. But after the scandal broke, the material was just too close to home—the plot revolves around a horse-trainer's friendship with a streetwise twelve-year-old Latino kid. I called Al and said, "Maybe somebody else can star, I don't mind, or you can hold it for me a little longer."

He'd already talked to the investors. "They'll make any other movie with you. But not this one," he said.

Just as after my heart surgery, Hollywood initially pulled back. The phone stopped ringing. But by summer my nephew Patrick Knapp, who serves as my entertainment lawyer, reported that studios and producers had begun calling again. "Is Arnold's career still on hold?" they were asking. "We don't have to talk to Arnold directly, because we understand if he's still going through this family crisis, but can we talk to you at least? We have this great film we want to do with him . . ."

By autumn I was back to shooting action movies—*The Expendables 2* in Bulgaria with Sylvester Stallone, *The Last Stand* in New Mexico with director Jee-Woon Kim, and *The Tomb,* another film with Stallone, near New Orleans. I'd wondered what being in front of the cameras again would feel like. When I was governor and I would visit a movie set, I would think, "Boy, am I glad that I am not hanging upside down in a harness having to do a fight scene." My friends would ask,

"Don't you miss this?" And I would say, "Not at all. I'm so glad I'm in a suit and tie and I'm about to have a meeting about education and digital textbooks and then give a speech about keeping crime down." But the brain always surprises. You start reading scripts and visualizing the scene and how to direct it, how to choreograph the stunt, and then you get into it and then you look forward to doing it. The mind unwinds from the political stuff and shifts to the new challenges.

Sly was shooting *The Expendables 2* in Bulgaria, and when I arrived on location in September 2011, it was my first time back as an actor, except for cameos in *The Kid and I* and *The Expendables* while I was governor. I was eight years out of practice with shoot-outs and stunts. The other veteran action heroes in the cast—Sly, Bruce Willis, Dolph Lundgren, Jean-Claude Van Damme and Chuck Norris—were really nice to me and kind of protective. Normally an action star keeps to himself on the set, practicing his martial arts and looking studly. But these guys really went out of their way. Someone would come over and say, "The safety of that gun is here . . . This is how you load the shells." I felt like I was being welcomed back into the craft of action and acting.

The stunts were hard. The work is very physical and it takes conditioning because you have to do each stunt over and over: slamming into some desk, running around with weapons, dropping to the floor, staying low because you're being shot at. You realize there's a difference between being thirty-five and almost sixty-five. I was glad that *The Expendables 2* is an ensemble movie, where I was one of eight or ten stars. I was only on the set for four days, and never felt that the pressure to carry the movie was on me.

I went from Bulgaria to the American Southwest to shoot *The Last Stand.* With that movie, a lot of the pressure did fall on me. In fact, the script had been written for me. I play an LAPD drug cop who is near retirement. After my partner gets crippled in a bungled raid, I decide I can't handle the job anymore. So I go back to my hometown on the Arizona-Mexico border and become sheriff. Then suddenly a major drug gang is headed my way after escaping the FBI. They're hardened criminals and ex-military warriors, I'm supposed to stop them from crossing into Mexico, and I have only three inexperienced deputies. We're the last stand. It's a great, great role. The sheriff knows if he succeeds, it will mean everything to the town. His reputation is on the line. Is he really over the hill or can he do it?

For my next movie, *The Tomb*, I shift from being the law to being an outlaw. I play Emil Rottmayer, a security expert who gets locked up and put under interrogation for plotting cyberterrorism. The prison is a nightmarish, privately owned super-high-tech dungeon in an unknown location, where Western governments remand people who pose a threat to the establishment. Rottmayer is tortured because he won't betray his boss, the rebel mastermind, who is still at large. Into this scene comes Sylvester Stallone as the prison world's top "structural security" expert, Ray Breslin. His specialty is going undercover into ultramax prisons and exposing their weaknesses by breaking out. Only this time, he's been betrayed by a business partner who stands to make a fortune if the Tomb is escape-proof and Sly never succeeds in escaping. After some confrontations Sly and I team up, and the action takes off from there. To get the hardcore huge industrial prison look, our director, Swedish filmmaker Mikael Håfström, is shooting most of *The Tomb* in a former NASA plant in Louisiana. The common area for the prisoners, called Babylon, is a cavernous 200-foot-tall chamber where until recently rocket-makers assembled the external fuel tank for the space shuttle. Today the space is empty and intimidating, the perfect backdrop for a movie that pits the heroes against the evils of the global establishment.

Back in real life, I'm taking on a big, fresh challenge. This summer we announced a major new institute at the University of Southern California, the USC Schwarzenegger Institute for State and Global Policy. So even though I left office, I will continue to promote the policies that were closest to my heart: political reform, climate change and the environment, education reform, economic reform, and health care and stem cell research.

Just as presidential libraries continue the legacies of former presidents with research and scholarship, our institute will seek to add to the public discourse and inspire change. We will work with some of the best minds in public policy to produce studies and offer recommendations on a world stage.

USC is a perfect fit: it prides itself on being neither conservative nor liberal but open minded. It operates by promoting discussion to draw the best ideas from the brightest minds across the political spectrum. We'll host summits and workshops and sponsor research in areas where I focused as governor and where California has made historic progress.

I will also have the great honor of being appointed the first Governor Downey Professor of State and Global Policy, a chair named after California's first immigrant governor, USC cofounder John G. Downey. Professorship will enable me to travel the world and give lectures representing USC and the Schwarzenegger Institute.

My term as governor had to end, but with the institute, I will extend and expand on the work I started in office. I find this compelling because I'm never happy until I can share what I've learned and experienced. I think back to Sarge and Eunice, and the way that they always encouraged me to focus on causes bigger than myself. Sarge said it best in a great speech he gave at Yale in 1994. He told the graduating class, "It's not what you get out of life that counts. Break your mirrors! In our society that is so self-absorbed, begin to look less at yourself and more at each other. You'll get more satisfaction from having improved your neighborhood, your town, your state, your country, and your fellow human beings than you'll ever get from your muscles, your figure, your automobile, your house, or your credit rating. You'll get more from being a peacemaker than a warrior." I think about those words all the time. The great leaders always talk about things that are much bigger than themselves. They say working for a cause that will outlive us is what brings meaning and joy. The more I'm able to accomplish in the world, the more I agree.

CHAPTER 30

Arnold's Rules

I ALWAYS WANTED TO be an inspiration for people, but I never set out to be a role model in everything. How could I be when I have so many contradictions and crosscurrents in my life? I'm a European who became an American leader; a Republican who loves Democrats; a businessman who makes his living as an action hero; a tremendously disciplined superachiever who hasn't always been disciplined enough; a fitness expert who loves cigars; an environmentalist who loves Hummers; a fun-loving guy with kid-like enthusiasm who is most famous for terminating people. How would anybody know what to imitate?

People often assume I should be a role model all the same. When I ride my bicycle around Santa Monica without a helmet, there's always someone who complains, "What kind of an example is that?" It isn't meant to be an example!

Usually the objection to my cigars is that I've been on a fitness crusade for decades. But I remember once in Sacramento a reporter said, "We zoomed in with the camera on the label of your cigar. It said Cohiba. That's a Cuban cigar. You're the governor. How can you flout the law?"

"I smoke it because it's a great cigar," I said.

The same with movie violence. I kill people onscreen because, contrary to the critics, I don't believe that violence on-screen creates violence on the street or in the home. Otherwise there would have been no murders before movies were invented, and the Bible is full of them.

I do want to set an example, of course. I want to inspire you to work out, keep yourself fit, lay off junk food, create a vision and use your will to accomplish it. I want you to throw away the mirror like Sargent Shriver said, get involved in public service and give back. I want you to protect the environment rather than mess it up. If you're an immigrant, I want you to embrace America. In these ways, I'm very happy to take the torch and be a role model for others because I've always had great role models myself—Reg Park, Muhammad Ali, Sargent Shriver, Milton Berle, Nelson Mandela, and Milton Friedman. But it's never been my goal to set an example in everything I do.

Sometimes I prefer being way out there, shocking people. Rebelliousness is part of what drove me from Austria. I didn't want to be like everyone else. I thought of myself as special and unique and not the average Hans or Franz.

Being outrageous is a way to succeed. Bodybuilding was a nowhere sport when I was Mr. Olympia. We were struggling to get media coverage. So I started telling reporters that pumping up your muscles was better than coming. It was a crazy statement but it made news. People heard that and thought, "If working out is better than sex, I'm going to try it!"

No one could put me in a mold. When I was governor and people would say, "This is what other governors do" or "You can't do that if you're a Republican" or "No one smokes in the capitol, it's not politically correct," I'd take that as a signal to go the other way. If you conform, then people complain you're acting like a politician. The way we ran the governor's office was unique. How I dressed, how I talked—I always looked for my own way of doing it. People elected me to solve problems and create a vision for our state, yes, but also they wanted things to feel different. They wanted a governor *and* a Governator. Of course, being different was right up my alley. I didn't have the same body as everyone else or drive the same car as everyone else.

I've never figured this all out. I'm sure a shrink would have a good time with it. Definitely Sigmund Freud, my fellow Austrian, would have a good time talking about the cigars—he smoked stogies too. But life is richer when we embrace the multitudes we all contain, even if we aren't consistent and what we do doesn't always make sense, even to us.

When I talk to graduating classes, I always tell a brief version of the story of my life and try to offer lessons everybody can use: have a vision, trust yourself, break some rules, ignore the naysayers, don't be afraid to fail. Woven through the stories in this memoir are some of the principles of success that have worked for me:

- ***Turn your liabilities into assets.*** When I wanted to star in movies, the Hollywood agents I talked to told me to forget it—my body and my name and my accent were all too weird. Instead, I worked hard on my accent and my acting, as hard as I'd worked at bodybuilding, to transform myself into a leading man. With *Conan* and *The Terminator*, I broke through: the things that the agents said would be a detriment and make it impossible for me to get a job, all of a sudden made me an action hero. Or as John Milius said when he directed *Conan the Barbarian,* "If we didn't have Schwarzenegger, we would have to build one."
- ***When someone tells you no, you should hear yes.*** Impossible was a word I loved to ignore when I was governor. They said it would be impossible to convince Californians to build a million solar roofs, and to reform health care, and to do something decisive about global warming. Tackling these challenges appealed to me *because* no one had been able to do them before. The only way to make the possible possible is to try the impossible. If you fail, so what? That's what everybody expects. But if you succeed, you make the world a much better place.
- ***Never follow the crowd. Go where it's empty.*** As they say in LA, avoid the freeway at rush hour—take the streets. Avoid the movie theater on a Saturday night—go to the matinee. If you know the restaurant will be impossible to get into at nine, why not have an early dinner? People apply this kind of common sense all the time, and yet they forget when it comes to their careers. When every immigrant I knew was saving up to buy a

house, I bought an apartment building instead. When every aspiring actor was trying to land bit parts in movies, I held out to be a leading man. When every politician tries to work his or her way up from local office, I went straight for the governorship. It's easier to stand out when you aim straight for the top.

- ***No matter what you do in life, selling is part of it.*** Achieving my goal of becoming Mr. Olympia was not enough. I had to make people aware there was such a thing as a competition for the most muscular man in the world. I had to make them aware of what training does, besides creating a muscular body—I had to make them aware that fitness promotes health and enhances the quality of life. This was about selling. People can be great poets, great writers, geniuses in the lab. But you can do the finest work and if people don't know, you have nothing! In politics it's the same: no matter whether you're working on environmental policy or education or economic growth, the most important thing is to make people aware.

Every time I meet a great person—and I never pass up the chance—I try to ask how they made good and to figure out the angle that has worked for them. I know that there are a thousand keys to success and I love distilling new rules from my experiences and theirs. So here are ten principles I want to pass along:

1. ***Never let pride get in your way.*** Muhammad Ali and I did a lot of talk shows together. I always admired him because he was a champion, had a great personality, and was generous and always thoughtful toward others. If all athletes could be like him, the world would be better off. He and I would meet in green rooms and joke around. Once he challenged me to shove him against the wall if I could. I think somebody in boxing must have told him he should start lifting weights like George Foreman, because Ali was more known for his speed and his use of psychology. He was thinking about adding a little "strong as a bull" to "float like a butterfly, sting like a bee," and he wanted to see how powerful a bodybuilder really was. I was able to shove him to the wall, and he said, "Wow, this weight-lifting stuff really works. Cool. That's really cool."

The next time I saw him, he had some buddies with him and he said, "Watch this. Hey, Arnold, try to push me."

"This must be a setup," I thought. "Nobody wants to get pushed around in front of his friends."

I started pushing Ali and backed him up all the way to the wall again. He said, "I told you guys, I told you! This guy's really strong. This weight stuff is really good."

He didn't care about losing a pushing match. He just wanted to show his friends that resistance training worked. It gave you stronger legs and hips and could be useful for boxing.

2. ***Don't overthink.*** If you think all the time, the mind cannot relax. The key thing is to let both the mind and the body float. And then when you need to make a decision or hit a problem hard, you're ready with all of your energy. This doesn't mean that you shouldn't use your brain, but part of us needs to go through life instinctively. By not analyzing everything, you get rid of all the garbage that loads you up and bogs you down. Turning off your mind is an art. It's a form of meditation. Knowledge is extremely important for making decisions, for a reason that's not necessarily obvious. The more knowledge you have, the more you're free to rely on your instincts. You don't have to take the time to learn about a subject. Yet in most cases, people who have the knowledge get bogged down and frozen. The more you know, the more you hesitate, which is why even the smartest people blow it big-time. A boxer brings a huge amount of knowledge to the ring—when to duck, punch, counter, dance back, block. But if he were to think about any of this when a punch comes, it would be over. He has to use what he knows in a tenth of a second. When you are not confident of your decision-making process, it will slow you down.

Overthinking is why people can't sleep at night: their mind is racing and they can't turn it off. Overanalyzing cripples you. Back in 1980, when Al Ehringer and I wanted to develop a block at the end of Main Street in Santa Monica, the investors we were bidding against for the property let their worries hold them back. We'd done the research, too, and realized there were uncertainties that might limit the upside potential. The land was an old trolley right-of-way and wasn't available for sale, just for long-term lease. Land nearby was contaminated with chemical waste—suppose this land had a problem too? The property straddled the border of Santa Monica and Venice, so it was unclear which local tax laws and regulations applied. We didn't dwell on these challenges, but the rival bidders did, and after a while all they could see was red flags. So they dropped out when we raised our bid, and we got the property. Within two years, we were able to convert the lease into a purchase, and our gamble started to pay off; 3100 Main Street turned out to be a phenomenal investment. Many movie deals are made under pressure, and if you freeze, you lose. On *Twins* we had a deadline: Universal needed to know if Danny, Ivan, and I were all committed. There was no time for the agents to dialog. Danny and Ivan and I made the deal on a napkin at lunch. We all signed it and left the table. Danny later had it framed.

3. ***Forget plan B.*** To test yourself and grow, you have to operate without a safety net. The public opinion numbers were very low in early 2004 for my newly announced ballot initiatives, in which we were asking the voters' permission to refinance $15 billion of debt. Our budget experts were already wringing their hands. "What are we going to do if these initiatives fail? We need a plan B."

"Why take a defeatist attitude?" I said. "If there is no plan B, then plan A has to work. We just announced the initiatives. There's a lot we can do to get ourselves closer to the goal."

If you're anxious, instead of making fallback plans, think about the worst that can happen if you fail. How bad would it be? You quickly find out it's really nothing. If you fail at running for governor, you may be humiliated, but that is the worst that can happen. Think of all the presidential candidates who bow out. People understand that's how it works. I thought that if I lost the election for governor, I would just go back to being in movies and making a lot of money. I'd be a free guy, eating good food, riding my motorcycle and spending more time with my family. So I did everything I could to make it happen—putting the best team together, raising the money, running an excellent campaign. If it didn't happen, then I'd have said, "It just didn't work out this time." When I did lose all my ballot initiatives in 2005, it didn't kill me. Life went on and I led a fantastic trade mission to China. And a year later I was reelected.

My standard for misery is the guys who worked in the diamond mines in South Africa when I visited in the sixties. The mines were something like 1,400 feet down and it was about 110 degrees and the workers were getting paid a dollar a day and were allowed to go home to their family only once a year. That's being in deep shit. Anything better than that and you're in good shape.

4. ***You can use outrageous humor to settle a score.*** In 2009 my friend Willie Brown, the former mayor of San Francisco and the longest-serving assembly speaker in California history, was hosting a fund-raiser for the California Democratic Party at San Francisco's Fairmont Hotel, and he and I thought it would be funny for me to drop in.

I showed up unannounced and gave Willie a big hug and a smooch in front of everybody, which freaked out half the Democrats and made the other half laugh. Then a freshman state assemblyman from San Francisco named Tom Ammiano stood up at his table and started heckling me. "Kiss my gay ass!" he yelled. The press wrote about it. Ammiano was a professional comedian besides being a politician. I didn't make any comment. Very funny, ha ha. But in my mind I said, "There will come a time when I'm signing bills and I'm going to get one sponsored by him . . ."

Sure enough, a few weeks later I got one of Ammiano's bills. It was a routine measure about the San Francisco waterfront but it meant a lot to him. I instructed my staff to put together a nice veto message.

GOVERNOR ARNOLD SCHWARZENEGGER

To the Members of the California State Assembly:

I am returning Assembly Bill 1176 without my signature.

For some time now I have lamented the fact that major issues are overlooked while many
unnecessary bills come to me for consideration. Water reform, prison reform, and health
care are major issues my Administration has brought to the table, but the Legislature just
kicks the can down the alley.

Yet another legislative year has come and gone without the major reforms Californians
overwhelmingly deserve. In light of this, and after careful consideration, I believe it is
unnecessary to sign this measure at this time.

Sincerely,

Arnold Schwarzenegger

STATE CAPITOL • SACRAMENTO, CALIFORNIA 95814 • (916) 445-2841

No one picked up on the message spelled out by the first letter of each line, so a suggestion was leaked to a few reporters: "Are you sure you read the governor's veto message the right way? Maybe you should read it vertically." Then everybody saw it and there was a big public fuss:

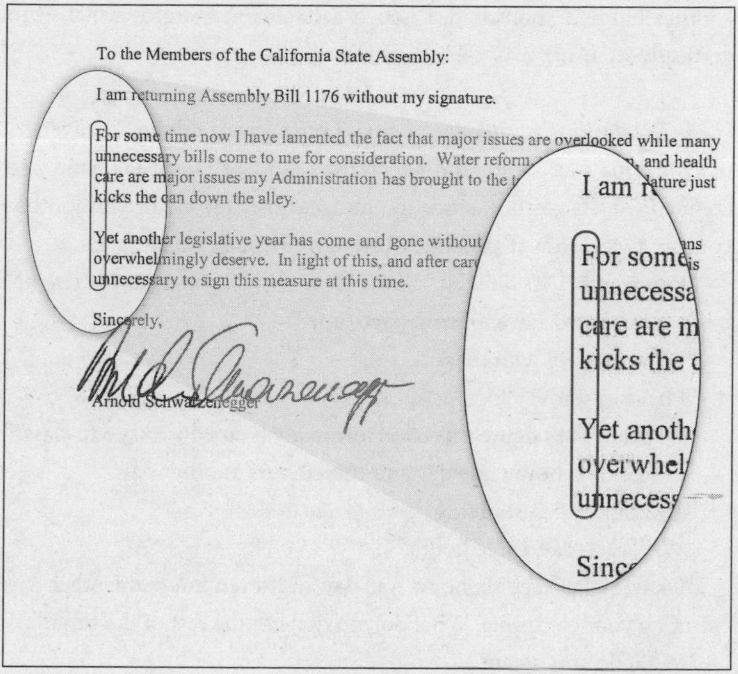
To the Members of the California State Assembly:

I am returning Assembly Bill 1176 without my signature.

For some time now I have lamented the fact that major issues are overlooked while many unnecessary bills come to me for consideration. Water reform, [illegible], and health care are major issues my Administration has brought to the [illegible] lature just kicks the can down the alley.

Yet another legislative year has come and gone without [illegible] ans overwhelmingly deserve. In light of this, and after care [illegible] is unnecessary to sign this measure at this time.

Sincerely,

Arnold Schwarzenegger

Journalists asked my press secretary if the fuck-you message had been intentional and he said, "No, we had no idea. It must have been an accident." But at the next press conference I held, a reporter raised his hand and said, "We gave this message to a mathematician. He said the odds of it being accidental are more than two billion to one."

"Okay," I answered. "Why don't you go back to that same expert and ask what the odds are for an Austrian farm boy to come to America and become the greatest bodybuilding champion of all time, to get in the movie business, marry a Kennedy, and then get elected governor of the biggest state of the United States. Come back to me at the next press conference and tell me those odds."

The reporters laughed. Meanwhile Tom Ammiano was quoted as saying in effect, "I was a schmuck so he has a right to be a schmuck too." It defused the whole thing. (A year later, after signing into law another bill he'd sponsored, I issued a statement about it which read vertically, "Y-o-u-r-e W-e-l-c-o-m-e.")

5. ***The day has twenty-four hours.*** I once gave a talk in a University of California classroom, and afterward a student raised his hand and complained, "Governor, since the budget crisis hit us, my tuition has gone up twice. Now it's too high. I need more financial aid."

"I understand, it's difficult," I said. "But what do you mean, too high?"

"I mean now I have to work part-time."

"What's wrong with that?"

"I have to study!"

So I said, "Let's figure this out. How many hours do you go to class?"

"I've got two hours one day and three hours another day."

"And how much studying do you have to do?"

"Well, each day, three hours."

"Okay. So far I see six hours one day and seven hours the other day, counting your commute. What do you do with the rest of the time?"

"What do you mean?"

"Well, the day is twenty-four hours. Have you ever thought about working more? Maybe even taking more classes? Rather than wasting your life away?"

The class was shocked to hear me say this. "I'm not wasting my life away!" said the student.

"Yes, you are. You're talking about six hours a day. The day is twenty-four hours, so you have eighteen hours left. Maybe you need six hours for sleeping. So if your part-time job takes four hours, you still have time for dating and dancing and drinking and going out. Why are you complaining?"

I explained how as a student I'd trained five hours a day, gone to acting classes four hours a day, worked in construction several hours a day, and gone to college and done my homework. And I was not the only one. In my classes at Santa Monica College and at UCLA Extension there were people who were also working full-time jobs. It's natural to hope for someone else to foot the bill. And government should be there to help if there is genuine need and provide education. But if government is not taking in enough revenue because of an economic slowdown, then everyone should chip in and sacrifice.

6. ***Reps, reps, reps.*** When you walked into the Athletic Union in Graz where I lifted weights as a kid, to the left was a long plywood wall covered with chalk marks. That was where we wrote down our training program each day. Each of us had his own little section on the wall, and before you undressed you'd make a list:

DEAD LIFT:	5 SETS OF 6 REPS	/ / / / /
CLEAN AND JERK:	6 SETS OF 4 TO 6 REPS	/ / / / / /
SHOULDER PRESS:	5 SETS OF 15 REPS	/ / / / /
BENCH PRESS:	5 SETS OF 10 REPS	/ / / / /
DUMBBELL FLYS:	5 SETS OF 10 REPS	/ / / / /

And so on, for a total of maybe sixty sets. Even though you didn't know how strong you were going to be that day, you'd also write down the weight. After each line would be a row of hash marks, one for each set you had planned. If you'd written down five sets of bench press, you would put five lines on the wall.

Then, as soon as you were done with the first set, you went to the wall and crossed off the first line so it became an X. All five lines would have to be turned into Xs before that exercise was done.

This practice had a huge impact on my motivation. I always had the visual feedback of "Wow, an accomplishment. I did what I said I had to do. Now I will go for the next set, and the next set." Writing out my goals became second nature, and so did the conviction that there are no shortcuts. It took hundreds and even thousands of repetitions for me to learn to hit a great three-quarter back pose, deliver a punch line, dance the tango in *True Lies,* paint a beautiful birthday card, and say "I'll be back" just the right way.

If you look at the script of my first address to the United Nations in 2007 on how to fight global warming, here is what you will see:

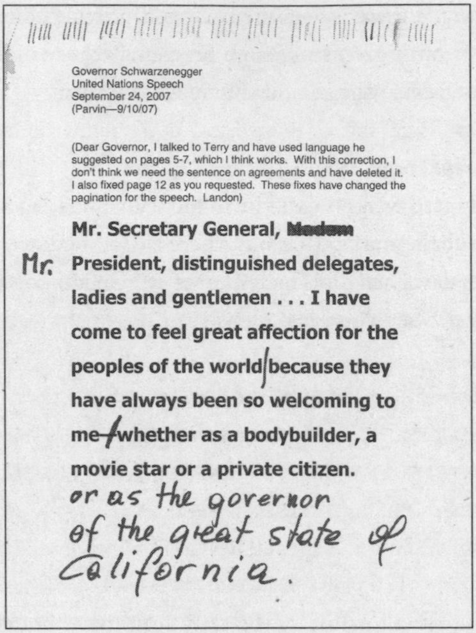

Governor Schwarzenegger
United Nations Speech
September 24, 2007
(Parvin—9/10/07)

(Dear Governor, I talked to Terry and have used language he suggested on pages 5-7, which I think works. With this correction, I don't think we need the sentence on agreements and have deleted it. I also fixed page 12 as you requested. These fixes have changed the pagination for the speech. Landon)

Mr. Secretary General, [redacted]
Mr.
President, distinguished delegates, ladies and gentlemen . . . I have come to feel great affection for the peoples of the world because they have always been so welcoming to me, whether as a bodybuilder, a movie star or a private citizen.
or as the governor of the great state of California.

Each stick at the top of the page represents one time I rehearsed delivering the speech. Whether you're doing a bicep curl in a chilly gym or talking to world leaders, there are no shortcuts—everything is reps, reps, reps.

No matter what you do in life, it's either reps or mileage. If you want to be good at skiing, you have to get out on the slopes all the time. If you play chess, you have to play tens of thousands of games. On the movie set, the only way to have your act together is to do the reps. If you've done the reps, you don't have to worry, you can enjoy the moment when the cameras roll. Filming *The Tomb* in New Orleans recently, we shot a scene with seventy-five people in a prison brawl. The choreography was so complicated, with dozens of fistfights and wrestling matches and prison guards coming in clubbing people, that just the rehearsals took half the day. By the time we shot, everyone was tired but at the same time really pumped. The take was a success. The moves had become second nature to us and it really felt like a fight.

7. ***Don't blame your parents.*** They've done their best for you, and if they've left you with problems, those problems are now yours to solve. Maybe your parents were too supportive and protective and now you feel needy and vulnerable in the world—don't blame them for that. Or maybe they were too harsh.

I loved my father when I was little and wanted to be like him. I admired his uniform and his gun and the fact that he was a policeman. But then later on I hated the pressure he put on my brother and me. "You have to set an example in the village because you're the children of the inspector," he would say. We had to be the perfect kids, which of course we were not.

He was exacting, which was his nature. He was also brutal at times but I don't think that was his fault. It was the war. If he had lived in a more normal way, he'd have been different.

So I've often wondered: What if he'd been warmer and nicer? Would I have left Austria? Probably not. And that is my great fear!

I became Arnold because of what he did to me. I recognized that I could channel my upbringing in a positive way rather than complain. I could use it to have a vision, set goals, find joy. His harshness drove me from home. It made me come to America, and work for success, and I'm happy it did. I don't have to lick my wounds.

There's a passage near the end of *Conan the Barbarian* that has always stuck with me. The lines are said not by Conan but by Thulsa Doom, the sorcerer who makes Conan as a young boy watch his father be devoured by dogs and who slaughters Conan's mother before his eyes. As Conan is about to kill him and avenge his parents, Thulsa Doom says, "Who is your father if it is not me? Who gave you the will to live? I am the wellspring from which you flow."

So it's not always obvious what you should celebrate. Sometimes you have to appreciate the very people and circumstances that traumatized you. Today I hail the strictness of my father, and my whole upbringing, and the fact that I didn't have anything that I wanted in Austria, because those were the very factors that made me hungry. Every time he hit me. Every time he said my weight training was garbage, that I should do something useful and go out and chop wood. Every time he disapproved of me or embarrassed me, it put fuel on the fire in my belly. It drove me and motivated me.

8. *Change takes big balls.* While on a trade mission to Moscow during my last year as governor, I took a little time out to visit former Soviet president Mikhail Gorbachev at his home. We'd become friends over the years and I'd given a speech for him and sat with him at his eightieth birthday party in London a few months before. Gorbachev's daughter Irina made lunch for us and several friends from the Gorbachev Institute. We ate for at least two and a half hours.

I've always idolized Gorbachev because of the courage it took him to dismantle the political system that he grew up under. Yes, the USSR had financial troubles, and yes, Reagan outspent them, and they were backed into a corner. But for Gorbachev to have the guts to embrace change rather than further oppress his people or pick fights with the West has always amazed me. I asked how he did it. How could he change the system after being indoctrinated from childhood to view Communism as the solution to every problem, and after rising to leadership in the party, where you had to show passion for the system all the time? How could he be so open minded? "My whole life I worked to perfect our system," he told me. "I couldn't wait to get to the most powerful position, because I thought then I would be able to fix problems that only the leader can fix. But when I got there, I realized we needed revolutionary change. The only way things got done was if you knew somebody or you paid somebody under the table. So what system did we have? It was time to dismantle the whole thing." Maybe it'll take fifty years for people to understand his achievement. Scholars will always be debating whether he did it the right way. I'm not going to debate it; I just thought it was great that he did it. I'm amazed by the courage it took to not go for immediate gratification but to look for the best direction for the country in the long run.

To me Gorbachev is a hero, at the same level as Nelson Mandela, who overcame the anger and despair of twenty-seven years in prison. When given the power to shake the world, both of them chose to build rather than destroy.

9. ***Take care of your body*** **and** ***your mind.*** Some of the earliest advice that stuck in my head was Fredi Gerstl channeling Plato. "The Greeks started the Olympics, but they also gave us the great philosophers," he would say. "You have to build the ultimate physical machine but also the ultimate of the mind." Focusing on the body was no problem for me, and later on, I became really curious to develop my mind. I realized that the mind is a muscle and we should train it too. So I was determined to train my brain and get smart. I became like a sponge, absorbing everything around me. The world became my university, I developed such a need to learn and read and take it all in.

For people who are successful with their intelligence, the opposite applies. They need to exercise the body every day. Clint Eastwood exercises even when he's directing and starring in a movie. Dmitri Medvedev worked endless hours when he was president of Russia, but he had a gym at home and worked out two hours each day. If world leaders have time to work out, so do you.

Many years after hearing it from Fredi Gerstl, I heard the same idea of balance from the Pope. I visited the Vatican with Maria and her parents in 1983 for a private audience with John Paul II. Sarge was talking spiritual talk because he was an expert in that. Eunice asked the Holy Father about what kids should do to become better people and he said, "Just pray. Just pray."

I talked to him about his workouts. Just before we went, I'd read a magazine story that described how athletic the pope was and what good shape he was in. To him, besides religion, life was about taking care of both your mind and your body. So we talked about that. He was known for getting up at five in the morning and reading newspapers in six different languages and doing two hundred push-ups and three hundred sit-ups, all before breakfast and before his workday began. He was a skier too, and he skied even after he became pope.

And he was already in his sixties, twenty-seven years older than me. I said to myself, "If that guy can do it, I've got to get up even earlier!"

10. ***Stay hungry.*** Be hungry for success, hungry to make your mark, hungry to be seen and to be heard and to have an effect. And as you move up and become successful, make sure also to be hungry for helping others.

Don't rest on your laurels. Too many former athletes spend their lives talking about how great they were twenty years ago. But someone like Ted Turner goes from running his father's outdoor advertising business to founding CNN, to organizing the Goodwill Games, to raising bison and supplying bison meat, to having forty-seven honorary degrees. That's what I call staying hungry. Bono starts as a musician, then buys others' music, then works to combat AIDS and to create jobs. Anthony Quinn was not happy just being a movie star. He wanted to do more. He became a painter whose canvases sold for hundreds of thousands of dollars. Donald Trump turned his inheritance into a fortune ten times as big, then had a network TV show. Sarge traveled the world till he died, always hungry for new projects.

So many accomplished people just coast. They wish they could still be somebody and not just talk about the past. There is much more to life than being the greatest at one thing. We learn so much when we're successful, so why not use what you've learned, use your connections and do more with them?

My father always told me, "Be useful. Do something." He was right. If you have a talent or skill that makes you happy, use it to improve your neighborhood. And if you feel a desire to do more, then go all out. You'll have plenty of time to rest when you're in the grave. Live a risky life and a spicy life and like Eleanor Roosevelt said, every day do something that scares you.

We should all stay hungry!

My son Patrick and I flew to Europe in 2011 for the unveiling at the Graz Museum of an eight-foot tall, 580-pound bronze of me as Mr. Olympia in a favorite pose, the three-quarter back. © Heinz-Peter Bader/Reuters

ACKNOWLEDGMENTS AND SOURCES

MEMOIRS ARE ABOUT LOOKING back, but I've lived my life by the opposite principle. So when people over the past two decades asked me to write a memoir, I always answered, "At home I have a hundred photo albums starting with my childhood in Austria, and I never look at them. I'd rather do another project or make another movie and learn from looking forward!"

Digging up and piecing together memories proved to be as difficult as I imagined, and yet what made the work unexpectedly enjoyable was the help I got from others. I found myself swapping stories with old friends from the worlds of bodybuilding, business, sports, Hollywood, and politics—a large cast of characters, too many people to name here. I'm grateful to all of them for helping me re-create the past and for making it immediate and friendly.

I want to thank first my coauthor, Peter Petre. Books like this require a collaborative partner with not just writing skill but also endurance, tact, judgment, and a great sense of humor, and Peter has them all.

My friend and close colleague of many decades Paul Wachter was generous in sharing recollections and editorial suggestions and providing practical acumen. Danny DeVito, Ivan Reitman, and Sylvester Stallone added funny Hollywood stories (Sly added Planet Hollywood stories also). Susan Kennedy, from 2005 to 2010 my gubernatorial chief of staff, gave us the benefit of her encyclopedic knowledge of my time in office. Her master's thesis, an inside analysis of turning around my governorship in late 2005 and 2006, was of great use. Albert Busek in Munich, one of my oldest friends and the first journalist ever to single me out, provided advice and photos. Bonnie Reiss contributed her recollections and notes to the accounts of my governorship and of the environmental and after-school movements. Steve Schmidt, Terry Tamminen, Matt Bettenhausen, and Daniel Zingale also helped reconstruct aspects of my governorship. Fredi and Heidi Gerstl, Franco Columbu, and Jim Lorimer reminded me of shared experiences from our lifelong friendships.

Because my life has been extraordinarily well covered by the media, we had the benefit of almost fifty years of books, magazine and newspaper stories, interviews, videos, photos, illustrations, and cartoons about me documenting my careers in the muscle world, the movie world, the business world, and the world of politics and public service. Three people were key in organizing these troves of material: my executive assistants Lynn Marks and Shelley Klipp and my archivist Barbara Shane. Lynn and Barbara, with help from my former assistant Beth Eckstein, also tackled the massive challenge of transcribing hundreds of hours of recorded conversations between Peter and me as well as other interviews conducted for this book. Rebecca Lombino and Chris Fillo supervised logistical and legal support.

Peter's wife, Ann Banks, speeded our writing by selecting and refining the research. His literary agent, Kathy Robbins, did excellent work getting this project launched.

Joe Mathews, who covered Sacramento for the *Los Angeles Times* and whose book *The People's Machine* details my first term in the statehouse, gave generously of his time and wisdom to help shape the political chapters of *Total Recall*.

I'm grateful to the other journalists, too numerous to mention, who have chronicled the accomplishments and adventures and dramas of my life—the writers from muscle magazines, entertainment publications, and political writers who interviewed me over the years and captured on the page jokes and conversations and observations and outrageous remarks that I'd forgotten all about and loved being reminded of. Among the books and publications we consulted, I will list some that proved particularly helpful: *Arnold hautnah* by Werner Kopacka and Christian Jauschowetz; *Arnold Schwarzenegger: Die Biographie* by Marc Hujer; *The People's Machine: Arnold Schwarzenegger and the Rise of Blockbuster Democracy* by Joe Mathews; *Fantastic: The Life of Arnold Schwarzenegger* by Lawrence Leamer; and *Arnold and Me: In the Shadow of the Austrian Oak* by Barbara Outland Baker.

To help bring back the bodybuilding days, we drew on the extensive coverage in *Muscle Builder/Power, Muscle, Muscle & Fitness*, and *Health and Strength*, as well as in *Sports Illustrated*—and of course the book *Pumping Iron* by George Butler and Charles Gaines and the film *Pumping Iron* by Robert Fiore and George Butler. We also consulted my own book/training manual about becoming a champion, *Arnold: The Education of a Bodybuilder*, cowritten with Douglas Kent Hall. Brooke Robards's filmography *Arnold Schwarzenegger* was especially useful in reminding me of details from my movie career, as was the coverage of my work in *Variety, Cinefantastique,* and other movie journals. *Seven Years,* a commemorative volume that my office published privately in 2010, was an invaluable resource in revisiting the governorship; Gary Delsohn, who worked on that book, contributed notes and recollections from his time as one of my speechwriters.

I'm grateful to Audrey Landreth for helping make sense of scores of photo albums and tens of thousands of photos and guiding me through the selection of images to illustrate my story. Kathleen Brady handled the fact-checking challenges with outstanding skill, speed, and judgment.

Adam Mendelsohn and Daniel Ketchell provided communications support and managed our presence on the internet; Greg Dunn contributed valuable practical backup; Dieter Rauter not only opened up his trove of videos and photos but also was there to challenge me at chess when I needed a breather.

Simon & Schuster provided the expertise and enthusiasm that a book like this needs. From the beginning, editor in chief and publisher Jonathan Karp shared my vision for *Total Recall.* He did me the favor of recommending Peter as my coauthor. He edited the manuscript and orchestrated the entire publication. As an editor, Jon is lively and imaginative and engaged and never loses sight of the big picture. His questions and suggestions were astute and always on target.

The political chapters of *Total Recall* also reflect the fast, deft work of Simon & Schuster executive editor Priscilla Painton, who refined them. My thanks also to Richard Rhorer, associate publisher; Tracey Guest, director of publicity; Emer Flounders, senior publicist; Elina Vaysbeyn, online marketing manager; Rachelle Andujar, marketing specialist; Nicholas Greene, assistant editor; Marcella Berger, Lance Fitzgerald, Mario Florio, rights directors; Jackie Seow, art director; Jason Heuer, jacket designer; Nancy Inglis, production editor; Phil Bashe and Patty Romanowski, copy editors; Joy O'Meara, design director, and Ruth Lee-Mui, senior designer.

For helping make *Total Recall* an international event, I'm grateful to my publishers abroad: Ian Chapman and Mike Jones of Simon & Schuster UK; Günter Berg, Hoffmann und Campe (Germany); Joop Boezeman and Joost van den Ossenblok, A.W. Bruna (the Netherlands); Abel Gerschenfeld, Presses de la Cité (France); Tomás da Veiga Pereira and Marcos Pereira, Sextante (Brazil); Agneta Gynning and Henrik Karlsson, Forma Books (Sweden); Michael Jepsen, Forlaget Turbulenz (Denmark); Elin Vestues, Schibsted Forlag (Norway); and Minna Castren and Jarkko Vesikansa, Otava (Finland); Javier Ponce Alvarez of Martínez Roca/Planeta (Spain).

Finally I thank my family. They were generous in helping me make sure that this memoir delivers on its name. And thanks especially to Maria, for her patience with the project and for remaining as always the person I could go to whenever I got stuck.

INDEX